# 100 GREATEST WELSH WOMEN

### TERRY BREVERTON

### Glyndŵr Publishing

ISBN: 978-1-903529-30-0

Book cover design by Dave Lewis

I bob Cymru – Yr ydym eisiau gwybodaeth am hanes y Brythoniaid i achub
am byth yr iaith Brydeinig

For the people of Wales – We need to know the history of the Britons to
forever save the British language

*About the author*

Terry Breverton was educated at Manchester and Lancaster universities, and is a Fellow of the Institute of Consulting and a Fellow of the Chartered Institute of Marketing. He has spoken on Wales at the North American Festival of Wales at Vancouver and Washington and across Wales, given academic papers in Paris, Thessaloniki, Charleston and Seattle and taught in Milan and Reggio Emilia. He has given the Bemis Lecture at Lincoln, Massachusetts and been awarded a Helm Fellowship at the University of Indiana. Breverton has appeared in several television documentaries about the Welsh, including in Los Angeles, and has worked and consulted in over thirty countries.

After a career in international business and acadaemia, he is a full-time non-fiction writer of over fifty books, and has won five Welsh Books Council 'Book of the Month' awards. He has spoken across Wales upon Welsh heritage, a particular interest being Welsh pirates and privateers such as 'Black Bart' Roberts and Admiral Sir Henry Morgan. His A to Z of Wales and the Welsh was an acclaimed 'first Welsh encyclopaedia', and Archbishop Rowan Williams commented upon his *The Book of Welsh Saints*: 'this book is a really extraordinary achievement: a compilation of tradition, topography and literary detective work that can have few rivals. I have enjoyed browsing it immensely, and have picked up all sorts of new lines to follow up... an enormous work of research.'

Richard Booth MBE, (King Richard Coeur de Livre, the 'King of Hay'), states that 'Breverton has done more for Welsh tourism than the Welsh Tourist Board.' His books have been published across the world, and translated into over twenty languages from Polish and Turkish to Chinese and Japanese. Breverton played rugby until he was 38, and says his proudest achievement is being on the committee of Llanybydder Rugby Football Club. Breverton's *100 Great Welshmen* (2001) was a Welsh Books Council Book of the Month reviewed as 'a fascinating compendium' with 'painstaking research'. His second edition of 2006 was called: 'a veritable goldmine of a book'; and 'a massive treasure chest of facts and figures which no collector of books on Wales can overlook'.

# CONTENTS

i

# INTRODUCTION

A companion to my recent *100 Greatest Welshmen*, this is a revised edition of my *100 Great Welsh Women* of 2002. This itself was a companion volume of my *100 Great Welshmen*, the Welsh Book Council's 'Book of the Month' in June 2001. I have realised that there were errors of fact and omission in both of the original volumes – as writer, proof-reader and publisher, while having one full-time and three part-time jobs at that time, it was difficult to achieve the standard I wished. In particular I was unaware of the outstanding literary contribution by Welsh female writers in the last few decades, far outshining any male output. Gillian Clarke and Ruth Bidgood were in my previous volume, but to this are added Eleanor Puw Morgan, Eluned Phillips, Menna Elfyn, Gwyneth Lewis and Mererid Hopwood – mea culpa for omitting them. I also had left out the deserving Maria Jane Williams, Jane Brereton, Martha Hughes Cannon and Frances Elizabeth Hoggan. After speaking several times with her daughter Nina, Dilys Cadwaldr (1902-1979), the first woman to win the Bardic Crown, has been omitted. It is to be hoped that other writers do not pursue this wonderful lady for information about her mother or father, for reasons I cannot disclose. It has been a real pleasure contacting the women included in this book – one can only hope I have done them justice, as I will not be revisiting this work. Thus, I have replaced some women with lesser contributions or who are only partially Welsh – these ten entries include Saint Helena, the Ladies of Llangollen (neither Welsh), Mary Harris Jones, Mary Hopkin, Charlotte Church, Elizabeth David, Catherine Zeta Jones, Sian Philips, Esther Williams and Mary Edwards Walker. I have included the story of the 'Maid of Cefn Ydfa', not because she is a 'great Welsh woman', but because of the childhood resonances it brings. I was tempted to add the Lady in the Lake, but that legend is recounted in full in my *The Physicians of Myddfai*. Thus this book is not perfect in its choice of women, but hopefully will achieve its overall effect of making us proud of our Welsh heritage. For instance, few other countries in the world, including England and our other European neighbours, have anything like the first twenty or so entries in this boo. I would revisit and update my The Book of Welsh Saints to expand the 200 or so early female entries from our 'Age of the Saints' when the rest of Europe was barbarian, but publishers are unwilling to produce a two-volume work.

This book helps bring to light the history and achievements of Welsh, i.e. British, women. Before the English Conquest, Wales fortunately has many more important female leaders, opinion formers and icons than countries of a similar size. Many of our early saints, in the Dark Ages which spread over the rest of Europe in the 6th century, were women. Indeed, it was this country's 'Age of the Saints'. Britain's greatest monarch, Elizabeth Tudor, was part-Welsh, and surrounded herself with trusted Welsh advisors. Two of our royal princesses were incarcerated by the French rulers of

England until they died. Our greatest heroine, Gwenllian, was executed by the Normans after battle. A Welsh woman was possibly the sister of the second Bishop of Rome. Britain's greatest female novelist, George Eliot was Welsh. Boudica was a Celtic-speaking Briton, i.e. what we now call Welsh. (The word Welsh has a Germanic root, meaning 'foreign', applied by the pagans when they invaded England and pushed the native Britons westwards. Thus the Welsh are called 'foreigners' in their own land. The English were never described as 'British' until late Elizabethan times, as the Welsh were always known as the Britons until that time.) We have suffragettes, bacteriologists, politicians, athletes, actresses, philanthropists, round-the-world yachtswoman, artists, hymn-writers and Hollywood stars like Bette Davis and Myrna Loy. The book even shows that Lucy Walter of Pembrokeshire is an unacknowledged Queen of England. Today, in the author's view, our most important poets and writers, after the death of R.S. Thomas, are women.

The original book had excellent reviews and sold its limited run of 1,000 copies fairly quickly. Meic Stephens in *The Western Mail Magazine*, reviewing both *100 Great Welshmen* and *100 Great Welsh Women*, said: 'Both are really extraordinary achievements by a single author whose industry and enterprise seem to show no bounds ... Terry Breverton is to be congratulated.' The late Dr Peter N. Williams, in *Ninnau* (The North American Welsh Newspaper) called the author 'an astonishing worker... Perhaps the most prolific Welsh author today is T.D. Breverton, of Glyndŵr Publishing, in the Vale of Glamorgan, South Wales. This astonishing worker has recently produced such practical reference books as An *A-Z of Wales and the Welsh, The Secret Vale of Glamorgan, The Book of Welsh Saints* and *100 Great Welshmen*, as well as published important books by other Welsh authors. Now Terry has done it again. His latest book has finally arrive to fulfil the enormous gap in our knowledge of the enormously important, but sadly unheralded contribution of women, not only to Welsh society and Welsh history, but to Western civilisation itself. Titled *100 Great Welsh Women*, it gives short biographies to those of the fairer sex who deserve to be added to out pantheon of Welsh heroes.

Acknowledging that women have so often played subordinate roles in our male-dominant society (and Wales is no exception), Breverton's list of suitable candidates is purely a personal one, but all those included are those who have connections with Wales and who have been an inspiration for all women, everywhere. Included are queens, princesses, writers, mothers of famous men, poets, civil rights activists, politicians, and so on to include women of every imaginable activity and social status.

This most invaluable addition to every bookshelf and library begins with the little-known Saint Almedha (5th-6th century) and ends with Jane Williams (19th century) ...The book is an absolute must for all those who value their Welsh heritage, and for all those who wish to see Welsh women accorded their rightful place in history...'

The book was even reviewed in the *Daily Mail, Daily Express* and *The Daily Mirror*, headlined a two-page review: 'New Book: 100 Great Welsh Women contains some surprises! OZ Diva Kylie is a Valleys Girl! What do Guinevere, Nell Gwynn, Bette Davis, Lady Llanover and Kylie Minogue all have in common? ... Ever wondered which movie stars or historical figures have Welsh ancestry? Then Terry Breverton's new book, *'100 Great Welsh Women'* is the one for you... Famous figures stand alongside equally illustrious but lesser-known names. Each entrant enjoys a detailed biography which flags up their links to Wales, and it is a fascinating read.' *The Sunday Express Books Review* told us that 'Breverton's breadth, generosity and sheer enthusiasm about Wales are compelling', and *Yr Enfys* noted 'Let's admit it - one would be hard-pressed to think of 50 Welsh women who could be described as 'great'. Terry Breverton, however, has just proved that to be a fault with us rather than the contribution made over the years by the women of Wales.'

Of course, the history of our male-dominated society has meant that women have played a subordinate role until recently, and there are still major problems of female equality to be addressed. It is interesting to note how many Victorian females appearing in this book had to be single to gain any professional status. Marriage meant subservience (just as some males expect today). In all honesty, I cannot state that this is an 'original' book. T.J. Llywelyn Pritchard, for instance wrote *The Heroines of Welsh History* in 1854, and I repeat his dedication:

To
The Virtuous Votaries
Of
TRUE WOMANHOOD,
In all
Its Graces, Purity, and Excellence
As contra-distinguished from
The Fantastic Fooleries and Artificial Characteristics
Of
FINE LADYISM
In the Middle Walks of Life,
This Work is Dedicated
By their Ardent Admirer,
The Author

# PRINCESS BRANWEN ferch LLŶR - 1st century

## QUEEN BRONWEN of IRELAND

Branwen's legend links the first-century Welsh King Brân and the *Mabinogion\**, and is recounted in the *Red Book of Hergest*, the *White Book of Rhydderch* and elsewhere. Princess Branwen was said to be the daughter of Llŷr (King Lear), with brothers Bendigeidfran\*\* (Brân the Blessed) and Manawydan. On Llŷr's death, Brân became High King of the 'Island of the Mighty'. Branwen married Matholwch, King of Ireland, to help stop the incessant wars between Ireland and Britain. He had come to Harlech with thirteen ships to seek her hand from Brân, to form an alliance across the Isle of Britain (Ynys Prydein). Indeed, the ancient name of Harlech is Twr Bronwen, Bronwen's Tower. It was later called Caer Collen denoting an ancient site, before it became Harlech.

Branwen's story is given in the *Second Branch of the Mabinogion*. Her half-brother Efnysien was furious that she has been given to Matholwch without his consent, and insulted Matholwch by maiming his men's horses. Matholwch returned in anger to Ireland, but was pacified by the gifts of new horses and the 'Cauldron of Rebirth'. One of the 'Treasures of Wales', it would restore dead warriors to life, but without the power of speech. Matholwch was pacified, Brân gave a great feast at the marriage in Anglesey, and Matholwch and Branwen sailed to Ireland. In the first year of their marriage, a son Gwern fab Matholwch was born, but the Irish reminded Matholwch of

**Sculpture by Ivor Roberts-Jones outside Harlech Castle**

their humiliation in Wales, and Queen Branwen was forced to live and work in the royal kitchens as a baker for three years, being was beaten daily by the butcher.

Irish ships, boats and vessels were forbidden from sailing to Wales and any Welsh visitors were imprisoned, so that Branwen's family would not hear of the insult against her. Three years went by and Branwen befriended a starling in the kitchen, taught it her language and described Brân to it. Branwen sent the starling to find Brân, with a letter expressing her treatment, tied around the starling's wing. The starling found Brân in Caer Saint, Arfon. It was decided that Branwen's family and their men should sail to Ireland and leave Caradog fab Brân as the leader of Britain, with seven knights to support him. With his brother Manawydan and men from the 154 cantrefs of Britain, Brân sailed to Ireland. Brân waded across the Irish Sea, being a giant of a man to big for any ship. Indeed, Branwen's marriage at Aberffraw had been held in a tent because Brân was too tall for any house. Matholwch's men were watching the coast one day, and told Matholwch that they had seen trees on the sea and a mountain with a tall ridge and a lake at each side of the ridge, all moving across the sea. No one knew what the wonder was, so Matholwch ordered his messengers to ask Branwen if she knew anything about it. She was asked and told them that they were her brother's men, coming over the sea after hearing about the insult against her. They asked her 'What are the trees we see on the sea?' She replied 'The masts of the ships.' They then asked 'What was the mountain we saw alongside the ships?' Branwen told them 'That is Bendigeidfran, my brother. There is no ship big enough to contain him.' The messengers asked 'What was the ridge and the lake on either side of the ridge?' to which Branwen replied 'They were his two eyes on either side of his nose'.

Matholwch gathered his men and decided to retreat to the other side of the Shannon and demolish the bridge across the river, to obstruct Brân and his men from reaching them. When Brân's fleet arrived at the river, his men said to him 'Lord, you know the size of the river: we cannot cross it and there is no bridge across it. What is your advice for a bridge?' Brân answered with a saying which has become a Welsh proverb '*A fo ben bid bont*' - 'Let he who is leader be a bridge'. His men crossed over their king's body.

The Irish offered to make peace and build a house big enough to entertain Brân but hung a hundred bags inside, supposedly containing flour but actually containing armed warriors. Efnisien, suspecting a trick, reconnoitred the hall and killed the warriors by crushing their heads inside the bags. Branwen tried to reconcile the two sides, and Matholwch offered to abdicate in his son Gwern's favour, and it looked at if there may be peace, but the hateful Efnisien grabbed Gwern and threw him into a fire to burn to death. The Irish were nearly destroyed, but are helped by the 'Cauldron of Rebirth' to regroup, and the Welsh lost Bran and most of their army. Seeing that the Irish are using the cauldron to revive their dead, Efnisien hid among the corpses and destroys the cauldron, sacrificing himself in the process, and enabling the Welsh survivors to withdraw. Only seven of the Welsh returned from Ireland***, including Prince Manawydan, but they rescued the fatally-injured Bran. They landed at Aber Alaw in Anglesey, where Branwen died heart-broken, and was buried on the banks of the River Alaw****. The seven brought Brân's head back for burial, first staying at Harlech and then on Gwales (Grassholm Island), before burying it at Gwynfryn, White Mount, to face Fance and protect against invasion. This is where the Tower of London now stands. Brân is Welsh for raven, and this may be the origin of

2

the story of the end of the nation when the ravens leave the Tower of London. Caswallon fab Belli succeeded Brân to the British throne.

* For further information upon the *Mabinogion*, see the entry upon Charlotte Guest and the footnote in Gwenllian's entry.

** Brân was the father of Caradog (Caractacus), who was led in triumph in Rome by Claudius. He was supposed to have spent seven years in Rome as a hostage for Caradog, where he became a Christian and met St Paul. Brân was said to have brought Christianity back to Britain, to Trefran, near Llanilid, and was thus sainted as Brân Fendigaid, or Bendigaidfran, Brân the Blessed.

*** Every living soul in Ireland had been killed in the fighting, except for five pregnant women in a cave. Five sons were born to them and they were raised by their mothers until they were strong men who wished to have wives of their own. The men took their peers' mothers as wives and children were born to them. Ireland was divided between the five sons, forming the five districts of Ireland.

**** There are some fascinating burial mounds left that have legends attached to them. Taliesin was also said to be one of the seven warriors who survived Bran's invasion of Ireland. Bedd Taliesin, the Grave of Taliesin, is on the slopes of Moel-y-Garn, near Talybont. Taliesin was a famous bard and warrior, perhaps a contemporary of Merlin. The barrow only consists now of a long stone slab and cairn, as many stones were removed for building. In the nineteenth century, local people tried to remove Taliesin's bones to re-inter them on a Christian burial site. During excavation, lightning struck the ground nearby, and the workers fled, never to try again.. The story is recounted in the *Mabinogion*. Bedd Branwen (Branwen's Grave) is on the banks of the river Alaw, a mile north of Anglesey's Treffynon Church. This cromlech was excavated in 1813. In it a Celtic urn, inside a stone chest (cist), with the cremated bones of a woman were found, now in the British Museum. Unfortunately, local farmers carried away most of the stone for building after 1813, and one large stone remains there, Carreg Branwen (Branwen's Stone).

In the *Mabinogion* we can read 'a square grave was made for Bronwen the daughter of Lear, on the banks of the Alaw, and there she was buried. Fenton described the discovery of Branwen's grave as follows: 'Happening to be in Anglesea soon after this discovery, I could not resist the temptation of paying a visit to so memorable a spot... I found it... the tumulus raised over the venerable deposit was of considerable circuit, elegantly rounded, but low, about a dozen paces from the River Alaw. The urn was preserved entire, with the exception of a small bit out of its lip, was ill-baked, very rude, and simple, having no other ornament than little pricked dots; in height about a foot to fourteen inches... never was there a more interesting discovery, as it greatly serves to give authenticity to our ancient British documents...'

Evangeline Walton rewrote the *Mabinogion* series as novels, and one review reads: *'The Children of Llŷr'* is the second part of the *Mabinogion*, following the retelling of the fourth book of the *Mabinogion* in 'The Island of the Mighty'. In stark, gaunt prose, it chronicles the years of Bran the Blessed - he was so vast a man that no house could hold him or ship bear his bulk - and of the tale of his beloved sister Branwen, his brother Manawyddan, and of his half-brothers Nissyan and the ghastly Evnissyen. It is a tale of change and storm, of love beyond death, of high courage at the end of an era, and the beginning of another. It is epic fantasy in its purest form - marvellous in its compass and power.'

# BOUDICA d. 60 or 61

## BUDDUG - QUEEN OF THE ICENI

The Christian Arviragus had escaped from the last battle of Caradog (Caractacus) in 52 and carried on the fight against Rome, as Pendragon. The Romans are said to have fought thirty battles against him, from Anglesey to the Isle of Wight, without any major gains. In 53, the year after the battle of Clunbury Hill, where Caradog was defeated, Ostorius Scapula was badly defeated at 'Caerfelin', Llanmelin hillfort, the Silurian tribal capital near Caerwent and Caerleon. A crack Roman legion was wiped out here. In 57 Scapula petitioned the new emperor, Nero, to be relieved of this worst command in the Empire, and he was succeeded by Aulus Didius, also known as Didius Gallus. It may well be that the Roman Castle of Didius became Caer Dydd, or Cardiff. Didius deposed Cartimandua, Queen of the Brigantes, who had treacherously surrendered her cousin Caradog. Didius also lost several battles with the Silures and so was replaced by Veranius in 57. Nero ordered huge reinforcements to be sent to Britain, under his army's finest general, Suetonius Paulinus. Suetonius brought with him the II Augusta Legion, and the famous IX, XIV and XX legions, but still could not overcome the British.

**Boudica and her army**

Two of the three legionary fortresses in Britain were to be placed on the Welsh borders at Chester and Caerleon, with the third at York. Tacitus complained that Rome was sending their most capable generals and finest

4

legions to this extremity of the Empire, and stated 'in Britain, after the capture of Caractacus, the Romans were repeatedly defeated and put to rout by the single tribe of the Silures alone... the race of the Silures are not to be changed by clemency or severity.' Suetonius Paulinus now followed a scorched-earth policy from 59-62, with the centre for European druidism, Anglesey, being targeted first.

Meanwhile, the Britons in the east of Britain were stirring, when Queen Boudica (Budigga, Boadicea) led her British Iceni against the Romans. After her husband, the wealthy King Prasutagus had died, he left his kingdom to two daughters with the Emperor of Rome as co-heir, the usual practice for a client-king of Rome. While the governor of Britain, Suetonius Paulinus, was fighting in Anglesey, his procurator, Catus Decianus took over the Iceni kingdom in 60. Buddug protested at the breaking of the Claudian Treaty, and was flogged and her daughters raped. Roman writers graphically reported that the Romans were stunned by the savagery of the British reaction. Tacitus wrote of the rape and whipping and licentiousness of the Romans, and concluded 'The Menai [Anglesey] massacre [of the druids] ...followed closely on the heels of this bestiality. These combined monstrosities infuriated the British beyond restraint.'

Boadicea's chariots crossed the Grimsdyke, crushing a small Roman force near Newmarket, on her way to vengeance at Colchester. The Iceni attacked Colchester, although its temple held out for two days, defended by Roman veterans before they succumbed. The IX Legion under Petilius Cerealis was almost annihilated at Coggeshall after marching from Lincoln to try and relieve the city. Cerealis escaped on horse, and Colchester was now destroyed. The Trinobantes, who had fought against Julius Caesar a century before, had also joined the Iceni. Next the 40,000 Roman defenders of London were killed and the city razed to the ground. Verulanium, St Albans was next to feel the force of Boadicea's army, and the city was levelled. According to Dion Cassius, from 60-61 many battles were fought, 'with the heavy balance of disaster borne by the Romans.' Tacitus recorded that 70,000 civilians and soldiers died in this wave of attacks, including one legion being wiped out to a man. This massive uprising from a previously quiescent tribe took the weight off the attacks on the Silures and other western tribes, and Paulinus hurried back from North Wales with 10,000 hardened troops to deal with the revolt.

Not until 61 was the revolt ended, possibly at a great battle at Trelawnyd in Flintshire. Dion Cassius records her speech to the British before the battle as follows: 'I appeal to you as a woman. I rule not, like Nicrotitus, over beasts of burden, as are the effeminate nations of the East, nor like Semiramis, over tradesmen and traffickers, nor like the man-woman Nero, over slaves and eunuchs - such is the precious knowledge that foreigners introduce among us - but I rule over Britons, little versed in craft and diplomacy, but born and trained in the game of war, men who, in the cause of liberty stake down their lives, the lives of their wives and children, their lands and property. Queen of such a race, I implore your aid for freedom, for victory over enemies infamous for the wantonness of the wrongs they inflict, for their perversion of justice, for their contempt of religion, for their insatiable greed; a people that revel in unmanly pleasures, whose affections are more to be dreaded and abhorred than their enmity. Never let a foreigner bear rule over me or these my countrymen; never let slavery reign in this island. Be thou forever O Goddess of manhood and victory, sovereign and Queen in Britain.' Dion Cassius stated that she had long golden hair, was wearing a tartan dress with a military cloak, and carried a spear when she addressed the Iceni.

The narrowness of the field of battle meant that Boudica could use only as many troops as the Romans could at a given time. The lack of manoeuvrability of the Britons also put them at a disadvantage to the Romans, who were skilled at open combat due to their superior equipment and discipline. The Romans stood their ground and used volleys of *pila* (heavy javelins) to kill thousands of Britons who were rushing toward the Roman lines. The Romans were then able to engage Boudica's second wave in the open, advancing in a wedge formation. Britons attempted to flee, but were impeded by the presence of their own families, whom they had stationed in a ring of wagons at the edge of the battlefield, and were slaughtered. Tacitus reported that 'according to one report almost eighty thousand Britons fell' compared with only four hundred Romans. According to Tacitus, Boudica poisoned herself, but Dio Cassius says she fell sick, died and was given a lavish burial. Fearing Suetonius' actions would provoke further rebellion, Nero replaced the governor with Turpilianus, and one Roman historian reported that the crisis almost persuaded Nero to abandon Britain.

The Romans quickly came to peace terms with the Iceni leaders, restoring the illegally-confiscated wealth of their nobility and people. Welsh place-names at Trelawnyd (called Newmarket from 1710-1954) have survived through the years as 'Cop Paulinus', 'Hill of Arrows', 'Hollow of Execution', 'Field of the Tribunal', 'Knoll of the Skirmish', 'Hollow of No Quarter', 'Hill of Carnage' and 'Hollow of Woe'. *The Comprehensive Gazetteer of England and Wales* of 1894-5 tells us: 'A very large tumulus, the highest in the country, covering more than an acre, is at the Gop, and is supposed to have been erected for a burial-place to Queen Boadicea of the Britons. The summit of the tumulus is called the "Clip of the Gop." There is a most interesting cave on the side of the hill a little below the tumulus. A carved pillar is at Maen Achwynfan, and many barrows are on the heights.'

Two miles from Trelawnyd is Maen Achwynfan, the 'Stone of Lamentations', the tallest disc-headed cross in Wales at twelve feet above the ground, and carved from one block of stone. It is supposed to mark the spot where Boadicea took her life, and on the road to Caerwys was 'Carreg

Bedd Buddug' (The Stone of Buddug's Grave), since moved to Downing. Maen Achwynfan features Christian and pagan orthography, with representations of a man, dog, donkey and coiled serpent, with some beautiful ribbon-plait carvings. Chwyfan is the aspirate mutation of Cwyfan, so it may have one time been dedicated to that early saint. Boudicca's fateful last stand against the Romans may have been between here and Newmarket. The Stone of Lamentations stands near an important junction of the Sarn Helen Roman road and the Holywell road, near Offa's Dyke. With Carew Cross and Penmon Cross it is the largest such structure in Wales. Perhaps the Romans marching from Anglesey to their fort at Chester met the Britons marching from London at this spot, but the actual site of this British queen's last battle is still unknown.

*Footnote:*
From Westwood's *Lapidarium Walliae* we read: 'The Maen Achwynfan is here seen with its top towering over the hedges of the field in which it stands, far removed from any village or any remains either of a religious or civil nature, and devoid of any tradition on the spot which would give a clue to the reason of so remarkable a monument being placed in such a situation. The surrounding district, however, has been the scene of many conflicts. Close to Newmarket is the Cop'r'leni, with an immense carnedd of limestones on its summit. On the brow of another adjacent hill is Bryn Saethau ("the Hill of Arrows"). Near to this is Bryn y Lladdfa ("the Hill of Slaughter"). Below this, again, is the Pant y Gwae ("the Hollow of Woe"); and, indeed, says Mr Pennant, the tract from this place to Caerwys was certainly a field of battle, as no place in North Wales exhibits an equal amount of tumuli; - all sepulchral, as is proved by the urns discovered in them.'

## SAINT CLAUDIA c.36-c.110

## GWLADYS ferch CARADOG

Arviragus ruled as Pendragon of the Britons, while Caradog was in Roman captivity, and Juvenal stated that the Romans feared him greatly: 'Hath our great enemy Arviragus, the chariot borne British King, dropped from his battle throne?' According to Jowett, he was the first king of any country to fight with the cross as his battle flag. St Clement (30-100), the second Pope after Linus, referred to the disciples in Britain in *The Epistle to the Corinthians*, as did Eusebius of Caesarea.

In 42, Emperor Claudius sent the largest army in the history of Rome, to subdue the Silures and Christian Britain. It was led by Aulus Plautius, the most brilliant commander of his day, who made his headquarters in Colchester in 43. The elder brother of Arviragus, Guiderius, was king of the Silures, but was killed in the second battle against the invaders, and then his cousin Caradog took over battle command as Pendragon. The first battle had been won by Arviragus and Guiderius in 43. The series of battles was so intense that Agricola wrote that it would be no disgrace to fall in battle against so brave a people. The Claudian campaign lasted nine years, with one brief interlude, during which Tacitus said 'the fierce ardour of the British increased.'

In 45, after the Silurian-Roman battle at Brandon Camp, there was said to be a six-month armistice when Caradog and Arviragus were invited to Rome to discuss peace. Claudius offered Arviragus his daughter Venus Julia as his wife. At the same time Caradog's sister Gwladys was said to have married the Roman commander Aulus Plautius in Britain. Gwladys, with Arviragus, Guiderius and Caradog's daughters Eurgain and Gwladys had been converted by Joseph of Arimathea. Tacitus recorded the marriage of Caradg's sister Gwladys, when she took the name Pomponia, the clan name of Aulus Plautius. She was henceforth known as Pomponia Graecina Plautius. In 47, Plautius and his British wife were recalled to Rome. It seems that Claudius did not trust the conduct of the war when his commander was related to Rome's greatest enemies. Pomponia was later brought to trial in Rome for helping Christians, but acquitted.

**The Church of St Pudentiana on the site of Claudia's 'British House' in Rome**

The new Roman leader was Ostorius Scapula, and the wars continued until Caradog lost a great battle at 'Clune', possibly at Llanymynech in Powys in 51. Scapula was reinforced by Geta, the conqueror of Mauretania, who brought with him the II and XIV legions from Gaul. Vespasian, a future Roman Emperor was another general on the field, along with his brother, and his son Titus (who later burned Jerusalem and scattered the Jews). Caradog's entire family was taken captive, and Caradog was later handed over in chains by Cartimandua, queen of the Brigantes, to whom he had fled for assistance. In the *Roman Records* of Eutropius, he states that in nine years, 32 pitched battles were fought, with victory swaying from one side to the other. *The British Annals* give 39 battles, and still Rome had not conquered Britain. The British *Triads* state that Caradog was betrayed at the battle, when the Coranaid (Coritani) tribe, in the secret pay of the Romans, attacked his rear.

Tacitus records that 'three million people' watched the triumphal procession leading Caradog and his family to his trial. He records also that Caradog's daughter Gwladys never left his side, although it was against the law for a woman to enter the Senate. After Caradog's famous speech for mercy, the Senate applauded, and Queen Agrippina congratulated Caradog and his daughter. The only restriction imposed was that the British royal family was exiled in Rome for 7 years, and were never to bear arms against Rome again. When Caradog returned home, possibly to Dunraven (Dundrafan) or St Donat's (Abergwerydd) in 59, he kept out of the war still being fought by Arviragus and Galgacus. Dundryfan indicates a triangular fortress and on the headland is an Iron Age hillfort with hut sites and pillow mounds. It was said to be the principal residence of the lords of the Silures, and of Bran ap Llyr and his son Caradog ap Bran, Caractacus. It is mentioned in *Bonedd y Saint* and a nearby farm is called Cae Caradoc.

St. Claudia's feast date is 7 August, and it is claimed she was the daughter of Caradog and wife of Pudens. Her sister was St. Eurgain, who was said to have brought the gospel back to Britain. (However, another theory is that Eurgain and Gwladys were the same person). Claudia was said as a child to have been baptised by Joseph of Arimathea, and died at Pudens' villa in Sabium in Umbria, Italy in 110. Other sources give her death date as 97 and 107. Her body was taken back to Rome to lie alongside his. However, Tacitus calls her the daughter of the British king Cogidubnus. A marble tablet discovered at Chichester notes that Pudens, under the sanction of Cogidubnus, erected a temple to Neptune and Minerva. Whether she was the daughter of Cogidubnus or Caractacus may be uncovered in the future - suffice it to say that this British woman was extremely important in the very early Christian church in Rome, three centuries before Rome officially stopped its persecution of Christians. The house of Pudens in Rome was the first to be used for Christian worship, and the church of St Pudentiana now stands on the site. Claudia and Pudens were the parents of the saints Timothy, Pudentiana and Praxedes, and Claudia and Pudens were said to have received St Peter into their house.

Her brother Cyllin was also said to be a saint of this time, and some sources make him Pope Linus, the second pope (c.65-c.76) after Peter. Some believe that she was Gwladys Ruffyth (Gruffydd), Romanised to Claudina Ruffina, and born in Penllyn Court, Glamorgan, another fortified site associated with the Silures. Much more research is needed upon the legends concerning Wales and first century Rome, but it may be well to elucidate what is known to the author. From 51 Caradog was in Rome. His father Bran also seems to have been held hostage with him for seven years, although many sources place Caradog as the son of Cunobelinus, Cymbeline. Around this time St Paul was in Rome, and was executed in 67 or 68. Paul converted a wealthy Roman couple, Quintus Cornelius Pudens and Priscilla, and the faithful including St Peter assembled at their house, now in Via Urbana, for worship. Quintus Pudens was martyred and Priscilla had a catacomb, still known by her name, made as the family cemetery.

9

Their son Cornelius Pudens appears to have been in Britain in the reign of Claudius. The stone found at Chichester reads: 'The College of Artificers and they who preside over sacred rites or hold office there by the authority of King Cogidubnus, legate to Tiberius Claudius Augustus in Britain, dedicated this temple to Neptune and Minerva for the welfare of the Imperial Family, Pudens the son of Pudentinus giving the ground.' Pudens seems to have returned to Rome as a member of the imperial household around 65, and like Gwladys (Claudia) and Eurgain probably came into contact with Paul and was baptised. It is thought that Gwladys took the name Claudia at baptism in gratitude to the Emperor Claudius for sparing her father's life. (A Roman tradition was that those given mercy or pardon took the name of their benefactor). Cornelius Pudens married Claudia, and Martial wrote several odes to her in 66 including in *Book II, Epigram* 54:

'From painted Britons how was Claudia born?
The fair barbarian how do arts adorn?
When Roman charms a Grecian soul commend,
Athens and Rome may well for her contend.'
Lines in *Book IV, Epigram 13* also read:
'My Pudens, with the stranger Claudia wed,
Demands thy torch, O Hymen, light to shed,
Then rare cinnamon with spikenard join,
And mix Thaesean sweets with Massick wine.'

As well as Martial, Seneca also mentions the bright blue eyes of the Britons in Rome: 'The British lady, Claudia, to whom Martial addressed two or three of his epigrams, and others to Linus and Pudens, is supposed to be the Claudia mentioned with Pudens and Linus, in Paul's *Second Epistle to Timothy*. She is believed by Cambrian writers to be of the family of Caractacus, and, perhaps, the first British Christian.' The connection between Pudens, Linus and Claudia mentioned by Martial is replicated by St Paul (*II Timothy 4:21*). Martial was living in Rome from 49-86, when he went to Spain. He would have been about 38 years old when Paul wrote his Second Epistle to Timothy, at the height of his intellectual powers in Rome, around 67.

In the *Roman Martyrologies*, Pudens and Claudia had six children: Pudentiana, Potentiana, Praxedes, Linus, Timotheus and Novatus. St Paul in his *Second Epistle to Timothy at Ephesus* (iv.21) reads 'Eubulus greeteth thee, and Pudens, and Linus, and Claudia, and all the brethren.' Timotheus and Novatus held services in Rome at the baths they had built. It was said that St Timotheus came to Britain, and a letter from Pastor Hermas telling him of death in his family still exists. He returned to Rome and was martyred. When Justin the Martyr was forced to tell the place where Christians assembled he answered 'in the baths of Timotheus.' Linus, according to the Apostolic Constitutions, was made first Bishop of Rome, so Peter's successor, like St Timotheus, was half-British.

When her five siblings were all dead, Praxedes asked Pope Pius I to erect a church on the site of her brothers' baths. The church was eventually founded around 145 in Pudens' house and dedicated *Pudentis*. Rebuilt around 780 by Hadrian I, it has been called 'The Cradle of the Western Church.' In this church the author has found very early Celtic Christian knotwork which predates the rebuilding. No other church in Rome seems to have such a collection.

In Rome, Caradog had lived in the Palatium Brittanicum, with his sons, Cyllin and Cynon. The eldest son, Cyllin, was allowed to return to Britain to act as regent for his father in Wales. According to Iolo, he was a saint. Cynon took a religious life, and seems to have been renamed Linus in Rome. Caradog's grandfather Llyr had died shortly after arriving in Rome, and Bran, Caradog's father, offered to replace him as a hostage. Bran's seat was at Trefran, in the parish of Llanilid, Glamorgan, and Llanilid has the reputation as the oldest church in Britain. Bran returned from Rome in 58, a year before Caradog, with Eurgain, Aristobulus, Manaw the son of Aristobulus, Brennus, Ilid and Cyndaf, the latter two being Judaeans. Eurgain, married to the Roman Lucius [Salog, Lord of Salisbury], founded Cor Eurgain at Llanilltud Fawr, the oldest Christian monastery in the world.

In 44 Peter first went to Rome, eight years after Joseph came to Britain, and in 56 Paul arrived in Rome. Baronius states that Peter was received in the Palatium Brittanicum, later Pudens' house, on Viminalis Hill in 44. The *Bible* refers to two churches in Rome, the Jewish Church for the circumcised, and the Gentile Church controlled by Hermas Pastor. The first Christian group met secretly at the house of Aquila and Priscilla. St Paul backed the Gentile church of the Britons, which gradually absorbed the Jewish church in Rome. Aulus Plautius and Venus Julia, or Venissa, from 45 had returned to Rome, both now Christians, Venissa being related to Caradog. Caradog had his two daughters with him in Rome, the eldest Eurgain and the youngest Gwladys born in 36AD (Gwladys means 'princess'). Eurgain returned to Britain and devoted her life to missionary work in South Wales.

The Emperor Claudius, impressed by Gwladys, adopted her, and she was then known as Claudia. The Christian Claudia (possibly baptised by Joseph of Arimathea) in 53 married Rufus Pudens Pudentius, a former aide-de-camp of Aulus Plautius, in a service performed by Hermas Pastor. Pudens had served in the Claudian campaign in Britain, and owned vast estates in Umbria, but stayed with Claudia in the Palatium Britannicum, which Caradog had given them as a dowry. (The Chichester Stone records Pudens' stay in Britain, when he was still a pagan). The *Roman Martyrology* states that Pudens brought 400 servants from his Umbrian estates to serve him at the British Palace.

Claudia and Pudens had four children according to Roman sources. Next to the Palace were the two largest baths in Rome, called after two of their children Thermae Timotheus and Thermae Novatianae. Timothy was the eldest son. In his will he left his estates and palace to the First Christian Church at Rome, the only properties owned in Rome by the church up to the time of the Emperor Constantine. Hermas Pastor regarded the palace as the home of hospitality for Christians, a sanctuary, where no Roman soldier dared to enter to arrest any member, or guest, of the Pudens household. Martial was a constant visitor from his coming to Rome in 65, who extolled the beauty of the British-born Claudia Rufina, who had won the hearts of the Roman people, and whose scholarship even surpassed her famous aunt, Caradog's sister Pomponia.

Martial also wrote poems about Claudia's marriage and the birth of her daughter Pudentiana. From the age of marriage at 17, to the age of 21, Claudia bore Timotheus and Pudentiana. Her daughter Praxedes and son Novatus were born some time later. Timotheus was named after a frequent visitor to the Pudens household, known to use as the Apostle St Timothy, Bishop of Ephesus. According to Baronius, the martyr Justin was staying at this time in the Pudens home. (However, his dates of 100-165 mean that he stayed at the Titulus Pudentis much later). St John and St Paul were closely associated with St Timothy, and Jowett makes a case for Paul being the brother of Pudens. Thus Claudia was sister-in-law to the Apostle to the Gentiles, and Paul stayed at the Pudens household in his few years in Rome. Paul's mother, Priscilla, was also staying in the Palatium Brittanicum. In the *Roman Martyrologies* we read that from 56 'the children of Claudia were brought up at the feet of St Paul.'

The Palatium Britannicum was later variously known as the Titulus Pudentis and the Hospitium Apostolorum before it became the Ecclesia Pudentiana, the church of the martyred daughter of Claudia, by which name it is still known. Smithett Lewis believed that the building, upon Viminalis Hill, was where Praxedes hid martyrs, and then it became a hospice for pilgrims from the East, before Pope Evaristus (100-109) built a church named Pastor's after Pastor Hermas.

*The Apostolic Constitutions* refer to Linus: 'Concerning those Bishops who have been ordained in our lifetime, we make known to you that they are these; of Antioch, Eudius, ordained by me, Peter, Of the Church of Rome, Linus, brother of Claudia, was first ordained by Paul and after Linus's death, Clemens, the second ordained by me, Peter.' Peter also confirmed that Linus was the princely son of a British king. Clement stated that Linus was British, and the brother of Claudia. Clementus Romanus (Clement), the second Pope, had been one of Joseph of Arimathea's followers in Britain, according to Jowett. Clement also affirmed that St Paul lived in the Palatium Britannicum and instructed Linus, that the First Church of Rome was founded by the British royal family and that St Paul had preached in Britain.

*Footnote:*
Pope Linus died in 76 and was feasted upon 23 September. Pope from 64, he was the first Bishop of Rome according to the records of St Irenaeus, Julius Africanus, St Hippolytus, Eusebius, and the *Liberian Catalogue* of 364. These all place him as the successor of Peter the Apostle. St Irenaeus wrote in 174, less than a hundred years after his death: 'After the Holy Apostles (Peter and Paul) had founded and set the Church in order (in Rome) they gave over the exercise of the episcopal office to Linus. The same Linus is mentioned by St Paul in his *Epistle to Timothy* (*St Paul II, Timotheus iv.21*). His successor was Anacletus.' He was buried alongside St Peter at the foot of Vatican Hill. Other authorities place Clement as the first Bishop of Rome, but the *Catholic Encyclopaedia* firmly refutes this later attribution. Linus was the son of Claudia, grandson of Caractacus and nephew of Eurgain, which means that this first Pope was half-British. Near Pisa, an 11th century fresco in S. Piro de Grado shows Linus burying St Peter. He was celebrated in the west as a martyr.


# SAINT EURGAIN c.40-c.90

## VIRGIN FOUNDRESS OF WALES

According to *Catholic On-Line Saints*, Eurgain was the 'virgin foundress of Wales' with a feast-date of 30 June. However, it gives this 'daughter of Caradog', who founded Côr-Eurgain, the feast date of June 30th, and a 6th century date, so seems to have confused her with the 6th century St Eurgain, the daughter of Maelgwn Gwynedd. She was also feasted on 30 June 30. This later Eurgain married Elidyr Mwynfawr who was killed near Caernarfon, and founded Llaneurgain in Flint, now known as Northop. Her body is supposed to lie under a tumulus at Criccin, near Rhuddlan.

According to Iolo Morganwg's *Genealogy of Iestyn ap Gwrgan*, 'Caradog built a palace, after the manner of the Romans, at Abergwerydwyr, called now Llandunwyd Major, or St Donat's. His daughter, Eurgain, married a Roman chieftain [Lucius, a noble], who accompanied her to Cambria. This chieftain had been converted to Christianity, as well as his wife Eurgain, who first introduced the faith among the Cambro-Britons, and sent for Ilid (a native of the land of Israel) from Rome to Britain. This Ilid is called, in the service of commemoration, St Joseph of Arimathea. He became principal teacher of Christianity to the Cambro-Britons, and introduced good order into the côr (monastic college) of Eurgain, which she had established for twelve saints near the place now called Llantwit; but which was burnt in the time of King Edgar. After this arrangement, Ilid went to Ynys Afallen in Gwlad yr Haf (Somerset), where he died and was buried.' Côr Eurgain, or Côr Worgorn, appears to be the Romano-Celtic villa outside Llanilltud Fawr. It was not rediscovered until 1887, so Iolo would not have known it existed, as it was covered by grass.

In 51 CE Caradog had been marched in chains with his brother, wife and daughters in the triumphal procession for the Emperor Claudius in Rome. Such captives were always publicly executed as enemies of Rome, but Caradog's proud bearing and speech to the tribunal is recorded by Tacitus: 'To you the situation is full of glory; to me full of shame. I had arms and soldiers and horses; I had sufficient wealth. Do you wonder that I am reluctant to lose them? Ambitious Rome aims at conquering the world: does the whole human race then have to bend to the yoke? For years I resisted successfully: I am now in your hands. If vengeance is your intention, proceed: the scene of bloodshed will soon be over, and Caradog's name will fall into oblivion. If you spare my life, I shall be an eternal memorial to the mercy of Rome.'

Uniquely, Caradog was pardoned by the Emperor Claudius, and after seven years' captivity is said to have been allowed to return to his camp at St. Donat's near Llanilltud Fawr (Llantwit Major), and was buried in the latter. Not only did his daughter Eurgain marry a Roman, but his other daughter Gwladys also married a Roman noble. Eurgain was said to have brought Christianity to Wales, possibly accompanying her grandfather Bran, founding a monastic settlement called Côr Eurgain in Llanilltud Fawr. Another version is that Eurgain remained in Rome, and the côr was set up in her honour, first at Llanilid, then transferring to Caer Mead (Côr Eurgain) Roman villa at Llanilltud.

St Paul was said to be a friend of Eurgain and Gwladys, and in legend came to Wales as St Ilid with Eurgain in 61 an 68. Gwladys is mentioned in *Epistle 2, Timothy 4-21* as Claudia. Paul was said to have visited Galicia, which may be Wales rather than the Spanish province. Other versions relate Ilid as Joseph of Arimathea. Llanilid has the reputation of being the oldest church in Britain. When the author recently visited it, a buzzard was making an unholy row in the graveyard.

Côr Eurgain, where Illtud's later monastery stood, was endowed by King Cyllin whose son had been converted by Eurgain. It was burned by Irish pirates in 322 and rebuilt by St Theodosius, Tewdws or Tewdrig. Then it was known as Côr Tewdws, or 'the college of Theodosius in Caer Wrgan', and associated with Emperor Theodosius. Other sources tell us that Tewdws is an alternative of Tewdrig*, the martyred grandfather of Arthur. There is a record that the Irish attacked and destroyed Caer Wrgan in the fifth century, which would fit with Tewdrig's dates. Caer Wrgan is the old name for Caer Mead, the huge Romano-Celtic villa just a mile north of Llanilltud Fawr. Côr is a very early version of Llan, meaning choir now but a monastic college in the past, giving Llantwit Major the 'oldest university in the world'. Remember that the Roman Church was extinguished throughout Europe for decades, but the British Church survived, giving the Irish Christianity and St. Patrick. Cor Tewdws is marked on an 18th century map of Llanilltud as being a field north of the monastery site of Illtud.

*Achau y Saint* notes that the College of Caerworgorn was founded by Cystennyn Fendigaid (Constantine the Blessed) and soon destroyed by the Irish, at which time its principal was Padrig. This was Padrig Maenwyn, son of Mawon of the Gower peninsula, who was taken into captivity, but the tradition is probably fictitious. However, Caer Worgan was just a few hundred yards north of Cor Tewdws (which is still marked as such on maps). Perhaps after the sacking of the villa, a new building was erected, just north of the existing Llantwit (Llanilltud Fawr) church. Theodosius II, the Great, was a contemporary of Cystennin and supposed to have founded it, but it was more likely to have been named in his honour by a Romano-British principal such as Tewdrig.

Garmon then supposedly restored the foundation in 447, when he appointed Illtud as its principal and Bleiddian as its chief bishop. However, this is far too early for Illtud, who fought with Hywel for Arthur. Bleiddian was earlier, and accompanied Garmon on his first visit to Wales. *The Book of Llandaf* states that Illtud received the first principalship of the college that bore his name from Dyfrig. It would appear that Illtud was included in the Garmon story by mistake, and that Garmon re-consecrated the building as Cor Worgan, if he had any connection at all with it.

It is probable that, as well as the monastery (re-founded later by Illtud) the pagan Irish destroyed the fabulous fifteen-room Roman villa at Caer Mead, a mile from Llanilltud. After Macsen Wledig left with the legions in 383, this was taken over by the local prince or king, and

**Saint Eurgain is associated with the huge Roman villa at Caermead**

there was evidence of forty-one Christian burials on the site in the 'Age of the Saints'. This may have followed a recorded Irish pagan attack in the 5th century. It is thought that the kings of Glamorgan and Gwent, from Tewdrig through his son Meurig to his son Arthmael or Arthrwys, may have used it as their palace. Arthmael, the Arthur of legend, has always been associated with being born at nearby Boverton, which claims to the Caput Bovium of the Romans (Cowbridge being Bovium). The L-shaped Caer Mead site covers two acres, and one room (the court?) was a massive 60 by 50 feet. There are mosaics there, and coins pottery and glass were discovered. Excavated in 1888 and a couple of times since, it has since been covered over and ignored, when it could hold the key to the legend of Arthur.

Caemead is a mixture of the Welsh for field and the honey drink. However, 'cae mellitus' means the honey-coloured field, and could be associated with Camelot. A gold torc was found in the next field early in the 19th century, but sold for £100 and melted down. CADW should excavate this priceless site, at present merely humps in the ground.

* King Tewdrig controlled much of south-east Wales, and fought with Constantine the Blessed against the invading Saxons. He is also said to have founded the college of Côr Tewdws on the site of Côr Worgan, (Côr Eurgain), later to become famous as Llanilltud Fawr. After Constantine's death, he allied with Vortigern to keep the peace, and passed on his kingdom to his son Meurig. (Pentre Meurig is north of Llanilltud Fawr, on the old Roman Road from Cardiff to Neath). Tewdrig retired to Tintern, where he was attacked by Saxons. A stone bridge in the nearby Angidy valley is called Pont y Saeson, 'Bridge of the Saxons', and this may be where the fight took place. The enemy were driven off, but not before Tewdrig was mortally wounded. His son Meurig arrived and took his father on a cart to a well in Mathern. A plaque there reads 'By tradition at this spring King Tewdrig's wounds were washed after the battle near Tintern about 470AD against the pagan Saxons. He died a short way off and by his wishes a church was built over his grave'. Mathern is the corruption of 'Merthyr Teyrn', 'the site of martyrdom of the sovereign'. In 822, Nennius described the well as one of 'the marvels of Britain', and also referred to the nearby Well of Meurig.

## SAINT ELEN LLUYDDOG 4th century

### ELEN OF THE HOSTS, HELEN OF CAERNARFON, ELEN FERCH EUDAF, PATRON SAINT OF TRAVELLERS

Her Feast Days are 22 May and 25 August. This saint is supposed to have been the daughter of King Coel ('Old King Cole'), and is often confused with the Elen who 'brought the True Cross to Wales'. However, that saint was St Helena the British wife of Constantine the Great, responsible for his conversion to Christianity. Much Welsh legend also interlinks Elen ferch Eudaf (Octavius, Lord of Ewyas), the British wife of the Emperor Maximus (Macsen Wledig), with the former St. Helena. However, Elen ferch Eudaf was the mother of Cystennin (Constantine) and Peblig (Publicius), and the progenitor of the Royal House of Dyfed. The fact that they both had first sons named Constantine also adds to the confusion. Elen's cousin, the great warrior Cynan Meriadoc was said to have vied with Magnus Maximus* for her hand in marriage, but other genealogists make Cynan her brother)

Raised by the legionaries in Britain to the title *Imperator*, Maximus joined with Cynan Meriadoc to invade Europe, and their army was known in the Welsh *Triads* as one of the three 'emigrating hosts' of the island of

16

Britain. Emperor Gratian, after the disaster of the Battle of Adrianople, aroused the contempt and resentment of his troops and was assassinated in 383. Magnus Clemens Maximus took advantage and led his British legions to become Emperor of Gaul, Britain and Spain from 383. He held his Imperial Court at Treves, and was in contact with St Martin of Tours. The Franks were defeated by Macsen's forces. Flavius Clemens Magnus Maximus Augustus was now known as Emperor Maximian, but Gratian's brother Valentinian II retained Italy, Spain, Pannonia and Africa. In 387 Maximus invaded Italy, but the Roman Emperor of the East, Theodosius, raced from Constantinople and defeated him in 388. In reality, the death of Macsen Wledig at Aquileia marked the end of direct imperial presence in Northern Gaul and Britain.

Many of his Welsh troops then seem to have gone to Brittany to settle there. One tradition is that Elen did not go to Europe but stayed in Caernarfon (Segontium) with her son Owain Finddu. Ffynnon St Elen was a famous well near her ruined chapel in the Roman fort of Caernarfon (Segontium). Very many of the earliest Welsh saints are associated with Roman sites. There are North Wales churches dedicated to Elen and also the extinct Llanelen near Llanrhidian in Gower, and Llanelen near Abergavenny in Monmouthshire. There was a Capel Elen in Penrhosllugwy in Anglesey, and Bletherston Church in Pembrokeshire is a dedication. Bletherston is now St Mary's, but the village was known as Tref Elen. Bletherston Church has two holy wells, one used for children's ailments and one for baptismal water. There is also Elen's Well in nearby Lawhaden (Llan Aidan).

She is said to have returned to Wales on the death of Macsen Wledig, with her sons who became saints, Cystennin (Constantine)** and Peblig (Publicius). Other records show that Elen had other sons - Owain Finddu, Gwythyr and Ednyfed also were counted as saints. Even more sons may have been Anhun (Antonius) and Dimet. From tradition, Elen's father Eudaf held Caernarfon (Segontium) for Rome. She married Macsen before he left for Gaul, and her brothers (or cousins) Cynan Meriadog and Gadeon went with Maximus. The *Notitia Dignitatum* of 429 records a regiment of the *Segontientes* serving in Illyricum, and the other claimant for Macsen's wife is Helen 'of Illyricum', so we have the *Mabinogion* tale based upon ancient facts. Recent evidence also backs up the *Mabinogion* story of Cynan Meriadog completing his service for the Emperor and settling in Europe, with the discovery that he settled near Nantes.

Sarn Helen, Ffordd Elen and Llwybr Elen are associated with her, and she is the Celtic patron of travellers, the (older) Welsh equivalent of St Christopher. There is a Ffynnon Elen in Cwm Croesor, on Fford Elen in Snowdonia. A giant called Cidwm is supposed to have killed her favourite son with an arrow where the well sprung forth. Castell Cidwm is the name of the crag on the Cnicht Mountain, near Nantmor, from where Cidwm loosed the arrow. When Elen heard she shouted 'Croes awr – croes awr i mi!'

('Cursed hour – cursed hour to me!'). She suspected a jealous elder brother of killing her son. The spot was called Croesawr or Croesmor ever after, and the small village that grew up around the well was called Croesor. The spring was diverted to make a water-supply for Croesor village, but its mossy mouth can still be seen and after heavy rain still flows. It is on the side of Sarn Helen, the Roman road in Llanfrothen parish, Merioneth.

Near the Seiont river at Llanbeblig is Ffynnon Helen, approached by steps as the ground around it has been raised. Jones noted that it was still being used by people who filled bottles for use as medicine in the 1950's, and that there once was a Capel Helen near the well. There was also a Ffynnon Elin holy well near Llanilar in Cardigan, and St Ellen's Well near Cydweli in Carmarthen. St Helen's Well has given its name to a district of Swansea, a chalybeate spring said to cure wounds and cancers, and still regularly used in the 1850's. There were two holy wells in Pembroke named Ellen's Well, one near Angle and one near Llawhaden. As stated, Blethersone, the neighbouring parish to Llawhaden, was originally Tref Elen. Over the years Trefelenstown became Bletherstone in this part of

St. Elen, like many Welsh saints, was associated with Roman sites, like Segontium Fort, Caernarfon

'Little England Beyond Wales.' There are several old Roman roads and pathways known as Sarn Elen. One leads down to the Roman camp at Nidum (Neath), there is another near Festiniog and another near Dolwyddelan. Llwybr Cam Elen runs between Llandderfel and Llangynog. The 'baldmoney' (spignel, meum) plant is known as Amranwen Elen Lluyddog (Elen's whitewort) or Ffenigl Elen Lluyddog (Elen's fennel).

* In the *Dream of Macsen*, in the *Mabinogion*, the future Roman Emperor, Magnus Maximus, dreams of King Eudaf Hen's beautiful daughter, and sent emissaries across the empire to find her. She was discovered at her father's palace at Caer-Segeint (Caernarfon), where the old man sat, carving *gwyddbwyll* pieces for an ancient Welsh game similar to chess. Maximus/Macsen came to Britain, married the girl and eventually inherited her father's kingdom, much to the disgust of her cousin and Eudaf's heir, Conan Meriadoc. Eudaf (the Welsh form of Octavius) was the ruler of North Wales, but later Geoffrey of Monmouth made him the 'Duke of the Giwissei' or 'Iarl Ergyng ac Ewias', the Earl of the area of the Silures, stretching from Hereford to Glamorgan. Perhaps Elen and Macsen moved from Caerleon or Cardiff to Caernarfon.

** King Cystennin Gorneue, who died in 443 or 448, was also known as Cystennin Fendigaid (the Blessed), and Constantine. The son of Magnus Maximus and St Elen ferch Eudaf, and the brother of St Peblig, he is remembered at Llangystennin in Caernarfonshire, and at Welsh Bicknor in Herefordshire, which was formerly called Llangystennin Garth Benni. Near the former is Llangernyw, the Church of the Cornishman. It is dedicated to the saints Erbyn and Digain, who were Cystennin's sons by the daughter of Peibio, King of Ergyng. He seems to have been the first 'Pendragon', or warleader, to assume the actual monarchy of Britain. Other sources say that he was a prince of Armorica. Welsh Bicknor (Llangystennin/Garthbenni) had a notable monastery between 575 and 866, possibly the seat of Dyfrig's original bishopric.

Macsen Wledig's son Constantine was murdered in 448 by Vortigern (Gwrtheyrn), and was avenged by Emrys Wledig (Ambrosius Aurelianus). Cystennin was the great-great-grandfather of the saints Cybi and Gildas. Geoffrey of Monmouth made Cystennin the father of Uther Pendragon and grandfather of Arthur. At Caernarfonshire's Llangystennin is Ffynnon Llangystennin (near Llandudno Junction). On the outskirts of Caernarfon (Segontium Roman town) is Llanbeblig, said to have been founded by Peblig, a son of Macsen Wledig and Elen. Nennius wrote that the 'son of the great, the very great' was buried at Segontium, i.e. the son of Magnus Maximus. Matthew of Westminster informs us that in 1283, the body of Emperor Constantine was transferred to Llanbeblig, the mother church of Caernarfon, on the orders of King Edward I.

*Footnote:*
There are many legends about the flower of the British army that went to help Magnus Maximus become Roman emperor by defeating Gratian. Known in Brittany as Conan Meriadoc, a British prince was given lands in Armorica by Magnus as a reward for assisting him. Conan's army did not participate in the last two battles of Macsen Wledig. Upon Magnus' death in 388, Cynan stayed as Duke of Armorica ('Brytein Fechan' or Prydain Fychan, Little Britain), submitting to Emperor Valentinian II. In 409 he claimed independence for Brittany and died in 421. Cynan lived at Castel Meriadoc (Plougoulm outside Morlaix), and 'divided the land into plous and trefs and thenceforth by the grace of God the country was called Little Britain'. He seems to have also settled near Nantes. Cynan features in the *Dream of Macsen Wledig* in *The Red Book of Hergest*, as the son of Eudaf ap Caradog and thereby the brother rather than the cousin of Elen Luyddog, the wife of Magnus Maximus (Macsen Wledig).


## SAINT DARERCA c.380 - c.440

## SISTER OF ST PATRICK

Welsh authorities state that this was Patrick's Welsh sister, whose sons included the saints Mel, Rioch (Rioc, who was consecrated a bishop in

Ireland by Patrick), Sechnallus (Secundinus), Menni (Muin) and Auxilius (probably Maelchu). Mel was consecrated Bishop of Ardagh by his uncle Patrick, and is recorded as a British evangelist in Ireland, celebrated on 6 February. Mel made St Bridget a priest, and then a bishop, and was immensely important in Ireland's early days of Christianity. Some Irish sources make Darerca a virgin, closely associated with Patrick and Bridget, and the foundress of Killeevy in County Armagh. She was captured with Patrick and her sister Lupidia, in a raid by Niall of the Nine Hostages.

From the *New Advent Catholic Encyclopaedia* we read: 'Her fame, apart from her relationship to Ireland's greatest apostle, stands secure not only as a great saint but as the mother of many saints. When St Patrick visited Bredach, as we read in the *"Tripartite Life"*, he ordained Aengus mac Ailill, the local chieftain of Moville, now a seaside resort for the citizens of Derry. Whilst there he found the "three deacons", his sister's sons, namely St Reat, St Nen and St Aedh, who are commemorated respectively on 3 March, 25 April and 3 August. St Darerca was twice married, her second husband, Chonas (Cynan, Conan), founded the church of Both-chonais, now Binnion, Parish of Clonmany, in the barony of Inishowen, County Donegal. She had families by both husbands, some say 17 sons, all of whom, according to Colgan, became bishops. From the *"Tripartite Life of St Patrick"* it is evident that there were

St. Darerca's son,
St. Mel of Ardagh

four sons of Darerca by Chonas, namely four bishops, St Mel of Ardagh, St Rioc of Inisboffin, St Muin of Forgney, County Longford, and St Maelchu.

St Darerca had two daughters, St Elche of Kilglass and St Lalloc of Senlis. Her first husband was Restitutus the Lombard, after whose death she married Chonas the Briton. By Restitutus she was mother of St Sechnall of Dunshaughlin; St Nectan of Killunche, and of Fennor, near Slane; of St Auxilius of Killossey (near Naas, County Kildare); of St Diarmaid of Druim-corcortri (near Navan); of Dabonna, Mogornon, Drioc, Luguat, and Coemed Maccu Baird (the Lombard) of Cloonshaneville, near Frenchpark, County Roscommon. Four other sons are assigned to her by old Irish writers, namely St Crummin of Lecua, St Miduu, St Carantoc, and St Maceaith.'

Darerca is honoured on 22 March, and is the patroness of Valencia Island. On this day in 2001, World Water Day was celebrated in the Kerry Diocese at her holy well on Valencia. A 5th - 6th century stone in St Patrick's Churchyard on Inchagoll Island records her grandson, reading

'Lugnaedon, son of Limenueh'. Some sources place her sister as St Tigridia, and say that Darerca was Patrick's youngest sister.

The *Catholic Online Saints* directory tells us that of Darerca's fifteen sons, ten became bishops across the whole of Ireland, helping to Christianise that country. Some sources also make Darerca an ancestor of Arthur. A son by Conan was Urbien, whose son was Solomin, whose son was Constantine, said to be Arthur's grandfather. Whatever the tangled facts about her progeny, it is clear that this Welshwoman's descendants contributed greatly to the evangelisation of Ireland. Professor Hewis, in his *Royal Saints of Britain*, names Darerca as the wife of Conan Meriadoc, (a Roman office, of Duke of the Armorican [Breton] Frontier) under the Emperor Maximus, who was supposed to have been first King of the Bretons. However it is difficult to reconcile Conan's movements with those of Conan Meriadoc at this time.

*Footnote:*

Darerca's brother Padrig (c.373-461), is St Patrick, who has been called 'the most famous Welshman in the world'. The following is the entry from the author's *The Book of Welsh Saints*. 'Born in Bannaviem Tabarniae, Bannventa, possibly modern Banwen near Neath, (near the village of 'Enon') he was the grandson of a priest named Potitus, and the son of a deacon and decurio (town councillor) called Calpurnius. Padrig was captured as a 16-year-old by Irish pirates organised by the (pagan) High King of Ireland. He was treated as a slave by a Pict in Antrim for six years. Padrig either escaped or was freed, returned to Wales, received some training as a priest, and returned to Ireland around 430-433. From his Armagh base, he wrote the first literature identified with the early British church, following the simple Welsh monastic life and attempting to abolish paganism and sun-worship.

Another version is that Saint Patrick was born in Pembrokeshire in 389, and was carried off by Irish raiders in 406, becoming Bishop of Armagh in 432, being consecrated by St Garmon at Auxerre. Recent evidence seems to point to his birth in Banwen. In St. Patrick's *Confessio* he states he was born at Banaven Taberiar, a small-holding near a Roman fort, which could be Tafarn-y-Banwen, a farm near an old Roman stronghold. This is also on the strategically important Sarn Helen, once a major Roman road through Wales. Local tradition says that Patrick came from Banwen, and there are placenames such as Hafod Gwyddelig (Irish Summerhouse) and a Nant Gwyddelig (Irish Stream). George Brinley Evans also points to the nearby Hirfynydd Stone, the extremely rare early Christian carving of a man in prayer, surrounded by Irish symbolic patterns. (Note that 'Gwyddelig', the Welsh for 'Irish', is identical to 'Goidelic'. The Welsh were the Brythonic Celts, and the Irish were the Goidelic Celts).

Cressy states that Patrick was born in Glyn Rosina, the valley of St Davids, in 361, and died at Glastonbury in 472, aged 111. Eisteddfa Padrig is a chair-like rock in the sea cliffs of Pembrokeshire near St David's Cathedral, where God showed Padrig the view of Ireland and told him that it was now all in Padrig's care. An angel had told Padrig that he could not settle at Glyn Rhosyn, as that place was reserved for David's birth in thirty years' time. Under the sandy

21

shoreline of Whitesands Bay lies the sixth century St Patrick's Chapel, which itself lies upon an older burial ground. A rectangular mound now stands in the field called Parc-y-Capel near the shore. Excavated in 1924, it is a single cell chapel with human remains below the west wall. There is a nearby rock called Carn Patrick. There was also a Paterchurch, or Patrickchurch, in Monkton, Pembrokeshire. One of the gates to St David's Cathedral is still known as Porth Padrig. Cefn Padrig is a ridge of coastline between Burry Port and Llanelli.

Iolo Morganwg names a Padrig as the son of Maewan, Principal of the monastery at Bangor Illtud, who was carried away by Irish pirates. Evans, in his *History of Glamorgan*, tells us: '.other writers doubt the existence of Eurgain, but all agree that a college was founded by the Roman General Theodosius (called by the Welsh, Tewdws) some time between the years 368 and 395 AD. The principal and chief teacher of this college (Llanilltud Fawr), now called Cor Tewdws, was one Balerius, a learned Roman Christian. He was succeeded by Patrick, a native of Glamorgan, and a former student of the college. The college prospered exceedingly until it was attacked, despoiled, and destroyed by some Irish pirates, who, when they retired, carried Patrick with them a prisoner. Patrick continued his good work in Ireland, preaching the Gospel boldly, and he is still loved by the Irish as their Patron Saint.'

Pawl Hen traditionally founded the great monastery at Whitland in Carmarthen, variously known as Alba, Rosnat or Tŷ Gwyn (being whitewashed), but some say that it was founded by Padrig before he went to Ireland. Perhaps Pawl Hen founded the famous school there in Patrick's monastery, which would explain the large numbers of Irish monks said to have studied there. In preparing a book upon St Tathan, the author discovered another link between Patrick and Wales, recorded by Marie Trevelyan in 1910. According to her, Padrig was known as Maenwyn (Holy Rock) and educated at Caerworgan (Llanilltud Fawr), where the Latin honorary name of Patricius was given to him. A very old folk lament was remembered by two people who lived far apart in the Vale of Glamorgan. The lament was sung at 'Mal (sic) Santau' and was familiar at the firesides of Penmark, St Tathan and Llanilltud Fawr in the 19th century. The song was about a boy named Maenwyn who was born at Nant-y-Tirion, Treberfaydd (Boverton), and who was caught in a nearby bog when the Goidels (Irish Picts) burned Caerworgan. Wales' most important Roman villa, at nearby Caermead, was burnt by the Irish at about this time. Another antiquarian states that Maenwyn was born at the village of Pedr Onen (Peter's Ash), now called Broadway, near Bonafon (Cowbridge). It appears that Patrick's name may have been 'Succat', and the name Patricius or Patrick means 'of noble birth'.

# BRYCHAN'S DAUGHTERS

## THE PEREGRINI (WANDERING SAINTS)

King Brychan (c.480-550) was feasted on his saint's days of 5 and 6 April. He was the son of the Irish prince Amlech and the Welsh Saint Marchell, was born at Bannium, the Roman camp now known as Y Gaer near Brecon. His father was buried near the door of Ynyspyddid Church. In the churchyard is the ancient monument known as 'The Cross of Brychan Brycheiniog', and the church is dedicated to Cadog, his grandson. The inscription 'Broccagni' was found on a fragmented stone at Capel Mair, Llangeler, Carmarthenshire, and also at Porthqueene, near Camelford in Cornwall. He was said to be buried on Ynys Brychan, Lundy Island.

    Brychan Brycheiniog was the first king of Brecon after the Romans left, and the founder of a long line of saints*, including his daughters or grand-daughters Gwladys (the mother of Cadog, who married King Gwynlliw), Arianwen, Bechan/Bethan, Tanglwst (Ynystanglws, near Swansea), Mechell, Nefyn, Gwawr (the mother of the soldier-poet Llywarch Hen), Gwrgon (who married Cadrawd), Eleri, Lleian, Nefydd, Rhiengar, Gwenddydd, Tybie (Llandybie), Elined, Ceindrych, Gwen (Gwenllian or Gwenhwyfar, who may have married King Arthur), Cenedlon, Cymorth, Clydai, Dwynwen (q.v.), Ceinwen (q.v. Cain),

One of Brychan's daughters, St. Marchell is commemorated at her foundation at St. Marcella's Eglwys Wen, Denbighshire

Tudfyl (q.v., martyred at Merthyr Tydfil), Enfail, Hawystl, Tybie, Callwen, Gwenfyl, Ceingar (the mother of Cynidr), Goleuddydd, Meleri (the grandmother of Dewi Sant), Ceneu (q.v. Cain), Ellyw, Keneython, Nectan, Mwynen, Cain (Llangain and Llangeinor), Endellion, Clether and Morwenna. There is a major problem of tangled genealogies, as many appear alongside known people of the sixth century, probably grand-children and great-grandchildren, but still referred to as 'Brychan's daughters'.

    Gerald of Wales writes of Brychan's 24 daughters, 'dedicated from their youth to religious observances', who 'happily ended their lives in sanctity'. Michael Drayton in *Polyolbion* refers to the legend of Brychan's 24 daughters remaining virgins and being transformed into rivers flowing into the Severn (Hafren) on their deaths, no doubt a tale linked with the Celtic river goddesses of folk memory.

The descendants of Brychan, with those of his instructor Byrnach, and of Gastayn, (the spiritual advisor of Brychan's eldest son Cynog), are responsible for around sixty ancient church sites in Wales, and many in the West Country. About 22 are in Brecon and on its borders. There are around 16 in Carmarthen and Pembroke, at that time much of it occupied by the *Gwyddyl Fichti* (Irish Picts). There are 5 churches in Anglesey, 3 on the Isle of Man, and others in Denbigh. Leland, in his *Life of St Nectan*, listed their influence in Dumnonia (the West Country) – 'Nectanus, Joannes, Endelient, Menfre, Dilic, Tedda, Maben, Weneu, Wensent, Merewenna, Wenna, Juliana, Yse, Morwenna, Wymp, Wenheder, Cleder, Keri, Jona, Kanane, Kerhender, Adwen, Helic, Talamanc. All these sons or daughters were afterwards holy martyrs and confessors in Devon and Cornwall, where they led an eremetical life.' It seems that there was a missionary movement from Brycheiniog along the Roman roads in the 5th and 6th centuries.

From Brychan's female descendants, we have the 5th century Christian foundations of Clydey in Pembroke, from St Clydau, feasted 1 November. Clydau's sisters Cymorth and Cenedlon had llannau at Newcastle Emlyn, and Cenedlon, as Endelentia, also founded St Endellion near Tintagel, plus Tregony in Cornwall and was associated with Lundy Island. At St Clears in Pembroke and Clether in Cornwall, Saint Clether (Cler) was feasted on 19 August, 23 October and 3 and 4 November. At Capel Callwen near Defynog, Brecon, Saint Callwen was feasted upon 20 April. Llandegwyn, Merioneth and possibly Cedris near Abergyynolwyn are associated with Ceindrych. Tanglwst/Tudglid was celebrated at Awst, Llan Awstl near Machen, and Peterston-super-Ely (formerly called Tanglwst) on 9 May. Tybie was martyred at Llandybie, and was feasted upon 26 December and 30 January, and is also remembered at Llandebia near Dinan in Brittany.

Mwynen was remembered at Marhamchurch and Morwenstow in Cornwall, feasted on 5 July 5th and 14 August. Gwenfyl was remembered at Gynfil in Brecon. Nefyn was feasted upon 13-15 August and 24 March at Nefyn, and St Nyven, near Crick. Nefydd was associated with Llanefydd in Denbighshire, Goleudydd at Llanhesgyn and Ellyw at Llanelieu, Brecon; Enfail was martyred at Merthyr Enfail, Carmarthen and Gwendydd is remembered at Tywyn and Nevern. Lluan was feasted at Llanlluan Chapel, near Llanarthney, and Keneython at Llangynheiddion, near Llandyfaelog, Carmarthen. Rhiengar is remembered at Llech, in Maelienydd, Radnorshire. St Ceingar was the mother of St Cynuidr, and Gwawr was Llywarch Hen's mother. Meleri married King Ceredig and was thus St David's grandmother. Bethan evangelised the Isle of Man (Manaw) with two brothers, and full information upon all of these female saints and other descendants of Brychan can be found in the author's *The Book of Welsh Saints*.

Llangors Lake in Brecon is now known as Llyn Syfaddan, but was called Breccanmere in the *Anglo-Saxon Chronicle*. The only known crannog (fortified island) in Wales is here, and it is held to be the place of Brychan's court. Crannogs are well-documented in Ireland. In 916 it was raided by Aethelflaed, and King Tewdwr's wife and 33 captives taken. Nearby is the ancient church of St Paulinus. There was a place-name near Pol-de-Leon named 'Brochana pars', and Doble notes how many of the dedications of Brychan's descendants are near those of Peulin. There was also a place seven miles west of Llanddeusant named Llys Brychan (Brychan's Palace), which is surrounded by the foundations of Brychan's children at Llandingad, Capel Tudyst, Capel Cynheiddon, Llandybie, Llanceinwyry, Llanlluan and Llansteffan (Cynog).

*Among Brychan's sons or grandsons, Arthen, Berwyn, Clydwyn, Clydog, Cynog, Gwen, Gwynau, Gwynws, Cyflefyr, Rhain,Dyfnan, Gerwyn, Cadog, Mathaiarn, Pasgen, Neffai, Pabliali, Dedyn, Llecheu, Cynbryd, Cynfran, Hychan, Dyfrig, Cynin, Dogfan, Rhawin, Rhun, Clydog, Caian and Dingad were saints. St. Cynin was either a son or grandson of his. Many of his children went to Cornwall from Brecon, where they were venerated. There are many lists extant of his descendants, but all vary. Brychan's family forms one of the 'Three Saintly Tribes of the Isle of Britain', along with those of Caw and Cunedda. Brychan is depicted in a stained glass window at St Neots in Cornwall, and his wives were said to be Eurbrawst, Proestri and Rhybrawst.

The three earliest Welsh records list these sons of Brychan, by his wives Banadl, Prawst, Rhybrawst and Eurbrawst: Cynog, Rhain Dremrudd, Clydwyn, Arthen, Papai, Dingad, Berwyn, Rhydog. The same sources sometimes relate the following as sons, and sometimes as grandsons: Cynon, Pasgen, and Cylflifer. Other Welsh sources claim the additional sons: Marthaerun, Rhun, Caian, Cynbryd, Cynfran, Cynin, Dogfan, Dyfnan, Dyfrig, Hychnan, Llecheu, Neffei, Rhawin, Llofan, Llonio, Heilin, Afallach, Gwynnen, Gwynnws. The *De Situ Brecheniauc* also lists these daughters: Meleri, Hunydd, Gwladys, Ceingar, Tudglid, Nyfain, Gwawr, Marchell, Lluan, Arianwen, Bethan, Ceinwen, Cerddtch, Clydai, Cynheiddon, Dwynwen, Eiliwedd, Goleudydd, Gwen, Lludd, Tudful, Tudwystl and Tybie. Other Welsh sources add these daughters: Beiol, Tydieu, Eufail, Hawystl, Edwen, Gwenrhiw, Tudwn, Callwen, Gwenfyl, Gwennan and Mwynwen. Cornish sources, based upon the *Life of St Nectan*, list 24 children by his wife Gwladys: Adwen, Canauc (Cynog), Clether (Cleer), Dilic, Endelentia, Helie, Johannes (Sion), Iona, Juliana (Ilid), Kenhender (Cynidr), Keri (Curig), Mabon (Mabyn), Menfre (Menfrewy), Morwenna, Nectan, Tamalanc, Tedda, Wencu, Wenheden (Enoder), Wenna (Gwen), Wensent, Wynup (Gwenabwy) and Yse (Ide). An Irish record gives us his sons by Dina, daughter of the King of the Saxcns as: Mo-Goroc, Mo-Chondoc, Diraid, Duban, Cairinne, Cairpre, Iast, Elloc (Dilic), Paan, Caeman and Mo-Beoc. In Breton tradition, Brychan married Menedoc, daughter of Constantine, King of Scotland, and their progeny included Nennocha (Ninnoc).

*Footnote:*
This author has long asked for the links between Arthur and Welsh 6th century

saints to be further researched, to help Welsh tourism. Any visit to Devon and Cornwall, counties with tenuous Arthurian links, shows what can be achieved for this son of Meurig ap Tewdrig. Just some of Arthur's links with the daughters of Brychan, from a Hay-on-Wye website, are recounted here: 'Between the rivers Wye and Usk is a land, which in the Dark Ages was illuminated by characters of Arthurian Romance and the Grail Quest. The daughters of Brychan Brycheiniog (King of the region roughly equating with the present day Brecknockshire), formed a powerful group of landowners in the area as a form of matriarchal inheritance prevailed at that time. They included: NYFEIN, or Vivian, who occupied the palace on Llyn Syfadden, now known as Llangorse Lake. She was the mother of Urien of Gorre (Gower), grandmother of Owain. She enchanted Merlin in the Forest of Brocielande, in Brittany. (The family of Brychan owned land in the Celtic lands of Brittany, or Armorica, Cornwall, Scotland and Ireland). GWLADUS, whose abduction caused King Arthur to intervene, and whose son, Cadoc, was one of the three knights of the Holy Grail. TUDGLIG, mother of Meugan the Poet, schoolmaster of Merlin, (although there are those who say that he was Merlin). He founded the monastery of Brocielande where legend tells us Vivien enchanted Merlin. His settlement (llan) can be found at Llanfeigan near Talybont-on-Usk. ELUNED, whose Stone and Ring (with which she saved Owain in the tale *Iarlles y Ffynnawn*) are included in the '13 Treasures of Britain' taken by Merlin to his Tŷ Gwydr, or House of Glass. Some sites of interest - Arthur's Stone, Dorstone. Nennius' 'Wonder of Britain', Llygad Amir. Llangors Lake, with crannogs and legends of the drowned city, Loventium. Tretower Court, Ystrad Yw in the *Mabinogion* tale *Culhwch and Olwen*. Moccas, site of a Palace, once the residence of Llacheu son of King Arthur, and site of the monastery of Saint Dubricius (Dyfrig), who crowned Arthur.'

## SAINT TUDFUL d.c.480?

## MARTYR

23 August was *Mabsant* Merthyr, when Tudful was feasted at Merthyr Tydfil, and 24 September was the 'Apple and Pear Fair' there, originally another of her feast days. This 23rd daughter of Brychan by his 4th wife was said to have been assassinated, with her brother Rhun, by a band of Saxons and Irish Picts. Rhun's son Nefydd put the warband to flight. Merthyr means shrine as well as place of martyrdom, so she may not have been martyred, however. Her holy well Ffynnon Dudful seems to have disappeared.

Llysworney Church in the Vale of Glamorgan is dedicated to this female saint, as was a chapel of Llanilltud Fawr until it was given to the Abbey of Tewkesbury. From William ab Ieuan ap Morgan of Llysworney came the Williams family of Llanishen, Cardiff, from whom Oliver Williams was descended. This Williams changed his surname as a young man to that of Cromwell, after Thomas Cromwell, his father's benefactor. Thus we have the only two successful insurrections by the British people since the Norman Conquest were headed by the Welshmen Henry Tudor and Oliver Cromwell. However, Llysworney seems to have been called Llysyronen at one time, and Tudful may not have been associated with it. It is more likely that St Dial's under Llanfihangel Llantarnam near Caerleon may have been Tudful's church, as it seems to be the place called Llandudful mentioned in the *Book of Llandaff.*

Brychan's many daughters (q.v.) were educated in the Christian tradition at Gwenddwr-on-Wye, and founded churches in Wales, Cornwall and Brittany, being known as *peregrini* or wandering evangelists. Tudful was said to be Brychan's 23rd daughter by his fourth wife, and set up her *llan* in the Taff Valley. The legend is that in his old age Brychan decided to visit his children one last time. He took with him his son Rhun (Rhain) Dremrudd, Rhun's son Nefydd, and Nefydd's own son, with servants and warriors. They visited his 3rd daughter Tangwstl at her llan at Hafod Tangwstl, now called Aberfan, just south of Tudful's community. Wishing to linger with his daughters, Brychan sent Nefydd and most of his warriors home to Garth Madrun (Talgarth), and went on to visit Tudful. Rhun and Nefydd's son stayed with Tangwstl.

The party was now spread out 7 miles apart, and vulnerable to pagan raiders. One legend tells us that the invaders were Scottish Picts who had settled in South Radnorshire, but they were more likely to have been a Saxon warband. It may be that the Gwyddel Fichti (Picts) had allied with a Saxon party. Rhun Dremrudd was attacked by the raiding party, a mile from Hafod Tangwstl, and died valiantly defending the bridge now known as Pont-y-Rhun, near where the village of Troedyrhiw now stands. The Saxons now split into two groups, one of which devastated the religious community at Hafod Tangwstl. The other chased after King Brychan, and caught up with him and his followers at Tudful's llan.

While others panicked and ran, Tudful knelt and prayed, and she was killed. The warband retreated but was caught by the avenging Nefydd and his men on 'Irishman's Hill' nearby. A Celtic Cross was erected in her llan's clearing near the River Taff, which became a meeting place for the people of the valley, and Merthyr Tydfil (Tudful) came into being. In the 13<sup>th</sup> century the cross and its wattle and daub church were replaced by a stone church dedicated to St Tydfil the Martyr, and the church was again rebuilt in 1807 and 1894. When the Norman church was demolished, a stone coffin was discovered, forming part of the foundations. Also, there were two stone pillars, one of which was dedicated to Brychan's son Arthen, who also died in the battle. He himself had founded the religious community of Llanarthen (now extinct), near Marshfield, between Cardiff and Newport.

Tudful's brother, the martyred Rhun Dremrudd (Red-Eyed) was lord over Eastern Brecon and was buried at Llandefaelog Fach outside

Brecon. He may have been Brychan's second son. His sons were Nefydd and Andras. He had a church at Mara, near Llangors Lake in Brecon. Nefydd Ail ap Rhun ap Brychan, father of St Nefydd and brother of St Andras, was himself feasted upon 8 September. He put to flight the Saxons who killed his father, and become a bishop in the North of Britain (Llechgelyddon?), where he was himself killed by Picts or Saxons. Llanefydd in Denbigh may be his, or his son's dedication, and it is now dedicated to the Virgin Mary, with her feast date of 8 September. Tradition says that it was called St Effydd's, but Edward Lhuyd in 1699 thought it was dedicated to St Ffrymden or St Frymder, as the locals referred to Bedd Frymder as the saint's grave in the churchyard. Ffynnon Ufyod here was used in the 17th century, where one could be cured of an illness by bathing upon three successive Fridays. It was reconstructed in 1604, but is now dilapidated.

The great Saturday market of Merthyr Tudful was lovingly described by the US consul, Wirt Sikes in 1881, and is notable for its description both of Welsh costume (including the old beaver-skin hats) and the 'spoon-food' tradition: 'But women reign at most of the stalls. Here is a brisk Welshwoman selling lace caps to a crowd of elderly Welsh dames, who gravely remove their bonnets, untie their old caps, and try on the new with religious care; and a lively trade drives the cap-seller, for here every woman wears a cap of lace or muslin under her bonnet or hat. There is a noticeable change, too, in the costumes of the market-women. The peasants of Wales, like those of most lands, cling less strenuously to their distinctive costume in these latter days than they were wont to do. Formerly a farmer's wife or daughter who should make her appearance at market or church (or on any like occasion which calls for the donning of one's best) without wearing a tall hat, would have been deemed careless of her personal appearance, or peculiar in her tastes; so that twenty years ago these were seen in every

**Saint Tudful commemorating her martyrdom**

direction in Merthyr market, as well as the distinctive long cloaks of bright colours, and the occasional scuttle-shaped bonnets. Nowadays this custom is so greatly relaxes that we see but few of these in Merthyr market. The head-coverings of the women are chiefly mushroom hats of dark straw, or close-fitting bonnets of black crepe, always with a lace or muslin cap underneath.

There are, however, some specimens still to be seen of the Welsh peasant costume as it has been for generations past; notably a comely young woman behind a vegetable stall, who wears the full costume in all its glory.

She is a pink of neatness, and her beaver is superb. I at once christen her the Pride of the Market, and if ever I go to live in Merthyr Tydfil, I shall buy my vegetable marrows off none but her. Her hat is prodigiously tall, and shines with a gloss that betokens careful brushing; it has a broad rim, and a peaked crown, and is adorned about the base of its chimney with a twist of some pinky stuff. Underneath it is seen a muslin cap of snowy whiteness, with blue ribbons, and the woman's hair is drawn back smoothly from her shining forehead. A short semi-coat of red flannel reaches to her knee, and over her shoulders is pinned a gay green kerchief, striped with yellow. A blue chequered apron hangs from her waist, and a dark stuff gown reaches to her ankles, clearing the ground by some inches, and showing her stout shoes tied with a bit of ribbon. All these stuffs were home-made, I judged. The hat looked as if it were new, just out of the shop, but she told me that she had had it some years. Such a hat will last the wearer a life-time, with care, but it is likely to grow wrinkly at its peak as the burden of years grows heavy on it. Later in the day, while rambling about in the neighbourhood of Merthyr, I came upon two elderly dames before a cottage door; whose hats were as old as themselves, to all appearance; one of the beavers indeed awakened the suspicion that it had been sat on in some dark hour of its existence…

At a stall near the great entrance a buxom Welsh dame in the forties presided over a display of eatables. In pursuit at once of information, experience, and luncheon, I sat on the wooden settle behind the bench on which the viands were spread, and surveyed the board. A bouquet of flowers in a pot-bellied white pitcher, with blue rings around it, stood surrounded by pies and tarts of various sorts; a huge rice pudding in a deep dish, a bowl of eggs, square cuts of German-looking pastry, and certain round boulders of black plum pudding. A pile of what I took to be sausages were steaming furiously over a brazier of burning coals on one end of the bench, with a teapot leaning lazily against it and thinking aloud. Choosing what seemed to be the least formidable specimen of the food before me, I pointed to the brazier and sad, but in a tone so low I was not heard, "I will take a sausage." Obeying my gesture, the woman served me a saucer-full of the black balls, swimming in hot gravy, and gave me a pewter spoon with which to eat it, instead of the knife and fork which might have been expected with meat. The balls proved to be not unpalatable eating, and were, according to my best judgement, made of liver. What they were actually made of, however, is a question upon which I subsequently learned to entertain doubts; they are a savoury compound locally called "faggits" or fagots. (Query, fag-ends?)

My hostess addressed me in the Welsh language this question: "Will you have some bread?" This being the first Welsh I had heard spoken out of doors in Wales afforded me profound satisfaction; and thinking perhaps my hostess could not speak English, I made bold to ask for *cwrw da*, which means good ale. She had no ale, but proceeded to mention other beverages with Welsh names to an extent that threw me into a perspiration. I concluded that I would conduct the remainder of the conversation in English, if possible. The good woman knew English well enough, it appeared, but uttered it in a fashion I could hardly understand better than her Welsh; she recommended me, for instance, to have a bottle of "pup" which I should certainly have never taken to mean ginger-pop, had I not gathered the fact from her showing a bottle. I took a cup of tea. In my cup was a curious little spoon of brass, worn thin like the old silver teaspoons which come down to us from our grand-mothers, and stamped on its handle with a sheaf of wheat. Concluding my feast with rice pudding, what was my surprise at seeing the woman cut it from the dish with a knife, serve it on a plate instead of a saucer, and give me with it an iron-pronged fork instead of a spoon? A fork to eat rice-pudding; a spoon to eat liver balls? Why this revolution in one's notions respecting table-ware? I asked myself. It was not due to any carelessness or poverty of outfit; the woman was scrupulously attentive of my comfort, and had an abundance of utensils. The luncheon cost me sixpence, and was very filling at the price.

At the adjoining stall I saw several glasses standing on a neat slab, containing drinkables, some of which were white, and some bright red. Inferring that the white liquid was "pup", and the red lemonade (such as the Germans sell, colouring it with some harmless essence), I put a glass of the red liquid to my lips. It tasted like some nasty medicinal draught; I set it down again, but drew my purse; whereupon the girl in attendance plumped a teaspoonful of white powder (more medicine, thought I) into the red liquid, causing it to fizz and bubble in a surprising manner. Price a ha'p'ny. I did not drink it; it seemed too eccentric in its habits. Subsequent better acquaintance again enlightened me regarding this beverage, which is a favourite of the poorer classes at fairs and the like.'

There is a wonderful verse in *Gwalia Deserta* by Idris Davies that describes Merthyr Tydful after the ravages of industrialisation:

'Ride you into Merthyr Tydfil
Where the fountains have run dry,
And gaze upon the sands of fortune
But pray not to the sky.

If you will to Merthyr Tydfil,
Ride unarmed of dreams;
No manna falls on Merthyr Tydfil,
And there flow no streams.

Pints of pity give no healing,
Eyes go blind that will not see,
Ride you into Merthyr Tydfil
With salt of charity.'

# DWYNWEN d.c.460

## PATRON SAINT OF LOVERS, WALES' VALENTINE

She is also known as Dwyn, Donwenna, Dunwen and Donwen, and her Feast Date is 25 January, which has become the Welsh equivalent of Valentine's Day. Said to be the youngest daughter of Brychan Brycheiniog, King of Brecon, this virgin moved to Anglesey and her name is commemorated at Llanddwyn and Porthddwyn. A young man called Maelon Dafodrill wished to marry her, but she refused him and prayed for deliverance. She then dreamed that a drink cured her of her longings and turned Maelon to ice. Dwynwen thus prayed for three things: that Maelon was unfrozen; that all true lovers should succeed in

**Saint Dwynwen's priory and holy well can be found on Llanddwyn Island**

their quest for love, or be cured of their passion, and that she should never wish to become married. She then became a nun. Her church was a focal point for young men and women, and for the sick.

St Dwynwen built an oratory and hermitage in the sixth century. Another legend is that this was after she had been turned down in love. Dafydd ap Gwilym called her 'holy Dwynwen, goddess of love, daughter of Brychan'. The ruins of 'St Dwynwen's Abbey', on Llanddwyn Island, are cut off at high tide from Malltraeth Bay in Snowdonia. A rock shaped like a bed on the island is known as *Gwely Esyth*, and those who slept on it would be cured of rheumatism, if they carved their names on the surrounding turf when they awoke. Another boulder on the cliff edge has a strange 'spy-hole' in it, which opened for the dying Dwynwen to finally look at the magnificent sunset over the Irish Sea.

St Dwynwen's Well on Llanddwyn Island (unfortunately since renamed Ffynnon Fair, Mary's Well) had a sacred eel. Pilgrims to it sprinkled breadcrumbs on the surface of the water, and covered them with a piece of cloth. If the eel took the cloth as well as the crumbs, the pilgrim's loved one was unfaithful. Another version is that if bubbles appeared during the 'ceremonies', lovers would find happiness. Because of the fame of the well, Llanddwyn became rich. Ffynnon Ddwynwen was also known as Crochan Llanddwyn (Llanddwyn's Cauldron), but it was mainly destroyed by Calvinistic Nonconformists in the 19th century. There was a custom of invoking Dwynwen to cure sick animals, which also lasted until the 19th century, probably because Llanddwyn (near Newborough) was formerly a fairly remote island. There was also a Ffynnon Dafaden holy well on the headland near her church.

In 'The Sayings of the Wise' there are the lines:

'Hast thou heard the saying of St Dwynwen,
The fair daughter of Brychan the Aged
"There is none so loveable as the cheerful"'
Dafydd ap Gwilym wrote a famous cywyd that he read to her image, asking her to take the message to his beloved Morfudd:
'Dwynwen, beautiful as tears of frost,
In your candle-lit choir
Your golden statue knows well
How to soothe the pain and
Torment of sad men.
He who keeps watch in radiant holiness
In your choir, shining Indeg,
Can never depart from Llanddwyn
With love-sickness nor a troubled mind.'

Thomas Pennant, in his 1778 *A Tour in Wales*, noted: 'I soon reached Newborough (or more properly Rhosfair, the Welsh name) about three miles from the shore. Here had been one of the residences of our princes. In Mr Rowlands' time, the foundation of the Llys, or palace, was to be seen a little to the south of the church. Newborough now subsists by a manufacture of mats and *rhofir morhesg* ropes, made of sea reed-grass. Queen Elizabeth wisely prohibited the extirpation of this plant to prevent having half the parish buried in the unstable sands by the rage of the tempests. Such is the case with Llanddwyn, almost the whole is at present covered with sand-hills. In the reign of Henry VIII it was one of the richest prebends in the cathedral of Bangor. Its wealth arose not from the real fertility of the place but from the superstition of the common people: from pilgrimages to crosses, relics, holy wells, ordeals and divination from fishes. On the peninsular are the ruins of the church, dedicated to St Dwynwen, daughter of Brychan, one of the holy Colidei or primitive Christians of Britain. From Newborough, I several years ago made an excursion to Aberffro [Aberffraw], about 7 miles to the north, in search of another palace of our ancient princes. They took one of their titles from this place, Princeps de Aberffro, which preceded that of Dominus de Snowdon. I crossed at low water the arm of the sea called Malltraeth and rode by the church of Llangadwaladr, said to have been founded by Cadwaladr, last king of the Britons, and made one of the sanctuaries of the island...'

At Tresilian Cove in Glamorgan, where the notorious Breton pirate Colyn Dolphyn was buried up to his neck to face the incoming tide, is a huge fissure Ogof Dwynwen, known as the cave of Dwynwen. There is a natural archway in the cave, called her Bow of Destiny. Local people used to throw a stone to pass over the arch. If it took ten times to achieve this, it would be ten years before one married. If one was married, it would be ten years before one's partner died. Marriages were also celebrated in the cave. A scribbled note by John Prosser of St Tathan was that Colyn Dolphyn's cries could be heard 'especially on the nights of the February full moon. However, Tresilian Bay has also been the scene of more pleasant happenings. In her book *Land of My Fathers* Miss Edith Picton-Turberville asserts that the parents of her famous ancestor, General Thomas Picton (see this author's *The 100 Greatest Welshmen*), were actually married in Tresilian Caves. The bridal couple were Miss Cecil Powell of Llandow and Thomas Picton of Poyston.'

*Footnote:*
Be careful if visiting Ynys Llanddwyn, as visitors to her holy well and chapel may be cut off by the tide. The breakwater connecting the island to Anglesey has slowly disintegrated, so that the tide forms a deep channel, which cannot be forded for up to six hours at high tide. Swimming is not recommended - the currents around islands such as Llanddwyn and Sully are among the most vicious in Britain, and can carry away the very best swimmers.

## SAINT ALMEDHA 5th-6th century

## ELINUD, A DAUGHTER OF BRYCHAN

Said to be born around 468, and also known as Eiliwedd, Elined, Elinud, Aled, Alud, Ailed, Elud, Elyned, Aluned and Lludd, her feast day is 1 August in Brecon (12 August Old Style). She was also celebrated on 9 October, and upon 17 March in Cornwall. Giraldus Cambrensis states that Almedha, a daughter of Brychan*, was martyred by Saxons on a hill named Penginger near Brecon, and he noted her 'basilica' on the hill a mile east of Brecon. Slwch, where there used to be an Iron Age hill-fort, was identified as the site in Jones's *Brecknockshire*. The stone where she died was near a mound at Pencefngaer**, a mile east of Brecon, near Slwch Farm. The place was also called Crug Gorseddawl ('the hill of judgment'). Almedha's holy well is named Penginger Well by Francis Jones, who states that she was buried at Usk. Cressy states 'This devout virgin, rejecting the proposals of an earthly prince, who sought her in marriage, and espousing herself to the eternal king, consummated her life by a triumphant martyrdom. The day of her solemnity is celebrated every year on the first day of August.'

Llaneleu, under Llangattock Crickhowel in Brecon, is attributed to Almedha/Elinud rather than Ellyw or Elli. In the Middle Ages Llaneleu Church was associated with the Austin Canons of Llantony Abbey, but is now unfortunately no longer used for services. Two 7$^{th}$-century pillar stones stand outside the porch, indicating the antiquity of this beautiful site at the foot of the Black Mountains. The very remoteness of the church ensured that its roodscreen was spared the excesses of Cromwell's followers.

**Saint Almedha's Well at Llanddew is now named Bishop Gower's Well after rebuilding**

The *Harleian MS.* related her legend that a prince wanted to marry her, but she fled to Llanddew where she was badly treated, then moved to nearby Llanfillo where she was treated as a common thief because of her ragged clothes, then to Llechfaen where she was made to sleep in the road ever since called Heol Sant Alud. Her holy well is now overgrown, and the chapel has vanished, but there is a field in Llanhamlach called Clos Sant Ailed.

Giraldus Cambrensis noted the roofless condition of her Brecon chapel in the 12$^{th}$ century, but noted that her festival dance was still held there. The men and women came from far away for 1 August, and formed a circle around the churchyard, singing as they danced. 'Then on a sudden falling on the ground in a fit, then jumping up in a frenzy, and representing with their hands and feet before the people whatever work they have unlawfully done on feast days'. Some mimed cobbling, tanning, spinning, weaving or even ploughing with oxen. It was the community demonstrating that they worked for the communal welfare, but also that all such work should only be done at the appropriate times and season. 1 August was also the start of the season of Lammas, held in honour of the Celtic God, Lug. This day was always associated with the making of corn dollies in Wales

According to Cressy, Almedha had lived at Ruthin, a tiny hamlet in the Vale of Glamorgan, not the North Wales town, before her martyrdom. Her sister Tudful (q.v.) and her brother Cynog*** were also slain by the pagan Saxons and became saints. She is also remembered as 'Luned' in the *Mabinogion*, and she is the 'Lynette' of Tennyson's *Gareth and Lynette*. She seems also to be identical with 'Enid' of the *Mabinogion* and of Tennyson's *Idylls of the King*.

* The descendants of Brychan Brycheiniog, king of Brecon in the 5th-6th century, who spread the gospel across Wales and the West Country, were known as 'the daughters of Brychan', and in old texts, Almedha is his 23$^{rd}$ daughter.

** Pen Cefn y Gaer (the summit of the ridge of the camp) was transmuted over time to Pencefngaer and Penginger - the remains of a British camp can still be seen there. Near this ancient camp was her monastery, where Llywelyn Pritchard noted its remains and an ancient yew tree in 1854, near the farmhouse known as Slwch. Owen Pugh believed that another church in Mold in Flintshire had also been dedicated to her.

*** Her brother Abbot Cynog, also known as Saint Canoc, or Cynawg Ferthyr, died around 492. He was feasted upon 7-11 October, also later in that month, and also on 11 February, and upon 24 January in Padstow. One of Brychan's sons by Banhadlwedd, and a claimant to be the eldest, he was celebrated at Defynog, Ystradgynlais and Penderyn in Brecon and Llangynog in Montgomery. Battle Chapel and Llangynog under Llanganten were also his chapels. Just south of Battle Church is a twelve foot menhir on a small tumulus. There are two Llangunnocks, in Hereford and Monmouthshire, also associated with him. He was supposed to have been murdered by Saxons or Irish Picts upon Van mountain (Y Fan Oleu) in Brecon, in the parish of Merthyr Cynog, where the church of Merthyr (the Martyr) was built over his grave. However, it is more likely that he was killed in a skirmish between Brychan's Irish tribe and other local chieftains, after which many of the family of Brychan fled to Cornwall. His name is seen on a 7th-century inscribed stone near Tremadoc, as *CUNACI*.

Giraldus Cambrensis described the armlet that Brychan gave to Cynog: 'I must not be silent concerning the collar which they call St Canauc's; for it is most like to gold in weight, nature and colour; it is in four pieces wrought round, joined together artificially, and clefted as it were in the middle, with a dog's head, the teeth projecting. It is considered by the inhabitants so powerful a relic, that no man ventures to swear falsely upon it when laid before him. It bears the marks of heavy blows, as if made by an iron hammer; for a certain man, it is said, endeavouring to break the torque for the sake of he gold, experienced divine vengeance, was deprived of his eyesight, and lingered out the rest of his days in darkness.'

At Defynnog, his *Gŵyl Mabsant* was commemorated at the time of Cynog's Ffair a Bwla on the second Thurday in October. At this fair, purchases were made for his wake, on the following Sunday. The wake lasted a week, with feasting and celebrations taking place in front of the Bull Inn. The custom only finished in 1835, except for several decades after there was a goose fair on the Sunday. On the Monday, *Dydd Llun Gŵyl Gynog*, there was a custom of 'carrying Cynog' where a stranger or local volunteer was dressed in a suit of old clothes, carried through the village, and thrown into the river. He was jeered at by the crowd as he tried to clamber out. The last record was of a drunken farmer being carried in 1822. On Tuesday, a tithe was taken of cheese, which was brought to the churchyard, displayed on the gravestones, and sold for the benefit of the church. Defynnog has a tall Celtic pillar-cross with Latin and Ogham inscriptions which are now illegible.

# SAINT CAIN 5<sup>th</sup>-6<sup>th</sup> century

## A DAUGHTER OF BRYCHAN, KENYA THE VIRGIN

Also known as Keyne, Cenue, Cenai, Keina and Kenya, her Feast Date is 8 October and also its eve, 7 October. This beautiful hermit went to Cornwall where she met her nephew Cadog at Mount St Michael. He asked her to return to Wales, where she died. At St Keyne's Well in Cornwall, the tradition was that the first to drink the water after marriage will attain mastery over the other partner. One man left his bride on the church porch to drink the water first, whereupon she outwitted him by quickly producing and drinking a bottle that she had hidden under her wedding dress. This well, near Liskeard, was so famous that it inspired Robert Southey to write:

'I hastened as soon as the wedding was o'er
And I left my good wife in the porch,
But i'faith she had been wiser than I
For she took a bottle to church'

Near this well are the foundations of her brothers, Clether, Cynog and Cynin. The same powers of spouse dominance were said to be bestowed by Keyne on the stone seat in the castle at St Michael's Mount.

Associated with South Wales and Herefordshire, Cain was supposed to have been an itinerant evangelist, who moved between Brecon and St Michael's Mount. Llangeneu (Llangenny) in Brecon is ascribed to Ceneu, the daughter or grand-daughter of Brychan, but others place it earlier with Ceneu ap Coel (Cenedlon). Her feast day is the same as that of her sister Ceinwen. Cressy recorded that 'when she came to ripe years, many nobles sought her in marriage, but she utterly refused that state; having consecrated her virginity to our Lord by a perpetual vow; for which cause she was afterwards by the Britons called Keyn wiri (Cein-wyryf), that is Keyna the virgin: at length she determined to forsake her country and find out some desert place, where she might attend to contemplation. Therefore directing her journey beyond the Severn, and there meeting a woody place, she made her request to the prince of that country, that she might be permitted to serve God in that solitude. His answer was, that he was very willing to grant her request, but that the place did so swarm with serpents that neither man nor beast could inhabit it: but she constantly replied, that her firm trust was in the name and assistance of Almighty God to drive out all that poisonous brood out of the region. Hereupon the place was granted to the holy virgin, who presently prostrating herself to God obtained of him to change the vipers and serpents into stones; and to this day, the stones in that region do resemble the windings of serpents through all the fields and villages, as if they had been framed so by the hand of the engraver.'

The religious community at Keynsham on the Avon near Bristol was said by Camden to be founded by Cain, on account of the number of 'snakes', ammonite fossils found there which she destroyed. However, the name comes from 'Caega's Hamlet', although its church was dedicated to Keyne before St John.

Near Abergavenny, Ysgyrid Fawr is also known as The Skirrid, The Holy Mountain or St Michael's Mount. At its tops are the remains of the pilgrimage centre of St. Michael's Chapel. Cain's nephew St. Cadog ap Gwynlliw made a pilgrimage to the Mount of St Michael where he met

**St. Cain's Well, at St. Keyne, near Liskeard**

Ceneu, but the local inhabitants wanted her to stay in the region. However, she later returned to her birthplace in Breconshire where she built an oratory on the top of a mountain and prayed to God who provided a spring there. Last century the traces of her oratory and holy well Ffynnon Geneu (St Geney's Well) could still be seen near the church of Llangeneu in Brecon, a chapel under Cadog's foundation at Llangattock Crickhowel. The well water cured sore eyes, and the first of a newly-married couple to drink its waters would be 'dominant' in the marriage, exactly the same tradition as in her Liskeard foundation. When her oratory was demolished around 1790 a farmer found an iron bell, a 'bangu' used by Celtic saints to call worshippers.

At Llangeneu, Golden Grove Standing Stone is between Druid's Altar and the Dragon's Head public house. Nearby is 'The Growing Stone', almost 14 feet high, surrounded by oak trees. Kentchurch in Hereford was formerly called Llangain, then Keynechurch, and its priest was the famous Welsh 'magician' and cleric Sion Cent. He was said to be buried half-in and half-out of his church. Llangeinor* in Mid-Glamorgan is also associated with Cain. Its original name, Llan Gain Wyryf, means the Church of Cain the Virgin. St Kenya's Church, Runston, is in the care of CADW and is freely accessible near Chepstow. The ruined church is in the centre of a deserted village of twenty-two houses, and the site of a medieval manor house can be made out. At Cilcain (Holy Retreat of Cain) in Clwyd, in Penbedw Park, there still stands a Neolithic stone circle with five stones, in an oak copse.

Traditionally, Cain was buried in her own oratory, by her nephew Cadoc (see *The Book of Welsh Saints*). She had shortly before been visited by angels, and she prophesised to Cadoc: 'this is a place above all others, beloved by me; here my memory shall be perpetuated: this place I will often visit in spirit, if it may be permitted me - because our Lord hath granted me this place as a certain inheritance. The time will come when this place shall be inhabited by a sinful people which, notwithstanding, I will violently root out of this seat. My tomb shall lie a long time unknown, until the coming of other people, whom by my prayers I shall bring hither; them I will protect and defend, and in this place shall the name of the Lord be blessed for ever.' Llywelyn Prichard added his comments in 1854: 'These good strangers are not yet arrived, nor has the tomb of the saint been discovered; but we must have patience - who knows what time may bring to pass?'

* There may have been a saint named Ceinor. There is a Ffynnon Geinor holy well noted at Pontsian near Llandysul in Cardigan, and Ceinor was once a popular female name in that county. The once popular name Gaynor probably stems from this saint.

## SAINT NON 5th – 6th century

## SAINT DAVID'S MOTHER

Also known as Nonna, Nonnita and as Melaria in Brittany, her Feast Day was the day after her son David's, on 2 March. 3 and 5 Marchand were also her days in Wales, with 15 June at Altarnon and Tavistock, and 3 July at Launceston (formerly Lansteffan) in Cornwall. Some sources say that she was a noblewoman, the daughter of Gynyr (Cynyr) of Caer Gawch and his wife Anna ferch Gwrthefyr Fendigaid. Rhygyfarch's *Life of David* states that Non was a nun at Tŷ Gwyn monastery at Maucan, near Whitesand Bay in Pembrokeshire, who was seduced or raped by Prince Sant (Sandde) and gave birth to St David.

Sant ap Ceredig ap Cunedda was the former king of Ceredigion who had possibly become a monk. Other records state that she and Sant were married, but he was never sanctified, so the former story may be true. Non seems to have the attributes of the Celtic goddess Anna, Nonna or Dana, mother of the gods and ancestress of Celtic nobility. In the Northern Tradition, she is Nanna, mother of the slain god Balder, and in the Roman deology she is Annona, goddess of the Harvest. This ancient Celtic goddess became St Anne, the mother of Our Lady and the grandmother of Jesus, after the conversion to Christianity. The cult of St Anne is still strong in British-speaking Brittany.

Gildas was said to have lost the power of speech, being overwhelmed with the presence of the unborn baby David. Non left the monastic school when pregnant, to live among standing stones on the cliffs behind Bryn y Garn. The birth was accompanied by thunder and lightning, and the stone upon which she lay was split apart by the force of the birth, leaving the imprint of her hands on it. Part of the stone was later used as the altar slab in her chapel. St Non's Chapel is on the coast of St Bride's Bay, and is said to be where she gave birth to St David. A slab with a ring cross in the ruins has been dated from 600-800. David was supposed to have been born dead, but the bishop St Ailbe (Eilfyw, Elvis) resuscitated him and fostered him. St Ailbe then christened him at St Elvis holy well next to his llan at St Elvis Farm, between St David's and Solva.

St Non's Well* near her chapel, sprang from the ground during St David's birth, and the holy waters were said to cure rheumatism, eye illnesses and headaches. George Owen wrote during the reign of Elizabeth I that every St Non's Day people offered pins, stones and the like to the well. In 1811 Fenton wrote 'the fame this consecrated spring had obtained is incredible, and still it is resorted to for many complaints. In my infancy... I was often dipped into it, and offerings, however trifling, even of a farthing or a pin, were made after each ablution, and the bottom of the well shone with votive brass. The spring... is of a most excellent quality, is reported to ebb and flow, and to be of wondrous efficacy in complaints of the eye.' To cure a lunatic, he had to be persuaded to stand upon the well wall, and then be knocked down into the water. He was then tossed up and down in the

Saint Non's Well near St. David's Cathedral, said to have sprung forth in a thunderstorm when David was born

water until his strength was sapped, a procedure known as 'bowsenning'. The madman was then taken to the nearby church for mass. If he was not cured, the bowsenning was repeated, and so on. The well was restored by the Roman Catholic Church in 1951, re-dedicated and a pilgrimage made to it.

It appears that Non became a nun after the death of Sant, and moved to Altarnon in Cornwall around 527 at the request of her sister St Gwen, where there is also a chapel and well named after her. There is a Celtic cross of this period by the churchyard gate. The insane were also 'precipitated' into this Altarnon well to cure them. There are also dedications in Pelynt in Cornwall and Bradstone in Devon. Llannerch Aeron and Llansanffraid on Cardigan Bay are dedicated to Non, with the latter formerly being known as Llan Non. There is also a Llan-Non in both Carmarthen and Radnorshire. Carmarthen's Llannon has a fifteen feet high pillar stone known as Bryn Maen, and a holy well, Ffynnon Non, where the saint drew water. At Ilston in Gower and Eglwys Newydd near Margam Abbey in Glamorgan are two more dedications.

Her tomb survives in Dirinon in Finistère, and her statue is in a niche behind her holy well there. A mystery play, *Buhez Santes Nonn* was performed for centuries at Non's *pardon* in Dirinon. A *pardon* is a Breton pilgrimage, one of the most traditional demonstrations of popular Catholicism in that Celtic nation. It probably dates back to the conversion of the country by British monks, and occurs on the feast of the local Breton patron saint, at which an indulgence is granted, hence the use of the word *pardon*.

Within a mile of Dirinon are holy wells dedicated to both David and Non. In Brittany Nonna is regarded as a male companion of St David, rather than his mother. She came to be regarded as the mother of the church in Wales, and as a peace-maker and healer is attributed to have said that 'There is nothing more stupid than argument.' A 1717 *Survey of St David's* recorded that for the first three days of March, dedicated to David, Non and Lily 'if any of the people had been known to work upon any of these Days, it would have been esteemed a very heinous Offence.'

* St Non's Chapel and Holy Well can still be seen, idyllically sited above St Non's Bay, along the coastal footpath from St David's Cathedral. The earliest reference to the chapel is in 1335, but early Christian stone coffins and a 7th century pillar-cross were found there. Aligned north-south, like many of the oldest foundations, the chapel traditionally marks the spot where Non gave birth to David. In medieval times, two pilgrimages to St David's were accounted as the equivalent of one to Rome, and pilgrims to the chapel gave money, which was then taken to the Cathedral. The chapel lost its pilgrims after the Reformation, and became a house, then a vegetable garden. The Holy Well, just east of the chapel, was famous for healing until long after the Reformation, and in the 18th century a stone vault was built over it, probably replacing a previous well-building.


## SAINT GWLADYS 6th century

## QUEEN CLAUDIA OF GWYNLLIWG

Also referred to as Gwladus or Gwlawys, her feast date is 29 March, the same as her husband's. She was raised at King Brychan's court at Garthmadrun (Talgarth). A beautiful young woman, she soon came to the notice of Brychan's southern neighbour, King Gwynlliw* of Gwynlliwg (roughly Glamorgan and Monmouthshire). There is a legend that she wished to marry Einion Gam (Einion the Lame). The beautiful Scwd Einion Gam waterfall in the Vale of Neath is named after him, as it follows a crooked path as it crashes 70 feet down the rocks. Gwynlliw sent envoys to Brychan requesting the hand of his daughter (or grand-daughter), but Brychan did not want a barbarian to marry her, and sent them away. Gwynlliw then decided to take her by force, and made a raid with 300 men into Breconshire (Brycheiniog) to seize the princess. Brychan caught up with the war-band at Fochriw and demanded the return of Gwladys. The High-King, Arthur, was said to have raced to the battle to mediate and was himself struck by the beauty of Gwladys, and wanted her for himself. Two of his knights had rescued her from the skirmish. However, his advisors eventually talked him around to support King Gwynlliw's cause, and Brychan agreed to the dynastic marriage.

**Gwladys and Gwynlliw, the parents of St. Cadoc, remembered at St Cado's, Bretagne**

The Christian Gwladys and King Gwynlliw Filwr (the Warrior) married and she gave birth to the saints Cadog, Eigion, Cyfyw, Maches and Glywys. Cadog had been raised a Christian at Caerwent by St Tathan at his mother's insistence. She and her pagan husband lived on Newport's Stow Hill (where there was an Iron Age camp), until persuaded to separate by Cadog when he converted Gwynlliw to Christianity. Gwladys then moved as a hermit to Pencannau (Pencarn) near Bassaleg. A mound near Rock Cottages is said to be her grave, as is Capel Glwadys (Wladus) at Gelligaer. The ruined Capel Gwladys is now hardly visible, but there was a Celtic Cross found there (now in Gelligaer parish church) and it is surrounded by Roman training camps.

In Tredegar House Park**, Newport, the ancestral home of the Morgans, is her holy spring, where she used to bathe naked with Gwynlliw. Now known as Lady's Well (a modern corruption of Gwladys Well), it had a bath-house erected over it in 1719. A rock on the nearby Ebbw River probably had her chapel on it, as it was known as 'The Chapel' until recently. Ffynnon Wladus is a holy well in Llangynllo parish, Cardigan, and there was also another St Gwladus martyred near Aberffraw on Anglesey.

* Gwladys' husband, Gwynlliw Filwr, was also known as Gwynlliw Farfog (the bearded), and the Latinised versions were Gundleus or Gunleus. He was prince of Gwynlliwg (Wentloog) and son of Glywys ap Tegid ap Cadell. His mother was said to be Gwawr (Gwal) ferch Ceredig ap Cunedda. As the eldest of seven sons, he was acknowledged the superior over the territories passed by *cyfran* (gavelkind) to his brothers, so was acknowledged as King of Glamorgan and Gwent*. He and Gwladys ferch Brychan are the only married couple to share a feast day. The legend is that he took Gwladys by force from the Court of Brychan and Arthur (who also wanted Gwladys) was asked to mediate at

Fochrhiw. Arthur wanted her for himself. Gwynlliw is also linked with St Tathan, whose cow he stole at Caerwent. The father of the great Welsh saint Catwg, or Cadog, Gwynlliw has his own *Life* and is also mentioned in the *Life of Cadog*. He was known as the 'Prince of the Southern Britons.'

According to the *Life of Cadoc*, Cadoc's behaviour brings about Gwynlliw's conversion, but in Gwynlliw's *Vita*, he is a respected man who is converted by an angel, and leaves his wife to pursue a religious life. He was visited on his death bed by St Dyfrig. St Woolos is the Anglicisation of St. Gwynlliw's Cathedral, which stands on the remains of a Celtic camp on Stow Hill, overlooking Newport. This may well have been the site of Gwynlliw's court. It is said that Gwynlliw saw a white ox on the top of the hill, and built his cell there. There is a 'protection curse' on the site which says anyone who desecrates the church (cathedral) will die. A field on Stow Hill had a moated mound on it, known as Bedd Gwynlliw, but this was probably not his grave but his fort. He was buried by his son Cadog at St Woolos, and the district of Pillgwenlli in Newport means Gwynlliw's Creek.

**Saint Gwladys ferch Brychan**

Apart from Cadog, the sons of Gwynlliw and Gwladys seem to have included the saints Cammarch, Glywys Cerniw, Bugi, Cyfyw, Cynfyw, Gwyddlew, Cyflewyr, Cammab, and Maches. Bugi's son was St Beuno and Gwyddlew's son was Cannen. The son of Glywys Cerniw was Gwodloew. However, older sources give as sons of Gwynlliw only Cadog, Bugi and Cemmeu (Cynfyw). Pedrog, who became a Cornish saint, was either a brother or nephew of Gwynlliw. Gwynlliw's 'Saying of the Wise' is: 'Hast thou heard the saying of Gwynlliw, / In mutual acrimony? / "It avails not to reason with a madman".'

Lands at this time were said to be apportioned almost on a Roman pattern of each district under a *regulus*. It appears rather than be sucked into fratricidal wars for territories, the seven sons of Gwladys power-shared on the following basis. Gwynlliw was in charge of the area Gwynlliwg, (named after him and later adulterated to Wentloog), the district between the Usk (Newport) and Rhymni (Cardiff) rivers. His brother Etelic took the eastern lands of Monmouthshire, and the famous Paul Penychen ruled the Vale of Glamorgan from a base at Penllyn or Pentremeurig. North of Gwynlliwg and Paul, Seru held the lordship of Senghenydd (which later passed down to the famous Welsh hero Ifor Bach). Travelling west across Glamorgan from Paul, Mar had Margam, Guria ruled the Neath area, Cetti took Cydweli and Cornouguill ruled the rest of Carmarthenshire.

\*\* In Tredegar Park is a statue dedicated to Sir Briggs, a truly remarkable horse that carried Captain Godfrey Morgan, later Viscount Lord Tredegar, to victory at the principal race on Cowbridge race-course at Penllyn Castle. Thousands from all over South Wales attended. This partnership also took part in cavalry charges in the Crimean War at the battles of Inkerman and The Alma. It possibly goes without saying that the pair returned from the first line of the Light Cavalry Charge at the battle of Balaclava also. If any horse deserved a fitting resting place from a grateful owner, it was this celebrated charger. Sir Briggs died in 1874, aged 28 years.


## SAINT TATHANA 6<sup>th</sup> century

## PRINCESS BRAUST


In some local histories of the Vale of Glamorgan, Tathana is posited as the founder of St Tathan (now Anglicised to St. Athan, and previously called Llandathan), not Tathan. The author fortunately came across *The Welsh Outlook*, November 1924, which gives the legend of the female saint, in an

article by Augusta F. Jenkins, wife of the vicar of St. Athan. An intriguing part of the legend places the court of Meurig ap Tewdrig at 'Treberfaidd' (Boverton, wrongly named Trebeferad in recent years. The meaning seems be 'sparkling', 'perfect' or 'beaver' town). As local legends and Breton writings constantly place Boverton as the birthplace of Arthur, and Athrwys ap Meurig ap Tewdrig was the

**Saint Tathana's Grade One listed church, founded by St Tathana**

real Arthur of history, perhaps the ruins of Boverton Castle should attract tourism into the area. There is a 'World of Camelot' in the west of England, but while Dumnonia (Devon, Somerset and Cornwall) was a subject princedom under Arthur, Boverton in the Vale of Glamorgan seems to have been his home. Penllin, just five miles north, was the palace of Pawl Penychen, prince of Glamorgan, and Llanilltud Fawr is just a mile away from Boverton. St Illtud was one of Arthur's knights. Half a mile from Penllin is Pentre Meurig (Chief Town of Meurig).

According to Jenkins, when Arthur's father Meurig was dying in Boverton, his sons and daughters gathered around him, including his daughter Anna, and her children St. Samson and Princess Braust. Braust, because of her kinship with Illtud the Knight (Illtud Farchog) had been dedicated to the Lord, and was destined to rule as abbess at Amesbury.

However, Meurig feared for her safety, and his dying wish was that she was sent for protection to her great-grandfather Gwgan, who ruled the West Country from his court at Bath. She sailed from the old port of Aberddawen (Aberthaw) to Caer Brito (Bristol), then travelled the Roman road to Bath. At Gwgan's court, she fell in love with a pagan Irish slave, Diarmait, cup-bearer to Gwgan. Gwgan was seeking a peace between the invading Saxons from the east, to deal with the Irish threat from the west, and accordingly arranged for Braust to marry a Saxon prince. The wedding turned into a riot as the Irish slaves, led by Diarmait, revolted and Diairmait escaped in the confusion with Braust. However, Diarmait soon abandoned his now-pregnant wife, and returned to Ireland, leaving only a bronze armlet. Braust named their child Conan, and noticed a strange mark on his shoulder which Diarmait also had possessed. Diarmait had told her was the sign of kingship.

After many adventures, Braust and Conan returned to Britain and crossed the Severn (Hafren) to Caerwent (Bangor Tathan), staying near Tathan's tomb. Tathan appeared to her in a vision that night, telling Braust to live a holy life, succouring the poor and pilgrims. On her journey the Archbishop at Caerleon also blessed her, and she followed the Via Julia Maritima from Caerwent. Braust turned south at Cowbridge (Bovium) to pass through Llanfeithyn and Llandathan, both dedicated to St. Tathan, tutor of the great St Cadog.

Following the coastal road west, Braust thus returned to Boverton (Treberfaidd), where she was met by her uncle Prince Ffrioc, Arthur's brother. Ffrioc granted her the villa of Eurgain in Llanilltud Fawr (Eurgain ferch Caradog q.v., had built a villa in the Roman style, which is possibly that at Caer Mead, excavated over a century ago, with Christian burials there). This is marked as Caer Worgan on all old maps, and only seems to have been renamed Caer Mead in the 19th century. Braust stayed here for 16 years helping the poor and weak, and was now called Tathana in honour of her vision of Tathan, while her son grew up into a lawless man. He told his story to the Irish slaves at Llanilltud's great abbey, and he stole the keys to the great gate to allow Irish pirates to sack and pillage Llanilltud Fawr. He cut off his mother's hands to take her rings and bracelets before escaping with the pirates to Ireland. Her villa burnt, Tathana's slaves built her a hut of mud and reeds at Pont Newydd, where there was a well of pure water. This is near where the ruined East Orchard Castle Mill stands on the River Thaw on the Barry-Llanilltud road today. The sea used to come up to this point.

To truncate the story, Conan killed his father Diarmait, who had become king, in trial by combat. They only found out each other's true identity as Diarmait lay dying. Famine struck Ireland, and Conan led a force that was repulsed by the men of Glwyssing (Glamorgan) at Aberddawen (Aberthaw). Conan's disillusioned pirates tied him to a stake near the tidal river Thaw, next to Tathana's hut, and left him to drown. His cries for help alerted Tathana, who took her coracle out to him. Conan asked her to take his dagger and cut his cords, and the water swirled around his waist, but then he saw that she only had stumps instead of arms. At the same time she saw that he was wearing Diarmait's bronze armlet and had his father's mark on his shoulder. Tathana forgave her son, and the wave that covered his face also overturned her coracle so that they died together. Her body was found on the Leys, and she was taken by villagers and buried in the church of Tathan 'which they called after her name from that day, but the village after the old abbot, as it is to this day. Thus was the sin washed out in tears and the waters of the Ddawen, which had begun in fire and blood at the burning of the Church of Bath.'

The author was looking for church remains in a Chapel Field, or Chapel Cross Field, where a chapel was marked on old maps, in April 2000. From East Orchard Castle I found a series of thick stepping slabs across the stream which flows from West Orchard castle through Rills Valley to join the River Thaw. They were of a different stone to that locally occurring. Our local limestone would dissolve and crack over time in such a wet situation. The chapel field was supposed to be the triangular field above the woods on Castleton Farm lands, with one edge overlooking Flemingston Moors and one edge along the Rills Valley. Not finding any traces, I cut down through the woods, finding a dead dog fox in a fork of a tree on the way, and half-way down saw a rectangular shape in the valley.

Made up of a mixture of dressed stone with traces of mortar, and rubble, the ground-level walls were aligned approximately 25 feet East to West, and 15 feet North to South. The Thaw meandered through the wide valley, and this building would have been close to the high tide level - could this have been the site of Tathana's 6th century church? The earth is still full of sea shells around the site. The site has been verified by the Glamorgan-Gwent Archaeological Trust as a previously unknown medieval chapel, just a mile from St Athan. In 1535, the church was referred to as Ecclesia Sancta Tathana, indicating that Braust or Tathana was the saint remembered, rather than Tathan. The church was then valued at £16-10-6d.

Nearby West Aberthaw Chapel is a mediaeval building, which was dedicated to St Nicholas, now a cattle shed and part of West Aberthaw Farm. Iolo Morgannwg noted it, along with the other ruined chapels at Castleton, West Orchard and East Orchard, but it was 'lost' for many years. It measures 21 feet in length and has an inserted upper floor, cutting across a large blocked window which used to illuminate the altar. Another blocked window can be seen in the south wall, above the small aumbry or piscina. (An aumbry is a mural recess, or a cupboard in which an icon or relic was kept. A piscina is a stone basin for washing sacramental vessels, usually located in the wall beside the altar.) This could have been a pre-Norman site, but earthworks in the adjacent field have been ploughed out. The nearby well could make it a Celtic Christian foundation, but the name of the founding saint may never be known. Perhaps, however, this is where

Tathana lived. West Aberthaw, with its farm buildings, earthworks and chapel, was once one of the most romantic places in Wales, prior to the building of the power station. Surface traces of two platform houses are visible of the deserted mediaeval village in West Aberthaw, and ancient stone wall foundations are still below the earth there. It seems that it was a Roman site, with the vestiges of vine terraces in the fields. It may be that the Via Julia Maritima actually passed along the coast from Cardiff to the Roman building at Cold Knap, Barry, to Caer Mead at Llanilltud Fawr. There was within living memory the vestiges of a road from Aberthaw harbour along the coast to Boverton, which adjoins Llanilltud Fawr. (The author's *The Secret Vale of Glamorgan* gives more details on the area described above).

## GUINEVERE 6th century

### ARTHUR'S QUEEN GWENHWYFAR

Just like her husband Arthur, Gwenhwyfar was lifted from British history and placed effortlessly into the greatest medieval legends of Europe. Her husband was Arthwys ap Meurig ap Tewdrig, based in south-east Wales, who spent most of his life, with his West Country and Breton allies, fighting the Saxon invasion from the east, the Irish invasions from the west, and finally against his own Welsh cousins from the north.

The Lady Guinevere by Howard Pyle, from "King Arthur and his Knights', 1903

A series of old *englynion* called *Ymddiddan Arthur a Gwenhwyfar* have been lost, and survive only in a more recent version. They link Cai (Sir Kay), Melwas and Gwenhwyfar, who was possibly the daughter of Ogrfran Gawr. They were composed, by their construction, prior to 1100, and the prose accompaniment seems to have been lost. We read that Gwenhwyfar speaks to Arthur after the battle of Camlan:

'Arthur son of Uther of the long sword
I will tell you now the sad truth
There is a master over every strong man'.
Arthur replies:
'Are you Gwenhwyfar? My little white lady?
I have never been healed of lovesickness for you.

Medrawd (Mordred) is dead. I am at death's door.
A surgeon has never seen a scar
When Caledfwlch (Excalibur) struck once.
I have struck Medrawd nine times.'

Gwenhwyfar is first named as Arthur's queen in the *Culhwch and Olwen* tale
from the *Mabinogion*, written down in the 11th century, but passed down
orally from the 6th century. Also, in Caradog of Llancarfan's *Life of Gildas*,
written in the 1120's or 1130's, we see that Melwas abducted Gwenhwyfar to
Glastonbury and imprisoned her for a year: 'Ynys Wydrin [The Isle of
Glass]...was besieged by the tyrant Arthur with an innumerable host because
of his wife Gwenhwyfar, whom the aforesaid king Melwas had violated and
carried off bringing her there for safety, because of the invulnerable
position's protection, provided by the thicketed fortifications of reed, rivers
and marshes. [Glastonbury was once literally an island, surrounded by lakes
and marshland]. The war-like king had searched for the queen throughout
the cycle of one year, and at last heard that she resided there. Thereupon he
called up the armies of the whole of Cornwall and Devon and war was
prepared between the enemies.
    When the abbot of Glastonbury - attended by the clergy and Gildas
the Wise - saw this, he stepped in between the contending armies, and
peacefully advised his king Melwas, that he should restore the kidnapped
lady. And so, she who was to be restored was restored in peace and good
will. When these things had been done, the two kings gave to the abbot
many territories; and they came to visit the church of St Mary to pray; the
abbot sanctioning the dear fraternity in return for the peace they enjoyed and
the benefits they bestowed and which they were about to bestow yet more
plentifully. Then reconciled, the kings left, swearing reverently to obey the
most venerable abbot of Glastonbury, and not to violate the holiest part nor
even the lands bordering on the land of its overseer.'
    Chrétien de Troyes later copied this story, when Meleagant abducts
Arthur's queen 'Guenievre' (the French version of the Welsh Gwenhwyfar,
which later became the English 'Guinevere'). He writes that Mealeagant (or
Meleagaunce) took her to the otherworldly kingdom of Gorre and was killed
by Lancelot. Geoffrey of Monmouth made the abductor Mordred, Arthur's
nephew, and in the *Vulgate Romances*, the abductor became Lancelot.
According to Geoffrey of Monmouth, Gwenhwyfar fled the fatal battlefield
of Camlan to become a nun in Caerleon.
    Welsh tradition is that she had a sister called Gwenhwyfach (in the
*Mabinogion*), and from 1136 Geoffrey of Monmouth started off the Arthur-
Merlin-Guinevere-Lancelot-Camelot-Excalibur-Round Table industry with
his writings, based upon an old Welsh book that no-one else knew of. With
the later embellishments of Chrétien de Troyes, linking Arthur's knights with

the search for the Grail, a series of historical Welsh warriors and saints were transmogrified into the most potent stories for hundreds of years.

Gawain, St Gwalchmai, one of Arthur's knights and a 6th century historical character, tells us of Guinevere in Chrétien de Troyes *Perceval le Gallois* (Percival being based upon Arthur's Welsh knight, Peredur): 'Ever since first woman came to be, there has never been a lady of such renown, which she deserves, for just as the wise master teaches young children, my lady the queen teaches and instructs every living thing. From her flows all the good in the world, she is its source and origin. Nobody can take leave of her and go away disheartened, for she knows what each person wants and the way to please each according to his desires. Nobody observes the way of rectitude or wins honour unless they have learned to do so from my lady, or can suffer such distress that he leaves her still possessed of this grief.'

One Welsh tradition was that Morgan was Arthur's youngest son, born of the third of the ladies named Gwenhwyfar that Arthur married. His rise to favour irked Modred, who was Arthur's nephew, foster-son and hopeful successor. The same story tells us that Modred was the incestuous offspring of Arthur and his sister Gwyar (Morgan le Fay). In *Triad 80, The Three Faithless Wives of the Island of Britain*, Gwenhwyfar is listed as the fourth and most faithless of all, not a helpless victim, but this seems probably a later addition to the other three women. In Welsh sources, she was only faithless in relation to Mordred (Medraut), but the Melwas story allowed later French writers to portray her as having lax morals.

Chrétien makes her the source of troubles in the Round Table, and Arthur is finally prevailed upon to execute her for her adulteries, but she is rescued by Lancelot. Malory said that she was childless* in a marriage to a man she did not love, and that she fell for Lancelot, ending her days in a convent in Amesbury, realising that her deeds had ruined the noblest group that the world had ever known, but 'she was a true lover and therefore she had a good end'. Malory wrote that she married Arthur despite Merlin's warnings that she would one day betray him, and as a dowry brought the Round Table, capable of sitting 150 knights.

The earliest Welsh legends make her a prime cause of Arthur's fatal last battle at Camlan, but the *Triads* place the blame on a feud between Gwenhwyfar and her half-sister Gwenhwyfach. *Triad 84, The Three Futile Battles of the Isle of Britain* blames the enmity, and *Triad 53, The Three Harmful Blows of the Isle of Britain* tells us that Gwenhwyfach struck Gwenhwyfar, which led to the battle.

*Triad 54* tells us of *The Three Unrestrained Ravagings of the Isle of Britain*: 'the first occurred when Medrawd came to Arthur's Court at Celliwig in Cernyw'. This was the ancient fort of the Silures at Llanmelin in Gwent. Cornwall was not known as 'Cerniw' until the 10th century, but Cernyw was the name for part of south-east Wales in Arthur's time. Medrawd ransacked the court, dragged Gwenhwyfar from her throne and hit her. The second 'ravaging' was Arthur's counter-attack on Medrawd's court. Whether Guinevere left voluntarily with Medrawd or was abducted, we are not told.

Giraldus Cambrensis commented on the 'finding' of the graves and cross of Arthur and Guinevere by the monks of Glastonbury (a medieval 'scam') and that the cross stated that Guinevere was Arthur's second wife. This is echoed in the 'false Guinevere' of the later French romances. In these it was an identical half-sister, the *doppel-ganger* Gwenhwyfach, born on the same night, who persuaded Arthur that she was his true wife and lured him away from court while Gwenhwyfar went to Lancelot. Another ancient *Triad, The Three Chief Queens of the Isle of Britain* tells us that Arthur actually married three Gwenhwyfars, being the daughters of Cywryd, Gwythyr ap Greidiol and Ogrfan Gawr respectively. Arthmael ap Meurig ap Tewdrig married Gwenhwyfar, the sister of Prince Gwythian of Cornwall. His place as the 'real Arthur' is explored in the author's *The Book of Welsh Saints*.

\* Gwenhwyfar's son Lacheu fab Arthur appears in the *Black Book of Carmarthen* in battle against Cai Wyn. Also Gwyddno Garanhir claims he was present when Llacheu was killed. He is often mentioned elsewhere as a fearless warrior, and was supposed to have died 'below Llech Ysgar'. An early poem commemorates this:

'I have been where Llacheu was killed,
Son of Arthur, marvellous in songs,
When the ravens croaked over blood .....
I have been where the warriors of Britain were slain,
From the East to the North;
I am alive, they are in their grave.'

Stones called the 'Sons of Arthur' may indicate that others of Arthur's offspring died, just leaving the young Morgan, causing the leadership of Britain to pass to Constans, then to Maelgwn. These two standing stones, Cerrig Meibion Arthur, stand near Cwm Cerwyn in the Preseli Hills, where Arthur fought the Twrch Trwyth and his son Gwydre and another son died. Near here is the unusually elliptical stone circle, Bedd Arthur. A tradition is that Morgan was Arthur's youngest son, born of the third of the ladies named Gwenhwyfar that Arthur married. His rise to favour irked Modred, who was Arthur's nephew, foster-son and hopeful successor. The same story tells us that Modred was the incestuous offspring of Arthur and his sister Gwyar (Morgan le Fay).

*Footnote:*
A story that many people are familiar with comes from Malory's *Gawain and the Green Knight*. Morgan le Fay sent the Green Knight to Camelot to frighten Guinevere. At the beginning of Arthur's reign, Guinevere had banished one of Morgan's lovers from court. Morgan le Fay represents Morrighan, the dark

goddess of winter and warfare, while Guinevere the Fair is the Flower Bride, representing spring and new life. The two women are constantly in opposition, and as Guinevere's champion, Lancelot becomes the bitter enemy of Gawain, the knight of the Goddess, who is Morgan's champion. In myth, the Flower Bride is stolen by one of her suitors, and then rescued by another, to represent the change in seasons. Thus, as in *the Life of Gildas*, Melwas of the Summer Country carries off Guinevere and she is rescued by Arthur. (Somerset gets its name from the translation of the Welsh, as it was known as Gwlad Haf, the land of the Summer). The abduction is repeated in several stories, where the kidnapper is Sir Meliagraunce, and the rescuer Lancelot.

Lancelot and Guinevere fall in love, and in one story the 'False Guinevere' takes her place when she takes refuge with Lancelot in Sorelois. The False Guinevere and her champion Bertholai admit their deception, and on the False Guinevere's death, Guinevere is restored to Arthur. However, Guinevere and Lancelot are too deeply in love for this state of affairs to last, although Lancelot spends all his time away from court, pursuing knightly deeds. Just as they have decided that the affair must end forever, Mordred, Arthur's illegitimate son, finds the pair in the queen's chamber. Lancelot flees and Mordred forces Arthur to condemn Gunievere at the stake. Lancelot charges in for a last-minute rescue but accidentally kills Gareth and Gaheris, the brothers of Sir Gawain, sparking a war. While Arthur is away fighting Lancelot, Mordred declares himself as king and announces that Guinevere will be his wife. She refuses and locks herself in the Tower of London, and Arthur returns for the final battle with Mordred at Camlan.


## ABBESS MELANGELL d.590

## SAINT MONACELLA

A life of c. 570 – 641, and a death date of 607 are also given for Melangell. Also known by her Latin name as Saint Monacella, Melangell is given feast days of 31 January, 27 and 28 May, and is the 'Patroness of hares and the natural environment'. The daughter of King Cyfwlch Addwyn (or Iochwel) and Ethni (Eddni) Wyddeles (the Irishwoman), on her father's side she was related to St Elen of Caernarfon. Melangell fled from Ireland to Wales to escape a forced marriage, and settled at Pennant, in the beautiful Vale of Llangynog. Another source states that she was the daughter of Tudwal (Tugdual) and descended from Macsen Wledig, the sister or niece of Rhydderch Hael, King of Strathclyde.

In 604 Prince Brochwael of Powys was hunting a hare with his hounds. The animal fled into a bramble thicket. Brochwael's men tramped through the undergrowth to see Melangell kneeling in prayer. She had protected the hare by hiding it in the sleeve of her gown. Brochwael urged on his dogs, but they stayed behind him. He tried to blow his hunting-horn, but it stuck to his lips. This Brochwael was at the disastrous Battle of Chester in 613. The legend usually relates that it was Prince Brochfel Ysgythrog* (Brochwael the Fanged, the father of St Tysilio) but he died around 560.

When the hare peeped out to look at the dogs, they fled, and Brochwael acknowledged the presence of this holy woman, giving her the land across which he had hunted. She lived here, at Pennant Melangell, for

**Saint Melangell's Church at Pennant Melangell lies in a circular Celtic churchyard**

another 37 years, and no animal was killed in her sanctuary. Hares were known as '*wyn bach Melangell*' or Melangell's little lambs, and to kill a hare in her parish was regarded as an act of sacrilege. To call after a hunted hare 'God and Melangell go with thee' was thought to save it from a pack of hounds. Brochwael's successors confirmed the privilege of 'perpetual sanctuary, asylum and safe refuge of the wretched' to her convent lands.

Llanfihangel-y-Pennant near Llangynog is probably Melangell's foundation, but then became one of the ubiquitous Norman re-dedications to Michael. Hares can be seen on its mediaeval rood screen, and her 12th century shrine survives there, until recently in a 17th century room, Cell-y-Bedd in the east end of the church.

Her 12th-century coffin-shrine, supported on pillars, is a unique survival in Britain. It was dismantled after the Reformation and its stones, carved with a strange blend of Romanesque and Celtic motifs, were built into the walls of the church and lych-gate. They were reassembled in the last century and have now been re-erected in the chancel. The result is an impressive monument, recently described by a leading scholar as 'of pan-European significance'. Hidden bones, said to be those of the saint, were reinterred within the shrine.

In the church of Pennant Melangell are also two recumbent stone figures, the local tradition being that one is the Celtic prince Iorwerth Drwyndyn and the other St Melangell. According to Pennant, 'she is buried in Pennant Melangell. Her hard bed is shown in a cleft of the neighbouring rock. Her tomb was in a little chapel, or oratory, adjoining the church, which is now used as a vestry room. This room is still called cell y bedd, cell of the grave; but her relics as well as her image have long since been removed; but I think the last is still to be seen in the churchyard.'

The following pun on her name was ancient even when it was recorded in the registers of her church in 1723: 'Mil engyl a Melangell /

Trechant lu fyddin y fall.' – 'Melangell with a thousand angels / Triumphs over all the powers of evil.'

\* In 615 or 616, a successful attempt was made to cut Wales off from the northern British of Cumbria and Strathclyde, by the Angles at Bangor-is-Coed, the great monastery of Dunawd at Bangor-on-Dee, near Chester. The Welsh were said to be led by Brochwel (the 'Fanged', but he was dead by now), Selyf Sarfgaddau of Powys (the 'Slayer of Serpents'), Prince Bledrws of Cornwall, King Meredydd of Dyfed and King Cadfan ab Iago of Gwynedd. Brochwel escaped with his life, but hundreds of monks were slaughtered by the pagans, much to the glee of the Venerable Bede, who hated the British church and its antecedence to Rome in the religious life of Britain. The Anglo-Saxons went on to conquer Cumbria and Cornwall, leaving Wales to fend for itself at the last outpost of the British people and its independence. Sir Walter Scott wrote *The March of the Monks of Bangor* to commemorate the massacre, the last verse of which reads:

'Bangor! O'er the murder wall,
Long the ruins told the tale;
Shatter'd towers and broken arch
Long recall'd the woeful march;
On thy shrine no tapers burn,
Never shall thy priests return;
The pilgrim sighs and sings for thee,
O misere Domini!'


## SAINT HELEDD 6th – 7th century

## THE FIRST WOMAN POET

The church of Llanhilleth is now dedicated to Illtud, but before the 16th - 17th centuries it was spelt Llanhilledd Vorwyn, dedicated to Hilledd the Virgin (*morwyn*). 'Llan Helet' is also mentioned in the *Stanzas of the Graves* (*Englynion y Beddau*), possibly dating from the late 6th century. Hilledd ferch Cyndrwyn, a princess of Powys, and therefore of a saintly family, was the aunt of Aelhaiarn, Cynhaiarn and Llwchaiarn. Importantly, she was the sister of Cynddylan\*. His death in battle against the Saxons, and the burning of his palace on the great Roman site of Wroxeter (or Shrewsbury-Pengwern or Whittington/Trefwen)\*\*, is commemorated in a magnificent saga poem finally written down in the 9th century. Wroxeter had been built on the River Severn crossing of Watling Street, as the base for the Roman invasion of Wales. It became the fourth largest town in Roman Britain, and has been much improved as a visitor centre in the last few years. The most unusual find was the skull of a man, who suffocated while hiding under the floor of one of the hot-air rooms when the city was attacked. He was clutching a bag containing his savings of 132 coins. The fugitive Heledd's elegy begins:

'Stand forth, maidens and look upon
The land of Cynddylan;
The court of Pengwern is blazing,
Woe to the young who desire rich garments'.

Some of the following lines from *Stafell Gynddylan (Cynddylan's Hall)* from the saga *Canu Heledd* are:

'Dark is Cynddylan's hall tonight
With no fire, no bed.
I will weep awhile, then I will be silent

Dark is Cynddylan's hall tonight
With no fire, no candle.
Save for God, who will give me peace?

Dark is Cynddylan's hall tonight
With no fire, no light.
Tears wear away cheeks.

The hall of Cynddylan, its vault is dark
After the bright company;
Alas for him who does not do the good which falls to him!

Hall of Cynddylan, you have become shapeless,
Your shield is in the grave;
While he lived you were not mended with hurdles.

The hall of Cynddylan is loveless tonight,
After him who owned it
Ah, Death, why does it spare me?'

The poem was traditionally attributed to Llywarch Hen, whose poems in their 9th century form were gathered in *The Red Book of Hergest*, but the poem is so intensely personal that this author favours the authorship of Princess Heledd. Her brother Cynddylan has been killed in battle and his hall at Pengwern is in flames, while an eagle tears at his corpse:

'The eagle of Eli is screaming tonight
After feasting on blood,
The heart's blood of fair Cynddylan.

The eagle of Eli, I hear him tonight,
He is bloodstained, I dare not go near him,
He is in the trees, my grief is heavy upon me.

The eagle of Eli, from his haunts
He seeks not the fish in the estuaries,
He demands a feast of men's blood.

The eagle of Pengwern, with grey tufted head tonight,
Loud is his cry,
Eager for the flesh of Cynddylan

The eagle of Pengwern, with grey tufted head tonight,
And talon uplifted,
Eager for the flesh of the one I love.'

What used to be included in the Llywarch Hen canon of work, is a series of 113 *englynion* now known as *The Heledd Poems*. Apart from Shrewsbury, Trewern (near Welshpool) and Wroxeter, the Wrekin hill-camp in Shropshire has also been posited as the

site of Cynddylan's Court, the capital of Powys. Heledd laments, like Llywarch Hen, in the first person. Her brother Cynddylan has been killed defending Trenn (the border area of the river Tern in Shropshire) from a Mercian invasion. After he has been buried in Baschurch (Eglwys Basau)***, Heledd calls upon women to gaze from a height

**The church of St. Heledd with Castle Hilleth remains in the foreground**

overlooking the desolation of the kingdom, and the blazing remains of Pengwern. Heledd mourns the death of the 8 sisters and 7 brothers, and laments her fate having to sleep on rough goatskin in old clothes. Before this disaster, she had fine horses and gowns of crimson decorated with yellow feathers. Anthony Conran described the scene thus:

'She watches in terror as an eagle feasts upon Cynddylan's dead body in the woods. She does not dare to go near, in case the birds turn on her. She has seen them before, these eagles fishing in the estuaries; now they swim in blood. She thinks of her victorious enemy, the one that slew Cynddylan; the eagles are pampered by him, and he prospers. Then she looks up, hears another eagle scream and hover in the sky, talons down for the swoop. It is jealous of the flesh that she loves and would like to save, and jealous of its rival's feast. Her splintered mind remembers Trenn, the luckless, glittering town, that Cynddylan died defending, and the eyes of the eagles watch on the blood.'

Heledd next sings an elegy to her sister Ffreur, who had died in Pengwern's devastation, blames herself for the tragedy as she has lapsed a few times from true Christianity, and becomes a homeless wanderer:

'I am called wild Heledd
O God! To whom will be given
My brothers' horses and lands?'

Heledd's *Saying of the Wise* is:
'Hast thou heard the saying of Heledd,
The daughter of Cyndrwyn, of extensive wealth?
"Prosperity cannot come from pride".'

The recent 'Anglo-Saxon Horde' complete with Celtic knotwork and Christian devices, was very possibly looted in this attack – see footnotes.

* St Issui was martyred at Patrishow (Patricio), a chapel under Llanbedr in Brecon. Fenton described this fascinating church as follows: 'below the church saw the Sainted Well of Isho, being a very scanty oozing of water, to which, however, was formerly attributed great Vertue, as within the building, that encloses it are little Niches to hold the Vessels drank out of and the offerings they left behind.' This is one of the most famous churches in Wales, with a celebrated 'Doom Figure', a wall painting of a skeleton with an hour-glass and spade. A small 13th century chapel is built over the saint's grave, abutting the Norman nave. The internal furnishings, screens, nave roof, rood staircase, rood loft, doorway and porch all somehow survived the Reformation, making this possibly the most 'complete' of all the old parish churches in Wales. The full name of the church is Merthyr Issui at Patricio. In connection with Heledd, there is a pre-Norman stone font here with the inscription 'Menhir made me in the time of Genillin', possibly referring to Cynddylan's rule of the princedom of Powys before its capital at Pengwern was destroyed in the early 7th century.

** Paul Remfrey makes a persuasive case for Cynddylan's Hall being at Whittington in Shropshire, a castle on a Dark Age site. Baschurch – see below – is only 5 miles away and may be the 'fair town' of the poem.

*** Cynddylan's death is the subject of one of the greatest of the early Welsh poems, and Pengwern has been placed variously as Shrewsbury, nearby Atcham (also on the River Severn) and Wroxeter Roman city. However, there is another candidate for the site of his court, the strangely shaped Iron Age fort at Baschurch, called The Berth. A bronze cauldron was unearthed there, and Cynddylan, after his defeat in 'the battle in the marshes' was carried to burial at

'Eglwys Basau', possibly this Baschurch near Shrewsbury. Baschurch makes Whittington a likely site.

*Footnotes:*

1. It seems absurd that the 2009 discovery of 'Saxon treasure' in Staffordshire has been trumpeted by all archaeologists and newspapers as 'proof' that the Anglo-Saxons accepted Christianity far earlier than was thought. A cursory examination of the finds reveals many Celtic knotwork designs. There were 1,500 artefacts, the greatest find since Sutton Hoo, found near Lichfield, with around 5kg and 2.5kg of gold and silver items. (Ironically, Lichfield Cathedral still houses the so-called *Gospel of St Chad*, in actuality the *Book of St Teilo*, stolen from Wales and claimed as English. At the time of its writing, England was barbarian, but that is another story.)

The largest cross was folded, indicating a pagan burial. A gold strip reads, in Latin, 'Rise Up, Lord - May your enemies be scattered and those who hate You be driven from Your face.' The objects are dated between 650 and 750 CE, which was around the time that the barbarian Penda and Aethelred of Mercia were invading Christian Wales. The Christian inscription on the buried hoard indicates a 'Christian Saxon king' according to English experts. The horde is contemporaneous with the sacking of the court of Cynddylan, Prince of Powys at Wroxeter or Whittington, and the taking of his other capital of Powys, Pengwern (Shrewsbury). The gold was quite possibly taken from the destruction of British (i.e. Welsh) monasteries and churches, and its provenance to Welsh gold mines can probably easily be made. A similar occurrence happened on a TV documentary analysis of Irish gold - they could not link it to any Irish gold mines, because it was pillaged from Wales when the Irish were pagan and the Welsh were Christian.

Why does no academic realise that the Romans came to Britain to get at the largest gold and copper mines in Europe, at Dolaucothi and the Great Orme, mines worked by the Celts for centuries? Welsh slate, copper, gold, silver and lead was exported on a huge scale. Why does no English academic understand that there were three Roman legions stationed in Britain, compared to one in each of Rome's other far-flung provinces. Of those, one was in York, safeguarding most of England and Scotland. The other two were stationed on the Welsh borders, at Caerleon and Chester, with the most intensive network of Roman roads in Europe emanating from them to other major forts at Carmarthen and Caernarfon.

2. It seems the tide is turning at last. I watched a repeat of *Time Team*, where the 'experts' stated that the occupation of a newly discovered Roman villa in the south-west transferred from Romans to Anglo-Saxons, totally ignoring the Roman-British era, as do most history books. The continuum of British history is always 'Nothing Worth Considering' – Romans – 'Nothing Worth Considering' – Anglo-Saxons – Normans – Angevins – Plantagenets – Tudors and so on. However the next day in *The Times* (10 July 2015) a headline read *Celts were history's real horny beasts*, with an item about the Celts wearing intricate horned helmets, not the Vikings. (The myth probably stems from the first stagings of Wagner's *The Ring* cycle). The British Museum is looking at

reattributing many Viking/Anglo-Saxon artefacts as British-Celtic, with the Celts being regarded by both Greeks and Romans as the best metal-workers in Europe.

## SAINT GWENFREWI c.615 – 3 November 660

### WINIFRED OF HOLYWELL, GUENEVRA, BREWI

**St. Gwenfrewi's well at Holywell**
*courtesy of castlewales.com*

3 November is the feast of her 'second' death, and 22 June the feast of her martyrdom. 4 November and 19 and 20 September were also celebrated. Gwenfrewi was the daughter of Prince Tefydd of Tegeingl (modern Flintshire) and Gwenlo (Gwnlo), St Beuno's sister. Beuno had come from his foundation at Clynnog in Caernarfonshire, to build a church on land granted by Prince Tefydd, probably at Sychnant. While Gwenfrewi's parents were at Mass in Beuno's new chapel, the legend is that Gwenfrewi suffered from the unwanted attentions of Prince Caradog ab Alan, from Hawarden (Penarlag in Flintshire). He had been hunting nearby and called at her parents' home for refreshment. Seeing that Gwenfrewi was alone, he attempted to ravage her, on Mid-Summer's Day.

She fled from him but he caught up with her at the church door before she could gain sanctuary with Beuno. Because she had spurned him, Caradog cut off her head, whereupon the earth opened up and swallowed him. Her uncle, St Beuno, restored her head to her shoulders and she lived the rest of her days as a nun at Gwytherin in Denbighshire. For the rest of her life, Gwenfrewi had a pure white circle around her throat. Where her head fell to the earth at Holywell (Treffynnon, Welltown), a spring of water gushed forth. Some sources say that she became abbess of a nunnery at Holywell for seven years, (before going to Gwytherin) and others that she then followed Beuno to Clynnog, and then moved on to Bodfari, Henllan before finally becoming a nun under St Eleri in Gwytherin near Llanrwst. St Eleri's mother, St Theonia was the abbess there. The *Vitae Sanctae Wenefredae* tells us that Gwenfrewi asked to be buried alongside Theonia.

She died at Gwytherin fifteen years after her head was restored to her body. This may have been about 660, as she was spoken of as a 'girl' when Cadfan was King, and he died about 630.

A legend says that Beuno asked Gwenfrewi to send him a rain-proof woollen cloak each year on the feast day of John the Baptist, the anniversary of the day upon which she was brought back to life. She placed it on a stone in the river, and each year the stone would sail down the river and across the sea to her uncle, and reach him in a perfectly dry condition. St Beuno's chapel was erected just above where St Margaret's Chapel now stands in Holywell, but the site is now rededicated to St James.

In 1138, her relics were removed from Gwytherin and enshrined in Shrewsbury's Benedictine Abbey church (Pengwern)*. As a result, St David became patron saint of Wales in her stead. Her cult was confined to North Wales and the Marches, and to Ewyas and Ergyng in South Wales until 1398. From Dafydd ap Llywelyn's gift of 1240, the Cistercian monks at nearby Basingwerk Abbey were in possession of her holy well and church at Holywell until the Dissolution of the Monasteries. In 1398, Archbishop Roger Walden of Canterbury ordered her feast to be kept in the province of Canterbury. Archbishop Chichele of Canterbury commanded in 1415 that she be registered as one of the more important feasts, along with those of David and Chad. In Wales, a famous pilgrim route was from St David's through the Cistercian monastery of Ystrad Fflur with its Holy Grail, to Holywell.

In 1416 Henry V walked on foot from Shrewsbury to Holywell, to give thanks for his victory at Agincourt. Pope Martin V entrusted indulgences to the monks for all who visited the chapel in 1427. In 1437 the Earl of Warwick ordered an effigy of himself made of twenty pounds weight of gold, to be placed at the shrine. In 1439 his wife gave her velvet gown to clothe the image of Gwenfrewi. Edward IV is said to have made a pilgrimage there in 1461 just before the great battle of Towton Moor, and placed some soil on his crown. Richard III paid for a priest to maintain the well until his death at Bosworth in 1485.

Because the cult spread widely that the well waters cured disease, Henry Tudor's mother, Margaret Beaufort, enclosed it in a stone shrine in 1490. Her son Henry VII some years before had a lucky escape from Richard III at Mostyn after visiting the shrine. The window he fled through can still be seen. It seems that the shrine was not smashed during the Dissolution as she was Henry VIII's grandmother, and because the waters were seen as 'medicinal'. Over 1,500 Roman Catholics gathered at the well on 3 November 1629. In 1686 King James II and his Queen Mary of Modena visited, desperate for an heir to the throne. Soon after the queen became pregnant. To achieve a wish, they had to duck under the water and kiss the wishing stone, 'Beuno's Pillow', near the steps. Unfortunately for

James and the Stuart dynasty, the consequent birth ten months later of a male Catholic heir, hastened James' expulsion from England, never to return.

Father Gerard, one of the few men to escape from the Tower of London, bathed in the well on 3 November 1593. In 1605 'Little John' (Nicholas Owen) made a pilgrimage with the Jesuit Superior, Henry Garnet. Both were executed within two years, as was Edward Oldcorne, who had come to Holywell in 1601 to cure cancer of the tongue. Interestingly, throughout the Reformation and after, pilgrimages never ceased, despite sporadic attempts at suppression. Pilgrims still travel to the well, which has been described in two poems by Gerard Manley Hopkins. It is the best-preserved medieval pilgrimage centre in Britain, and may be the longest unbroken centre of well-worship in Europe. Some of the stones in this holy shrine have strange red marks, said to be the blood of Gwenfrewi.

The Welsh bard Tudur Aled of Llansannan (c.1465-c1525) wrote:

In the earth, red-marked stones,
Musk and balm within the world,
A pure white stone with a pure place,
Stones marked with the blood of a white neck.
Which mark endures forever?
The band of her blessed blood.
A shower of tears like rose-hips,
Droplets of Christ,
From the wounds of the Cross;
It is good for a man's body –
To accept tears of blessed water;
Bloody droplets, like water and wine,
Bringing miracles of laughter.
The laughter of the seething sweet water
Is a sign of health – the bells of the water.
A burning stream from the fiery foam,
The powerful support of the Holy Ghost,
The waters of baptism are
The life support of the world,
It is the fountain of the oil of faith.'

Caxton wrote that the well 'heleth al langours and sekenesses as well in men as in bestes', and in August 1774 Samuel Johnson witnessed people bathing in its waters. He remarked also that it turned no fewer than nineteen mills, as Afon Wenfrewi rushed the mile from the spring to the sea. The bell in Holywell's church was dipped in the well, then wrapped in a christening robe, before being mounted, to keep lightning, evil and storms away from the site. The well was the most copious natural spring in Britain, but the rate of flow is now restricted to a fifth of its previous flow into the well. Its flow was 100,000 gallons per minute in 1917, but it was diverted in 1917. The water is a chilly 10 degrees C, all the year round.

Open morning to dusk, pilgrims are expected to pass through the water three times, perhaps a derivation of the old Celtic custom of triple immersion (three was the holy number). By a miracle, the shrine was not destroyed in the reformation, only the sacred images, but a priest remained to guard the well. Not until 1688 did Protestants sack the chapel and expel the guardian priest. However, people continued to use the well and in 1851 and in 1887 the pope granted indulgences to pilgrims using the well. Unfortunately Gwenfrewi's great tomb and shrine at Shrewsbury

**St Winifred's Well, Woolston, Shropshire**

were destroyed in the Reformation. 'Oh Winifred' was a popular expression in the 1890's, meaning disbelief, and stemming from the reputed miracles at Holywell.

It is fairly certain that Daniel Defoe never went to Wales, but he records the toleration shown to Catholics at Holy Well: 'The stories of this Well of St Winifred are, that the pious virgin, being ravished and murthered, this healing water sprung out of her body when buried; but this smells too much of the legend, to take up any of my time; the Romanists indeed believe it, as tis evident from their thronging hither to receive the healing sanative virtue of the water, which they do not hope for as it is a medicinal water, but as it is a miraculous water, and heals them by virtue of the intercession and influence of the famous virgin, St Winifred, of which I believe as much as comes to my share…There is a little town near the well, which may, indeed, be said to have risen from the confluence of the people hither, for almost all the houses are either public houses, or let into lodgings; and the priests that attend there, and are very numerous, appear in disguise. Sometimes they are physicians, sometimes surgeons, sometimes gentlemen, and sometimes patients, or anything as occasion presents… Nobody takes any notice of them, as to their profession, though they know them well enough, no not the Roman Catholics themselves; but in private, they have their proper oratories in certain places, whither the votaries resort; and good manners has prevailed so far, that however the Protestants know who and who's together; no body takes notice of it, or enquires where another goes, or has been gone.' (From *The Tour of the Whole Island of Great Britain* published anonymously in 3 volumes between 1725 and 1726.)

Large pilgrimages were undertaken to the well at Holywell during the 17th century. When a man was found dead near the well in 1603 after denigrating its powers, a local jury brought a verdict of 'death by divine judgement.' Until recently, when the authorities clamped down, it was customary for those cured to leave their crutches and callipers on the wall at the back of the well. Thousands still take the waters every year, from countries as far as Australia and Canada. More people should know about the shrine – there is nothing like it in Europe – over 1300 years of unbroken pilgrimage has taken place here.

We can compare the shrine favourably to Lourdes, dating from a vision by a 14-year-old shepherdess named Bernadette in 1828, not 190 years ago. From the anti-Semitism of the shrine's early political supporters, via the need for income in a poor part of the Pyrenees, Ruth Harris describes the manipulation by the church for Bernadette to achieve sainthood and the place to become a centre of pilgrimage. The following anecdote tells us far more about the 'holiness' of Lourdes compared to Holywell than any of its 'glow-in-the-dark' plastic Madonna lighters: 'At the height of the sentimental hysteria surrounding the new shrine of Lourdes in the late 19th century, a priest called Père Ricard who was visiting the shrine asked for a drink. Not ordinary water – instead, he asked a Lourdes stretcher-bearer to fill his glass with the infected blood and scabs of sick pilgrims. He made the sign of the Cross and drank it. "The water of the good Mother of Heaven is always delicious", he said with a beatific smile.' (Ruth Harris, *Lourdes,* 1999).

One can stay at another St Winifred's Well, hidden away in the woods at Woolston near Oswestry. Her body was taken in the 12th century from its Denbighshire grave by the monks of Shrewsbury Abbey – they believed that more people would receive benefit from her relics being in a greater centre of population, and of course this would bring greater revenues to their abbey (- a theme explored by Ellis Peters in her *Brother Cadfael* stories). The story is that the saint's body was rested at Woolston, where a spring gushed forth, just as it did at Flintshire's Holywell. The well has been venerated for centuries, and the innermost pool, with a niche for a statue, is presumably the medieval well chamber. A mediaeval timber well chapel stands over it, which was adapted for use as a Court House until 1824, after which it became a cottage. The well had been enlarged to form a bath, open to the general public, but conduct became so riotous that it was closed to them in 1755, together with the ale-houses which had opened nearby. The Woolston well is in the care of the Landmark Trust, and can accommodate two people. Being near to Shrewsbury, Sycharth (Glyndŵr's Court), Wroxeter Roman City, Valle Crucis and Llangollen, it is a perfect place to take a vacation.

It is worthwhile noting one of the lesser-known poems by Gerard Manley Hopkins (1844-1889), a beautiful verse called simply *St Winefride's Well*:

Oh now while skies are blue, now while seas are salt,
While rushy rains shall fall or brooks shall fleet from fountains,
While sick men shall cast sighs, of sweet health all despairing,
While blind men's eyes shall thirst after daylight, drafts of daylight
Or deaf ears shall desire that lipmusic that's lost upon them,
While cripples are, while lepers, dancers in dismal limb dance,
Fallers in dreadful frothpits, waterfearers wild,
Stone, palsy, cancer, cough, lung-wasting, womb not bearing
Rupture, running sores, what more ? in brief, in burden,
As long as men are mortal and God merciful,
So long to this sweet spot, this leafy lean-over,
This dry dene, now no longer dry nor dumb, but moist and musical
With the uproll and the downcarol of day and night delivering
Water, which keeps thy name, (for not in rock written,
But in pale water, frail water, wild rash and reeling water,
That will not wear a print, that will not stain a pen,
Thy venerable record, virgin, is recorded)
Here to this holy well shall pilgrimages be,
And not from purple Wales only nor from elmy England,
But from beyond seas, Erin, France and Flanders everywhere,
Pilgrims, still pilgrims, more pilgrims, still more pilgrims
What sights shall be when some that swung, wretches, on crutches
Their crutches shall cast from them, on heels of air departing,
Or they go rich as roseleaves hence that loathsome came hither !
Not now to name even
Those dearer, more divine boons whose haven the heart is.
As sure as what is most sure, sure as that spring
primroses shall new-dapple next year, sure as tomorrow
morning, amongst come-back-again things, things with
a revival, things with a recovery,
Thy name Winefride will live.'

* There is still recounted in Holywell the following story about Gwenfrewi's relics. When Shrewsbury's 'Black Monks' (disliked by the Welsh, unlike the Cistercian 'White Monks') tried to find Gwenfrewi's coffin, only one monk at Gwytherin disclosed its whereabouts. The bones were reverentially disinterred and placed in a fine coffin to be ceremonially transferred to Shrewsbury. That night, the monk who betrayed her resting-place was poisoned and placed in the coffin, while Gwenfrewi's bones were once again interred at Gwytherin. However, two of her finger-bones were left in the new coffin by accident. Holywell claims one finger bone as a relic, and the other was allowed to stay

with the body of the treacherous monk and is in Shrewsbury Cathedral. In the Dissolution of the Monasteries, the Shrewsbury finger-bone was taken to Powys Castle, then to Rome, only returning to Shrewsbury in 1852. However, the Holywell bone was not known about by Henry VIII's agents, and has been venerated in Britain for centuries.

** Sir Gawain may have stayed at Basingwerk Abbey when searching for the Green Knight, when Holywell was known as 'Holy Head', before he went on to the Wirral Peninsula.

## QUEEN ANGHARAD ferch OWAIN ab EDWYN c.1066 - 1162

### WIFE OF GRUFFUDD AP CYNAN, 'THE POSSESSOR OF BRITAIN'

Watercolour by T. Prytherch (1864-1926) - 'Gruffydd ap Cynan yng yngharchar Hugh d'Avranches yng Nghaer'

Angharad, the grand-daughter of Edwyn, Lord of Englefield, was wooed by Gruffudd ap Cynan (1055 - 1137) who became King of Gwynedd, and was known by the bards as 'the Possessor of Britain'. It was a marriage made for love, as Gruffudd could have had an arranged marriage with a more powerful dynasty, giving him a more secure base of alliances. The monk who wrote Gruffudd's life tells us that Angharad 'was an accomplished person - her hair was long and of a flaxen colour - her eyes large and rolling, and her features brilliant and beautiful. She was tall and well-proportioned - her fingers long, and her nails thin and transparent. She was good-tempered, cheerful, discreet, and witty - gave advice, as well as alms to her needy dependants, and never transgressed the laws of duty.'

From Gruffudd ap Llywelyn ap Seisyllt's death in 1063, there had been almost permanent fighting between the Welsh princes. The laws of Gavelkind meant that kingdoms and princedoms were constantly being broken up between all male heirs, legitimate and illegitimate. Gruffudd ap Cynan, grandson of Iago of Gwynedd, landed in Anglesey to reclaim his lands from Trahaiarn, in 1075. (His father had died fighting with Gruffudd ap Llywelyn against Harold of

63

Wessex in 1063, when Gruffudd ap Cynan was just eight years old). Gruffudd defeated Trahaiarn at the Battle of Waederw and recovered Merioneth as well as Gwynedd, but there was a revolt against him because of the conduct of his Irish mercenaries. Gruffudd attempted again in 1076 to regain his lands, but was forced off Anglesey. In 1081, he returned once more, allying himself with Rhys ap Tewdwr to try and heal the land after the depredations of the Earl of Chester and vicious Robert of Rhuddlan.

Angharad married Gruffudd around 1079, on his accession to the throne of North Wales. Their son Owain was born in 1080, known to history as the great warrior Owain Gwynedd. The carnage in Wales only relented with the victory of Rhys ap Tewdwr (of the royal house of Deheubarth), and Gruffudd ap Cynan (of the royal house of Gwynedd) at the battle of Mynydd Carn (Carno) in 1081, when Trahaiarn ap Caradoc was killed. William the Conqueror, on a pilgrimage to St David's in 1081, then recognised Rhys ap Tewdwr's right to Deheubarth.

However, in his attempts to gain the throne of Gwynedd, Gruffudd ap Cynan was captured by Hugh the Fat, Earl of Chester and held as a prisoner in chains for twelve years. Hugh the Fat had bribed Meirion Goch to bring Gruffudd to a meeting at Rug, in Edeyrnion, in 1082, where peace might be arranged between the Welsh and Normans. Gruffudd arrived at the meeting lightly armed with a few Irish retainers, and was surprised by the heavily armed contingents of the earls of Shrewsbury and Chester. Gruffudd was incarcerated in Chester Castle. His Irish followers had their thumbs cut off and were released. They were now useless as fighting men, as they could no longer draw a bowstring or grasp a sword, spear or battle-axe. For the next twelve years, Queen Angharad probably sought shelter with her son Owain at her father's court in Englefield (Tegeingl, modern Flintshire), as North Wales and Powys had been over-run by the Normans upon Gruffudd's treacherous seizure.

In 1094, the Earl of Chester ordered that Gruffudd be displayed in chains at Chester market place so the people could see the fall of the great Prince of Gwynedd. In the bustle of the market, he was rescued by Cynwrig Hir. A blacksmith knocked the chains off and the small rescue party managed to escape to Aberdaron, and sail back across to Ireland. Gruffudd soon returned to Wales, with his fellow prince, Cadwgan ab Bleddyn. He ravaged parts of Shropshire and Cheshire, and defeated the Normans in the woods of Yspwys. William II (William Rufus) invaded Wales in 1095 to restore order, but the Welsh retreated to the hills, and William returned to England.

In early 1096, Angharad and her 16-year-old son Owain eventually met with Gruffudd at his court at Aberffraw on Anglesey, the last piece of Wales that he held. Gruffudd's son had never known him, and Angharad had only spent two years of the last fifteen with him. Owain grew up not trusting the French-English - two of his own sons were later blinded by the English king when held as hostages. It had been difficult for Angharad to join Gruffudd up to this point, as her own father Owain ab Edwyn had sided with the English, sending forces to destroy Gruffudd ap Cynan. Their journey across Wales had not been easy, as all the land except Anglesey was held by the Normans, and her father had sent out search parties to capture her and his grandson. However, in 1096, Gruffudd defeated Norman armies at Gelli Trafnant and Aber Llech, and started to regain all his lands in North Wales, demolishing Norman forts on his way. William II led another fruitless invasion in 1097 against Gruffudd and Cadwgan, being beaten back into England.

In 1098 the earls of Chester and Shrewsbury again campaigned in a concerted attack against Gruffudd and Cadwgan, and invaded Anglesey, but Gruffudd and Cadwgan managed to flee to Ireland. Angharad's father Owain ab Edwyn had joined Gruffudd's cause, but deserted him at the last moment, siding with the Norman Marcher Lords. For two years, Angharad and her son Owain stayed at the king of Dublin's court with Gruffudd, and Angharad bore another prince and a princess of Gwynedd, Cadwaladr and Mared. Norman cruelty in Wales led to a fresh revolt, and just then the Scandinavians descended upon Anglesey. The Norman earls were beaten on the banks of the Menai River by the force led by Magnus Barefoot, King of Norway, who personally killed Red Hugh, the Earl of Shrewsbury. Gruffudd now moved back to Wales to restore and consolidate his Gwynedd power base as the Normans retreated, reigning over Anglesey and the kingdom known as Gwynedd uwch Conwy.

Angharad bore Gruffudd another son, Cadwallon, and four more daughters, Susanna, Ranullt, Nest and the ill-fated Gwenllian (q.v.) Owain Gwynedd made a dynastic marriage to Gwladys ferch Llywarch ab Trahaearn, Lord of Pembroke. (Trahaearn had been killed in battle by Gruffudd ap Cynan). At some time Angharad's young son Cadwallon was taken prisoner on the border with England, and put to death. Her daughter Gwenllian married Gruffudd ap Rhys, Prince of South Wales in 1116.

In 1114, Henry I invaded with three forces; in South Wales under Strongbow, Earl of Pembroke; in North Wales under Alexander of Scotland, and a force under himself against Powys. In a difficult holding campaign Gruffudd fought no battles, and lost no land, but decided to parley with Henry. As a result, Gruffudd submitted to the English king, and promised to give up his son-in-law Gruffudd ap Rhys, the other patriotic leader, in order to keep the peace. However, it appears that Gruffudd ap Cynan warned Gruffudd ap Rhys of his agreement. He and Angharad had no wish to see Gwenllian's husband tortured and murdered. The *Chronicles* tell us that Gruffudd ap Cynan quietly sent a messenger to Pembroke Castle to tell Nest that her brother's life was in danger. Gruffudd ap Rhys was staying with Nest and Gerald de Windsor, and first fled to Aberdaron, before hiding in the great forest of Ystrad Tywi in Deheubarth. Gruffudd ap Rhys was the son of Rhys ap Tewdwr, the co-victor of Mynydd Carn. He later avenged the murder of his wife Gwenllian ferch Gruffudd ap Cynan, defeating the Normans outside Cardigan.

Gruffudd ap Cynan ruled Gwynedd quietly until 1121, when he moved in collusion with Henry I to quickly take over Powys, which was riddled with internal disputes. Gruffudd later took over Deheubarth. In 1135 Henry I died, and in the disputed succession of Stephen, Gruffudd's sons Owain and Cadwaladr cemented his grip on most of Wales. Gruffudd now ruled over a peaceful Wales until his death, blind and ailing, in 1137. The work of some poets of his time is preserved in *The Black Book of Carmarthen*, and some of the court poetry of his bard Meilyr survives. His biography was written just twenty years after his death, declaring Gwynedd to be the 'primus inter pares' ('first among equals') of Welsh kingdoms. Gruffudd was buried in Bangor Cathedral to the left of the high altar, and his son, the

**Arms of Gruffydd ap Cynan, King of Gwynedd**

heroic poet-prince Owain Gwynedd succeeded peacefully. During Gruffudd's lifetime, his sons took Meirionydd, Rhos, Rhufoniog and Dyffryn Clwyd for Gwynedd.

Gruffudd's wife Angharad ferch Owain ab Edwyn was said to have survived him by 25 years, receiving half his personal estate, as was Welsh custom. Her daughter Gwenllian and grandson Morgan were executed in 1136* by the Normans after the battle of Maes Gwenllian. In 1137 Angharad also lost her son-in-law, Gruffudd ap Rhys, killed fighting the Normans. Gwenllian's son, Rhys ap Gruffudd (Yr Arglwydd Rhys) fought with his uncle Owain Gwynedd against the Normans, and took over leadership of Welsh resistance upon Owain's death. Thus the descendants of Angharad and Gruffudd carried on the fight for Wales for sixty years after Gruffudd's death, to the death of Rhys ap Gruffudd in 1197. Just thirteen years after this, Welsh leadership had passed to Llywelyn the Great, of the House of Gwynedd. In 1485, Angharad's descendant, Henry Tudor, became the first Welsh King of England.

* After the murder of Gwenllian, 'alive to an injury so singular and atrocious, her brothers, Owain Gwynedd and Cadwaladr, laid waste with infinite fury the province of Cardigan. Among a people whose manners seem to have been little refined by chivalrous feeling, we are surprised at the appearance of characters whose individual qualities and bravery of spirit, whose courteous and gentle

demeanour, might have entitled them to dispute the palm with the most distinguished knights of feudal ages. These distinguished persons were the sons of Gruffudd ap Cynan.' (from Pritchard's *Heroines of Welsh History*).

## PRINCESS NEST 1080? - 1145?

## 'THE HELEN OF WALES'

Rhys ap Tewdwr (d. 1093) was the last king of Deheubarth, a direct descendant of Hywel Dda, and had been assisted in reclaiming his territories in 1081 at the battle of Mynydd Carn by Gruffudd ap Cynan. Killed by Norman treachery near Brecon, his kingdom was revived by his grandson,

**Princess Nest – 'The Helen of Wales'**
*courtesy of castlewales.com*

The Lord Rhys. Rhys ap Tewdwr had married Gwladus ferch Rhiwallon ap Cynfyn. Her father Rhiwallon was killed at the Battle of Mechain in 1069. Rhys and Gwladus had three children, Hywel, Gruffudd ap Rhys (who married the ill-fated Gwenllian, q.v), and a daughter named Nest. In 1093, the beautiful Nest was placed into the care of William II as a royal ward. At court, she was seduced by the crown prince Henry, later Henry I, and their first son Henry was made the Duke of Gloucester. He was known as *filius regii*, the King's son', and was the first of the line of Fitzhenrys.

Nest grew up in turbulent times, and her first marriage in around 1100 to the king's friend Gerald Fitzwalter, Gerald de Windsor (c.1175-1135), the Norman castellan of Pembroke Castle, seems to have been diplomatically arranged by the new king, Henry I, to keep the peace between the Normans and the Welsh. By Gerald of Windsor, Nest had two daughters and three sons, William, Maurice and David Fitz-Gerald. David Fitzgerald became Archbishop of St David's Cathedral, a compromise appointment to satisfy Welsh and Norman clerics. He assisted in the consecration of Thomas Beckett at Canterbury, and met Pope Alexander III at Tours. David prevailed upon The Lord Rhys (Rhys ap Gruffudd) to release his half-brother Robert Fitzstephen, from a three-year captivity. Robert was released upon condition that he left Wales, and thus became one of the conquerors of Ireland.

Another of Nest's sons Maurice Fitzgerald, Lord of Llansteffan, had with William Fitzgerald, Lord of Emlyn, instigated a Norman war against the native princes in 1136. However, they lost territory, and were still trying to regain Llansteffan castle in 1146. Frustrated in his attempts to gain lands in Wales, Maurice led an invasion from Wexford into Ireland, taking the area around Dublin. He was granted Kildare for his services to the English crown. Nest's daughter Angharad married William of Manorbier, and one of Angharad's sons was the great Giraldus Cambrensis, Gerald de Barry.

Gerald de Windsor maintained an uneasy truce with Prince Cadwgan of Ceredigion and Powys, but Owain ap Cadwgan saw the beautiful Nest at his father's eisteddfod at Cardigan Castle, and resolved to elope with her. From his manor at Plas Eglwyseg* near Llangollen he broke into Cilgerran Castle** in 1109, fired it, and escaped with Nest. From *The Chronicle of the Princes*, we read: 'Owain had heard that Nest was in the castle, and he went with but a few of his men to visit her as a kinswoman... And then he came to the chamber in which Gerald and Nest were sleeping. And they raised a shout around and about the chamber in which Gerald was, and kindled tapers and set fire to the buildings to burn them. And when he heard the shout, Gerald awoke, not knowing what to do. And then Nest said to him, "Go not out to the door, for thine enemies await thee, but follow me.' And that he did. And she led him to the privy which adjoined the chamber. And there, as is said, he escaped by way of the privy hole. And when Nest knew that he had escaped, she cried out from within and said to the men who were outside, "Why do you cry out in vain? He whom you seek is not here. He has escaped."... They seized Nest and her two sons and her daughter and another son of Gerald's by a concubine, and they sacked and plundered the castle. She told Owain "If thou wouldst have me faithful to thee, and keep me with thee, have my children escorted to their father".'

Prince Cadwgan was ordered to restore Nest to Gerald, but Owain refused his father's wishes, and Norman barons eventually wrenched Powys and Ceredigion from Cadwgan. They closed in on Owain, who escaped to Ireland twice between 1109 and 1111. Owain had succeeded to the princedom of Powys upon Cadwgan's death by assassination in 1111. In 1112, Nest's brother Gruffudd ap Rhys, the husband of Gwenllian, returned from Ireland, spending most of his time with Gerald and Nest. When Gruffudd was denied the inheritance of his father Rhys ap Tewdwr, he accused to the king of conspiring against him, and allied with his father-in-law. War broke out, and in 1114 Gruffydd ap Cynan agreed to submit to Henry I, promising to give up Nest's brother Gruffudd ap Rhys as part of the agreement. A messenger rode from Gruffydd ap Cynan to Pembroke Castle to warn Angharad, and her brother escaped to fight another day.

Owain ap Cadwgan had, by now, been pardoned by Henry I, who seems to have looked upon Owain favourably as a counter-balance to over-powerful Norman barons. Henry took Owain with him to Normandy in 1115, where he was knighted. Owain was ordered to rendezvous with a Norman force to proceed against Gruffudd ap Rhys in Ystrad Tywi. En

68

route, he and his force chanced to run into none other than a group of Flemings under Gerald de Windsor. Despite Owain being a royal ally, Gerald chose to avenge his wife's abduction, and killed Owain in 1116. Nest now returned to Gerald de Windsor, but he shortly after died at Carew Castle.

After Gerald's death, Nest's sons married her to Stephen, her husband's Constable at Cardigan Castle, by whom she had another son, possibly two; the eldest was Robert Fitz-Stephen (d. 1182), one of the Norman conquerors of Ireland with his half-brother Maurice Fitzgerald. Robert helped Henry II against Owain Gwynedd in 1157, and was badly wounded. He then held Cardigan Castle for the king against the de Clares, and later against Hywel ab Owain Gwynedd. However, the castle was betrayed to the Lord Rhys, who razed it to the ground in 1165, and had imprisoned Robert. Maurice Fitzgerald had decided that it was easier to exist in Ireland than Wales, and Robert Fitzstephen was also forced out of Wales, playing a significant role in the conquest of Ireland, being given lands around Wexford and a joint grant of the kingdom of Cork.

Nest then married the Sheriff of Pembroke, having at least another son. Thus the great families of Fitzgerald, Carew, Fitzroy, Fitzhenry, Barry and Fitzstephen were descended from Nest. In all she was reputed to have had 17 children by her husbands and lovers, including another son by King Henry in 1114 when he visited Wales. No less that seven of her offspring were known as 'the race of Nesta' and involved in the conquest of Ireland.

* Owain ap Cadwgan's manor of Plas Eglwyseg is now named Plas Uchaf, near the quaintly named World's End, and according to a previous owner, Goering and Churchill stayed there on a shooting holiday in 1936-37. More intriguingly still, there was a very strong local tradition that Elizabeth I, the Virgin Queen, bore a baby there by Robert Dudley. A large inscription upon the present Tudor building reads LX III ELIZABETH REGINA. Perhaps she had a child there in 1563, as in 1564 she raised Robert Dudley to be Earl of Leicester in 1564. (q.v. Elizabeth Tudor).

** Some sources say Carew Castle, and others Pembroke Castle, but it was Cenarth Bychan, on the site of Cilgerran Castle.


## GWENLLIAN ferch GRUFFUDD ap CYNAN 1098 - 1136

## WALES' GREATEST HEROINE, WRITER OF THE MABINOGION?

Gwenllian was the youngest daughter of the warrior king of Gwynedd, Gruffudd ap Cynan, and Angharad ferch Owain ab Edwyn (q.v.) and her son was 'The Lord Rhys' (Yr Arglwydd Rhys, Rhys ap Gruffudd)*. Sister of the great Owain Gwynedd, Wales was under unceasing attack from the Normans during her lifetime. Owain Gwynedd had succeeded his father in leading the Welsh defence against the Marcher Lords. In 1114 Gruffudd ap Rhys had first come to the royal court at Aberffraw, after his long exile in Dublin. His father Rhys ap Tewdwr, the last King of Deheubarth, had assisted Gruffudd ap Cynan at the great battle of Mynydd Carn, so the young prince was welcomed with open arms. It seems that Gwenllian fell in love with Gruffudd. Soon after Hywel ap Rhys escaped from a long Norman captivity in Montgomery Castle and joined his brother Gruffudd ap Rhys at court in Aberffraw. Gruffudd visited his sister Nest (q.v.) and her husband Gerald de Windsor at Cydweli Castle to ascertain if there was any support for him to regain his father's kingdom of South Wales. Henry I was alarmed by the reuniting of the brothers Hywel and Gruffudd, and when Gruffudd ap Cynan was agreeing peace terms against three invading armies, he was forced into promising to deliver Gruffudd ap Rhys ap Tewdwr up to Henry's forces.

**Princess Gwenllian**
*courtesy of Kidwelly Council*

Somehow or other, the message of impending betrayal was passed by Gruffudd ap Cynan in London to Gerald and Nest in Pembroke Castle, who then sent messengers to North Wales to warn the brothers to flee. A ship from Pembroke had come to take them to a refuge in South Wales. Gerald de Windsor was the king's lieutenant and representative in South Wales, and must have acted in this manner out of love for his wife. Gwenllian then left her father's court to join Gruffudd, to join him in his hiding-place in the wild forests of Ystrad Tywi. The outlawed brothers collected a force of disaffected Welshmen to their cause, to regain the kingdom of their father, Rhys ap Tewdr, but kept well away from attacking any of Gerald de Windsor's estates.

The Welsh retook most of Pembroke and Carmarthen, sacking castles and pushing the Normans back into Glamorgan. Even Carmarthen Castle was taken, the principal seat of Henry's governance of South Wales, and the town burnt. Gwenllian married Gruffydd ap Rhys ap Tudor in 1116, when she was eighteen.

Gruffudd took Cydweli Castle next, the base of the hated Maurice de Londres, one of the cruelest Norman barons. At last he and Gwenllian could leave the forests of Ystrad Tywi and they made this their first court. However, a reverse at Plas Crug and another outside Aberystwyth Castle forced Gruffudd to fetch Gwenllian from Cydweli, and they returned to their Ystrad Tywi lair. Their twins Maelgwn and Morgan were born in 1118, Maredudd in 1130 and their youngest son Rhys in 1132. (Gruffudd also had sons Anarawd and Cadell by a previous marriage).

In order to rid himself of Gruffudd's constant threat, Henry I now engaged the services of Owain ap Cadwgan as a paid assassin, a favourite ploy of the Norman monarchy. Again Gerald of Windsor's wife, Nest, passed the news to her brother that his life was in danger, and Gwenllian and her young family left their refuge just before Owain's force arrived. Owain was killed soon after by Gerald's men.

In 1121, Henry invaded Wales but could not capture Gruffudd or his family. For the next six years, Gruffydd kept quiet, not incurring the king's wrath, and was allowed to live peaceably at Dinefŵr Castle, with Gwenllian and their four sons, Morgan, Maelgwn, Mareddud and Rhys. However, in 1127 Henry levelled a false charge against Gruffudd and the family decamped yet again to the fastnesses of Ystrad Tywi.

For the next eight years, Gruffudd waged guerrilla warfare upon the Norman barons, until 1135 when Henry I died. In the ensuing civil war in England, Wales rose in revolt. The sons of Gruffudd ap Cynan, Owain Gwynedd and Cadwaladr, took most of North Wales back from the French. Gruffudd hosted his flag, the red dragon on a field of green, and led the uprising in the south. Ceredigion was wrenched back from the Normans, giving Gruffydd control of much of the ancient kingdom of Deheubarth.

On New Year's Day, 1136, Gwenllian's husband and his eldest son Anarawd joined other Welsh forces in an attack upon the Norman invaders, allying with Owain Gwynedd. Gruffudd ap Rhys was thus away in North Wales, at the court of Gwenllian's father, Gruffudd ap Cynan.

Maurice de Londres, the detested Norman Lord of Cydweli took the opportunity to attack the Welsh in South-West Wales. Gwenllian led the few defenders that were left in the area, and her youngest son, Rhys, was only four years old. Giraldus Cambrenis stated that 'she marched like the Queen of the Amazons and a second Penthesileia leading the army'. In 1136, Gwenllian led her army against the Normans at Cydweli. A Norman army had landed in Glamorgan, and was marching to join the force of Maurice de Londres. Gwenllian stationed her rapidly assembled volunteers at the foot of Mynydd-y-Garreg, with the river Gwendraeth in front of her, and Cydweli Castle nearby. She sent some of her forces to delay the oncoming invasion force, but it evaded them and her remaining army was trapped between two Norman attacks.

One son, the 18-year-old Maelgwn, was killed at her side, his twin Morgan, imprisoned and lost from history, and towards the end of the fighting, Gwenllian ferch Gruffydd ap Cynan was captured and executed, over the body of her dead son. The wounded woman had pleaded for mercy, but was beheaded on de Londres' express order. The battlefield is still called Maes Gwenllian, a mile from the castle, and a stone marks the place of her death. The battlefield has still not been fully explored, and should be preserved as a heritage site.

Gwenllian left the 6 year-old Maredudd and the 4-year-old Rhys, to be known as The Lord Rhys, the grandson of Rhys ap Tewdr who was slain by the Normans at Brycheiniog in 1093, and the nephew of the great Owain Gwynedd. Gwenllian's daughter Nest married Ifor ap Meurig, Lord of Senghenydd, the Welsh hero 'Ifor Bach' who scaled the walls of Cardiff Castle to kidnap Earl William and regain his stolen lands. Her husband Gruffudd ap Rhys partially avenged her death in defeating the Normans in a great battle at Cardigan a year later. With her brother Owain and his brother Hywel he had led a force from North Wales. However, Gruffudd died just a year later, possibly poisoned, a severe blow to the reunification of Wales.

Dr Andrew Breeze (*Medieval Welsh Literature*, 1997) believes that the author of *The Four Branches of the Mabinogion***\*\*** is Gwenllian, around 1128, making her the first British woman author. Breeze says that the *Four Branches of the Mabinogion* 'are remarkable for two particular qualities. First is the extraordinary power and variety of their incident, often violent, irrational, bizarre or enigmatic. Second is the excellence of the lucid, untroubled prose in which their author wrote them'. To truncate his analysis without his proof is unfair, and interested readers should really purchase his excellent book, but the relevant references to Gwenllian are as follows: 'What kind of author wrote the *Four Branches*? Here we may say first that our writer was almost certainly a woman. A woman writer of fiction can usually be detected in the way she

Cydweli Castle, near the site of Princess Gwenllian's murder

presents male and female characters, fighting, weapons, jewels, clothes, love, and (above all) babies and children... In fact, it seems now that we can identify the author... as Gwenllian (1098-1136), daughter of Gruffudd ap Cynan (c.1090-1137) and wife of Gruffudd ap Rhys (1090-1137). She was a remarkable lady... All the evidence we can point to indicates her authorship of the *Four Branches*. Though circumstantial, it amounts to a very strong case...

First, only a woman of high rank would be in a position to write an early medieval vernacular text and have it transmitted after her time.

Gwenllian was a king's daughter; her descendants, through her son the Lord Rhys (1132-97), dominated life in West Wales for generation; and the *White Book of Rhydderch*, in which the *Four Branches* appear, was actually written for the grandson of her grandson's great-grandson.

Second, the author of the *Four Branches* had an intimate knowledge of courts and a royal attitude to life, especially clear in her women characters. Rhiannon and even Branwen (who negotiates peace between the Welsh and Irish) organise their lives with confidence...

Third, the writer had a detailed knowledge of Gwynedd, a more limited knowledge of Dyfed (effectively, just the valley of the Teifi), and a shadowy knowledge of Gwent and the rest of Britain. Both Gwynedd and Dyfed are praised. The defeat of a Dyfed army by one of Gwynedd in the fourth branch is described with tact. This geographical picture tallies with Gwenllian's experience as a princess of Gwynedd living with her husband in the region of Caeo, eight miles south-east of Lampeter...

Fourth, the use of Irish sources in Branwen accords with the fact that both Gwenllian's father and husband lived in Ireland as exiles (their situation as political refuges perhaps accounts for the tale's somewhat negative view of the Irish). Branwen's brother Bendigeidfran successfully invades Ireland from Wales; in 1081 Gwenllian's father Gruffudd had successfully invaded Wales from Ireland...

Fifth, the tales stress royal descent and status. The first branch begins with a statement of Pwyll's princely rank; the second, with one of Bendigeidfran's exaltation with the crown of London. Such references would be natural for the daughter of a king and wife of a prince. Equally natural, too, would be the knowledge of Welsh law shown in the texts (especially as regards insult and honour-price), contrasting with the complete lack of evidence of Latin book-learning (another reason for rejecting ascription of the Four Branches to a priest.)

Sixth is the incoherence of the tales' narrative structure, in striking contrast to the masterly ease, refinement, and limpidity of their style. The *Four Branches* cannot be the work of a professional story-teller. Jackson saw them as written by "antiquary literary men", working up half-forgotten tales. But the author's familiarity with the ceremonies and luxuries of court does not suggest an antiquarian at work. The curious blend of supreme stylistic skill, and indifference to matters of construction, is due probably to a royal excursion into authorship.

Seventh is the known literary activity of the royal houses of Gwynedd and Dyfed...

Eighth is the note of Dyfed irredentism running through the work. Gwenllian's husband Gruffudd ap Rhys was a prince of Dyfed who was somewhat down on his luck, living in reduced circumstances at Caeo. In the *Four Branches*, the line of Dyfed gains territory and prestige, until by the beginning of the last tale Pryderi is ruling most of South Wales... It was an attempt to revive the fortunes of Deheubarth (South Wales) that led to Gwenllian's death at Kidwelly in 1136. The expansionism of Dyfed in the *Four Branches* must rule out authorship by anyone from Glamorgan or Gwent...

Ninth is the textual context of the *Four Branches. The White Book of Rhydderch* was compiled for Rhydderch ab Ieuan. He was the great-great grandson of Maredudd ab Owain, whose children Efa and Gruffydd have already been noted as literary patrons. Maredudd himself was the great-grandson of Gwenllian. If the *Four Branches* were published as a "limited edition", having little or no circulation except amongst the descendants of the Lord Rhys, it would explain why allusions to them are so rare in the work of medieval Welsh bards... The *Four Branches* were read in a limited court circle...

Tenth is the dating of the *Four Branches*.... Gwenllian married in 1116 and was killed in 1136. If she wrote these tales in the 1120's, it would suit the chronological arguments used by Ifor Williams and others, a crucial item of which is the use of at least one loanword from Old French: "pali" (brocaded silk), from "palie". Had the tales been written much later than the 1120's, we would expect more signs of French influence in terms of vocabulary and the institutions of feudalism... If these aspects of the Four Branches were due to Gwenllian's possible exile in Dublin in 1127, we might date them to between then and 1136, perhaps to 1128 or a little later. This evidence tallies with the subjective feeling that such a literary masterpiece is more likely to be written by a mature woman of 30 or so than by someone younger.

Eleventh is the relation of the *Iron House* legend in Branwen to the Irish tale *Mesca Ulad*... the evidence of Branwen, which hardly predates 1120, strengthens the case for taking the *Book of Leinster Mesca Ulad* as a product of the first quarter of the 12th century... Perhaps Gwenllian came across *Mesca Ulad* in 1127, as an exile in Dublin.

Breeze goes on to develop other aspects of the *Four Branches*. Wales' greatest heroine, the mother of the great Arglwydd Rhys, not only could have written this true classic of European literature, a work of world renown, but also be the first British woman author.'***

* Rhys ap Gruffudd, with his surviving brother Maredudd, fought the Normans (see the author's *100 Greatest Welshmen*), and Rhys burnt Kidwelly Castle in 1139 before rebuilding it 30 years later. It was back in Norman hands by 1201, but in the first half of the 13th century was partially destroyed on two more occasions by Welsh attacks on their French overlords. The castle is well worth visiting. It stood as the Norman gateway into West Wales, the royal base in Carmarthenshire. In 1106 Henry I asked Bishop Roger of Salisbury to build a castle there, next to the River Gwendraeth, and it later passed to the de Londres family, who had built Ogmore Castle. By 1244 it was again recovered from the Welsh, and held out in 1257-58 against a Welsh rising which destroyed the

town. Payn and Patrick de Chaworth began a major stone reconstruction in the 1270's, inspired by the castles they had seen on crusade. Henry of Lancaster than added a concentric construction, and in 1403 it held out for 3 weeks against the Welsh and French forces of Owain Glyndŵr. In the 15th century the great Sir Rhys ap Thomas owned it.

** The power of this cycle of stories should not be underestimated. In the USA, the prestigious *Saturday Review* commented on Evangeline Walton's rewriting of the *Mabionogion* as a series of novels, *Prince of Annwn, Children of Llyr, Song of Rhiannon,* and *Island of the Mighty*: 'These books are not only the best fantasies of the 20th century, but also great works of fiction. They are actual retellings of the diverse legends of the Mabinogion in novel form...dealing with Good and Evil, quest... and the nature of love.... Only C.S. Lewis has matched Walton's subtle depiction of the forces of Good and Evil'.

*** Footnote: Ernest Renan, the noted 19th century French philosopher called the *Mabinogion,* in his *The Poetry of the Celtic Races* (1896) – '... a manifestation of the romantic genius of the Breton (British) races (Cornwall, Wales, Brittany). It was through them that the Welsh imagination exercised its influence upon the Continent, that it transformed, in the twelfth century, the poetic art of Europe, and realised this miracle, - that the creations of a half-conquered race have become the universal feast of imagination for mankind... Do we now understand the intellectual rôle of that little race which gave to the world Arthur, Guinevere, Lancelot, Perceval, Merlin, St. Brandan, St. Patrick, and almost all the poetical cycles of the Middle Ages?

It was above all by the creation of woman's character, by introducing into mediaeval poetry, hitherto hard and austere, the nuances of love, that the Breton romances brought about this curious metamorphosis. It was like an electric spark; in a few years European taste was changed. Nearly all the types of womankind known to the Middle Ages, Guinevere, Iseult, Enid, are derived from Arthur's court... In the Mabinogion, on the other hand, the principal part always belongs to the women...' A case can be made that Gwenllian's book altered attitudes of Western men towards women more than any other piece of literature or legislation.

*Footnote:*
Giraldus Cambrensis wrote in his *Itinerary*: 'In this district (Kidwelly), after the death of King Henry, whilst Gruffydd, son of Rhys, the Prince of South Wales, was engaged in soliciting assistance from North Wales, his wife Gwenllian (Like the Queen of the Amazons and a second Penthesilea) led an army into these parts; but she was defeated by Maurice de Londres, lord of that country, and Geoffrey, the bishop's constable. Morgan, one of her sons, whom she had arrogantly brought with her in that expedition, was slain and the other, Malgo (Maelgwyn), taken prisoner; and she, with many of her followers, was put to death.'

## GWENLLIAN ferch LLYWELYN ap GRUFFUDD 19 June 1282 – 7 June 1337

## A PRISONER FOR 54 YEARS

Another Gwenllian was the tragic daughter of *Ein Llyw Olaf* (Our Last Leader) Llywelyn ap Gruffudd. Gwenllian's mother was Eleanor, the daughter of Simon de Montfort, who led the Second Barons' War in 1263-64, becoming *de facto* ruler of England. De Montfort was Earl of Leicester and called two parliaments, the first stripping Henry III of unlimited authority, and the

The remains of Gwenllian's birthplace at the llys of the Princes of Gwynedd, Abergwyngregryn *courtesy of Roger Richards*

second including ordinary citizens from towns. Just as his grandfather Llywelyn ab Iorwerth (Llywelyn Fawr) had sided with the English barons to force John to sign the Magna Carta in 1215, Llywelyn ap Gruffudd, Prince of Wales, sent Welsh infantry to assist Simon de Montfort, when the earl defeated and captured Henry III at Lewes in 1264. Henry's son Edward never forgot the humiliation of the defeat, and determined on revenge. Llywelyn's men were also in de Montfort's army when he was killed at Evesham in 1265. Heavily outnumbered by royalist forces, the battle was described as the 'murder of Evesham, for battle it was none.'

Prince Edward deliberately picked twelve of his most powerful warriors as an assassination squad, and they stalked the battlefield, independent of the main army, with their sole aim being to kill de Montfort. Roger Mortimer killed Montfort by stabbing him in the neck with a lance, and the body was frenziedly mutilated. 'The head of the earl of Leicester ... was severed from his body, and his testicles cut off and hung on either side of his nose', and Edward sent it as a gift to Roger Mortimer's wife at Wigmore Castle.

In 1238 de Montfort had secretly married (the widow) Eleanor Plantagenet, 'Eleanor of England' (1215-1275), the youngest daughter of King John, and the sister of King Henry III. The relationship between King Henry and his brother-in-law was frequently strained, even before the Barons' War. Their daughter Lady Eleanor de Montfort was born in 1252. Her father's ally Llywelyn ap Gruffudd, Prince of Wales made a treaty with

Earl Simon shortly before Evesham when the earl was killed, and Llywelyn pledged to marry Lady Eleanor.

After de Montfort's death, his family was forced to flee from England, with Countess Eleanor taking her 13-year-old daughter Lady Eleanor to the safety a Montfort foundation, the Dominican nunnery at Montargis near de Montfort's great castle. Countess Eleanor died in Spring 1275, and shortly afterwards Llywelyn ap Gruffudd and Eleanor de Montfort married by proxy. The Prince of Wales was said to have been born around 1223, but judging from the treaties he sealed, it may have been nearer 1217 or even earlier. Thus Llywelyn was around 58 and Eleanor 23. Eleanor began the sea voyage from France to north Wales, avoiding travelling through England.

However, the two ships carrying Eleanor, her brother Amaury and a bodyguard of Welsh and French knights, were captured just off the Isles of Scilly. Edward, now king of England and at war with Llywelyn, had been forewarned of their departure, and had sent four ships to intercept them. Edward's paybooks record that he paid Thomas L'archdeacon £20 for carrying out the mission. *'The Demoiselle'* Eleanor was taken to Bristol, and then held prisoner at Windsor for nearly three years. She was not released until 1278, following the Treaty of Aberconwy between Edward and Prince Llywelyn.

Eleanor and Llywelyn were formally married at Worcester Cathedral in that year, and Edward I gave his cousin the bride away, and paid for the wedding feast. Before the wedding mass was celebrated, Edward insisted that Llywelyn should put his seal to an adjustment to the agreement that they had previously made. Llywelyn had no alternative but to comply, and he later stated that he did it under duress, 'moved by the fear that can grip a steadfast man'.

Following the ceremony, Eleanor became officially known as Princess of Wales and Lady of Snowdon. On the Feast Day of Gervasius and Protasius, 19 June 1282, she died in childbirth, giving birth to a daughter, Princess Gwenllian in the Welsh royal home on Garth Celyn. Lady Eleanor's body was carried across the Lafan Sands, and she was buried in the Franciscan Friary on the sea shore at Llanfaes, alongside Lady Joan, the wife of Prince Llywelyn ab Iorwerth.

In Spring 1282, King Edward had moved a massive army into north Wales. Having suffered two major defeats, and Prince Llywelyn's rejection of a bribe of £1,000 a year and a baronial estate in England, Edward sent an assassination squad led by Roger LeStrange. Upon Friday 11 December, Prince Llywelyn, having been lured into a trap near Builth Wells, was killed. The following morning, some 3,000 infantry, with their arms laid down under truce waiting for the return of the Prince, were massacred. Roger Le Strange wrote to the King immediately afterwards to inform him of the success of the mission. Edward then moved his army across the river Conwy, to circle the heartland of Gwynedd.

Bards were killed to prevent the news spreading, the subject of one of Hungary's favourite poems, recounted in this author's *The 100 Greatest Welshmen*. The effect of Llywelyn's death upon Wales was dramatic. The people and the bards grieved. Part of Gruffudd ab yr Ynad Coch's despairing elegy shows us the emotion felt towards Gwenllian's father (- translated by Professor Joseph Clancy):

'With Llywelyn's death, gone is my mind.
Heart frozen in the breast with terror,
Desire decays like dried-up branches.
See you not the rush of wind and rain?
See you not the oaks lash each other?
See you not the ocean scourging the shore?
See you not the truth is portending?
See you not the sun hurtling the sky?
See you not that the stars have fallen?
Have you no belief in God, foolish men?
See you not that the world is ending?
Ah God, that the sea would cover the land!
What is left us that we should linger?
No place to flee from terror's prison,
No place to live; wretched is living!
No counsel, no clasp, no path left open.
One way to be freed from fear's sad strife.'

In June 1283, Llywelyn's brother Prince Dafydd ap Gruffudd, and his family that is believed to include the infant Gwenllian, were captured at Bera, in the uplands above Aber Garth Celyn. Prince Dafydd, 'seriously wounded' in the struggle, was taken to King Edward who was waiting at Rhuddlan castle. On 3rd October 1283, he was tied to the tail of a horse, dragged through the streets of Shrewsbury, then hanged, drawn and quartered. The royal children were locked away, never to be set free. Brutality and the ruthless hunting down of the bloodline brought a virtual end to Welsh resistance to the invasion.

Edward seized Welsh royal fortifications including Castell y Bere, Harlech, Cricieth, Caernarfon and Rhuddlan, and extensively refortified and extended them. He removed the Cistercian Abbey from Conwy, and built a castle on the rock, gaining a key foothold into the ancient kingdom of Gwynedd. The series of castles, now a World Heritage Site, were built girdling Snowdonia, almost bankrupting the English economy. Edward paid for his wars with punitive taxes upon Jews, and only achieved victory by bankrupting two Italian banks, reneging upon his loans. Draconian laws were passed, taking away Welsh human rights.

At this time, the heads of Gwenllian's father and uncle were being exhibited on spikes at the Tower of London by the Norman-French-speaking monarch of England. Llywelyn's body was possibly buried at Abbey Cwm-Hir, but the quarters of Dafydd's body went on display at Bristol, Northampton, York and Winchester. It is thought that Edward I first arranged for Gwenllian to be killed, but he was prevailed upon to desist because there was a close family tie (she was his cousin's daughter). Instead, he arranged for Princess Gwenllian to be sent 'in her cradle' to the Gilbertine Priory at Sempringham Priory, asking for her to be admitted to the order 'having the Lord before our eyes, pitying also her sex and age, that the innocent and unwitting may not seem to atone for the iniquity and ill-doing of the wicked and contemplating specially the life of your Order'.

The king gave the Gilbertines £20 a year, a huge sum at the time, for their services in hiding Gwenllian from the rest of the world. Four years later, Edward sent a mandate to Thomas Normanvill 'to go to the places where the daughters of Llywelyn and David his brother, who have taken the veil of the Order of Sempringham, are dwelling, and to report upon their state and custody by next Parliament'. Later, when the abbey was beset by financial difficulties, Edward appealed to the Pope to assist, reminding him that the abbey was the custodian of the daughter of Llywelyn, Prince of Wales.

Gwenllian grew up never knowing the Welsh language, her native tongue, nor any familial love. From her cradle to her grave all she knew was austerity, (behind high walls, in bleak, windswept, Lincolnshire.) The Gilbertines never even knew how to pronounce her name, recording it as 'Wencilian', and it seems that she signed herself 'Wentliane'. Prince Dafydd's sons Llywelyn and Owain, the heirs to the Principality, were taken under armed guard to Bristol castle, locked away, and never released.* Princess Gwladys ferch Dafydd was imprisoned in the Gilbertine Priory at Sixhills, Lincolnshire. Gwladys died in 1336. Her cousin Gwenllian died in 1337, having spent 54 years as a prisoner in the Priory.

The Gilbertian Order was allowed to acquire certain lands, including Cottesmore, Ketton, Stamford and Casterton, because Edward I had endowed them on Gwenllian. In 1301, when Princess Gwenllian, was 19, Edward I made his son the first English 'Prince of Wales' (later Edward II), to try to give credence to right as a conqueror. In 1327, the new king Edward III granted the 45-year-old Gwenllian a yearly pension to pay for her board and lodgings in the Priory.

The records state: '1337. Wencilian, daughter of the Prince of Wales Llywelyn, died, after 54 years of life in the Order. The King excuses the prior and the Convent from a payment of £39 15s 4d...' The payment waived was for tax owed by the Abbey, because the King was grateful that yet another Royal Welsh child had died. Piers Langtoft, in his rhyming chronicles noted that in 1337:

'More than a year before he met his shame,
A daughter was born, Wencilian her name,
In her cradle young to England she came;
Through counsel of the king was brought to Sempringham;
And there she was in four and fifty year,
Nourished with wynne, nun and secular.
Nor have we new lattles, dead is Wencilian,
Llywelyn's daughter of Wales, that on England ran.
Her death was much mentioned, for she was full courteous,
Amongst the ladies gentle they tell of her loss,
The seventh day of June, Whitsun even the time,
Died that lady between midern and prime.'

In 1993 a plaque was placed in the ruins of Sempringham. The late Captain Richard Turner of Caernarfon and Angharad Thomas had led the campaign to commemorate this 'lost' Princess of Wales. The Norman church of St Andrews at Sempringham is a mile along an uneven cart-track at Pointon village, near Bourne in Lincolnshire. It is on the site of a famous priory founded by the crippled priest St Gilbert around 1130 for his white-robed Gilbertian order. This was the only purely English monastic order, and the only one which cared for men and women alike. The foundations, fish ponds and holy well have been excavated. Just south of the church is the slate and stone memorial to Princess Gwenllian. It simply reads:

'In memory of Gwenllian
Daughter of the last Prince of Wales
Born at Abergwyngregyn 12.6.1282
Died at Sempringham 7.6.1337
Having been held prisoner for 54 years.'

* The two sons of Prince Dafydd ap Gruffudd had been imprisoned in Bristol Castle. Prince Llywelyn ap Dafydd died of malnutrition in 1288 (aged ten?) but Prince Owain ap Dafydd was still alive. After almost thirty years of incarceration, he asked to be allowed outside his cell to play. In 1312, Owain wrote to Edward II: 'Owain, son of Dafydd ap Gruffydd, shows that whereas he is by order of the King detained in the Castle of Bristol in a strong and close prison and has been since he was 7 years old for his father's trespass. He prays that the King that he may go and play within the wall of the Castle if he cannot have the better grace.' The letter was read and the King's Council vindictively refused his request: 'As the King wills that Owain, son of Dafydd ap Gruffudd who is in the Constable's custody in the Castle, should be kept in future more securely, he orders the Constable to cause the strong house within the castle to

be repaired as soon as possible, and to make a wooden cage bound with iron within that house, in which Owain might be enclosed at night.'

*Footnotes:*

1. In 1991, Byron Rogers wrote an article, *Gwenllian and the Lost Children* in *The Guardian*. Captain Richard Turner of Caernarfon, having read the article, and also Sharon Penman's novel *The Reckoning* and Edith Pargeter's *The Brothers of Gwynedd*, in 1993 decided to erect a memorial to Gwenllian at Sempringham. Together with Angharad Tomas and Kathryn Pritchard Gibson, they raised the funds to have a stone engraved. Captain Turner took the stone to Sempringham and erected it himself (and without permission) near the church. In 1996, shortly before Captain Turner's death, and at his insistence, The Gwenllian Society was founded to look after the memorial and to keep alive Gwenllian's memory. The Society's first AGM was held at Garth Celyn in 1998, the site of the Welsh royal home, Gwenllian's birthplace. In a 1999 telephone poll the *Daily Mirror* asked 'Should the day of Gwenllian's birth become a national holiday?', and 96% answered 'Yes'. However, in 2000 the memorial at Sempringham was vandalised, and in 2001 a new, more substantial memorial stone was set up to her in Sempringham. In 2008 an inscribed stone in honour of Gwenllian was set up at Snowdon summit, and in 2009 a peak in the Carneddau range was renamed Carnedd Gwenllian.

2. Following the capture of Prince Dafydd ap Gruffudd in June 1283, the Welsh royal home was seized by Edward. The king and his entourage stayed in the Welsh palace of Garth Celyn, Abergwyngregryn, twice, for brief periods, in July 1283 and again in August 1284. The Palace and its farmland was retained by the English crown until 1553, although no member of the English royal family stayed there again. In 1303 and again in 1306 the documentary evidence shows that extensive repair works were carried out to Gwenllian's birthplace. A total of 12,640 gallons of lime and 37,920 gallons of sand were used to make mortar and plaster. The walls and windows were repaired, doors were rehung, new wooden chests made for the solar and garderobe, and the garden was cleared. Priests continued to be paid to say masses in the Royal Court Chapel. Repairs continued to be made to the royal home until the reign of Henry VI, but then they were left to gradually fall into disrepair and crumble.

   In 1537, Henry VIII's Antiquary John Leland noted 'the Palace on the hille still in part stondeth.'

   In 1553 Rhys Thomas of Aberglasney and his wife Jane acquired the property in an underhand deal with the Earl of Pembroke shortly before the death of the young king Edward VI. The Thomas family and their descendents turned the medieval buildings into an Elizabethan complex known as 'The Manor of Aber'. It was later acquired by the Bulkeley family of Anglesey, who in turn sold it in 1862 to Penrhyn Estate.

   Parts of the walls of the medieval buildings, dating to the 12th and 13th centuries, still remain in the present buildings. Carved sandstone fragments are found in front of the house. The turret, known locally as Tŵr Llywelyn, dating to c.1200, has later windows cut into the structure.

In the 1890s letters appeared in the newspapers, pleading for a Memorial to the Princes and their families to be erected on the hillside behind the house. The Manor of Aber was at that time owned by Penrhyn estate, and the suggestion was rejected.

From 1926 when Penrhyn estate sold off many of its landholdings, the house (known as Pen y Bryn from the 17th century), on the promontory of Garth Celyn, has been in private ownership.

On 2 May 1230, Lord William de Braose was hanged in the marshland at the foot of Garth Celyn, having been found together with Lady Joan in Prince Llywelyn's chamber. Lady Joan was held under house arrest here following the incident. This forms the basis for the drama *Siwan* by Saunders Lewis, studied by Welsh A level students. Lady Joan, wife of Prince Llywelyn ab Iorwerth died here in 1237; Prince Dafydd ap Llywelyn died here in 1246; and Lady Eleanor de Montfort died here on 19 June 1282, giving birth to Princess Gwenllian. The late Gwynfor Evans described Garth Celyn as 'A place that holds the Soul of the Nation', and the last Palace of the Princes needs to be properly recognised for its role in the history of the nation.

# CATRIN GLYNDŴR 1380? - 1413

## WALES' LOST PRINCESS

By Isabel Monnington-Taylor

The greatest of all Welsh heroes was Owain Glyndŵr (28 May 1354 or 55 – 20 September 1415), a man who fought the English crown for 15 years, repelling no less than six fullscale invasions, and who then vanished from history. Owain's daughter Catrin was probably born at her father's splendid moated manor house at Sycharth, near Oswestry. This grand house had many rooms and pillars, and a tiled roof. It even boasted a chimney, a very modern feature for these times. The bard Iolo Goch wrote of it as:

*'Llys barwn, lle syberwydd*
*Lle daw beirdd aml, lle da byd*
(The court of a baron, a place of courtesy
Where numerous bards come, a place of the good life)
… Each side full, each house at court,
Orchard, vineyard, white fortress;
The master's rabbit warren;
Ploughs and strong steeds of great frame;
Near the court, even finer,
The deer park within that field;
Fresh green meadows and hayfields;
Neatly enclosed rows of grain;

Fine mill on a smooth-flowing stream;
Dovecot, a bright stone tower;
A fish-pond, enclosed and deep,
Where nets are cast when need be,
Abounding, no argument,
In pike and splendid whiting;
His land a board where birds dwell,
Peacocks, high-stepping herons....
His serfs do the proper work,
Fill the needs of the region,
Bringing Shrewsbury's fine beer,
Whisky, the first-brewed bragget,
All drinks, white bread and wine,
His meat, fire for his kitchen.'
And Owain's wife Margaret is described as:
A knightly line's bright daughter,
Proud hostess of royal blood,
His children come, two by two,
A fine nestful of princes.'

Sycharth was indeed a plentiful estate, where Glyndŵr distilled his own *chwisgi*, and his house-bard Iolo Goch delighted in the beer from Shrewsbury. It was set in prosperous and fertile land, with many timbered buildings and nearby market towns.

Through Owain, Catrin Glyndŵr was descended from Madog ap Maredudd, last prince of Powys, and also from the princes of Deheubarth. There were also vast family estates at Glyndyfyrdwy near Llangollen, an enclave of Welsh rule in Edeirnion and Dinmael. These were near the ruined remains of the magnificent hilltop castle, Castell Dinas Bran, and also the great Cistercian monastery of Valle Crucis. Here, Catrin could have seen the tomb her great-great-grandfather Madog ap Gruffudd Fychan, of the dynasty of Powys, under a fine heraldic slab. She could have run her fingers over the carved single lion rampant - the lion of the dynasty of Northern Powys, later taken up by her father as his standard. If she had visited all her father's lands, she would have gained an understanding of the different landscapes of Wales, as Iscoed lay north of the river Teifi, in Ceredigion.

Marriage to English families of the borderlands (The Marches) was quite usual. Owain's grandfather Gruffudd had married Elizabeth le Strange, and Catrin's own mother Margaret was the daughter of Sir David Hanmer of Maelor Saesneg. The Hanmers' integration with their Welsh neighbours was comfortable and complete. Catrin's maternal grandmother, the wife of Sir David Hanmer, was Angharad ferch Llywelyn Ddu. No doubt these families were thoroughly bilingual, as shown by the ecclesiastical favour given to Catrin's mother under her Welsh name Marred ferch Dafydd. Her brothers were Gruffudd, Philip and John Hanmer. Catrin's was probably an intellectual household. Her father Owain had received legal training at London's Inns of Court. Her grandfather Sir David Hanmer was Governor of South Wales in 1381, and one of the chief justices of the King's Bench by 1383. He was also retained as a legal advisor to families in the Marcher borders. However, he died in 1387 and Catrin lost some valuable links and activity with society across Wales and the borderlands.

After David Hanmer's death, the family must have been marginalised. Owain Glyndŵr progressively lost influence, a factor in the dispute with his neighbour Reginald de Grey. De Grey, a notably treacherous character, claimed land which had been held as common grazing rights for Owain's Welsh tenants. Owain felt obliged to appeal to the courts and travelled to London to affirm his rights to this land, on behalf of his tenants. He was 45 years-old, a cultured linguist, legally-trained and had faithfully served the Franco-English crown in battle. Coming to the end of his years, he had retired to a life of luxury on his estates. However, this nobleman was sent packing from the court, with the judge's words ringing in his ears 'What care we for barefoot Welsh dogs!' Catrin must have seen him leave angry, but expecting right and legal precedence to prevail. She now saw him return, exhausted from the journey, frustrated and seething at Norman 'justice'.

**Catrin Glyndwr's father Owain - statue at Corwen**
*courtesy of Dr. Ed Conley*

The sense of injustice was shared by all his family, and de Grey asked Owain.to meet for peace talks, but hid armed men in the nearby forest to kill him. Warned in Welsh by a bard, Owain narrowly escaped with his life. As a result, upon 16 September 1400 (Glyndŵr Day), he was proclaimed Prince of Wales by his supporters. He adopted on his seal the four lions passant of Gwynedd, the arms of the last Prince of Wales, the murdered Llywelyn ap Gruffudd. However, Owain altered them to lions rampant upon the seal, and upon his scarlet and gold flags and trappings. Catrin's uncles Gruffudd and Philip Hanmer, and Tewdwr ap Gruffudd (Glyndŵr's brother) were amongst those whose names were included in the declaration. Catrin and her brothers and sisters must have experienced a chill of excitement. The arguments and emotions were strong - there was no choice but to risk all - the alternative was a slow disintegration of all they valued. Once fighting had broken out, there was no satisfaction of success in the field for Catrin and her family, only the watching and hoping for news.

Things must have appeared bleak when Henry IV marched into Sycharth and destroyed it completely. Everything Catrin had known and loved had gone.

No-one knows where the family spent this time - presumably in the houses of supporters, never knowing how welcome they might be or when they might need to move on. Any invading forces of Henry IV followed a scorched-earth policy. But increasing support and the news of battle successes must have helped keep their spirits high. And then sometime around late-June 1402 the news must have reached them - of a superb battle success, both militarily and psychologically. The 'barefoot Welsh dogs', a volunteer army, unlike the larger professional forces of Henry and his Marcher Lords, had destroyed the king's army and captured important prisoners, taking them to Owain's 'fortress' of Snowdonia. At the great Battle of Pilleth on June 22nd, over 2,000 of the king's men died in a crushing victory. Their commander, Lord Edmund Mortimer was an heir to the throne, and came from one of the most powerful families in the realm. With her connections amongst the Marcher families, Catrin would have known of Edmund and the power and influence of his family. In the brief 3 months that followed, Edmund changed from Owain's captive to an important ally. By October 1402, Catrin and Edmund were married*. This may have been a political marriage, but it could also have been a romantic one. Shakespeare suggests this in *Henry IV - Part 1*, where Owain describes his daughter's love and her fighting spirit to Mortimer:

'My daughter weeps; she will not part with you,
She'll be a soldier too; she'll to the wars'.

She was 'one that no persuasion can do no good upon'. So this was a potentially stormy relationship! But in spite of a language problem: 'my wife can speak no English, I no Welsh', Shakespeare writes that Mortimer returned her feelings:

'I understand thy looks: that pretty Welsh,
Which thou down-pourest from these swelling heavens...
I understand thy kisses, and thou mine.'

It was thought at the time that Glyndŵr could command the elements, and well as possessing a magic Raven's stone that made him invisible - even the English troops ascribed magical properties to this guerrilla partisan. Again, this is referred to in *Henry IV Part 1*:

'Three times hath Henry Bolingbroke made head
Against my power. Thrice from the banks of the Wye
And sandy-bottomed Severn have I sent
Him bootless home, and weather-beaten back.'

A 1402 entry in *Annales Henrici Quarti*, the English recording of the times, reads that Glyndŵr 'almost destroyed the King and his armies, by magic as it was thought, for from the time they entered Wales to the time they left, never did a gentle air breathe on them, but throughout whole days and nights, rain mixed with snow and hail afflicted them with cold beyond endurance.'

The next few years after her marriage would have been busy for Catrin. She started her family early, but she was still without a permanent home for her young family. By the third year of Catrin's marriage this had all changed. The great and unconquerable Harlech Castle was taken by the Welsh! The capture was sometime after April 1404 - a major boost to the whole campaign. It was her new home - a home which should have been fit for a royal family. But it was certainly not as luxurious as Sycharth, and the previous occupants had not cared for the castle. Like many of the English castles in Wales, Harlech had fallen into a state of disrepair. Lead had not been replaced, so that the roofs leaked and timbers rotted. There were no stocks of any kind, so Catrin and her children would have to rely on anything that the surrounding country could provide - and blockaded Wales had been ravaged by war and Henry's scorched-earth policy. Provisions were meagre. The traditional trading routes with Herefordshire were badly disrupted and little must have got through to Harlech. But with another home to replace the destroyed mansions at Sycharth and Glyndyfrdwy, and her with mother Marred to help, Catrin will have started to look forward to a settled future. By the spring of 1405, the family's hopes must have been high. The winter storms and winds in the cold, damp castle, would have passed, and now there was more to eat, and fresh food.

But May 1405 brought terrible news, of the Battle of Pwll Melyn where Catrin lost a brother and her uncle. The family must have been devastated by the news. Her uncle Tewdwr was three years or so younger that Owain. Like Owain, he was a dynamic, experienced knight. Tewdwr and Owain had first fought together at Berwick and in Scotland. Tewdwr was so like Owain that at first it was thought that Owain had been killed in the battle. There was more awful news. Catrin's brother Gruffudd had been captured and taken to the Tower of London (- he was later to die of disease, incarcerated in Nottingham Castle). The news must have had a devastating effect upon Marred, Catrin's mother, who must have started to wonder at the course Owain was taking.

Hopes were now dashed, and there was an increasing sense of foreboding as the summer heat increased. But Owain was determined not to let one setback undermine all the progress he had made. In July, he called for all his supporters to come to an Assembly. The preparations for such a gathering must have been immense, for it took place just a month later in August. Was it on this occasion that Owain wore the royal gilded helmet, cuirass and sword given to him by Charles VI, King of France, just the year before? But in spite of this gift French support was waning, and by the following year was finished. The following spring, with the Pennal Declaration, the family's hopes were high, but mixed with doubt and fear as support diminished. The English siege of Aberystwyth started in early summer 1407. Its defender, Rhys Ddu, was threatened with beheading by Owain himself if he surrendered it. When it finally fell in later 1408, the siege engines (including a massive cannon known as 'The King's Daughter') were brought up to besiege Harlech Castle.

1408 saw another blow for Glyndŵr. His ally, the old Earl of Northumberland, Hotspur's father, was killed at the Battle of Braham Moor by Prince Henry's forces. The Prince then re-entered Wales, bombarded Aberystwyth into submission, and by 1409 had also taken Harlech,

**Catrin Glyndwr's memorial in London**

Glyndŵr's last bastion, capturing his wife and family. Edmund Mortimer, the former enemy who became his son-in-law in captivity, died (probably of starvation) in Harlech, fighting for Glyndŵr. Owain had just managed to escape from Harlech as the besiegers moved in. It must have been a difficult decision to leave his family there, while he tried to round up support rather than be cornered. A sad footnote has been the discovery noted in John Lloyd's 1931 book *Owen Glendower* – he 'left behind him in the castle one little personal relic which has recently been unearthed in the course of excavations, viz. a gilt bronze boss from a set of horse harness, bearing the four lions rampant which he had assumed as Prince of Wales'. The four lions rampant, counter-changed in gold and red, were the ancient arms of the princes of Gwynedd. Glyndŵr was more a descendant of the Houses of Deheubarth and Powys than Gwynedd. He had needed that provenance though, which had died out with the vicious assassination of Owain Llawgoch, to be accepted throughout Wales.

The winter of 1408 had been exceptionally severe, with an abundance of snow from December to March, so cold that blackbirds and thrushes dropped dead from the trees. At that time, the sea washed right up to the castle crag, and Catrin and her children would have seen the siege engines, men and supplies coming ashore. Wales had no sea power, since the French and Bretons had left them to their fate a few years earlier. Her children saw death and starvation, heard the crashing cannon, and hid from the arrows of longbows and the bolts of crossbows. 1,500 crossbow bolts were fired in the sieges of Aberystwyth and Harlech. Llywelyn ap Madog ap Llywelyn, the commander of the castle's defences, was killed, and Catrin's saw her husband, Lord Edmund Mortimer, die of starvation. The remaining defenders had no supplies or armaments left, during one of the most terrible winters on record. After being besieged from 1407, the castle fell in February 1409. Marred, Catrin and her son Lionel and three daughters were captured by Gilbert Talbot of Goodrich Castle, and transported on a cold, difficult journey to London. The children were potential heirs to the throne, so Catrin knew that their future was bleak. Here she heard of the execution of Owain's bravest lieutenants.

The last gasp of Glyndŵr's revolt occurred near Welshpool Castle when a raiding party under Phillip Scudamore, Rhys Tudur and Rhys Ddu was beaten and the leaders captured. After the usual revolting, slow, barbarous executions, Scudamore's head was placed on a spike at Shrewsbury, Rhys ap Tudur's at London, and Rhys Ddu's at Chester. By 1413, the force of Owain Glyndŵr 's uprising was spent, and the new King Henry V took the throne in March. By December, after four long years in captivity, Catrin and two of the children were dead. Their burial, in 1413 at St Swithin's Church in the heart of the City of London, is recorded in Exchequer documents: 'To William del Chambre, valet of the said Earl (Arundel). In money paid to his own hands, for expenses and other charges incurred for the burial and exequies of the wife of Edward (sic - Edmund) Mortimer and her daughters, buried within St Swithin's Church London... £1'. It is interesting to note that when King Henry V came to the throne he restored Thomas FitzAlan, 12th Earl of Arundel to a place of influence, immediately appointing him Lord Treasurer. Thomas FitzAlan owed much to the new king but was also anxious to prove his loyalty - the Beauforts, with whom he had previously been closely associated, having fallen out of favour. We do not know what happened to Catrin's son Lionel – he had more right to the crown than Henry V, the son of the usurping Henry IV, so he was possibly simply starved to death.

In 2001 Menna Elfyn (q.v.) was asked to write an inscription for Catrin Glyndŵr's sculpture set in Swithin's Graveyard, London, and later relocated in Wallbrook Gardens, near Cannon St, London. She said 'Somehow her miserable life and death gnawed at me until I had finished a whole sequence. It began with simple lines in my head: *Aria ei rhyw yw hiraeth* (The aria of her kind/sex is longing) and 'An exile's silent song'. The sequence is, of course, as meaningful today as it was back then with the wars that continue to silence people-speaking in tongues and hushed tones'. The inscription reads:

Catrin Glyndŵr
GODRE TWR – ADRE NID AETH
At the tower end, far away from home
ARAI EI RHYW YW HIRAETH
longing is a woman's song

alaw dawel yr alltud
An exile's silent song
*Menna Elfyn*

In 2003 an exhibition was held at the National Library of Wales to celebrate
Catrin's legacy. A play, *Catrin Glyndŵr*, by the estimable Heledd Bianchi,
was premièred in 2004, which this author was lucky to see. For a brief
moment in history, Owain Glyndŵr's daughter Catrin might have become
Queen of England.

* In 1402, the imprisoned Edmund Mortimer married Owain Glyndŵr's
daughter, Catrin. Mortimer's nephew, the young Earl of March, had a far better
claim to the English throne than Henry IV, and no doubt Glyndŵr was hoping
that Henry Bolingbroke would be killed and Wales made safe with an English
king as an ally. (The nephew was the young son of Roger Mortimer, and he died
in 1425, his massive estates passing to Richard, Duke of York. Roger Mortimer
had been officially appointed his heir by the childless Richard II. The Welsh
people wanted a Mortimer to succeed to the crown, instead of the usurper, Henry
Bolingbroke).

Although Glyndŵr had briefly won political, cultural and ecclesiastical
independence, before final defeat and the harshness of the laws of a revenging
English king, the wars had been a personal disaster for him. His brother Tewdwr
had died at the Battle of Pwll Melyn in 1405. His son Gruffydd was captured
there, and spent the remainder of his years imprisoned in the Tower of London
and Nottingham Castle. Some sources say that he died of the plague in the
Tower of London in 1410 - he just vanished from history, like so many other
captured descendants of Welsh princes. Glyndŵr's wife, two daughters and
three grand-daughters were taken into imprisonment after the fall of Harlech
Castle, and all died shortly in captivity. His son-in-law, Edmund Mortimer, with
a good claim to the English crown, died at Harlech. Mortimer's wife, Owain's
daughter Catherine, died in prison with two of her daughters, and all were buried
in St Swithin's Church in London around 1413. Only the churchyard remains.
Her son Lionel, Owain's grandson and a claimant for both Welsh and English
crowns, died, where or when is unrecorded, but probably by neglect or murder.
Owain Glyndŵr's closest lieutenants and comrades-in-arms, Rhys Ddu, Rhys ap
Llywelyn, Rhys Gethin and Phillip Scudamore had all been tortured to death
Only one son, Maredudd, somehow survived the carnage.

*Footnotes:*
1. There is a memorial sculpture to Catrin Glyndŵr and her children at their
burial site at St Swithin's garden opposite Cannon St Station in London. The
huge 14-tonne block of bluestone from Gelligaer carved free-form by Richard
Renshaw and topped by a bronze casting by Bryn Chegwidden stands as a
reminder of the suffering of all women and children in war. Isabel Monnington-
Taylor, a direct descendant of Glyndŵr, unveiled the monument on Glyndŵr

Day, September 16th, 2001. Details and directions can be found on www.londonremembers.com/memorials/catrin-glyndwr.

2. There is also information upon Hereford's Wigmore Castle, Mortimer's great base, in the superb website castlewales.com. The Marcher Lords were allowed to raise their own armies, exact taxes and build castles without the king's consent, in return for acting as a defensive cushion between Wales and its adjacent shires, with many Welsh-speakers. By 1328, Roger Mortimer's acquisitions had earned him the title Earl of March, signifying his ownership of lordships all along the Welsh border and in the English enclave of southern Pembrokeshire. Ludlow Castle was the Mortimers' administrative centre, but Wigmore was the family seat, reinforced by the Mortimer endowment of Wigmore Abbey. After Roger Mortimer's liaison with Queen Isabella, and their murder of King Edward II in Berkeley Castle, he became de facto ruler of England until executed by Edward III. The 4th Earl of March, another Roger Mortimer, was named heir to the throne by the childless Richard II. However, the crown was usurped when Henry Bolingbroke captured and murdered Richard II. The new Henry IV held Roger's son Edmund at Windsor, to ensure that his own son, Prince Hal (later Henry V) succeeded him. On Roger Mortimer's death, Edmund Mortimer was in a difficult position. When he was captured by Glyndŵr, Henry IV knew that the powerful uncle to the real heir to the throne was out of the way, and made no attempt to ransom him, as was usual. Declaring his allegiance in the summer of 1402 to Glyndŵr, he married Catrin upon November 30th of that year. His nephew Edmund survived to serve the new king Henry V and was rewarded with the return of the earldom of the March, but died childless and the family's possessions reverted to the crown.

## GWLADUS FERCH DAFYDD GAM c.1390-1454

## SEREN-Y-FENNI, THE STAR OF ABERGAFENNI

Her mother was Gwenllian ferch Gwilym ap Llewelyn, born in 1355 in Traean Glas, Breconshire. Her father was Dafydd ap Llywelyn ap Hywel Fychan, born in 1351, in Peytyn (Peytin Gwyn, Petyn Gwyn, Peutun, Peyton), near Llanddew and Llandyfaelog, Breconshire. Gwladus was also born at Peytyn, and had 6 siblings: Thomas, Catrin ferch Dafydd and four others. Her mother was Gwenllian ferch Gwilym ap Howel, an affluent country gentleman, residing at his seat called Grach, in Elval, on the banks of the Wye, Radnorshire. Gwladus and her brothers and sisters were brought up near Brecon, at Petyn Gwyn, in the parish of Garthbrengy. Another residence of theirs was Old Court, in the county of Monmouth, 'the site of which is in a field adjoining Llandeilo Cressanwy House, on the Lanvapley road, midway between Abergavenny and Monmouth. She had two brothers older than herself, of the respective names of Morgan and Thomas; and it is probable they were all born at Petyn Gwyn, previous to the year 1402, a period very disastrous to the father of this family; fatal to his wife, and most perilous and distressing to the children'. (- Pritchard, *Heroines of Welsh History*)

Gwladys' father, Dafydd, was a gentleman of considerable property and a celebrated military figure, descended from the native Welsh rulers of Brycheiniog. A noted warrior, whose father's castle stood at Pen-Pont on the River Usk. '*Gam*' signified that he was lame (from which we have the word gammy, referring to a limp), or more likely he squinted or had lost an eye. He may have fled from his county after killing a relative, Richard of Slwch, in the High Street of Brecon. 'Davy Gam' first appears in records, as a king's esquire, in April 1400, receiving forty marks a year. The new usurper Henry IV had been for some years previously in control of the marcher lordship of Brecon, and

**Gwladus, Seren-y-Fenni, alongside her husband in St Mary's, Abergafenni**

Dafydd remained a loyal Lancastrian until his death. Dafydd opposed the Glyndŵr Rising of 1400-1415, and in November 1401 he was rewarded with rebel lands.

In 1402, Dafydd's lands in and around Brecon became a target for Glyndŵr's attacks. Owain is recorded to have arrived at the family's principal residence at Petyn Gwyn where he captured and assaulted Lady Gwenllian. After taking her for ransom, he burnt the mansion to the ground. Driven from their last home in Wales, Gwladys, with her father, grandfather, and her two brothers, found refuge at Henry IV's court. She served as a Maid of Honour to the usurper Henry IV's second wife, Queen Joan. Dafydd Gam was said to be in the force that beat Glyndŵr's at Pwll Melyn near Usk, on 5 May 1405. He may also have tried to assassinate Owain at the Machynlleth Parliament in 1404. Dafydd fell into Glyndwr's hands in June 1412 and Henry V paid his ransom. Glyndŵr could have killed him, but desperately needed money to equip his men. The release was effected, and Dafydd was killed at Agincourt in 1415, possibly being knighted as he lay dying. Through the marriage of his daughter Gwladys to Sir William ap Thomas of Raglan, Dafydd Gam was forefather of the Herbert dynasty.

Gwladys had first married Roger Vaughan 'The Younger' in 1413, aged 23. He was 36 and owned estates around Bredwardine, Herefordshire.

After her marriage to Vaughan, she returned to Wales with her family. Roger was a great friend of her father's and would later fight and die with him at Agincourt. From the period of her marriage she never again left Wales. Gwladus was lauded as a supporter of Welsh culture, especially of the bards and minstrels. In Lewys Glyn Cothi's elegy, Gwladys is called 'the strength and support of Gwentland and the land of Brychan' (Monmouth and Brecon).

In contrast to Gwladus and Roger Vaughan's allegiance to the House of Lancaster, their three sons were solidly Yorkist during the Wars of the Roses during the Wars of the Roses (1455-1487), fighting in alliance with her sons by William Herbert at Edgecote Moor. They took residence at the main Vaughan holdings of Bredwardine, Hergest, and Tretower. Watkin (Walter) Vaughan of Bredwardine married a daughter of Sir Henry Wogan. He was murdered at Bredwardine Castle in 1456, for which half-brother William Herbert and Walter Devereux forcibly ensured prosecution of execution of the culprits at Hereford. Thomas Vaughan of Hergest married Ellen Gethin, daughter of Cadwgan ap

**Remains of the Herbert's Raglan Castle**

Dafydd and in 1461 Thomas died at the Battle of Edgecote. Gwladus' third son Roger Vaughan of Tretower Court was knighted for his activities supporting the Yorkist regime.

After the Battle of Mortimers Cross in 1461 Sir Roger had personally ensured that Owen Tudor, the father of Jasper and grandfather of Henry Tudor, was beheaded at Hereford. After the victory at Tewkesbury in 1471, he was sent with a force by Edward IV to kill Jasper and Henry Tudor at Chepstow. However, he was captured by Jasper Tudor and beheaded in revenge at Chepstow, before Jasper and Henry escaped to the Continent. Gwladus daughter Elizabeth Vaughan married a gentleman Griffith ab Eineon. Her other daughter Blanch Vaughan married a wealthy Englishman John Milwater, who was commissioned by Edward IV to accompany Blanch's half-brother, William Herbert, to the siege of Harlech Castle.

Six years after the death of her husband, and aged 36 Gwladus married the 29-year-old Sir William ap Thomas in 1421. He had also fought at Agincourt, and had known her husband and father. William was the son of Thomas ap Gwilym ap Jenkyn, a local landowner and his wife Maud, daughter of Sir John Morley. He was knighted in 1426 and was known, because of the colour of his armour, as *Y Marchof Las o Went* (The Blue Knight of Gwent.) By 1432 William was able to purchase Raglan Manor for about £667 and afterward, he vastly expanded the manor to become Raglan Castle.

Sir William was appointed to the position of High Sheriff of Cardiganshire and Carmarthenshire in 1435, and in 1440, also to the position of High Sheriff of Glamorgan. About 1442 or 1443, William became Chief Steward of the estates of Richard Plantagenet, 3rd Duke of York. He also served as a member of the Duke of York's military council.

As Lady of the imposing Raglan Castle, Gwladus was able to entertain her guests and assist the needy and afflicted on an even greater scale than when the mistress of Bredwardine, and their court became famous for its entertainment and hospitality. The bards called her 'the star of Abergafenni' and Lewys Glyn Cothi named her 'Gwladus the happy and the faultless... like the sun... the pavilion of light.'

Gwladus and William's children were raised with her five Vaughan children. They included William ap William, a Yorkist warrior responsible for the death of Henry Tudor's father Edmund, who Anglicised his surname to Herbert (see this author's *100 Greatest Welshman*). He was the first full-blooded Welshman to enter the English peerage and he was knighted in 1452. William Herbert has been called 'the first statesman of the modern era', and replaced Warwick (the 'Kingmaker') as Edward IV's major supporter, forcing Warwick into rebellion. Like his brother Sir Richard Herbert of Coldbrook House near Abergafenni, William Herbert, Earl of Pembroke, died at Edgecote Moor in 1461. Her daughter Elizabeth Herbert married Sir Henry Stradling, and their son Sir John Wogan was killed fighting for the Herbert brothers at Banbury in 1465.

Lady Gwladus mourned at length when her husband died in London in 1445, and died herself in 1454. They were patrons of Abergafenni Priory, and their alabaster tomb and effigies can be seen in St. Mary's Church. She was said to be so beloved by her people that 3,000 knights, nobles and weeping peasantry followed her body from Coldbrook House (her son Richard's manor) to the Herbert Chapel of St. Mary's Priory Church where she was buried.


## QUEEN MARY TUDOR 18 February 1516 – 17 November 1558

### MARY I (19 July 1553 – 17 November 1558), 'BLOODY MARY', QUEEN-CONSORT OF SPAIN, ENGLAND'S FIRST FEMALE RULER IN HER OWN RIGHT, QUEEN OF JERUSALEM

Of the Welsh Tudor dynasty, Mary was England's first female ruler in her own right, without a male consort or acting as regent for an infant son. Empress Matilda (1102-1167), Henry I's heir, had been expelled by the English barons and her cousin Stephen of Blois was made king. Matilda was never formally declared Queen of England, but instead had been titled 'Lady of the English'. Henry VIII was pleased with her birth in 1516, proudly displaying the infant Mary to visiting ambassadors and noblemen, and expecting that a male heir would soon follow. She was considered one of the most important European princesses and Henry used her as a pawn in political negotiations. She was also well-educated with a fine contralto singing voice and great linguistic skills. Her mother, Catherine of Aragon, was deeply devoted to Mary, a reflection of Catharine's strongly domestic nature as well as the numerous miscarriages she suffered.

Educated by her mother and a ducal governess, Mary became betrothed to her cousin, the Holy Roman Emperor Charles V, Charles I of Spain. Charles made the unfortunate demand that she come to Spain immediately, accompanied by a huge cash dowry. Henry VIII ignored the request, so Charles refused the marriage, concluding a match with a more accommodating princess. Meanwhile, Henry invested Mary as Princess of Wales in 1525, and she held court at Ludlow Castle. Henry meant to soothe Catherine's fears that Mary's position as the only legitimate Tudor heir was being undermined. Only a few weeks before the investiture, Mary had attended a ceremony in which her father ennobled his illegitimate son, Henry Fitzroy, as Duke of Richmond. Henry sharply rebuked Catherine for criticizing his open affections for Fitzroy, and the bastard's accompanying titles and wealth. Mary was not only the first Princess of Wales in the English royal family, but the first female royal to hold court at Ludlow. However, sending Mary to the Welsh Marches was not the same as sending a son and heir. Henry never intended her to rule England, at least not as its sole ruler, and the role was simply symbolic.

When Catherine fell from favour, Mary suffered. The schism between England and Rome had begun. Catherine of Aragon was shut up in a room in Kimbolton Castle and separated from Mary. Henry never saw Catherine again, and Henry cruelly forbade Mary to ever contact her, even by letter. From 1531, aged fifteen, Mary was kept separate from her mother, and developed a lasting hatred of Anne Boleyn which extended to Anne's daughter, Elizabeth. She never openly blamed her father for his actions, though she considered them unlawful. Instead, she persuaded herself that he had been Anne Boleyn's pawn. Henry now sent Catherine to one decaying residence after another, dismissing several of her devoted servants. Although deprived of her title, home, jewels, and companionship, Catherine never recognized the divorce. She refused the title of Princess Dowager, offered by Henry as recognition of her previous marriage to his deceased brother Arthur, Prince of Wales. In 1533 when Anne Boleyn bore Elizabeth, Mary was asked to accept that her mother's marriage was not valid, and so she was illegitimate. Stripped of her title of Princess by Henry, and instead called Lady Mary, she given to the care of an aunt of Anne Boleyn, who was instructed to beat her if she was troublesome. Mary was always locked in her room when Henry came to visit his new daughter Elizabeth. Mary was gravely ill in 1534, and desperately needed her mother by her side, but this was refused With Henry's Oath of Supremacy, Mary had been declared illegitimate, and she heard that unless she took the oath, she would be beheaded. Her mother became ill in 1535, and died in January 1536 without being able to see or even write to her only child. Mary was now totally alone, and was sent to be lady-in-waiting, aged seventeen, to her recently born half-sister Elizabeth.

Unlike Mary, Elizabeth was recognized as a Princess of the realm. For the teenaged Mary, the complete reversal of her fortune was devastating. She began to suffer from a variety of illnesses, undoubtedly stress-related. These plagued her until her death, causing such symptoms as severe headaches, nausea, insomnia, and infrequent menstruation.

Anne Boleyn had taken an equal dislike of Mary, because, Elizabeth was legitimate only if Mary was not, and vice versa. After Anne Boleyn's fall from grace, Henry offered to pardon Mary and restore her to favour in 1536, but only if Mary acknowledged him as head of the Church of England and admitted the 'incestuous illegality' of his marriage to Catherine. Mary refused to do so until her cousin, Charles V, persuaded her otherwise, an action she was to always regret. Meanwhile, Catherine of Aragon had died at Kimbolton Castle. She had not seen Mary for years although they had written one another, against Henry's orders, in great secrecy.

Anne Boleyn's execution on charges of incest and treason had now illegitimized Elizabeth, and Mary was named godmother to Henry VIII and Jane Seymour's son, Prince Edward, born in October 1537. When Jane died shortly after her son's birth, Mary was the chief mourner. Jane had desperately tried to reconcile Mary with her father, but Mary's adamant refusal to acknowledge Henry as Supreme Head of the Church had made it impossible. Indeed, the Duke of Norfolk told her that if she had been his daughter, he would have knocked her head 'against the wall until it was as soft as baked apple.' Only in 1544 did a statute restore Mary as heir to the throne, after her half-brother Edward.

Mary did not like the executed Catherine Howard, but Henry's final wife, Catherine Parr, treated her as a sister, being only four years older than Mary. Mary was at her father's side when he died in 1547 - he apologised for not finding her a suitable husband. Edward VI succeeded, aged just nine, and during his reign, Mary was unfairly suspected of plotting against him, and her life was in danger once more. When Edward became king, Mary continued to attend Catholic mass in her own private chapel. When Edward ordered her to desist she appealed to her cousin, Emperor Charles V, and he threatened war with England if she was not left alone. Edward died in 1553, aged 15, to be succeeded (with difficulty and danger) by Mary. Like her mother, Mary was a devout Catholic and she detested the religious changes of her father and her brother Edward VI. Catherine of Aragon was the youngest daughter of Ferdinand of Aragon and Isabella of Castile, the 'Catholic Kings' who united Spain geographically and spiritually. Through her mother, Mary could trace her lineage to John of Gaunt, and grew up as an *Infanta* of Spain.

Unlike Henry VIII, her claim to royalty was not a mere few decades old. As such, she was naturally proud and dignified. Mary inherited Catherine's pride and sense of destiny, as well as her mother's enduring love for Spain. When she became queen, this affection was to have terrible consequences. Mary had no real idea of how the nation had changed. She had spent the last few years in the countryside, surrounded by a Catholic household, and sympathetic nobles. She never realized the extent of Protestantism in the vital areas of London and its surrounding countryside. Mary assumed that all of England wished to return to the early 1520s, the years before the break with the Roman church. Unfortunately, she assumed that the popular support which had given her the throne indicated support for Catholic rule as well as her rightful queenship. Mary attended Mass with her Privy Councillors but, on 12 August 1553, told her council that she would not 'compel or constrain other men's consciences.' She hoped her subjects would open their hearts to the truth and soon return to the true faith. On Mary's succession, about 800 Protestants fled to the Continent.

Mary believed that she must marry, as no woman had ruled England in her own right before. Mary, whose life had possessed little peace after her adolescence, had always turned to her mother's family for advice and support. She was advised that Philip of Spain, heir to the Hapsburg Empire, was the most sought-after prince in Europe. She was deeply religious and had spent the past twenty years essentially alone and unloved. Thirty-seven years old, and chaste, she wondered whether the twenty-six-year-old widower Philip would want her. Her advisor Renard assured her that Philip was delighted to wed Mary, adding that they would have children together, and ensure that England had a Catholic succession. Mary replied that she had never considered marriage until God had raised her to the throne. However, now that she was queen, she would lead her subjects down the path of true righteousness. With the might of the Holy Roman Empire behind her, her faith would be triumphant. Thus she agreed to marry Philip in 1553 and their engagement was made official.

Mary had no idea that there would be a hostile reaction, both from her subjects and the King of France. Englishmen believed that Charles V wanted to drag England into another costly and ineffectual war against France. Charles wanted control of the vital sea route between Spain and his holdings in the Netherlands, and needed to control the English coast in order for his trade route to operate at its maximum profitability. With Protestant propagandists, and the French ambassador spreading rumours about Spanish invasions and imminent wars, there was uproar. Philip was eleven years Mary's junior and heir to the throne of Spain. Mary's choice was opposed both in the Privy Council and in Parliament. In a patriarchal age, wives were expected to obey their husbands, and Spain was far more powerful and wealthy than England at this time.

The English did not want their country to become a Spanish dependency, and her officials worked together to limit Philip's powers in England. Under the terms of her marriage act, Philip was to be styled 'King of England', and Parliament was to be called under the joint authority of the couple, for Mary's lifetime only. England would not be obliged to provide military support to Philip's father in any war, and Philip could not act without his wife's consent or appoint foreigners to office in England. Philip was unhappy at the conditions imposed, but he was ready to agree for the sake of political and strategic gains from the marriage. Philip's aide wrote to a correspondent in Brussels: 'the marriage was concluded for no fleshly consideration, but in order to remedy the disorders of this kingdom and to preserve the Low Countries.' To elevate his son to Mary's rank, Emperor Charles V ceded the crown of Naples, as well as his claim to the Kingdom of Jerusalem, to Philip. Thus Mary became Queen of Naples and titular Queen of Jerusalem upon marriage. Their marriage took place just two days after their first meeting. After the wedding, they were proclaimed: 'Philip and Mary, by the grace of God, King and Queen of England, France and Naples, Jerusalem and Ireland, defenders of the faith, Princes of Spain and Sicily, Archdukes of Austria, Dukes of Milan, Burgundy and Brabant, Counts of Habsburg, Flanders and the Tyrol.' In January 1556, Mary's father-in-law abdicated and Philip became King of Spain, with Mary as Queen-Consort of Spain. Philip was declared king in Brussels, but Mary stayed in England.

After her marriage, there were riots across the country, and when Sir Thomas Wyatt reached London, he found the bridges closed to him. Wyatt surrendered, and was tried and executed along with approximately 90 rebels, many of whom were hanged, drawn and quartered. Wyatt himself, after being severely tortured in the hope of extracting a confession implicating Elizabeth, was beheaded at Tower Hill and his body quartered. Mary had refused to let the Tower guns be turned on the traitors. Mary was now advised by others including Renard to be harsher, to show a stern example, which sealed the feat of Lady Jane Grey, still imprisoned after claiming the crown after Edward VI's death.

Mary became determined to undo the religious changes of the Henry and Edward. Catholic mass was restored in December 1553, and in 1554 married clergy were ordered to leave their wives or lose their posts. In November 1554 the Act of Supremacy was repealed. The first Protestant martyr was John Rogers, burned on 4 February 1555, followed by the burning of the bishops Hugh Latimer of Worcester and Nicholas Ridley of London. Neither Ridley nor Latimer could accept the Roman Catholic mass as a sacrifice of Christ. Both Ridley and Latimer were burned at the stake in Oxford on 16 October 1555. Mary believed that she was carrying out the will of God, and her constant saying was: 'In thee, O lord, is my trust, let me never be confounded: if God be for us, who can be against us?'

Mary's first Parliament of 1553 had abolished all Edward VI's religious legislation, turning the clock back to 1547. During 1554-55, Parliament undid most of the religious legislation of Henry VIII's reign and restored the papal supremacy. However, MPs refused to restore of monastic lands, and only with great difficulty were persuaded to restore the payment of annates to the church. Late in 1554, Reginald Pole, with his attainder reversed, arrived in England as papal legate and formally restored England to obedience to Rome In 1555, he was appointed Cardinal, and 1556 became Archbishop of Canterbury. Despite her age of thirty-seven, Mary announced in 1555 that she was pregnant. When it became clear that she was not, and indeed would never have a child, Mary became all the more determined to extirpate 'heresy' from England before she died. She seemed to think that the ill-success of her marriage was owing to God's divine vengeance for not uprooting the heresies still practised in England.

In all about 275 Protestants were executed between 1555 and 1558, and were later included in John Foxe's *Acts and Monuments of the English Martyrs*. Most of them were artisans from Southeast England where Protestantism had spread most widely, under the energetic administration of Edmund Bonner, Bishop of London. To history, mainly because of Foxe's book, she became known as 'Bloody Mary'. It was the godliness of many of her victims made them stand out, but these deaths were not numerous in comparison with the violence that characterized the Reformation on the Continent, or indeed the ten thousand or so of her father's reign. The people in general were hostile to the executions, and over the course of Mary's reign sheriffs and Justices of the Peace grew increasingly unwilling to participate. Many more Protestants fled abroad. In 1556 Thomas Cranmer, the former Archbishop of Canterbury, went to the flames. The burnings gained sympathy for the Protestants, alienating nobles and commons alike. 1555 and 1556 saw extremely poor harvests and were followed by a serious influenza epidemic which killed thousands (perhaps 6% of the population).

From 1556, Philip tried to overcome the resistance of the Privy Council and involve England in war with France. Philip's cause was helped by the abortive invasion of Thomas Stafford - a Protestant exile in France. Although Henry II of France denied initiating the raid, England declared war on France, and the English navy lent Spain important support at sea. Nevertheless, the war was regarded as disastrous because in January 1558, England lost Calais. It actually cost more to maintain than it was worth economically or militarily, but Mary and the English regarded its loss as a massive humiliation. English prestige abroad also suffered because it was evident that English resources were not adequate to mount a serious attempt to regain the lost territory. Calais had stayed in English hands for over two centuries, since 1347.

With this loss came good news for the beleaguered Mary, who was sure she was pregnant again, at the age of forty-two. She entered seclusion in late February 1558, and on 30 March drafted her will, worded in such a way to portray that she thought she was pregnant. After the symptoms began to fade, Mary was left quite ill, and became progressively worse, possibly suffering from stomach cancer. She was lucid enough to agree to pass the crown to her half sister, adding that she hoped Elizabeth would maintain the Catholic faith in England. On 16 November 1558, Mary's will was read aloud, in keeping with custom. The queen was lucid during the Mass held in her chamber the next morning, after which her priest performed the Last Rites, and she died. Elizabeth gave her a royal funeral and he body was interred in Westminster Abbey in the chapel built by her grandfather, Henry VII. Her heart and bowels were placed in the Chapel Royal at St. James's. Half Spanish, married to a Spaniard, and desperate for a child, Mary never understood her people properly. Mary was unmourned by most of the nation because of the burnings and the loss of Calais. Her last words were said to have been: 'when I am dead and opened, you shall find Calais lying in my heart.' Her sister Elizabeth was to be buried alongside her.

*Footnote:*
The above entry is from the author's *'Everything You Wanted to Know about the Tudors but were Afraid to Ask.* The old nursery rhyme, 'Mary, Mary quite contrary, how does your garden grow? With silver bells and cockle shells, and pretty maids all in a row' refers to Mary's reign. Silver bells and cockle shells were worn by pilgrims, especially to Compostela, and the pretty maids were the nuns who were allowed to return to England under her rule.


## KATHERYN OF BERAIN 1534 or 1535 – 27 August 1591

## CATRIN O FERAIN, 'MAM CYMRU' (THE MOTHER OF WALES), KATHRYN TUDOR

Catrin o Ferain was later called *Mam Cymru*, the Mother of Wales, because of her many descendants. A grand-daughter of Henry VII, she allegedly had six wealthy husbands, killing five of them by pouring molten lead in their ears as they slept, and burying them in Berain orchard. The story is that the sixth locked her up and starved her to death. In Lloft y Marchog (the Knight's Bedroom) at Berain are irremovable 'stains of blood' on the wall, where Catrin is supposed to have attacked her second husband, Sir Richard Clough. A more dispassionate reading of history reveals that she was born Katheryn Tewdwr in the mansion of Berain, Llanefydd in 1534 and died in 1591. She married four times, all to men influential in Welsh affairs, and had six children, so founding several dynasties of the Welsh upper classes.

Her father was Tewdwr ap Robert Fychan of Berain, Denbighshire, and her mother Jane, the daughter of Sir Roland Velville. Velville was quite possibly a bastard son of Henry VII, by a Breton lady he had met in exile, and Henry appointed Roland as Constable of Beaumaris Castle. Certainly Catrin and her descendants believed this to be so. As an only child, she was an heiress of a large estate, which combined with her beauty made her an attractive proposition for many men. The fact that she married four times to men of rank ensured that her descendants formed some of the richest families in Wales.*

Catrin's first marriage was in February, 1556, to the devout Catholic John Salusbury, MP for Denbigh, and the heir of Sir John Salusbury of Lleweni, Denbighshire. They had two sons, Thomas (executed at Shrewsbury for his alleged part in the Babington Plot on September 21st, 1587) and John, before Salusbury died in 1566. It may be that Thomas was 'framed' by the Elizabeth I's 'favourite' the Earl of Leicester, who was also Governor of Denbigh at the time. John was nicknamed, on account of his unusual strength, 'Syr John the Lion Killer', and was supposed to have killed with his bare hands a white lioness, in the Tower of London zoo which was started by Henry VIII. (John also had two thumbs on each hand, and was said to have kept up his strength by pulling up full-grown trees!)

Shakespeare's poem *The Phoenix and the Turtle* was dedicated to John Salusbury, who was knighted by Elizabeth the same year of 1601. The Llewenni estate passed to John, then through an heiress into the Combermere family. At the funeral of Catrin's first husband, she was led out of the church by Maurice Wynn of Gwydir, who asked her

**Katheryn of Berain's portrait by Adriaen de Cronenburgh**

to marry him. She politely declined, as she had already accepted a proposal from the Welsh merchant Richard Clough on the way to the funeral. However, she told Wynn 'that in case she performed that same sad duty to the knight, he might depend upon being the third (husband)'.

Clough had been working for Sir Thomas Gresham, and on account of his abilities was made Gresham's correspondent and agent in Antwerp in 1561. In 1563 Clough had written to the Welshman William Cecil (Elizabeth I's chief advisor, Lord Burghley) and had been leased large estates across Wales and England. In 1565 he wrote to Gresham advising the building of a 'Royal Exchange' in London for the benefit of merchants, like the fine stock exchange in Antwerp. He said that the accommodation for merchants in London was nothing short of a disgrace, so Greshan acquired some tenements, demolished them and laid the foundations of the Royal Exchange (now the Stock Exchange) on 7 January 1566. Thus we can say that the two premier elements for making London a financial capital, the Stock Exchange and Lloyds of London, were the foundations of Welshmen.

After their marriage in April 1567, Catrin went with Sir Richard Clough to Antwerp. He spent some of his fortune in building great houses including Bachygraig and Plas Clough**, introducing wherever possible the Flemish gable. These were the first Welsh houses constructed of brick, with bricks brought from Holland, 'a mansion of three sides enclosing a square court, the first consisting of a square hall and a parlour, the rest rising in six storeys, including a cupola.' The cupola was for Richard's interest in astronomy. Clough and Catrin then moved from Antwerp to Spain, and in 1569 they settled in Hamburg, where Clough died in 1570. He was buried in Hamburg, but his heart and hand were brought back in a silver urn to be buried at Whitchurch, Denbigh. Whitchurch is a particularly fine Perpendicular-style church, with many Salusbury family tombs. Their two daughters Anne and Mary later married into the powerful Salusbury and Wynne families. One of their descendants was Hester Lynch Salusbury Piozzi (q.v.) Clough left Catrin a small fortune to provide for their young daughters and his two stepsons.

Returning to Berain, Catrin asked the bard William Cynwal to compile a genealogy of her family, and sometime before 1573 she married her third husband, Maurice Wynn of Gwydir. He was of the famous family of the 'Princes in Wales' at Gwydir, twice a widower himself, and owner of 'one of the fairest estates in Wales'. Much more frugal than Clough, he was also a strict Protestant. He was the son of John (Wyn) ap Maredudd ap Ieuan ap Robert ap Maredudd, in a line going back to Owain Gwynedd, and had been the first to take the surname of Wynn. As MP for Caernarfonshire and its High Sheriff, when he died in 1580 he left Catrin a wealthy woman, and she had two children Edward and Jane with him, to add to her previous four children.

In 1583, Catrin married the (younger) Edward Thelwall (d.1610), of Plas y Ward, Ruthin, her fourth husband and a widower. The great Welsh courtier-scholar, Edward Herbert, first Baron Cherbury, praised Thelwall thus: 'After I had attained the age of nine, during all of which time I lived in my grandmother's house at Eyton, my parents thought fit to send me to some place where I might learn the Welsh tongue, as believing it necessary for me to treat with my friends and tenants who understood no other language. Whereupon I was recommended to Mr Edward Thelwall of Plas-y-Ward, in Denbighshire. This gentleman I must remember with honour as having of himself acquired the most exact knowledge of Greek, Latin, Italian and Spanish and all other learning, having for that purpose neither gone beyond seas nor so much as had the benefit of any university. Besides he was of that rare temper in governing his choler, that I never saw him angry during the time of my stay there and have heard the same of him many years before. When occasion of offence was given him, I have seen him redden in the face, and after remain for a time silent, but when he spake his words were so calm and gentle that I found he had digested his choler; yet, I confess, I could never attain that perfection, as being subject to passion and choler more than I ought, and generally to speak my mind freely, sought rather to imitate those who, having fire within doors, choose rather to give it vent than to suffer it to burn the house. I commend much more the manners of Mr Thelwall; and certainly he that can bear speaking for some while will remit much of his passion.'

Catrin predeceased this placid man of 'rare temper', having seen her son Thomas Salusbury beheaded for treason just five years earlier. She lies in Llanefydd Church. According to Pennant, she was buried with a gold chain and locket which contained the hair of her favourite husband, Richard Clough.

* There is an absolutely riveting account of the intermarriage policy pursued by the Welsh aristocracy to protect their wealth, recounted by Llywelyn Pritchard in his *Heroines of Welsh History*: 'Catrin's daughter, by Maurice Wynn of Gwydir, married Simon Thelwal the eldest son of her last husband by a former marriage. Simon Thelwal's son Edward married Sydney the daughter of William Wynn of Garthgynan, the fourth son of Sir John Wynn of Gwydir, the historian; and their daughter and heiress married Sir William Williams of Llanforda, the eldest son of the Speaker of the House of Commons in the reign of King James II. Hence the connection with Sir John Wynn of Wynnstay, who was first cousin to Sidney, and who left his great property to Mr Williams, her grandson, afterwards Sir Watkin Williams Wynn, the great grandfather of the present Sir Watkin Williams Wynn.'

** Bachygraig was built in Tremeirchion, Flintshire, in 1567, and was the first house in Wales to be built of bricks, being erected so quickly that local people thought it to be the work of the Devil. When the builders ran short of materials, it was said that new supplies would arrive each night beside the local stream known today as Nant y Cythraul ('The Devil's Brook'). A legend is that Sir Richard studied the stars with the Devil in an attic room, and when discovered by Catrin, the Devil took Sir Richard in his arms and they escaped through the walls of the house. It was demolished by Hester Lynch Piozzi (q.v.) when she returned to Wales to live there, and her new mansion was built nearby. The Grade II* Plas Clough in Denbigh survives.

*Footnote:*
The fine painting of Catrin that used to hang in Llewenni Hall is dated 1568, and was thought to have been painted by Lucas de Heere. It is now in the National

Museum of Wales, attributed to Adriaen van Cronenburg. A 1799 copy by Joseph Allen can be seen at Erddig.

## QUEEN ELIZABETH TUDOR 7 September 1533 - 24 March 1603

### THE VIRGIN QUEEN, ENGLAND'S GREATEST MONARCH

Elizabeth was the grand-daughter of Henry VII, the Welsh Earl of Richmond who led the last successful invasion of British soil, and overcame the greater force of Richard III at Bosworth Field. Her lifetime companion was her Welsh nurse, Blanche Parry, who taught her some of her native Welsh language. Blanche's brother Thomas looked after Elizabeth's household accounts. Under Elizabeth, Britain became a power on the world stage, and her reign saw the greatest flowering of culture - the Elizabethan Age - in the history of the islands.

**Princess Elizabeth Tudor, artist unknown**

Catherine of Aragon's child-bearing days were numbered, when Henry VIII fell madly in love with the young Anne Boleyn, the sister of one of his mistresses. Henry desperately needed a male heir, and wished for his marriage to be annulled. To do this he had to oust the power of the Pope, break up the great monasteries, abbeys and churches, and effectively start a new religion. The Reformation made Henry Tudor the Supreme Head of the Church in England, in order that he could achieve the annulment, to marry the heavily pregnant Anne in January 1533. Anne was given a magnificent coronation, and the astronomers assured Henry that his son was about to be born. When his daughter Elizabeth was born in Greenwich Palace, there was little celebration and Anne became extremely unpopular. She was blamed for the religious changes, and the bitterly disappointed Henry transferred his feelings to other women in the Court.

In 1539 Anne Boleyn was sentenced to death by decapitation or burning for a trumped-up charge of 'incest' and Henry chose the swordsman for her. Her head was chopped off on Tower Green in May 1536. Elizabeth was not yet 3 years old, and was sent away from Court as she served as a reminder to Henry of her mother. Elizabeth was stripped of her title of

103

Princess, as had happened to her half-sister Mary previously. After a while she was neglected to the point that her governess had to ask Henry VIII for new clothes to replace the ones she had outgrown. Jane Seymour, Ann Boleyn's maid-of-honour, now gave birth to Henry's long-awaited son, Edward, but she died a few days later.

Next, Henry married and divorced without consummation Anne of Cleves, before marrying Katherine Howard, who was decapitated for adultery. About this time, Elizabeth told her childhood companion Robert Dudley that she would never marry. She was just eight years old, had lost her mother and had had three stepmothers, two of which were dead. Henry's sixth wife, Katherine Parr, brought Elizabeth into the family home. Katherine protected Elizabeth from Henry when he fell into a great rage at a question that Elizabeth had asked him. She was thirteen, and with her nine-year-old brother Edward at the royal palace of Enfield, when told of Henry's death. Elizabeth went to live with the Queen Dowager and her new husband, Lord Thomas Seymour, Lord-Admiral. Katherine had actually hoped to marry Seymour before Henry decided that she was to be his new queen. He was the brother of Edward Seymour, Lord Protector of England, who was running the realm on the young Edward's behalf.

Seymour took an extremely unhealthy interest in the 14-year-old princess. It is recorded that both Katherine and Thomas used to rise early to 'tickle' Elizabeth in bed. It was thought best that Elizabeth left the household after several scandals involving her and Seymour. Soon after this, Katherine died shortly after she gave birth to a daughter. Thomas Seymour now planned to marry Edward VI to Lady Jane Grey, and for himself to marry Elizabeth. Thomas formally asked for Elizabeth's hand in marriage. He arrested the young king, but the plot failed and Seymour was executed, and Elizabeth placed in the Tower of London. Edward VI henceforth saw Elizabeth as a threat, and she responded by wearing plain black and white gowns, and building up such an attitude that he later called her 'sweet sister temperance'. Elizabeth called Thomas Seymour 'a man of much wit and little judgement'.

Northumberland took over from Edward Seymour as Protector, and it seemed certain that Edward VI was ailing. Northumberland was the father of Robert Dudley, Elizabeth's childhood friend, and did not want the Catholic Mary Tudor to succeed to the throne. He 'bastardised' Elizabeth and Mary, as the claim to the crown naturally fell on his family if the half-sisters were excluded. He married his youngest son, Guildford Dudley, to the other crown claimant Lady Jane Grey and proclaimed her queen after Edward's death, on July 6, 1553. However, there was no popular support. Nine days later Mary and Elizabeth rode into London to a rapturous reception, and Northumberland and later Lady Jane were executed.

After Mary's accession on 19 July, she was always suspicious of the Protestant Elizabeth, and set about restoring the Catholic faith in England.

However, her marriage to Philip of Spain was extremely unpopular. A plot in 1554 for Edward Courtenay to marry Elizabeth and depose Mary was revealed, and Elizabeth was taken by boat to the Tower of London. The boat stopped at the Traitor's Gate, at night. Elizabeth, cold and wet, just sat in the boat for hours, refusing to get out, and there was an impasse. No-one could lay hands on the royal princess. She feared that she would never come out, but her governess eventually convinced her that she was safe, and she was confined in the Bell Tower. Her life hung in the balance, but Mary refused to sign her death warrant, believing that there could be a popular rising. Elizabeth was released from the Tower, but kept a virtual prisoner in the dilapidated Palace of Woodstock for a year. Elizabeth's early life had been full of uncertainties, and her chances of succeeding to the throne had seemed very slight once her half-brother Edward had been born in 1537. She was then third in line behind her Roman Catholic half-sister, Princess Mary, who was 17 years her senior. Roman Catholics, indeed, always considered her illegitimate.

Mary could not have children, and her husband Philip of Spain recommended that she installed Elizabeth as her heiress to the crown. Next in line was Mary Queen of Scots, and it was in the Spanish interest that England did not pass into the hands of a monarchy with close links with France. Elizabeth succeeded to the throne on her half-sister's death of stomach cancer on 17 November 1558. Elizabeth had heard the news of Mary's death while eating an apple under an oak tree at Hatfield palace. She knelt to the ground and whispered in Latin 'This is the Lord's doing, and it is marvellous in our eyes.' The new queen was very well-educated (fluent in six languages), and had inherited intelligence, determination and shrewdness from both parents. Her 45-year reign is generally considered one of the most glorious in English history, and during it a secure Church of England was established. Its doctrines were laid down in the *39 Articles* of 1563, a compromise between Roman Catholicism and Protestantism. Elizabeth herself diplomatically refused to 'make windows into men's souls... there is only one Jesus Christ and all the rest is a dispute over trifles'; she asked for outward uniformity. Most of her subjects accepted the compromise as the basis of their faith, and her church settlement probably saved England from religious wars like those which France suffered in these times.

Autocratic and capricious, Elizabeth had astute political judgement and chose her ministers well, especially her closest advisor William Cecil, Lord Burghley. Overall Elizabeth Tudor's administration consisted of some 600 officials administering the great offices of state, and a similar number dealing with the Crown lands (which funded the administrative costs). Social and economic regulation and law and order remained in the hands of the sheriffs at local level, supported by unpaid justices of the peace. Elizabeth's reign also saw many voyages of discovery, including those of Francis Drake, Walter Raleigh and Humphrey Gilbert, particularly to the Americas. These expeditions prepared England for an age of colonisation and trade expansion, which Elizabeth herself recognised by establishing the East India Company in 1600.

Elizabeth fell in love with Lord Robert Dudley*, and made him Master of Horse, but her advisors were strongly against a marriage. The sudden death of his wife Amy Robsart, in 1560, destroyed any chance of a wedding. She was found with a broken neck at the bottom of a staircase, and Dudley was believed to have been responsible. However, he and Elizabeth were very close for the next ten years, and some think they may have had children. When Elizabeth was not busy with Cecil on political business, she enjoyed her court entertainment, having a troupe of actors called The Queen's Players. She particularly liked Shakespeare's work and great English musicians such as Purcell, Tallis and Byrd flourished under her. She loved to ride horses, worrying her advisors, and hunted deer and stags with her courtiers. She also enjoyed cock-fighting, bear-baiting and tennis. A skilled musician and dancer, Elizabeth also enjoyed classical literature and wrote poetry.

**Elizabeth I in her coronation robes**

The arts flourished during Elizabeth's reign. Country houses such as Longleat, Burghley and Hardwick Hall were built, miniature painting reached its high point, and theatres thrived. The Queen attended the first performance of Shakespeare's *A Midsummer Night's Dream*.

The image of Elizabeth's reign is one of triumph and success. The Queen herself was often called 'Gloriana', 'Good Queen Bess' and 'The Virgin Queen'. Investing in expensive clothes and jewellery, to look the part, like all contemporary sovereigns, she cultivated this image by touring the country in regional visits known as 'progresses', often riding on horseback rather than by carriage. Elizabeth made at least 25 progresses during her reign. At home she wore simple gowns, but fashion indicated social status, so Elizabeth had to set the standards in her favourite colours of black and white, which represented virginity and purity. Elaborate neck ruffs were the height of the fashions set by her, as starch had been discovered. Dudley gave her a watch placed in a bracelet, possibly the first wrist-watch in the world. She wore little make-up until an attack of smallpox in 1562, after which it was needed to cover her facial scars. The bewigged monarch painted her face with white lead and vinegar, rouged her lips, and covered her cheeks with red dye and egg-white. The lead had long-term effects on her health.

However, Elizabeth's reign was one of considerable danger and difficulty for many, with threats of invasion from Spain through Ireland, and from France through Scotland. Much of northern England was in rebellion in 1569-70. A Papal Bull of 1570 specifically released Elizabeth's subjects from their allegiance to her, and in return she passed harsh laws against Roman Catholics after plots against her life were discovered. One such plot involved Mary, Queen of Scots, who had fled to England in 1568 after her second husband's murder, and her subsequent marriage to a man believed to have been involved in his murder. As a likely successor to Elizabeth, Mary spent 19 years as Elizabeth's prisoner, being was the focus for rebellion and possible assassination plots, such as the Babington Plot of 1586. Mary was also a temptation for potential invaders such as Philip II. Philip II believed he had a claim to the English throne through his marriage to Mary. In a letter of 1586 to Mary, Elizabeth wrote, 'You have planned ... to take my life and ruin my kingdom ... I never proceeded so harshly against you.' Despite Elizabeth's reluctance to take drastic action, on the insistence of Parliament and her advisers, Mary was tried, found guilty of treason and executed in 1587, at Fotheringhay Castle. One of her son James I's first acts on his accession to the English throne was to raze the castle to the ground.

Mary I's former husband Philip II of Spain had long wished to invade the small, weaker England and recover the nation for the Catholic faith. Elizabeth had encouraged English privateers such as Francis Drake to attack Spanish ships, and some of this treasure had been used to bolster the Dutch revolt against Spanish rule. After three years of shipbuilding, the Spanish Armada sailed towards England. Elizabeth, on a white horse, addressed her soldiers and sailors on the shore:

'My loving people, we have been persuaded by some that are careful for our safety, to take heed how we commit ourselves to armed multitudes for fear of treachery. Let tyrants fear. I have always so behaved myself that, under God, I have placed my chief strength and safeguard in the loyal hearts and goodwill of my subjects. And therefore I am come amongst you all, as you see at this time, not for my recreation and disport, but being resolved, in the midst and heat of the battle, to live or die amongst you all, to lay down for my God, and for my Kingdom, and for my People, my honour, and my blood, even in the dust. I know I have the body of a weak and feeble woman, but I have the heart and stomach of a King, and of a King of England too, and think foul scorn that Parma of Spain, or any Prince of Europe should dare to invade the borders of my realm! I myself will be your general, judge and rewarder of every one of your virtues in the field.'

In 1588, aided by bad weather, the English navy scored a great victory over the massive Spanish invasion fleet of around 130 ships. The defeat of the Armada was the beginning of the end of the great Spanish Empire, the 16th century's greatest power, and the start of the rise of the English Empire, the greatest the world has seen. It was only in Elizabeth's reign that England turned from being a peripheral player in world affairs to a major one. However, during Elizabeth's long reign, the nation also suffered from high prices and severe economic depression, especially in the countryside, during the 1590s. The war against Spain was not very successful after the Armada had been beaten and, together with other campaigns, was very costly. Although she kept a tight rein on government expenditure, Elizabeth left large debts to her successor. Wars during Elizabeth's reign are estimated to have cost over £5 million (at the prices of the time) which Crown revenues could not match - in 1588, for example, Elizabeth's total annual revenue amounted to some £392,000. Despite the combination of financial strains and prolonged war after 1588, Parliament was not summoned more often. There were only sixteen sittings of the Commons during Elizabeth's reign, five of which were in the period 1588-1601. Although Elizabeth freely used her power to veto legislation, she avoided confrontation and did not attempt to define Parliament's constitutional position and rights.

Elizabeth chose never to marry. If she had chosen a foreign prince, he would have drawn England into foreign policies for his own advantage (as in her sister Mary's marriage to Philip of Spain). However, marrying an English lord could have drawn the Queen into factional infighting. Elizabeth thus used her marriage prospects as a political tool in foreign and domestic policies, and the 'Virgin Queen' was presented as a selfless woman who sacrificed personal happiness for the good of the nation, to which she was, in essence, 'married'. Late in her reign, she addressed Parliament in the so-called 'Golden Speech' of 1601 when she told MPs: 'There is no jewel, be it of never so high a price, which I set before this jewel; I mean your love.' She seems to have been very popular with the vast majority of her subjects. Overall, Elizabeth's always shrewd and, when necessary, decisive leadership brought successes during a period of great danger both at home and abroad. She died at Richmond Palace on 24 March 1603, having become a legend in 45 years on the English throne. Her death day was the same as that of her father, Henry VIII. Her magnificent funeral on 28 April saw national mourning, and the date of her accession was a national holiday for 200 years.

* Near Llangollen is Plas Uchaf, linked forever with the Welsh 'Helen of Troy', Nest ferch Rhys ap Tewdwr. Plas Uchaf used to be named Plas Eglwyseg, the manor to which Owain ap Cadwgan abducted Nest. It is close to the quaintly named World's End, and according to a previous owner, Goering and Churchill stayed there on a shooting holiday in 1936-37. More intriguingly still, there is a very strong local tradition that Elizabeth I, the Virgin Queen, bore a baby there. A large inscription upon the present Tudor building reads LX III ELIZABETH REGINA. This date of 1563 could denote her baby being born. If so, it could have been Robert Dudley's. There was no way that she could marry Lord

Dudley, because of the scandal surrounding the mysterious death of his wife, Amy Robsart. He was also the son of the hated Duke of Northumberland. It seems that Elizabeth loved Dudley, later the Earl of Leicester, but was unable to marry him. Her principal suitors, which were given serious consideration by her advisors, were: 1534 the Duke of Angoulême (3rd son of Francis I), c.1542 a Prince of Portugal; 1543 the son of the Earl of Arran; 1544 Prince Philip (Philip II of Spain); 1547 Sir Thomas Seymour; 1552 the Prince of Denmark; 1553-4 Edward Courtenay, Earl of Devonshire; 1554 Philibert Emanuel, Duke of Savoy; 1554 the Prince of Denmark (again); 1556 Prince Eric of Sweden; 1556 Don Carlos (the son of Philip II mentioned just 12 years earlier!); 1559 Philip II (again); 1559 Prince Eric of Sweden (again); 1559 the son of John Frederic, Duke of Saxony; 1559 Sir William Pickering; 1559 the Earl of Arran (previously a suitor before he inherited the title); 1559 Henry Fitzalan, Earl of Arundel; 1559 Robert Dudley; 1560 King Eric of Sweden (a third attempt); 1560 Adolphus, Duke of Holstein; 1560 King Charles IX; 1560 Henri, Duke of Anjou; 1566 Robert Dudley (again); 1570 Henri, Duke of Anjou (again) and from 1572-1585 Francis, Duke of Alençon, later Duke of Anjou. The last named was the only one of Elizabeth's foreign suitors to court her in person. He was 24 and Elizabeth was 46, and presumably flattered, Elizabeth became close to him, calling him her *petit grenouille* (little frog), on account of a frog-shaped brooch or earring he gave her. This is probably the origin of the derogatory term for the French some use today.

We can see the virtual 'feeding frenzy' of 1559-1560, as Elizabeth and her advisors realised that she was coming to the end of her child-bearing years, and wished for an heir and stability. The probable answer is that Elizabeth could never marry without destabilising the realm - as long as she was uncommitted, there would be no disorder between powerful courtiers. These nobles would fight against each other and possibly disrupt the Tudor dynasty, but equally would not brook a foreign king over them. Some sources state that she had 3 children, and others two by Lord Dudley, with research linking Sir Francis Bacon, 'The Father of Modern Science' as her son. His putative father Nicholas Bacon had married the sister-in-law of William Cecil, Lord Burghley and achieved high honours in 1559.

*Footnotes:*

1. Just as 'The Virgin Queen' allegedly bore a child, we must mention the queen's half-brother Sir John Perrot, who was given massive estates in Pembrokeshire by his father, Henry VIII. One of history's intriguing elements was the failure of Henry VIII to have a son by Catherine of Aragon, the former wife of his brother Arthur. However, he did have two sons, Henry Fitzroy and Sir John Perrott, who was born in 1527. His mother was Mary Berkeley, a lady of the royal court and wife of Sir Thomas Perrott. Her success in giving Henry a male heir turned him against all of his wives in turn. Edward VI, Mary and Elizabeth I all acknowledged John Perrott as a half-brother, and a giant of a man, he strongly resembled his father. Sir John was one of the four knights who carried Elizabeth I's canopy at her coronation. In 1554, at a tournament for his half-sister Queen Mary Tudor and her husband Philip of Spain, he 'fought best

of all' of the Spanish and English grandees and Mary herself gave out the prizes, including 'a diamond ring of great value'. Perrot made vast wealth from his time as Vice-Admiral for West Wales, much from collusion with pirates, and built a great manor at Haroldston outside Haverfordwest, and rebuilt Laugharne and Carew castles as manor houses.

Elizabeth appointed him Lord President of Munster, to suppress a rebellion there, which he did within a year. He was then appointed by Elizabeth Lord Deputy of Ireland from 1584 to 1588, but was arrested on a false charge of treason in 1591 and sentenced to death. She had sent him to Ireland in command of a fleet to intercept a possible invasion of Ireland by the Spanish, but he had acted in a high-handed manner there, just as the Earl of Essex did when he followed him. Perrot's comments about his half-sister were reckless. She had appointed a Mr Errington to be clerk of the Exchequer in Ireland, and Sir John exclaimed 'this fiddling woman troubles me out of measure. God's dear Lady, he shall not have the office! I will give it to Sir Thomas Williams!' Again, at the time of the Spanish Invasion of 1588, he was reported to have said 'Ah silly woman, now she will not curb me! Now she shall not rule me! Now, God's dear Lady, I shall be her white boy again!' He added, when Sir John Garland brought him a letter from the Queen, 'This it is, to serve a base-born woman! Had I served any price in Christendom, I had not been thus dealt with!' When told he must die, he exclaimed 'God's death! Will my sister sacrifice her brother to his frisking adversaries?' Queen Elizabeth refused to sign the death warrant of her half-brother and planned to pardon him, but he died in 1592 in the Tower of London, aged 65.

2. In 1576, the Privy Council ordered the mayor of Chester to discharge a man confined in Northgate Prison for asserting that Elizabeth had two bastards by the Earl of Leicester. A 1940 book by Alfred Dodd, *The Marriage of Elizabeth Tudor* makes a persuasive case for Francis Bacon being the illegitimate son of Leicester and Elizabeth. Lady Anne Bacon was chief lady-in-waiting to Elizabeth at the time of Francis' birth, and Sir Nicholas Bacon was Lord Keeper of the Great Seal. Sometime in January, about 4 months after her alleged marriage to Leicester, Elizabeth was supposed to have had a baby, which the Bacons took on as their own. Unfortunately, this is tangential to this book, but Dodd's arguments are difficult to refute. The Duke of Norfolk wrote of a child playing with Leicester and Elizabeth in the Queen's private apartments. Francis Bacon spent most of his time at court, until the queen suddenly sent him France, and on his return in 1578 her private portraitist painted miniatures of both her and the 18-year-old Francis for Elizabeth. Nicholas Hilliard wrote on the back of his Bacon portrait 'could I but paint his mind'. Nicholas Bacon left all his children provided for, except Francis, who became a 'queen's gentleman pensioner' as a young man, with his studies paid for at Gray's Inn. Sir Edward Coke, his lifelong enemy, always referred to Francis as 'the Queen's bastard'. His mother, in letters to her son Anthony, calls Francis her 'ward', not her son. Bacon had a high-flying career, and became personal adviser to Elizabeth and a great friend and Chancellor to King James I.

# LUCY WALTER c.1630 - 1658

## QUEEN OF ENGLAND

Like Nell Gwyn (q.v.) Lucy was another of Charles II's mistresses. She met him in 1648 when he was a refugee from Oliver Cromwell. Her father was William Walter*, of Roch Castle, Pembrokeshire, and his grandfather had married Jane Laugharne, whose own mother was Janet Philipps of Picton Castle. Lucy's mother was Elizabeth Prothero, whose parents were John Prothero of Hawksbrook (Nantyrhebog) Carmarthenshire, and Eleanor Vaughan of Golden Grove. Thus Lucy was part of the Royalist gentry of West Wales, being related to the Laugharnes, Phillips and Vaughans. (John Vaughan was first Earl of Carbery.) Lucy was brought up at Ravensdale (Cwmcigfran), a few miles from Carmarthen.

**Lucy Walter by Sir Peter Lely,** *courtesy of Scolton Manor Museum, near Haverfordwest*

When Lucy was just eleven, her parents began legal proceedings against each other, with Elizabeth securing a deed of sequestration on Walter's estate, upon the grounds of desertion, and being left without maintenance. He presented a counter-petition, claiming that he had never been paid his £600 share of a bond which his father-in-law John Prothero had entered into at the time of the marriage. He went on to claim that he suspected 'incontinency' on his wife's behalf, and that he only had £100 a year for his own support. Also in the same year of 1641, the House of Lords ordered that Elizabeth should return to her husband. Elizabeth reported back that she could not find her husband, but that he intended to sell his estate, and petitioned for support from his estate. The Lords then granted her £60 a year from the estate, to be increased when his mother and grandmother died and left him as their heir. Walter still evaded payment, and the Lords ordered that his estates be sequestrated in 1642. However, events overtook legislation, with the outbreak of the Civil War upon 13 May 1642.

After more contradictory evidence, and a part-settlement to Elizabeth in 1646, the order against Walter was revoked in 1647, when Walter was given custody of their children Richard, Justus and Lucy. In the meantime, in the English Civil War, Roch Castle was held for King Charles by Richard Vaughan, second Earl of Carbery, from 1643. However, Rowland Laugharne took it for the Parliamentarians in 1644 after he had defeated the royalist army at Pill, near Milford Haven, in 1644. Later that year, Roch Castle was taken again for the king by Sir Charles Gerard. William Walter and his family seem to have been in London during this period of conflict, and William later claimed losses of income and damages of £3,000 for this period.

Lucy went to France, under the protection of a kinsman, John Barlow of Slebech. She was an adherent of Lord Edward Somerset, Marquis of Worcester and Earl of Glamorgan, and possibly accompanied him. Lucy was at the exiled Charles Stuart's court in The Hague in the early 1648, and was with him when the court-in-exile moved to Paris. Charles I was executed on 30 January 1649, and Charles Stuart became *de facto* king. Lucy's son James was born a few weeks later in Rotterdam on April 9th, 1649. A daughter Mary was later born at The Hague in May 1651, who also appears to have been fathered by Charles. Although Mary's father was rumoured to have been Colonel Henry Bennett, later Earl of Arlington, Charles settled an annual pension of £600 a year on the little girl, so he obviously thought that Mary was his. (Charles did not become *de jure* king until his return to England in May 1660, after the deposition of Richard Cromwell.)

Lucy returned to London during Charles' exile, in 1656. The king in exile was impoverished, and she was out of favour. It was said that Charles had returned from the Second Civil War and his narrow escape at the Battle of Worcester, and had been enraged by Lucy's infidelity, refusing to see her. However, the infidelity story seems to have been a smokescreen - Charles was still close to Lucy and her son and daughter at least six years later. A great expense at his court-in-exile, with a pension of 5,000 livres a year, it appears that some of his friends had promised her a pension of £400 a year if she would return to England, and get out of his life.

Algernon Sidney told the Duke of York that he had given 50 gold pieces for her, but having to rejoin his regiment handed her over to his brother, Colonel Sidney. These facts are shown to be a tissue of lies by Lucy's latest biographer. Sidney was later executed for supporting Monmouth's Rebellion. James Duke of York later became King James II and was terrified of Lucy's son by his elder brother Charles being recognised as the *de facto* king instead of him. His court and followers thus spread malicious rumours about Lucy's character whenever able. Blackened in reputation as a prostitute by James and his cronies, Lucy was still living with Charles' sister, the Countess of Orange as late as 1655, six years after Charles had become King. Charles never denied that he was married to Lucy until 1678, 20 years after her death. Edward Hyde wrote in 1680 that 'His Majesty had a lawful son of his own by a former marriage to succeed to his dignity', i.e. Lucy's son, James, Duke of Monmouth.

Lucy sailed from Flushing as 'Mrs Barlow' and took humble lodgings over a baker's shop near Somerset House, where she was traced by Cromwell's men. Lucy was arrested as a suspected spy and placed with her maid Anne Hill in the Tower of London. At first she pleaded that she was the widow of a Dutch sea captain, and had returned to collect an inheritance of £1,500 from her mother, who had recently died. However, when her true identity was discovered, she openly disclosed that she was the mother of Charles II's son. She allegedly had a Pension Warrant, and 'a paper containing something relating to a Marriage, a Dowry, or Pension or Maintenance from his Majesty… taken away by Bradshaw'.

Being discharged, Lucy was deported back to Holland, Lord Protector Cromwell saying 'by those that hanker after him (Charles II) may see they are furnished already with an heir apparent, and what a pious charitable Prince they have for their master, and how well he disposeth of the collections and contributions which they make for him her, towards the maintenance of his concubines and royal issue. Order is taken forthwith to send away this lady of pleasure and the young heir, and set them on the shore of Flanders which is no ordinary courtesy.' Thus it seems that no less a man than Oliver Cromwell believed that Lucy's son was the true heir to the Crown of England.

Charles, now, after several attempts, abducted his son from Lucy along with several official papers, and gave the seven-year-old boy to his widowed mother, Queen Henrietta Maria, to bring up in Paris. Lucy tore her hair out with anger at this treatment, and died just a few months later, in 1658. After the Restoration, Lucy's son James was made Duke of Monmouth**, and aged 14 married Anne Scott, *de jure* Countess of Buccleuch, taking the Scott surname (April 20th, 1663 in the King's Chamber at Whitehall). It was widely believed that Charles had married Lucy***, and she was said to have died in extreme poverty in Paris in 1658. Most sources state that there was no money to pay for her burial, but in her last days she was befriended by William Erskine, son of the Earl of Mar, who paid for it (possibly at Charles' prompting). However, recent research shows that her aunt took out letters of administration to look after Lucy's estate. Thus it was impossible that she died impoverished. Erskine was the king's cup-bearer, and uncle of Lucy's future daughter-in-law the Countess of Buccleuch. She was probably buried in the Huguenot Cemetery at Faubourg Saint Germain. There are several portraits of her, one by the court painter Sir Peter Lely. A novel by Rhydwen Williams, *Liwsi Regina*, based on her life, won the Daniel Owen Prize in 1988. All the blackening of Lucy's name with affairs and misdemeanours came from the philandering Duke of York's faction, when Lucy and Charles were safely dead - they could not afford for her son James, Duke of Monmouth to be recognised as the true king.

A recent book by Gerry Lamford OBE, a former Assistant Chief Constable of Manchester Police and Commandant of Bramhill's Police Staff College, has made the most persuasive case for Lucy being Charles II's legal wife. It is entitled *The Defence of Lucy Walter - Putting Right a Towering*

*Injustice.* Very briefly, some of the points he makes are as follows. The allegations against her arose over two decades after her death, in the days when her son the Duke of Monmouth was James II's implacable enemy. It seems that Lucy and Charles married once in Wales at Lucy's father's house and again in Liège or Paris. When Lucy escaped to the Continent, there was a warrant for her arrest as she was suspected of taking royal treasure to Charles. She travelled under the name of Mrs Barlow, and Charles used the pseudonym of Mr Barlow when escaping after the Battle of Worcester.

A member of the Privy Council wrote in 1645 that Lucy was repeatedly called his wife by Charles in letters to him from his sister the Countess of Orange.*** Monmouth was beheaded swiftly and illegally without trial, before he could make his case as Charles II's legitimate son. Monmouth was treated very differently from any of Charles' dozen or so illegitimate children, with his wife being created Duchess of Buccleuch and raised to the peerage. His other sons married heiresses. King Charles' mother especially favoured Lucy's young son, and referred to Lucy as Charles' wife. There were witnesses of Charles wedding to Lucy in Paris, and Baron Gerard was positive that Monmouth was the rightful heir. Lucy told her relatives that she had married Charles. There is so much research in Lamford's book that it is almost certain that Lucy was Queen of England and Wales.

**Lucy Walter's son James Scott, Duke of Monmouth, by Sir Peter Lely**

Even some of the entries in Samuel Pepys' *Diaries* seem to confirm Charles' feelings towards the 14 year-old Monmouth. Remember that the Duke of York was Pepys' patron as regards the Admiralty preferment, so Pepys was not in favour of Monmouth:

'May 14th, 1663 Met Mr Moore and with him to an ale-house in Holborne; where in discourse her told me he fears the king will be tempted to endeavour the setting of the crown upon the little (14 years-old) Duke, which may cause troubles, which God forbid, unless it is his due!
November 9th, 1663- Mr Blackburne and I fell to talk of many things, wherein he was very open with me...He tells me that it is much talked of that the King intends to legitimate (sic) the Duke of Monmouth.
January 20th, 1664 Dr Pierce (the Surgeon) tells me... that the Duke of Monmouth the King do still dote on beyond measure, insomuch the King only, the Duke of York, and Prince Rupert, and the Duke of Monmouth do now wear deep mourning, that is long cloaks, for the Duchess of Savoy: so

that he mourns as a Prince of the Blood, while the Duke of York do no more, and all the nobles of the land not so much

February 8th, 1664 Dr Pierce told me... that the King do dote infinitely upon the Duke of Monmouth, apparently as one that he intends to have succeed him. God knows what will be the end of it!

February 22nd, 1664 This evening came Mr Alsopp the King's brewer with whom I spent an hour talking... He (the King) is so fond of the Duke of Monmouth that everybody admires it; and he says that the Duke hath said that he would be the death of any man that says that the King was not married to his mother

December 16th 1666 The Duke of Monmouth, Lord Brouncker says, spends his time the most viciously and idle of any man, nor will be fit for anything; yet he speaks as if it were not impossible but the King would own him for his son, and that there was marriage between his mother and him.'

* Around 1490, Henry VII appointed a John Walter of Essex to be an 'approver' of certain Pembrokeshire lordships. He married Alison Mendus of Fishhguard, and their son Morris Walter was Mayor of Haverfordwest in 1579 and 1587. He married Jane Warren of Trewerne. Their son was William Walter, who married Francis Laugharne of St Brides, and purchased the manor of Roch and other major properties. His son Richard was Sheriff, as was Richard's grandson another Richard, in 1727. William's daughter Lucy bore James Duke of Monmouth, from whose marriage comes the line of the Dukes of Buccleuch.

** Upon being made Duke of Monmouth and Buccleuch, Baron Tyndale and Earl of Doncaster, Lucy's son James was made in quick succession: MA Cambridge; Knight of the Garter; MA Oxford; Member of the Inner Temple; Master of a Troop of Horse; Captain in Prince Rupert's Regiment; Colonel in the Life Guards; General of the British Forces in France; Ambassador to the Court of France; Warden and Chief Justice on Royal Parks South of the Trent; Great Chamberlain of Scotland; Governor of Kingston-on-Hull; Lord-Lieutenant of East Riding; Lieutenant-General in the French Army; Lord of the Admiralty; High Steward of Kingston-on-Hull; Master of the Horse; Chancellor of the University of Cambridge; Colonel of the Royal English regiment of Foot in the French Army; Governor of Charterhouse; Joint Registrar of the Court of Chancery; Lord-Lieutenant of the County of Stafford; General of the British Forces in Flanders; Captain-General of the Forces; and Privy Councillor for Scotland. The sheer density of titles and honours makes it unlikely that he was illegitimate.

*** A letter from the Princess of Orange to her brother Charles Stuart refers to Lucy as Charles' 'wife', asking Lucy's forgiveness for the affair and pregnancy with Henry Bennett: 'Your wife desires me to present her humble duty to you, which is all she can say. I tell her it is because she thinks of another husband and does not follow your example of being as constant a wife as you are a husband. 'Tis a frailty, they say is given to the sex, therefore You will pardon her I hope'.

Also, in the *Journal* of John Paterson, Archbishop of Glasgow, we find an entry on February 20th, 1696: 'Sir John Cook told me that E. Newburgh told him that he was witness to King Charles' marriage with the Duke of Monmouth's mother, and that Pogers and Anoyr also were so too.' Edward Podgers, Groom of the Bedchamber, was responsible for the abduction of the infant James from Lucy into Charles' mother's care. According to Davies and Edwards' *Women of Wales* (1935), 'a Caernarvonshire Squire wrote against his grand-daughter's name in his genealogical tree "married King Charles y Second of England". The grand-daughter was Lucy Walter.'

During the 1745 Rebellion which threatened to topple the Hanovers, the Home Office issued a High Warrant for the Marriage Register of St Thomas, Haverfordwest, where the Walter family marriages were commemorated. It was never returned, and no reason given for its disappearance. It was asserted however, that a marriage in the 1640's had been solemnised at St Thomas's which could have affected the House of Hanover's succession. We must remember that the current royal family is an unbroken line from the Hanovers, and the Elector of Hanover, George I, was 58th in line to the succession. The first 57 were Catholic and ineligible. If Lucy's marriage was legal, her descendants would have a far better right to the crown.

Edward Pogers had known Charles for years, and was his Gentleman to the Bedchamber. An ardent Royalist, he was Groom of the Bedchamber and an attesting witness at the wedding of Charles and Lucy. He was chosen by Charles to abduct James from Lucy. Charles' reputed second marriage to Lucy in Paris was carried out by Dr John Cosin, who upon the Restoration was made Lord (Bishop) of Durham. Cosin was in 1648-49 the Protestant Chaplain to the suite of the Queen Mother in Paris, and confided in the marriage to his son-in-law, Sir Gilbert Gerrard. Charles never denied the marriage in Lucy's lifetime. A Mr Forder of Houghton-le-Spring also claimed to be at the marriage, and was Dr Cosin's steward when he was Bishop of Durham.

There are three accounts of the Duke of Buccleuch's destruction in 1879 of a record of the marriage of Lucy Walter and Charles, given in Lamford's excellent book. Lord Mersey records Queen Victoria telling Dean Stanley that Buccleuch had found the mysterious black box from Montague House in Whitehall. Upon being told that he was therefore the real King of England, he threw the deeds into the fire, as 'that might cause a lot of trouble'. Another version from the Duke of Abercorn is that this same Fifth Duke of Buccleuch found the papers in the muniment room at Dalkeith, and burned them for the same reason in 1875. The third version recorded by Lamford is that Sir Hew Dalrymple, during the lifetime of the 7th Duke of Buccleuch (who died in 1935), copied the following manuscript from the family papers: 'The certificate of the marriage was found by Henry, Duke of Buccleuch (Henry, the 3rd Duke, was the 5th Duke's grandfather) and President Hope (Lord President of the Scottish Court of Sessions) amongst some old papers at Dalkeith and the Duke thought best to burn it. It does not seem clear whether it was the original or a copy of one at Liege, where they were married by the Archbishop of Canterbury. I believe it is supposed that the other copy or original, whatever it was, might be found at Liège if looked for. And it is said, Charles II would have acknowledged the

Duke of Monmouth as his heir, if it had not been prevented by James II. And it is said that James never left him on his deathbed for fear he should then do it.' (However, there was no Archbishop of Canterbury at this time, and the most senior churchman on the Continent with Charles was Dr John Cosin.)

*Footnote:*
James Scott, Duke of Monmouth, was the son of Charles and Lucy, born in 1649. He was much favoured by his father, and made Commander-in-Chief of the army in 1674, at the same time that Charles' younger brother James of York had the lesser post of Admiral of the Fleet. Lord Shaftesbury and the Whig opposition party urged King Charles to recognise the popular Protestant Monmouth as his heir, rather than let the Catholic convert James follow him as king. In April 1663, Monmouth was given the Order of the Garter, and on 28 March 1663 was empowered to use the royal arms, with tellingly no 'bar sinister' indication of illegitimacy. After James II's accession in 1685, Monmouth was exiled, and people were terrified of another Catholic persecution. James had made a deeply unpopular second marriage to another Catholic, the 15 year-old Mary of Modena. (This was at the time of the riots concerning the Exclusion Bill from 1679-1681.) Monmouth landed at Lyme Regis, Dorset, in May 1685 to claim his 'rightful' crown. Many people believed him to be the legitimate heir, and there were rumours of a 'black-box' with the marriage papers of Charles and Lucy. His poorly-armed rebellion was mercilessly crushed at Sedgemoor, and he was quickly executed with 320 of his followers. Monmouth's last letter, written in his condemned cell, before he was executed, may be read as an appeal for his children to be saved in return for denouncing their legitimate claim to the throne: '....the late King told me he was never married to my mother. Having declared this, I hope that the King, who is now, will not let my children suffer on this account. And to this I put my hand July 1685, Monmouth.' It seems that Monmouth wrote this letter to save his children from harm, and that his rebellion was badly mistimed. Later, the hated James was forced to flee Britain forever, in the 'Glorious Revolution'.


## KATHERINE PHILIPS 1 January 1632 - 22 June 1664

## 'THE MATCHLESS ORINDA', 'BRITAIN'S FIRST RECOGNISED FEMALE WRITER', 'THE FIRST OF THE ENGLISH POETESSES'

Katherine's father was John Fowler, an eminent merchant and member of the Clothworkers' Company. His second wife was a daughter of Dr Daniel Oxenbridge. (Some sources give Katherine's birth year as 1631, not 1632, and she was born in the parish of St Mary Woolnoth Haw in London, not Brecon as some claim). Aged 8 she went to Mrs Salmon's Puritan school for girls in Hackney. When Katherine was 15, her mother married Sir Richard

Philipps of Picton Castle (where that family still lives today), and Katherine's association with Wales began. Picton Castle had been ransacked by the Royalist army, and only restored to the Parliamentarian Sir Richard in the year before he married Mrs Fowler. Thus Katherine grew up surrounded by Puritans. John Aubrey remarked that at this time she was 'pretty fatt, not tall, reddish faced' with a 'read pumpled face'. However, by the age of 16 she was a vivacious girl, and James Philips of Cardigan Priory married Katherine Fowler of London in 1648. He was a 54 year-old kinsman of Sir Richard, both descended from Sir Thomas Philips, and from the Porth Eynon, Ceredigion, branch of the family. Katherine was his second wife. (His first wife had been Frances, a daughter of Sir Richard Philips). James and the young Katherine had a son, Hector, who died in childhood*. They then had a daughter also named Katherine. This latter Katherine had 15 children with Lewis Wogan of Boulston, but only a daughter survived.

Katherine Philips

Katherine Philips - 'the matchless Orinda'

When Katherine married, Cardigan was just a village, and in the 12 years until the Restoration of the Monarchy seems to have changed from a Parliamentarian Puritan to a Royalist Episcopalian town, although her husband remained devoted to Cromwell's cause. Already an important landowner in the counties of Cardigan and Pembroke, James Philips had also made his mark in London before the return of King Charles II. In 1650, Orinda wrote the following lines regarding her move from cosmopolitan London to the country:

'How sacred and how innocent
A country life appears
How free from tumult, discontent
From flatterye and feares.
That was the first and happiest life,
When man enjoyed himselfe;
Till pride exchanged peace for strife,
And happiness for selfe.'

In 1649 her husband was High Sheriff for Cardiganshire, and in 1653 sat in the 'Barebones's Parliament' as the only Moderate from Wales, representing either Pembroke or Cardigan. In 1656 he was Mayor of Haverfordwest. It may be that Katherine wrote poems celebrating the return of the Stuart monarchy in order to soften the blow against her husband. He survived the charges brought against him by the King's new Parliament, but had to leave the House of Commons and he was never as prosperous again.

Katherine lived partly in London and partly in Wales, and wrote poems to Henry Vaughan, Anne Owen and in praise of the Welsh language. She was surrounded by a coterie of admirers, and was the centre of London's most noted literary 'salon'. According to *The New Companion to the Literature of Wales*, 'it has been claimed for her, at least, that she was the first woman writer in Britain to win professional and public recognition in her own right. *Orinda* was her nom-de-coterie, as *Antenor* was her affectionate husband's, while 'the Matchless' came from her admiring friends and panegyrists'. The latest edition of her *Collected Works* was published in three volumes in 1993.

**The sculpture also featured in the prefaces to 'Orinda's' poetical works**

In her lifetime her writings were in vogue, and she counted among her friends and critics some of the leading literary men of the 17th century. Cowley, Waller, Henry Vaughan, the miniaturist Samuel Cooper and the musician Henry Lawes were in her circle. Jeremy Taylor dedicated his *Discourse of the Natural Offices and Measures of Friendship* to 'the most ingenious and excellent Mrs Katherine Philips'. It seems that Katherine started writing around 1651, with verses to Henry Vaughan and Anne Owen of Landshipping surviving from that year. Anne Owen's name in Katherine's *Society of Friendship* was *Lucasia*. Another member, the diplomat-courtier-scholar Sir Charles Cottrell of Glamorgan's Cottrell Manor, went by the name of *Poliarchus*. Mary Aubrey, the daughter of Sir John Aubrey of Llantrithyd Place, was *Rosania*. The great Keats praised Katherine's writings to his friend Reynolds, especially one poem dedicated to *Rosania* (who became Mrs Montagu): '... a book of Poetry written by one beautiful Mrs Philips, called "The Matchless Orinda", a friend of Jeremy Taylor's. You must have heard of her, and most likely read her poetry - I wish you had not, that I may have the pleasure of treating you with a few stanzas - I do it at a venture - you will not regret reading them once more. The following to her friend Mrs Montagu at parting - you will judge of.' The final two verses of the poem dedicated to *Rosania* are as follows:

'Thus our twin souls in one shall grow
And teach the world new Love,
Redeem the age, and sex, and show
A Flame Fate dare not move:

And courting death to be our friend,
Our lives together too shall end.

A Dew shall dwell upon our tomb
Of such a Quality
That fighting Armies thither come
Shall reconciled be.
We'll ask no Epitaph, but say
Orinda and Rosania.'

Anne Owen (*Lucasia*) was widowed at 22, and Katherine was determined that Anne should marry the dashing Sir Charles Cottrell (*Poliarchus*), who was probably responsible for her own movement towards the Royalist cause. He fought at Edgehill, Newbury and Alresford, and besieged and took Oxford, joining Charles Stuart's court-in-exile when Charles I was executed. He had lived on the Continent for ten years before his return with Charles II, acting as Steward to Elizabeth, Queen of Bohemia. For 15 years he represented Cardigan in Parliament, owing to the influence of Katherine and her husband, and courted Anne Owen during this time. Much of the correspondence between *Orinda* and *Poliarchus* is concerning his chances with *Lucasia*. However, she chose Colonel Marcus Trevor, afterwards first Baron Dungannon, and it was left to Katherine to break the news to Sir Charles.

Katherine went to Ireland with Anne Owen and her new husband in 1662, trying to claim some estates for her husband which had been granted under the Parliamentarians. She was celebrated in Dublin, with the Earls of Roscommon and Orrery and the Countess of Cork becoming close friends. Her translation of Corneille's *Pompey* was performed with great success in London in 1663, and published in Ireland and London. The first impression sold out in a fortnight, and an unscrupulous publisher traded in on her new-found popular fame by printing a collection of her poems which had only been meant for private circulation, causing her some distress.

Meanwhile, she had been successful in the two most important of three lawsuits concerning her husband's estates, and returned to Cardigan and then London where she started working on a translation of Corneille's *Horace*. Katherine was welcomed back at Charles II's Court and in London society, and wrote more poems, including one to Cowley on his retirement from Court. Another poem was to Charles Rich, only son of the Earl of Warwick, who 'dyed of the small Pox 1664'. Unfortunately, Katherine caught the same disease, and died a few weeks later. There was an outburst of eulogies, from Abraham Cowley, James Tyrell, Thomas Flatman and William Temple amongst others, placing her as the prime example of the perfect English poetess. There is an excellent small book in the *Writers of Wales* series on *Orinda*, by the Rev. Patrick Thomas.

* Hector was born in 1655 after 7 years of marriage, and Katherine composed a poem in his remembrance, one verse of which is:

'-I did but see him, and he disappeared
I did but pluck the rose-bud and it fell;
A sorrow unforeseen and scarcely feared
For ill can Mortals their afflictions spell.'

## NELL GWYN 2 February 1650 - 1691

### ELEANOR GWYNN, MISTRESS OF CHARLES II AND MOTHER OF CHARLES BEAUCLERC, THE FIRST DUKE OF ST ALBANS

Nell's father was Thomas Gwyn, a Welsh royalist soldier, who died in a debtors' prison, possibly in Oxford. She was reported in a 1688 manuscript to have been a daughter of Thomas Guine, a Captain of 'ane antient fammilie in Wales'. Oxford, Covent Garden and Hereford all have claims that Nell was born there, with Pipe Well Lane in Hereford being renamed Gwyn Street. She was brought up in London by her alcoholic mother, who ran a brothel there after her husband's death, and who fell drunk into the Thames and drowned in 1679. Nell had grown up carrying drinks to customers in the brothel, but obtained a job working in the new King's Theatre in Drury

**Nell Gwyn by Sir Peter Lely**

Lane. Aged 14, with her elder sister Rose she sold oranges to the patrons, and by 1664, she made her first appearance on the stage, becoming a major success at the age of 17. She acted in the King's Company of Comedians, under Killigrew's patent, at the New Theatre in Drury Lane. Her beauty and vivacity had attracted her first lover, a comedian called Lacy. Then the most handsome and famous actor of her day, Hart, also favoured her, and both admirers assisted in her tuition as an actress. The poet Dryden wrote parts for her. Before the Restoration, no woman had acted upon the English stage, female parts being all played by men. The novelty and attraction of seeing beautiful women led to a huge upsurge in the popularity of the English theatre, and Nell was the most famous of our early actresses.

Nell soon attracted the attentions of Charles II, and became his favourite mistress aged 19, carrying on with her acting career as the greatest comic actress of her era. Samuel Pepys called her 'pretty, witty, Nell', and recorded often watching her in theatre. At the Admiralty, he had a print of Nell, naked and portrayed as Cupid, above his desk. Her forte was not in serious roles, but in comic ones, where she could sing and dance. Having previously been the mistress of Charles Hart and Charles Sackville, Gwyn called the king her 'Charles the Third'. Nell bore the king two sons, and was the only one of Charles' many mistresses from a humble background. 'Nelly' was known as Madame Ellen on the play bills, but retired from the theatre completely in 1671 to bring up her children. Charles II made her one of the ladies of the queen's privy chamber, and gave her a house in Pall Mall, where

**Nell Gwyn as Venus, by Sir Peter Lely, c.1668**

they both entertained foreign diplomats and ambassadors. A natural wit, she was extremely popular at court, where the Duchess de Chaulnes called her a 'femme d'ésprit, par la grace de Dieu'. Another contemporary wrote 'she alone had the patent from Heaven to engross all hearts'. However, Bishop Burnett said she was 'the wildest and indiscreetest creature that was ever in a court.' Nell appears to have been the only one of Charles' lovers to have been completely faithful to him, and is credited with converting him from Catholicism to the Church of England.

Nell had the reputation of being kind-hearted, and never used her position to gain advantage. Once, she saw a clergyman in the hands of the sheriff's officers on Ludgate Hill. She asked her carriage driver to halt, ascertained that the crime was debt, and paid his fine to release him. She then ensured that the clergyman's family never went into debt again. She also pressurised the feckless Charles to complete the building of the Chelsea Hospital. In 1681, a mob surrounded her carriage, baying for the blood of the Duchess of Portsmouth, another of Charles' mistresses. The Comte de Gramont recorded: 'Nell Gwynn was one day passing through the streets of Oxford, in her coach, when the mob mistaking her for her rival, the Duchess of Portsmouth, commenced hooting and loading her with every opprobrious epithet. Putting her head out of the coach window, "Good people", she said, smiling, "you are mistaken; I am the *Protestant* whore." The 'Catholic whore' was still the French noblewoman Louise de Kérouaille, created Duchess of Portsmouth in 1673. Nell's ccoachman once was fighting with another man who had called her a whore. She broke up the fight, saying, 'I *am* a whore. Find something else to fight about.'

Charles planned to make Nell Countess of Greenwich, but died suddenly, his last words being 'Let not poor Nelly starve.' Bishop Burnet, at his bedside, was scandalised that the king should have thought 'of such a creature' at that moment. Nell continued to live in Pall Mall, surviving on a pension of £1,500 a year from James II, living with strict decorum and regularly attending church. In 1687, Nell had two strokes, and died at the age of 37, possibly severely affected with syphilis.

When Nell died, St Martin-in-the Fields was packed for the service held by her friend Thomas Tennison, then vicar of St Martins. 'He praised her kindness to the needy - she left all her money to her nurses, her porter and the poor of the diocese - and ordered that £20 should be given annually on Christmas Day for the release of debtors'. Tennison enlarged on her benevolent qualities, sincere repentance and exemplary end. Charles Beauclerk was born to Nell and Charles in 1670, just before she quit the stage, in Lincoln's Inn Fields. Her other son James Beauclerk died in his childhood, in Paris, having been sent to school there. Charles was created baron of Heddington and Earl of Burford, and in 1683 Duke of St Albans, Registrar of the High Court of Chancery, and Grand Falconer. He married Lady Diana Vere, only daughter of the twentieth and last Earl of Oxford, and the greatest heiress in rank and descent in the three kingdoms, ensuring that poor Nell's descendants did not ever have to work too hard for a living.

## LADY NITHSDALE c.1680 - May 1749

### HEROINE OF THE ESCAPE FROM THE TOWER OF LONDON

Lady Winifred Herbert was the youngest daughter of William Herbert, first Marquess of Powis, a leading Roman Catholic implicated in the 'Popish Plot' and of Lady Elizabeth Somerset, a daughter of the Marquis of Worcester. Her father had taken his family to France to follow James II into exile. Upon reaching the age of twenty-one in 1697, William Maxwell, 5th Earl of Nithsdale visited the Jacobite Court a Saint-Germain to give his allegiance to the exiled king, where he met his future wife Lady Winifred. After their marriage at Saint-Germain in 1699, they settled at his family seat at Terregles Castle near Dumfries. As a prominent Catholic in the predominantly Protestant Lowlands, he was often the object of Presbyterian attacks on his estates. Winifred and her husband were devout Catholics, but their home at was ransacked by a rabble led by local ministers in 1703, on the pretext of hunting for Jesuits and priests. The Earl went to Justiciary Court for recompense, but instead was stripped of his office of hereditary steward of Kirkudbright. Financially struggling, the Earl signed an agreement to rebel to help the exiled House of Stuart, which he believed would revive his own fortunes. In 1712, however, Nithsdale realised that his estates could be forfeited in these dangerous times, and signed a contract giving all his estates to his infant son, reserving only a life-long rent. While resident at Terregles, the couple had five children.

In 1715, when the Earl of Mar raised the standard of rebellion in the Scottish Highlands, the Northumbrian Jacobites took up arms under the Earl of Derwentwater, and the adherents of the Stuart cause in Dumfriesshire and Galloway joined them on the Borders. The Earl of Nithsdale was a Roman Catholic, so it was deemed unpolitical to place him, as would otherwise have been done, at the head of the combined forces, and the chief command was given to Viscount Kenmure of the Galloway Gordons, who was a Protestant. However, the memory of the cruel persecutions of the Covenanters was too strong in the district to permit the great body of the people to show any zeal on behalf James Stuart 'The Old Pretender', the son James VII of Scotland (James II). Even the tenants of the Jacobite leaders took up

**Winifred Herbert, form a portrait at Everingham Park**

arms in support of the English Government, and the Earl of Nithsdale, as he himself stated, was attended by only four of his own domestics when he joined the insurgents. The insurrection was so wretchedly mismanaged that it never had the slightest chance of success. The combined force advanced as far as to Preston, where Nithsdale was in command of the 'gentleman volunteers', and was there surrounded by the royal troops, and compelled to surrender at discretion.

The noblemen and principal officers were conveyed to London, and committed to prison. On 27 November 1715, Nithsdale wrote to Winifred asking for money, and for her to come to London. It was a terrible journey in a bad winter, and she sent her young daughter to stay with Winifred's sister-in-law, the Countess of Traquair. The family papers were buried to prevent them being destroyed in her absence, and she borrowed £50 and a letter of empowerment for another £50 off a local land agent. Most of Nithsdale's family had taken no part in the rising and did not want to be associated with his misfortunes. Winifred took a groom and her Welsh maid, Cecilia Evans with her to London. Cecilia had been with her since her marriage, and had become a great friend. The trio went on horseback on the long journey to Newcastle, but there were no seats on the stage coach, so they carried on to

York. A Jacobite supporter managed to get Winifred a single seat at York, but Cecilia continued riding.

The snow was so bad in this winter, that several post-boys were found frozen to death, the rivers were blocked with ice, and when the coach reached Grantham in Lincolnshire, it could proceed no further. The countess again took to her horse, but she and Cecilia could only travel a short while before stopping at Stamford, where she wrote on Christmas Day to Lady Traquair 'I must confess such a journey I believe was scarce ever made, considering the weather, by a woman. But an earnest desire compasses a great deal, with God's help; and I may say the delays and stops I have unavoidably met with to my more speedy performance of it, has been by far the greatest difficulty I have had, though if I had known what I was to have gone through, I should have doubted whether I was able to have done it. However, if I meet my dear lord well, and am so happy as to be able to serve him I shall think all my trouble well repaid.' On arriving eventually in London, Winifred called upon all those who she thought might help her husband, but as a Catholic and a devoted adherent of the Stuarts, he had no supporters. Although ill, Winifred went to the Tower and met her husband upon several occasions.

The Earl of Nithsdale and another five lords had been sent to the Tower of London, and were brought to trial on 19 January 1716, before the House of Lords, on a charge of treason. They pleaded guilty, no doubt with the hope that a confession of guilt along with their speedy surrender might possibly incline the King to grant them a pardon. Sentence of death was pronounced upon Nithsdale, Kenmure, Derwentwater, Carnwath, Widdrington and Nairn by the Lord Chancellor Cowper, who acted as High Steward at the trial, and their execution was appointed to take place on 24 February. The last three lords however, were reprieved. Winifred had a Welsh friend at Court, a Mrs Morgan, who was acquainted with the Duke of Montrose, who had promised to do all he could to assist her. Mrs Morgan went to the Court with Winifred to present a petition for clemency to the king. They waited in the drawing room, through which the king would pass from his apartment to the Court, Winifred dressed in mourning. When the king was abreast of her, she fell to her knees in front of him and offered the petition, explaining in French what it was.

George I was a Hanoverian who never learned English, but who spoke some French as well as his native German. Hanover was about the size of the Isle of Wight, and the Germanic dynasty's kings always mistook arrogance for grace and intelligence. George ignored her, and she clutched his coat and was dragged along the floor before attendants took her away. An onlooker picked up the petition and passed it to Lord Dorset to give to the King. Dorset was another friend of Mrs Morgan.

Winifred wrote to Lady Traquair that she did not think that her actions would have any effect, but that she had done everything in her power, and was going to take a chamber near the Tower of London, to be next to her husband in his hour of need. She knew 'A Catholic upon the Borders and one who had a great following and whose family had ever proved on all occasions stuck to the royal [Stuart] family, could not look for mercy' [from the new Hanover line]. In a later letter she referred to her young son, who had joined her in London, saying that she was going to send him to France out of harm's way as soon as possible.

Another petition failed to be presented by the Duke of St Albans to the House of Lords on 22 February, two days before the beheading of Nithsdale, by which time Winifred had laid her plans to save her husband. On the last day before the execution, she implored Montrose and Pembroke to intercede, and there was a debate in which Pembroke stated that the king could over-rule Parliament and grant a reprieve.

Winifred took her lodgings-keeper, Mrs Mills into her confidence, and the following is a transcript of a letter she wrote later to Lady Traquair: 'I told her that I trusted she would not refuse to accompany me, that my Lord might pass for her. I pressed her to come immediately, as we had no time to lose. At the same time I sent for a Mrs Morgan, then usually known by the name of Hilton, to whose acquaintance my dear Evans had introduced me, which I look upon as a very singular happiness. I immediately communicated my resolutions to her. She was of a very tall and slender make; so I begged her to put under her own riding-hood, one that I had prepared for Mrs Mills, as she was to lend hers to my Lord, that, in coming out, he might be taken for her.

Mrs Mills was then with child; so she was not only of the same height but nearly the same size as my Lord. When we were in the coach, I never ceased talking, that they might not have leisure to reflect. Their surprise and astonishment when I first opened my design to them, had made them content, without even thinking of the consequences. On our arrival at the Tower, the first I introduced was Mrs Morgan; for I was only allowed to take in one at a time. She brought in the clothes that were to serve Mrs Mills, when she left her own behind her. When Mrs Morgan had taken off what she brought for my purpose, I conducted her back to the stair-case; and in going, I begged her to send me in my maid to dress me; that I was afraid of being too late to present my last petition that night if she did not come immediately. I went partly downstairs to meet Mrs Mills, who had the precaution to hold a handkerchief to her face, as was very natural for a woman to do when she was going to bid her last farewell to a friend, on the eve of his execution. I had indeed, desired her to do it, that my Lord might go out in the same manner.

Her eyebrows were rather inclined to be sandy, and my Lord's were dark and very thick: however I had prepared some paint of the colour of hers to disguise his with. I also brought an artificial head-dress of the same coloured hair as hers; and I painted his face with white, and his cheeks with rouge, to hide his long beard which he had no time to shave. All this provision I had before left in the Tower. The four guards, whom my slight liberality the day before had endeared me to [Winifred had given them money to drink to the health of the King and her husband], let me go quietly with my company and were not too strictly on watch as they usually had been; I made Mrs Mills take off her own cloak and put on that which I had brought for her. I then took her by the hand, and led her out of my Lord's chamber; and in passing through the next room, in which there were several people, with all the conern imaginable I said "My dear Mrs Catherine, go in all haste, and send my waiting-maid: she certainly cannot reflect how late it is: she forgets that I am to present a petition tonight, and if I slip this opportunity I am undone..." Everybody in the room, who were chiefly the guards' wives and daughters seemed compassionate to me exceedingly; and the sentinel officiously opened the door.

When I had seen her go out, I returned to my Lord and finished dressing him. I had taken care that Mrs Mills did not go out crying, as she came in, that my Lord might the better pass for the lady who came in crying and affected. When I had almost finished dressing my Lord in all my

petticoats, excepting one, I perceived that it was growing dark, and was afraid that the light of the candle might betray us; so I resolved to set off. I went out leading him by the hand; and he held his handkerchief to his eyes. I spoke to him in the most piteous and afflicted tone of voice, bewailing bitterly the negligence of Evans, who had ruined me by her delay. Then, said I, "My dear Mrs Betty, for the love of God, run quickly and bring her with you. You know my lodging; and if ever you made despatch in your life, do it at present - I am almost distracted with this disappointment."

The guards opened the doors; and I went downstairs with him, still conjuring him to make all possible despatch. As soon as he had cleared the door, I made him walk before me, for fear the sentinel should take notice of his walk.... At the bottom of the

C.L. Doughty's painting of Lady Nithsdale pleading with George I for the release of her husband

stairs I met my dear Evans, into whose hands I confided him. I had before engaged Mrs Mills to be in readiness before the Tower to conduct him to some place of safety, in case we succeeded. In the meanwhile, as I had pretended to have sent the young lady on a message, I was obliged to return upstairs, and go back to my Lord's room, in the same feigned anxiety of being too late: when I was in the rook [cell], I talked to him as if he had been present, and answered my own questions in my Lord's voice, as nearly as I could imitate it.

I walked up and down as if we were conferring together, till I thought they had time enough thoroughly to clear themselves of the guards. I then thought proper to make off also. I opened the door and stood half in it, that those in the outward chamber might hear, and held it so close that they could not look in. Then before I shut the door, I pulled through the string of the latch, so that it could be only opened on the inside. I said to the servant as I passed by, that he need not carry in candles to his master till my Lord sent for him, as he desired to finish some prayers first. I went downstairs, and called a coach and drove home to my lodgings, where poor Mr Mackenzie had been waiting to carry the petition, in case my attempt failed. I told him that there was no need of any petition, as my Lord was safe out of the Tower; but that I did not know where he was. I then desired a servant to call for a Sedan chair, and I went to the Duchess of Montrose, who had always borne a part in my distresses.....

I ran up to her in my transport of joy. She appeared to be extremely shocked and frightened - she advised me to retire to some place of security; for that the King was highly displeased, and even enraged at the petition I had presented to him. I sent for another (sedan) chair; for I always discharged them immediately, lest I might be pursued.

Her Grace said that she would go to court, to see how the news of my Lord's escape were received. When the news was brought to the King, he flew into an excess of Passion and said he was betrayed.' Thus on 23 February, Winifred and her husband escaped from the Tower. The letter goes on to tell how she stayed with her husband in a poor woman's lodgings opposite the guards' house at the Tower, not moving off the bed for fear of being heard on the floorboards, subsisting on a bottle of wine and a loaf from Thursday until Saturday, until Mrs Mills conducted Lord Nithsdale to the Venetian Ambassador's house, where he was concealed in a servant's room until the following Wednesday. The Ambassador was not told, and Nithsdale donned livery and went down with the Ambassador's coach to Dover, where a small boat was hired to sail to Calais.

Winifred and Evans made their way back to Scotland, first to Traquair and then to Terregles. She had no permit to be in the country, as the wife of an escaped traitor, and was liable to imprisonment. At her deserted house, she unearthed the family papers. She knew that the Lord Lieutenant of the county would warn her if there was to be a search instituted for her. Winifred went through the mansion, noting what could be sold to sustain her family in exile, and left her husband's relative, a Major Maxwell in charge of the estate. Her friends bought the furniture, and she had to leave Traquair as Dumfries magistrates were asking her to provide evidence that she had government permission to be in Scotland. Once again she rode to London, again with Cecilia Evans, although the Countess was expectant.

In London she was given letters from the Earl, imploring her to join him in Paris with their daughter. Soldiers and spies swarmed over the city looking for her, under the Hanoverian king's orders, as he claimed that she had done him 'more mischief than any woman in Christendom'. A fortnight later she made a dash for the coast, and in a terrible crossing not only miscarried but almost died herself. Cecilia Evans wrote to the Countess of Traquair from Bruges: 'I have seen many a dangerous illness with her, but never like this...'

Winifred joined the Earl at Lille in October, then went to Mary of Modena, the wife of King James II, to ask for financial assistance. Unfortunately, neither Mary nor her son, James 'The Old Pretender', could take the earl into their Courts, as they were likewise suffering financially. However, Winifred managed to extract a pension of 100 livres a month for herself, and 200 livres a month for the Earl. It was still very difficult, as he was a spendthrift, and Winifred appears to be glad that he had now left for the James Stuart's court in Rome. She later joined him there, but it was not a happy time for her.

Although Lady Nithsdale continued to suffer from financial troubles and illnesses, probably brought on by the conduct of her husband, several events occurred to cheer her. After long litigation in the Court of Session and the House of Lords, the entail which Lord Nithsdale had executed in 1712 was sustained, and Lord Maxwell, his sole surviving son, would succeed to the family estates at the earl's death. Practically, he came into possession of them even before that event, since the life interest of his father was purchased from the Government for his benefit. Lady Anne Maxwell, the only daughter of Lord and Lady Nithsdale, was married to Lord Bellew, an Irish nobleman, at Lucca, in 1731. Lord Maxwell, who was now resident in Scotland, had become attached to his cousin, Lady Catherine Stewart, daughter of Lord and Lady Traquair, and made her an offer of marriage. The old connection between the two families, their constant friendship, and their agreement both in religion and politics, rendered the proposed marriage agreeable to Lady Nithsdale and Lord and Lady Traquair. But for some unmentioned reason, Lord Nithsdale for a considerable time withheld his consent. The marriage at length took place, however, in the course of the year 1731, and appears to have been as happy as Lady Nithsdale anticipated. As no sons were born from it, the male line of this ancient family ended at Lord Maxwell's death. The last we hear of the faithful Cecilia Evans is in 1732, in a letter from Countess Nithsdale to Countess Traquair, stating that Evans is still with her.

Lord Nithsdale continued to live at Rome in debt and difficulties, still hoping that the exiled Stuart family might be restored to the throne of their ancestors, but he did not live to witness the last uprising on their behalf. He died at Rome in March, 1744. After his decease his widow was induced to accept an annuity of £200 a year from her son, who then came into full possession of the family estates. Of this annuity she resolved to apply one-half to the payment of her husband's debts, which would then be paid off within three years. When this was attained, in harmony with her generous character, she told her agent to tell Lord Maxwell that 'as his father's debts are now quite extinguished, his lady mother will have no occasion for more than one hundred pounds sterling per annum from him henceforth. She is now quite easy, and happy that she is free of what was a great and heavy burden upon her.' Nothing further is known of Lady Nithsdale's declining years, but she appears to have grown very infirm. She survived her husband five years, and died in the spring of 1749 at Rome, still in attendance of her exiled king. Both she and Lord Nithsdale were probably buried in Rome, but no trace can be found of their last resting-place. The 'Nithsdale Cloak', the brown cloak worn by Nithsdale to disguise his escape is now in the possession of the Duchess of Norfolk, who represents the Nithsdales in the female line.

## MARY SCURLOCK November 1678 – 26 December 1718

## LADY STEELE

Mary Scurlock's father was Jonathan Scurlock JP, alderman and Sheriff for Carmarthenshire in the year of her birth. A Norman, William de Scurlog, had been noted in Ireland in 1184. One of his descendants came to Wales and Jonathan was his descendant. He married Elizabeth Stylt on 3 August 1677, at St Peter's Church, Carmarthen, and their daughter Mary was born in Carmarthen or adjacent Llangunnor in November 1678. She cannot have been expected to live, as she was christened the day after her birth, but not received into the church until she was two years old.

The next we hear of Mary Scurlock is when she is sued for breach of contract of a marriage, by Henry Owen of St James, Westminster. The proceedings began on 18 February 1703, and the 1704 libel proceedings make fascinating reading:

'1. That in 1700, 1701, 1702 and more particularly in 1704 Henry Owen and Mary Scurlock were free from all matrimonial contracts, he being a widower, and she a spinster; and that they often treated of a marriage between them, as is public and notorious.
2. That in 1703 they, having known each other for several years, became more particularly acquainted, and often frequented each other's company in Wales, at Bath, etc., and in London.
3. That he courted her, and she did not refuse, but in divers ways encouraged him.

130

4. That while they were lodging in the same house in St James's parish he became very much indisposed and made a will, leaving a considerable estate to her; this will he gave sealed to her mother, who gave it to her daughter, who by opening the cover or otherwise, found what he had bequeathed. On his recovery, he renewed his addresses, which were received with favour.

5. That she accepted presents, some of value, and gave him presents in return; she also admitted him to her bedchamber at twelve at night and other late hours, and declared to several persons her affection for him, saying that she would let him embrace her and that they might tell this to another person who was supposed to be courting her.

6. That in November, December and January, 1703, they, being in the same lodgings, frequently dined and supped together, and visited friends, and were often alone together for hours early and late.

7. That she would often resort to his bedchamber where they discussed plans for their future married life.

8. That she freely agreed to enter into a marriage contract in the terms he might think most binding; and that about January 1703 they contracted themselves in marriage, using the words from the *Book of Common Prayer*, and he put a silver ring on her finger, which she readily accepted, and they embraced.

9. That she wore the ring for a considerable time, confessing that she had received it from him, and the contract they had entered into; but that when it came to her mother's knowledge, Mary, by her mother's direction, threw the ring into the fire, and said that there was an end to the contract.

10. That she, being sensible that the contract was really valid and obligatory, endeavoured to prevail with him not to insist upon it.

11. That he was a barrister-at-law and JP in the county of Carmarthen and had an estate of at least £500 a year, and was 30, 35 or 40 years of age at most.

12. That Mary Scurlock was and is within the jurisdiction of the Court.

She defended herself in a 'Personal Answer' to the court on the grounds that Owen was after her fortune, and was 'much in debt'. Being an only child, she had inherited her father's Llangunnor estate, so was a wealthy woman. She also argued that there was no marriage contract, that Owen was only an 'old acquaintance' and most importantly that he had he had previously 'paid addresses to' (courted) her widowed mother. The judge agreed with her, and Owen appealed to the Court of Arches, but again lost.

Owen was still chasing Mary when aged twenty-nine she married the Irishman Sir Richard Steele at St Margaret's, Westminster on 9 September 1707. They appear to have met at the funeral of his first wife Margaret. Steele seems to have secured his mother-in-law's approval for the marriage by estimating his future income from writing (he founded *The Tatler*) at over £1,000 a year. The newly-weds bought a house in Bury Street in the expensive neighbourhood of St James, near St James Church, Westminster, which they both attended. The location was crucial to Steele in his role as a Gazetteer, as he was close to the palace and also the 'Cockpit', where the Secretary of State had his office.

Steele's pet name of 'Prue' for Mary seems to have come from her prudence with money compared to his extravagance. Steele's first wife, an elderly widow (whom he seems to have married for money), left him estates in Barbados which she had inherited from her brother. The property was said to be worth £800 a year, but had debts attached of £3,000. Steele earned another £100 as Gentleman-Waiter to Prince George of Denmark. In 1707, the year of his marriage to Prue, he had received the appointment of Gazetteer, which meant another £300 a year. Prue herself was the only heiress to her father's extensive property estate when her mother died, and their marriage seems to have been a constant squabble about Steele's spending habits. His business and literary interests meant that he spent quite a time away from home, but hundreds of letters between the couple record their arguments and making-up.

**Sir Richard Steele by Godfrey Kneller c.1712, National Portrait Gallery**

On 7 June 1708, we read: 'Dear Prue, I enclose to you a Guinea for your pocket - I dine with Lord Halifax. I wish I knew how to court you into Good-Humour, for Two or Three Quarrels more will dispatch me quite [kill me]. If you have any Love for Me believe I am always pursuing our Mutual Good. Yours ever, Richard Steele'.

Another from 6.30 in the morning of 9 August 1708, sent from Bury Street, reveals that Prue had left the house: 'Dear Prue, Thou art such a foolish Tender thing that there is no living with Thee. I have broke my rest last night because I knew you would be such a fool as not to sleep. Pray come home by this morning's Coach if you are impatient; but if you are not here by noon I will come down to you in the Evening, but I must make visits this morning to hear what is doing. Yours ever, Richard Steele.'

Obviously Prue did not return on the stagecoach, as he sent another note that same night: 'Dear Prue, I cannot possibly come expecting Orders Here which I must overlook and having not half done my other business at the Savoy. Dear Creature come in the morning Coach and if I can I will return with you in the evening. Please wrap yourself very Warm. Yours ever, Richard Steele.'

Around this time Steele asked Prue to go with him to visit a boarding school for young ladies, where he paid a great deal of notice to one of the children. Prue asked if the child was his, and when Richard affirmed this, Prue said 'Then, I beg she shall be mine too'. They took the girl home with them and brought her up as their own. Also in the summer of 1708 Steele's fortunes turned for the better, and he took a house at Hampton Court. Prue was given a chariot with four horses, a saddle-horse of her own, a footman, gardener, a young boy for errands, a maid and a boy who could speak Welsh. However, a letter from Richard of 11 August 1708 shows that again she was still worrying about their finances: 'Dear Wife, I shall make it the business of my life to make you easy and happy. Consult your cool thoughts and you'll know that tis the glory of a Woman to be her husband's Friend and Companion and not his Sovereign Director'. Lady Steele's worries proved correct. At the end of 1708 an order for arrears of rent on Bury Street appeared, shortly before the birth of their daughter Elizabeth on 26 March 1709.

A week later, Steele and Joseph Addison (godfather of their daughter) founded *The Tatler*. Steele also collaborated with Addison in founding *The Spectator* in 1711, and *The Guardian* in 1713. *The Tatler* was an immediate success but did not solve the family's cash-flow problems, mainly caused by Steele's lavish hospitality and love of expensive wines. In May 1709 Richard was arrested for debt, and vowed vengeance on 'that insufferable brute', their landlady at Bury Street. In December another letter was sent to pacify his wife: 'My Dear, I shall not come home to dinner, but have fixed everything and received money for present uses. I desire, My Dear, that you have nothing else to do but to be a darling; the way to which is to always be in good humour, and believe I spend none of my time but to the advantage of you and Your Most Obedient Husband, Richard Steele.'

1710 saw another upturn in the couple's fortunes. Richard was made a commissioner of the Stamp Office, giving him £1,000 a year. Unfortunately, he voluntarily renounced the money so that he could attack the Government in defence of his Whig principles. In 1713, Prue's mother died, which released an estate worth £500 a year to Steele. The couple were yet again living above their means, in a grand house in Bloomsbury Square, and Steele was entertaining recklessly, with a retinue of servants. The king knighted him in 1715, but in January that year they could not even afford coal, as Steele wrote: 'Dear Prue, I have that in my Pocket, which within a few days will be a great sum of money, besides what is growing at the Play-House. I prefer your ease to all things. I beg of you to send for coals and all things necessary for this Week and Keep Us only to the end of it out of Your Abundance and I shall ever add to it hereafter instead of attempting to diminish it. I cannot indeed get money, immediately without appearing most scandalously indigent which I would avoid for the future. Ever Yours, Richard Steele.'

In 1716, Lady Steele travelled to Wales to sort out the leases upon their Scurlock estates, an action made necessary by eight court actions against Steele for debt. He wrote to her 'We had not when you left us an Inch of Candle and a pound of Coal or a bit of Meat, in the House'. Prue's resolve must have been critical, as her younger daughter Molly was ill at the time, but luckily recovered unmarked from smallpox. Prue stayed at Llangunnor and in Wales for almost a year, missing Christmas Day in London with her children Betty and Molly. When she returned to London, she had decided to leave Sir Richard. Steele's drinking, gambling and living above his means had constantly made it difficult for him to keep up the rent, always being forced to move to properties in less fashionable districts or to use houses that belonged to the Scurlock family.

Arrangements were made for the family to return to Wales in autumn 1717, but she died in the following December aged only 40. Her sons Richard and Eugene had died in childhood, and Molly was to die of consumption in 1730. Her surviving daughter Elizabeth married the Welsh Judge John Trevor, who became 3$^{rd}$ Baron Trevor of Bromham. Steele retired to Carmarthen to end his days, living at Ty Gwyn, near Llangunnor, being buried in St Peter's, Carmarthen in 1729. However, Prue is buried in the South Transept of Westminster Abbey. All the notes that Richard sent Prue were published in 1787, and form an invaluable insight into the early 18th century.


## JANE BRERETON 1685 – 7 August 1740

## JANE HUGHES, *MELISSA*

Jane was born in 1685 the daughter of Thomas Hughes of Bryn Gruffydd near Mold, Flintshire and his wife Anne Jones. She was the younger of two daughters, but her sister died early. Unusually for a girl at the time, Jane was educated at least up to the age of sixteen, when her

Jane Brereton is burind near the altar at St. Giles Church, Wrexham

father died in 1801, and she showed an early interest in poetry. Her friends encouraged her 'peculiar Genius for poetry, which was her chief Amusement.'

In January 1711 she married Thomas Brereton (1691-1722), a 'commoner' of Brasenose College, Oxford. He turned out to have a violent temper – 'his first Fit of Passion, after their Marriage – was like a Thunderclap to her.' The Breretons moved to London for Jane to pursue a literary career, writing prose, plays and poetry. Her husband soon spent his considerable fortune, left by his father, an officer under Marlborough. Their two sons died in infancy but two daughters survived. He left for Paris, and some time after this, a separation took place and Jane retired in 1721 to Flintshire, where she led a solitary life, seeing little company but some intimate friends. She lived in seclusion as she was 'well aware what a critical Case it is to behave without the Censure of the World, when separated from an Husband.' About this time Thomas Brereton obtained from the Earl of Sunderland a post belonging to the customs at Parkgate, Cheshire, but in 1722 drowned in the River Dee at Saltney, as the tide was coming in.

She possessed talents for versification, if not for excellent poetry, which she displayed for some years as a correspondent to the *Gentleman's Magazine*, under the signature *Melissa*. There she had a competitor who signed himself FIDO, a wealthy Wrexham wine-merchant, Thomas Beach, who in 1737 slit his throat. In 1722 the 37-year-old Jane had moved to Wrexham for the benefit of her children's education, where she died aged 55, leaving two daughters, Lucy and Charlotte. Charlotte recorded in an anniversary poem published in the *Gentleman's Magazine*. The cause was said to be 'gravel', or urinary problems. She is buried near the altar at St Giles Church, Wrexham.

Thirty-five years after her death a volume of her *Poems on Several Occasions; with letters to her friends; and an account of her life, was published* (1744). A number of her poems were reprinted in subsequent collections. Her entry by Kathleen Turner in the *Oxford Dictionary of National Biography* reads: 'Brereton's body of poetry displays a flair for tactful occasional writing, and represents a transitional moment in women's writing in the eighteenth century, a moment at which being a published writer while retaining respectability was becoming a real possibility.'

The following lines have been attributed to Jane, in Dyce, *Specimens of British Poetesses,* and by Robert Southey in his *Specimens of the Later English Poets, Volume I.* Southey includes three poems by Jane, including one to Richard Steele, on the death of his friend Addison, and also the commemorative poem on Jane's death by Charlotte Brereton. Beau Nash is a Welshman featured in this author's *100 Greatest Welshmen:*

'On Beau Nash's Picture at full length between the Busts of Sir Isaac
Newton and Mr. Pope.
The old Egyptians hid their wit
In Hieroglyphick dress,
To give men pains to search for it,
And please themselves with guess...
Moderns to tread the self same path,
And exercise our parts,
Place figures in a room at Bath:
Forgive them, God of Arts!...

Newton, if I can judge aright,
All wisdom doth express;
His knowledge gives mankind new light,
Adds to their happiness...
Pope is the emblem of true wit,
The sun-shine of the mind;
Read o'er his works for proof of it,
You'll endless pleasure find...
Nash represents man in the mass,
Made up of wrong and right,
Sometimes a knave, sometimes an ass,
Now blunt, and now polite...
The picture, placed the busts between,
Adds to the thought much strength;
Wisdom and Wit are little seen,
But Folly's at full length.'

## MARGED ferch IFAN 1696 – 1788, 1788 or 1801 (claimed)

### 'THE WELSH AMAZON', MARGARET EVANS OF PENLLYN

Marged Evans was born at Dyffryn Nantlle, Caernarfonshire, possibly at Talmignedd Ucha farm. She was the keeper of the Telyrniau Inn, Gelli, during the great Drws-y-Coed copper-mining operations of the mid-18th century. The six-foot-tall Marged is recorded as singing and playing the fiddle or harp, which she made herself, while her customers danced. Prosperous days for the Drws-y-Coed mining district eventually came to an end and Marged was forced to move to search for work and a way to make a living. She moved with her husband to Nant Peris where copper mining was still flourishing, settling at Penllyn, Llanberis near Cwm y Glo. Marged now built her own rowing boat and got a job ferrying copper ore and passengers across Llyn Peris and Llyn Padarn to Penllyn.

Marged soon became well-known and admired, amongst the locals earning the title of 'Queen of the Lakes.' Her job rowing copper all day ensured that she stayed strong for her wrestling and Thomas Pennant claimed that she was still wrestling in her seventies and could take on and beat even the youngest men. One story says that she built the bridge at Pont Meibion, Nant Peris which is made from one huge piece of slate. Legend has it that Marged held up one end while a gang of young men held the other whilst it was fixed in place. Another story is that a passenger argued with Marged after she had agreed to row him across the lake, possibly over his fare. 'Mr Smith' soon found himself in the lake and had to agree to pay her a guinea to save him.

Thomas Pennant, the Flintshire scholar who corresponded with the eminent Linnaeus, and with Gilbert White of Selborne, kept diaries of his travels through Wales, Ireland and Scotland. His *A Tour of Wales 1778 and 1781* is a fascinating assemblage of three volumes to which we are indebted the following information. Pennant tried to visit Marged in 1786, but she was away, and he recounts several tales of her. It is worthwhile noting his description of the beginning of his route from Llanberis to Beddgelert: 'On the loftiest part, over one of the lakes, stands the remains of Castell Dolbadarn, consisting of a round tower and a few fragments of walls. It was constructed with the thin laminated stones of the country, cemented with very strong

**Dolbadarn Castle, built by the Princes of Gwynedd, overlooks Llyn Padarn**

mortar without shells. The inner diameter of the tower is only 26 feet. This seems to have been built to defend the pass into the interior parts of Eryri (Snowdonia) and was likewise used as a state prison. The founder was evidently a Welsh prince. I am informed that it was Padarn Beisrudd, son of Idwal.

In this valley are two groups of wretched houses. The farthest is near the end of the upper lake, with its church dedicated to St Peris who was, we are told, a cardinal. Here is to be seen the well of the saint, inclosed with a wall. The sybil of the place attends and divines your fortunes by the appearance or non-appearance of a little fish which lurks in some of its holes. From hence I took a ride above the lakes to their lower extremity. The upper is the lesser but much the most beautiful piece of water. It is said to be in places 140 yards deep and to have abounded with char before they were reduced by the streams flowing from the copper mines which had been worked on the sides of the hills.

The lowest lake is about a mile and a half long, narrows gradually into the form of a river called the Rhyallt, and flows in a diffused channel to Caernarfon where it assumes the name of Seiont. Near this end of the lake lived a celebrated personage whom I was disappointed in not finding at home. This was Marged uch Ifan of Penllyn, the last specimen of the strength and spirit of the ancient British fair. She is at this time (1786) about 90 years of age. This extraordinary female was the greatest hunter, shooter and fisher of her time. She kept a dozen at least of dogs, terriers, greyhounds and spaniels, all excellent in their kinds. She killed more foxes in one year than all the confederate hunts do in ten, rowed stoutly and was queen of the lake, fiddled excellently and knew all our old music, did not neglect the mechanic arts for she was a very good joiner, and at the age of 70 was the best wrestler in the country; few young men dared to try a fall with her.

Some years later she had a maid of congenial qualities but death, that mighty hunter, at last earthed her faithful companion. Marged was also a blacksmith, shoemaker, boat-builder and maker of harps. She shoed her own horses, made her own shoes and was under contract to convey the copper ore down the lakes. All the neighbouring bards paid their addresses to Marged and celebrated her exploits in pure British [Welsh] verse.'

Pennant noted that, after rejecting many local suitors 'at length, she gave her hand to the most effeminate of her admirers, as if predetermined to maintain the superiority which nature had bestowed on her.' This was Richard Morris. On the evidence of his family, she gave him two fearful beatings, the first shortly after the wedding. After his second beating, he became 'one of the chief leaders of Methodism in the parish'. (Others state that her unfortunate husband was one William Richards). At least two accounts place her death in 1801, aged 105. Marged possibly died around the year 1789, aged 93 years old, a short time after the death of her favourite maid who had served her for over forty years. Pennant believed she was 90 when he met her in 1786. A legend has it that she is buried under the altar stone of Nant Peris church.

Beryl H Griffiths, in *Merched Gwyllt Cymru - Wild Welsh Women* (2007) gives us an old poem about Marged, which reads translated into in English:

'Marged fwyn 'ach Ifan has
a big tub and a small tub
One to wash shirts and bedclothes
Another just for porridge

Gentle Marged daughter of Ifan
Has a big clutch and a little clutch,
One to drag the dogs from the corner
Another to break people's bones.

Iron Marged daughter of Ifan
Has a big clog and a little clog,
One to kick the dogs by the corner
Another to kick her hubby to the devil.

Gentle Marged daughter of Ifan
Has a big clutch and a little clutch,

One to drag the dogs from the corner
Another to break people's bones.

Dear Margaret daughter of Ifan
Has a big harp and a small harp,
One to play within Caernarfon
Another to keep her hubby fond.

And she has, besides a sheepfold,
A big horse and a small horse
One to carry hubby from the tavern,
Another to carry the pouch of money.

She bides in Bala
Her breasts like driven snow
Send my regards to her
She is Marged fwyn 'ach Ifan


## BRIDGET BEVAN 30 October 1698 (christened) - 11 December 1779

### MADAM BEVAN, EDUCATIONIST AND PHILANTHROPIST

**Bridget Bevan
by John Lewis 1745**

Bridget Vaughan was the youngest daughter of John and Elizabeth Vaughan, of Derllys Court, Carmarthen. John Vaughan was the organiser of SPCK schools in Carmarthenshire from 1700-1722. The Society for Promoting Christian Knowledge, an Anglican mission to distribute Christian education and literature, had only been formed in 1698. Derllys Court was a great religious and educational centre, and Bridget's rector, Thomas Thomas of Merthyr, in 1700 had written a letter to the SPCK advocating a charity school in every parish in Britain. From this time Griffith Jones (q.v. in *The 100 Greatest Welshmen*) was in charge of the schools at Laugharne (1709) and Llanddowror (1716), and it seems that Bridget must have known him since her childhood. Griffith Jones was also linked to the

Vaughan family, and he and Richard Vaughan (Bridget's uncle) married two of the daughters of Sir John Philipps of Picton Castle, a great SPCK benefactor.

Bridget married Arthur Bevan, a Laugharne barrister, on 30 December 1721. Bevan became Recorder for Carmarthen from 1722-1741, and an MP from 1727-1741. In 1735, Arthur Bevan was appointed Judge of Equity in South and North Wales, dying in 1743. Bridget Bevan had been deeply affected by the work towards education carried out by her father and rector, and herself had opened two schools at Llandybie and Llandeilo Abercywyn. In turn she greatly influenced Griffith Jones, and became his chief patron and advisor when he began his circulating schools between 1731 and 1737. In these years Jones wrote 175 letters to her, and upon his wife's death in 1755 went to live at Mrs Bevan's home in Laugharne, dying in 1761.

In 1731 Griffith had written to the SPCK proposing a 'Welch School' at Llanddowror, as the number of SPCK charity schools (for poor children aged 7-11) in Wales had started to decline. Griffith Jones began his 'circulating schools' movement around between 1731 and by 1737 there were 37 schools with 2,400 scholars. Schools were held for three months in the same place, usually in winter when farm-workers and children had more time available to study. Often the village church was used, if the rector would agree. Schools were also run in barns, storehouses and even a windmill. Night schools were also available for those who could not get any time off in the day, and pupils were taught to read the Welsh *Bible* and to learn the *Church Catechism*. SPCK religious texts were used to teach literacy, and any funds raised were spent on teaching, not on buildings. All the schoolmasters were trained by Griffith Jones personally at Llanddowror, and he insisted that they were members of the Church of England.

The movement was essential in giving the Welsh opportunities for literacy - by the time he died in 1761, it was estimated that 158,000 people between the ages of 6 and 70 had learned to read, out of an estimated Welsh population of 480,000 (in 1750). This percentage of literate Welsh people was probably higher than any other European nation of the time, and probably the world, despite the grinding poverty. By 1764 news of the success of this Welsh educational initiative had reached Catherine the Great of Russia, who ordered her ministers to make enquiries about the scheme. The annual report, *Welch Piety*, recorded that over 3,495 schools had been set up by Jones's death in 1779, a wonderful success story. In that actual year, the 210 existing schools taught 8,023 pupils.

Griffith had bequeathed to Mrs Bevan the funds of his schools and his private fortune, a huge sum of £7,000, asking her to carry on the religious and educational work of his schools. Madam Bevan continued his work with great success, so that in the year 1773 there were 242 schools and 13,205 pupils, the highpoint of the popularity of the movement. She died in

1779, and was buried near Griffith Jones in Llanddowror, although her husband had been buried in Laugharne. She left £10,000 for the continuation of the schools, but the will was disputed by two of her relatives who were also trustees, Lady Elizabeth Stepney and Admiral William Lloyd. Not until 1804 was the money released from Chancery for the schools, now worth £30,000. The schools survived until 1854 when they were absorbed into permanent National Society schools.

## ANN MADDOCKS 8 May 1704 (christened) – 6 June 1727 (buried)

### THE MAID OF CEFN YDFA

Ann Thomas was the daughter of William Thomas of Cefn Ydfa, Llangynwyd, near Maesteg, and her mother was Catherine Price, of Tynton, near Llangeinor, Glamorgan. Catherine's niece was Wales' greatest thinker, the philosopher Richard Price, and Richard's father, Rees, was to sign Ann's marriage settlement in 1725. Her father William Thomas died in May 1706, around the time of Ann's second birthday, and she was allegedly placed in the wardship of Anthony Thomas, a Cwmrisga lawyer. It was said that this lawyer forced Ann to marry his son Anthony Maddocks on 4 May 1725. From these brief details we have perhaps the most beautiful Welsh folk song, *Bugeilio'r Gwenith Gwyn* ('Watching the White Wheat').

The legend of the Maid of Cefn Ydfa has appeared in many books

It is said that she had fallen in love with a local poet, and soon after her forced marriage, died of a broken heart, pining for her true love. On her death bed she asked to see Will Hopcyn, and when he arrived she died in his arms. She is buried in St Cynwyd's Church, Llangynwyd. Her true love, Will Hopcyn, had composed the haunting verses, *Bugeilio'r Gwenith Gwyn* just for her. Iolo Morganwg said that Wil Hopcyn (1700-1741) was the author of the haunting poem, but it seems that Iolo himself wrote the finished version of the poem and song, based upon a far earlier tradition. Around 1745, Iolo's son Taliesin told the tragic tale of the poet Wil Hopcyn and Ann Thomas of Llangynwyd, the 'Maid of Cefn Ydfa', and connected the song to this story. Griffith John Williams said that Taliesin ab Iolo found the words in his father's works, and gave them to Maria Jane Williams

(*Llinos*), and they were published in *Ancient National Airs of Gwent and Morgannwg* in 1845. Several books

**Old Postcard showing the ruins of Cefn Ydfa farmhouse**

were written on the tragic love story between the heiress and the impoverished poet, and Joseph Parry wrote an opera in 1802 on the maid of Cefn Ydfa.

William Hopcyn was buried in Llangynwyd Churchard in 1741, and Iolo claimed that he and Will were fellow-pupils in *Cadair Morgannwg*, the bardic chair of Glamorgan, in 1760. It is known that a 'Wil Hopkin' wrote a poem satirising the bards at the 1735 Cymer Eisteddfod.

The first verse of *Bugeilio'r Gwenith Gwyn*, a slow traditional air, is as follows:

| | |
|---|---|
| *Mi sydd fachgen ieuanc ffol,* | I'm a young and carefree boy, |
| *Yn byw yn ol fy ffansi:* | Who lives and follows his fancy: |
| *Myfi'n bugeilio'r gwenith gwyn,* | I tend the fair white wheat, |
| *Ac arrall yn ei feid.* | Another reaps the harvest. |
| *Pam na ddeui ar fy ol,* | Why not come and follow me |
| *Ryw ddtdd ar ol ei gilydd,* | One day, and then another? |
| *Gwaith rwy'n dy weld y feini'r fach* | For I see thee, my little maid, |
| *Yn lanach, lanach beunydd* | Fair and ever fairer. |

*Footnote:*
There seems to be an overlap, or confusion, of this story with that of Elizabeth Williams, 'The Maid of Sker' c.1747 - 1776. This tragic heroine was the heiress of Sker House, Porthcawl, who fell in love with the harper, Thomas Evans. He composed the song *Y Ferch o'r Sger*, (The Maid of Sker) for her. Her father made her marry a rich English industrialist, Thomas Kirkhouse, and she died of a broken heart. It is recorded that she was engaged to another man, shortly before her 1768 marriage. The story was first recorded in 1806, and then recounted in greater detail by Jane Williams (*Ysgafell*) in 1838. Again it became the basis of several novels. R.D. Blackmore, the author of *Lorna Doone*, used to stay in Sker House, and also wrote a novel entitled *The Maid of Sker*, but it does not concern Elizabeth Williams.

**The 1741 Grave of Wil Hopcyn at Llangynwyd**

## DOLLY OF PENTREATH 17 May 1714 (baptised) – 27 December 1777 (buried)

## DOROTHY JEFFERY, LAST SPEAKER OF THE CORNISH LANGUAGE

 Dolly is an 'Eminent Briton' as in the sub-title of this book, in that she spoke the British language, Celtic-P. Cornish, like Breton, is a very close relative of Welsh, unlike the Celtic-Q branch of Scottish Gaelic, Manx and Irish. She is celebrated as the last of the Britons of Cornwall who spoke their native language, and for her longevity. Dolly is said to have lived to 102, with the monument in Paul churchyard giving this dubious fact. (Paul was founded by the 6th century Welsh saint Pol de Leon). Pentreath means the same as the Welsh 'pen' and 'traeth', 'head' of the 'beach', or 'strand-head'. Her father was Nicholas Pentreath, also of Paul, the neighbouring parish to Mousehole*, and she was generally known as Dolly Pentreath rather than her married name of Jeffery. Prince Lucien Bonaparte, who studied ancient languages, was intrigued by her story and paid for a monument with a lengthy inscription in Paul churchyard. The newspaper, *The West Briton* reported in March 1888 that her real grave had been found, and 'the big memorial stone erected by Prince Lucien Bonaparte in the wrong place has been transferred to where the bones rest of the last talker of old Cornish.' Her strangely-shaped skull had made its way to the surface, and contained only three teeth.

The memorial reads: 'Here lieth interred Dorothy Pentreath who died in 1777, said to have been the last person who conversed in the ancient Cornish. The regular language of this county from the earliest records till it expired in the eighteenth century in this Parish of Saint Paul. This stone is erected by the Prince Louise Bonaparte in Union with the Revd John Garret Vicar of St Paul. June 1860. Honour thy father and thy mother, that thy days may be long in the land which the Lord thy God giveth thee. Gwra pethi de taz ha de mam: mal de Dythiow bethenz hyr war an tyr neb an arleth de dew ryes dees. Exod. xx. 12'

A Truro engineer named Tompson wrote an epitaph for Dolly:

'Coth Doll Pentraeth cans ha deau
Marow ha kledyn ed Paul pleu:
Na ed an eglos, gan pobel bras,
Bed ed eglos-hay, coth Doly es'
- 'Old Doll Pentraeth, one hundred and two,
Deceased and buried in Paul parish too:
Not in the church with people great and high,

But in the churchyard doth old Dolly lie'.

Welsh and Breton speakers will note the language similarities – in Welsh *eglwys* is a church, and *plo* or *plou* is a prefix symbolising an old parish in Breton.

Dolly was a humble fishwife, born and buried in Paul, with a voice that could be heard 'as far away as Newlyn'. It was said that when a naval press-gang landed in search of seamen, Dolly chased them back to their boats with a hatchet, cursing them in Cornish, and that they never returned to the port after that time. Her old house overlooked the quay, and she hid a sailor sentenced to hanging in her chimney cavity, where she also kept smuggled goods. The man was wanted for desertion by the navy, and had been sentenced in his absence to be hung from the yardarm. The deserter escaped on a lugger to Guernsey after an unsuccessful search of Dolly's cottage. There is a room in the Keigwin Arms in Mousehole where Dolly smoked her pipe and drank her ale. (This is now a private residence, with a plaque outside, reading 'Squire Jenkin Keigwin was killed here, 23rd July 1595, defending this house against the Spaniards. Mousehole was burned but the house spared. It is now the oldest in the village. Built circa 14th century'.

From her window she could see any fishing boats coming in, bought a basket of fish and trudged into Penzance with a wicker basket on her back to sell the fresh catch. From 1772, towards the end of her life, she seems to have acquired fame among visitors and tourists, who used to seek her out as the last speaker of the language. In her turn, she used to affect to knowing no English, in return for money. Whether she was a monoglot Cornish-speaker we may never know. Dolly may

**Dolly's commemoration stone**

merely have been a three-toothed old charlatan spewing out a few phrases to make money. Whatever the truth of the matter, she stands as a symbol that languages matter. Cyrus Redding, in his *Itinerary of the County of Cornwall* wrote: 'In the death of a language there is something painfully striking - as being the medium through which, for perished ages, perished generations of men communicated alike wants the most trivial, or the thoughts that wander through eternity.' Despite official reports to the contrary, Welsh is dying out as a living language, with over a third of the population no longer Welsh, and in-migration making up 90% of Wales' population increase in the last three decades.

Because of the Saxon westward pressure, and the conquest of Devon and Somerset, in the 7th and 8th centuries, only Cornwall remained as the rump of the old Celtic kingdom of Domnonia. During the next couple of centuries, Cornish evolved into a distinct language from Welsh, as Breton did. Cut off from Wales, Cornwall remained a distinct kingdom until its last ruler was killed in 936 and it became an earldom of Wessex under Athelstan. By 1362 the English language was being used for matters of state in Cornwall, but Cornish was still the language of the people, and in the 15th century miracle plays in Cornish were produced to teach the people about the church. From 1400 to 1500 the important medieval works consisting of three mystery plays known as the *Cornish Ordinalia* were produced. In 1504 *Bewnans Meriasek* (The Life of St Meriasek) appeared for the first time and is still performed today. However, Henry VIII's break from Rome in 1534 was the start of a systematic attempt to eradicate Cornish in order to enforce Anglican *Liturgy* in the battle against Catholicism. The introduction of the *English Prayer Book* was a severe blow to the language, and after a Cornish Rising in 1548, the Cornish language was greatly suppressed (just as in Wales).

By 1602, the language had been driven into the western extremities of the Duchy, just as it was pushed westwards in Brittany and Wales. Richard Carew in around 1600 stated that Cornish was more easy to pronounce than Welsh, and 'not so unpleasing in sound.' In 1640 however, the sacrament was still administered in Cornish at Feock, near Truro. At this time it is claimed that Cornish, Breton and Welsh speakers could still understand each other. In 1689, William Scawen wrote that the language was dying because of the following reasons: loss of contact with Brittany; the lack of a prayer book and Bible in Cornish; the cessation of the miracle plays (*Plen-en-gwary*, performed in open spaces); discouragement from the gentry; failure to preserve Cornish manuscripts; and general apathy. In 1700, the language was still spoken by the tinners and fishermen of St Just and on the western side of Mount's Bay. In 1707, the Welsh polymath Edward Lhuyd published his *Archaeologica Britannica* which described Cornish grammar.

Daines Barrington (1727-1800) was an English antiquary who made a journey to look for Cornish speakers in 1768. After finding no-one around Lands End, he was told about Dolly, and meeting her recorded that she 'spoke in an angry tone of voice for two or three minutes, and in a language which sounded very like Welsh'. Two old women nearby told Barrington that Dolly had been abusing him, for supposing that she did not understand her native language. She had lived in poverty all her life, but became something of a celebrity in her remaining decade. One of her recorded phrases is of an insult she gave to a local squire who upset her basket of fish

- she called him *an cronnack hagar du*, an ugly black toad. Barrington wrote 'She is very poor and maintained partly by the Parish and partly by fortune-telling and gabbling Cornish. I have thus thought it right to lay before the Society of Antiquaries this account of the last sparks of the Cornish tongue.'

Was Dolly really the last Cornish speaker? Borlase reckoned that it had ceased to be spoken by 1758, but in 1768 at least those two old ladies in Mousehole could understand Dolly Pentreath, according to Daines Barrington. The Rev. Robinson preached in Cornish, near the Lizard Point, in 1768. However, in 1776 a Mousehole man named William Bodener (also spelt Bodinar) wrote: 'My age is three score and five. I am a poor fisherman. I learnt Cornish when I was a boy. I have been to sea with my father and five other men in the boat, for a week together. I never saw a Cornish book. I learnt Cornish going to sea with old men, there is not more than four or five in our town can talk Cornish now, old people four-score years old. Cornish is all forgot with young people.' He died in 1789. A Mr Polwhele stated that Bodener used to converse with Dolly, but his two sons did not know the language. John Nancarrow of Marazion was another Cornish speaker of this time.

In 1790, William Pryce published his *Archaeologica Cornu-Britannica*, giving examples of Cornish Language poetry and prose. An tombstone in Zennor churchyard, near St Ives, commemorates John Davey (1812-1891) and his father, also John Davey, of Boswednack and St Just (1770-1844) as 'the last to possess any considerable knowledge of the Cornish language.' The Cornish language had all but died out, but Henry Jenner's *A Handbook for the Cornish* led to a revival, described on the homepage of the Cornish Language Learning Centre. There are now about 3,000 claiming fluency in the language, and it is no longer classified as extinct. There is excellent information upon the history and survival of the Cornish language on the website *'kernewek'* which asserts that the language never truly died out with Dolly's death.

Indeed, after her death Barrington Daines received a letter, written in Cornish with an English translation, from a Mousehole fisherman, William Bodener (or Bodinar), stating that he knew of five people who could speak Cornish in Mousehole alone. Barrington also wrote informing him of John Nancarrow of Marazion, who was a native speaker and survived into the 1790s. According to Wikipedia, there was a known traditional Cornish speaker, 'John Mann, who as a child in Boswednack, Zennor, always conversed in Cornish with other children, and was alive at the age of 80 in 1914. He was the last known survivor of a number of traditional Cornish speakers of the 19th century including Jacob Care of St Ives (d. 1892); Elizabeth Vingoe of Higher Boswarva, Madron (d. 1903 and who taught at least some Cornish to her son); John Davey junior (d. 1891) and senior, of Boswednack; Anne Berryman (1766–1854), also of Boswednack. Matthias Wallis of St Buryan certified in 1859 that his grandmother, Ann

Wallis, who had died around 1844, had spoken Cornish well. He also stated that a Jane Barnicoate, who had died about 1857, could speak Cornish too.'

* Mousehole, pronounced 'Muzzle' is a delightful fishing village just outside Penzance, and was famous for its 'stargazey pie'. The heads of 7 different types of fish pop out of the pastry top, gazing at the sky. A plaque at 3 Keigwin Place reads 'Here Lived Dolly Pentreath, One of the Last Speakers of the Cornish language as her native tongue. Died December 1777'. Dylan and Caitlin Thomas spent their honeymoon here, and the now empty Lobster Pot Inn on the harbour. He called it 'the loveliest village in England'.

*Footnote:*

In January, 1880, the Rev. W. Lach-Szyrma wrote of the death of the Cornish language, and of Dolly in particular: 'The death of a language is not an unparalleled event in our 19th century, but the death of an Aryan language is one of which, in modern times, we have few instances. Savage languages die out as savage tribes die out; the bullet and the "fire-water" clear off the last speakers of the old barbarous speech, or, as in Russia, the enforced decrees of the conqueror stamp out the old tongue and supersede it with the more polished language of the Government and the governing bodies. But for all that, as we have said, in modern times the death of an Aryan language is rare. It is true that the old Gaulish is lost, it may be beyond recovery; but that event occurred more than a thousand years ago. The Cumbrian (allied to Welsh) also of our own northern counties has gone - gone utterly and hopelessly. Some European languages also at the present time are in great danger. Manx is narrowed to a few parishes, and is known only by a few thousand persons... In the 18th century an Aryan language did then die out; and that language was Cornu-British, of the south-western promontory of Great Britain. The history of the decay and decline of the old Cornish has again and again been written. Even at the period of the Reformation it appeared to be doomed, though under Henry VIII we have the rough and very brief Cornish dictionary of Dr Andrew Borde. Carew wrote thus under Elizabeth, when some Cornishmen spoke Cornish, and some a "naughty English".

Most of the inhabitants can speak no word of Cornish, but very few are ignorant of the English, and yet some so affect their own as to a stranger they will not speak it; for if meeting them by chance you enquire the way or any such matter, your answer shall be, *"Mee a navidna cawza sawnech"*- I can speak no Saxonage. (Saesneg is the Welsh for the Saxon-English language). Norden, in 1584, says much the same. And from other sources we are told how the last sermon was preached at Lawednack, in 1678; how in the reign of Charles II there were only some old people who could speak only Cornish; and how Sir Francis North regretted the decay of Cornish in 1678.

Whether we should say that last the language died out when it passed away with the only person who remembered it as a vernacular - one old woman at Mousehole; or whether we should say that a few persons after her death still recollected some sentences, and that thus it lingered a few years after her; or whether we deny, as some do, that it can be called really extinct while its accent affects common speech in West Cornwall, and while so many Celtic words remain in use, depends on the definition of the life or death of a language we choose to adopt ... After Dolly Pentreath there may have been a few persons who could express a few ideas in Cornish, as to this day there are to be found two or three old people who recollect a sentence or two in the old tongue, or can count up to twenty, or who use Cornish words for certain things, not knowing what the proper English name of that thing is...

One the one hand (Dolly) has been denounced as an arrant impostor; nay, some hypercritical persons have gone so far as to affirm that she was a merely mythical personage, although the entry for her burial, a hundred years ago, is to be clearly read in Paul register, and everything about her life and death - even to the particulars of the making of her coffin - is treasured in local Mousehole tradition. That a myth could possibly form itself so definitely since 1777 is an extreme view, worthy only of the most enthusiastic mythological theorists. If we accept the weight of local evidence, and acknowledge that there is no more reason to doubt the existence of Dolly Pentreath than of any other minor celebrity of the last century, we still have to consider the question whether she was an impostor.

Now, to detect an imposture at the time is difficult, and a century after the death of the person it is manifestly more so. On the other hand, to prove "bona fides" is difficult. The probability is that old Dolly Pentreath was neither quite an impostor nor quite as remarkable a personage as her contemporaries and admirers supposed. When she was a child, it is certain that there was some Cornish spoken at Mousehole, and this she learnt. Other boys and girls may have done the same. They found it of little use to them as the old folks died off, and so they forgot it. Either from vanity, from patriotism, or from the possession of a retentive memory, Dorothy recollected what other people forgot. Her case is not singular. In the history of the decay of the language there are two somewhat similar instances of persons retaining interest in the subject and memory of it when others had cast it over.

They are both Mousehole cases. The one is anterior to Dolly Pentreath. I refer to John Keigwin, to whom we are indebted for the preservation of much that is still known of the Cornish language. His edition of *Mount Calvary* was published, with an English translation, in 1682. When others rejected Cornish as barbarous, Keigwin collected the last relics of the language. Perhaps from a literary point of view the old Celtic tongue might be said to have died out with him in 1710, though in the vernacular it lasted half a century later. He was the last educated Cornishman to whom Cornish was his mother-tongue. The other is Mr Bernard Victor, a Mousehole fisherman, still living, who has just written the Prize essay on old Cornish. By a retentive memory, Mr Victor has preserved words and sentences which others in the village have forgotten.'

148

## SIDNEY GRIFFITH 1715? – 31 May 1752

## MADAM GRIFFITH, SIDNEY WYNNE

Her parents were Jane Griffith of Caernarfon and Cadwaldr Wynne IV of Voelas, Yspysty Ifan. Her ancestors in this famous Welsh family of the Wynnes of Voelas included Rhys Fawr, Henry VII's standard-bearer at Bosworth Field and the famous Dr Elis Pryce. Her grandmother was Sidney Thelwall of Plas-y-Ward, Ruthin, from whom she received her Christian name. In 1741 she married William Griffith of Cefn Amwlch, Caernarfonshire, unfortunately a drunkard with whom she had a miserable life. They had a son in 1742, and in 1746 came the turning point in her life. Sidney was transfixed by a sermon from Peter Williams (see this author's *Secret Vale of Glamorgan*), and she rapidly became prominent in the Methodist Revival, meeting Howel Harris in 1748. In 1749 she accompanied Daniel Rowland to Methodist Association meetings, and was at his base in

**Howell Harris, associated with Madame Griffith**

Llangeitho, and in that same year accompanied Howel Harris to Trefecca. Harris admired her greatly, although she sided with Daniel Rowland against Griffith Jones of Llanddowror (see Bridget Bevan).

In that same year, Harris returned from preaching in London to find 'Madam Griffith' waiting for him at Trefecca. Her husband had drunk his way into bankruptcy, and had beaten Sidney and thrown her out of their marital home, for refusing to give him some of her savings. However, George Whitefield, the great English Methodist leader, and a colleague of Harris's, disliked Madam Griffith's position of influence in Welsh Methodism, and had estranged Harris's wife from her. Harris wanted Sidney to stay at Trefecca, but his wife adamantly opposed it, so Sidney headed back north to Cefn Amwlch. However, she was taken ill on the journey, and Howel and Ann Harris brought her from Llanidloes back to Trefecca. Whitefield unjustly placed an immoral interpretation upon Wynne's stay, which caused a rupture in relations between him and Harris.

Many Methodist exhorters opposed Madam Griffith, because she claimed to be a prophetess, and for her growing influence upon Harris, who was adopting Moravian tendencies at this time, leading to the great schism between the supporters of Rowland and those of Harris in 1750. The 'scandal' of Madam Griffith staying with the Harris family, instead of returning to a dissolute wife-beater, hurt Harris's reputation, although neither Daniel Rowland nor William Williams* of Pantycelyn thought that there was anything 'immoral' in his relationship with Madam Griffith. However, one of Harris's major followers, Morgan John Lewis, deserted him after the Llanidloes session of 1751, joining Rowland's faction, because of his unease at the power of Sidney Wynne. In May 1750, Lewis had tried to reason with Harris about her power over him. The rank and file who made up most of Rowland's supporters also believed that there was an immoral relationship in place, although relations between Sidney and Ann Harris were now cordial. Harris believed Madam Griffith to be 'the eye of Christ's body', a term he had previously applied to Morgan John Lewis, took her advice on all matters, and she was at his side in all his preaching.

Madam Griffith failed to reconcile Daniel Rowland and Howel Harris in June 1750. She had been formerly a wealthy woman, contributing to Harris's cause, but her funds had now run out. She may have paid up to £900 for the establishment of the 'Family' commune at Trefecca by 1752. However, by September, she was relying upon Harris for financial support, and he was also paying for her 8-year-old son's education. By September 1752, her health was failing, and Harris took her to London to stay with her brother Watkin. Watkin Wynne was the son of Cadwaladr Wynne IV, High Sheriff of Denbigh, who had built Pentrefoelas Church. Madam Griffith died at his London home in on 31 May 1752. It was not until 1762 that Harris and Rowland healed the split between the Methodist factions.

* William Williams Pantycelyn wrote *Bywyd a Marwolaeth Theomemphs* (The Life and Death of Theomemphus), which has been called the first great poem of the European romantic movement. It seems to describe the spiritual pilgrimage of Howel Harris, and some believe that Madam Griffith is the '*Philomela*' of the poem. It seems that she regarded herself as the spiritual mother and prophetess of the Welsh Methodist movement.

*Footnote:*
For more information upon the Trefecca 'family', and the massive and lasting influence of the great Methodist Revival in Wales, see the entries on Howel Harris and William Williams in this author's *100 Greatest Welshmen'*.


## HESTER LYNCH PIOZZI 16 January 1741 - 2 May 1821

## MRS THRALE, AUTHOR AND BELLE-LETTRISTE

Hesther was genuinely proud that she was descended from Catrin o Berain (q.v.) through her father John Salusbury of Bachygraig, Flint, and also through her mother Hester Maria Cotton of Combermere and Lleweni. The

Salusburys had originally been centred at Lleweni Hall outside Denbigh from the early 14th century, until the estate passed from the deceased last baronet through his sister to the Cotton family in 1684. Hester's father John Salusbury was the governor of Nova Scotia. Her grandfather Sir Thomas Cotton married Philadelphia Lynch, and Hester Salusbury took her unusual middle name from this grandmother.

In her autobiography Hester noted of her parents: '...my mother had £10,000, an excellent fortune in those days, besides an annuity for her mamma's life of 125 per annum, and was living gaily with her brother, Sir Robert Salusbury Cotton, and his wife, Lady Betty Tollemache, (and) refused all suitors attracted by her merits and beauty for love of her rakish cousin, John Salusbury of Bachycraig. He, unchecked by care of a father

**Hesther Lynch Piozzi**

who died during the infancy of his sons, ran out the estate completely to nothing, so completely that the £10,000 would scarcely pay the debts and furnish them out a cottage in Caernarfonshire, where - after two or three dead things - I was born alive, and where they were forced by circumstances to remain until my grandmother Lucy Salusbury - an exemplary creature - should die, and leave them free at least to mortgage or sell, or to do something towards reinstating themselves in a less unbecoming situation.'

Born near Bodfel Manor, outside Llannor, Pwllheli, and an only child, Hester Lynch Salusbury excelled in learning foreign languages, loved writing and assiduously kept journals. At the age of six, she was something of a prodigy, becoming a favourite of Lord and Lady Leeds in London. Her father was not a rich man, and she spent most of her time in London, at Lleweni or at Offley Park, in Hertfordshire, the home of her wealthy uncle Sir Thomas Salusbury. Her father strongly opposed her wishes to marry a rich London brewer, Henry Thrale, but died in December 1762, and Hester married the following year. However, her journals reveal that she also had reservations about the wedding. Upon her father's death, Hester's mother inherited Bachygraig House and estate, charged with £5,000 a year for hester, which her uncle Thomas made up to £10,000. Obviously in 1763, Thrale had redoubled his efforts to woo this heiress worth £10,000 a year, who would eventually inherit Bachygraig and an even more substantial income. According to her autobiography, Thrale did not love her – 'he deigned to accept my undesired hand' and had never spent more than five minutes in her company until their wedding day. She also wrote 'he loves money and is diligent to obtain it... his servants do not much love him... he is extremely reserved and uncommunicative.'

Soon after her marriage, Hester was in the exalted company of Sir Joshua Reynolds, David Garrick, Oliver Goldsmith and the cream of the artistic society of London. She was an attractive and witty conversationalist, and is best remembered for her long-lasting friendship with Samuel Johnson. James Boswell noted that she was 'a lady of lively talents, improved by education. She could appreciate a classical allusion or quotation, and translate at sight a Latin epigram into idiomatic English.' She was also familiar with French, Italian and Spanish. The Doctor was captivated with Hester, and dined with the Thrales upon every Thursday from 1764. In 1766 a long illness left Johnson severely depressed, and near a breakdown, and Hester persuaded him to come for a change of air, and stay with them in Streatham for a few months. After this event, a room in the house was set apart for him for the next 16 years.

In 1772, Thrale was duped by a man named Henry Jackson, and disaster was only averted for his brewing business by Hester obtaining a loan of £6,000 from an old friend, supplemented by her mother's savings. The brewery, on the site of the Globe Theatre, slowly recovered, and Hester carried on entertaining lavishly, one of her friends being Fanny Burney. Johnson accompanied the Thrales on their two-month tour of North Wales in 1774, and published a *Diary* of it, as did Hester Thrale. Hester used to stay up until four in the morning with Johnson, feeling sorry for him as he was an insomniac (no doubt because he used to consume 14 cups of tea each evening).

Sir William Pepys noted that she was the only human being who possessed the talent of conversation to the same extent as Johnson. The threesome also visited France in 1775. Henry Thrale had become morose on the death of their two sons, and died in 1781. In 1784 Samuel Johnson and her daughters remonstrated against Hester when she wished to marry Gabriele Piozzi, an Italian music-master. However, as previously, Hester went ahead with the marriage. It was a far happier period of her life than with Mr Thrale, and she and Piozzi obviously loved each other deeply.

Dr Johnson was vehemently against the marriage, writing to her '...You are to consider, Madam, that it is our duty to maintain the subordination of civilised society; and when there is a gross and shameful deviation from rank, it should be punished so as to deter others from the same perversion!' For some months, Hester put off the marriage, but called Piozzi back from Italy and married this man of 'below her rank in society'.

Hester replied to more letters from Johnson, saying that 'I have this morning received from you so rough a letter in reply to one which was both tenderly and respectfully written, that I am forced to desire the conclusion of a correspondence that I can continue no longer. The birth of my husband is not meaner than that of my first; his sentiments are not meaner; his profession is not meaner, and his superiority in what he professes acknowledged by all mankind. It is want of fortune then that is ignominious; the character of the man I have chosen has no other claim to such an epithet... Till you have changed your opinion of Mr Piozzi; let us converse no more. God bless you.' Johnson went on to call Piozzi 'an ugly dog without particular skill in his profession'.

The Piozzis visited Italy, not returning until 1787, and the resentment from her circle of inner friends and family now softened towards the marriage. They left London for Bachygraig (outside Tremeirchion) in 1795, built the new mansion of Brynbella nearby, and Gabriele Piozzi died of gout there in 1809. Hester wrote poems, and her *Anecdotes of the late Samuel Johnson during the last Twenty Years of his Life* was published in 1786. Boswell, for obvious reasons, criticised the publication, but undaunted, Hester later published *Letters to and from Dr Johnson*. Amongst her other publications were descriptions of her tours in France, Italy and Germany. In 1794 she published *British Synonymy or an attempt at regulating the choice of words in familiar conversation*, and in 1798 *Three Warnings to John Bull before he dies, by an old acquaintance of the public.* In 1801 was published *Retrospection*, a survey of civilisation since the time of Christ.

In Wales, Hester was friendly with the writer Thomas Pennant, Sarah Siddons (q.v.), the notorious 'Ladies of Llangollen' (q.v.) and Lewis Bagot, Bishop of St Asaph. Her closest friend in Wales was another confidante of Samuel Johnson, Margaret Owen of Shrewsbury. Margaret Owen was also close to William Boswell and Fanny Burney, and Joshuah Reynolds painted Margaret's portrait. She did not think it was a good likeness, saying: 'In these features so placid, so cold, so serene, / What trace of the wit of the Welshwoman's seen?'

Hester spent her later years at Bath, and died at Clifton, Bristol in 1821, being buried at Tremeirchion in Flintshire. Her letters form collections in several libraries. Hester's adopted son with Piozzi, John, later became Sir John Piozzi Salusbury, and died in 1858. He was Piozzi's nephew, whose family had been ruined by the rebellion in Lombardy, and to him she left the whole of her property. Of her 13 children with Henry Thrale, only four survived childbirth, one son surviving until he was ten and two daughters reaching adulthood. The daughters received much of their father's fortune.

From Mrs Thrale's memoirs of Dr Johnson, we read: 'At the age of two years Mr. Johnson was brought up to London by his mother, to be touched by Queen Anne for the scrofulous evil which terribly afflicted his childhood, and left such marks as greatly disfigured a countenance naturally harsh and rugged, beside doing irreparable damage to the auricular organs, which never could perform their functions since I knew him; and it was owing to that horrible disorder, too, that one eye was perfectly useless to him; that defect, however, was not observable, the eyes looked both alike. As Mr. Johnson had an astonishing memory, I asked him if he could remember Queen Anne at all? "He had," he said, "a confused, but somehow a sort of solemn, recollection of a lady in diamonds, and a long black hood." The christening of his brother he remembered with all its circumstances, and said his mother taught him to spell and pronounce the words 'little Natty,' syllable by syllable, making him say it over in the evening to her husband and his guests. The trick which most parents play with their children, that of showing off their newly-acquired accomplishments, disgusted Mr. Johnson beyond expression. He had been treated so himself, he said, till he absolutely loathed his father's caresses, because he knew they were sure to precede some unpleasing display of his early abilities; and he used, when neighbours came o' visiting, to run up a tree that he might not be found and exhibited, such, as no doubt he was, a prodigy of early understanding.

His epitaph upon the duck he killed by treading on it at five years old— "Here lies poor duck That Samuel Johnson trod on; If it had liv'd it had been good luck, For it would have been an odd one"— is a striking example of early expansion of mind and knowledge of language; yet he always seemed more mortified at the recollection of the bustle his parents made with his wit than pleased with the thoughts of possessing it. "That," said he to me one day, "is the great misery of late marriages; the unhappy produce of them becomes the plaything of dotage. An old man's child," continued he, "leads much such a life. I think, as a little boy's dog, teased with awkward fondness, and forced, perhaps, to sit up and beg, as we call it, to divert a company, who at last go away complaining of their disagreeable entertainment." '

*Footnote:*
In 2001, *According to Queeney* by Beryl Bainbridge was published by Little, Brown, based on the fictional memoirs of Hester's daughter. It examines the strange 20-year relationship of Dr Johnson with Hester. Bainbridge draws upon a 1949 article, *Johnson's Vile Melancholy*, which pointed out a Latin entry in his diary referring to 'insane thoughts about fetters and handcuffs'. In the 1823 sale of Hester Thrale's effects there was a padlock, catalogued as Johnson's.


## JEMIMA NICHOLAS c.1750 - 1832

## THE HEROINE OF THE LAST INVASION OF BRITAIN


The last invasion of British soil was by a Franco-Irish force in 1797 at Carregwastad Point, near Fishguard. A forty-seven year old cobbler, Jemima Nicholas ('The Welsh Heroine') was said to have single-handedly captured fourteen French soldiers, armed just with a pitchfork. The force surrendered in The Royal Oak Inn in the centre of Fishguard, which still retains mementoes of the time. She was known as Jemima Fawr, Jemima the Great, not because of her inherent nobility, but because she was a very tall and large lady for that time.

For the 1797 French Invasion of Britain, most of the soldiers were kitted out from a stock of British uniforms which had been captured earlier. However, these would only take dark brown dye so *La Séconde Legion des Francs* became known as *La Légion Noir*, or the Black Legion. The force of over 1,200 men consisted of a mixture of republicans, deserters, royalist prisoners and grenadiers, very well armed, with some Irish officers. The quality of the four ships was impressive, *Le Vengeance* and *La Résistance* being two of the largest and newest French frigates, the latter on her maiden voyage. The corvette *La Constance* and the lugger *Vautour* were also new. Having burnt Bristol, Britain's second largest city, the force was intended to land on the Welsh side of the Bristol Channel or failing this, in Cardigan Bay and then make for Chester or Liverpool. Apart from this, the

**Jemima Nicholas capturing French troops**

working classes were to be encouraged to rebel. Britain's trade was to be dislocated and French prisoners of war liberated, causing such chaos as to make the full-scale invasion of Britain possible.

The inhabitants of Ilfracombe sounded the alarm as the French fleet passed and the local volunteers were mobilised. By noon on 22 February 1797, the fleet was spotted rounding St. David's Head in Pembrokeshire, having swapped its Russian flags for British colours. At 4 p.m. the French anchored off Carregwastad, three miles west of Fishguard. By 2 a.m. on 23 February, 17 boatloads of troops, 47 barrels of powder, 50 tons of cartridges and grenades and 2,000 stands of arms had been brought ashore.

A company of grenadiers under an Irishman, Lieutenant St. Leger rushed a mile inland and took over Trehowel Farm, which became Tate's headquarters. *La Séconde Legion des Francs* had succeeded in making the last landing by enemy soldiers on the British mainland. When one of the French ships entered Fishguard Bay to reconnoitre, Fishguard Fort fired a blank shot, and the ship promptly hoisted the French *tricolour* and sailed away to rejoin the others. Although Fishguard Fort had eight nine-pounders, there were only three rounds in the magazine and the small port could have easily been taken.

William Knox was attending a social function at Tregwynt Mansion when news of a suspected enemy landing was brought to him. He instructed his Fishguard Volunteers to march the seven miles to his headquarters at Fishguard Fort. Lord Cawdor was 30 miles away at Stackpole Court when he received the news. He had been commissioned captain of the Castlemartin Troop of the Pembroke Yeomanry Cavalry, which fortunately was assembled for a funeral on the following day. He immediately mobilised all the troops at his disposal and crossed the Pembroke Ferry with the Pembroke Volunteers and the Cardiganshire Militia. Lieutenant Colonel Colby of the Pembrokeshire Militia gathered about 400 soldiers and sailors at Haverfordwest, then galloped 16 miles to Fishguard to assess Knox's situation.

The French had moved a further two miles inland and occupied two strong defensive positions at Garnwnda and Garngelli, high rocky outcrops giving an unobstructed view of the surrounding countryside. On the morning of 23 February, a hundred of Knox's men had still not arrived and he soon learned that he was facing an enemy of over 1,200 men, who could have been seasoned veterans. Knox decided to retreat slowly towards Haverfordwest. He gave orders to spike Fishguard Fort's cannons (which the Woolwich Bombadiers refused to carry out), and left Fishguard now completely to the French. Knox and his 194 men met the reinforcements led by Lord Cawdor and Colby at Trefgarne, 8 miles from Fishguard, Colby being surprised to see he had left his post. After a short dispute Cawdor was accepted as commander-in-chief and he led the Welsh forces back towards Fishguard.

600 men, dragging their cannons, marched towards the French position on Garngelli, then Cawdor decided to withdraw to Fishguard, since they were losing their bearings in the darkness. The force prepared to spend the night in Fishguard and the officers were based in the Royal Oak Inn. However, many of the French foraging parties had resorted to pillaging the local farms and Llanwnda Church. Indiscipline was prevalent with drunken and mutinous men threatening their officers. The French General Tate became aware that the local Welsh were hostile to his force of 'liberators', and many of his Irish officers were counselling surrender. The departure of their fleet for Ireland demoralised the men who had seen their escape route vanish over the horizon.

The French were severely deceived by the appearance in the neighbourhood of large numbers of local womenfolk wearing the traditional dress of red shawls and black hats, which at a distance resembled infantry uniforms. It is certain that inhabitants over a wide area were flocking towards Fishguard to attack the enemy. The formidable local cobbler,

Jemima Nicholas, alone captured a dozen or so demoralised French soldiers and secured them in St. Mary's Church.

That evening, two French delegates arrived at the Royal Oak to negotiate a conditional surrender, but Cawdor bluffed that with the superior numbers at his command, which were increasing hourly, he would only accept an unconditional surrender. He gave an ultimatum of 10 a.m. the following morning, otherwise the French would be attacked. On the following morning the British force was lined up in battle-order on the high ground overlooking Goodwick, reinforced by hundreds of civilians from all parts of the region, to await General Tate's response. Tate accepted the terms and at 4 p.m. the French prisoners were marched through Fishguard on their way to temporary imprisonment in Haverfordwest.

To place Jemima's activities in context we are enlightened by a report made by Lord Milford, who had been reluctant to assume leadership of the British forces, which as Lord Lieutenant had been naturally his responsibility. Writing from Haverfordwest on Thursday 23 February 1797 (the day after the landing), he stated, '... fifty more prisoners have been brought in and it is believed the whole will surrender today.'

**Gravestone of Jemima Nicholas**

It was probably one of these incidents that brought fame to Jemima Nicholas. H.L. Williams, who was present as a member of the Fishguard Volunteers, writing his memoirs in 1842, described her as 'an heroic single woman' and went on to describe her actions: 'On her approach she saw in a field, about twelve Frenchmen; undaunted she advanced to them, and whether alarmed al her courage, or persuaded by her, she conducted them to and confined them in, the guard house in Fishguard Church'. Early accounts place this in a field in the Henner area, above Goodwick.

In 1832, the Vicar of Saint Mary's, Samuel Fenton, noted on her burial record: 'This woman was called Jemima Fawr or Jemima the Great from her heroine acts, she having marched against the French who landed hereabout in 1797 and being of such personal powers as to be able to overcome most men in a fight. I recollect her well. She followed the trade of a shoemaker and made me, when a little boy, several pairs of shoes.'

A memorial stone was erected in 1897 as part of the centenary celebrations, and stands near the entrance of Saint Mary's churchyard facing Main Street. It reads: 'In Memory of JEMIMA NICHOLAS of this town. THE WELSH HEROINE who boldly marched to meet the French invaders who Landed on our Shores in Febrary 1797. She died in Main Street in

February 1832, aged 82 years. At the date of the Invasion she was 47 years old, and lived 35 years after the event.

Harri Webb wrote *The Women of Fishguard*, a poem of which the final verse is:

'I'll make the proclamation
Though a conqueror I am,
You can conquer all creation
But you'll never conquer MAM'

In 1853 Lord Palmerston conferred upon the Pembroke Yeomanry the battle honour 'Fishguard.' This regiment has the unique honour of being the only one in the British Army, regular or territorial, that bears the name of an engagement on British soil and it was the first battle honour to be awarded to any volunteer unit. The unit has merged and is now called 224 (Pembrokeshire Yeomanry) Squadron, Royal Logistics Corps (Volunteers). Thus it is now the only Territorial Army unit with a 'battle honour'. In 1797, Fishguard celebrated the bicentenary of the invasion, with a huge tapestry in St Mary's Hall depicting the invasion, on the lines of the Bayeux Tapestry. The lower town of Fishguard was also the harbour setting for the Gregory Peck movie, *Moby Dick* and the Richard Burton film *Under Milk Wood*.

The most interesting and long-lasting effect of this invasion was that the run it caused on the Bank of England. Investors panicked and wanted to recover their gold sovereigns from the Bank, which was forced, for the first time, to issue paper bank-notes, to the value of £1 and £2. It seems symbolic that the printing of all the UK's money is now carried out in Wales at The Royal Mint in Llantrisant.

*Footnotes:*
1. A Letter in *The Spectator* 21 March 1940, Page 21, reads: 'There is, as it happens, a letter in existence, of which I made an exact copy, that was written five days after the invasion. This letter, which contains no punctuation of any sort, reads: Narberth Febry 27 1797 Dear Sister I write to you hoping that you are in good health as I am at present thanks be to God for it the French invaded near fisgard Last wednesday wick put the Contry in Great Confusion because they wear 14 hundard and the Contry gathard from all parts of Pembrokeshire near four hundard Women in Red Hanes and Squier Cambel went to ask them were they to fight and they said they were and when they com near the french put down thair arms and they weas all tok presoners that time and are bhrought to haverfordwest friday night Last not one kild But too of our men and five of the french by been to Bould please to give my love to my Brother and recive the same your self and we are wel so hoomore at present from your loving Brother and Sister John & Mary Mathias We had no more than about four hundard men under arms and they thought the women to Be a Ridgment of Soldiers and they 14 hundard and the Lord tok from our Enemes the Spirit of War and to him be

158

the Prais God save the King From this one must conclude that the women in their red Hanes were more of a reality than are most legends.' The French obviously thought the women were an English regiment.

2. There is also a letter from Anne Knight written just after the French surrender, which states: 'on [Wednesday] evening the first news came of their arrival at fishguard and the next day all the Soldiers and Militia round about the country gatherd as fast as they could and the english or rather Welsh got together all the women and children as fast with the red flannels over their shoulders and placed them in such a position that the french could only see their heads and they thought it was a large army of men ... '

Ann Knight is saying that on the Thursday, the day before the surrender, the women and even the children were deceiving the French into believing that they faced a red-coated army. Her statement that the women and children were 'placed... in such a position that the French could only see their heads' gives additional weight to the idea that women, together with the other peasantry, were in the Duke of Rutland's words, 'artfully arranged' in the sight of the French as the surrender took place and that the traditional story that the French mistook Welsh women in their red shawls and tall black hats for an army of Redcoats is substantially true.

## SARAH SIDDONS 5 July 1755 – 8 June 1831

## THE MOST FAMOUS ACTRESS OF HER AGE

Sarah was born in Wales, her sister Julia Anne Hatton (q.v.) settled in Wales, and Sarah maintained close links with the country, especially with her friend Hester Lynch Piozzi (q.v.), all her life. The Shoulder of Mutton, in Brecon's High Street, has now been renamed The Sarah Siddons as she was born there. Sarah was the eldest of the twelve children of Roger Kemble* and Sarah 'Sally' Ward, members of John Ward's band of strolling players who performed in Wales and along the Welsh Borders. Their eleventh child, the actor and playwright Charles Kemble, was also born in Brecon, twenty years after Sarah. Five of Roger Kemble's children and many of his grandchildren became famous actors.

**Mrs Sarah Siddons by Thomas Gainsborough**

Sarah acted with the troupe from her early years (a playbill lists her acting in *Charles I*, aged twelve in 1767), and aged seventeen she wished to marry William Siddons, who had joined the actors in 1772. The marriage was opposed by her parents, and by a Brecon man named Evans. Siddons appealed in verse to the Brecon audience that he could wed Sarah, and was dismissed from the company. Her mother boxed his ears, and also sent Sarah out of his reach, to work as a lady's maid at Guy's Cliffe House in Warwickshire. However, she soon married Siddons, in Coventry in 1773, and in 1774 the couple obtained an acting engagement in Cheltenham back in Kemble's company. A party of gentry went to the theatre, hoping for amusement, including Lord Aylesbury and his step-daughter the Honourable Mrs Boyle. However, Sarah so impressed them, acting in *Venice Preserved*, that Mrs Boyle sought her out at her lodgings and congratulated her, beginning a life-long friendship. On their return to London, the Earl and Countess brought Sarah Siddon's name to the attention of the great actor-manager David Garrick, who sent a man to Cheltenham to watch her act. Garrick then invited her to appear at Drury Lane, on the huge salary of £5 a week (which included her husband), which she accepted. However, her husband William Siddons was a handsome, but dull, actor, and never thrived in the demanding London theatre scene.

Garrick was kind to Sarah, but the critics less so. A first night critic condemned her Portia in the *Merchant of Venice*: 'on before us tottered, rather than walked, a very pretty, delicate, fragile-looking young creature, dressed in a most unbecoming manner, in a faded salmon-coloured sack and coat and uncertain whereabouts to fix either her eyes or her feet. She spoke in a broken tremulous tone; and at the close of a sentence her words generally lapsed into a horrid whisper, that was absolutely inaudible.' After playing a few more parts for Garrick, he abruptly ended his stage career, and Sarah returned to the country, expecting to be summoned to Drury Lane for the next season. However, while appearing in Birmingham, she was informed by letter that her services were no longer required. She said 'It was a stunning and cruel blow, overwhelming all my ambitious hopes, and involving peril, even to the subsistence of my babies. It was very near destroying me.'

Her son was only three, and her daughter Sarah had been born just two weeks before her first Drury Lane appearance. In her own words, Sarah had been 'banished from Drury Lane as a worthless candidate for fame and fortune.'

However, she pulled herself together, spending years touring the provinces, and received acclaim from audiences in Birmingham, Bath, Manchester, York and Liverpool, before reappearing in Drury Lane in 1782. Sarah had become famous on the English stage through her incessant touring of the provinces. Sheridan was now the leading figure (writing and producing) in London, and he chose Sarah to play in Southerne's *The Fatal*

*Marriage*. She was determined not to repeat the poor showing of her previous London appearance, and her father came for her first night, comforting her in her dressing-room.\*\*

As a tragic actress, she had no peers, and her performance as the wronged Queen Isabella had the audience in tears. The triumph made her name, and she became the theatre's 'Queen of Tragedy'. Her cold, sad beauty and immersion in the role meant that the audience rose to applaud her death scene, and the performers were unable to complete the play. Burke, Gibbon and Sheridan praised her. Sarah now recounted the names of great statesmen who visited her dressing-room after plays, to make their bow and congratulate her. The Prince of Wales and Sir Joshua Reynolds were admirers. At evening parties, fine ladies stood upon chairs to obtain a view of her, and others called at her house to see her. George III said that he admired her for her repose, adding with typical Hanoverian perspicacity that 'Garrick never could stand still - he was a great fidget'. A perfectionist, actors playing with her were frequently terrified of her glance, and one ran off stage, never to return. Samuel Johnson noted her as a person of great propriety and modesty: 'Neither praise nor money, the two powerful corrupters of mankind, seem to have depraved her.' In 1783 she was appointed to teach oratory to the royal children.

Sarah's fame grew in such roles as Queen Katharine in *Henry VIII*, Desdemona in *Othello* and as Volumnia to the *Coriolanus* of her brother John Philip Kemble, with whom she often starred. Other famous roles were as Belvidera in *Venice Preserv'd*, Constance in *King John*, Zara in *The Mourning Bride* and the lead role in *The Tragedy of Jane Shore*. Lady MacBeth was her greatest role, which she first took in 1785 and chose as her farewell performance. Her rich voice and majestic presence held audiences (and other actors) in awe, although she shunned publicity. She was painted by Gainsborough, Lawrence, and by Reyholds as *The Tragic Muse*, and a statue of her is in Westminster Abbey. From her glittering career in London, Sarah sometimes returned to Wales to stay with Hester Piozzi at Brynbella. She seems to have been the only one of Hester Piozzi's circle who did not despise her husband Signor Piozzi - 'I left them with great regret; and between their very great kindness, their wit and their music, they made me love, esteem and admire them very much'. Her own marriage ended in an informal separation, with her husband living in Bath, while Sarah lived in London.

With her brother, the actor John Philip Kemble, Sarah withdrew from Drury Lane in 1802, and took shares in the new Covent Garden Theatre. There was a fire there in 1809 and it was rebuilt. Sarah's last performance was as Lady Macbeth on 29 June 1812, with a massive black market in tickets, and huge crowds surrounding the theatre. Sarah invented the 'hand-washing' gestures in the sleep-walking scene, which have been repeated by all actresses since that time (most notably in Kurosawa's incredible film version, *Throne of Blood*.) The play could not be continued at the conclusion of this scene, as the audience were uncontrollable with admiration. Her farewell to the stage was written by her nephew, Horace Twiss, who knew that she preferred Tragic to Comic parts:

'Judges and friends, to whom the magic strains
Of nature's feelings never spoke in vain,
Perhaps your hearts, when years have glided by
And past emotions wake a fleeting sigh
May think on her whose lips have poured so long
The charmed sorrows of your Shakespeare's song;
On her, parting to return no more
Is now the mourner she but seemed before.'

Aged 56, she retired to a country cottage at Westbourne - now the site of Paddddington Railway Station. Until a year before her death, she was regularly summoned to Windsor to give Shakespearian readings to Queen Charlotte. She sometimes gave benefits for theatre friends and family members such as her brother Charles, who had fallen on hard times, however. Of her seven children, she outlived five of them. Her son Henry became an actor and manager of the Edinburgh Theatre and died aged just 40. Cecilia married, and Maria and Sarah died young. George worked for the government in India. Sarah Siddons died from erysipelas, aged 75, and was buried in Paddington Church.

* It is thought that her father Roger Kemble, born in Hereford, was descended from the family of John Kemble (1599-1679), the Welsh border priest who is one of the 40 Martyrs of England and Wales, canonized in 1970. From his brother's house at Pembridge Castle, he set up Jesuit mission centres in Gwent and Hereford, including at the Llwyn, Coedanghred, the Craig and Hilston. After the Popish Plot he was taken to London to face Titus Oates, tried for being a seminary priest, and sentenced to be hung drawn and quartered. (See the author's *The Book of Welsh Saints* for further details). Kemble was a Catholic, as was Roger Kemble, but Sarah Kemble was a Protestant. Thus the sons of the Kemble family were brought up as Catholics, and Sarah, Ann and the other daughters as Protestants.

** Two other attendees on this memorable first night were a Mr Keith and a Mr Prowse, who together ran a musical instruments shop in Berkeley Square from 1780. This was in the days before one could book theatre tickets, and some rich clients asked the partners if they could send their boys down to London to see Mrs Siddons, asking Keith and Prowse to sit in the seats until the boys arrived. The partners saw the advantage of being able to book seats, and persuaded the London theatres to number seats for the first time, thus inventing the need for a theatre ticket. They then ensured that their clients received the best seats in the house, and the famous Keith Prowse ticket agency company was founded.

## MARY DARBY ROBINSON 17 November 1758 - 26 December 1800

### *PERDITA*

Mary Darby's mother was Hester Seys, of Boverton Castle, near Llanilltud Fawr (Llantwit Major). The Seys were a noted family in the history of the Vale of Glamorgan, and Mary was the third of five children brought up in Bristol. However, when she was seven, her American father Captain John Darby left his wife and family to establish a whaling station in Labrador. He took his mistress with him, and from then on did little to support his family, formally separating from Hester. He never lived with his family again. The precocious Mary loved poetry, and when the family moved to Chelsea, went to the alcoholic Meribah Lorrington's seminary for her education. When the school closed, she briefly went

**Mary Robinson as Perdita,
by John Hoppner**

to another school, but had to leave when her absent father failed to pay his expected remittance.

Now a desperately poor Hester Darby started her own school to support her family, taking in between ten and twelve girl boarders. Mary was teaching at her mother's school by the age of 14. However, Captain Darby returned for a few days and closed the school. According to English law, any property or business of a wife legally belonged to the husband. Mary, aged 15, then went to Mrs Hervey's finishing school in Oxford Street, Marylebone. The great actor David Garrick met her, and proposed that, aged 15, she take to the stage. She wrote 'Garrick was delighted with everything I did. He would sometimes dance a minuet with me, sometimes request me to sing the favourite ballads of the day; but the circumstance which most pleased him was my tone of voice... Never shall I forget the enchanting hours which I passed in Mr Garrick's society; he appeared to me as one who possessed more power, both to awe and to attract, than any man I ever met with. His smile was fascinating...'

However, the attractive and talented girl was being pursued by another. She had had her first proposal of marriage when aged just 13, and now the eligible Thomas Robinson was courting her. With the approval of her mother, Mary married Robinson on April 12th, 1774, aged just 15. However, Robinson wanted the marriage to be kept secret. He had misrepresented his prospects - he was an articled clerk and had not finished his articles to be a solicitor, and was illegitimate, with no prospects of any inheritance. He was also a roaring drunkard.

When Mary became pregnant, Mary insisted that the façade be ended, and that her marriage was to become public knowledge. Mary and Thomas travelled to Wales to tell his family, and then returned to London. The couple now lived far above their means. Thomas acquired a mistress, Harriet Wilmot, and incurred huge gambling debts. One of his betting and drinking cronies, the notorious rake Lord Lyttelton, made no secret of his interest in Mary Darby Robinson. Thomas and Mary now escaped back to his family in Wales, fleeing his creditors, and there Maria Elizabeth was born on 18 November 1774. When creditors caught up with Thomas, the couple again fled, to Mary's grandmother in Monmouth, but Thomas was finally arrested with enormous debts of £1,200.

Thus aged 16, Mary had had a baby, a feckless father and a useless husband, and had been surrounded by money troubles all her short life. Thomas, Mary and Maria lived in the King's Bench Prison for over a year. Thomas had another affair with an Italian prisoner, while Mary cooked, cleaned, looked after the baby and earned a little money in copying legal documents. Mary also had some assistance from the Duchess of Devonshire, to whom she sent a copy of her *Poems* in 1775. The slender volume made little money, but Mary then wrote *Captivity, A Poem: and Celadon and Lydia, A Tale* in 1777, dedicating it to the Duchess.

After 15 months, Robinson negotiated their release, and the young Mary now met David Garrick, Richard Brinsley Sheridan and William Brereton. She wished to support her family by acting, and the trio engaged her at Drury Lane. Appearing as Juliet in December 1776, aged just 18, her talent was recognised. Over the next four seasons, there was increasing acclaim, and she appeared in a musical farce that she had written, *The Lucky Escape* in 1778. However, her second daughter, Sophia died when only a few months old, and her husband was once more descending into a morass of debts, leading to possible imprisonment. Aged 21, she took her most famous role as Perdita in *A Winter's Tale*. On 3 December 1779, the 17-year-old Prince of Wales (later George IV) decided that the 21-year-old Mary had to be his mistress. He sent Lord Malden to negotiate with her. There was an exchange of excited letters between 'Perdita' and 'Florizel' (the prince), and he started paying her marked attention in public. The press of the day, such at the *Morning Post* and the *Morning Herald*, were quick to uncover the scandal.

George sent letters of love, gifts such as a miniature portrait set in diamonds, and a bond worth £20,000 when he came of age. The daily newspapers followed the progress of the courtship with glee, and had a field day when she eventually agreed to become his mistress. Their affair lasted less than a year, but 'Perdita' was now public property - the 'hot news' of the day. She regretfully wrote in her memoirs 'Every event in my life has more or less been marked by the progressive evils of a too acute sensibility'. The *Morning Herald* reported in June 1781: 'Fortune has again smiled upon Perdita; on Sunday she sported an entire new phaeton, drawn by four chestnut-coloured ponies, with a postillion and servant in blue and silver liveries. The lady dashed into town through Hyde Park at four o'clock, dressed in a blue great coat prettily trimmed in silver; a plume of feathers graced her hat, which even Alexander the Great might have prided himself in.' However, the end of the royal affair once again put her in an extremely difficult financial situation. She and Thomas were deeply in debt to the sum of £7,000, living on borrowed money.

Mary's reputation had gone, as had her career as an actress. She appeared in several productions in the early 1780's, but had lost her former popularity. The prince had made no provision for her, so Mary decided she had nothing to lose. She demanded that Prince George paid £25,000 for the return of his love-letters. She accepted £5,000 from the German monoglot King George III 'to get my son out of this shameful scrape', and she paid off the creditors. In 1782, she negotiated a £500 annuity for herself, and a £200 annuity during the life of her daughter Maria, in return for surrendering the prince's promised £20,000 bond.

Lord Malden now became her lover, and Thomas Robinson drifted out of Mary's life, his debts cleared by her. She was also strongly rumoured to be a mistress of the politician Charles James Fox, who had negotiated her annuity settlement. In 1782, an impoverished army officer and Revolutionary War hero, Colonel Banastre Tarleton, joined the gambling circle of Lord Malden and the Prince of Wales. They gambled on anything, including racing geese and turkeys. One night, Malden bet Tarleton 1,000 guineas that he could not seduce his mistress, Mary. Several weeks later, Tarleton won the bet. Mary found out and was furious with both men.

Once again the gutter press had a field day. The *Morning Post* marvellously recorded in September 1782: 'Yesterday, a messenger arrived in town, with the very interesting and pleasing intelligence of the Tarleton, armed ship, having, after a chase of some months, captured the *Perdita* frigate, and brought her safe into Egham port. The *Perdita* is a prodigious fine clean bottomed vessel, and had taken many prizes during her cruise, particularly the *Florizel*, a most valuable ship belonging to the Crown, but which was immediately released, after taking out the cargo. The *Perdita* was captured some time ago by the *Fox*, but was, afterwards, retaken by the Malden, and had a sumptuous suit of new rigging, when she fell in with the *Tarleton*. Her manoeuvring to escape was admirable; but the *Tarleton*, fully determined to take her, or perish, would not give up the chase; and at length, coming alongside the *Perdita*, fully determined to board her, sword in hand, she instantly surrendered at discretion.'

Malden left her, feeling that she had betrayed him, as well as having cost him a massive 1,000 guineas. Tarleton's family wanted to stop his excessive gambling, and also keep him away from the notorious Perdita. They offered to pay his worst gambling debts, on condition that he left, alone, for the Continent. The papers crucified Perdita, saying that she had 'corrupted' the Prince, and he was well rid of her. Otherwise faced with social ruin, Banastre Tarleton set out for France in July, 1783.

The desperate Mary, still only 24 years old, borrowed money for his debts and set out in a post-chaise for Dover, to intercept him. However, she was pregnant, and the rough journey caused a miscarriage. The attendant midwife caused injuries that partly paralysed Mary's legs, and this brought on increasing paralysis and acute rheumatism for the rest of her life. She was bed-ridden for six months. Colonel Tarleton, away in France, was upset by the news, but decided to remain there and write a history of the 1780-1781 military campaigns. Mary visited baths and spas, trying to regain her health, and wrote *Ode to Valour, Inscribed to Colonel Banastre Tarleton*. In 1784, he decided to return to England to stand as an MP, and moved in with Mary. However, he was neither elected, nor gained a political appointment, and yet again Mary was in dire financial straits. All her possessions were seized by creditors and auctioned off, but somehow she managed to hide and keep the diamond-studded miniature of the Prince of Wales. Fortunately, in the autumn of 1784, the Duc de Lauzun offered hospitality to Mary and her beloved 'Ban', and they went to France.

Living in France and Germany, Mary assisted Tarleton in writing his *History of the Campaigns of 1780 and 1781*. In 1786, Tarleton was excoriated by letters in the London papers criticising his handling of the Battle of Cowpens. However, he returned to London for its publication in 1787, and was feted but made little money from the book. He opened a gambling-den with a partner, dedicated to the game of *faro*, and known as a *faro-bank*, to try to make his fortune. Mary continued writing poetry, and in 1788 with her health improved for a time, returned to live at 42 Clarges Street. 'Ban' lived at number 30. Her relationship with Tarleton continued on and off until 1798, by which time he had become an MP and been promoted to general. Tarleton was appointed a Knight of the Bath in 1833 and died in great wealth, a major-general. Her poetry and fiction made her famous once again during these years. Her first poems were published anonymously in *The World* and *The Oracle*, and when they were well-received, she claimed them in her own name.

Her *Poems* of 1791 had 600 subscribers, the list being headed by her former lover, George, Prince of Wales. Crippled and ailing, her second collection of poems was published in 1794, the sonnet collection *Sappho and Phaeon* in 1796, and *Lyrical Tales* in 1800. Many of her poems feature the themes of sadness, isolation and alienation. *Sappho and Phaeon* has been seen by some critics as a 'manifesto for modern poetry, a poetry that negotiates between romantic sensibility and enlightened reason'. However, Mary made far more money from her prose, which helped to support her, her mother Hester, her daughter Maria and often Banastre Tarleton. She wrote the novels *Vancenza* (1792), *Angelina* (1795), *The Widow* (1796), *Hubert de Sevrac* (1796) and *Walsingham* (1797). Witty, sharp and liberal, they all went into multiple editions and were published in France and Germany. Other novels followed. *The False Friend* and *The Natural Daughter* are thinly disguised attacks on 'Ban' when he finally left Mary, after 15 years together, and married a rich young heiress. Mary's circle of friends at this time included William Wordsworth, and especially Samuel Taylor Coleridge*, who like her contributed to the *Morning Post* newspaper.

Mary wrote a book criticising marriage, *A Letter to the Women of England, on the Injustice of Mental Subordination*, reflecting the thinking of her friends Mary Wollstonecraft and William Godwin. She argued for the right of women to leave their husbands, as she had done with the wastrel Thomas Robinson. She could not complete her autobiography, as her health was broken, and died of a pulmonary oedema in 1800, shortly after her 42nd birthday. However, her daughter Maria completed Mary's *Memoirs of the Late Mrs Robinson, Written by Herself.* Coleridge carried on a correspondence with Maria, advising her how to preserve her mother's reputation as a poet, while glossing over her image as a fallen woman. He also lamented Mary's death: 'O Poole, That that Woman had but been married to a noble Being, what a noble Being she herself would have been'. What a marvellous film her life story would make. Stronger than all her male partners, beautiful, multi-talented, she was much neglected during Victorian years because of her infamy.

Perdita's most popular poem, *'The Snowdrop'*, was originally published in *'Walsingham: or, The Pupil of Nature'*, and is too long to reproduce here, but the first two and final verses are:

'The snow-drop, Winter's timid child,
Awakes to life, bedewed with tears;
And flings around its fragrance mild,
And where no rival flowerets bloom,
Amidst the bare and chilling gloom,
A beauteous gem appears!

All weak and wan, with head inclined,
Its parent breast, the drifted snow;
It trembles while the ruthless wind
Bends its slim form; the tempest lowers,
Its emerald eye drops crystal showers

On its cold bed below...

Where'er I find thee, gentle flower,
Thos still art sweet, and ear to me!
For I have known the cheerless hour,
Have seen the sun-beams cold and pale,
Have felt the chilling wintry gale,
And wept, and shrunk like thee.'

\* Some of Coleridge's poems were influenced by Mary Darby Robinson,
Perdita. Also, an article by Betsy Bolton, *Romancing the Stone: "Perdita"
Robinson in Wordsworth's London* argues that her experiences as both artist and
fallen woman had a direct influence on Wordsworth's *Prelude*, which in this
author's opinion is possibly the most important poem in the English language.
Wordsworth almost changed the title of his 1800 opus *Lyrical Tales* because of
Perdita's use of the same title.

*Footnote:*
Banastre Tarleton's father was Mayor of Liverpool. 'Ban' studied at Oxford
University and the Middle Temple of the Inns of Court. He sailed for America in
1776 with Lord Cornwallis, commander of the British forces in the colonies.
Banastre Tarleton participated in the battle for New York City, and in the attack
on Fort Moultrie in Charleston, South Carolina (the author has visited the Fort
Moultrie site and drunk Samuel Adams ale in the Moultrie Tavern in Charleston,
and recommends the area wholeheartedly). While serving in a unit of dragoons
in 1776, Tarleton captured General Charles Lee, second-in-command of the
colonial Continental Army. Tarleton was promoted to commandant of the
British Legion, a mixed force of cavalry, which became famous as 'Tarleton's
Green Horse' because of the colour of their uniforms. Tarleton distinguished
himself in the campaigns of 1780 and 1781 in the South. Following a battle with
Colonel Abraham Buford's regiment at Waxhaw Creek, South Carolina, he
earned the epithet 'Bloody Tarleton'. He fought at Camden, South Carolina, and
routed Brigadier General Thomas Sumter at Catawba Fords at Fishing Creek,
South Carolina. Tarleton chased Lieutenant Colonel Francis Marion into swamp
country unfamiliar to the British and gave Marion the nickname of 'Swamp Fox'
when he could not capture him.

Halted by Brigadier General Sumter at Blackstock, South Carolina,
Tarleton was defeated by the Welsh-American, Brigadier General Daniel
Morgan at the Battle of Cowpens at Chesnee, South Carolina, on 17 January
1781. Tarleton continued to fight gallantly until the British surrender at
Yorktown on 19 October 1781. Returning to England in 1782, Tarleton fell in
with the set of people around the Prince of Wales and became a notorious
gambler. Fleeing from his gaming debts, he went to France in 1786 and wrote
*History of the Campaigns of 1780 and 1781 in the Southern Provinces of North
America* (1787). Tarleton then returned to England where he was elected to
Parliament from Liverpool in 1790 and served for 22 years. As the

representative of shipping interests, he led the reaction against social reformer William Wilberforce's antislavery movement. Tarleton was promoted to general in 1812 and made a baronet in 1815.

## JULIA ANN HATTON 29 April 1764 - 26 December 1838

### *ANN OF SWANSEA*, JULIA ANN KEMBLE

**Portrait of Ann of Swansea**

The sister of 'the incomparable' Sarah Siddons (q.v.), she was the seventh child of Roger Kemble and Sarah Ward. However, her lameness and a squint meant that her parents discouraged her from becoming part of their troupe of family actors. Aged 11, she wrote a play that her father's company performed at Brecon. She became apprenticed to a costume maker. After a brief marriage in 1783 to an adventurer named Curtis, who proved to be a bigamist and deserted her, the 19-year-old Mrs Curtis published *Poems on Miscellaneous Subjects*. Also in 1783, Ann lectured at London's 'Temple of Hymen', run by the quack doctor James Graham, 'on chastity and other delicate subjects'. She placed in all the London newspapers notices calling for *'Donations in Favour of Mrs Curtis'*. She was desperately impoverished, aged 21, because her famous brothers and sister 'Messrs Kemble and Mrs Siddons, whom she has repeatedly solicited for relief... have flatly refused her.' In 1789, as Ann Curtis, Julia Ann attempted suicide in Westminster Abbey. Whether she meant to succeed or whether it was a plea for help is unknown. Ann was then accidentally shot in the face in a brothel, where she was a 'model', which led to much newspaper speculation about her activities. She wrote to the press, however, stating that the shooting was not due to neglect by her family.

Aged 28, marrying a maker of musical instruments, William Hatton, in 1792, she went with him to America. In New York, Ann Hatton had success as a songwriter and librettist for two productions staged in the John Street Theatre. The second of these, *Tammany - or, The Indian Chief: A Serious Opera* was produced in 1794, and was performed several times in Boston and Philadelphia as well as New York. In 1795, reduced from 3 acts to 2, it was retitled *America Discovered: or, Tammany, the Indian Chief*.

Members of the Republican-Democrat Tammany Society* packed the house for all its performances, jeered by Federalist Party onlookers. She was acclaimed as 'poetess to Tammany Society', and gave programmes of readings at 'Tammanial Hall' in 1794.

The Hattons returned to Britain, and leased the Swansea Bathing House from 1799 to 1806, and also operating a hotel in Swansea. Hatton died in 1806, whereupon Ann moved to Cydweli where she now opened a dancing school. By 1809 she had returned to Swansea, and devoted herself to full-time writing, being at last financially supported by her brother John Philip Kemble and Sarah Siddons. For the great actor Edmund Kean, she wrote the play *Zaffine*, and her *Poetic Trifles* was published in 1811. During these years, she also wrote over a dozen novels. She now called herself 'Anne of Swansea', and between 1810 and 1831 published thirteen works of fiction and a volume of poetry.

She died in Swansea, her small income assisted by an annual stipend of £20 given by Sarah Siddons, on condition that Ann lived at least 150 miles from London. She also had an annual bequest of £20 from her father and £60 a year from the will of her brother John Philip Kemble. Her London publications include: *The Songs of Tammany* (1783); *The Indian Chief* (1794); *Cambrian Pictures, or, Every One has Errors* (1810); *Poetic Trifles* (1811); *Sicilian Mysteries: or, The Fortress of Vecchii: A Romance* (1812); *Conviction, or She is Innocent! A Novel* (1814); *Secret Avengers, or, The Rock of Glotzden: A Romance* (1815); *Chronicles of An Illustrious House: or, The Peer, The Lawyer, and The Hunchback: A Novel* (1816); *Gonzalo de Baldivia, or, A Widow's Vow: A Romantic Legend* (1817); *Secrets in Every Mansion, or, The Surgeon's Memorandum Book: A Scottish Record* (1818); *Cesario Rosalba: or, The Oath of Vengeance; A Romance* (1819); *Lovers and Friends, or, Modern Attachments: A Novel* (1821); *Guilty or Not Guilty, or, A Lesson for Husbands: A Tale* (1822); *Woman's a Riddle: a Romantic Tale* (1824); *Deeds of the Olden Time: A Romance* (1826); *Uncle Peregrine's Heiress: A Novel* (1828); and *Gerald Fitzgerald: An Irish Tale* (1831).

A prudish 1822 review in the *Monthly Censor* of her *Guilty or Not Guilty* of that year states: 'We do not know what to point out as very engaging in the production of a lady, who seems so satisfied with the character of an author by trade, that she not only refers you to a list in her title page of eight novels and two romances, (besides two &c's.) with which she has supplied the novel market, but complains bitterly in her epistle dedicatory, that she has never yet been benefited by "the great men, and liberal encouragers of Genius", to whom she had before inscribed her works. The ground work of *'Guilty, or Not Guilty'* is this: General Fitzallen suspects the infidelity of his wife, Lady Caroline, and goes abroad with his daughter Rosella. They are supposed to be lost on their passage from India. Rosella first reappears, and presents herself to her half-sister Lady Clarisford, who rejects and treats her as an impostor. There are some high wrought scenes, in which Ornville, as the lover of Miss Fitzallen takes of course a very conspicuous part, particularly when he is pestered and plagued, and then persecuted and carried off from a masquerade by the Countess of Clarisford. The innocence of Lady Caroline Fitzallen forms one of the principal features of the eclaircissement.

We cannot be much impressed in favour of the moral tendency of a book in which there are so many details of intrigues and profligacy, and if ladies must write novels for circulating libraries, they ought to take care to avoid subjects which administer to anything rather than to reserved and correct feeling. One of the chapters is headed by a quotation from the seventh chapter of Proverbs, in which Solomon describes the artifices and allurements of a wanton, and the chapter itself presents you with a highly coloured picture of a beautiful intriguante. An unfit one surely to place before readers of any description. The reader might suppose that a writer, who publishes under the romantic name of 'Ann of Swansea', placed most of her scenes in some sequestered spot upon the sea-shore, and selected her heroes and heroines from a marine villa, or fisherman's hut. This however is not the case; we are introduced into the most busy and fashionable circles, and there is scarcely a page which does not teem with dukes, or countesses, masquerades, balls, operas, or concerts. How the retired and distant Swansea could furnish the authoress with opportunities of describing such persons and scenes, with the requisite degree of accuracy, may be a little problematical...'

**Plaque to Ann Julia Hatton on the site of her bathing house**

Anne was painted in 1835, at the age of 71, by William Watkeys, and her portrait is in Swansea Museum. There is another painting in the Glynn Vivian Art Gallery. She died aged 74 in Swansea, being buried in St John's churchyard (now St Matthews), and there is a blue plaque commemorating her at the site of her former bathing house, now the new Civic Centre.

* Tammany Hall, also known as the Society of St. Tammany, the Sons of St. Tammany, or the Columbian Order, was a New York City political organization recently founded in 1786 and incorporated in May 1789, as the Tammany Society. It became the Democratic Party political machine which played a major role in controlling New York City and New York State politics and helping immigrants, most notably the Irish, rise up in American politics from the 1790s to the 1960s.

# ANN GRIFFITHS April 1776 - 12 August 1805 (buried)

## HYMN-WRITER, MYSTIC AND THEOLOGIAN, 'THE GREATEST OF WELSH WOMEN POETS'

The daughter of John and Jane Thomas, she was born at Dolwar Fach, two miles from Llanfihangel-yng-Ngwynfa, Montgomeryshire. John Evan Thomas was renowned as a *bardd gwlad\**, and Dolwar Fach was renowned for its hospitality and its *noson lawen\*\**. Her parents were devout church-goers, and Ann was an intelligent, gregarious child who  loved dancing but was cursed by poor health. Ann received a religious upbringing, with her father being more zealous than was the norm among Anglicans. He attended services regularly at his parish church and held family devotions at home every morning and evening. According to tradition an old dog at Dolwar would follow its master to Llanfihangel Church every Sunday morning, lying quietly under the pew until the service was over. A sign of Ann's father's regularity at the morning service is that the dog would attend every Sunday morning through force of habit, even if no member of the Dolwar family were present. Yet despite the family being, by all accounts, sincere and conscientious Anglicans, almost each of them in turn came to the conviction that they did not possess true experiential faith. Four of the five children experienced conversion as adults, and their father also followed the same spiritual path before his death. They all joined the Welsh Calvinistic Methodists, and Dolwar Fach became a preaching station for the Methodists for some years.

When her mother died in 1794, Ann at the age of 17 had to look after her elder and younger brothers. Both her older sisters were already married, and Ann remained mistress of this household until her death. As a young girl, known as Nansi Thomas, she is known to have loved parties and dancing, probably at the nearest market town of Llanfyllin, six miles away. She only had a couple of years' schooling, from Mrs Owen 'y Sais' at Dolanog, and probably from John Roberts in the local circulating school, but it appears not enough to read English.

Ann's elder brother John was the first to experience a religious conversion to Methodism, soon followed by his father, his brother Edward and the rest of the family. Like most Welsh people of the period Ann was a faithful Anglican. She would tirade against all types of Nonconformist religion, and would refer with derision to those going to the Methodist Association meetings at Bala, 'Look at the pilgrims going to Mecca'. However, Ann was converted after hearing Benjamin Jones of Llanminio, Carmarthenshire, preaching. He was preaching from his base in Pwllheli, at Pendref Chapel, Llanfyllin, when Ann saw him on Easter Sunday, 1796. At Christmas, she found herself alone at the parish church, the rest of her family going to the Methodist meeting. Ann consulted her parish priest after being so deeply moved by Jones. We know that she went to the church well before the special early morning Christmas service, the *plygain*, and his utterly hostile response drove Ann into the Methodist community forever. Now every Sunday she travelled the 22 miles over the Berwyn Hills to Bala, to receive communion from Thomas Charles, and repeated his sermons to her friends, word-for-word on her return.

In his memoir of Ann Griffiths, published in 1865, Morris Davies includes a number of anecdotes relating to a group of Methodists from her area, and Ann prominent among them, who would cross over the mountains to attend meetings at Bala. Returning home on Sunday evenings, says one of her fellow-travellers, 'our work along the way was to listen to Ann Thomas reciting the sermons. I never saw anyone like her for remembering.' Ann Griffiths would often stay on Saturday nights at Tŷ Uchaf, Llanwddyn, the home of a godly man by the name of Humphrey Ellis, in order to break her journey to Bala for Communion on Sunday mornings.

From 1796, Ann's home Dolwar Fach had become a centre of Methodist preaching, becoming officially registered as a place of worship in 1803. In 1797, she joined the Methodist seiat (fellowship meeting) at Pontrobert, and from around 1800 she was in regular contact with the noted cleric, hymn-writer, author and teacher of the circulating schools, John Hughes of Llanefydd, with whom much correspondence remains. John Hughes (1775-1854) had lodged at Dolwar Fach.

The following description by a woman who was well acquainted with the Dolwar family, clearly demonstrates the central place Ann afforded the in her life following her conversion: 'There would be a very pleasant appearance to the family at Dolwar while spinning, with the old man [Ann's father] carding wool, and singing carols and hymns. At other times, a solemn silence would reign among them. Ann would spin with her *Bible* open in front of her in a convenient place, so she could snatch up a verse while carrying on with her task, without losing time. I saw her at the spinning wheel in deep meditation, paying heed to hardly anything around her, and the tears flowing down her cheeks many times.'

One of the most notable aspects of Ann Griffiths's life is the deep spiritual experiences which characterised it, experiences which resulted in her rolling on the floor on occasions and going into a deep trance-like meditation at other times. She called them 'visitations, and stated in a letter to one of her Methodist friends, Elizabeth Evans, that she would sometimes become so absorbed in spiritual matters that she would completely fail 'to stand in the way of my duty with regard to temporal things'. In such a state, she says, 'the Lord sometimes reveals through a glass, darkly, as much of his glory as my weak faculties can bear'. It was deep spiritual experiences such as these that led Thomas Charles to declare during a visit to Dolwar Fach that he was of the opinion that Ann 'was very likely to meet with one of three things – either that she would meet severe trials; or that her life was almost at an end; or else that she would backslide'.

The handling of wool had been one of the main activities in Ann's daily life. Around the time of her death, there was a loom, five spinning wheels and about eighty sheep on the family farm, Dolwar Fach. Ann was reasonably well-off, being a farmer's daughter. Although not rich, her father was in a fairly easy financial position and played a prominent role in local parish life. In October 1804, eight months after the death of her father, the 28-year-old Ann married the Methodist elder Thomas Griffiths, a Meifod farmer and leading local Methodist. Their daughter Elizabeth was born in July 1805, but died a fortnight later, in August. Ann died of problems associated with the birth soon after, and both were buried at Llanfihangel.

When Ann married, she married into a quite wealthy family. Her husband, Thomas Griffiths, had brought with him to Dolwar Fach, on his marriage to Ann, six silver spoons. Until then, the kitchenware at Dolwar had been of pewter and wood, with no silverware. From Elizabethan times onward a family's status depended on having at least six silver spoons, and it is indicative that when the time came for Thomas Griffiths to leave Dolwar Fach, following Ann's death, he took the six spoons with him!

It was common at that time for Methodist maidservants to include in their agreement of employment a clause which allowed them to attend the Bala Methodist Association meetings every summer. In return for that privilege they would take a reduction of five shillings a year in their wages. It seems that such an arrangement obtained in the case of Ruth Evans, who became maidservant at Dolwar Fach in 1801, since there is mention of Ann offering Ruth five shillings on one occasion so that she could go to Bala instead of Ruth. However, by all accounts, the devout Ruth preferred to go to the Association meetings than accept the money.

Ann used to recite the hymns that she had composed to Ruth Evans, her maid at Dolwar Fach, who had memorised them. In 1805, Ruth Evans married the Calvinistic Methodist minister John Hughes, the friend of Ann. They now gave the hymns to Thomas Charles of Bala to publish them, saving Ann Griffiths' hymns and letters for the nation. Robert Jones*** of Rhos-lan prepared them for publication in 1805 as *Grawn-Syppiau Canaan*, and in 1806 as *Casgliad o Hymnau gan Mwyaf heb Erioed eu Hargraffu o'r Blaen*. R. Saunderson of Bala published this second edition. In 1807 there was a third edition by J. Evans of Carmarthen, and another by Saunderson of Bala in 1808 entitled *Hymnau o Fawl I Dduw a'r Oen*. John Hughes' most famous memoir is of Ann Griffiths, which appeared in *Y Traethodydd* in 1846, and as a book in 1854.

Of her letters, only eight survive, seven to John Hughes and one to Elizabeth Evans, the sister of Ruth Evans. They include passages of religious prose said to be among the finest examples in the Welsh language. Only 74 of her hymn verses have survived, with only one in her own hand, as they were personal expressions of love for God, not intended to be sung in congregations. However, they are comparable with those of the great William Williams *'Pantycelyn'*, and Saunders Lewis claimed that her longest hymn, *Rhyfedd, rhyfedd gan angylion* was one of the greatest religious poems in any European language. In it Ann sees Christ, 'a worthy object of my love' among the sweet myrtles, and expresses the wish 'Hail! The morning/ I shall see him with no veil.' Her entry in *The New Companion to the Literature of Wales*, edited by the inestimable Meic Stephens, gives an excellent reading list on this much-studied young woman, and states 'Owing to the unusual intensity of her life, some critics have discerned mystical qualities in her work, while others have demonstrated the similarities between her work and that of other writers of very different traditions. But a proper understanding of her genius must rely on the fact that she was a poet in the Calvinistic Methodist tradition.'

The great Sir Owen M. Edwards, who wrote the most moving account of the 'Welsh Knot', published John Hughes' correspondence with Ann Griffiths, and the contents of his note-books in 1905, in *Gwaith Ann Griffiths*, with the original versions of her hymns. She is given the Holy Day of 12 August by The Church in Wales. One of her letters, translated by Gwyn Williams, reads 'It isn't strange that the sun hid its rays when its Creator was under nails. It astonishes me to think who was on the cross, he whose eyes are like a flame of fire piercing heaven and earth at the same time unable to see his creatures, the work of his hands.... And thanks be for ever that the furnace and the fountain are so near each other.'

Ann wrote down none of her hymns - its is nothing short of a miracle that Ruth Evans remembered their vivid phrasing of thirty of them, e.g. one verse reads:

'Gwna fi fel pren planedig, O! fy Nuw,
Yn ir ar lan afonydd dyfroedd byw:
Yn gwreiddio ar led, a'I ddail heb wywo mwy,
Yn ffrwytho dan gawodydd dwyfol glwy.'
'Make me feel as a tree planted, O! my God,
Sappy on the bank of the waters of life:
Rooting widely, its leaves no longer withering,
Fruiting under the showers of a divine wound.'

The best introduction to the works of Ann Griffiths is by A.M. Allchin, *Ann Grifiths: Furnace and Fountain*, 1986, a re-edition of the 1976 *Writers of Wales* series. Tony Conran called Ann 'the greatest of Welsh women poets', and A.M. Allchin wrote that she was 'A central figure in the Christian tradition of vision and song.'

* A *bardd gwlad* was a 'country poet', an expert in traditional metres and the intricacies of *cynghanedd*, with little education but a gift for verse about his or

her own locality. *Cynghanedd* means 'harmony', and is the ancient and intricate system of sound-chiming within a line of verse. First noted in the 6th century, there are four main types of cynghanedd (*groes, draws, sain* and *lusg*), each involving the serial repetition of consonants in precise relationship to the main accents in a line, together with the use of internal rhymes. More intricate, overlapping forms can also be used, such as *cynghanedd groes o gyswllt, cynghanedd anghytbwys, cyhghanedd sain gadwynog,* and *cynghanedd sain drosgwl.* Gerard Manley Hopkins also used *cyghanedd* as a basis for some of his brilliant poetry.

** *Noson Lawen* means 'merry evening', an informal entertainment by locals around the hearth on winter evenings for neighbours, similar to the original Irish/Scottish *ceilidh.*

*** The preacher and author Robert Jones (1745-1829) of Llanystumdwy, Caernarfonshire, had attended one of Griffith Jones' circulating schools, and it was he who persuaded Bridget Bevan (q.v.) to reopen the schools across North Wales. He organised a strong Methodist association around his cottage at Tir bach, Rhos-lan, and was instrumental in persuading the great Thomas Charles of Bala not to leave Wales for America.

*Footnotes:*
1. The plaque on the memorial chapel at Dolanog commemorates *Prif Emynyddes Cymru* (The foremost female hymn-writer in Wales). Visitors are welcome to her home at Dolwar Fach. If one buys the memorial pamphlet there, the proceeds go towards the restoration of Pontrobert Chapel. Because the Methodist Church had no rights at this time to bury its members, Ann's grave is in the beautiful churchyard of Llanfihanel-yng-Ngwynfa.

2. Menna Elfyn (q.v.) has recorded how Ann inspired her to write: 'After all, wanting the language to survive and flourish was only one part of my identity. As a young girl, I discovered the remarkable hymnist Ann Griffiths whose work was only published posthumously. A woman who wrote hymns, a female poet? It was my epiphany. If she could, so could I. I was already drawn to the poetry of Marianne Moore, Elizabeth Bishop, Emily Dickinson and later Adrienne Rich and others. Slowly, another political consciousness was emerging within me - the need for a Wales that was not based on patriarchy or dependent on the stereotypical "Welsh Mam". Again, though I campaigned and voiced feminist values, I still relished the solitude of being "the other", distant and aloof.'

## MARY JONES 16 December 1784 – 24 December 1864

## THE INSPIRATION FOR *THE BIBLE* SOCIETY

At Bryn-Crug Chapel is an inscription at the chapel reading: 'In Memory of MARY JONES Who in the Year 1800, At the age of 15, Walked from Llanfihangel-y-Pennant to Bala to procure a copy of a Welsh *Bible* from Rev Thomas Charles, BA. This incident led to the formation of the British and Foreign Bible Society.' This barefoot journey took Mary 25 miles over the rocky paths of Cader Idris and back, with the three shillings and sixpence (13 pence for the post-decimalisation generation) that she had painstakingly saved from the age of ten to almost sixteen.

Mary Jones was born the daughter of weavers, in Tyn-y-Ddol cottage, the remains of which can be seen just a few hundred yards from the evocative remains of Castell-y-Bere, near Llanfihangell-y-Pennant village (see St Melangell) and the Afon Cader Bridge. There are a plaque and obelisk at the site. Her parents were strict Calvinistic Methodists. As a young child, after helping her parents with weaving and household chores all day, in the evenings Mary thrilled to her father's stories from the *Bible*, of Daniel and the Lion, of David and Goliath, and of Peter in Prison. Mary had a very poor upbringing, after her father died when she was four, and being raised by her widowed mother in a small cottage. These were years when the poor in Wales became even more impoverished, owing to the Napoleonic wars and poor harvests. Mary was poor as a child and remained poor to the grave. Aged eight, she asked her mother for her own *Bible*, but her mother replied that none of them could read, and that *Bibles* were far too expensive. However, a school came to the village two miles away, and Mary learned to read over the next two years.

Mary came to personal faith at eight years of age, and was received into membership of the local Methodist *seiat* at that time, sometime in 1793. It was unusual for children to become seiat members at such an early age, but since Mary attended other religious meetings of an evening with her widowed mother, in order to carry the lamp for her, she was also allowed to accompany her mother to the *seiat* meetings. Early in life, therefoe, she had become very familiar with the content and message of the *Bible,* much more familiar than most children in her area at that time. When she was about ten years of age, one of Thomas Charles's circulating schoolmasters, John Ellis, came to keep day-school at Abergynolwyn, two miles from Mary's home, and soon a Sunday school was also established there.

Mary was one of the most punctual and regular attendees at both these schools, to the extent that her circumstances allowed. Earnestly sought scriptural knowledge, and it is obvious from the surviving evidence that she was a capable pupil, and even in old age she could still recite faultlessly large portions of Thomas Charles's catechism, the *Hyfforddwr* (Instructor). Her biographer, Robert Oliver Rees, wrote: 'She distinguished herself especially in the Sunday school by treasuring in her memory, and reciting aloud in public, entire chapters of the Word of God, and in her "good understanding" of it.'

Apart from the copy of the *Bible* in the parish church, the *only* Bible in the vicinity at that time, it would seem, was the one at Penybryniau Mawr, a farmhouse about two miles from Mary's home. The *Bible* was kept on a table in the small parlour, and Mary was given permission by the farmer's wife to go and read it, on condition that she removed her clogs before venturing in. It is said that Mary would walk there every week, whatever the weather, over a period of some six years in all, to read the *Bible* and commit portions to memory.

However, Mary longed for a *Bible* so that she could read it at home to her mother, and worked hard at small jobs to earn extra money. She sold eggs, picked up sticks for firewood for an elderly woman, and washed and ironed or bathed the children to ease a neighbour's burden. At long last, she had saved enough, and the day before her trip went to borrow a bag from her neighbour Mrs Rees, to protect and carry the Bible back home from Bala. 'I want to know if you will lend me that nice wallet you have,' Mary said, 'I must carry some food for the day, and my mother's purse with the precious pennies in it. I must also carry my shoes, for they would be worn out if I wore them all that long way.'

Next morning, she slung the bag with her shoes over her shoulder. She was looking forward to meeting Thomas Charles, described by great Methodist preacher Daniel Rowland as 'the Lord's gift to the North' when Charles moved to Bala. When she finally met the great man (q.v. Ann Griffiths), Charles unfortunately gave her the news that there was no *Bible* to be bought. Moved by her sadness, he gave her his own personal *Bible*, and her zeal and endeavour inspired Charles to create *The Bible* Society to make free *Bibles* available to all those who wanted them, all over the world.

Another version of the story is that Thomas Charles was so moved by the girl's faith and determination that he arranged lodgings for her until a new supply of *Bibles* arrived two days later. Then he sold her three copies for the price of one. Two copies of Mary Jones' *Bible* still exist. One is in the archives of the British and Foreign *Bible* Society in Cambridge, another in the National Library of Wales at Aberystwyth, and the third copy, if it existed, has disappeared. In the Cambridge copy, Mary Jones wrote the following (in English) on the last page of the *Apocrypha* (- the spelling is her own):

'Mary Jones was born 16th of December 1784.
I Bought this in the 16th year of my age. I am Daughter of Jacob Jones and Mary Jones His wife. the Lord may give me grace. Amen.
Mary Jones His [is] The True Onour [owner] of this Bible. Bought In the Year 1800 Aged 16th.'

This meant that she was fifteen, because at the time people counted the number of new years they had each had, 'in the 16th year of my age' meaning that she was in the year leading up to her sixteenth birthday.

The American *Bible* Society was formed in 1816, in New York. There are now *Bible* Societies in almost 200 countries. At least one book of the *Bible* is now available in over 2,000 different languages, and millions of *Bibles*, testaments and selections of scripture are distributed each year.

There are Mary Jones Societies amongst Christian children across the world, from Mexico to Indonesia. A French-Canadian website, translated by the author, has the following version of her story: 'Mary Jones and her Bible - Happy News: In 1794, in Wales, a little 10-year-old girl, called Mary Jones, lived with her parents close to a small village. Mary and her parents were very religious. They went to the village chapel each week to pray. But, like most people, they could neither read nor write. One day, they learned that a school will soon open in the village. What happy news!

The Decision: Mary rose early each day to do the housework. Then, she walked 3km to the village school where she learned to read. Finally came the day when Mr John Ellis, the schoolmaster, asked her to read to the other children from the school's large Welsh *Bible*. At that point, Mary decided that she would do anything to be able to buy her own *Bible*.

The *Bible* of Mrs Evans: *Bibles* were very expensive. Mary knew that it would be necessary to save for years to have enough money. So what could she do in the meantime? Mrs Evans was the farmer's wife who lived close to Mary's house. As she knew Mary loved reading the *Bible*, she invited Mary to come and read the family *Bible* at her farm. Thus, each Saturday mid-day, straight after helping her mother with the housework all morning, Mary walked happily to the Evans farm to read their *Bible*.

A Great Deal of Work: Mary worked as hard as she could to gain money to purchase her *Bible*. She knitted socks, grew vegetables and sold them, and collected honey from hives. Mrs Evans gave her some hens, so Mary could sell eggs. She also helped the local farmers harvest their crops. Sometimes she felt discouraged, but then she remembered how happy she felt on Saturday afternoons when she could read Mrs Evans' *Bible*. She

179

thought of the joy she would have when she eventually had her own *Bible*, and could read it whenever she wished!

One Marvellous Day: Mary worked hard, for long hours, saving all her money for six years. Finally, counting her money one day, she realised that she had enough for her *Bible*.

Mary Goes on a Journey: Mary saw her clergyman and asked where she could buy a *Bible*. She was told that Thomas Charles of Bala (a great man in Welsh history) will be able to sell one, the same man who engaged Mr Ellis to be her schoolmaster. But Mr Charles lived in Bala, 40km away! Far from being discouraged, Mary hurried to tell her parents, and with little delay, started walking. Such a trip was very dangerous. Robbers often watched for travellers on the roads and stole their money. Mary trusted in God to protect her. [Author's note: Mary walked barefoot. It was custom as this time to have a single pair of shoes for 'best' to wear to church only. The poor used to walk barefoot to church, wash their feet nearby, sometimes in the local holy well, don their shoes for the service, and reverse the process when going home. The author's *The Book of Welsh Saints* has more details.]

Mary has her *Bible*: She walked all day and arrived at Bala late in the evening. She spent the night with a friend before seeing Mr Charles the next morning. Very excited, she had woken early and knocked his door. Mary told Mr Charles her story of saving for years. Mr Charles was full of kindness, but could do nothing for Mary. He had sold all of his Welsh *Bibles* except for one he was keeping for a friend. Mary was so disappointed that she burst into tears. However, Mr Charles also had an English *Bible*, which he said that he would give to his bilingual friend, and he sold the Welsh *Bible* to Mary, who spoke no English. Full of joy, Mary thanked Mr Charles for the *Bible*, and also for the school where she learned to read. With the *Bible* wrapped tightly in her grasp, she began the long journey back to her village. Mary read her *Bible* every day. The more she did, the more she loved God and his Word.

*Bibles* for Everyone: Mr Charles remembered Mary for a very long time. It made him very sad that Welsh people like Mary could not buy *Bibles*, even if they saved for years, because *Bibles* were so rare. He decided to do all in his power to ensure that more *Bibles* were printed to spread the word. Four years later, in about 1804, he went to London, and helped for a society for religious affairs. There were many like-minded people who wished to help people like Mary obtain their own *Bibles*. Thus was created the British and Foreign Biblical Company whose first religious publication was the *Gospel of St John*, published in the language of the Mohawk Indians of North America. Later, one saw the creation of the Canadian Biblical Company, whose work was similar to that of the BFBC. The French-speaking Biblical Company of Belgium works with other Biblical Companies in more than 180 countries throughout the world, so that people like Mary Jones can now buy their own cheap *Bibles* in their own language.'

The counties of Merioneth and Montgomery were the main centres of the woollen industry in Wales from the middle of the sixteenth century to the beginning of the nineteenth, and wool played a prominent role in the lives of its people. Mary was the daughter of weavers, and she and her husband were weavers all their married life. In old age, she would enjoy reminiscing of how in her youth she would walk all Saturday night in order to reach Bala in time for communion on Sunday morning, of the group prayer meetings on the way, and of the powerful preaching and rejoicing she witnessed in the open-air meetings on the Green in Bala. It is quite probable that Ann Griffiths and Mary Jones, for a few years at the beginning of the nineteenth century, actually attended the same meetings at Bala, and knew one another. They both belonged to the same religious community, a community which centred on Bala and on Thomas Charles. All the elements which characterised the Calvinistic Methodism of North Wales at the end of the eighteenth century were at work in both their lives. Their spiritual experiences were essentially the same, as were their beliefs. 'As regards religious practice, they both spoke the same language, followed the same customs, and attended the same type of meetings. They heard the same preachers, read the same books, sang the same hymns. Both knew Thomas Charles personally, and although Ann had not, like Mary, been a pupil in one of Charles's circulating schools, both were deeply indebted to Thomas Charles's educational efforts. For example, the chief spiritual mentor in both cases were teachers in Charles's circulating schools: William Hugh of Llanfihangel-y-Pennant in the case of Mary Jones, and John Hughes of Llanfihangel-yng-Ngwynfa (later of Pontrobert) in that of Ann Griffiths.'

Mary Jones had a long life. It was a poor and a grim one in many ways. She married in 1813. At least six children were born to her and her husband, but most of them died young. Only one child seems to have survived her, and he had by then emigrated to the United States. Around 1820, Mary and her husband, Thomas Lewis, moved a few miles nearer the coast, to the village of Bryn-crug near Tywyn. She kept bees to supplement their meagre earnings. Her local cleric, Robert Griffith of Bryn-Crug noted: 'She [i.e. Mary Jones] had only a small garden of land, and that was very full of fruit, and a myriad of bees, and she would be like a princess on a fine summer's day, in their midst, and she could pick them up in her hands like corn, or oatmeal, without any one of them using its sting to oppose her.' Mary kept the income from selling the honey for her own livelihood, but she divided the income from the beeswax, which could be a considerable sum, between the *Bible* Society and her denomination's Missionary Society. She attributed the fact that the bees did not sting her, and that they were so productive, and that their produce was of such high quality, to the fact that they knew that Mary dedicated a substantial portion of that produce to the work of their Creator.

Despite her poverty, she contributed regularly to the work of the *Bible* Society, and donated half a sovereign to the special collection made in 1854 to send a million *New Testaments* to China, to celebrate the fiftieth anniversary of the founding of the British and Foreign *Bible* Society. Thomas Charles visited her whenever he could. In her old age, Mary Jones would enjoy telling the tale of her walk to Bala to obtain a *Bible*, and made good use of the *Bible* she received from Thomas Charles. She read it from cover to cover four times during her lifetime. She memorised substantial sections of it, which proved of great benefit and comfort to her after she lost her sight. And when she died aged 80, the Bible she had bought in Bala over 60 years previously was on the table by her side.

A memorial obelisk was erected among the ruins of her cottage, *Tyn y Ddol. Cartref Mari Jones,* but gives her age on her walk as 16 rather than 15. Mary Jones World, at St Beuno's Church, Llanycil, Bala, is an interactive exhbition, demonstrating how her life changed the lives of millions across the world.


## ELIZABETH CADWALADR 24 May 1789 – 17 July 1860

## BETSI DAVIES, THE HEROINE OF THE CRIMEA, ELIZABETH OF BALACLAVA, BETI PEN-RHIW, 'THE REAL LADY OF THE LAMP'

Betsi Cadwaladr was born at Pen-rhiw farm near Bala in 1789 and christened at Llanycil. Her paternal grandfather was known as Cadwaldr Dafydd, and the family had been on the same land for hundreds of years. His five sons all had different names, as at that time Welsh surnames were so unsettled. Elizabeth's father merely changed the order of his father's name, and was known as Dafydd Cadwaladr. Elizabeth was known as Beti Cadwaladr or Beti Pen-rhiw. Dafydd Cadwaldr was a famous Calvinistic Methodist preacher, the son of Cadwaladr and Catherine Dafydd of Erw Ddinmael, Llangwm, Denbighshire. Even aged over 70, he thought nothing of walking 28 miles in a day to preach. His walking-staff was given to him by Selina, Countess of Huntingdon, and had a watch set into a silver case it its top. Before he died in 1834, aged 82, and was buried in Llanycil, he had fathered 9 sons and 4 daughters, and our knowledge of her extraordinary life comes from Jane Williams of Ysgafell, who compiled notes of Betsi's conversations for a two-volume *The Autobiography of Elizabeth Davis, a Balaclavan Nurse, Daughter of Dafydd Cadwaldr*, published in 1857.

Betsi's mother, Judith, died in 1795 or 1796, and she was left in the care of an elder sister whom she hated. Thomas Charles of Bala knew her at this time. A rebellious child, she ran away from home aged just nine, and was taken into the service of Dafydd's landlord, the cleric Simon Lloyd at the great house Plas-yn-Dref in Bala. Here she was well-treated and learned to read, write, play the harp and practise Welsh folk dance. However, she appears to have run away, aged just fourteen, to become a domestic servant in Liverpool. She recounted 'A sudden thought occurred to me that I was not to stay there any longer, and that I must see something more of the world. I instantly got up and tied a few clothes in a bundle. Before Monday morning dawned, I had thrown my bundle out of my bedroom window, and jumped out after it.' She reached the house of her aunt in Chester, who gave her money to take a coach back home, but Betsi instead took the packet boat for Liverpool. Her relatives there found her work, as her father was well-known and liked, being one of Lady Huntingdon's 'Connection' of itinerant ministers.

As they could not say 'Cadwaladr' in Liverpool, she called herself Elizabeth Davis. She regularly attended the Calvinistic Methodist church there, and also travelled around Britain with her employer. She saw Sarah Siddons (q.v.) act at Edinburgh, and visited the continent between 1815 and 1816. Betsi returned to Bala, but again ran away, via Chester, to escape an arranged marriage. In London she sought refuge at the home of John Jones of Glan-y-Gors, a distant relative, before finding a post in the service of a fashionable tailor. 'Jac Glan-y-Gors' was a satirical poet, who ran The King's Head tavern in Ludgate Street, Southwark, now the Canterbury Arms, and was at the hub of London Welsh societies.

Betsi combined regular attendance at chapel with her passion of theatre-going, before returning again to Bala in 1820, aged thirty-one, which she found extremely dull compared to London society. She now became a maid to a sea-captain's family, travelling the world for years, and refusing several marriage proposals. Bitten by the travel-bug, she and worked on ships travelling to the West Indies, Australia, Tasmania, China, India, Africa and South America. She is accredited in saving a ship, the *Denmark Hill*, under Captain Foreman, by lowering the sails while the crew cowered below decks. She met the missionaries William Carey and Bishop Heber in India, and John Davies in Tahiti. Reginald Heber was astonished to find that she was the daughter of the poet Dafydd Cadwaladr.

Betsi had acted in Shakespeare on board ship, and had lost her savings upon returning to London, when Charles Kemble heard her acting *Hamlet* in her employer's kitchen. She joined his company on £50 a week, performing across Wales from 1844 to 1849. She alleged that he left her a fortune, but she was cheated out of it, and took up a nursing career in Guy's Hospital. Betsi had returned to London to live with her sister, and was accepted by Guy's Hospital to train as a nurse, in her fifties at the time. In September 1854, at the age of sixty-five, she read in *The Times* about the terrible Battle of Alma in the Crimean War, and that hundreds of British troops were dying from cholera and the intense cold, as well as from untreated wounds. She just missed Florence Nightingale's first group, but joined the second to go to Scutari. Scutari was 300 miles from the front, the modern Uskudar, near Istanbul. This group of 'Miss Stanley's nurses' left England in December 1854, being coldly received by Nightingale. The nurses under Miss Stanley had been sent out against Nightingale's wishes, who thought many of them unsuitable for the work.

The wounded had to be taken in ships, with unattended wounds, across the Black Sea to Scutari. Betsi was one of the very few women who

 actually nursed in the war. Nightingale only visited there twice, not nursing but only organising the Scutari hospital*. Betsi did not like Nightingale's set-up and wrote a personal letter to Lord Raglan asking to nurse at the front line in Balaclava. He granted permission, and Betsi took a troopship to the base hospital there. As she said, 'By the time the wounded soldiers get across the Crimea to Turkey and the Scutari hospital they are dead. I want to be there close to the battlefield'.

**Betsi Cadwaladr's grave**

'Her work saved hundreds of lives. She supervised the feeding of the wounded men and their medication.' The beds were so close together, that nurses had to pass sideways to attend the exhausted, verminous and filthy men, who were clothed only in rags. Many of the wounds had received no attention for six weeks, and were full of maggots. The hand of one man fell off at the wrist when Betsi was about to dress it. She was put in charge of the Extra Diet Kitchen, where food was supplied for the very worst cases, and remained in sole charge for ten months.

Her bedroom was rat-infested, unsanitary and not even rain-proof. She took eleven other nurses with her to the front line, and took charge of the kitchens by day and the wounded at night. Betsi fought hard against Nightingale's Requisition System. *The Times* had a Fund of Free Gifts, including medical stores, which had been handed over to Nightingale, and she adhered steadfastly to the military hospital rule whereby anything had to be subject to two written acquisition orders, often signed by different medical officers. This mismanagement helped add chaos to disorder as men were lying in filthy rags and could not receive clean shirts or bed-linen which were in stock. Against Nightingale's wishes, Betsi had left Scutari to organise Balaclava Hospital, cutting through the hated red tape, and distributing the stores at her own discretion where they were best needed.

When her health broke under the deplorable conditions, many soldiers and officers came to thank her in person for saving their lives, before she was invalided home to London. Lord Raglan looked favourably on her work, and the Principal Medical officer at Balaclava wrote: 'I cannot speak in too high terms of Mrs Davis' universal good conduct and her unremitting attention to the sick.' Betsi's true opinions of the saintly Florence Nightingale* were said to be unprintable, and she had left after yet another quarrel with the haughty and imperious woman. Betsi had never accepted Nightingale's authority, saying that it did not extend to the front line at Balaclava Hospital. She knew that Florence, 'The Lady of the Lamp', had little practical nursing experience. Nightingale's original appointment only gave her authority in Turkey, but was later altered to extend her powers. The utter disaster of the Crimean Campaign meant that the press had to mediate the story, making Nightingale a 'heroine' and the terrible Charge of the Light Brigade into something 'glorious'.

Eirionedd Baskerville wrote '...as a result of reading one of William Howard Russell's newspaper accounts from the Crimean War of the suffering of the soldiers, she volunteered in 1854 for nursing service in the Crimea... She joined a party of nurses and "Sisters of Mercy" under a Miss Stanley and eventually reached Scutari. This was the main British Hospital and was under the control of Florence Nightingale. Strong-willed Betsy did not like Florence Nightingale and was angry at being made to mend old shirts and sort rotting linen instead of being allowed at the centre of the action, the Crimean peninsular. She therefore left for the hospital at Balaclava and immediately set to work to treat the infested wounds of the soldiers. She nursed the men for six weeks before being put in charge of the special diet kitchen. Being an excellent cook she made sure that the soldiers had good food produced from the best ingredients. However, overwork and ill health meant that she was forced to return to Britain, leaving with a recommendation from Florence Nightingale for a government pension. However, her comments on affairs in the Crimea are extremely scathing and she had little good to say about Florence Nightingale'.

Betsi died in 1860, and leaves behind no gravestone, just a two-volume autobiography of her adventures. History again is fascinating – those with the best public relations and access to the media are remembered fondly. The real heroes and heroines are ignored. Betsi spent her last years in extreme poverty, at her younger sister Bridget's** home in London. She was still devoutly religions, keeping the small Welsh *Bible* that had been given to her by the great Thomas Charles of Bala, as her 'constant companion.'

The penniless and obscure Betsi Cadwaladr was buried in 1860 in Abney Park Cemetery, either laid above, below, or sandwiched between, three complete strangers in a pauper's grave dug deep enough to take four cheap coffins. There were probably not many mourners at her funeral and no marker or memorial was erected over the burial spot. The headstone now over her grave is new, put up in 2012 by the Royal College of Nursing and a Welsh Health Board that had adopted her name and proclaimed Betsi a Welsh national heroine. In Wales there were letters accusing the former nurse of having worked as a prostitute in the Liverpool Docks, and the Welsh Daily Post felt obliged to defend her honour against her detractors, reporting that there was no evidence that she had ever sold herself on the streets of Merseyside.

* Florence Nightingale's reputation has taken a real hammering in the past few years - a BBC2 *Reputations* documentary of 17 July 2001 stated that she was driven 'more by ambition than compassion', and she was called 'a seething bundle of neuroses, just as prone to seeing female colleagues as her enemies as stuffy military sexists' (*Sunday Times* 15 July 2001). The TV commentator called her 'the ultimate domineering, bossy, ruthless woman', so it was no small wonder that the independently-minded Betsi wrote scornfully of her. Nightingale's war record was appalling - records reveal that troops who arrived at her hospital in Scutari from the Crimea were twice as likely to die than those who were kept in a regimental hospital tent at the front. Of the 300 members of the Grenadier Guards who were sent there, none came back. Her hospital was built over a contaminated cesspit, soldiers were inadvertently drinking their own sewage, she knew little of nursing, refused to delegate, had a low opinion of her fellow women and was opposed to female suffrage.

According to her biographer, Mark Bostridge, 'she relied much more on men, was much more interested in men, thought of herself as a man and had an almost total contempt for the human race'. On her return from the Crimea she had a breakdown and lived as a recluse, but this did not stop Lytton Strachey criticising her in his *Eminent Historians* (1918), written just eight years after her death. 'The Iron Maiden', who 'believed in order, in command... who could only lead... and was not interested in delegating' (*Weekend*, 7 July 2001) seems to have been eerily resurrected in another English heroine, 'The Iron Lady', Mrs Thatcher. According to Mark Bostridge 'She [Nightingale] was built up by the Victorians during the Crimean War partly because Britain needed a hero, having not had one since Nelson and Wellington... she was very like Margaret Thatcher. Very bossy, a cutter of red tape, who hated other women and could only work with men. She was really a manipulative politician herself.'

** Bridget was born in 1795, shortly before her mother's death, and was a maid to Lady Llanover (q.v.) in London and Llanover, dying in 1878 and being buried at Llanover.

## FELICIA DOROTHEA BROWNE (FELICIA HEMANS) 25 September 1793 - 16 May 1835

## THE AUTHOR OF *THE BOY STOOD ON THE BURNING DECK*

Born in Duke Street, Liverpool in 1793, Felicia Browne lived in this bustling city until 1800. Her merchant father, suffering business reversals, then moved the family to Gwrych, near Abergele, when she was seven years old. Their first home in Wales was Hen Wrych, near Gwrych Castle. The family then moved to Bronwylfa Hall, her mother's home, near St Asaph Cathedral. Felicia Browne lived here for most of the period from 1809-1828, grew up to speak five languages besides her own, and made a serious study of German literature before she produced *Lays of Other Lands*. Her childhood, and the greater part of her adult life, was spent in Wales (1907-1828). Only the first seven and last seven years of her life were spent outside the country, and she always regarded it as 'land of her childhood, her home and her dead'. When she left Wales forever in 1828, she wrapped her face in a cloak so she could not see the hills fade out of sight.

If the beauty and serenity of Wales were an important influence on the young girl, so too was her mother, whose devoted care included encouraging her to use the large home library. The mother of the golden-haired Felicia was the cultured daughter of Benedict Park Wagner, formerly of North Hall, near Wigan. Felicia read avidly, memorised poetry, studied music and art, and learned French, Portuguese, Spanish, and Italian from her mother. She also learned Latin from the local vicar, and later, German. Felicia Browne began to write poetry, her first subjects being her mother and Shakespeare. Aged 14, with her mother's management, she published a handsome illustrated quarto, *Poems* (1808), undertaken to help pay for her education.

The book was sold by subscription, and on its list appeared Thomas Medwin and Captain Alfred Hemans, an army friend of her brothers, who were in Spain fighting against Napoleon. Medwin reported the poet's talents and beauty to his teenage cousin Percy Shelley, who began writing to Felicia. Although Mrs. Browne intervened in this correspondence, possibly saving her daughter from the fate of some of Shelley's other infatuations, Shelley offered sympathy to the young poet in the wake of the disappointing reviews of her *Poems*. Felicia had taken to her bed as a response to the adverse criticism, but when older did not worry about reviews.

*England and Spain, or, Valour and Patriotism* appeared in 1809 (to no sales and no notice), just as she was finishing another long poem, *War and Peace*, an impassioned plea for peace in an age of war. She fell in love with Captain Hemans when they met in 1809 and she was sixteen. In 1810, Felicia's father deserted the family to seek a fresh start in Canada, where he died two years later. Captain Hemans returned to England in 1811, weakened and scarred from war, and the couple married in 1812, the year she turned nineteen. In the same year her third volume, *The Domestic Affections*, including *War and Peace* appeared. (This was the same year that Byron changed the literary landscape with his epic of alienation, *Childe Harold's Pilgrimage*.)

Felicia Hemans's volume did not attract notice, and when the captain's post-war appointment ended in a discharge without pay, they and their baby boy joined her mother's household in Wales. Her son George was born at Bronwylfa Hall in 1814, and had a successful career in civil engineering. Felicia kept writing, and her first genuine success came with a poem lauding Britain's triumphant emergence as world power after the fall of Napoleon. This was her topical poem, *The Restoration of the Works of Art to Italy* (1816), which Byron praised, and John Murray purchased for a second edition. Soon after, Murray published her *Modern Greece* (1817) and a volume of translations and original poetry (1818). Aged twenty-five, she had four boys by this point, and Felicia Hemans was pregnant again.

In 1818, just before the birth of their fifth son, Captain Hemans, after five years of marriage, left for Italy. The reasons were unclear. The story given was his health, but Hemans' friend Maria Jewsbury suggested that he was uncomfortable living off his wife's income, and a later memoir reports his complaint that 'it was the curse of having a literary wife that he could never get a pair of stockings mended'. Thus, her husband repeated the vanishing trick of her father. The captain's departure strengthened her determination to support her family with her writing.

In 1822 this mother of five boys, ages three to ten, wrote to a friend that she felt herself in 'the melancholy situation of Lord Byron's "scorpion girt by fire... Her circle narrowing as she goes", for I have been pursued by the household troops through every room successively, and begin to think of establishing my métier in the cellar'. However, there were some practical advantages. She had a sister, a mother, and brothers to help her, and no husband to press for wifely service and obedience. Felicia could now just about find time to read, study, and write, and her career took off. *Tales, and Historic Scenes* (1819), a wide-ranging critical view of politics and culture, was well reviewed and commercially successful. By 1820 she was winning prize competitions and further favour with the public and the reviewers. In rapid succession she produced *Wallace's Invocation to Bruce, The Sceptic,*

*Stanzas to the Memory of the Late King* (which expressed sympathy for the suffering of George III), *Dartmoor* and *Welsh Melodies*. New venues for publishing poetry opened with the founding of *Blackwood's Edinburgh Magazine* in 1817, and the inauguration of the annuals craze with the publication of *Forget Me Not* in 1822. Hemans quickly grasped the importance of these journals, especially for women's poetry. She wrote several poems on Welsh themes, such as *The Rock of Cader Idris*, and *Chant of the Bards before their Massacre by Edward I* (the author includes a famous Hungarian poem on this topic for *The 100 Greatest Welshmen*). *Owain Glyndŵr's War-Song* takes up arms for the Welsh nation in its 15th century war against the English crown.

Her Welsh patriotic verses had been published in the 1821 volume *'Welsh Melodies'*, which led to her contemporary Welsh audience hailing her as 'a poet for Wales'. According to her own testimony, she regarded herself as a naturalised Welsh woman. Cefn yr Ogof Pass, overlooking her Welsh home in the years 1800-1828 when she lived in Wales, was a natural battle-ground between the Welsh and the invading English over the centuries. In the 19th century, Jane Williams (*Ysgafell*) said 'no other spot in the Principality has been more thoroughly saturated with blood'. Some of Felicia's verses in *'Welsh Melodies'* are translations, so she probably could read Welsh, if not speak it fluently.

Throughout the 1820s she sold her work to magazines and annuals, then gathered many of these pieces for volumes published by John Murray and then William Blackwood. Her fame was assured with *The Forest Sanctuary* (1825 and 1829), *Records of Woman* (1828, with several subsequent editions) and *Songs of the Affections* (1830). Among all the acclaim, her family life also gave her an important public advantage. 'Mrs. Hemans' was seen as a poet not only of home but sited at home, under 'the maternal wing', a phrase used throughout the nineteenth-century biographies. The professional woman who would dismay Wordsworth (also a poet at home, whose work was materially enabled by the labour of the women of his household) by seeming 'totally ignorant of housewifery' thus avoided the stigma of 'unfeminine' independence. W. M. Rossetti called Felicia an 'admired and popular poetess', a 'loving daughter' and a 'deeply affectionate, tender, and vigilant mother', and George Eliot (q.v.) called Hemans' *Forest Sanctuary* 'exquisite'.

Frances Wilson (*London Review of Books*, 6 November 2000) noted 'Mrs Hemans - or Hewomans, as Byron called her - was lavishly praised in her own lifetime, and second only to Byron in popularity and sales. But while Byron was disowned by the Victorians, embarrassed that this "huge sulky dandy", as Thomas Carlyle called him, should have received so much adoration and respect, Felicia Hemans' reputation grew, and her work went out of print only after the First World War. Her importance in dictating the taste for patriotism, obedience and sacrifice in generations of readers cannot be underestimated.'

The Times Literary Supplement tells us that 'Hemans' poetry pivots between Romantic internationalism and Victorian patriotic nationalism in fascinating and complex ways', and Documentary Editing noted in 2000 that a new edition of her collected poems 'Will help restore Hemans' place in the Romantic canon with Wordsworth, Shelley, Scott and Byron, all of whom respected and admired her poetry.' To many of her readers, she was the 'exemplar of womanliness'. With her small figure and long flowing hair, her friend Geraldine Jewsbury called her 'a muse, a grace, a variable child, a dependent woman - the Italy of human beings'. Among other lines, she gave us:

'The stately homes of England,
How beautiful they stand,
Amidst their tall ancestral trees,
O'er all the pleasant land!'

The death of her own mother in 1827 was a devastating loss, deepened by the break-up of the household, as older sons left for school and siblings married or moved away. To escape the emptiness, Hemans now moved from Bronwylfa with her younger sons to a village near Liverpool in 1828. Here she found schooling for them, and literary and musical society for herself. She met Wordsworth and Sir Walter Scott and enjoyed summer holidays with each. From Wordworth's Rydal Mount, she wrote: '...I am charmed with Mr Wordsworth, whose kindness to me has a soothing influence over my spirits. Oh! What relief, what blessing, there is in the feeling of admiration, when it can be freely poured forth! - The whole of this morning he kindly passed in reading to me a great deal from Spencer, and afterwards his own Laodamia, my favourite Tintern Abbey and many of his noble sonnets. His reading is very peculiar, but to my ear very delightful; slow, solemn, earnest, in expression, more than any other I have heard...'

And from Scott's Abbotsford home she wrote: 'I have now had the gratification of seeing Sir Walter in every point of view I could desire: we had one of the French Princes here yesterday with his suite - the Duc de Chartres son of the Duc d'Orleans, and there was naturally some little excitement diffused through the household by the arrival of a royal guest. Sir Walter was, however, exactly the same in his own manly simplicity - kind, courteous, unaffected - I was a little nervous when he handed me to the piano on which I was the sole performer...' However, aged 38, her health was weakening from emotional and physical stress, and in 1831 she sent her two oldest boys, Arthur and George, to their father in Italy and moved to Dublin, to be near her brother George and his wife.

Although she again found good society and continued to write and publish, the Irish climate proved a disaster. She became very ill with scarlet fever and bed-ridden with complications which turned to 'dropsy' (possibly rheumatic fever) in 1834. She died a few months before her forty-second birthday, in 1835, only eight years after her mother, and regreting about the poetry she never finished: 'My wish ever was to concentrate all my mental energy in the production of some more noble and complete work.' Her great friend Wordsworth wrote on her death:

'Mourn rather for that holy spirit,
Sweet as the spring, as ocean deep -
For her who, ere her summer faded,
Has sunk into a breathless sleep.'

Apart from her best-known poem *Casabianca*, other works by Hemans which were very popular in her lifetime include *Welsh Melodies* and a play called *The Vespers of Palermo*. She also translated Portuguese poems into English. William Wordsworth and Sir Walter Scott were admirers of her work.

\* These lines come from her poem *Casabianca*, about a 13 year-old boy, the son of the Admiral of the Orient, who remained at his post in 'The Battle of the Nile':

'The boy stood on the burning deck
Whence all but he had fled;
The flame that lit the battle's wreck
Shone round him o'er the dead.
Yet beautiful and bright he stood,
As born to rule the storm;
A creature of heroic blood,
A proud, though child-like form.
The flames rolled on, he would not go
Without his father's word;
That father, faint in death below,
His voice no longer heard...'

## MARIA JANE WILLIAMS 1794 or 1795 – 10 November 1873

### *LLINOS*, FOLK MUSICIAN AND FOLKLORIST

This musician and folklorist was born at the great Aberpergwm House, Glynneath, and rescued many Welsh songs from obscurity. Her ancient home was gutted by fire and is being restored by CADW. She was the second daughter of Rees Williams (d. 1812) and his wife Ann Jenkins of

Fforest Ystradfellte. Southey corresponded with Rees Williams in 1802. Maria's brother, William Williams (d.1855), was a considerable traveler and linguist, and was the first to suggest, in 1836, the formation of the Welsh Manuscripts Society.

Maria lived in Blaen Baglan but in her later years, at a house called Ynys-las, near Aberpergwm House. Maria Jane Williams was well educated, a great supporter of Welsh language and traditions and had an extensive knowledge of music. She was acclaimed for her singing, and was an accomplished player of the goitre and harp. Henry Fothergill Chorley called her 'the most exquisite amateur singer he had ever heard' She acquired the name *Llinos* (Linnet), and was associated with the Welsh cultural society known as *Cymreigyddion y Fenni\**, making his home a focus for supporters of the 'Celtic Renaissance'.

In 1826–7 Maria made a collection of the fairy tales of the Vale of Neath, which was published in the supplemental volume of *Irish Fairy Legends* and subsequently reprinted in an abridged form in the *Fairy Mythology*. In thee 1837 Abergavenni eisteddfod, Maria became friendly with Lady Lanover, and was awarded the prize for the best collection of unpublished Welsh music. It was published in 1844 as *The Ancient National Airs of Gwent and Morgannwg*, and remains an important contribution to the knowledge of traditional Welsh music. The book contains 43 songs with Welsh words and

**The decaying ruins of Maria Jane Williams' great mansion at Aberpergwm**

accompaniments for the harp or piano, and also provides notes on the songs and a list of persons for whom copies of the work had been printed. The book has since been re-issued by the Welsh Folk Songs Society with a contemporary introduction and notes by Daniel Huws. Through the collection she rescued many songs, the best known being *Y Deryn Pur* (The Gentle Dove) and *Y Ferch o'r Sger* (The Maid of Sker). Maria claimed that: 'The songs were given as... obtained, ...in their wild and original state; no embellishments of the melody have been attempted, and the accompanying words are those sung to the airs.' In October 1838, at the ensuing Eisteddfod, she won a prize for the best arrangement of any Welsh air for four voices. Maria subsequently noted down many additional airs, which after her death were delivered to Lady Llanover with a view to publication.

She assisted John Parry (*Bardd Alaw,* 1776–1851) to produce the *Welsh Harper* (1848), and John Thomas (*Pencerdd Gwalia,* 1795–1871) also consulted her before he published his two volumes of Welsh airs, as did Brinley Richards for his songs. During her last years she lived in a house called Ynys-las, near Aberpergwm, and died there in 1873 (press notices at the time of her death gave her age as 79, thus giving the date of her birth as 1794). She was buried at St Cadoc's Church in the grounds of Aberpergwm House.

In the reprint of her book of airs, Daniel Huws's Introduction contains background information, for example on other relevant folk song collectors, on Jane Williams's singers, and on how the words and music were published and edited. Near the beginning of the book Huws reproduces a painting of Jane, aged about 20 to 25, which indicates that she was far from unattractive. In his Introduction, he establishes that Jane's maidservant, Fanny Baker, was almost certainly her illegitimate daughter. He questions who was the father. It could have been the Earl of Dunraven, who married a Welsh heiress, 'witty, refined and shy', or John Randall 'the handsome gardener' from Ireland. One contemporary witness testifies that the Earl was the culprit, and that the scene of crime was 'a so-called shooting box,' built by the Earl for amatory purposes, where the couple 'used to meet for their blisses.'

\* Abergavenny (Abergafenni) became a centre of Welsh learning, helped by Lady Lanover and Maria Williams. Provincial eisteddfodau came to an end at Cardiff in 1834 but a new movement, under the auspices of the new *Cymreigyddion Y Fenni,* began to hold *eisteddfodau* from 1835 to 1851. They were sponsored by Lady Llanover (q.v.), who had already played her part in the provincial eisteddfodau. She had sponsored Maria, collator of the melodies in *Ancient National Airs of Gwent and Morgannwg.* She had also sponsored the famous Thomas Stephens, who won a fabulous prize, the Prince of Wales's Prize, for *The Literature of the Cymry,* a particularly influential book in its time. Lanover had the support of her husband, Sir Benjamin Hall, and assistance from the Reverend Thomas Price, Carnhuanawc, and Tegid, who won a handsome cup in Cardiff in 1834. It was with the help of people such as these that Lady Llanover and her husband created a series of ten *eisteddfodau* at Abergavenny. They were remarkable in that nothing else of that kind has really been seen in the Eisteddfod's history since then. They were not 'poor' *eisteddfodau,* but offered very substantial prizes, sometimes as much as eighty guineas. Prizes such as these could be won for essays on Celtic philology, and attracted some of the greatest European Celtic scholars, such as Karl Meyer and Albert Schultz of Germany.

# LADY LANOVER 21 March 1802 - 17 January 1896

## AUGUSTA WADDINGTON, *GWENYNEN GWENT*, PATRON OF WELSH CULTURE, 'THE LIVING PATRON SAINT OF WALES'

Augusta was the younger daughter of Benjamin and Georgina Waddington, of Tŷ Uchaf, Llanover. When in 1823 she married Benjamin Hall, Lord Llanover, MP for Monmouth and then Marylebone, the great neighbouring estates of Llanover and Abercarn were united. Hall was Commissioner of Works, when the great new clock at Westminster was erected in 1855, and it has always been known as 'Big Ben' after 'Ben' Hall. Benjamin Hall engaged in bitter controversy with the bishops, on the state of the church in Wales. He championed the right of the Welsh to have church services in their own language; challenged the exploitation of Church revenues, which were allocated nepotistically; and demanded that any new bishop should be Welsh-speaking and reside in Wales. Augusta's elder sister married Baron Bunsen, later German ambassador to Britain, whose circle was also interested in all things Celtic.

By 1834, Lady Llanover had learned Welsh so well that she won a prize in a Cardiff eisteddfod for an essay on the Welsh language, under the pseudonym of *Gwenynen Gwent* (the Bee of Gwent, symbolising her desire to be seen as hard-working and productive). Augusta proudly used this epithet for the rest of her life. Like Charlotte Guest (q.v.), she was closely associated with Thomas Price (*Carhuanawc*), and she organised her household on traditional medieval Welsh lines, giving Welsh titles to her servants. At all times only Welsh could be spoken, and everyone had to wear Welsh traditional dress. Another influence was Lady Coffin Greenly of Herefordshire, one of the patrons of Iolo Morganwg. Augusta had a harpist* and a bard in residence at Llanover Court, and was responsible for the revival of interest in traditional Welsh dress, costume and folk-dancing**.

A patron of the Welsh Manuscripts Society and of Llandovery's Welsh Collegiate Institute, she purchased Iolo Morganwg's writings from his son Taliesin. Lady Llanover also collaborated in collecting Welsh folk songs, which were in danger of dying out after the great Methodist Revival. The Llanover manuscripts that she had bought and collected were given by her grandson, Baron Treowen, to the National Library of Wales in 1916, a fabulous legacy for the nation.

Indeed, apart from the renewal of the custom of patronage of harpists and bards, the Halls reinstated ancient Welsh customs such as the *Mari Llwyd*, the *plygain*, folk dancing and folk songs, and even opened a Welsh woollen mill. Augusta gave annual prizes of Welsh costumes to pupils in the Llanover School, for knowledge of Welsh customs. The Halls had built the school and employed a Welsh-speaking headmaster from Bethesda. (Most of Monmouthshire was still Welsh-speaking at this time - the speeches to the Chartist rebels were in Welsh).

She was an avid teetotaller, buying up all the seven local taverns that her husband had established on their estates, giving them Welsh names, and turning them into tea houses. The Halls held 10 eisteddfodau between 1834 and 1853, with lavish prizes, and they sponsored a Welsh dictionary and a Welsh magazine for women. She helped collate and translate the *Mabinogion* and collected Welsh folk tunes, with Maria Jane Williams, which otherwise would have been lost forever. Augusta even established a school for harpists on her estate. It was at Llanover Court that her harpist Thomas Gruffydd composed his *Llanofer Reel*.

The Reel was danced by the Manor's servants to entertain the Hall family and its guests. In 1918, the harpist's daughter and the old school headmaster recalled the dance so that it could be revived in the school and village. The dance is for a man and two women, an unusual form of the Queen Elizabeth style of dancing. There are 14 dance figures, each having a traditional name such as *Tua'r Delyn* (Towards the Harp). It was probably usual to dance the reel in a long column of threes in the narrow Banqueting Hall. The dancers would progress along the hall to where the head of the family sat, underneath the musicians' gallery. *Rhif Wyth* is a longways Triple Minor Dance from Llanover, recalled by the harpist's daughter, Mrs Gruffydd Richards, in 1926.

Lady Llanover endowed two Calvinistic Methodist churches at Abercarn and Capel Rhyd-y-Meirch, on condition that services were conducted in Welsh, and wrote *The Autobiography and Correspondence of Mrs Delaney*. Her 1867 traditional Welsh cookbook *Good Cookery... and recipes communicated by the Hermit of the Cell of St Gover*,\*\*\* was recently reprinted. She was responsible in 1867 for the important book of coloured illustrations of regional Welsh female costumes, carrying out the drawings and colouring them herself.\*\*\*\* Lady Lanover became interested in their recording and survival as one of her older retainers had been distressed by their dying out. Her cousin, Horace Waddington, left an account of his many visits to Llanover: '...I was invited to stay there at the New Year 1859, with Sir Benjamin and Lady Hall in the magnificent house built in the park some little way from the old 'White House' - the arrangement of the household was quaint, maids in old-fashioned style with white cross-overs, early dinner at two (announced by the butler in Welsh), high tea in the dining room at eight. Lady Hall took me all around the grounds, shrubberies, the seven springs of St Gover, the Cromlech, and then the walled gardens, hot-houses, etc., and I saw the famous old giant rhododendron about 85 paces round.

On Sunday morning Sir Benjamin and I to the English services in the little church, in the afternoon Lady Hall to the Welsh service, she in strict Welsh dress - pointed tall hat with feather and close frilled cap under it, scarlet mantle fur-bordered and a shortish skirt. She always spoke Welsh with her servants - she had a family harpist, old Griffiths, who was a celebrated player of the old triple-stringed Welsh harp - a most difficult art as instead of putting the single row of strings into different keys by the pedals, each tone and half tone had its own string; he used to come in of an evening, in the gallery of the great hall, to play to us delightfully, old Welsh airs.'

Griffiths afterwards was appointed Chief Harper to the Prince of Wales, later Edward VII. 'Lady Hall was so active that her bardic name of *Gwenynen Gwent* - the bee of Gwent, was singularly apposite. I was driven out to see the great places round about - Llanarth, Clytha, The Hendre, Raglan, etc., and was sent shooting on my own with keepers and dogs - including old Lewis aged 80, head keeper, who remembered my father there as a youngster before he went to India in 1813...Later in the year I used to visit the Llanovers at their fine London house - 9, Great Stanhope Street. Becoming intimate my wife and I in July, 1872, went to brilliant balls at Llanover. After this I stayed often with them.'

Her 1867 book, *The First Principles of Good Cookery* is a superb volume, recently reprinted, with Lady Llanover's Salt Duck probably its signature dish. The recently retired Franco Tarushchino at the Walnut Tree, Llanddewi Skirrid, offered a superb version. Her version of Welsh Leek broth uses a trussed chicken for stock, and a dozen plums which are added in the last half-hour of cooking. Lady Lanover's book on national dress gives us costumes based on the clothing worn by Welsh countrywomen in the early 19th century - a striped flannel petticoat, worn under a flannel open-fronted bedgown, with an apron, shawl and kerchief or cap. The style of bedgown varied, with loose coat-like gowns, gowns with a fitted bodice and long skirts, and also the short gown, similar to a riding habit style. She encouraged the wearing of costume in her own home and at eisteddfodau. In the 1870's, paisley cotton shawls became common, sometimes replacing the traditional shawls, which were also used to wrap around and carry babies. The tall 'chimney' hat did not appear until the late 1840's, based on an amalgam of men's top hats and a form of high hat worn from 1790-1820 in Welsh rural areas. Apart from her court harpist, Lady Llanover was not interested in men's costume, so Welshmen have not had a traditional national dress until recently.

Her husband Benjamin Hall died in a gun accident in 1867, and was himself a champion of the Welsh people's rights to have religious services carried out in the Welsh language. He was the first industrialist to leave the established church, and in 1831 he introduced the 'Truck Act' to help stop the 'truck' system which had mainly caused the bloody Merthyr Rising. Living for thirty years after her husband's death, Lady Llanover was so industrious in supporting the revival of Welsh culture that her reputation grew to the point that she was termed 'The Living Patron Saint of Wales'. She helped establish a factory to manufacture Welsh harps, and encouraged the breeding of Welsh Black cattle and Welsh Black Sheep. It is possibly apocryphal, but she was supposed to have popularised the verse 'Baa Baa Black Sheep' to advertise the merits of Welsh sheep. Her work, with Lady Charlotte Guest, led to the Welsh Revival of 1835-45, and to the foundation of the National Eisteddfod, Welsh Manuscripts Society and the Society of Cymmrodorion. She also endowed churches and chapels where Welsh was the only language to be used, and befriended and supported Welsh poets and antiquaries. Lady Lanover helped to save the remnants of Welsh culture from their Calvinistic destruction.

\* Different types of harp used are the large Gothic, the Grecian (Orchestral) Harp, the small Harp and the very difficult Triple Harp with three sets of strings. One can see harp makers exhibiting at the National Eisteddfod, and the annual festival, *Gŵyl Cerdd Dant*, ensures the continuation of the old tradition. Until the sixteenth century, the harp (*'y delyn'*) had the highest social status of any instrument in Welsh culture, but its close associations with dance made it offensive to puritanical Non-conformists by the eighteenth century. There was still a harpist employed at Llanover Court until his death in 1888. The massive concert pedal 'Welsh' Harp came over from Austria in the seventeenth century, ousting in popularity the authentic portable Welsh harp, that had been described by Giraldus Cambrensis in the twelfth century. Before the Nonconformist fever, the harp was often used with a *'pibgorn'* (pipe) and *'crwth'* (Celtic violin, from which we get the surname Crowther, a crwth player). There was also a primitive Welsh bagpipe, the *'pibacawd'*. From over eight centuries ago, Giraldus Cambrensis gives us the following description in his *The Journey Through Wales...* 'Guests who arrive early in the day are entertained until nightfall by girls who play to them on the harp. In every house there are young women just waiting to play for you, and there is certainly no lack of harps. Here are two things worth remembering: the Irish are the most jealous people on earth, but the Welsh do not seem to know what jealousy is; and in every Welsh court or family the menfolk consider playing on the harp to be the greatest of all accomplishments.'

*The Laws of Hywel Dda*, codified around 940-950, specify that each master must employ a *'pencerdd'* (chief musician) and give him a harp, *pibgorn* and *crwth*. These traditionally accompanied dancing until the eighteenth century, when the harp and fiddle became the main accompaniment. The *pibgorn* was last commonly played by Anglesey shepherds in the early 1800's. The *crwth* was originally plucked like a lyre but from the eleventh century played with a bow (with some plucking). The last Welsh *crwth* player, or 'crowther', travelled through Anglesey in the eighteenth century. *Crwths, pibgorns* and harps can be seen at The Museum of Welsh Life in Saint Fagans. The last household bard, or poet, in Wales seems to have been Dafydd Nicolas (d. 1774) at Aberpergwm, the home of Rees Williams.

A famous 1612 manuscript by Robert ap Huw notates traditional harp music, using five scales, and no-one has yet interpreted it correctly – Wales' own *Rosetta Stone*. This is in the British museum, and part had been copied from an earlier manuscript of the Elizabethan harpist, William Llewelyn. Arnold Dolmetsch has transcribed it, believing that it is 'the only source of knowledge of the polyphonic music of pre-Christian civilisations'. Gustave Rees, the American author of *Music of the Middle Ages*, states that 'if the contents of the manuscript are as ancient as have been claimed, that fact would revolutionise both our notions concerning the development of music in medieval Europe, and the general belief that the concept of harmony as a system governing musical combinations from the vertical standpoint did not make itself felt with any radically great strength until the seventeenth century.' He admits that the older part of the manuscript contains the twenty-four measures of Welsh string music, mentioned in even older Welsh manuscripts.

** Welsh folk dance was extremely exacting and complicated, as Richard Warner commented in *A Walk Through Wales* in 1799, 'Men and women individually selected us to dance. As the females were very handsome, it is most probable we would have accepted their offers, had there not been a powerful reason to prevent us - our complete inability to unravel the mazes of a Welsh dance. 'Tis true there is no great variety in the figures of them, but the few they perform are so complicated and so long, that they would render an apprenticeship to them necessary in an Englishman.' Traditional Welsh dance falls into two categories, of which one is 'stepping'. Similar to Irish dancing, there is film of this dance in The Museum of Welsh Life, and stepping competitions between two men at a time were very popular. Clog and step dancing was also known as 'jigs and hornpipes'. There has been a renaissance in the dance, and excellent 'steppers' of all ages can now be seen in eisteddfodau. Because of the energetic nature of the heel and toe clogging, with high leaps and Cossack-style dancing, dancers or 'jiggers' often followed each other individually at wakes and revels until the instrumentalists were too tired to play. The second type of dance is 'folk dancing', which survived the Nonconformist attack by the thinnest of threads. To know the history of Welsh dance is to realise how important it is to preserve the Welsh language. The *Llanover Welsh Reel* was recalled in 1918 by Mrs Gruffydd Roberts, daughter of Thomas Gruffydd, the last harpist at Llanover Court. He was employed there from 1844 until his death in 1888. The reel was then revived by local schoolchildren, and for many years was regarded as the only genuine Welsh folk dance. However, the publication of the old Llandagfan dances in 1936 gave fresh impetus, along with many people researching the dances before time and memories ran out.

Then Mrs Margaret Thomas of Nantgarw, born 1880, remembered her childhood at local Sunday school tea parties, and dancing at homes and Caerphilly and Tongwynlais Fairs. She also remembered when 'stepping' was popular in the Long Room in the local tavern. Her daughter, Dr. Ceinwen Thomas, painstakingly committed these memories of tunes and dances to paper. Now, only since 1954 we have the 'Nantgarw Dances' forming part of all folk dance group repertoires. They include the Flower Dance (with a beautiful costume), the Dance of St. John's Eve, *Rali Twm Sion*, the Grasshopper Dance, Caerphilly Fair, the Snowball Dance and the Ball Dance. *Dawns y Pelau* (the Ball Dance) is spectacular, with each man and woman holding a multicoloured ball on elastic string, and each ball is decked with long ribbons in the national colours of Red, White and Green.

Mrs Thomas said of the present dancers '... they've a long way to go before they can dance the way the old people danced. The boys dance too much like women, you see. They're not muscular enough. The boys years ago would jump higher than the women, and because they were so energetic, the women looked more feminine.' Her family came to regard dancing as a one-way ticket to hell and damnation. Her husband's grandfather, Ifan Tomos, a well-known 'stepper' until his conversion in 1859, used to 'run past the tavern in the dark when he heard the harp and dancing outside, because the urge to join in was well nigh intolerable.' Many of the dances were performed at *taplasau haf* or *mabsantau*, assemblies of dance and song held most weekends in the summer months. For many centuries the most popular festival in Welsh calendars was the *gŵylmabsant*, a wake or revel associated with the feast day of the parish saint. Work could be suspended for days. These in time were replaced by *twmpathau*, which often took place after the taverns shut, and so were disapproved of by 'respectable' folk. The feast days of local saints are still celebrated across all the towns and villages of Brittany, and these also feature religious processions in local costume – *'pardons'*, with folk music and dance following. It may be that some Celtic-Welsh dances can also be rescued from the Breton traditional dances.

*** Saint Gofor (Gover) is probably Myfor, but according to Iolo Morganwg Gofor was the patron of Lanover, now dedicated to Bartholomew, in Monmouth. There is a large tombstone there with a poorly carved cross. There were also eight wells, all flowing into a bath known as Ffynnon Over or Gofor. *Gŵyl Ofer* was celebrated on 9 May, but the *Book of Llandaff* informs us that the previous spelling of Llanover was Lanmouor, which gives us Myfor as the saint. Previous spellings of Merthyr Mawr near Bridgend also are Merthyr Myour, Mouor and Momor.

**** The current Scottish kilt was only invented 200 years ago, and there is a movement to wear the Welsh cilt, a development of the *brycan*. The *brycan* was a length of hard-wearing wool, two yards by six, that served as the Celt's dress by day and blanket by night. When hunting or in active pursuits, the *brycan* was belted at the waist to kilt (tuck) up the folds, and the resulting skirt falling to the knees was the kilt in its embryonic form. Welsh costume, with the tall 'stovepipe' hat for women, is an adaptation of eighteenth century peasant dress. Traditional colours of women's woollen shawls and skirts varied between areas, but were usually a mixture of black, brown, white and red. Men wore plain woollen breeches and waistcoats, with heavy black shoes. Llanuwchllyn, near Bala, was the last place where the national costume, of tall beaver hat and a scarlet cloak, was regularly worn by ladies going to market and religious services. William Coxe, in his 1801 *An Historical Tour in Monmouthshire*, tells us of a typical scene in Pontypool market:

'It was a pleasing amusement to mix in these crowded meetings, to observe the frank and simple manners of the hardy mountaineers, and endeavour, in asking the price of their provisions, to extort a Saxon word from this British progeny. The women were mostly wrapped in long cloth coats of a dark blue or brown colour; all of them wore mob caps neatly plaited over their forehead and ears, and tied above the chin; several had also round felt hats like those worn by the men, or large chip hats covered with black silk, and fastened under the chin. This head-dress gives an arch and lively air to the younger part of the sex, and is not unbecoming.'

At Landyfan Forge, near Trapp and the fabulous Carreg Cennen Castle, William Lewis used a cannon ball to grind indigo to make dye. It was bought by Carmarthen Museum in 1892. Different herbs were used to dye Welsh costumes, explaining the regional variations in colours. Welsh black wool was very popular for stockings as it did not fade. The following is from Ken Etheridge's lovely little book on *Welsh Costume*: 'Each area specialised in its own kind of cloth; Gwallter Mechain tells us that blue cloth was woven on Anglesey and sold at Chester Fair; while the people of Caernarfon produced two kinds of cloth – a blue cloth to sell in Merioneth, and a grey (called *"brethyn Sir Fôn"* – the cloth of Anglesey) to sell at the Anglesey fairs. The finest flannel was made in the district between Dolobran and Llanidloes, which was called the Welsh flannel country. A kind of slate-blue flannel was produced in the Carmarthen district, while the coastal regions of Gower, Llanelli and southern Glamorgan specialised in the production of a brilliant scarlet cloth; in Pembroke it was dark red, almost claret; in Gower it was more scarlet; in Carmarthen and Llanelli (Penclawdd) it was more of a crimson colour; all were sometimes striped with narrow lines of black, cream, white or dark brown.

In Montgomery cloths of blue, drab and brown – all with stripes of darker self-colour – were produced...Perhaps this choice of colour had a good deal to do with local products; the red, obtained in earliest times from the cockle, was a colour predominating near the coast; while blacks and browns from rock lichens were the colours worn by shepherds and their families in the mountain regions. The relation between dye and the vegetation of the locality was probably much more distinct in the olden days of restricted communications. With the advent of industrial amenities the local idiosyncrasies tend to vanish... The wool then passed to the weaver, who was a craftsman venerated by all for his skill, which took a lifetime to learn. He was practised not only in the weaving, but also in dyeing and fulling the cloth.

The dyeing varied in different regions (as indicated above); checks and stripes were also peculiar to certain localities and not to others. Checks were popular in eastern parts of the country and in the northern parts of Cardigan, while plaid patterns were prevalent in Gwent. Altogether South Wales patterns and colourings were considerably gayer: scarlet, crimson, blues and orange and bright brown were seen; while in the North drab greys and black, with greens, Prussian blues and violets (in the Bangor area) were more prevalent. Herbs, plants and wild fruit, such as blackberry and bilberry were used; onion skins gave a rich brown; indigo gave a variety of blues and greens; chemical dyes superseded the vegetable, but it is doubtful whether any more beautiful or lasting colours were achieved.'

## JANE WILLIAMS 1 February 1806 – 15 March 1885

### *YSGAFELL*

Born the second of seven chidren in Riley Street, Chelsea, her parents were David and Eleanor Williams. Her father held an appointment in the navy office, and was descended from Henry Williams (d.1684) of Ysgafell, near Newtown, Montgomeryshire. For most of her life, Jane lived in at Neuaddd Felin*, Talgarth, because of poor health, not returning to Chelsea to live until 1856. Jane became extremely friendly with Lady Lanover (q.v.), and developed a great love of Welsh literature after she learned Welsh, taking the Bardic name *Ysgafell*.

Jane was only 18 when her *Miscellaneous Poems* were privately printed at Brecon in 1824. In 1838, her *Twenty Essays on the Practical Improvement of God's Providential Dispensations as Means to the Moral Discipline to the Christian* was published in London. A decade later she published a pamphlet in Llandovery and London, strongly disputing the *Blue Books* commissioners' findings: *Artegall; or Remarks on the Reports of the Commissioners of Inquiry into the State of Education in Wales.*

In 1854, Jane edited the work and wrote the life of that great Welshman Thomas Price, *The Literary Remains of the Rev. Thomas Price, Carhuanawc... with a Memoir of his Life.* Also in 1856, she published *The Origin, Rise, and Progress of the Paper People,* with illustrations by Lady Llanover, which describes the world of paper people created by herself and her siblings during her childhood.

1857 saw her remarkable biography of Betsi Cadwaladr (q.v.), *The Autobiography of Elizabeth Davis, a Balaclava Nurse, Daughter of Dafydd Cadwaladr.* Her extremely critical *The Literary Women of the 17th Century* and *Celtic Fables, Fairy tales and Legends versified* followed in 1861 and

1862, the latter reprinted from her contributions to *Ainsworth's Magazine* between 1849 and 1850.

Jane's ambitious *A History of Wales derived from Authentic Sources* of 1869 was published in London, and not superseded as a source of reference on Welsh history until Sir John Lloyd's superb *A History of Wales to the Edwardian Conquest* in 1911. Jane also wrote a local history of Glasbury-on-Wye, translated French work on Celtic philology and was thanked for her work in helping Brinley Richards to prepare his *Songs of Wales* (1873). Jane died at 31 Oakley Street, Chelsea and was buried in Brompton Cemetery, having lived in London for the last 29 years of her life.

\* Neuadd Felin (New Mill) has its origins in the 15th century, and internally parts of the house remain plastered with a combination of mud and horse-hair.

## LADY CHARLOTTE ELIZABETH GUEST 1812 - 15 January 1895

## TRANSLATOR, DIARIST AND EDITOR OF *THE MABINOGION*

This honorary Welshwoman was born Lady Charlotte Elizabeth Bertie, daughter of Albemarle Bertie, 9th Earl of Lindsey. In 1833, aged 21, she married Sir Josiah John Guest (1785-1852), the iron-master of Dowlais, Glamorgan, twenty-seven years her senior. Within thirteen years  of marrying, Charlotte had ten children and had translated the *Mabinogion* folk tales. Guest was the third in a line of Dowlais iron-masters, who raised Dowlais to the position of the largest and most productive ironworks in the world. By 1849, he was sole proprietor, upon whom the welfare of 12,000 people depended, and became first MP for Merthyr Tydfil.

She cared greatly about the welfare of the workers, and assisted Guest to found schools in Dowlais which were considered the best in Wales. However, Charlotte's main claim to fame is her translation of the *Mabinogion*, which was published at Llandovery (1838-1849). She was helped by Thomas Price (whose bardic name was *Carhuanawc*) and John Jones (*Ioan Tegid*). Tegid transcribed *The Red Book of Hergest* stories for Lady Charlotte, from the manuscript in Jesus College, Oxford and he helped her with the translation. It seems that Thomas Price assisted with the *Taliesin* story which was added to the original eleven stories of the *Mabinogion*.

In her journal of 28 March 1839, we read 'Today I worked hard at the translation of *Peredur*. I had the pleasure of giving birth to my fifth child and third boy today', and on 30 March we read 'I was well enough in the afternoon to correct with Lord Merthyr's [her husband Sir John Guest's] assistance the proof sheets of my book sent up by Rees'.

15 May reads: *'Peredur* is, I may now say, quite ready for the press. Only a few pages of translation remain incompleted. I do think that it has been got up and brought through the press with great speed, considering that seven weeks ago I never dreamed of printing, anything but "*Geraint*". Since that time I have transcribed it, translated it, written the notes, provided the decorations and brought it almost to the printers hands'. Her hurry was brought on by a young Breton, de la Villemarque, who had visited her and then decided to forestall her translation by publishing *Peredur* in France.

For 11 November, we read 'Mrs Waddington (Lady Llanover's mother) brought me the essays written for the prize given at Abergavenny "on the influence of the Welsh Tradition on the Literature of Europe". The prize was given to Schulz, Villemarque also wrote for it. His was really amusing to me. He made great use of my *Mabinogion* and scarcely made me any acknowledgement. On the contrary, he deliberately insinuated that I did not write the book myself. (A degree of moral turpitude which he dare not openly accuse me of). The secret of all this is his anger at being able to forestall me in the publication of *Peredur*, March 1839). Villemarque next had the cheek to send Charlotte a copy of his *Contes Bretons*, containing a translation into French of the first three parts of the *Mabinogion*. She wrote 'he tries to make it appear that he has translated straight from the Welsh without any obligation to my version. He has followed me servilely throughout and taken my notes without any acknowledgement except in one unimportant instance. Altogether it is a most shabby proceeding, but the man is too contemptible to be noticed. During the morning Merthyr [her husband] sent me the most kind notes from the House of Commons, doing all he could to soothe my ruffled feelings, but though he might calm me about what had passed in the morning before he went out, he could not prevent my feeling very ill. At night I was hardly fit to move, but I took Mary (her half-sister) to Lady Powis's and stayed there at a ball with her till daylight.'

After the publication of *Peredur/Pryderi*, she went on to publish another six parts by 1845. In her 1877 version of all seven parts, she noted that Tennyson had used her translation of *Gereint and Enid* for *The Idylls of the King*. Thus a *Mabinogion* story returned to the public as the most popular poetic work of all the Victorian era. She now turned her back on her literary career, writing: 'Now that my seven babies are growing up and require so much attention, it is quite right that I should have done with authorship. I am quite content with what will have been done when the present work is concluded, and I am sure if a woman is to do her duty as a wife and mother, the less she meddles with pen and ink the better.' Her husband was tiring of managing 12,000 workers, and now moved to Canford because of his health. However, he decided to return to his native land to die, and the couple and their (by now) ten children came back to Dowlais.

Her husband had also been MP for Honiton from 1825-1831, then for the new seat of Merthyr from 1832 until his death. Charlotte met many of the greatest figures of her age, either in London or at their Dowlais mansion. Charles Babbage, the father of computing, was their guest in Wales when trying to arouse interest in his 'Analytical Engine'. Charlotte astutely noted in her journal 'He feels how much his invention is beyond the power of the age to appreciate and this mortifies him more than it should do.' Her husband was the owner of the world's largest ironworks, in Dowlais, and when he died in 1852, Charlotte took control of the business, and continued to run the works until she remarried in 1855.

On her husband's death, the 40-year-old Lady Charlotte now supervised her five sons and five daughters and managed the Dowlais Works successfully. She married Charles Schreiber, a former MP in 1855. He had been her son Ivor's tutor in Cambridge. She was a great collector of playing cards, fans and porcelain, writing books on fans and cards, and leaving her fabulous collection of porcelain to the Victoria and Albert Museum. In 1884, her co-collector and second husband had died, and her diary for 19 November 1885 reads: 'Before 10 o'clock the storekeepers from the South Kensington came to commence their labours and worked all day. They have packed and carried away all the Bow [porcelain] - and have packed most of the Chelsea. I have been in all day attending to the packers. The dear Chelsea aviary has gone.' She had written on Charles Schreiber's death 'So ends my life on earth. It has been a very happy one, and I have much to be grateful for. Henceforth I have but to bow the head in patience, working till it shall please my merciful Father to call me hence.' Her son edited the two volume set *Lady Charlotte Schreiber's Journals: Confidences of a Collector of Ceramics and Antiques*, which was published in 1911. In 1950, the Earl of Bessborough edited *Lady Charlotte Guest, Extracts from her Journal 1833-1852.*

Charlotte was a truly remarkable woman who found fame as a translator, linguist, writer, social benefactor, businesswoman and historian. Despite bringing up 10 children in 13 years, she brought *The Mabinogion* to a massive new audience, and wrote more than 30 volumes of diaries over a period of 71 years, from the age of 12 until her death. She was a benefactor to Merthyr, ensuring a decent water supply for the first time - the only alternative drink until then was alcohol - and she sponsored a recreation area for the thousands of employees of the largest ironworks in the world. She helped modernise schools and promoted adult education, unheard of at this time for the working classes. Visiting schools, she brought in new teaching methods, and the Guest schools have been called 'the most progressive in the industrial history not only of South Wales, but of the whole of Britain in the nineteenth century.'

*Footnote:*
*The Mabinogion* is a treasury of Welsh mythology consists of folk tales from the eleventh century and earlier, which were preserved by monks writing *The White Book of Rhydderch* around 1300-1325, and *The Red Book of Hergest* c.1400. These books are the source of much of the legend surrounding King Arthur, and the collection was first translated in full into English by Lady Charlotte Guest, and published in three volumes between 1838 and 1849. A cheaper, one-volume edition was printed in 1877. Charlotte used the *Red Book*, because the *White Book*, which has older, finer versions of the tales, had not been discovered at that time. Later translations are composites of both books.

Lady Guest divided the tales into three volumes: the *Four Branches of the Mabinogi*, the *Four Independent Native Tales* and *The Three Romances* and added the story of *Taliesin* from another old manuscript. These stories are 'among the finest flowerings of Celtic genius and, taken together, a masterpiece of mediaeval European literature' according to Professor Gwyn Jones in his introduction to the Everyman edition. *The Four Branches* are the *Mabinogi* proper, the stories of *Pwyll, Branwen, Manawyddan* and *Math*. There are two short stories, *The Dream of Macsen Wledig*, and *Lludd and Llefelys*. The other two stories are the incomparable *Culhwch and Olwen,* the earliest Arthurian tale in any language, and the romantic *Dream of Rhonabwy*. The three Arthurian romances are *The Lady of the Fountain, Peredur* and *Geraint Son of Erbin*.

*The Dream of Macsen Wledig* commemorates the time of Magnus Maximus, the fifth century Roman leader of Britain (Dux Britanniarum) who took the British garrison with him to campaign across and gain most of the Western Empire of Rome. He was eventually defeated by Theodosius. There is a theory that *The Four Branches* were written by Gwenllian ferch Gruffydd (q.v.) the Welsh heroine killed by the Normans outside Cydweli, making her the earliest known woman writer in Britain (save for five Anglo-Saxon nuns whose letters are preserved.

Around 1050 to 1150, the stories known as *The Mabinogion* were first written down, possibly by Gwenllian, as they are remarkable in their female view of events. Four Welsh manuscripts (*The Four Ancient Books of Wales*) are truly outstanding pieces of mediaeval literature, of international importance. They were all written down using far older material:

*The Black Book of Carmarthen*, dating from the third quarter of the twelfth century;
*The Book of Aneirin*, written in the late thirteenth century;
*The Book of Taliesin*, from the fourteenth century; and
*The Red Book of Hergest*, also fourteenth century. In *The Red Book* are to be found Welsh translations of *British Chronicles*, the famous *Triads*, ancient poems of Llywarch Hen, and the priceless *Mabinogi* stories.

The oldest surviving manuscript in Welsh, *Llyfr du Caerfyrddin* ('The Black Book of Carmarthen') dates from around 1250. About fifty years later, in the scriptorium at Ystrad Fflur (Strata Florida Abbey), the collection of mediaeval Welsh poetry *Llawysgrif Hendregadredd*, was collected.

It is interesting to study the work of the Breton philosopher Ernest Renan (1823-1892) as regards the interlinking ethnicity and attitudes of the Celts. His entry in *The New Companion to the Literature of Wales* includes the following lines: 'In his view the Celtic nature was reserved, inward-looking, lacking in initiative or political aptitude, fatalistic and given to defending lost causes, yet redeemed by a sensitivity and deep feeling for nature and all living creatures, exhibited in Brittany by the cult of forests, springs and wells. He emphasised the close bonds of blood-relationship which are manifested among all the Celtic peoples and are expressed in their "backward look" – their faithfulness to their past and to the memory of their dead. He described *The Mabinogion* as "the real expression of the Celtic genius" and regarded it, with the legend of Arthur, as the source of all the romantic creations which in the twelfth century had "changed the direction of the European imagination". In spite of the threat of modern industrialised civilisation, Renan believed firmly that the Celtic peoples had not yet "said their last word" but might still have a mature and unique contribution to make to European life and culture.' The Professors Gwyn and Thomas Jones said that the *Mabinogion's* author 'created a miniature masterpiece. He achieved the effect of illumination and extension of time and space which lies beyond the reach of all save the world's greatest writers.' We must remember that these few surviving manuscripts are all that survives of over a millennium of warfare, burning and pillage across the whole of Wales – just what has been lost?

## GEORGE ELIOT 22 November 1819 - 22 December 1880

### MARY ANN EVANS, 'THE GREATEST LIVING ENGLISH NOVELIST', AUTHOR OF 'THE GREATEST NOVEL IN THE ENGLISH LANGUAGE'

Mary Ann Evans was born at South Farm, near Griff, in the parish of Colton, Warwickshire, the youngest child of the Welsh land agent Robert Evans and of Christiana Pearson. Robert was a former carpenter who had moved to Warwickshire from working as a carpenter near Ashbourne. He then became a forester, before becoming a land agent and surveyor for five estates in the Midlands. The gentle Robert Evans had a reputation for trustworthiness across Warwickshire, when he was working for Sir Roger Newdigate of Arbury Hall. Evans had lost his first wife, by whom there was a son and daughter, and of his second wife Christiana, little is known. The family moved to Griff House in March 1820. Mary was described as a 'queer, three-cornered, awkward girl, who sat in corners and shyly watched her elders'. In 1924 she went to Miss Latham's Boarding School, then in 1928 to Mrs Wallington's Boarding School at Nuneaton. There she became a protégée of the Welsh governess, Miss Maria Lewis, who kept in touch with Mary for fourteen years after she left in 1932. Mary Ann Evans then went to Nant Glyn Welsh Baptist School in Coventry, now 29 Warwick Row, from 1832-35, where she probably made her first attempts at writing fiction. From 1935-39 she was at Miss Franklin's School at Coventry, where she worked to rid herself of her Midlands accent and 'cultivated the low, well-modulated, musical voice, which impressed everyone who knew George Eliot in later years.'

However, her mother had been ill for some time, and in 1839 died. The 19-year-old Mary Ann left school to take care of her father at Griff House, and they moved to a large semi-detached house, Bird Grove, on Foleshill Road near Coventry in 1841. It was then quite a rural setting, set well back from the road, but the area has now been developed and there is a

George Eliot Road there. She continued studying, especially Greek and Hebrew, and read Walter Scott in the evenings to her ailing father. In 1842, she stopped going to church, upsetting Maria Lewis and her father considerably. From 1841, she had become friendly with the like-minded Charles and Cara Bray, and met many important thinkers, such as Ralph Waldo Emerson, at their house. Emerson said 'that young lady has a calm and serious soul.' Mary Ann worked on the translation of Strauss' book on religious thought, *Das Leben Jesu*, which was published in 1844 under the name Marian Evans. She continued to nurse his father until his death in 1849, but Robert Evans had not softened his attitude towards his 29-year-old agnostic daughter, leaving her virtually nothing in his will.

She toured the Continent with the Brays, but stayed in Geneva alone before returning in 1850, resolving to move to London. She spent seven months with the Brays there, as she had nowhere else to stay, and met a London publisher named John Chapman. Impressed by her Strauss translation, he asked her to contribute an article for the *Westminster Review*. It was excellently received, and she moved to lodge with Chapman at 142 Strand, with Chapman's wife and mistress. After some time, the philanderer Chapman was caught with Mary, and his wife and mistress forced him to send her back to Coventry. In 1851, he purchased the *Westminster Review* and desperately needed an editor. Agreement was reached by all four parties that Mary could take up lodgings again, if her relationship with Chapman remained purely business. In two years, she transformed the *Review* back into the great intellectual journal it had been under John Stuart Mill. Her social circle now included the great thinkers of the day. Although she was not physically attractive, her friends loved her expressive face and eyes, her gentleness, intellect and beautiful, low voice.

Mary became tired of living with the Chapmans and of editing the *Review* by 1853. She had met George Henry Lewes in 1851, and fell in love with him. Lewes and his wife Agnes believed in 'free love', and his wife had five children by his friend, Thornton Hunt. Mary moved into lodgings in 1853 for her affair with Lewes to progress. In 1854, her translation of Feuerbach's *Essence of Christianity* was published, and it was the last time that 'Marian Evans' appeared on the title page of any of her books. She had now decided to live openly as Lewes' spiritual wife and lover, knowing that she would be an outcast forever if he left her.

They spent eight months on the Continent, and she took lodgings in Dover on her return in early 1855. Mary had asked George Lewes to separate permanently from his wife Agnes, as a divorce was impossible. When Agnes confirmed that a reunion was not possible, Mary moved to London, they took rooms as 'Mr and Mrs Lewes', and their 'marriage' officially started. The couple were ostracised at first by society, but Chapman asked Mary to take over the *'Belles Lettres'* section of the *Westminster Review* at £50 a year, and their social circle slowly enlarged.

In June 1856, the couple moved to Tenby and Mary thought seriously about writing fiction, encouraged by George. On their return to London, she began to write *The Sad Fortunes of the Reverend Amos Barton*, later to become a part of *Scenes from a Clerical Life*. Mr and Mrs Hackit in *Amos Barton* are based upon Mary's parents. Lewes sent the story to his publisher, John Blackwood, stating that it was the work of a friend (Blackwood presumed a male) who wished to remain anonymous. Writing was not seen as a female profession at this time.

It was published on New Year's Day, 1857, and the 37-year-old Mary adopted 'George Eliot' as her pseudonym, because 'George was Mr Lewes' Christian name, and Eliot was a good, mouth-filling, easily-pronounced word.' Shortly after she told her family that she was 'married' to George. However, when they pressed her for details, she disclosed that the marriage was not legal, and her two sisters and two brothers from this point shunned her. Apart from her half-brother Robert and half-sister Fanny, her sister Christiana [Chrissy] and brother Isaac also never communicated with her again, although they read her novels. Mary especially missed Isaac's friendship.

*Scenes from a Clerical Life* was a great success, and there was much talk about the identity of the author. 'George Eliot' now began work on the great novel *Adam Bede,* which she completed in 1858. It was hugely popular, with even Queen Victoria praising it. It was published in 3 volumes by Blackwood on February 1, with a second edition in March and a second impression of the second edition in April. There was a 3rd edition in June, and second, third and fourth impressions in July, August and October. This tragic love story was modelled on her father as the title character. In Griff House today is a painting of Robert Evans, referred to by the family living there as the picture of *'Adam Bede'.* In 1859, the 'Georges' bought their first home, outside London, and the literary circle discovered via John Chapman and others that Mary was 'George'.

Blackwood now refused to publish George Eliot's new novel about destructive family relations, *The Mill on the Floss* for a short time, worried about the controversy of Mary's life, and its effects on sales. However, the book was published, again with massive sales. It was published by Blackwood in 3 volumes in April, and there was a 3rd impression by May. The couple moved back to London, but Mary became depressed about the social ridicule surrounding her status. She was seen as the villain, while George Lewes' adulterous wife was seen as the long-suffering victim. There were still very few female intimates of their small social circle. From 1858 they lived at Holly Lodge, Wimbledon Park Road, Wandsworth, where *The Mill on the Floss* was written, probably the most beautiful of all her books. They then moved upmarket to The Priory, North Bank, St John's Wood, which became their London home from 1863 to 1880.

April 1861 saw the publication of *Silas Marner,* and then Mary went to Italy to research *Romolo,* which was to be set in 15th-century Florence. This was serialised in fourteen monthly instalments from 1862 in *Cornhill Magazine,* and by now Mary had accrued the massive fortune of £16,000 from royalties. In 1865 she visited Paris and Brittany, and in 1866 Blackwood published her *Felix Holt - The Radical.* In 1867 Mary went with George to Germany, and in 1868 her dramatic poem *The Spanish Gipsy* was published. *Middlemarch* was begun in 1869, and published in parts by Blackwood from 1871-72. It is her greatest work, inspired by her life at Coventry. We see the sexual and intellectual frustrations of Dorothea Brooke interwoven with other narrative lines, and the book is a sad comment upon female aspirations. Henry James called it 'a treasure-house of detail', and Martin Amis and Julian Barnes reckon it to be the greatest novel in the English language.

Apart from public acclaim, her literary and social circle grew with this esteemed work. Their social ostracism ended to the point that George and Mary looked for somewhere in the country to escape the constant stream of visitors. Mary was now seriously wealthy, the equivalent of a multi-millionaire in today's money. In 1874 she started to write *Daniel Deronda,* while suffering severely from kidney stones and depression. Upon its publication in 1876, she was regarded as 'the greatest living English novelist'. In her writing, she had developed the method of psychological depiction which we know in modern fiction. Her interest in the interior life of people, and their moral problems and pressures, anticipated the narrative methods we see today. D.H. Lawrence wrote 'It was really George Eliot who started it all. It was she who started putting action inside.'

The couple managed to prevent most people visiting them in London, but their 'business manager', American banker John Cross always visited on Sundays, and he found them the house of their dreams in the countryside in 1876. Lewes began to suffer from agonising cramps, however, and died at their London home on 30 November 1878. Mary refused to go to the funeral, locked herself in her room for a week, and refused to see any visitors. Cross wrote often to see her, but she would not meet him, writing 'each day seems a new beginning - a new acquaintance with grief'. However, she at last saw Cross on 23 February 1879. This year saw the publication of *Impressions of Theophrastus Such*. Cross grew close to Mary, and asked her to marry him three times. They eventually wed in May, 1880 and honeymooned in Italy. He was 40, and the bride 60 years old. In November she had her 61st birthday, and the couple moved to Chelsea on December 3$^{rd}$, where she contracted a throat infection, possible a double quinsy. Just 19 days after moving into her new house, she passed away at 4 Cheyne Walk, Chelsea, and was buried next to George Lewes in Highgate Cemetery.

*Footnote:*
Her 1715 mansion in Cheyne Walk was sold in 2015 to Michael Bloomberg, the billionaire former mayor of New York for £16 million in a bidding war, a million pounds more than the initial asking price.


## ANNA LAETITIA WARING 19 April 1823 - 10 May 1910

## HYMN WRITER

Born at Plas-y-Felin, Glynneath, Laetitia was the daughter of Elijah Waring (1788-1857), who had come to Wales in 1810. Such was Elijah's interest in Welsh history and culture, that he started and edited a magazine in 1813 to enlighten Englishmen. The periodical, *The Cambrian Visitor: A Monthly Miscellany*, was printed at Swansea over a period of eight months and he lost a great deal of money on the venture. In 1814, settling at Neath, he married Deborah Price, the sister of Joseph Tregelles Price, the ironmaster of the Neath Abbey iron-works. Price was a prominent Quaker, patron of the Anti-Slavery Movement, and first President of the Peace Society.

Elijah Waring was also a Quaker, and preached in Nonconformist chapels in the Neath district. Later a Wesleyan, he was a strong proponent of

Parliamentary Reform, and published several articles to this effect in *The Cambrian*. He became close to the great Iolo Morganwg, and published his famous biography of Iolo in 1850, *Recollections and Anecdotes of Edward Williams, the Bard of Glamorgan*. In 1835, he took his family to Cardiff, and then to Hotwells, Clifton, Bristol. In 1855 Waring returned to Neath and died there at the home of his son in 1857.

Laetitia was raised as a Quaker, moving with her father from Neath to Clifton when she was 12. She was baptised into the Church of England at

St Martin's, Winnal, Winchester in 1847. Deeply involved in philanthropic work, she worked hard for the Discharged Prisoners' Aid Society, spending much time visiting Bristol prisons. According to her friend, Mary S. Talbot, Waring 'visited in the prisons of Bridewell, and at Horfield, Bristol, for many years. To one who spoke to her of the painfulness of such work she answered, 'It is like watching by a filthy gutter to pick out a jewel here and there, as the foul stream flows by.'

**Laetitia Waring's birthplace is now apartments**

She read daily from the original *Hebrew Psalter* throughout her life, learning Hebrew in order to read and study the *Old Testament* in its original language. Anna published *Hymns and Meditations* in 1850, and *Additional Hymns* in 1854. According to *Julian's Dictionary of Hymnology*, 'These hymns are marked by great simplicity, concentration of thought, and elegance of diction. They are popular, and deserve to be so.' In 1864, they were published in Boston, America. Little is known of her life, but 33 of her best hymns are available on the website cyberhymnal.org. *In Heavenly Love Abiding* is one of her most popular works, and was published in a 1927 Scottish hymnal to the Finnish folk-tune *Nyland*:

'In Heavenly love abiding,
No change my heart shall fear;
And safe is such confiding,
For nothing changes here:
The storm may roar about me,
My heart may low be laid;
But God is round about me,
And I can be dismayed'.

## VARINA BANKS HOWELL DAVIS 7 May 1826 – 16 October 1905

## FIRST LADY OF THE CONFEDERATE STATES OF AMERICA

Varina was born of Welsh immigrant parents at 'The Briars', near Natchez, Mississippi. The Briars still exists, a beautiful mansion designed by Levi Weekes of Philadelphia. Varina's father, William Burr Howell, was a cousin of the politician Aaron Burr, and moved there in 1829. Varina was a deeply religious, intelligent woman, educated by a private tutor and close family friend, later attending finishing school to polish her social graces. In 1838 the Welsh war-hero Jefferson Davis had been elected to the House of Representatives, during which time he again served under Taylor in the Mexican-American War, and sat in the US Senate from 1847 to 1851.

Varina first met him aged just 17, when he made a memorable impression, as she wrote to her mother: 'I do not know whether this Mr Jefferson Davis is young or old. He looks both at times; but I believe he is old, for from what I hear he is only two years younger than you are [the rumour was correct]. He impresses me as a remarkable kind of man, but of uncertain temper, and has a way of taking for granted that everybody agrees with him when he expresses an opinion, which offends me; yet he is most agreeable and has a peculiarly sweet voice and a winning manner of asserting himself. The fact is, he is the kind of person I should expect to rescue one from a mad dog at any risk, but to insist upon a stoical indifference to the fright afterward.' On February 23rd, 1845 Jefferson Davis married Varina Howell at The Briars. She spoke French, played the piano beautifully, and was interested in politics and current affairs, quite unlike the other 'Southern Belles' of the time. Her parents, especially her mother, resisted the marriage, as the widower Jefferson Davis was 18 years her senior, but they attended the wedding. Varina abandoned her Whig convictions, deferred to Davis' politics, and eventually was to become the guardian of his beleaguered reputation.

Jeff Davis was Secretary of War under President Franklin Pierce from 1853 until 1857, when he returned to the Senate, becoming leader of the Southern Democrats. Varina's opinion was that politics was 'everything which darkens the sunlight and contracts the happy sphere of home', but was an excellent hostess in Washington DC. As well as her social duties, she helped Jefferson write his speeches and letters. The German-born abolitionist Carl Schurz said that Jeff Davis met every expectation of what 'a grand personage the War Minister of this great Republic must be'. As unofficial 'spokesman for the South', Jefferson however viewed the Southern states as 'a country within a country'.

In 1860 South Carolina issued a declaration of secession from the USA. By January 1861, Georgia, Florida, Alabama, Mississippi, Florida, Louisiana, Texas and Arkansas had also seceded from the union. Virginia and North Carolina soon followed. Jefferson Davis was elected in February 1861 as President of the Confederate States of America. Jefferson had not wanted the presidency, wishing instead to serve in the Confederate Army, and Varina proved to have considerable inner fortitude. Although they were both ambitious, she knew of his 'super-sensitive temperament', and that he would be deeply affected by office. The ensuing bitter Civil War lasted from 1861 to 1865, with the vast military capability of the Union North eventually overcoming the Confederate Southern states. During the whole war period, Varina had to tend to her sickly husband and helped manage many of his official affairs. She had many detractors and was seen as 'the power behind the throne' as she tried to protect him from his critics and a workload that weakened him. Such was her influence that some generals and cabinet ministers 'took pains to cultivate her good will.

The great and brutal battles of Manassas (where Davis took the field), Appomattox, Shiloh, Gettysburg, and the two battles at Bull Run echo through history, and the South has still not forgotten Sherman's devastation. 359,528 Union and 258,000 Confederate troops had died in the young republic. The turning point in the war, more than any other, was the mass-production of the Springfield rifle in Connecticut. It had greater accuracy and three times the range of the old smooth-bore rifle. On the fateful third day of Gettysburg, 12,000 Confederate soldiers had mounted one last, great, Napoleonic assault on the Union lines. All but 300 were mown down before they reached the Northerners. (Running out of footwear, the main reason for the horrific battle of Gettysburg was to obtain new boots for Robert E. Lee's troops).

As living conditions in the Confederate capital, Richmond, deteriorated from the second year of the War, with the effects of the Unionist blockade, some of the city's residents decried Varina's entertaining guests at The White House of the Confederacy. However, others complained that she did not entertain lavishly enough. Her loyalty to the South was also called into question, as her father had first settled in the North. One thing is certain, that she retaliated quickly and furiously when Jefferson's abilities as a politician and war-leader were questioned. Of her six children, one was born during the war years, and another one died tragically, falling off a balcony.

John Morgan's 'Alligator Horsemen' were the most hated and feared of all the Confederate soldiers. Courageous guerrillas, led by a

Welshman, and no atrocities can be held against their name in this dirty war. By 1865, Morgan's 'Second Kentucky Horse' had lost their horses and was a scattered regiment of foot soldiers, as the Union rampaged through the Southern States. Even now, they were so highly rated that they were the chosen élite troops, to assist the Welsh Confederate President Jefferson Davis, in his flight from Richmond, before his capture*.

After his capture near Irwinville, Georgia, Jefferson Davis was put in shackles and imprisoned. Varina was with him when he was arrested. Varina sadly sent their five children to Canada with her mother, and fought for her husband's early release after two years in poor conditions. Varina was prohibited from leaving Georgia without Federal permission. Davis refused to request the official pardon which would restore his citizenship. Varina's incessant lobbying led to Jefferson's release from prison in May 1867, and they returned to Mississippi.

The couple lived in near-poverty until the early 1870's, when they went to an estate called Beauvoir in Mississippi, which had been left to Jefferson Davis by a childhood friend. A private businessman and author after his release, Davis died in New Orleans aged 82, in 1889. Varina wrote her memoirs, and left Beauvoir to the state as a Confederate veteran's home, stipulating that it be preserved as 'a perpetual memorial sacred to the memory of Jefferson Davis'. She then moved to New York, supporting herself by writing articles for magazines and newspapers, where she died. Her final years were extremely sad for Varina, as she was survived by only one of her children.

* After Robert E. Lee surrendered the Confederate Army at Appomattox on April 9th, 1865, Jefferson and Varina fled southwards and westwards, with a $100,000 price on his head. President Johnson wrongly believed him to have been responsible for the assassination of Abraham Lincoln. His capture would close the sad saga of the Civil War. However, when finally apprehended in a dawn raid on 10 May, Jeff Davies was dressed in women's clothing, wearing Varina's 'raglan' and her dark shawl. He rushed from his tent as Union soldiers approached, and Varina explained 'Knowing that he would be recognised I pleaded with him to let me throw over him a large waterproof which had often served him in sickness during the summer season for a dressing gown, and which I hoped might so cover his person that in the grey of the morning he would not be recognised. As he strode off, I threw over his head a little black shawl which was around my own shoulders, seeing that he could not find his hat and after he started sent my coloured woman with him with a bucket of water, hoping that he would not be recognised.' Jefferson himself wrote: 'As it was quite dark in the tent, I picked up what supposed to be my "raglan", a waterproof, light overcoat, without sleeves; it was subsequently found to be my wife's, so very like my own as to be mistaken for it.'

Despite the Davis claims, Northerners saw this as a cowardly and ignoble action, one account saying that Mrs Davis and her sister, Mrs Howell, tried to disguise Jefferson as 'their poor old mother', to take her away from the firing. An account in Harper's shows Davis in a hoop skirt and bonnet, while a Union soldier looks on, saying 'She's the Bearded Lady... Where's Barnum?' (Barnum was a well-known showman and circus owner, who offered $500 for the 'petticoat' which Jefferson wore on his escape). A well-known song, 'Jeff in Petticoats' ended:

'Now, when he saw the game was up, he started for the woods,
His band-box hung upon his arm, quite full of fancy goods.
Said Jeff: They'll never take me now, I'm sure I'll not be seen,
They'd never think to look for me, beneath this crinoline!' ...
The ditch that Jeff was hunting for, he found was very near.
He tried to SHIFT his base again, his neck felt rather queer.
Just on the out-SKIRTS of a wood, his dainty shape was seen,
His boots stuck out, and now they'll hang old Jeff in Crinoline!'

## SARAH EMILY DAVIES 22 April 1830 – 13 July 1921

## FOUNDER OF GIRTON COLLEGE, EDUCATIONAL PIONEER, SUFFRAGIST AND FEMINIST

Strangely, Sarah Emily Davies does not appear in either *The Dictionary of Welsh National Biography*\*, nor *The New Companion to the Literature of Wales*. Her father was John Davies, born in 1795 at Llanddewi Brefi in Ceredigion. On his mother's death, his father emigrated to America, leaving John with his uncle. From inauspicious beginnings, John Davies went to Queen's College, Cambridge in 1820, and took his Bachelor of Divinity in 1831 and his Doctor of Divinity in 1844. John was a religious philosopher, publishing books on the *Testaments*, Swiss and French scenery, and his greatest work was *The Estimate of the Human Mind*. Apart from religious posts, he also ran a boarding school at Southampton for some time, which was where Sarah Emily Davies was born. She grew up in Chichester, and when she was 18, her brother Llewellyn gained a First in Classics and a Second in Mathematics at Cambridge. He became a curate at St Anne's, Limehouse, London, and was a lasting influence upon Emily.

Always known as Emily, she relied for her education upon her brother, and stayed with her parents. However, in 1855 her sister Jane contracted a lung disease and died just three years later. Her brother Henry contracted the same illness, and Emily went to tend him to Algiers, but he died on their return to England in 1858. In this same year her brother William died in China, after being invalided as a naval chaplain in the Crimea. Thus Emily was forced to remain with and help her parents, at their rectory in Gateshead. However, on John Davies's death in 1861, Emily and her mother moved to 17 Lanham Place, London, where Emily became involved in the Women's Movement. She already knew Elizabeth Garrett, whom she had advised to become a doctor. Also she had met Madame Bodichon (Barbara Leigh Smith) and her sister in Algiers. Her brother Llewellyn was now chaplain to Queen Victoria, and an advocate of higher education for women, and Emily now had the opportunity to 'qualify' herself in education, taking lessons in Latin and Greek. In London, Emily formed a committee for obtaining the admission of women to University Examinations.

At 19 Langham Place was the headquarters of the Society for the Employment of Women, and of the *Englishwoman's Journal*. One of the most active workers there was Madame Bodichon, and she was recognised as a leader of the Women's Movement, which itself had been inspired by the Married Women's Property Bill of 1857. In 1862, Emily wrote a paper on *Medicine as a Profession for Women*, presented at the National Association for the Promotion of Social Science in London. For six months she acted as editor of the *Englishwoman's Journal*, and started the *Victoria Magazine* in 1863. In 1864, she contributed a paper to the Social Science Congress, *On Secondary Instructions as Relating to Girls*. She stated 'A woman's reason, means, in the popular sense, no reason at all...probably only women who have laboured under it can understand the weight of discouragement produced by being perpetually told that as women nothing much is ever to be expected of them, and it is not worth their while to exert themselves'. George Eliot came into Emily's circle of friends and colleagues at this time.

Through Emily Davies' untiring efforts, the admission of girls to the Cambridge Senior and Junior local examinations was obtained in 1865. In 1866, she published the book *On the Higher Education of Women*. Also in 1866, Emily was one of the organisers of the first suffrage petition presented by John Stuart Mill. From 1867 onwards Emily worked wholeheartedly towards female suffrage, using her pen rather than taking part in demonstrations. However, her main focus was now in the establishment of a new college for women. Bedford College and other women's colleges already existed, but Emily wanted female students to be able to gain ordinary University degrees of Oxford and Cambridge. Money slowly came in for her proposed college, but by 1868 only £2,000 had been promised. Of this £100 was from Emily herself, £100 from Mrs Garrett-Anderson, £50 from George Eliot and £1,000 from Madame Bodichon. A press report ridiculed the scheme: 'It is difficult to treat with gravity this preposterous proposal of a University career for the potential wives of Englishmen without being betrayed into an indignation, such as, nowadays, is never effective, and is not infrequently ludicrous.'

However, in spite of the fact that the College would not be recognised by the Universities, a house for its premises was found in Hitchin, and five students had asked for enrolment in 1869. Aware of the inadequacy of her own education, Emily looked for a temporary 'Mistress' to run the college, and temporarily chose an old friend, Mrs Manning. By 1871 there were eleven young women studying at Hitchin and new premises had to be found. Emily saw her institution as a College, not an advance on existing girls' schools, and regarded it as essential that each student had her own private room for study. The College Committee appealed for another £7,000, and some of the press started to support her cause. Thus it was that in 1873 Girton College was opened in September, with the first newcomers being greeted by Emily Davies and the sound of carpenters' hammers.

Emily insisted upon a strict entrance examination for candidates (unlike many other colleges), that Girton should aim at being received into the University of Cambridge, and that it should be connected to the Church of England. For two years Emily was not only Secretary, but Mistress and on its Committee. In 1875 she wrote to Madame Bodichon 'I am 49 today - a good age for retiring into private life... as to your saying that the College is mine you know that is nonsense. It has taken all of us to get this far, and it wants us all still.' Thus in 1875 she resigned as Mistress, but remaining as Secretary for 30 years, she returned to London to live.

In 1896, she wrote a pamphlet *Women in the Universities of England and Scotland*, explaining the need for higher education: 'Let it be distinctly understood that the choice is not between a life wholly given up to study, and a life spent in active domestic duty. The dilemma thus stated is untrue on both sides; for while on the one hand, giving to women the opportunity of a complete education does not mean that they will spend all their lives in reading, so, on the other, denying them education does not mean that they will occupy themselves in household affairs... The aim of these new colleges will not be directed towards changing the occupations of women, but rather towards securing that whatever they do shall be done well. Whether as mistresses of households, mothers, teachers, or as labourers in art, science, literature... their work suffers from lack of training.' Until 1904 she was on the Girton Committee, where the Emily Davies Court is named after her.

In London, Emily worked with the London Schoolmistresses Association, and became Chairman of the London Society for Women's Suffrage. In 1906, aged 76, she led a deputation to Parliament demanding votes for women. Aged 80, Davies published *Thoughts on Some Questions Relating to Women*, and aged 90, she saw the enfranchisement of women in 1918. Emily was sent congratulations by the London Society, and she registered her first vote in the following year. She was one of the very few early members of the first Women's Suffrage Society still left alive to record their vote in a Parliamentary election. Glasgow University gave her an honorary LL.D, and her fifty years of work for Girton were commemorated by an address from over 1,300 subscribers, and an award of 700 guineas. A commemorative service was held at St Martin-in-the-Fields, after her death, aged 92.

* There is merely a footnote regarding Emily under her father's entry, as 'an early advocate of the higher education of women and founder of what later became Girton College, Oxford'. Girton was the first college in England to educate women, but its students were not allowed membership of Cambridge University until April 1948.

*Footnote:*
The papers of this amazing lady are held at Girton College, and her contribution to female advancement has been over looked. The papers include the *Family Chronicle* (an account of family and other matters written by Davies in 1905, covering the years 1847-68) and papers relating to the following: London University degrees for women; Elizabeth Garrett and medical examinations; the *Victoria Magazine*, 1863-4; the London School Board, 1870-73; the Schools Enquiry Commission, 1864-70; admission of girls to local examinations, 1858-69; the London Association of Schoolmistresses and the Kensington Society, 1866-69; Cambridge and Oxford degrees for women, 1880-97; Girton College, 1867-1903, and the College Jubilee, 1919; and women's suffrage, 1907-18. There are also presentations, obituaries, newspaper cuttings, pamphlets and letters to the press. The papers were given to Girton College by members of Emily Davies' family, the bulk being received from Miss Llewellyn Davies in 1930. In 1927, Barbara Stephen wrote *Emily Davies and Girton College –* perhaps someone can use the Davies papers to write a new book upon Emily.


## ANNA HARRIETTE LEONOWENS 5 or 6 November 1831 – 19 January 1915

## ANNA EDWARDS, TUTOR TO THE CHILDREN OF THE KING OF SIAM

Anna Harriette Leonowens is better known as the tutor to the royal children in Siam. How much *The King and I* with Yul Brynner and Deborah Kerr replicates the true story is a matter of debate. It had previously been filmed in 1946, as *Anna and the King of Siam*, starring Rex Harrison. The film was based on the Margaret Landon's 1943 novel, *Anna and the King of Siam*, and has recently been remade with Jodie Foster* starring. Her maiden name appears to have been Anna Edwards**, and she stated that she was born in Caernarfon. In Anna's autobiography, she wrote 'the Romans had not stamped the love of freedom out of our Welsh hearts, nor could the English do that in the centuries that followed.'

Anna had sailed to Bombay aged fifteen to join her mother and stepfather. Her drunken stepfather wished to marry her off quickly to a man twice her age, but she escaped the situation by going on a long tour of the Middle East with the Reverend Percy Badger. (Her sister Eliza had been similarly married off at 15 years-old, to a 38 year-old sergeant). Anna married a Welsh clerk, Thomas Leon Owens on her return to India, when she was aged just 18, although she called him an army major in her memoirs. Owens found it difficult to hold down a post, and they moved around a great deal, with Anna giving birth to a son named Louis*** and a girl named Avis (probably both were born aboard ships). Her husband died early of apoplexy, in Penang, Malaya, leaving her a penniless 27-year-old widow  with two infants on 8 May 1859. At sometime her husband had changed his name from Owens to Leonowens, possibly to escape his debts.

Friends now helped her to set up a small school for officers' children in Singapore, and Avis was sent back to England. According to Dr. W.S. Bristowe, Anna at this time deliberately began camouflaging her origins and her past. In the 1970's he wrote a biography of Louis Leonowens, called *Louis and the King of Siam*, and discovered most of the pertinent facts about Anna's background. Even her children did not know the truth, that Anna's mother was half-Indian, and Anna made a complete break with her sister Eliza back in India, to further conceal the fact. Such were social prejudices at the time that it would have been unthinkable for officers to send their children to a Eurasian's school, or that of a woman from the lower social classes. Thus, apart from inventing a captain father, she also transformed her feckless dead husband into a glamorous major, who had 'died in a tiger hunt'. Later, her sister Eliza's eldest daughter married a Eurasian named Pratt, and her youngest son took the stage-name of 'Boris Karloff'.

In Singapore, she received an invitation from the King of Siam. In 1862, we know that King Mongkut (Rama IV) was looking for a new English teacher for his wives and 64 children. The Christian missionaries he was using were boring his family, emphasising the *Bible* rather than secular learning, and he employed Mrs Leonowens to replace them. She went there with her son Louis, who is never mentioned by name in her writings, being referred to as the 'boy'. Her letter of appointment, signed by the king, still survives:

'English Era, 1862, 26 February
GRAND ROYAL PALACE, BANGKOK

To Mrs A.H. Leonowens:
MADAM: We are in good pleasure, and satisfaction at heart, that you are in willingness to undertake the education of our beloved royal children. And we hope that in doing your education on us and on our children (whom English call inhabitants of a benighted land) you will do your best endeavour for knowledge of English language, science, and literature, and not for conversion to Christianity; as the followers of Buddha are mostly aware of the powerfulness of truth and virtue, as well as the followers of Christ, and are more desirous to have facility of the English language and literature than new religions. We beg to invite you to our royal palace to do your endeavourment upon us and our children. We shall expect to see you here on return of Siamese steamer *Chow Phya.* We have written to Mr William Adamson, and to our consul at Singapore, to authorise to do best arrangement for you and ourselves. Believe me.
Yours faithfully,
S.S.P.P. MAHA Mongkut'

Anna worked at the king's court in Bangkok for five years. She does not seem to have been popular with the small British colony of merchants and consular officials, and was never asked into their social circle. Instead she mixed with the American Protestant missionaries, headed by Dr Dan Beach Bradley, who seemed to believe her stories. After King Mongkut's death, her services were no longer required by the new King Chulalongkorn, Rama V, and she returned to England in 1868 to take up a new career, writing books.

She thus recorded her first meeting with the Crown Prince: 'The Prince Somdetch Chowfa Chualalonkorn was about 10 years old when I was appointed to teach him. Being the eldest son of the queen consort, he held the first rank among the children of the king, as heir-apparent to the throne. For a Siamese, he was a handsome lad; of stature neither noticeably tall nor short; figure symmetrical and compact, and dark complexion. He was, moreover, modest and affectionate, eager to learn, and easy to influence.'

Anna's *The English Governess at the Siamese Court* (1870) and its sequel *The Romance of the Harem* (1872) were extremely popular and filmed a century later as *The King and I.* The 60-year-old king had around 600 women in his harem. He was a deeply religious man, who had spent most of his life as a monk, was educated in Western sciences and fluent in English. He is known as 'The Father of Thai Science'. During his 17 years on the throne, after 26 spent in a monastery, he fathered 82 children. The Inner Palace where he took up residence was a city of women - no males above the age of 11 were allowed in, and there lived the princesses of the blood, and the royal harem, all with female attendants. Anna despised the harem system, and wrote: 'How I have pitied these ill-fated sisters of mine, imprisoned without a crime! If they could but have rejoiced once more in the freedom of the fields and woods, what new births of gladness might have been theirs, - they who with a gasp of despair and moral death first entered those royal dungeons; never again to come forth alive! And yet have I known more than one of them who accepted her fate with a repose of manner and a sweetness of smile that told how dead must be the heart under that still exterior.'

Anna wrote of King Rama IV: 'Somdetch Phra Paramendr Maha Mongkut, late Supreme King of Siam, it may be safely said (for all his capricious provocations of temper and his snappish greed of power) that he was in the best sense of the epithet, the most remarkable of all the oriental princes of the present century, - unquestionably the most progressive of all the supreme rulers of Siam, of whom the native historians enumerate not less than forty, reckoning from the founding of the ancient capital (Ayudia or Ayuo-deva, "the abode of gods") in AD 1350. He was the legitimate son of the king P'hra Chow-P'hra Pooti-lootlah, commonly known as Phen-den-Klang; and his mother, daughter of the youngest sister of the king Somdetch P'hra Bouromah Rajah Pooti Yout Fah, was one of the most admired princesses of her time, and is described as equally beautiful and virtuous. She devoted herself assiduously to the education of her sons, of whom the second, the subject of these notes, was born in 1804; and the youngest, her best beloved, was the late Second King of Siam'.

The King's life was strictly regulated by palatine law over the centuries, and his daily routine was:

| | |
|---|---|
| 7am | The King rose from bed |
| 8am | He partook of a light repast consisting of rice gruel |
| 9am | He gave audience to the officers of the Royal Guards |
| 10am | He took his morning meal and retired again to bed |
| 11am | The ladies of the palace attended him |
| 1pm | He went out on an excursion |
| 2pm | He gave audience to his children and members of the Royal family |
| 3pm | He presided over a council of his ministers and the high officers of the realm and gave his decisions on affairs of state |
| 4pm | He went on an excursion |
| 5pm | He went to the Royal Chapel |
| 6pm | He decided on the affairs of the palace |
| 7pm | He studied the art of war |
| 8pm | He conferred with astrologers and pundits and discussed with them Religion and Philosophy |
| 9pm | A meal was served to the King |

| Midnight | Musicians and singers were brought before the King |
|----------|---------------------------------------------------|
| 1am | Storytellers were brought before the King |
| 2 or 3am | The King retired to bed |

Her books are sensationalist and entertaining, but full of errors. She was not hired as a governess, but as the king's letter makes clear, as a teacher of English. She makes mistakes about Thailand's past, does not understand Buddhism, and identifies a picture of Prince Chulalongkorn, the crown prince and her most notable student, as that of a princess. She claims to have spoken fluent Thai, but her language is full of errors. Her greatest mistakes are in *The Romance of the Harem*, when one historian commented that 'her store of pertinent facts was running low.' In it she claimed that the king threw wives who displeased him into underground dungeons at the Grand Palace, but there are no dungeons because of the watery soil. She also said that the king publicly tortured and burned a monk with whom Anna had fallen in love.

After leaving Thailand in 1868, Anna spent several years in America, where her books were written and she achieved great fame, before settling in Canada with her daughter in 1875. She spent the last 40 years of her life in Canada, 20 of those spent in Halifax, which she called home. Aged 66 in 1897, she founded the Victoria School of Design in Halifax (known as the Nova Scotia College of Art and Design, NSCAD since 1925). Anna was a well-known opponent of slavery, and also became an active suffragette, founding the Halifax Local Council of Women. She lived in Halifax until 1897. There is an Anna Leonowens Gallery in Halifax for displays of art. Its mandate reads: 'Anna Leonowens was a party to the founding of the (NSCAD) institution and the history of her life is a testament to a probing, creative spirit directed towards service.'

She died in Montreal aged 85, and her Mount Royal Cemetery gravestone reads:

'Anna Harriett Leonowens
Beloved Wife of
Major Thomas Lorne Leonowens
1834-1915
Duty was the guide to her life
And the love of her heart
To her life was beautiful and good
She was a benediction to all who knew her
A breath of the spirit of God.'

* This 1999 version, claiming to be a 'true story', was denounced for its inaccuracies by the Thai government and its release banned. The King of Siam's (Rama V's) response to her first book had been that she 'has supplied by her invention that which is deficient in her memory.' A website, thaistudents.com is

an excellent source of material upon her fabrications. The movie company Fox pronounced on its website: 'Set in 19th century Thailand, *Anna and the King* is the true story of the British governess Anna Leonowens, who is employed by the King (Chow Yun-Fat) to look after his many children. Soon after she arrives in this exotic country, Anna finds herself engaged in a battle of wits with the strong-willed ruler.' The film suggests that there was a romance between Anna and the King, and gives her credit for social reforms either carried out before she arrived, or initiated by other people. Fox had wanted to film the movie in Thailand, but it had to be made on location in Malaysia.

** She said that her name was Anna Crawford, born in Wales in 1834, and that her father was Captain Thomas Crawford who died in a Sikh uprising in India when she was just six years old. It appears, however, that her father was Thomas Edwards, a cabinet-maker who enlisted in the Bombay infantry in 1825. He married there Mary Anne Glasscock, the daughter of a gunner in the Bengal Artillery and a local Indian woman. Eliza was their first daughter, but Edwards died three months before Anna was born and her mother remarried a corporal in the Engineers. The corporal soon was demoted to private. Anna and her sister Eliza were then sent to school in England, possibly assisted by a charity and her father's relations, returning to India on the completion of her education, aged 14-15.

*** Her son Louis T. Leonowens returned to Bangkok where he built up a successful timber trading company, and the company can still be seen near the Oriental Hotel.

## ANNE ADALISA PUDDICOMBE 6 October 1836 - 21 June 1908

## ALLEN RAINE, ROMANTIC NOVELIST

Anne Adalisa Evans was born in Bridge Street, Newcastle Emlyn, the eldest daughter of the lawyer Benjamin Evans, and of Letitia Grace Morgan. Anne's father was the grandson of David Davis of Castellhywel, a famous minister, teacher, poet and supporter of the French Revolution. Her mother's father Thomas Morgan was a Newcastle Emlyn surgeon, and Anne's maternal grandfather was the great Methodist preacher Daniel Rowland of Llangeitho. Anne was known by her family as 'Ada'.

In 1839, aged thirteen, after attending school in Carmarthen, Anna was sent with her sister to live in Cheltenham and then Wandsworth with the family of Mr

Henry Solly, a Unitarian Minister, and friend of Charles Dickens, George Eliot, Bulwer Lytton and Mrs Henry Wood.

From 1851-56 the sisters stayed at Southfields near Wimbledon and Wandsworth, with the Solly family, and Anne became a capable musician and learned Italian and French. In 1856*, she returned to Wales, living in Newcastle Emlyn and Tresaith, a small port, until 1872. The family moved every summer from Newcastle Emlyn to their country house, Glandŵr, designed by John Nash in 1809, at Tresaith on the Cardigan coast. It is now a 5* country guesthouse, and you can stay in a king-size four-poster in The John Nash Room. In 1872, aged 36, Anna married Beynon Puddicombe, a distant relative and the foreign correspondent of London's Smith Payne's bank. Beynon had a Welsh mother, and may have met her at Tresaith. They married at Penbryn Church, Cardiganshire, and settled at Elgin Villas, Addiscombe, near Croydon.

However, Anne was in a state of almost permanent invalidity, confined to her sofa, for the first ten years of her marriage. They then moved to Winchmore Hill, London, a more open area and her health improved. The illness may have been more psychological than physical.** For 28 years they lived near or in London, but Beynon suffered a mental breakdown in 1900, and she took him to live at Bron-Môr, Traeth-saith, near Tresaith to recuperate. He died in 1906, and Anne in 1908, both being buried at Penbryn.

Her fame rests upon her writings. As a girl she had started a periodical at Newcastle Emlyn, and in 1894, aged 58, won a prize at Caernarfon National Eisteddfod for a story, *Ynysoer* upon Welsh life. Spurred by this late-life success, Anne wrote *Mifanwy* (sic), a novel which was rejected by six publishers in 1896. Undeterred, Anne changed her writing name to 'Allen Raine' (a pseudonym which came to her 'in a dream'), and its title to *A Welsh Singer*, and it was published by Hutchison in August 1897. Hutchison had wanted £20 to help defray the publishing costs, which Beynon Puddicombe only gave reluctantly, saying to his nephew 'Well, we must honour the little woman'. By July 1908, it had sold 316,000 copies. It is a love story, set in Tresaith, which is named *Mwntseison* in the book. Some authorities believe that Anne turned to writing in middle age to pay for her husband's early retirement, and to pay for Bron-Môr, their home in Tresaith in 1897. Beynon Puddicombe was given a pension of £25 a month by the bank, but was required to stay at times in a private asylum in North Wales, and had to have a constant attendant, a man named Ferriers.

In the following twelve years appeared another ten romantic novels, as well as a volume of short stories. She became one of the best-selling authors of her day, with excellent characterisation, understanding and humour. Her first novels tended to be more melodramatic, but as her style developed, she showed that she could handle difficult themes. Her books, in order of appearance, were *Torn Sails, By Berwyn Banks, Garthowen, A*

*Welsh Witch, On the Wings of the Wind, Hearts of Wales, Queen of the Rushes, 'Neither Storehouse nor Barn*, and, published posthumously: *All in a Month, Where Billows Roll* and *Under the Thatch. Where Billows Roll* is the translation of her first attempt at writing, the 1894 eisteddfod entry *Ynysoer*, which she did not seem to want published in her lifetime. *An Allen Raine Birthday Book* was published in 1909.

*Torn Sails* (1898) was her most popular book in Wales, made into a film in the 1920's, filmed at Llangrannog and Newquay. In *By Berwen Banks* (1899) Anne noted the 'would-be genteel (who) perfectly unconscious of the beauty of their own language, and ignorant of its literature, affect English manners and customs, and often pretend that English is more familiar to them than Welsh, a fatuous course of conduct which brings upon them only the sarcasm of the lower classes, and the contempt of the more educated.' She also deals with social pretensions in *Garthowen* (1900) and *A Welsh Witch - A Romance of Rough Places* (1902). *Garthowen* sold over 200,00 copies, but all her romances sold many more, so it seems that the publisher directed her to make *A Welsh Witch* more of a romance, and it is her longest and most ambitious work. Some of the material was drawn from the Welsh pit disasters at Tynewydd in 1877 and Morfa in 1890. *On the Wings of the Wind* (1903) is the story of a family feud, and *Hearts of Wales - An Old Romance* (1905) a historical novel set in the times of Owain Glyndŵr. The working title of the latter was the evocative *The Sin Eater*.

In 1904, Anne was affected by the massive Revival Movement, which originated around Newcastle Emlyn, and wrote to *The Western Mail* on 31 December: '...Public-houses deserted, happiness and love restored to ruined homes are glorious tributes to the force of the revival, to its undercurrent of spiritual strength. How great, therefore, will be our responsibility, more especially that of the ministers of religion, if this great spiritual awakening is allowed to pass away from our land without being followed by a real reformation in our national character. Let the leaders of this great movement, therefore, impress upon their converts what a true *diwygiad* [reform] means. There are many traits in the Welsh character of which we are bitterly ashamed. Let the full force of this Pentecostal wave be turned upon our national sins; let us lead cleaner and purer lives; then, indeed, the revival will have proved to be a blessed uplifter to our land.' The problems of this great religious revival are dealt with sympathetically in *Queen of the Rushes*, which appeared in May 1906, the month of her husband's death. This was her last major work.

All of this time she had been working under the constant pressure of her husband's mental fragility, and *Neither Storehouse Nor Barn* was published just before her death in 1908. She seems to have started the novel in 1903, the same time as *Hearts of Wales. Where Billows Roll - A Tale of the Welsh Coast* - her 1894 eisteddfod entry - was published in 1908 after her death. Anne dealt with her husband's breakdown in the book of previously published short stories *All in a Month* (1908), and with her own futile battle with cancer in the unfinished *Under the Thatch* (1910). She had consulted a London specialist and a Gwbert herbalist in a vain attempt to cure her breast cancer. *My People* was not published until 1915, seven years after her death, and predicts a bleak future for the people of Wales.

Her books sold around two million copies in the UK, and were also published in the USA and France, but the London Blitz destroyed Hutchison's sales records. 'The Bookman' ranked her one of the four best-selling novelists of the day, with Marie Corelli, Hall Caine and Silas Hocking. Allen Raine 'is unique in the annals of literature in Wales; not only did she become a best-seller whose sales were counted in millions, but she did so without ever ceasing to write chiefly about one small corner of Cardiganshire' (- *Allen Raine*, by Sally Jones). The novelist Owen Rhoscomyl wrote of her work in 'breaking down the antipathy to stories set in Wales.' The editor of *The Western Mail*, Arthur Mee, affirmed this point in 1908: 'England never really appreciated her Northern neighbour until Scott wrote for her and the world his immortal novels. Had he written them in Gaelic they would have been a sealed book to the Englishman till this day. Had Allen Raine written in Welsh her novels would no more have moved the Saxon than did "Rhys Lewis". Let the Welshman foster his native tongue; but to move the Saxon he must do it in English... her pages contain no false impression of a people who (as we know) are so easily misunderstood.'

* In May 1856, Anne joined in the London celebrations at the end of the Crimean War, recording 'Peace rejoicings. Went to Mrs. Case's and saw the fireworks on Primrose Hill. Did not get home till 3 next morning because the streets were so crowded.' Later that year her beloved brother Tom, a London medical student, died of typhoid after eating oysters, aged only 18.

** One of her characters in *Neither Storehouse Nor Barn* is the orphaned daughter of a Welsh country vicar, who goes to live with her aunt in Manchester. Her feelings may be those of Anne, stifled away from her natural rural surroundings: '"Poor things," she thought, "how dull their lives must be! Always the same wherever we go - the same talk, the same dresses; and if you look at the clock before you enter their houses, you can always tell what they will be doing: middle day - lunch, and the same things on every table; afternoon - tea, and the same talk everywhere; then in the evening, when we ought to be tired with the fresh air, walking or working, comes dinner and dressing up like a doll.'

# FRANCES ELIZABETH HOGGAN 20 December 1843 – 5 February 1927

## THE FIRST BRITISH WOMAN PHYSICIAN, SOCIAL REFORMER, PIONEER

Frances Elizabeth Hoggan is virtually unknown. In Zurich University however she is still is still known to this day as the first British woman physician and second woman in Europe to graduate with a medical degree from a European University. Frances was born at 19 High Street, Brecon to Richard Morgan, a curate of St Johns Priory, and Georgiana Catherina Philipps, of the Cwmgwili Estate in Carmarthenshire. When she was three years old her family moved to Cowbridge in Glamorgan, where she was brought up and educated in before moving to Windsor to continue her education. During her teens she also gave birth to an illegitimate daughter Because of the stigma associated with young unwed pregnant women, her mother Georgiana brought the baby up and passed her off as her daughter and Frances' sister.

In her early twenties Frances Morgan travelled to Europe to study in Paris and Düsseldorf. At some stage Frances decided to become a doctor, but in mid-Victorian Britain women were not permitted to study to become university trained doctors. Undeterred, Frances passed the examination to enter Zurich University, which was the only university in Europe in 1867 to accept women medical students. In 1870, aged 26 years, she obtained her medical qualification from the University of Zurich, and is still known today as one of the few people who completed the six-year course in three years. She also learnt Sanskrit in her spare time in addition to her language skills in French and German. Her remarkable doctoral thesis on muscular dystrophy also challenged the work and views of her supervisor. It is a common misconception that Elizabeth Garret was the first woman to receive a Doctorate in Medicine but in reality it was Frances Hoggan who obtained this degree three months before Garret who completed her course at the University in Paris in June 1870.

Following her graduation Frances went onto conduct post-graduate work in Vienna, Prague and Paris and in 1874 she married Dr. George Hoggan. Together the couple established the first husband and wife medical practice in Britain. Based in London they both published forty-two medical research papers in English, German and French and Frances herself became a specialist in women's and children's diseases. During this time she also became a campaigner and social reformer and has been cited as an important figure within books written on the suffragette movement in Britain. She never forgot her Welsh background and become heavily involved during the 1880s in debates concerning intermediate and higher education in Wales, particularly with emphasis on the importance of opportunities for women. She submitted a variety of papers on this subject, including her paper *The Present Condition of Intermediate and Higher Education in Wales* which she wrote to the Aberdare committee.

In 1882 she also wrote *Education for Girls in Wales*, which was an influential work that she spoke about in many meetings in Wales and London. The book was printed by the Women's Printing Society, which operated during the Women's Movement and examined the quality of education available to girls during the period. Before this time the Education Act of 1870 created a wider gap between the educations of the different social classes and aimed to stress the importance of the domestic subjects, such as cooking and sewing, within the education of young girls.

Frances also become very involved in the education and social reforms of South Africa, the Middle East, India and the USA in particular. She toured the United States and gave some very important lectures in which she campaigned against the lynching of African-Americans in the southern states. She also spoke about this issue at the first Universal Race Congress held in London in 1911 whilst also writing articles on this subject, with the most significant of these being *American Negro Women During the First Fifty Years of Freedom* which was published in 1913.

Frances died in 1927, and her ashes were interred with her husband's in Woking cemetery in an unmarked plot. In 1970, on the anniversary of Frances' receiving of her medical degree, the Cathedral in Brecon held a service dedicated to her and her amazing work. The Brecknock Society also presented the Cathedral with an inscribed font ewer in memory of the great woman. There have been several pamphlets and books written about or mentioning Frances. Dr. Gareth Evans described her as '… undoubtedly one of the leading feminist pioneers in Wales.' She should be remembered as being a woman who was ahead of her time in her campaigning for the rights of the oppressed whilst also using her medical knowledge to help others.

The surprisingly short *British Medical Journal* obituary for 19 February 1927 for this groundbreaking woman simply reads: 'Dr. FRANCES ELIZABETH HOGGAN, whose maiden name was Morgan, died at Brighton on February 5th. She was born in 1843; she received her medical education at Zurich, Prague, and Vienna, and graduated M.D. Zurich in 1870, six years before the passing of the Medical Act (1876) which opened the medical profession in England to women. She obtained the diplomas L.R.C.P.I. and L.M. in 1877, and the M.R.C.P.I. in 1880. She was one of the first women to practise in England, and, with Dr. [Elizabeth]

Garrett Anderson, was a physician on the staff of St. Mary's Dispensary in Crawford Street, which subsequently became the New Hospital for Women. Owing to the ill health of her husband she lived in the South of France until his death in 1900, when she returned to London. Soon afterwards she visited America, where she became interested in the colour, question, and published articles on this subject. When over 60 years of age she accompanied an exploring expedition to native villages of South Africa. For the last five years she had resided in Brighton. Her health failed during the last three months, but up to that time she had been very active in body and mind and took a deep interest in professional matters.'

## ELIZABETH AMY DILLWYN 16 May 1845 – 13 December 1935

### NOVELIST AND MANAGER, PIONEER OF WOMEN'S INVOLVEMENT IN BUSINESS AND PUBLIC LIFE

She was born into one of Glamorgan's leading families, a spoilt debutante who in later life climbed out of family bankruptcy to a point where 'her success as a Welsh industrialist was as astonishing as it was unique', according to her biographer, David Painting. She left seven leather-bound diaries from which we have a fascinating picture of this progressive woman's life. Her father was Lewis Llewellyn Dillwyn, MP for Swansea, an industrialist and land-owner, and her mother Elizabeth de la Beche. Amy grew up for the first five years of her life at Sketty Hall in Swansea, until her father built Hendrefoilan Mansion nearby. Taught privately, she was a tomboy, who loved swimming and fishing.

With the radical Liberal MP, Lewis Llewelyn Dillwyn, for a father, and pioneer photographer, John Dillwyn-Llewelyn, as an uncle, Amy had the fortune to be born into a family which encouraged enquiring, open minds in their children. Her maternal grandfather Sir Henry de la Beche, geologist and Fellow of the Royal Society, and her paternal grandfather was Lewis Weston Dillwyn, one of the founders of the Royal Institution of South Wales.

Amy was launched in society upon 28 February 1863, aged just 17. Her family set off in a carriage from their London home at 10 Prince's Terrace, Knightsbridge, and she recalled that Piccadilly was jammed with the carriages of the other 250 debutantes. She was irreverent about 'coming out', when she was presented at court, writing: 'I am at last fairly launched into the world. I have paid my respects to high and mighty majesty represented by a stumpy little Princess Royal. The poor little dear must have been tired by the time she had down with her mother's loyal subjects yesterday. I let down my train at the right moment, sailed up the room, came upon the royal trio considerably before I expected (partly because they were so short I could hardly see them down so low), made my three profound curtseys and nonchalantly had my train on my arm without doing any walking backwards at all.'

Two months after 'coming out', Amy went with her future fiancé, Llywelyn Thomas of Llwynmadoc, to a Covent Garden concert, chaperoned by his mother and sister. They had known each other since children. Llywelyn was a friend of Amy's elder brother Harry, and the sole heir of a landowner and colliery magnate. Both families approved the match, and in October 1863 he proposed and Amy accepted. However, his father died suddenly, and Llywelyn was now away looking after his new business interests, while Amy prepared for the wedding. In February 1864, the 24 year-old Llywelyn died unexpectedly in Paris, of smallpox. Amy was inconsolable, and mourned him in virtual seclusion for several weeks.

However, her mother was dying, and lingered on until 1866. Her 'summer season' in London, the highlight of Amy's year, was cancelled, and Amy became the new 'mistress' of Hendrefoilan and its dozens of servants. Also in 1866, there was a cholera epidemic in Killay, Swansea, and Amy toiled there unceasingly, despite the risk of fatal infection. For the rest of her life she worked for the welfare of the poor, sick and for her church.

Amy was now in effect her father's hostess and partner at social functions, often meeting the Prince of Wales and Queen Victoria at Buckingham Palace and social events. She knew Disraeli, Thackeray, Thomas Hughes and Robert Browning. Suitors circled her, notably the vicar of Sketty, Edward Bolney, whom she disliked. Indeed, he kept his word that he would marry no-one but her, and in old age died a bachelor. In 1872, she met Fulwar Craven, a Captain of the Grenadier Guards, who married her younger sister Essie. Amy was consumed with jealousy, and wrote despairingly in her diaries 'Why am I never to have the happiness of loving and being loved? Am I worse natured than other people that my life must be so much bitterer than theirs? I cannot go on living like this.'

Painfully aware, in her thirties, that she was now unlikely to marry (her fiancé Llewellyn Thomas had died when she was nineteen), Amy withdrew from the social circles she had frequented as a younger woman and began to suffer a form of invalidism. She became, in her own words, 'stuck to the sofa like a limpet on a rock'. She may have suffered from depression, a state familiar to many other women in her position. She was single, well educated and intelligent, yet with no outlet for her abilities or the prospect of marriage, any drive and determination she had came to naught. Amy's recovery began when, inspired in part by George Eliot's Middlemarch, she began writing. After several refusals, in 1880 she had *The Rebecca Rioters* published by MacMillan, under the name E.A. Dillwyn. Like George Eliot q.v., she decided that a female author would not be taken seriously. She was born just two years after the end of the riots, and her grandfather used to tell her stories about them. Her father and uncle had been instrumental in marshalling the forces of law and order, and her father had also written his own account of the raids on Pontarddulais toll-gate in 1843, the central event of her novel. Highly readable, the book was a success. The hero is Evan Williams, an intelligent young worker who cannot understand the injustices of society, and it was re-published by *Honno* in 2001.

In 1881 was published the novel *Chloe Arguelle,* based on her sister's experience of London, where a debutante marries her hero, and *A Burglary* in 1883. Her progressive outlook on life can be seen in her other novels dealing with contemporary society, *Jill* (1884), *Jill and Jack* (1887) and *Maggie Steele's Diary* (1892). According to David Painting, her novels are all variations on the same theme: Women ought not to be content to remain mere possessions of men but should assert themselves as intelligent human beings.' As a literary critic, her review of *Treasure Island* for the *The Spectator* helped establish Robert Louis Stevenson as a writer in 1884. She contributed over 60 articles to *The Spectator*, then a weekly magazine, and was also on its panel of reviewers.

Her younger sister Essie eloped with a 'penniless scamp' in 1856, leaving Fulwar Craven with 5 motherless children. Amy followed Essie to South Africa, but could not prevail upon her to return to her family. Fulwar was now drinking himself to death, and was her brother Harry. Harry died in 1890, aged only 46. Hendrefoilan was left in his will to his nearest male heir, his nephew. Amy had a home there as long as her father Lewis survived, but he died in 1892, and Amy now had to leave Hendrefoilan, her home for 40 years. However, Lewis Dillwyn left his faithful daughter Amy the residue of his estate, principally the Llansamlet Spelter Works. Unfortunately, Amy soon discovered that the Dillwyn Company was around £100,000 in debt. Amy's legacy had been placed in Chancery so that she could not receive any money before the creditors. She was expected to file for bankruptcy, but the thought of 200 unemployed men and their families stiffened her resolve.

Aged 47, she became manager of the works, and taking no profits, she used the margins from increased productivity and strict economies to start paying off the circling creditors. It was unheard of - a middle-aged eccentric spinster running a large organisation single-handed. In 1893, she was forced to sell all the contents of Hendrefoilan Mansion in a 5-day sale - long-case clocks, Jacobean furniture, Swansea and Nantgarw porcelain, guns - all went to part pay the creditors. 1894 saw a desperate entry in her diaries on her 49th birthday, possibly smudged by tears: 'For the first time in my life my birthday has passed without one single greeting. Papa and Harry always used to remember the day and Minnie (her other sister) always wrote a "many happy returns of the day" letter. But this year no living soul has remembered - it makes me feel terribly solitary in the world. Perhaps when one's as lonely as this a wish of "returns of the day" would necessarily be a farce.'

She was now living in lodgings in West Cross, Swansea, with just one maid. Amy caught the Mumbles train every morning to the company's office in Cambrian Place, and often travelled to Llansamlet to supervise the furnaces. She looked after all the accounts, and handled international correspondence as her two clerks knew only Welsh and English. Wisely, she employed a metallurgist, John Corfield, to look after the smelting. By 1896, she had paid back enough money to get her small inheritance out of Chancery, which she used to purchase her own estate. Dillwyn & Co was now legally hers.

In 1897, she generously gave a partnership in the firm to Corfield, despite the fact that he put no capital into the firm. By 1998, she was still living in cheap lodgings and paying off creditors, until the end of 1899 when she finally cleared all her father's debts. She now was given the actual deeds to the works. She no longer took the train to work, but strode out across the town, with new-found self-confidence. She owed nothing and her methods had turned around a bankrupt company. She was known to everyone in Swansea as 'Miss Dillwyn', and her small, lean frame, simple dress, trilby hat and walking stick made her instantly recognisable. No lady ever smoked in public, but she always lit a large cigar at the top table in social functions. Her favourite saying was the Spanish *'soy quien soy'*, I am who I am.

Tellingly, when she embarked on her task to rescue the family company from the brink of bankruptcy, Amy had announced: 'Altogether, I am becoming a man of business.' Amy's identification of herself as a man of business extended as far as her appearance, as she began to wear clothes which gave her a less feminine appearance, far removed from the crinolines and ballgowns of her youth. The fact that she felt she had to conduct herself as a man of business is important, because for all of Amy's remarkable achievements in writing, in business and in public life, she would still be hampered by her sex later in life. 'Criticism of Miss Dillwyn is summed up in a single sentence,' opined the *Cambrian Daily Leader*, after she had lost the Swansea Harbour Trust election in 1903. 'She is a woman, not a man'.

In 1902, *The Western Mail* ran a long article on her, calling her 'one of the most remarkable women in Britain', and the national press followed up. *Pall Mall Gazette* said she was 'one of the most original women of the age'. Amy was 57 and famous. She took up hockey in a mixed team, and water polo, and in 1902 took up the tenancy on a small house in West Cross. She called the house *Cadlys* (Battle Camp) as it was a temporary measure until her finances improved. She noted 'for the first time in 10 years I slept in my own bed, with my own sheets and my own blanket. I have had to furnish the tiny place and fell just like a child playing with a doll's house.' Two years later, she could afford to buy a bigger house, Tŷ Gwyn, just off the Mumbles Road, where she lived her last 31 years.

When Amy Dillwyn rescued the Llansamlet Spelter Works from £100,000 worth of debt over a century ago, Wales was a world leader in heavy industry. Often cited as the world's first industrial nation, with the 1851 census suggesting that it was the first country to have more people employed in industry than agriculture, it was in Wales that world prices in commodities such as coal, copper, iron, tin and zinc were set. Welsh coal and metals were exported around the world, and Welsh skills and labour followed, as places as far afield as Pennsylvania and Hughesovka, Russia sought the expertise of those who knew 'the Welsh way'.

Dillwyn Spelter Works was now making profits of £10,000 a year, and was one of the largest zinc producers in the UK. However, UK manufacturers were finding it difficult to get hold of high grade ores to compete with their much larger American and German competitors. Amy thus undertook the hazardous trip to Algiers in 1905 to source new supplies of zinc ore (calamine). She took Rice Dillwyn Nicholl, the heir to her company, and had to ride astride mules up into the mountains, as side-saddle was unknown in North Africa. On her return to Wales, she had an offer to buy her company from Metallgesellschaft of Frankfurt. Amy knew that the UK industry was in terminal decline, and sold her majority shareholding, on condition that her heir remained on the board of the new company.

The former managing director now threw herself whole-heartedly into civic life of Swansea, being elected for the Swansea School Board and becoming President of the Hospital Management Committee. She was instrumental in the building of a new convalescent home, supported a local shopworkers' strike, and stood as an Independent candidate for Swansea Council. She was an early supporter of women's suffrage, and caught up on the social life that she had missed in her years of debt repayment. Aged 75, she was seen playing bridge and poker with Lily Langtry's husband in Monaco. She died aged 90, was cremated and her ashes buried in the churchyard of St Paul's Church, Sketty, at the grave of her parents and brother Harry. She left £114,513 7s 9d in her will. Her Llansamlet Works closed in 1926, and was demolished in 1962. Hendrefoilan is now part of Swansea University. Her house, Tŷ Glyn, now Mumbles Nursing Home, still stands at West Cross, Swansea. Sketty Hall is the former home of Amy's grandparents, Lewis Weston Dillwyn and Mary Dillwyn. There are pictures and an article on Amy on display in the venue's Harry Secombe Lounge. The Amy Dillwyn Society was established in 1989 and aims to 'promote an interest in the arts, antiques and our local heritage and history'. It is thanks to the Amy Dillwyn Society that there is a blue plaque and tree dedicated to this grand old lady of Swansea, which can be seen from the Swansea to Mumbles cycle path, next to the West Cross Inn.

# ELIZABETH PHILLIPS HUGHES 12 July 1851 - 19 December 1925

## EDUCATIONALIST

Born in Carmarthen, her parents were the surgeon John Hughes and Ann Phillips. John Hughes was described by his grand-daughter, Dorothea Price-Hughes, as 'a Coroner, Chairman of the Board of Guardians, Chairman of the School Board, Borough Magistrate, County Magistrate, etc., etc., in the discharge of these offices he was feared as well as beloved, for he did not share the Welsh laxity, in certain slack quarters of the town he was known as Bismarck.' Elizabeth's elder brother, Hugh Price Hughes, became a prominent Wesleyan Methodist minister, and used to remonstrate with 'Bessie' to come to his prayer-meetings, threatening that he  would 'put his head into the fire' if she did not attend. As a child, she was extremely backward, being hardly able to read when aged ten. Her brother later wrote: 'Poor Bessie understood nothing, positively nothing, but I toiled and perspired and made it all clear to her. I should have been a coach. I have a great ability for making people see things.' However, her mother saw no reason for a 'lady' to be educated, which led to disagreements between her and Elizabeth, who through her brother's efforts, now aspired to be a teacher.

She was educated at Cheltenham Ladies College, and then taught at Cheltenham for four years, before studying moral sciences at Newnham College, Cambridge. She was over 30 when she started her course, and gained a remarkable First in 1884. Remarkably, the following year she also achieved a Second in a history degree. Thus in October 1885 she became the first Principal of the Cambridge Training College for Women Teachers. The Training College was initially housed in a few cottages near Newnham, and suffered from severe under-funding. One student wrote: 'We stepped from the stairs into the street, the Lecture-Hall was a sort of attic, in which a tall lecturer could hardly stand upright - the staff consisted of Miss Hughes alone.' Later, Elizabeth and her staff were referred to as 'those mad people at Cambridge'. Her work is now seen as being in advance of its time, and many of her ideas and systems were later adopted by Cambridge University. In 1887 the college moved to better premises, and in 1895 eventually into suitable purpose-built accommodation.

Hughes Hall, the oldest Graduate College in Cambridge, is named after her. It was unique in specialising in the admission of women graduates, at a time when the university itself did not even confer degrees upon women. It was originally Cambridge Training College in 1885, with Miss Hughes as Principal, and 14 female students in its small rented house. In 1894, she spoke before the Royal Commission on Secondary Education, saying 'We shall never get first-rate training until men and women are trained together... Mixed staff and mixed students' which to Elizabeth was the ideal institution. It is now a mixed college, and the 1895 building is still the centre of college life today. By 1899, there were 60 students in residence in the new buildings, and over 500 had already been trained.

Jurgen and Emily Pfeiffer made major bequests to Newnham College and Hughes Hall, as well as to Girton College. By 1902, Miss Hughes had visited Japan, and made Newnham and Hughes Hall centres for international students. Not until 1948 did the university give degrees to women, in which year the college became the Elizabeth Phillips Hughes Hall Company, in common usage Hughes Hall. In 1985 it became an Approved Foundation of the University, and the Cambridge Training College Council was replaced by a President and Fellows.

Elizabeth induced the College Council to allow the Labour Movement to use the lecture hall for Sunday evening lectures, despite the overwhelming suspicion of the new party. Working men and women could listen to Cambridge lecturers and speakers from a variety of fields. Through over-work, Elizabeth retired aged only 48 - she thought that teaching was only suitable for younger people with the necessary drive and energy. However, the success of this pioneering educational institution (which became Newnham College and Hughes Hall, Cambridge) was undoubtedly due to her hard work and enthusiasm before she retired to live in Barry in 1899.

She spent the rest of her years promoting higher education and the training of teachers and lecturers, lecturing in Britain and America, and holding a professorship in Tokyo for a time. She was the only woman on the committee which drew up the charter of the University of Wales. She said 'I felt that the quickest, most effective way of improving education was to induce teachers to be trained, and to try and improve training.' Interestingly, upon her many lecture tours, she noted that the Welsh were enthusiastic and receptive to new ideas, but tended towards impulsiveness, whereby the English people are slow to start, but can be relied upon to carry out any undertaking.

Elizabeth was 63 when World War I broke out, and served as commandant of a hospital, resultantly being one of the first recipients of an MBE. Elizabeth was given the bardic name of *Merch Myrddin* (Merlin's Daughter), and in 1920 the University of Wales conferred on her the honorary degree of LL.D. on account of her services to Welsh education and social progress. She sat on the governing body of Cardiff University, and was a member of the Education Committee and Glamorgan County Council until a few weeks before her death, at home in Barry, aged 75.

## HELEN HAMILTON GARDENER 21 January 1853 – 26 July 1925

## ALICE CHENOWETH DAY, AMERICAN WRITER, REFORMER AND FEMINIST

Alice was the daughter of the Reverend Alfred Griffith Chenoweth and Katherine A. Peele, born in Winchester, Virginia. She was Welsh of both sides of her family, her mother being descended from Morgan Williams of Llanishen, who married Elizabeth Cromwell. Their son was Richard Cromwell, alias Williams, and his great-grandson Oliver used to sign his name 'Oliver Cromwell alias Williams' before he became Lord Protector. Oliver's first cousins including Henry emigrated to Virginia around 1620, and Alice's direct ancestor William Cromwell married the Welsh woman Elizabeth Trahearne. On her father's side, John Chenoweth came from Wales about 1720 and married into the Cromwell family.

Alice graduated from Cincinnati High School and Ohio State Normal School, undertaking postgraduate work at Columbia University, New York. Aged only 19, she began teaching in Ohio State Normal School, becoming its Principal for two years. Alice married Charles S. Smart in 1875, aged 22, moving with him to New York in 1880. There, she studied biology at Columbia, wrote newspaper articles, and lectured on sociology at the Brooklyn Institute of Arts and Sciences. She came under the influence of the famous freethinker Colonel Robert G. Ingersoll, and gave a series of lectures on freethinking in 1884. These were published as *Men, Women, Gods and other Lectures* in 1885. In these married years in New York, she legally took the pen-name of Helen Hamilton Gardener, and wrote articles, stories and seven books.

She fought for the right of women to high school and college training, and later promoted the protection of children. In 1888, she carefully and scientifically refuted a claim by a leading neurologist, that the woman's brain was inherently and measurably inferior to the male brain, in *Sex in Brain*.

Her best-known and greatest book was *Sex in Brain*, a response to a statement by a prominent physician that the brain of a woman was inferior in

19 different ways to the brain of a man. Alice studied brain anatomy and proved the assertion to be false - the brain of a woman was not provably different from that of a man under the same conditions and with the same opportunities for development. Her synopsis was published in medical journals in eight languages.

In 1890 Helen gained further renown with a lurid novel, *Is This Your Son, My Lord*, which attacked male double standards. Her earlier collected works were published in book form as *Facts and Fictions of Life* in 1893. *Pushed by Unseen Hands* (1892) and *A Thoughtless Yes* (1890) were published, and *Pray You Sir, Whose Daughter* also appeared in 1892. Her 1894 *An Unofficial Patriot*

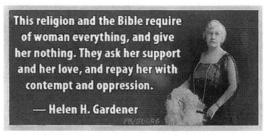

This religion and the Bible require of woman everything, and give her nothing. They ask her support and her love, and repay her with contempt and oppression.

— Helen H. Gardener

*courtesy of faithless feminist website*

was a fictionalised biography of her father, later dramatised by James A. Herne as *Griffith Davenport, Circuit Rider*.

Her husband died in 1901. Now an established suffragette leader, she married again, in 1902, Colonel Selden Allen Day. After Day retired from active service, they spent ten years touring the world, where she lectured at universities in Japan, France, England and Italy. She was decorated by the governments of France and Japan for her public work, and held the Peace Medal of France for her book *An Unofficial Patriot*. On her return to the USA, Alice lectured in universities on *Ourselves and Other People.*

In 1913, Helen was appointed to reorganise the Congressional Committee of the National American Woman Suffrage Association, which had been depleted by mass resignations of radical suffragists. She was elected vice-president, then president of the National Woman Suffrage Association. Now living in Washington, she was responsible for maintaining the *entente cordiale* with the White House, and is credited with having done much to secure the Amendment of the Constitution giving women the vote. Her contacts with President Woodrow Wilson and with Speaker of the House Champ Clark, along with her tact and wit, helped her to get the suffrage bill past many obstacles. In 1920, she became the first woman member of the US Civil Service Commission, a post she held until her death five years later. This was the highest federal position held by a female up to that time. This appointment by President Woodrow Wilson came to her 'unsolicited as recognition of her ability and was unanimously confirmed'.

*Footnote:*
Much of the above comes from a particularly gruesome article in *The American Journal of Physical Anthropology*, October-December 1927, which contains 60

pages of measurements and illustrations of her preserved brain, which she bequeathed to science. The beginning of the section of the article headed 'Purpose' shows that geneticism was seriously flawed in 1927: 'A study of the brain of Mrs Gardener has provided several points of interest. As her biography shows, her life was one of great achievement, and the interesting question is raised whether the mental endowment of a woman can be equal to that of a man. In a compelling way the question of the difference in structure of the brain of the two sexes is again submitted for solution. As her genealogy shows, she has in her ancestry two eminent lines of descent through Cromwell and Calvert (Baltimore) families. It is evident that a great mental talent resided in these families who combined the bloods of the Anglo-Saxon and Celtic races - a talent which was possibly inherent in her particular mental structure.

Since Pearl (1905) has shown that brain weight is not an essential factor, the question of the relation of brain pattern to mental functions has been definitely introduced into this study. There is good evidence that certain brain patterns as well as talents are transmitted characteristics. Though no sufficient anthropological data are available, she would probably classify as a member of the old American stock which the studies of Hrdlicka (1925) have defined. The study was made by comparing the brain of Mrs Gardener with that of forty other female hemicerbera and forty male hemicerbera, point for point, and tabulating the results.'

Part of the conclusion informs us 'The brain of Mrs H. H. Gardener belongs to the stenogyric type with highly developed and finely modelled convolutions in all regions. The primary fissural pattern is that of the usual type on both sides. The accessory secondary fissuration is due to the crowding and tortuosity of all the gyri which expresses a greater growth and differentiation of the cortex'... and so on... and so on.

## DR MARTHA CAREY THOMAS 2 January 1857 - 2 December 1935

### AMERICAN EDUCATOR AND FEMINIST

Martha was born into a family of prominent Baltimore-Welsh Quakers, the oldest of ten children. She attended a local 'dame's school' in the mid 1860's, and when the schooling thought appropriate for young ladies came to an end, she became jealous of the opportunities afforded her brothers. In 1872, Thomas persuaded her father to allow her to attend a newly opened school for girls in New York. While studying there her father asked her to investigate Cornell University for him. Although her father publicly approved of education for women, he did not approve of his daughter going to a co-educational college, but relented, and Thomas received her bachelor's degree in language and literature from Cornell in 1877. She then applied to John Hopkins University, being reluctantly admitted for a master's degree, the first woman to enter a Hopkins graduate course, but was barred from the classrooms.

Cornell insisted that she study privately with a professor and not mix with male students in classes or seminars, so she resigned. She went on to Leipzig in 1879, where after 3 years she was refused a degree, because she was a woman. Thomas was then accepted for an examination for linguistics at Zurich, gaining an unprecedented doctorate there, *summa cum laude*, in 1882. The *summa cum laude* was usually granted once in every two decades to a male student, and she was the first female to achieve the distinction. She then carried on with post-doctoral research for a year at the Sorbonne. However, her wealthy Quaker father still opposed her furthering her education.

Even as an adolescent Martha had decried the inequity that denied American women an education comparable to that of the men. She said 'I ain't going to get married and I don't want to teach school. I can't imagine anything worse than living a regular young lady's life.' Thomas noted in her journal, aged 18, 'There is so much opposition to the only thing I care for, it is impossible to get the highest culture by one's self, and I have to see thousands of boys enjoying and often throwing away the chances I would give anything for.' She went to Europe for further study as few American colleges would admit a woman. She now preferred to be known as 'Carey' Thomas (- her parents called her 'Minnie'). She had travelled to Europe with her 'devoted companion', Mamie Gwinn, but now decided that her academic achievement should serve as an  example to other aspiring women. Her mother now came round to Carey's point of view, and sympathised with her fight to realise women's equality in education.

While studying in Europe, Thomas heard of a proposed women's college at Bryn Mawr, Pennsylvania, and applied for presidency, which was given to a man.

In 1884 Carey was appointed to organise the new Bryn Mawr* College for women, serving as dean and professor of English. The Quaker women's college was just being founded, and its Board contained her father, uncle and several cousins. Carey quickly became its leading influence, being largely responsible for organising the undergraduate studies programme and starting the first graduate studies programme of any women's school. Although she was very busy with her work at Bryn Mawr, she often returned to Baltimore to work on other projects dear to her. One such project was the need for a school where girls could obtain an education which would prepare them to attend a good college. This filled another void in the American educational system, as an excellent preparatory school prior to college. In 1885, with her wealthy friend Mary Garrett, she founded Bryn Mawr School for Girls in Baltimore.

Thomas is perhaps best known for having facilitated the admission of women to the John Hopkins Medical School. With the help of Miss Garrett's millions, in 1889 the progressive Carey endowed the new Johns Hopkins Medical School, stipulating that women be admitted, as well as men. With the help of four of her friends, a total of $500,000 was raised to aid the Medical School in its financial struggle. The funds raised were used as a leverage to get the University to accept women. Thus, thanks largely to the efforts of these five women, women were to be admitted on precisely the same basis as men, and thhere were three women among the first class to enter the John Hopkins Medical School in 1893.

She was Bryn Mawr College's second president from 1894-1922, working to make it as good, if not better, than any men's college. Despite Thomas living with Miss Gwinn, the wealthy philanthropist Garrett had fallen in love with Carey. Carey Thomas had wanted the presidency, although only aged 25, and Garrett promised millions to the struggling new college if Carey became its president. In Horowitz' biography**, 'The Power and Passion of M. Carey Thomas', we read: 'By a vote of 7 to 5, the Bryn Mawr College board of trustees elected M. Carey Thomas president. She was not made a trustee… The board announced the decision to the press. In a faculty meeting Rhoads (James E. Rhoades, the first president) was overcome and "nearly wept, and altogether it was a most melancholy occasion". Carey Thomas shook hands with the professors, who "congratulated me, and many of them added the college also". Despite this reassurance, it was not the occasion of which she had so long dreamed… With her return to work in the Fall, M. Carey Thomas became the president of Bryn Mawr College. It was a sober prelude to a 28-year term.'

The Welsh philosopher, Bertrand Russell, visited Carey in 1896 and noticed that she was consummately balancing the needs of Garrett and Gwinn: '[Thomas] had immense energy, a belief in culture which she carried out with a businessman's intensity, and a profound contempt for the male sex… At Bryn Mawr she was Zeus, and everyone trembled before her. She lived with a friend, Miss Gwinn, who was in most respects the opposite of her… At the time we stayed with them, the relationship had become a little ragged. Miss Gwinn used to go home to her family for three days in every fortnight, and at the exact moment of her departure each fortnight, another lady, named Miss Garrett, used to arrive, to depart again at the exact moment of Miss Gwinn's return.' When Miss Gwinn ran off with a male philosophy professor in 1904, Miss Garrett moved in, staying with Carey until Miss Garrett's death in 1904.

Carey set high entry requirements, a demanding course of study, and only hired outstanding teachers. More than any other American, she set in motion the higher education of women on an irreversible upward course. An autocratic leader, her shaping of the curriculum led to frequent faculty revolts, but she held firm to her conviction that a female college must have the same exacting standards as any male counterpart: 'Girls can learn, can reason, can compete with men in the grand fields of literature, science and conjecture.' She wished to make Bryn Mawr 'a second Leipzig'...'a great university of women scholars, where publications and investigations done by women should prove original thinking power.'

In 1900 she finished *The Higher Education of Women*. She also wrote books on women's colleges (*Alma Mater*) and undergraduate culture (*Campus Life*.) In her 1901 article *Should the Higher Education of Women Differ from That of Men?*, she writes 'Women while in college ought to have the broadest possible education. This college education should be the same as men's, not only because there is but one best education, but because men's and women's effectiveness and happiness and the welfare of the generation to come after them will be vastly increased if their college education has given them the same intellectual training and the same scholarly and moral ideals'.

Thomas was a leader in the female-suffrage movement, and President of the National Collegiate Equal Suffrage League from 1906-1913. At a meeting in Buffalo, New York State, in 1908, she told the North American Woman Suffrage Association: 'The man's world must become a man's and woman's world. Why are we afraid? ... It is the next step forward on the path to the sunrise, and the sun is rising over a new heaven and a new earth.' A friend of the great American suffragette Susan B. Anthony, after 1920, Carey advocated the policies of the National Women's Party, and fought for the equal rights amendment to the American Constitution. In 1921 Thomas established a summer school for women in industry at Bryn Mawr, the first such course in the world, and a pioneering programme in liberal arts aimed at urban working women.

Gertrude Stein wrote a fictionalised account of Carey's life in *Fernhurst*, and her early journals and letters were published in 1979 as *The Making of a Feminist*. Her latest biographer, Helen Horowitz, tells us that she was a freethinker, suffragette leader and an 'impassioned lover, whose lovers were women'. She was a key figure in the development of American education and an icon for lesbian progress. By helping build the institution of the women's college, she enabled tens of thousands of women to develop the skills necessary for careers which could give them independent lives. As Horowitz says: 'The institutions that she created and the doors she opened for women remain a lasting legacy.'

* Some of the oldest and most prestigious American universities were founded by Welsh settlers, for instance Bryn Mawr, Brown, Johns Hopkins and Yale.

** An earlier biography, by Edith Finch in 1947, noted the following words by Carey Thomas: 'One thing I am determined on is that by the time I die my brain shall weigh as much as a man's, if study and learning can make it that way': 'My one aim and concentrated purpose shall be and is to show that women can learn, can reason, can compete with men in the grand fields of literature and science'; and '... a woman can be a woman and a true one without having all her time engrossed by dress and society.'

## MARTHA MARIA HUGHES CANNON 1 July 1867 – 10 July 1932

### PHYSICIAN AND SUFFRAGIST

'Mattie' Hughes was born in 1857 in Llandudno, and her parents emigrated to the USA. Peter and Elizabeth Hughes were converts to The Church of Jesus Christ of the Latter Day Saints. The left Liverpool on the *Underwriter* in 1860 and four weeks later landed in New York City. The Mormon Church assisted their move to Utah, but tragedy followed the family's three-month trip in a covered wagon to Salt Lake City. Shortly before the family's arrival in the Salt Lake Valley, in September 1861, Martha's 21-months-old sister Annie Lloyd Hughes died and was buried in an unmarked grave. Three days after the remaining family had arrived in Salt Lake City, Peter Hughes died. Elizabeth Hughes was left a widow with two young daughters at the age of 28. However, thirteen months later Elizabeth married James Patten Paul, a widower and had five additional children with him. After Elizabeth's marriage to Paul, Martha, at different times in her life, went by the surnames of both Paul and Hughes. Later in life, Paul encouraged Martha to follow her dream of becoming a medical doctor.

By the age of fourteen, Martha was a schoolteacher. She soon learned typesetting skills, landing a position at the *Women's Exponent*, a women's rights newspaper in Salt Lake City. She supported herself during her college years at the University of Deseret, now the University of Utah, completing a chemistry degree. Her academic prowess earned her admission to the medical school of the University of Michigan, from which she graduated as a physician at age twenty-three. Throughout her college and medical school years, Martha was a working girl, washing dishes, making beds, and working as a secretary to support her education. Martha entered pharmacy school at the University of Pennsylvania where she was the only woman out of seventy-five students. Unconventional and out of fashion, she cut her hair short to save time and wore men's boots to keep her feet dry during a period when women's fashions dictated undue discomfort and fuss.

Aged twenty-five, Martha returned to Salt Lake City to pursue her medical career. She established the first training school for nurses and became a resident physician at the newly founded Deseret Hospital. There she met Angus Munn Cannon, superintendent of the new hospital, and the couple married in October 1884. Martha Hughes became the fourth of six wives of Mormon elder. She married him despite an 1882 congressional act that outlawed polygamy. Shortly after the wedding, Angus was arrested by federal marshals for practising polygamy, sending Martha underground to avoid prosecution herself. With a new baby girl, Elizabeth Rachel, Martha hid in wagons travelling from town to town in Utah to avoid arrest. She spent two years in exile in England when she learned that Angus had married his fifth wife. Her marriage to Angus became more strained as the couple remained separated, although she wished to return to her home and husband in Salt Lake City.

Dr. Cannon finally returned to Salt Lake City with a new commitment to women's rights and self-sufficiency. She threw herself into the work of the Utah Equal Suffrage Association. By 1896, Utah women had regained the right to vote through passage of a suffrage clause in the new state constitution. The political life suited her so much that Cannon ran against her own husband, winning the first woman's seat in the Utah State Senate in 1896. Cannon's term in office was a success. She spearheaded funding for speech- and hearing-impaired students, establishment of a state board of health, and a law regulating working conditions for women and girls. The birth of Cannon's third child came at the end of her second term in office. Following her lawmaking career, Dr. Cannon served on the Utah State Board of Health until she retired from public life to move to California.

Aged seventy-five, Martha died in Los Angeles in 1932. The Martha Hughes Cannon Health Building in Salt Lake City was dedicated in her honour in 1986. The Utah Capitol Rotunda houses an eight-foot-high bronze statue of Dr. Cannon, dedicated in 1996, one hundred years after her path-breaking election as state senator. She wrote: 'I know that women who stay home all the time have the most unpleasant homes there are. You give me a woman who thinks about something besides cook stoves and wash tubs and baby flannels, and I'll show you, nine times out of ten, a successful mother.'

# ELUNED MORGAN 20 March 1870 – 29 December 1938

## PATAGONIAN WRITER

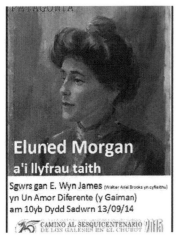

**Eluned Morgan**

**a'i llyfrau taith**

Sgwrs gan E. Wyn James (Walter Ariel Brooks yn cyfieithu)

yn Un Amor Diferente (y Gaiman)

am 10yb Dydd Sadwrn 13/09/14

CAMINO AL SESQUICENTENARIO
DE LOS GALESES EN EL CHUBUT

Although the daughter of Lewis Jones (1836-1904), she was christened with the Morgan surname. Lewis Jones was one of the Patagonian pioneers, a leader of the Welsh Colony movement, who wrote an over-flattering report on the area which encouraged many Welsh families to emigrate there. After three months in the colony, he left after a disagreement to become a printer in Buenos Aires. However, eighteen months later he heard that the settlers were proposing to return to Wales. He came back and persuaded the colonists to stay, becoming Governor of Patagonia, the only Welshman appointed by the Argentinean government to this post. He imported a printing press, and his newspaper *Y Drafod* is still in existence.

One daughter of Lewis Jones married Llwyd ap Iwan, the son of Michael D. Jones of Bala, and Llwyd was allegedly killed in a hold-up by Butch Cassidy and the Sundance Kid. Eluned was actually born on the *Myfanwy*, the boat that carried Lewis Jones and his family to Patagonia, hence her Christening with the Morgan surname, meaning 'from the sea' in Welsh.

Eluned was educated at the Welsh school in the settlement named after her father, Trelew. Her teacher Richard Jones Berwyn was the colony's first secretary to the council, first secretary to the Welsh courts, first postmaster, first registrar, first postmaster under the Argentine government and also the private secretary to the first governor. He was also the first to be imprisoned, in 1882-83, for organising a petition to protect the rights of the Welsh colonists. Eluned returned to Wales in 1885, and then again in 1888 to study at Dr Williams' school at Dolgellau.

In 1890 Eluned returned to Patagonia, to set up a boarding school for girls at Trelew until 1892. She began to become interested in writing by submitting essays to the colony eisteddfodau, and by 1893 was editor and compositor of *Y Drafod*, which had been founded by her father. Eluned again visited Wales in 1896 (remember the hazardous Atlantic crossing was by small sailing frigate), and had articles on *Y Wladfa* (Patagonia) published in *Cymru*.

In 1897 she was trying to establish an intermediate Welsh school in Caiman, and the next year travelled in the Andes mountain range. From

1903 - 1909 Eluned worked as an assistant at Cardiff Library, and made lecture tours across Wales. Eluned was strongly affected by the religious revival across Wales, forming a friendship with the evangelist Evan Roberts. She visited the Middle East before returning to Patagonia. She then came back to Cardiff from 1912-1918, again working in the Central Library. At the end of the Great War, she was able to return to Patagonia forever, where Eluned became a leader in its religious and cultural life.

Her publications include: *Dringo'r Andes* (Crossing the Andes, published 1904); *Gwynon y Môr* (an account of the voyage from Wales to Patagonia, 1909); *Ar Dir a Môr* (-the visit to Palestine, 1913) and *Plant yr Haul* (Children of the Sun, the story of the Peruvian Indians, the Incas, 1915). In *Gwynon y Môr* she describes being tied to the mast to witness the fury of storms at sea, during the sea voyage from Britain to Patagonia.

*Dringo'r Andes* is a wonderful account of early Welsh life in the Patagonian settlement, including accounts of the good relations between the Welsh, and the native Americans, the ruling Spaniards, and the immigrant Italians. An account of a flood that devastated the colony is 1899 reads: 'The frost was not as cold as usual, and not a whisper of wind stirred the small waves of the river, or in the tops of the trees: the cloudless, blue sky had turned into one huge, impenetrable cloud. For four months neither the sun in the day nor the stars at night were seen. The rain fell day after day and night after night with an awful quietness. Even the animals seemed to sense that something was amiss. They gathered together in large herds on the high lands, pawing miserably in the wetness that was so unknown to them. The sheep complained miserably on the boggy flat lands for solid ground and sheltering pens. And throughout the valley every heart beat with foreboding and fear.

On the 15th of July, on a never to be forgotten Sunday, disaster descended on the quiet valley with a terrifying roar, sweeping away in a few hours the labour and sacrifice of thirty years. It was dark, starless night in the depths of winter, with the rain still falling steadily, when the sharpest lads on their healthiest horses galloped all over the area, from house to house and village to village, and the cry was the same wherever they went "Flee for your lives, the water's coming!" Fathers hastened to the fields to roundup the horses to attach them to the wagons, and frightened mothers got their children up out of their cosy, warm coverlets, rushing to dress them as quickly as they could; the young men and women gathered together around the cattle to herd them towards the hills, so as not to lose them in the waters of the flood.

But who could describe the strangeness of all that bustle, only a quarter of an hour's warning was all that was had at times, and effort had to be made to pack provisions and clothes to keep hunger and cold away. But more often than not, before the wagon had set off, the water would arrive – the faithful horses were whipped onwards, and then it was away for their lives, with the waters of the flood like mountains behind them. This isn't the story of one person of one family, but of three thousand: men, wives and small children. And where were they to go, and what was to be their shelter? Only the bare rocky hills that surrounded the vale, where there were no sheltering trees or hedgerows, and remember that it was night, and the rain still pouring mercilessly on the terrified beings in flight.

By now there were thousands of animals on the hills too, and each one protesting in its own voice. But above it all the sound of the destroyer was clear: it roared like a lion roaming the forest in search of prey. The sound of houses collapsing, one by one, was heard, with each person wondering in their heart, in anguish, if that was their home, that had given them safety and shelter, and thinking of a thousand treasured family possessions that would never be seen again. But, thankfully, there was not much time or leisure to think. Some sort of shelter had to be built for the women and children, and … Imagine if you will the whole of the colony now camped out at the top of the hills, waiting for the dawn, and more anxious watchers there never were in any encampment. They were longing for the dawn and yet also dreading it greatly. As though in mockery, the sun rose in all its usual glory that first morning, or did it come as a herald of peace and hope? For its serene rays gave strength to many a burdened heart that day.

I'm losing heart, dear reader, at the task of describing the scene, so impossible to imagine except for those who were silent witnesses of the devastation. There was scarce anything to be seen but water, in the first days of the deluge, which spread from mountain to mountain, with no sign of canal or river, houses or land, only the tops of trees here and there like small islands in the middle of the sea. The children argued with each other over where their homes were situated. Every here and there one house, more stable than the others, was seen to have survived, with only its roof and chimneys in sight."

## GWEN JOHN 22 June 1876 – 13 September 1939

### 'ONE OF THE FINEST PAINTERS OF OUR TIME AND COUNTRY', 'RODIN'S STALKER'

The sister of Augustus John RA, he considered her a far superior artist. She was born in Haverfordwest, at 7 Victoria Place, now Lloyd's Bank. In 1884 her family moved to 5 Lexden Terrace, Tenby, where Augustus was born. Her mother died in that year, when Gwen was eight, leaving four children to be brought up by a strict solicitor father. They then lived in Victoria House, 32 Victoria Street, and some of her early works were of children at play on Tenby's beaches. The two had a studio in the attic, and in 1895 she followed

Augustus to attend the Slade School (now the Slade College of Art) until 1897, sharing rooms with him, and living near the poverty line. Augustus recalled in his autobiography: 'It wasn't long before my sister Gwen joined me at the Slade. She wasn't going to be left out of it! We shared rooms together, subsisting, like monkeys, on a diet of fruit and nuts. This was cheap and hygienic. It is true we were sometimes asked out to dinner, when, not being pedants, we waived our rule for the time being.'

Gwen was taught in a traditional style, which involved laborious copying of Old Master paintings. Her training shows through in the naturalism and carefully controlled colour range of her slowly worked paintings. In 1898, Gwen moved into a small room over a mortuary in the Euston Road, drawing water-colours of cats. She then moved to lodgings where the windows were always shuttered to avoid paying rates. She called this episode her 'subterranean life' in a letter to Augustus. However, she soon moved to France in late 1898, returning to Britain only for occasional visits. In late 1899 she exhibited in London, returning to Paris where she lived as a squatter in a derelict building from 1900-1901. In 1902 she was once again in London before returning to Paris.

In France, Gwen attended Whistler's School in Paris, developing her art. She shared a flat with two other women, one of whom Dorelia McNeill, soon became Augustus John's mistress. Gwen survived on a very small allowance from her father, living frugally, and when he visited her wore a dress for dinner that she had made herself, painfully copying one

**Self-Portrait by Gwen John, c.1900**

in a Manet painting. Her father, a strict solicitor whom Augustus John loathed, told her she looked like a prostitute, and she refused any further subsidy from him, saying 'I could never accept anything from someone capable of thinking so.'

Gwen supported herself by modelling at artists' studios in her spare time, Rodin describing her as having *'un corps admirable.'* Like many of Rodin's models, she became his mistress from around 1906, but left him in the evenings so he could return to his long-term companion, Rose Beuret, whom he married in his death year of 1917. Rodin, six years older than her father, seems to have been the true love of her life, and she posed for him, but Rodin often took steps to avoid her company. Her affair carried on painfully and intermittently, even after he had left her for the Duchesse de Choiseul. Chitty believed that her obsession with Rodin took years out of her working life. She often met Matisse, Braque, Picasso and others but was not affected by any other artist's style.

A devout Catholic, and thwarted in love, Gwen now lived a spare and simple life, finding greater comfort in solitude than congeniality, and painted a series of pictures of Dominican nuns and the orphans in their care.

The American John Quinn became her patron from 1910-1924, and she wrote to herself 'Don't be afraid of falling into mediocrity… you would never', and 'Be simple, expect nothing from circumstances' in her notebooks. In March 1922 she wrote to Quinn: 'I am quite in my work now and think of nothing else. I paint till it is dark … and then I have supper and then I read about an hour and think of my painting. … I like this life very much.' Quinn's death in 1924 closed this happy period and brought great financial insecurity. She painted less and, without Quinn's encouragement, was less eager to exhibit.

Rodin protested in letters to her that she was neglecting her health. The poet Rainer Maria Rilke was also an intimate friend and correspondent. Along with Rilke, she had an affair with Jacques Maritain. In early 1939 Gwen fell ill and wrote her will. It seems that she had not painted or drawn for the last six years of her life. She wished to be near the sea, heading for Dieppe, but arriving there she collapsed and was taken to a convent hospital where she died.

Her brother Augustus said that 'she utterly neglected herself for some bloody mystical reason', and Susan Chitty's 1981 biography confirmed a view of a reclusive, desperate, crazy painter who refused to exhibit. Gwen herself wrote 'a beautiful life is one led, perhaps, in the shadow, but ordered, regular, harmonious.' Langdale and Jenkins, in *Gwen John: An Interior Life* argued: 'Her lifelong tendency to form intense and smothering sentimental attachments to both men and women, by their very nature doomed to failure, became apparent at this time. Seemingly meek and self-effacing, she was in fact strong-willed and fiercely passionate. In appearance she was slight and pale, her brown hair carefully restrained, her dark eyes solemn and watchful; however… the firm set of her slightly receding chin hinted at her intransigent nature.'

In 1946 there was a Memorial Exhibition of 217 of Gwen's works in London, but her memory dimmed until recently. John Rothenstein, Director of the Tate, wrote in 1952 that 'the case of Gwen John provides a melancholy illustration of the neglect of English painting. I am not expressing an original opinion in saying that I believe her to be one of the finest painters of our time and country, yet - apart from her brother's eulogy and a discerning article on the Memorial Exhibition by Wyndham Lewis - her work has received no serious consideration whatever… Gwen John is, in fact, in danger of oblivion. It would be unjust to her contemporaries to suggest that they are solely to blame. She herself deliberately chose a life of seclusion. After her death a number of paintings disappeared from the little room she occupied. No work by her later than 1932 is known, and so withdrawn was her life during the closing years of it that it is uncertain whether she ceased to paint or whether the paintings she made were lost.'

In *Modern English Painters: Sickert to Smith,* Wyndham Lewis commented upon her exhibition for *The Listener* on 10 October 1946: 'Hers was a kind of art which is unlikely to recur... the personal world of this departed woman was chaste and bare and sad. These little fragments of experience testify to her beauty... the images of the "brute male force of the wicked world which marries and is given in marriage" are noticeably absent. Hardly a male is depicted here, only a handful of women: herself, Fanny, Dorelia, orphans, more children, and then the nuns, headed by the Mother Superior, the only one departing from the unsmiling rule.'

**Plaque to Gwen John and her brother in Victoria Place, Tenby**

Gwen was a superb painter, and Augustus John, at the height of his powers and fame, remarked that he would only be remembered at Gwen's brother. Tenby Museum and Art Gallery honoured her with a major exhibition in 2001 to commemorate the 125th anniversary of her birth. The museum's curator, John Beynon said 'She was a brilliant artist. It may well be that over the coming years she will become known more as a truly great artist than Augustus was', fulfilling Augustus John's prophecy. Of her paintings, the great man said he was 'flummoxed by their beauty'.

*Footnote:*

A recent article in *The Telegraph* (2 July 2015), entitled *Rodin's Stalker*, sheds some salubrious light upon Gwen's relationship. The details are from Sue Roe's marvellous *Gwen John: A Life*. 'AUGUSTE RODIN sculpted Gwen John in her twenties, larger than life and naked, standing on one leg with the other raised and splayed. The pose is majestically erotic and subversive. The model meekly bends her head with her arms snapped off at the shoulders, one bony knee level with her small firm breasts, her heel pointing directly at her crotch, which is barely concealed by what looks like a bed sheet, roughly modelled and tied across the top of her thighs. The piece suggests the sort of energetic and athletic sex Picasso painted in celebration of his own supple young mistress in the 1930s.

But it was in 1904 that Gwen first took off her clothes for Rodin. He had hired her to pose for a memorial, a Winged Victory commissioned by the

International Society of London to stand on Chelsea Embankment in honour of James Whistler's triumph over the enemies of Art. The Whistler Muse came as such a shock that the Society abandoned the project, and London lost a singular memorial commemorating three artists for the price of one. Gwen John was 27 when she met Rodin, who was 63. They made love on the floor of his studio, or in her rented room. Once he sent for her to have sex in front of another of his female assistants so that, as soon as he had finished, he could draw the two girls carrying on where he left off. Gwen was tickled pink. "I was a little solitaire," she wrote to him; "no one helped me or awoke me before I met you."

Once roused, her appetite proved insatiable. Rodin was soon pleading age and tiredness, and begging her to go back to painting. He said she made him feel like an old cracked vase that would fall to pieces at her touch. She waited for him every day and, if he didn't come, called at his studio. When he finally asked her not to, after the concierge had sent her away six times in one week, she hung around the station to watch him catch his train. She pursued him to the country, haunting his garden gate at Meudon and eventually renting a flat there herself. For more than a decade she wrote to him almost daily. "Letters are rather cowardly things sometimes," she noted shrewdly after Rodin's death in 1917, "like throwing stones that can't be sent back to you (at once)." It was a characteristically astute assessment of the demanding, one-sided, essentially autocratic relationships that she required of other people throughout her life. Parts of this book read like a stalker's charter. When Rodin died, Gwen was initially relieved. "I feel as if I have been ill, and am getting better." For the first time in 14 years, she could leave Paris without fear of missing a chance to see him.

## ALICE CATHERINE EVANS 29 January 1881 – 5 September 1975

## THE BACTERIOLOGIST WHO DISCOVERED THE CAUSE OF BRUCELLOSIS AND WAS RESPONSIBLE FOR PASTEURISED MILK

Alice Catherine Evans was born on a farm in Neath, Pennsylvania, the stronghold of Welsh settlers, to William Howell, a farmer and surveyor, and Anne B. Evans, a teacher. Her grandparents had emigrated to America in 1831, and this author cannot discover why she adopted her mother's surname of Evans, rather than Howell. Born on the farm in she was educated with her brother Morgan at a private school, Susquehanna Collegiate Institute, where she played for the female basketball team at a time when it was still seen as 'unladylike'. (There is a resonance of this is the game of netball played by females in the UK, rather than the more aggressive basketball). Her family could not afford for Alice to attend college, so she became an elementary school-teacher, one of the few professions open to women at this time.

Fortunately, she then learned of a free two-year course for rural teachers at Cornell University's College of Agriculture. Teachers were trained in nature study so that they could foster in rural children a love of nature and encourage them to remain in the country, rather than migrate to the towns. After four years in teaching, Alice had saved enough to pay for her subsistence, and enrolled in 1905. The new students shared some classes of basic studies with agriculture degree students, and Alice was fascinated by some of the science subjects, especially biology. When she ended her course, she won a scholarship to take a degree in agriculture. Again, tuition

fees were waived, as it was college policy to try and train more leaders for the agricultural industry. Alice chose to specialise in bacteriology, a discipline still in its infancy.

In 1909, she won a scholarship for graduate work at the College of Agriculture at Wisconsin University. The scholarship, for a student specialising in agricultural chemistry or bacteriology, had never been awarded to a woman. She achieved her master's degree there in 1910. Professor McCollum, who later discovered Vitamin A, wanted Alice to then take a PhD, but Alice's five years of higher education had been a physical and financial strain, and at that time a PhD was not essential for success in a scientific career. She was offered a post as a bacteriologist at Wisconsin University in Madison, in a team sponsored by the US Department of Agriculture, searching for methods to improve the flavour of Cheddar cheese.

Alice was in 1913 asked by the Department of Agriculture to work in their newly-completed Dairy Division laboratories in Washington DC. On her way there, she stopped at Chicago University and found out that it was not policy to hire female scientists. She realised that the Department of Agriculture believed that C.A. Evans must be a man, and that her hiring was a mistake. However, after spending three years as a Civil Service employee, it was difficult to dismiss her when she arrived at Washington. She recalled 'According to hearsay, when the bad news broke at a meeting of Bureau of Animal Industry officials that a woman scientist was coming to join their staff, they were filled with consternation. In the words of a stenographer who was present, they almost fell of their chairs'. Only one woman had been employed previously by the BAI, and she had lasted just a year in post.

Fortunately, her co-workers and immediate supervisors in the Dairy Division did not share the prejudices of those higher in authority. She was working as a junior collaborator on investigations in progress, when she was given her own research project, a study of the bacteria which multiply within the cow's udder and are excreted in milk. She initially concentrated on a species of bacteria, *Bacterium abortus*, which caused contagious abortion in cows (Bang's Disease). Evans decided to test if this organism could be dangerous to humans. She asked her Head of Pathology if there was any bacteria, carried by apparently healthy animals, which could be harmful to people. She was told that seemingly healthy goats could carry *Micrococcus melitensis*, causing Malta Fever (Human Undulant Fever). Alice then compared this *Micrococcus* with *Bacteria abortus*, to discover many similarities in culture tests on pregnant guinea pigs. Both organisms caused three out of four animals to abort. In effect, she believed the two micro-organisms to be almost, if not actually, identical. In her original studies on Malta Fever, her male superiors literally ordered her to stop her line of research, because she was claiming the source of contamination was the cow itself. Scientific wisdom said that the disease was caused by handlers, after the milk was drawn, and she was just wasting her time. Alice secretly continued with her tests, in her own time.

She reported her findings to a meeting of the Society of American Bacteriologists in 1917. Alice asked whether the bacteria which caused human undulant fever and bovine contagious abortion could cause disease, by being passed in raw milk. Scientists were extremely sceptical. They told her that if the two micro-organisms were so similar, this would have been noted by other (male) investigators. Alice was an unknown woman, without a PhD or reputation, and not for the first time (it happens today) the academic/scientific community closed ranks against a new idea. Besides, they argued that Human Undulant Fever was absent in the USA, so her relationship made no sense. What the scientists did not realise, however, is that the disease was very common in America, and all over the world, being mis-diagnosed as the potential fatal illness, Influenza. More severe cases of Human Undulant Fever had been mistaken for Typhoid, Malaria and other diseases. Hundreds of thousands of Americans were in reality affected by the potentially fatal disease, and it had killed millions all over the world.

The dairy industry also used its power to attack Alice's theory that raw milk could cause disease, and resisted her recommendations that all milk be pasteurised. Theobald Smith, the eminent bacteriologist who first isolated *Bacterium abortus* from raw milk, had warned against its possible pathogenicity in humans, but also now opposed her, drawing any waverers in the scientific community to side against Alice. However, she refused to back down, and her findings were confirmed in several laboratories around the world. The bacteria *Micrococcus melitensis* and *Bacterium abortus* were now together designated as the genus *Brucella*. Thus the term Brucellosis came to designate the terms Undulant Fever and Malta Fever.

Catherine's work led to the recognition of Brucellosis as a major global health problem, and the acceptance of pasteurised (heat-treated) milk which destroyed the bacteria. The dairy industry in the USA finally began pasteurisation across the country from 1928 to 1930, following the example of the brewing and wine industries for the previous forty years. The disease was all but eliminated in the USA as a result.

In 1918, her work recognised, Alice wished to help the war effort, and asked the Hygienic Laboratory (to later become the National Institute of Health and part of the Public Health Service) if they could use her services. She joined a team working to improve the serum treatment for epidemic meningitis. The Laboratory's Director, George McCoy, was an enlightened scientist who went out of his way to employ female scientists from 1916, but they still earned less, and were less likely to be promoted, than their male counter-parts. Alice also continued her studies on brucellosis, resultantly catching the disease in 1922, and her health was impaired for the next 20 years. 'Chronic Brucellosis' was not recognised at this time, and at first she had to put up with accusations that she was malingering. Periods of incapacity alternated with times of partial or complete recovery, similar to many auto-immune diseases. However, while she was undergoing surgery for another problem in 1928, surgeons found internal lesions from which *Brucella* were cultivated, supporting her diagnosis of Brucellosis. Her further research helped the understanding of her chronic form of the illness. Also in 1928, she was elected the first female President of the Society of American Bacteriologists.

Alice also contributed to the study of other infectious diseases, such as streptococcal infections and meningitis, and aged 65, she retired from the National Institute of Health. Aged 85, she protested in 1966 that the disclaimer of communist affiliation on the Medicare application violated her right of free speech. In 1967, the Department of Justice declared it unconstitutional. She received honorary doctorates from the Women's Medical College (later part of the Medical College of Pennsylvania), Wilson College and the University of Wisconsin. Alice never married and aged 94, she died of a stroke at a nursing home in Alexandria, Virginia.

## GWENDOLINE ELIZABETH DAVIES 11 February 1882 – 3 July 1951 and MARGARET SIDNEY DAVIES 14 December 1884 – 13 March 1963

## PHILANTHROPISTS AND CULTURAL BENEFACTORS

The sisters were brought up in the strict Nonconformist tradition favoured by their industrialist grandfather David Davies (1818-1890. Inheriting half a million pounds each, they remained strict teetotallers and Sabbatarians, and grew up in Montgomeryshire. Their brother David (1880-

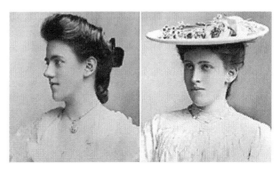

Gwendoline (on the left) and Margaret Davies, *courtesy of National Museum of Wales*

1944) was MP for Montgomeryshire, and was created Lord Davies of Llandinam in 1932. Their father Edward was weighed down by his responsibilities. He had wanted to go to Cambridge, but had to give up his dreams as he tried to balance his feeling for the miners during colliery unrest with his duties to his thousands of small share-holders. He also had problems at his great port of Barry Docks. His sensitivity led to a mental breakdown, and he died on New Year's Day 1898, just seven years after his father. The sister's mother had died in 1888, when they were aged just 4 and 6, followed by their beloved grandfather two years later. Gwen had asked if her mother was in Heaven. When told that she was, she asked 'Then why is everybody crying?'

Edward Davies married his deceased wife's sister, Elizabeth Jones, in Canada, as the marriage ceremony was not legal in Britain at that time. The young sisters' stepmother was strict Calvinist Methodist, who worked for good causes, and was Montgomeryshire's first woman magistrate. The girls attended Highfield Boarding School at Hendon, but also had a governess-companion, Miss Jane Blaker, who stayed with them until she died in 1947. It appears that there were suitors, but the girls had very high standards, they naturally assumed that their immense wealth (their father Edward died when the sisters were 15 and 17) would attract the wrong type of male, and they were fiercely protected by their stepmother and Miss Blaker. Gwen was an excellent violinist, but came to suffer from a blood disease affecting her fingertips.

At the start of World War I, the sisters went to work for the Red Cross in France, as they had previously travelled extensively there. They sent Thomas Jones and Major Burdon Evans to rescue fleeing Belgian artists and painters, whom they then settled at Aberystwyth and Barry until the war's end. One of the happiest times of their lives was opening a canteen for French soldiers in Troyes in 1916. *'Les Dames Anglaises'* were far away from the restrictions and formalities of life at home, and in their thirties had their first real taste of freedom amongst equals, scrubbing tables and singing to encourage the troops.

From 1908 they had been passionate art-collectors, guided by their advisors Hugh Blaker who was the brother of their governess (and curator of Bath's Holburne Museum) and John Witcombe (curator of Bath's Victoria Art Gallery). The sisters initially favoured works by J.M.W. Turner, Corot and Millet, but Blaker also encouraged them to purchase Daumier, Carrière, Monet and Rodin. By 1924 they had built up the largest collection of French Impressionist and Post-Impressionist works in Britain. In this year, their brother David had remarried, and asked Margaret, Gwendoline and their stepmother to vacate their family mansion at Plas Dinam, Llandinam, a few miles from Gregynog. Their stepmother Elizabeth Davies moved to Broneirion, the house built by the sisters' grandfather David Davies, to be near his chapel and Llandinam station. Elizabeth lived to be 90, and was always a strong influence upon Gwen and 'Daisy'. Gwendoline always called Margaret 'Daisy' because it had been her father's pet name for her. From 1924, Gwen had several long spells in hospital, eventually succumbing to leukaemia, possibly inter-related with her existing Raynaud's disease. One of her letters to TJ (Thomas Jones) from Ruthin Nursing Home in this year reveals the demands that were made on the sisters for funding: 'We have so much to give that isn't money and all that life seems to demand of us is money, money and yet more money. I am so weary.' Daisy, a keen artist, had problems with her voice, sometimes not being able to speak more than a whisper. She therefore spent many winters in the South of France to alleviate the condition.

Displaced from Llandinam, the sisters settled five miles from Newtown, Powys, at Gregynog Hall, with the fortune that they had inherited from David Davies' interests in contracting, Welsh coal-fields, railways and Barry Docks. Gwen Davies had first mentioned the hall as a 'white elephant' in 1919, and their brother David was going to auction its furniture and sell the unwanted building, possibly to an American. However, Walford Davies thought that it had potential as a centre for music, and the sisters soon took to the idea. There has been a hall on the site since at least the 12th century, but the present mock-Tudor building mainly dates from the 19th century, despite its older appearance.

Some parts of the older building have been incorporated, and the hall is surrounded by 750 acres of woodland and parkland. The estate used to comprise 18,000 acres at the beginning of the 19th century. From the 15th century it had been the home of the Blayney (Blaenau) family, and the home of bards and harpists, until Arthur Blayney died in 1795. Arthur regarded his tenants as 'his friends', shared his profits with them, assisted with their land and home improvements, and welcomed all who came to his 'plentiful table'. Ornate panelling carved with the Blayney coat of arms and dated 1636 can be seen throughout Gregynog Hall.

Gregynog's 'Great Wood' of oaks is a SSSI (Site of Special Scientific Interest) because over 140 species of lichens have been found there. This is one of the most important gardens and parks in Powys, dating from at least 1500. The house was rebuilt in 1830 and 1880. H.A. Tipping worked on the gardens 1930-33, and Dame Sylvia Crowe in 1972. Gwen was particularly interested in the gardens and their maintenance. The Davies sisters moved to live at Gregynog in 1924, four years after their purchase of the hall, numerous estate houses and 750 acres of land for £35,000. They did not originally intend to live there, but to make it a home for Welsh arts and crafts.

They created here a centre for the arts in Wales, and founded the prestigious Gregynog Music Festival, which attracted composers such as Vaughan Williams, Holst and Elgar. The many estate and hall staff were usually employed upon their singing capability, to form a choir that was often conducted by Walford Davies, then Sir Adrian Boult, and occasionally by Vaughan Williams and Gustav Holst. The festival is still held every June. Passionate about music, the sisters began by enlarging the former billiard room and installing a pipe organ, forming a music room able to seat an audience of 230. They were encouraged by their friend and mentor Dr Thomas Jones, known to all who knew him as TJ. The 'Gregynog Experiment' was the name popularly given to the centre for arts and crafts, music festivals and the printing press.

From 1922-1940 they ran a private press which produced 42 beautifully-bound fine print books. Fine hand-coloured illustrations, superb typography and wood engravings are features of the output, along with splendid bindings. TJ and Gwen were its driving forces, but the war ended production. In 1978, the University of Wales resurrected the press, and *Gwasg Gregynog* (The Gregynog Press) still produces superb limited edition books there. Some people recall walking into the dusty, cob-webbed workshops, closed off for over 30 years, and finding items of work and tools left laying as if the property had only just been vacated. Now, hot metal typesetting, letterpress printing and hand-binding is still carried out by time-served craftsmen; illustrations are commissioned from leading contemporary artists, and hand-made and mould-made fine papers are used, making every new edition collectible. Pouring money into the press, (and into the mining valleys for welfare schemes) the sisters' purchase of pictures virtually stopped, although Daisy bought some contemporary painters. However, on Gwen's death in 1951, Daisy started collecting in earnest again, selling some older paintings to acquire contemporary artists like Piper, Gill and Kyffin Williams.

The National Museum of Wales' website reads: 'After a good and progressive education, they developed a passion for the arts and music. Art history was in its infancy in Britain, so the sisters travelled widely in Europe, studying art in Germany and Italy before beginning their art collecting. Their sophisticated knowledge of art history was unusual for women of this period and their background. In 1908, the sisters began collecting art in earnest. Their early purchases included landscapes by Corot, peasant scenes by

Millet and also Turner's *The Storm* and *Morning after the Storm*. In the first six years of collecting, they amassed nearly a hundred paintings and sculptures. Their early taste was quite traditional, but in 1912 they turned to buying Impressionism. Their Impressionist purchases were generally less

**The Davies Sisters in France in WW1**

expensive than the works they had been acquiring by artists such as Turner and Corot. In 1913, Gwendoline acquired her most important painting, *La Parisienne*, for £5,000. The War transformed the lives of Gwendoline and Margaret. They worked as volunteers with the Red Cross in France.

However, they still managed to add to their collection during these years. They bought works by Daumier, Carrière, Renoir, Manet and Monet. In 1916 Gwendoline Davies also spent £2,350 on ten oil paintings and a drawing by Augustus John. In 1918, Gwendoline bought her two celebrated landscapes by Cézanne, Midday, L'Estaque and Provençal Landscape, which are among her most important and visionary purchases. In 1920, Gwendoline acquired perhaps her finest works, Cézanne's *Still-Life with Teapot* for £2,000 and Van Gogh's *Rain - Auvers* for £2,020. They also spent large sums on Old Masters, including Botticelli's *Virgin and Child with a Pomegranate*. Then their collecting suddenly reduced. Gwendoline wrote in 1921 that they could not continue to purchase so much 'in the face of the appalling need everywhere'. They still spent over £2,000 on Turner's *Beacon Light* in 1922 and £6,000 on a *Workshop of El Greco Disrobing of Christ* in 1923. In 1926, Gwendoline stopped collecting altogether.'

Like their noted brother, Lord Davies of Llandinam, the sisters were both also active social philanthropists, contributing to many educational and social causes. In the First World War, the sisters had run canteens in France for the troops, and in the Second World War willingly gave Gregynog for use as a Red Cross Convalescent Home. The Davies Memorial Gallery in

Newtown owes its existence to a bequest by the Davies charities, and fosters contemporary arts in Wales. Daisy was particularly concerned with helping Boverton Camp outside Llanilltud Fawr, which was used by youth clubs, and Tŷ Gwyn at Llwyngwril which provided long-term care for malnourished girls.

In 1950, Dr Thomas Jones, (the father of the Davies' biographer, Eirene White*) wrote: 'The home of Gwendoline and Margaret Davies is unique among country houses in Wales and I know of no parallel in England.' One of their closest advisors and friends, he could see Gregynog's joint function of devotion to the arts and the relief of social stresses of the times.

In 1951, Gwendoline died, and in 1960, Miss Margaret Davies made a gift of Gregynog and its contents to the University of Wales, which took it over on her death (as a tenant) in 1963. Her intention was that the Hall be used by the faculties of individual colleges for inter-collegial conferences. It is now a music, educational and residential conference centre. There is also a Welsh Learners' Centre at Gregynog, organised in conjunction with Powys County Council.

Collectors of 19th century French paintings, and patrons of contemporary artists, they were in the forefront of Europeans to appreciate the work of the French Impressionists and Post-Impressionists. Indeed, they amassed one of the finest art collections of the 20th century. 'The Davies Bequest' to the National Museum of Wales at Cardiff includes important works by Monet, Renoir, Pissaro, Sisley and Cezannes, and propelled Cardiff to the front rank of world art galleries. (The author still remembers vividly his first viewing of the Monets, aged ten). They bequeathed 256 important works to the National Museum in 1951 and 1963, completely transforming its character, range and quality.

It has been called one of the great British art collections of the 20th century. Among these were seven oil paintings that had been bought as Turners, of which three were subsequently judged to be counterfeit and withdrawn from display. These works were re-examined by the BBC TV programme *Fake or Fortune*, and were reinstated as genuine Turners. We can see in Cardiff a wall of Monet's paintings of water lilies, Venetian views and Rouen Cathedral, three paintings by Cezanne and Van Gogh's last painting, *Rain at Auvers*. There is also Rodin's famous *Blue Lady* ('*La Parisienne*') and his sculpture *The Kiss*. They also bought paintings from the workshops of Botticelli, El Greco's *The Disrobing of Christ*, Richard Wilson's *View of Windsor Pak*', five Turners and numerous Augustus Johns.

They also built up a fabulous collection from 1906 of watercolours by Turner, and others by Cezanne and Pissaro. Many were acquired in Paris during the First World War. Their 20th century acquisitions include the under-rated Welsh painter J.D. Innes, Frank Brangwyn, Eric Gill, Percy Wyndham Lewis, Stanley Spencer, Oscar Kokoscha, and Josef Herman. A small 1985 book by Lady Eirene White, *The Ladies of Gregynog*, pays tribute to their contribution to Wales. They both turned down honorary degrees from the University of Wales (which they had greatly endowed), but Gwen was made a Companion of Honour in 1937, and in 1949 Daisy at last accepted an honorary Doctorate of Laws.

\* Baroness Eirene White became Labour MP for Flintshire, and a tribute written to her was launched at Gregynog hall on August 28th, 2001, written by the House of Lords Librarian David Lewis Jones. Her father, Dr Thomas Jones, was Secretary to the Cabinet in several administrations, and a former chairman of Gwasg Gregynog.

*Footnote:*
The author has several treasured works from the Gregynog Press, and Thomas Jones noted its unique qualities in 1933: 'The feature which marks out the Gregynog experiment from others is that it attempts all the arts that go into the production of a complete book; it casts its own type and prints, it designs and cuts the initial letters, it designs and cuts all decorations and woodcuts, it makes marbled papers, designs and executes the bindings. The result is a unity and harmony in the final product, which is seen at its best so far in the superb *Ceiriog*. This book is being sold at a ridiculous price (one guinea) compared with its cost, in the hope that it may reach the schools and colleges of Wales and prove an inspiration to budding Welsh craftsmen...Every letter on the page has its fascinating story of turns and twists, of Gothic extravagance in this age and Roman austerity in that. The setting of the verses on the page, the size of the initials, the weight of the woodcuts, these and a hundred other problems have exercised the minds of craftsmen in their pursuit of perfection...They have sought after excellence and have made no compromise with meanness.'

## MARGARET HAIG THOMAS 12 June 1883 – 20 July 1958

### LADY RHONDDA, FEMINIST, SUFFRAGETTE AND PUBLISHER

Margaret's father David Alfred Thomas was born in Ysguborwen near Aberdare, in 1856, and her mother was Sybil Haig. After Cambridge University, David returned to Wales and eventually became the senior partner of a Cardiff firm, Thomas and Davies, which owned several Rhondda Valley collieries. In 1888 he was elected MP and held the seat until 1910. An only child and very close to her father, Margaret was educated at Notting Hill High School, St Leonards School of St Andrews and briefly at Somerville College, Oxford - this was at the time when women were not allowed to take degrees. According to her biographer, Deirdre Beddoe: 'She received a sound academic education, but there really never was any serious expectation that a girl of her class would work for a living. On leaving school she took the next logical step in the career progression of an upper-class girl and came out. Chaperoned by her long-suffering mother, she endured three successive London seasons. Paralysed by shyness and incapable of small talk, she found this an agonizing experience and she took herself off to Somerville College, Oxford, primarily to escape the horrors of a fourth London season, but gave that up and returned after less than a year.'

In 1908, the 25-year-old Margaret married a neighbour, Sir Humphrey Mackworth, a man twelve years her senior. The union was a mismatch from the start. He loved fox hunting, but Margaret thought hunting to be uncivilized and preferred to spend her hours reading. She found married life to be unfulfilling and her way of life too sheltered for her liking. In 1908 she joined the Women's Social and Political Union (WPSU, commonly known as the Suffragettes), becoming secretary of the Newport branch. During the 1910 General Election, she attacked the car of Herbert Asquith, and supporting the WSPU's arson campaign, was sent to prison for trying to destroy a post-box with a chemical bomb. However, a hunger-strike led to her early release after five days.

Upon the start of World War I, she accepted the WSPU leadership decision to restrain from militant action for the vote for women, and worked closely with her father. David Thomas was sent by Lloyd George to the United States to arrange the supply of munitions for the British armed forces, and at the same time took the opportunity of inspecting his coal mines in Pennsylvania. In May 1915, Margaret and her father were returning from the United States on the *Lusitania* when it was torpedoed by a German submarine. 1,198 out of 1,900 passengers and crew died. Margaret was rescued from the water, clinging to a wicker chair, and was thought to be dead, but came around several hours later. Margaret's brush with death left a deep impression on her, and she believed that her life had been saved to give it additional purpose and direction. Later in life, she became a deeply religious and very devout Christian

Awarded the title of Viscount Rhondda for his services to the country, David Thomas was appointed Minister for Food until his death in June 1918, just one month after being elevated to the Lords. His peerage passed, by 'special remainder' to Margaret, aged just 35. She tried to take her place in the House of Lords, but was kept out after extensive legal proceedings. She became Director of the Women's Department of the Ministry of National Service, and her 1918 report on the Women's Royal Airforce led to the dismissal of its commander Violet Douglas-Pennant and her replacement by the Welsh Helen Gwynne-Vaughan.

The British government recognized the right of women over thirty to vote in 1918. Margaret attempted to take her father's seat in the House of Lords as Viscountess Rhondda, citing the 1919 Sex Disqualification (Removal) Act as her birthright. The act stated 'a person shall not be disqualified by sex or marriage from the exercise of any public function.' The committee to which her petition was referred agreed that she had the right to sit in the House of Lords. This decision, however, alarmed many peers including Lord Chancellor Birkenhead, who set up another committee to reconsider the petition, constituting of himself and thirty other concerned peers. Margaret's claim was then swiftly rejected.

'Margaret inherited his [her father's] property, his commercial interests, and his title. *The Directory of Directors* for 1919 listed Viscountess Rhondda, as she now was, as the director of thirty-three companies (twenty-eight of them inherited from her father) and chairman or vice-chairman of sixteen of these. Already a famous figure whose activities were widely reported in the London press on account of her business career and of her increasingly leading role as a spokeswoman for feminism, her campaign to take her seat in the House of Lords attracted a great deal more publicity... But although in 1922 she seemed to have won, when the committee of privileges accepted her plea for admission, the decision was reversed in May 1922.'

George Bernard Shaw said that the House of Lords saw Lady Rhondda as a 'terror'... because of her political business acumen, 'the House of Lords has risen up and said, "If Lady Rhondda comes in here, we go away!"' Shaw said that if she had gained entry, 'there would be such a show-up of the general business ignorance and imbecility of the male sex as never was before.' However, Margaret persisted to change the law to accommodate women. She had her lawyer draft a bill to remove the sex bar and had Viscount Astor propose to Parliament. Although Astor proposed the same bill almost annually from 1924 to 1930, with the bill at times coming within two votes of passing, Viscount Astor would not succeed. The issue of women in the House of Lords was revived in the 1940s, and Margaret and others launched a petition to show there existed public support for women in the House of Lords. The first six months saw 50,000 signatures, including the principals of the women's colleges of Oxford and Cambridge. The Lords themselves finally passed a motion for women's admission in 1949, but the Labour government under Prime Minister Attlee refused to deliver the promised legislation. Four women were finally appointed to the House of Lords in 1958. It was much too late for Margaret, Viscountess Rhondda, who died that year, but her legacy had paved the way for women in generations to follow.

Soon after her father's death, in 1922 Lady Rhondda divorced her husband, using the most recent change in the divorce laws, and set up home with Helen Archdale. Archdale had three children and had also attended St Leonards School and been a Suffragette, leaving her husband for Margaret. According to Archdale's biographer, David Doughan: 'Helen Archdale had an intense relationship with Lady Rhondda, which seems to have begun in committee work during the First World War, though they also shared a background in suffrage militancy. By the early 1920s, she was sharing an apartment, and, together with her family, a country house (Stonepits, Kent) with Lady Rhondda.'

In 1920, Margaret founded, with Archdale as editor, *Time and Tide*, a feminist weekly journal of politics and literature, mainly publishing work that was boycotted elsewhere, such as George Orwell's expose of Stalinist repression in Republican Spain. Margaret took over the editorship when her affair with Archdale ended. Contributors included D.H. Lawrence, Vera Brittain, Virginia Woolf, George Bernard Shaw and Robert Graves. It was run by women, with an all female board of directors. It was a forum for women such as Winifred Holtby and Rebecca West to express their views, with articles including issues such as politics, health, birth control as well as literary pieces. The magazine, like its owner, gradually moved from the left-wing to a right-wing viewpoint, and it is estimated that over 38 years she lost over £500,000 in supporting its publication. Her savings having gone, she could not find any other funding and the publication folded.

In 1921 Margaret and Helen established the Six Points Group*, with the aim of campaigning for equal rights. She believed that the 1920's offered women boundless opportunities if only they would take them, and insisted that they needed to organise separately and independently from mainstream political parties. She encouraged younger women, and between the wars worked hard for peace and feminist goals. She wrote a memoir of her father, and an autobiography in 1933, *This Was My World*. After breaking up with Helen Archdale, she moved in with Theodora Bosanquet, the secretary of the International Federation of University Women.

* The Six Points were: pensions for widows; equal rights of guardianship for married parents; reform of the laws dealing with child assault; equal pay for teachers: reform of the law for unmarried mothers; and equal pay and conditions in the Civil Service.

## 'JEAN RHYS' 24 August 1890 - 14 May 1979

## ELLA GWENDOLEN REES WILLIAMS, AUTHOR OF *WIDE SARGASSO SEA*

Ella Gwendolen Rees Williams (Jean Rhys) was born at Roseau, Dominica, to a Welsh doctor William Rees Williams and a Creole woman. A 'white' girl in a black community, she was socially and intellectually isolated, and in 1907 left the Windward Isles for Perse School, Cambridge, where she was mocked for her accent and as being an outsider. (She returned only once to Dominica, in 1936). She attended two terms at the Royal Academy of Dramatic Art in 1909, but her instructors despaired of her ever learning to speak 'proper English' and advised her father to take her away. Now unable to train as an actress and refusing to return to the Caribbean as her parents wished, she worked with varied success as a chorus girl, adopting the names Vivienne, Emma or Ella Gray. Her beloved father died in 1910, and Rhys became the mistress of a wealthy stockbroker, Lancelot Grey Hugh ('Lancey') Smith. Though a bachelor, Smith did not offer to marry Rhys and their affair soon ended, but he continued to be an occasional source of financial help. In 1913 she worked for a time as a nude model in Britain to support herself, and received a small allowance from Smith.

In World War I she was a volunteer worker in a soldiers' canteen, and in 1918 was working in a pensions office. In 1919 Jean went to Holland and in that year married a French-Dutch journalist/songwriter Willem Johan Marie (Jean) Lenglet, a French-Dutch journalist, who was also seemingly a spy. He was the first of her three husbands. They first lived in Vienna and Budapest (1920-22), moving to Paris before settling in England in 1927. Their son died, just three weeks old, in mid-January, 1920, but a daughter survived.

In 1922 she had met the writer Ford Madox Ford in Paris, and began writing under his patronage. Ford recognized that her experience as an exile gave Rhys a unique viewpoint, and he praised her 'singular instinct for form... Coming from the West Indies with a terrifying insight and ... passion for stating the case of the underdog, she has let her pen loose on the Left Banks of the Old World'. Ford suggested she change her name from Ella Williams to Jean Rhys. Jean had an affair with Ford in 1923-1924, when her husband was in prison for illegal financial transactions. Rhys moved in with

Ford and his long-time partner, Stella Bowen, which she portrayed in her novel *Postures*, but the affair ended in bitterness and recriminations. Jean also was friendly with Ernest Hemingway and James Joyce during her Paris years. Distraught by events, including a near-fatal abortion (not Smith's child), Rhys began writing seriously.

Her first published major novel was *Postures* in 1928* (released as *Quartet: A Novel* in America). A film was recently made of her 1930 book, *Leaving Mr Mackenzie*. Its theme is a young woman recovering from sexual betrayal and attempting a futile liaison. She divorced Lenglet in 1932, and 1934 saw the publication of *Voyage in the Dark*. Its heroine, Anna Morgan, has come to England from Dominica, and gives a warm evocation of the Caribbean. Rhys continued to portray the mistreated, rootless woman, writing of a young chorus girl who grew up in the West Indies and was living in England, feeling alienated. It was the first novel she wrote, but the third to be published. In 1934 she married Leslie Tilden-Smith, an English editor. *Good Morning, Midnight* of 1939 tells us of the despair of the heroine, is written in first person narrative, alternating between the past and present, and is a technical tour de force. In it she uses a modified stream of consciousness to voice the experiences of an aging woman. All her novels were semi-autobiographical, featuring women protagonists adrift in Europe, in near-poverty, and hoping to be 'saved' by men.

With Tilden-Smith, she moved to Devon in 1939, where they lived for several years, but by the 1940's, however, the sad and lonely Rhys's work was unfashionable. Her husband died in 1945, and in 1947 Rhys married Max Hamer, another Englishman, a solicitor and cousin to Tilden-Smith. He was convicted of fraud and imprisoned after their marriage. From 1955 to 1960 she lived in Bude in Cornwall, where she was unhappy, calling it 'Bude the Obscure', before moving to Cheriton Fitzpaine in Devon until her death. In 1954, she wrote 'I must write. If I stop writing my life will have been an abject failure. It is that already to other people. But it could not be an abject failure to myself. I will not have earned death.' From 1958-1966 she worked on *Wide Sargasso Sea*, following interest in a radio broadcast by her in 1957, which displaced rumours of her death. Jean had literally disappeared from public view from 1939 to 1958, when the BBC dramatised *Good Morning, Midnight*.

After a long absence from the public eye, Jean published *Wide Sargasso Sea* in 1966, having spent years drafting and perfecting it. She intended it as the account of the woman whom Rochester would marry and keep in his attic in *Jane Eyre*. Begun well before she settled in Bude, the book won the prestigious WH Smith Literary Award in 1967. In it, she returned to themes of dominance and dependence, especially in marriage, depicting the mutually painful relationship between a privileged English man and a Creole woman of Dominica, made powerless on being duped and coerced by him and others. Both the man and woman enter into marriage under mistaken assumptions about the other. Her female lead marries Mr. Rochester, and deteriorates in England as the 'madwoman in the attic'. In this 'prequel', Jean portrays the woman from quite a different perspective from that drawn in *Jane Eyre*. *Wide Sargasso Sea* introduced her works to a new generation of readers and literary scholars.

She draws on the experience of her own great-grandfather's Dominican plantation being destroyed and the house burned down in 1844, following emancipation of the slaves. Coming of age, the Creoleheiress is married of to an Englishman, and he takes her from the only place she has ever known, a house with a garden where: 'the paths were overgrown and a smell of dead flowers mixed with the fresh living smell. Underneath the tree ferns, tall as forest tree ferns, the light was green. Orchids flourished out of reach or for some reason not to be touched.' The mad woman in Jean's story burns the house and herself after descending into madness, her husband noting: 'I watched her die many times. In my way, not in hers. In sunlight, in shadow, by moonlight, by candlelight. In the long afternoons when the house was empty.' After many rejections and revisions, it was published to bring Rhys critical acclaim which she said had come too late.

Her books have been described as telling the story of a lonely woman alienated in a male-dominated society, and a reviewer of the reprint of *Quartet* wrote in the *New York Times Book Review*, April 1971: 'Her heroines (there are no heroes) embody not so much a capacity for suffering as a thwarted capacity for joy.' She was made a CBE in 1978, and among her awards were the Royal Society of Literature Award and an Arts Council Bursary. Her final years bought fame and freedom from financial anxiety, with a new collection of short stories (*Sleep it Off, Lady*) and an unfinished autobiography, published posthumously as *Smile Please*. Her husband Max Hamer died in 1966. She had lived for many years in great poverty in the West Country. Living alone at her cottage at Cheriton Fitzpaine, Devon, she drank heavily. *'Ella'* died at home, alone, in Exeter, aged 84. Self-destructive and alcoholic, she described herself as 'a doormat in a world of boots'.

* Another novel, *The Left Bank* was published in a small edition in 1927. There are at least twelve books written upon this fascinating woman. The following quote by Jean should be used in campaigns to stop the closure of public libraries: 'Reading makes immigrants of us all. It takes us away from home, but more important, it finds homes for us everywhere.'

# DAME GWEN LUCY FFRANGCON-DAVIES 25 January 1891 - 27 January 1992

## AN ACTRESS FOR EIGHT DECADES

Both of her parents were Welsh, her Bethesda father moving to London to find work. Her father David Thomas Davies was a fine opera baritone, who had toured the Continent giving performances. He altered his name to David Ffrangcon-Davies, using an old spelling of the Snowdonia Valley of Nant Ffrancon, near his place of birth. Gwen began her stage career as a soprano, before changing to acting. She auditioned for the great Ellen Terry, who encouraged her. Gwen's debut was in April 1911 as a fairy in *Midsummer Night's Dream*, and she was in the Birmingham Repertory Company, taking leads by 1921.

1922 saw Gwen starring in *The Immortal Hour* by the composer Rutland Boughton. Birmingham Repertory Company took it to the West End where it ran for 219 performances, a record for a folk opera in the history of the English theatre. Such was Gwen's performance that the art critics of the day were reporting spotting more than 100 Etain lookalikes on the streets of London every day. She originated the role of Eve in George Bernard Shaw's *Back to Methuselah* (1923). By 1924, she was an established stage star, playing Juliet to a young John Gielgud's Romeo. She was hailed as 'the finest Juliet of her generation'. Gielgud was grateful to her for the rest of his life for the kindness she showed him, casting her as Queen Anne in *Richard of Bordeaux* in 1934.

In 1925, Thomas Hardy had scripted *Tess of the D'Urbervilles* as a play, and there was fierce competition between Sybil Thorndike, Gertrude Elliott (Lady Forbes Robertson) and Gwen for the role of Tess. Gwen played the role, first in Barnes Theatre before transferring to the Garrick in the West End. Apart from a brief run in 1928, after Hardy's death in 1928, the play was not performed again in the West End until 1993. In 1934, Gwen bought a 17th-century cottage in Halstead, Essex, where she lived for the next 57 years.

In 1938, she appeared with the Welshman Ivor Novello in *Henry V* at Drury Lane, and that same year appeared as Mrs Manningham in the first production of *Gas Light* opposite Gielgud. Gwen also starred with Gielgud in *The Importance of Being Earnest* in 1940 and as Lady MacBeth for almost an entire year in 1942. Gielgud himself died aged 96 in May 2000, and Sheridan Morley called him 'the greatest classical actor of all time'. Born in 1904, he was 19 when he played Romeo for the first time, opposite the 32 year-old Gwen, and recalled it as 'a baptism of fire'.

She went to South Africa with her life-long companion, the actress Marda Vanne, in 1942, to establish the country's first major classical theatre company. The playwright Nicholas Wright recalled her absolute determination to only accept the very highest professional standards there: 'My first theatrical experience was working for Gwen Ffrangcon Davies in *The Turn of the Screw* - she would direct in the most ferocious way, making me cry.'

The couple returned to England in 1947, and among Gwen's notable West End starring roles were appearances in *The Cherry Tree* (1954), *Becket* (1961) and *Much Ado About Nothing* (1965). She was a founder member of both the Royal Shakespeare Company and the Royal Court, and won *The Evening Standard* Best Actress Award for her performance in *Long Day's Journey Into Night*. Gwen was in her 70's when she debuted on Broadway in *The School for Scandal*. She also appeared in the films *The Devil Rides Out* (1968), *The Burning* (1968), *The Witches* and John Boorman's *'Leo the Last'* with Marcelo Mastroianni (1970). In the film *Tudor Rose*, the life of Lady Jane Grey, Gwen starred as Mary Tudor, alongside John Mills and Sybil Thorndike.

In Shakespeare's *oeuvre*, she played Cordelia, Cleopatra, Portia, Titania, Ophelia, Regan, Beatrice, Queen Katharine, Lady Macbeth and Juliet, which was her signature role. She displayed equal versatility in her other roles, most notably Elizabeth Barrett in *The Barretts of Wimpole Street* (1930, revived in 1935), Gwendolen in *The Importance of Being Earnest* (1940), Mary Tyrone in *Long Day's Journey into Night* (1958), and Amanda Wingfield in *The Glass Menagerie* (1965). She last appeared on stage in Anton Chekhov's *Uncle Vanya* (1970), but she continued to act on television and radio, taping her last television appearance at the age of 100. In the 1980s she appeared on the *Wogan* BBC TV chat show, in which she recited word for word Juliet's death scene. Aged 97 she was interviewed for *Desert Island Discs.*

Gwen was still acting in her 80's, and became a DBE in 1991. Her last stage appearance was in a Royal Court production of *Uncle Vanya* in 1970, and her last TV appearance in a Sherlock Holmes drama shown at Christmas 1991, 80 years after her acting debut. In her life, she played Lady MacBeth, Cleopatra, Mary Queen of Scots, Florence Nightingale and Eliza Dolittle, among many other main parts. Shortly before her death, she was asked if she was afraid of dying. Gwen replied 'My dear, I am always nervous about doing something for the first time.' The website 'women of achievement' notes her passing as an 'English (sic) actor who became a living legend. She continued acting on the stage into her 80's before turning to TV and taping her last segment when she was 100. A star on the classical stage, she was a leading Shakespearean actor and interpreter of Shaw and Tennessee Williams.' The website Hollwood.com reported the death of 'a legendary figure of the English stage, and in the words of the New York Times "a last link with the world of the Victorian theatre". Ffrangcon-Davies's career spanned 80 years, from a walk-on part in a 1911 performance of "*A Midsummer Night's Dream*" to an appearance in the 1992 Sherlock Holmes TV-movie *'The Master Blackmailer'*. She was hailed as the finest Juliet of her generation for her 1924 performance opposite the 19 year-old John Gielgud. Ffrangcon-Davies retired from the stage in 1970 but continued to work in radio and TV until the end of her life. She was made a Dame of the British Empire in 1991 after much campaigning by senior theatrical figures. At age 100, she was the oldest person to be so honoured.'

Her *New York Times* obituary called her 'a last link with the Victorian theatre... She told interviewers that one cherished memory of her girlhood was seeing the renowned actor and manager Sir Henry Irving playing Shylock in Shakespeare's *Merchant of Venice* on a stage lighted by gas footlights.' Her simple gravestone reads: Dame Gwen Ffrangcon-Davies, Actress, 1891-1992.

*Footnote:*

In her 1931 autobiography, Emma Goldmann noted: 'Shortly after my arrival in England Fitzi had appointed me her representative for the Provincetown Playhouse, to which she had already given years of labour and love. My credentials afforded me free access to some of the theatres, yet what I saw did not whet my appetite for further exploration of the London stage. English friends spoke highly of the Birmingham Repertory Theatre, the only outstanding group of artistic merit. It had grown out of amateur beginnings, they informed me, and it owed its first start and splendid development to the skill and generosity of its founder, Barry V. Jackson. My experience with British intellectual hospitality had made me somewhat sceptical. Opportunity to judge for myself came when the Birmingham Repertory Company opened in London with Shaw's *Caesar and Cleopatra*, and I made haste to present my credentials as Fitzi's European ambassador. At no theatre in the British metropolis had I been received with greater courtesy. The performance proved to be a revelation. Such settings, atmosphere, and ensemble acting I had not seen since the Stanislavsky Studio days, and even there the scenery did not compare with this feast for the eyes. Cedric Hardwicke's Caesar surpassed that of Forbes-Robertson, whom I had seen in New York. He succeeded in making the old Roman intensely human, with enough wit to laugh at himself. Miss Gwen Ffrangcon-Davies as Cleopatra was an exquisite creature. For the first time in England I was able to banish the gloom the travail of eight months had settled on my spirit'.

# KATE ROBERTS 13 February 1891 – 4 April 1985

## WRITER AND LITERARY JOURNALIST, THE 20TH CENTURY'S MOST DISTINGUISHED PROSE-WRITER IN WELSH, 'THE WELSH CHEKHOV', 'BRENHINES EIN LLÊN' (THE QUEEN OF OUR LITERATURE)

Kate was born the daughter of a quarryman, in the slate-quarrying village of Rhosgadfan, Caernarfonshire, when the industry was at its height, employing almost 20,000 men. It was an intensely Welsh cultural environment which always remained with her. She was educated at Bangor University (she gained a First in Latin, History, Welsh and Philosophy), and gained a teaching certificate. Following a period teaching at Dolbadarn, Llanberis and Conwy Elementary Schools, she became the Welsh teacher at Ystalyfera County School from 1915-1917, where the great *Gwenallt* (David James Jones) was one of her pupils. She also taught geography and history. She then taught in Aberdare Girls County School from 1917 until her marriage to Morris Williams in 1928. She had met him at Plaid Cymru meetings. They lived in Cardiff and Tonypandy until 1935, when they purchased Gwasg Gee, the publisher of the Welsh newspaper *Y Faner ac Amsera Cymru*, when they settled in Cilgwyn, Denbighshire.

Morris died in 1946, and Kate ran the paper for another 10 years, writing columns, political articles, literary criticism as well as running the business. Kate Roberts' written work is split into two definite periods. The early period starts with *Deian a Loli* in 1925 and ends with *Ffair Gaeaf* in 1937. Rural life and the slate-mining community provides the background for much of her work during this period, and she often draws on her childhood memories as a quarryman's daughter. This is true of her best-known novel *Traed mewn Cyffion* published in 1936. From 1923 she had been encouraged by W.J. Gruffudd, editor of the literary magazine *Y Llenor*, to write short stories, and this resulted in *O Gors y Bryniau* in 1925, followed by *Rhigolau Bywyd* in 1929 and *Ffair Gaeaf* in 1937. An English translation of some of these stories was published in 1946, as *Summer Day*. *Traed Mewn Cyffion* (*Feet in Chains*) in 1936 was her first novel, inspired by memories of the First World War, when her brother was killed.

The second period begins 12 years later, following the death of her husband in 1946. Saunders Lewis had not been as enthusiastic about her novel as he was about her short stories, and this seems to have stifled her creative muse, as her next book was not published until 1949, *Stryd y Glep*. Then the floodgates opened with novels and short stories, until her last book, *Haul a Drycin* was released in 1981. She was 90 years old. She published eleven books in this period, with the loneliness of old age being the dominant theme during this period, rather than poverty.

Before 1936 she wrote of the sufferings and misunderstandings of other people's lives, but after the war years wrote more of her own feelings. Gwyn Williams translated her feelings in 1958: 'In my later years I have had to go through bitter experiences alone, and the only way to be able to live at all was to write, not about those things as they happened to me but to write about other kinds of suffering and give them to other kinds of people. Suffering itself can turn into a kind of joy… to talk about people who go to the depth of suffering, who drink the bitter dregs and rise again, not victorious but with confidence to face life once more.' (*An Introduction to Welsh Literature*, 1992). Her Spartan, economical style has influenced many modern Welsh novelists.

Kate wrote in *Y Lôn Wen* in 1960, her 'piece of autobiography' that 'Everything important, everything of deep impression, happened to me before 1917.' Another passage in *Y Lôn Wen* gives us a flavour of her infallible childhood memory: 'How do children know when to change from one game to another? Children do not play all kinds of games indiscriminately, but there will come a hot fever of playing hoop, of playing marbles, playing top, or playing kite. No-one knows the hour or the day the fever starts, but it starts in every district at once. The children of Pwllheli and the children of Caernarfon, the children of Waunfawr and the children of Felinheli play the same thing at the same time of the year. For me this is one of Creation's mysteries.' All her books between 1925 and 1937 are set in Arfon, Caernarfonshire, in the slate-quarrying community, except for three stories of working-class life in the coal-mining valleys of Glamorgan. She lived from 1915-1935 in Glamorgan.

Then from her years living in Denbigh she was able to write about contemporary small-town life in North Wales from 1946. An anti-war nationalist, she wrote in *Traed Mewn Cyffion* in 1917: 'By now (the people of Foel Arian) did not believe at all that the war's purpose was to defend the rights of small nations, and that it was a war to end wars, nor did they believe one country was to blame more than another, but they had come to believe that there were people in every country who liked war, and that they used their sons to their own advantage. These were the aristocracy, the same people who oppressed them in the quarry, and sucked their blood and turned it into gold for themselves.'

Kate noted the difficulties of writing in Welsh in 1949: 'If a writer is a sincere Welsh writer, he cannot fail to be at one with his nation's past and at one with his nation's future also, and thus he strives to the best of his ability to keep his nation's literature and culture alive. Thus, he divides his life, interests and energy, and cannot give his whole life to literature.' In 1961 she noted 'it is not patriotism that should stimulate us to write... It is life that stimulates an author to write, life and all its problems, and people create those problems. When a man writes, he does not think of man as Englishman, but thinks of him as a human being, in relation to himself, or to his society, or to God... It is not patriotism that stimulates us... but something much greater, a longing to express ourselves on matters that pertain to the whole of Creation, things dark to us, or things that pain us, or things that interest us that are neither dark nor painful. We cry out, we howl at Life, most often because we do not understand it.'

By 1963, Kate Roberts was a lonely, disenchanted figure, giving a character in *Hyn o Fyd* the lines: 'We search for peace and contentment as if it were possible to have them; it's impossible to have them in a world so full of murder, thieving, dishonesty, prostitution, hypocrisy, niggardliness,... If we enjoy some part of our life, we enjoy it like seagulls skimming the surface of the water at the seaside, and forget, even in our profoundest moments, all the dirt and stink that's beneath us.' The best initial approach to an understanding of Kate Roberts' importance is *Kate Roberts* by Derec Llwyd Morgan (1974, republished in 1991 on the centenary of her birth.) Her many publications are analysed, and a list of those available in English translation is listed.

Kate worked until her death aged 94, and her wonderful illustrations of Welsh life captured the country in the 20th century forever. Her work was translated into many languages, but not until she was in her 70's and 80's was her real contribution to Welsh culture recognised. Derek Llwyd Morgan's short book on Kate demonstrates that 'her mastery of idiom and syntax was renowned, few of her fellows matched her sensitivity...the situations she invented possess the authoritative truth only the genius of imagination can produce.'

She was a regular contributor to *Y Faner*, one of the papers published by Gwasg Gee, under her directorship. Y Faner was prominent in its support of Plaid Cymru against the Ministry of Defence during the late 40s and 50s, and also against the drowning of Tryweryn Valley. She also contributed regularly to Plaid Cymru's newspaper, *Y Ddraig Goch.* She received a number of honours during her lifetime, and, in 1950, her commitment as a writer and prominent nationalist was recognised when she was awarded a University of Wales D.Litt. degree. Towards the end of her life, Kate was honoured by the Welsh Arts Council, the Honourable Society of the Cymmrodorion and the University of Wales, with a national testimonial in 1983. She was also successful in her bid to establish a Welsh-medium school in Denbigh, initially held at Capel Mawr Schoolhouse, before becoming Ysgol Twm o'r Nant in 1968

*Footnote:*
The plaque on Kate Roberts' cottage, Cae'r Gors, at Rhosgadfan, reads:

'*Hen Gartref Kate Roberts*
*Y Nofelydd*
*Y Lon Wen*
*Ffair Gaeaf*
*O Gors y Bryniau*
*Laura Jones*
*Deian a Loli*
*Rhigolau Bywyd*
*Te yn y Grug*
*Traed Mewn Cyffion* '

## ELENA PUW MORGAN 19 April 1900 - 17 August 1973

## THE FIRST FEMALE TO WIN THE LITERATURE MEDAL AT THE NATIONAL EISTEDDFOD

At the Cardiff National Eisteddfod in 1938, Elena was the first female to win the Literature Medal (*Medal Ryddiaeth*) for her novel *Y Graith* (The Scar). At that time, the medal was only awarded every three years for the best prose work of that period.

 *Y Graith* tells of the book's heroine, Dori, as she struggles with cruelty and poverty at the start of the twentieth century. The eminent adjudicator, D.J. Williams, wrote that 'this work is an important contribution to the novel in Wales, and will have a lasting place in our literature'.

Elena lived most of her life in Corwen, Meirionethshire. Her parents were Lewis and Kate Davies whose home was called Islwyn, where Elena spent her childhood. Her parents' only other child, Dewi Iwan, died in infancy before Elena was born. Lewis was a minister at the Independent chapel in Corwen but despite her sheltered and very religious upbringing, there is no trace of religious sentiment in Elena's novels. Most of her literary work was written in the 1930's. She published two children's books, *Angel y Llongau Hedd* (1931) and *Tan y Castell* (1937) under her maiden name of Davies, and wrote the (unpublished) *Bwthyn Bach Llwyd y Wig* and numerous short stories for children in the inter-war decades, when there was a dearth of attractive reading material in Welsh for children. These were published in periodicals and magazines and included for example *Kitty Cordelia*, a series about girls at a boarding school. Her work in the magazine *Cymru'r Plant* and her other stories helped to inspire the next generation of Welsh-language writers.

Her novels for adults included *Nansi Lovell* (1933) which describes the life of Welsh Romany gipsies. She was very sympathetic to and interested in Romany tradition and culture and had personal contacts amongst the North Wales Romany community. Alongside *Y Graith*, her other best-known work remains *Y Wisg Sidan* (The Silk Dress), published in 1939. It was enthusiastically received by the reading public, but less so by contemporary literary critics who considered it too 'popular', criticism which Elena took to heart and which greatly discouraged her. However, along with *Y Graith,* it is now recognised as a Welsh literary classic. Both novels are vivid portrayals of Welsh rural life, describing the harshness and suffering experienced by her young women protagonists, and are heavily imbued with the atmosphere and the natural landscapes of Wales. Both *Y Wisg Sidan* and *Y Graith* were updated by Catrin Puw Davies, Elena's daughter, in the 1990's, and both were made into powerful TV series by S4C. Elena married John Morgan, a local draper who, like herself, was prominent in the public life and Welsh culture of the area. They lived at Annedd Wen, close to Corwen town centre, and had one daughter, Catrin. Outside John Morgan's draper's premises, now a cafe, there is a plaque commemorating Elena and her work. Elena was a good friend of John Cowper Powys, who lived locally, and Annedd Wen was a frequent and lively meeting and discussion place in the area's literary and Welsh cultural scene. Elena suffered with ill-health both as a child (she missed an entire year of school) and later in life. She also took on a string of caring commitments, including nursing her uncle, her mother, and then her husband, as well as others. These constraints meant that, sadly, she did not continue her writing career much beyond the 1930's. She is buried, alongside her parents, husband, daughter and son-in-law, in Corwen cemetery.

*Footnote:*
Often, like the Bardic Crown and Chair, the Medal is not awarded, and the list of female winners shows the increasing influence of women in Welsh literature, and also how much of a pioneer Elena was:

1938    Caerdydd, Elena Puw Morgan - *Nofel: Y Graith*
1960    Caerdydd, Rhiannon Davies Jones - *Fe Hen Lyfr Cownt*
1964    Abertawe, Rhiannon Davies Jones - *Lleian Llanllŷr*

## LADY MEGAN LLOYD GEORGE 22 April 1902 – 14 May 1966

### FEMINIST AND RADICAL POLITICIAN

**Megan Lloyd George campaigning**

Born in Cricieth, the youngest daughter of the great statesman David Lloyd George, her brothers were Richard (1889-1968) and Gwilym (1894-1967), and her sisters Mair Eluned (1890-1907) and Olwen Elizabeth (1892-1990). She seems to be the first *Megan* recorded in history. She brought up, largely, at 11 and 10 Downing Street when her father was firstly Chancellor of the Exchequer and then Prime Minister. Until the age of four she spoke only Welsh and was at least partly educated by Frances Stevenson, Lloyd George's long-standing mistress. In 1911, Frances Stevenson had been appointed as Megan's tutor in French and piano in London, where her father was now Chancellor. Frances found Megan an 'enchanting child'. Lloyd-George became Prime Minister during the First World War, and was later referred to by Hitler as 'the man who won the war.'

274

It is no surprise that Megan developed an interest in politics, as she herself once said: 'I've had politics for breakfast, lunch, tea and dinner all my life'. She was encouraged by her father to join in conversations and he sought her opinion on the events of the period. In 1919 Megan accompanied Lloyd George to the Peace Conference at Versailles after the end of the First World War, and witnessed international affairs first hand. She became a fervent opponent of appeasement, the policy that, arguably, enabled Hitler to come to power in Germany. Megan spent a year at finishing school in Paris in 1919, and around 1920-21 became aware of her adored father's relationship with Miss Stevenson. She came to hate Miss Stevenson, and tried to do all she could to end the affair with her beloved 'Tada' (Tad = father in Welsh. Its mutation to 'dad' has passed into the English language, as has 'mam' or 'mum').

Her mother Margaret worked hard to secure the Welsh-speaking Megan's nomination as the Liberal candidate for Anglesey in 1928. When making a speech on agriculture, a farmer derided her from the crowd, saying that she knew nothing, not even how many ribs a pig possessed. Megan coolly invited him up to the podium - 'Come up here and I'll count!' Her slogan was: 'We can conquer unemployment' and in 1929 the 27-year-old won a thumping majority of 5,618 votes (13,181 voted for the Liberals against 7,563 for Labour and 5,917 for the Conservatives), and remained Anglesey's MP for 22 years, Wales' first female representative to sit in the House of Commons. There were just 13 female MP's, and she was the only Liberal, sitting with 8 Labour, 3 Tory and one Independent women. She began a long affair with the MP Philip Noel-Baker in 1929, but his wife would not divorce him. 25 years later, in 1954, he wrote to her: 'Always, all day, every day, ever since we first sat down together, I have longed to have you for my own, my perfect, my brilliant, lovely, exciting, famous, sweet & tender wife...'

As a Liberal MP, Megan Lloyd George was outspoken and forthright. In 1931 she refused to support the National Government of Ramsey MacDonald but this did not affect her popularity and she continued to hold the Anglesey seat until 1951. A noted feminist and radical, Megan fought for equal pay for women in the Second World War. In 1941 her mother Margaret died, and her father wanted to go back to Wales to live with Frances Stevenson in Bronawelon, the family home, and marry Frances. Megan was furiously and implacably opposed, although her brother Gwilym and sister Olwen were not against the marriage. However, David married Frances upon 23 October 1943. She had been his secretary for 30 years. Frances sent a kind letter to Megan after the wedding, but Megan was still consumed by anger and never responded. She was reconciled to her father in the next year, but only saw him on condition that Frances stayed away. Megan was also very much against her father becoming Earl Lloyd-George of Dwyfor, although she would now be entitled 'Lady' Megan Arfon.

Lloyd George died on March 26th 1945, at his new house of Tŷ Newydd, just a mile from Bronawelon. Megan was distraught. He was buried on the banks of the Dwyfor River. Frances Stevenson was not invited, but visited later and left a wreath of red roses. The following day Megan noticed the roses and threw them over a hedge into the road. The 16 year-old daughter of Lloyd George and Frances was sadly snubbed by the grieving Megan, when she went to greet her soon after. Megan now lived in Bronawelon.

In 1945, she only just defeated the young Cledwyn Hughes of the Labour Party to hold on to her Anglesey seat by 1081 (12,610 votes to 11,529). She was the only one of the 11 Liberals in the House of Commons who was a well-known personality, after this Labour landslide of an election. Her brother Gwilym was also a Liberal MP, and her London home was 13 Cromwell Place in South Kensington. In the 1940s and 50s she campaigned vociferously for a Welsh Assembly and for the appointment of a secretary of state for Wales. Megan was an excellent public speaker, relying more on improvised rhetoric than logical content. In 1950, the Labour Party organiser for North Wales had heard her speak during the 1950 election campaign: 'You could hear the emotion rising. I couldn't help feeling the desire to join her, and I had to remember that I was there to help defeat her.' In the 1950's Megan moved towards Welsh nationalism, and led the campaign for a Parliament for Wales. In 1944 she had managed to ensure that a Welsh Day, discussing Welsh matters, was held in Parliament.

She told the House 'Wales is not an area, not a part of England, but a nation with a living language of its own, hundreds of years of history behind it, and with its own culture... It is the Welsh way of life that we are determined to see maintained...No Englishman can understand the Welsh. However much he may try, however sympathetic he may feel, he cannot get inside the skin and bones of a Welshman unless he is born again.' She argued that the Atlantic Charter, signed by Roosevelt and Churchill, applied to Wales: 'That provision does not only apply to Poland, Czechoslovakia, Romania - countries far distant. It applies also to Wales... We have fought with you, we have also, many a time and for long centuries, fought against you, but we would now like to be in partnership with you in this greatest endeavour in our long history.'

As the 1940s drew to a close it was clear that Megan Lloyd George was moving further and further to the left in her political views and stance. Despite this, in 1949 she was appointed deputy leader of the Liberal Party, one of only 12 Liberal politicians in the House. She argued with Lord Beveridge that Wales had a 'national identity' and should not be treated as a region by the BBC. As Deputy Leader, in the 1950 election campaign, she made one of the three party political broadcasts allowed to the party. She argued for reduced taxation, and cost-cutting by the nationalised industries, before saying: 'We know that the men and women who tramped the streets of our great cities and the valleys of my country in dull, hopeless despair searching for work were not free men and women. Freedom must be the solid rock upon which we must build, but full employment must be the first pillar of our new society; social justice for all must be the other.' She ended her speech, not with the normal 'Goodnight' but with *'Nos da. Hunan llywodraeth i Gymru.'* English listeners would not have understood that this means 'Good night - self-government for Wales.' Her majority almost doubled in Anglesey, still then a predominantly Welsh-speaking county before the influx of English retirees, unemployed looking for a better environment, and holiday-homers. Just 9 Liberals were elected across Britain.

In 1950, Megan accepted the invitation to become President of the Parliament for Wales Campaign. She argued for 'a Parliament sitting on Welsh soil and answering to the Welsh people.' (What she would have thought of the present Assembly in Cardiff Bay is unthinkable.). Despite poor planning and a lack of manpower, over 250,000 signatures were gathered in a petition for a Welsh Parliament, 30,000 coming from the Labour heartland of the Rhondda Valley.

In 1951, Megan narrowly lost Anglesey to Cledwyn Hughes - his third attempt to unseat her, and the Liberal Party was down to 6 MPs in the

**Megan Lloyd George in 1956 with the petition of 250,000 people for a Welsh Parliament**

Commons. To many, it seemed as if her political career was over. Herbert Morrison congratulated Hughes on his Labour victory, but said 'Mind you, Megan is a great loss.' The Labour MP James Callaghan also commiserated and asked her to come into the Labour Party: 'I am genuinely sorry you are not in the House & I very much hope you will come back. We cannot sacrifice grace, charm, wit, passion as easily as that. But you must come back as a Member for our Party. First, because we are right about the malaise & the remedies for the 20th century. Secondly, because there is no other way back.' Megan toured Canada, the USA and Jamaica with Olwen, lecturing and trying to think about her future.

She knew she wanted to stay in politics, but was reluctant to join the Labour Party straight away. In Summer 1952, she lunched with the Labour PM, Clement Attlee, who wrote to his brother: 'I wish that she would join us, but she thinks it is her duty to keep the Liberal remnant away from the Tories.' In November, she wrote to the Anglesey Liberal Association, stating that she did not wish to be their candidate again - as 'the Radical daughter of a Radical leader, I have latterly been disturbed by the pronounced tendency of the official Liberal party to drift to the right.' Megan joined the Labour Party in 1955, writing to Clement Attlee that she would campaign across the UK for the Labour party in that year's election: 'It is only in the Labour Party that I can carry on the Radical tradition... the Labour Party exists to promote social justice and further our progress to a genuine welfare state. The Tories are the party of privilege...' Megan was a prominent member of the Tryweryn Defence Committee and featured strongly in the opposition to a hydro-electric scheme at Nant Gwynant in 1955.

In February 1956 Philip Noel-Baker was widowed, and the 76-year old went to Greece to recover. On his return he wrote to Megan, outlining his reasons for not marrying her and she wept uncontrollably. In November that year, the MP for Carmarthen died and there was a by-election in early 1957. Patricia Llewellyn-Davies commented on one of her speeches, 'She started in English, then she switched to Welsh, and everyone leaned forward as if they wanted to touch her physically. It was electrifying.' Plaid Cymru attacked her, as Labour policy was against a Welsh parliament, but she responded that policy called for a Welsh Secretary of State, and that she still would fight for her nationalist beliefs, within the party. Campaigning against the Suez invasion, she won in a massive 87.5% turnout, with 23,679 votes against the Liberals' 20,610 and Plaid Cymru's 5,741. In her victory tour of the constituency, one man called out 'You're as good as your father', to which Megan responded 'If I'm half as good that will do.' She was received into the House of Commons with rousing cheers from the Labour benches, her friends including Nye Bevan, Hugh Gaitskell, Jim Griffiths, Cledwyn Hughes and Desmond Donnelly. She spoke with passion for disarmament and against nuclear weapons. In 1958, Philip Noel-Baker received the Nobel Peace Prize for his book *The Arms Race*, an appeal for disarmament.

In October 1959, there was another election, with Macmillan trying for a third consecutive Conservative victory. Megan won Carmarthen again, from the Liberals, with the Tories holding on to their deposit by just 40 votes, and Plaid Cymru losing its deposit. She campaigned against the iniquities of the House of Lords system of inherited power. However, in 1962 her sister Olwen (a surgeon's widow) forced Megan to see a specialist about her weight loss and a lump on her breast. She also had what in Welsh is called a *dafad gwyllt*, (savage wart) a recognisable skin cancer. She had a mastectomy, and in 1963 a statue of David Lloyd George was unveiled at the House of Commons to mark the centenary of his birth. The family did not invite Frances, the Dowager Countess Lloyd George, and ignored her presence when she was invited by the Speaker of the House. In the election of 1964 Megan won again, and Plaid's candidate Gwynfor Evans* and the Tory Hilda Protheroe-Beynon lost their deposits. Labour's win ensured that there was a Secretary of State for Wales, the capable Jim Griffiths.

However, by 1965, Megan's period of remission from cancer was ending. Visible secondary carcinomas appeared, and the cancer had spread to her lungs, causing shortage of breath. Mervyn Jones, in his excellent biography of Megan, *A Radical Life*, noted her appearances in one week in October 1965, recorded by the *Carmarthen Journal*. On Monday she visited Carmarthen farms with a Ministry of Agriculture official; on Tuesday she attended a Young Socialists' meeting; on Wednesday she made a walkabout in the market and shopping centre, and made speeches in Cydweli and at a Pensioners' Association; on Thursday Megan went to a new factory in Cydweli, visited villages concerned about the bus service, and spent the evening with the women's section in the Gwendraeth valley; on Friday she went to Cefneithin secondary school, checked into opencast mining noise problems, and attended a party executive meeting in the evening. Carmarthen is a very large constituency, and for a dying woman, in pain, this was an astonishing schedule. Her doctor told her that the cancer was spreading, and she dismissed him. In November, she made her last speech in the House, on Welsh Day, stating that 'if any country ever suffered from having an unplanned economy, it is Wales', and regretting the wave of pit closures and unemployment. In 1966, there was another election, and she was returned with a record majority with 21,221 votes, a majority of 9,233. Gwynfor Evans received 7,000 votes for Plaid Cymru.

She became Lady Megan Lloyd George when her father became Earl David Lloyd George in 1945, a title she never embraced. She refused to call herself 'Lady Megan', and it was only after her death that she became known as such. Before her death she was appointed a CH (Order of the Companions of Honour). On 14 May 1966, Olwen visited Megan at Bronawelon, and found her too weak to sign a cheque at the first attempt. By 8 o'clock in the evening it was clear that she was dying, and she reached out with both arms and said *'Tada* - yes - I am coming.' She died at 8.30 that evening, and was buried on 18 May in the family vault with her mother Margaret and sister Mair Eluned. The cemetery was filled with friends and supporters, including Gwynfor Evans and Cledwyn Hughes. An elderly woman stood by the gates of the cemetery, not mixing with the mourners, the Dowager Countess Lloyd George - her old teacher, Frances Stevenson.

* Gwynfor amazingly reversed this defeat in the by-election to fill Megan's place by becoming Plaid Cymru's first MP in history. His margin was 2,436. He lost the seat to Labour in 1970 but regained it in 1974. This was the breakthrough for Plaid Cymru as a political party, but its 2015 General Election results were disastrous compared to the Scottish nationalists' performance.

## DOROTHY EDWARDS 18 August 1903 - 6 January 1934

### NOVELIST OF GENIUS

Dorothy was the daughter of Edward Edwards, a schoolmaster at Ogmore Vale, who could just afford for her to attend Howells School for Girls, Llandaff, and then Cardiff University, where she graduated in Greek and Philosophy. Her father claimed descent from Nell Gwyn, and her mother was the daughter of the famous writer Taliesin Jones (*Groeswen*). Dorothy grew up an avowed political revolutionary, as her father had strong Socialist links, and she strongly admired the American socialist Stit Wilson. However, her real passion was for literature, and in 1927 she published *Rhapsody* (a collection of short stories), and in 1928 the novel *Winter Sonata*. Apart from a couple of stories in *Life and Letters*, and a few critical articles, this was the

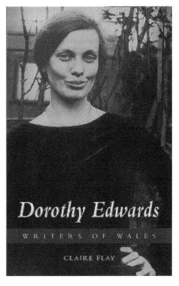

extent of her work. Her story *The Garland* starts perceptively: 'I am an old man now, and I do not know whether I am able any longer to tell a story without making unnecessary observations. Perhaps, too, I am seeing subtleties that were not really there, and yet it must be the fault of the old that they see too little in life, not too much.' She also wrote a short story, *The Conquered*, which was included in *A View Across the Valley*, an anthology of female Welsh nature writers.

The famous critic Gerald Gould said that *Winter Sonata* struck 'a new note in English literature' and hailed her as a 'genius'. It was a truly inventive and original novel, relying not on plot but on characterisations, situations and atmosphere, reflecting the influences of Turgenev and Dostoyevsky. Another great admirer of her work was Arnold Bennett, who spoke of her as a writer of genius with a 'subtle and intriguing talent'. He ranked her alongside Virginia Woolf and Vita Sackville-West. A strong socialist and Welsh Nationalist, Dorothy was an accomplished singer in Russian, German, Italian and Welsh, living for some time in London, Florence, and Vienna, as well as Cardiff.

According to the *Dictionary of National Biography*: 'She was also interested in politics and was a rare combination of ardent socialist and fervent Welsh nationalist, though she could not speak the language.' Dorothy wrote to S.R. Burstein: 'I think because I am Welsh that I am a kind of natural saint and genius mixed, as a compensation for being cut off from the action in the English sense of it - which I suppose means cutting a few niggers to pieces and stealing their rubber'. In another letter she said 'My God is language and the Welsh mountains', expressing a nationalist view of religion and literature. For those interested in Dorothy, Honno has republished her works, and Claire Flay's 2008 doctoral dissertation upon Edwards (*The Subversive Cinderella: gender, class and colonialism in the work of Dorothy Edwards*) is available on-line. Flay has also written a brief biography.

Edwards was noted by Michael Williams as 'that gentle creature', but had a fierce and changeable temper. Dorothy committed suicide, throwing herself under a train near Caerphilly railway station, aged just 31. Her 'collected papers' are held at Reading University. The collection contains letters from Dorothy Edwards to friends; letters to her from various correspondents including Keir Hardie, Dora Carrington and David Garnett; notebooks; diaries for 1932-1933; poems; short stories including *The Spirit of Music* and *The True Comedian* ; and a corrected proof of *Winter Sonata*. She left a suicide note stating: 'I am killing myself because I have never sincerely loved any human being all my life. I have accepted kindness and friendship and even love without gratitude, and given nothing in return.'


## MYRNA LOY 2 August 1905 – 14 December 1993

## MYRNA WILLIAMS, 'QUEEN OF HOLLYWOOD'

David Franklin Williams, the son of Welsh emigrants to the USA, noticed a train station named *Myrna* travelling by rail in early 1905. When he and his wife Della Mae had a daughter in that summer, they named her Myrna Adele Williams. David was a politician, banker and had business in real estate, and Della had studied music in Chicago. Myrna's early years were spent in Helena, Montana, also the home of the actor Gary Cooper. She was devastated by her father's death in 1918, and felt that she had to take on the responsibility of looking after her brother David and her mother. The family moved to Culver City, California, and Myrna enrolled at Venice High School, wishing for a stage career.

Aged 18, she left school and became a dancer at Sid Graumann's Egyptian Movie House. In the days of silent films, troupes of dancers were often the prologue for the movie. Rudolph Valentino spotted her in publicity photos for the prologue to Cecil B DeMille's *Ten Commandments* at the Egyptian Movie House, and tested her for his leading lady in the film *Cobra*. She failed the audition, but tested in a blonde wig for the role of the Virgin Mary is the silent version of *Ben Hur*. (Perhaps the blonde wig for a Jewish mother was a mistake). She failed again, but played an extra, wearing a black wig. In 1925 she changed her name from Williams to Loy and signed a

7-year contract with Warner Brothers, starting at $75 a week. She played exotic roles after her first major appearance in *Across the Pacific*. She then played a speaking role in *State Street Sadie*, and in 1929 was Azuri in the first all-sound movie, *The Desert Song*. The great director John Ford wryly said 'Wouldn't you know, the kid they pick to play tramps is the only good girl in Hollywood.'

However, the 1929 Wall Street Crash meant that she lost her Warner Brothers film contract, and she appeared in the Goldwyn Studios *The Devil to Pay* opposite Ronald Colman. She started an affair with the married Arthur Hornblow, Goldwyn's production supervisor, and starred in around 60 films between 1925 and 1931, appearing usually as a vamp, mistress, bad girl or in an exotic role. In 1931, Irvine Thalberg rescued her

from her freelance lifestyle and contracted her to MGM, where she played her first comedy role with Maurice Chevalier and Jeanette MacDonald in *Love Me Tonight*. Her next role was as a Javanese-Indian murderess in *Thirteen Women*. Leslie Howard, John Barrymore and Clark Gable were all chasing her at this time, while Hornblow kept assuring her that his wife would give him a divorce at any minute. Once Gable kissed her when his wife was not looking, and Myrna retaliated by pushing him over into some bushes. John Dillinger sneaked out of hiding in 1934 to see her star in *Manhattan Melodrama*, and was gunned down by the FBI as he left the cinema in Chicago.

In that same year came Myrna's really big break. She was cast opposite William Powell in Dalshiell Hammett's *The Thin Man*. Filmed in just 16 days, it was an amazing success world-wide. Together they starred in 13 films, 6 of them in *The Thin Man* series. After many vampish and exotic roles, she now became cast as the 'perfect wife', and 'Men-Must-Marry-Myrna' clubs were formed all over America. James Stewart commented 'I shall only marry Myrna Loy'. However, Myrna was disenchanted that Powell was receiving $3,000 a film to her $1,500, and she left Hollywood for Europe with Arthur Hornblow, refusing to return to the studios. After a year, L.B. Mayer lured her back to MGM at Hollywood from New York, by agreeing to her wage demands, plus a $25,000 bonus. In quick succession she starred in *Whipsaw* with Spencer Tracy, *Wife vs. Secretary* with Clark Gable, and *The Great Ziegfeld* with William Powell. At last Hornblow was divorced and they married in 1936. She recalled one evening in their home in Coldwater canyon, Hollywood, where Richard Rogers, Jerome Kern and George and Ira Gershwin squabbled over who was to play the piano.

From 1934-1939 Myrna made 21 films, including co-starring with Clark Gable in *Parnell* after which the pair were voted 'King and Queen of the Movies', in a poll of 20 million people in America. She made more films with Gable, including *Test Pilot* and *Too Hot to Handle*. She spent the early years of the war fund-raising for the Red Cross and War relief, and divorced from the demanding perfectionist Hornblow in 1942. Six days later she married a rich New York advertising executive, John Hertz junior, 'on impulse'. He did not want her to carry on working, and she spent her time visiting hospitals, before she realised that Hertz was possessive, neurotic and abusive. She left him in New York and returned to Hollywood to star in *The Thin Man Comes Home*. In 1945 she started going out with Gene Markey, the former husband of the film stars Joan Bennett and Hedy Lamarr.

She left MGM after 15 years - she and the studio had drifted apart during the war years, and she now played what she considered to be her best role, Milly in *The Best Years of Our Lives*. Cary Grant, who starred with her in two films (*Bachelor and the Bobbysoxer* and *Mr Blandings Builds His Dream House*) reaffirmed Jimmy Stewart's view that all Hollywood's leading men wanted Myrna as the perfect wife. 1946 saw Myrna being attacked in the Senator McCarthy witch-hunt against communists, while she was working with Grant on *Bachelor and the Bobbysoxer*. She threatened to sue for a million dollars and the newspaper involved printed a retraction. A solid Democrat, Myrna retaliated against the House Un-American Activities Committee by forming The Committee for the First Amendment, with other Hollywood personalities.

After the Russian murder of Jan Masaryk, her friend who was the Czechoslovak democrat leader, she began working for the American Association for the United Nations, and then for UNESCO. She spent most of the latter half of the 1940's working for UNESCO in Europe, and made *If This Be Sin* for Alexander Korda in Europe in 1949. She then returned to Hollywood to make *Cheaper by the Dozen* and divorced Gene Markey on the grounds of his repeated adultery in 1950. Becoming involved with Howland Sargeant, a UNESCO delegate, she settled in Washington and New York, and married him in 1951. Still working for UNESCO, visiting hospitals, making films and TV shows, she campaigned in the Adlai Stevenson and John F. Kennedy bids for the presidency. She divorced Howland in 1959. 1963 saw Myrna appear on the stage for the first time, and she was on Broadway in 1973. In 1990 she received an honorary Oscar in recognition of 'her extraordinary qualities, both onscreen and off, with appreciation of a lifetime's worth of indelible performances'.

# GRACE MARY WILLIAMS 19 February 1906 - 10 February 1977

## COMPOSER

 Grace was born in Wenvoe Terrace, Barry, the daughter of a Caernarfon schoolteacher William Matthew Williams and of another teacher from Llanelli, Rose Emily Richards. Grace's brother and sister, Glyn and Marian, were born later at 9 Old Village Road in Barry. William Williams led the famous Romilly Boys' Choir, and Grace grew up in a musical environment, Grace accompanying the choir on piano. At home she played the violin, her brother the cello and her father the piano in domestic music-making. After winning a scholarship, Grace went to Barry County Girls School, and then to Cardiff University to study music. She liked the social life, but found the Bachelor of Music degree course 'deadly' as there was little opportunity to write music there. Grace then attended the Royal College of Music in London, studying under the Ralph Vaughan Williams. It was at this time that Grace came into the circle of young women composers including Imogen Holst, Dorothy Gow, Elizabeth Maconchy* and, later, Elizabeth Lutyens. Grace and Elizabeth Lutyens remained life-long friends.

She won prizes for composition in 1928 and 1930, the latter enabling her to study under the Austrian Egon Wellesz in Vienna. Wellesz had been a pupil of Schoenberg, but it appears that Grace was more interested in the music of Wagner when she was there. Interestingly, she disliked Mahler's music at this time, only being 'converted' possibly because of her later friendship with Benjamin Britten. This was quite an odd relationship between the gentle, tolerant Grace and the arrogant, egocentric Britten. She met Britten during the 1930's, who introduced her to the film music industry, and they would often go to the cinema and the opera together. Not until Britten and his lover Peter Pears fled to the USA in 1939 did Grace realise Britten's true nature. Wellesz was a very different teacher to Vaughan Williams, his precision being of far greater value to Grace. Unfortunately, many of Grace's compositions from these times, and indeed later in her career, have disappeared.

Grace left Vienna in 1931, and became a visiting music lecturer at Southlands Training College, Wimbledon, and simultaneously part-time music mistress for Camden School for Girls, spending her vacations back 'home' in Barry. She was often home-sick, and this *hiraeth* was evident in her first major work. She wrote the orchestral piece *Hen Walia*, based on Welsh folk songs, showing the influences of Ralph Vaughan Williams, and which was broadcast several times in the 1930's. Her next major work was *Elegy*, a symphony for a string orchestra, again performed on BBC Radio. Also from this period are the *Cavatina* for string quartet (now lost) and the ballet music *Theseus and Ariadne*. The most ambitious of her pre-war orchestral works was *Four Illustrations for the Legend of Rhiannon*, using the tale of Pwll, Lord of Dyfed, from the first 'branch' of the *Mabinogi*.

She also composed solo songs with orchestra, of which the most notable was *Song of Mary*, showing the influences of Mahler and Strauss, and *Gogonedawg Arglwydd*, a choral work also in the 1930's. For the war years, Grace went with her school to Uppingham, Rutland, to escape the London Blitz. Unfortunately the disruption of war coincided with the time when the pacifist Grace Williams was at the peak of her creative powers, but she kept composing under difficult circumstances.

She finished her best-known work *Fantasia on Welsh Nursery Tunes* in 1940, which was broadcast. and then recorded by the London Symphony Orchestra under Mansel Thomas. Her *Sinfonia Concertante* for piano and orchestra was performed in 1943, and her *Symphony No. 1* in the form of *Symphonic Impressions of the Glendower Scene in Henry IV Part 1* completed in that same year. The four movements, with brass fanfares, show the different facets of Owain Glyndŵr's character as he rebelled against the Franco-English. It was not performed publicly until 1950, by the BBC Welsh Orchestra under Mansel Thomas.

The school returned to London in 1943, only to be faced with the new hazard of 'flying bombs'. Grace composed the excellent *Sea Sketches* in 1944, inspired by the Glamorganshire coastline, and dedicated to her 'parents who had the good sense to set up home on the coast of Glamorgan.' Its success rivalled that of her *Nursery Rhymes* suite, and it was published by the Oxford University Press. Trying to combine teaching with composing in the war years, contributed to Grace being physically ill by 1944, spending 11 days in hospital before being discharged. She resolved to give up composing to regain her emotional, physical and psychological well-being, after re-scoring *The Song of Mary*.

From 1944 followed the least productive creative period of her life. In Autumn 1945 she wrote: I don't want to stay in London - I just long to get home and live in comfort by the sea and have a well-paid full-time job which isn't teaching... I like the children and I've always liked teaching them - but I'm sick to death of the succession of school functions, dingy school buildings and - you know all the rest...' She found a job with the BBC in London after failing to be appointed at Cardiff University, and wrote radio scripts and arranged music, but her health was still failing and she was advised by her doctors to return to Barry. In February 1947, Grace returned to live with her parents, and remained there for the rest of her life. She scraped a living by freelance composing, mainly for the BBC and London film companies, and wrote scripts for school broadcasts. She did not regard this work as 'composing' but as 'jobbing'. However, by the summer of 1949 she was writing: 'I'll go to London next month, and it will probably be in search of another full-time job (which will really mean the end of composing this time). I've managed to keep going until now - but prospects aren't good and I can't live on air.'

Her only important orchestral work in this decade was her *Violin Concerto*, finished in 1950. She was again forced to teach, part-time at Cardiff College of Music in Cardiff Castle, to make ends meet from 1950. Her choral suite *The Dancers* was published in 1951, but from 1954 she had to work as a music copyist out of financial necessity. However, her greatest years as a composer were to come. She gave up her teaching job in 1954, and her agreement with the BBC came to an end. Her greatest work may be *Penillion* (1955), written for the National Youth Orchestra of Wales. It is a complex piece, based upon the *pennillion* chanting of Welsh tradition. Upon 5 June 1957, Grace's father William was presented with the freedom of Barry for his services to Romilly Boys' Choir, and he died 15 days later.

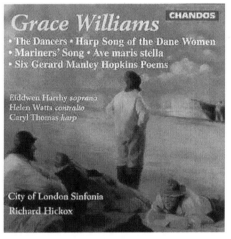

One of Grace Williams' recordings

She wrote her *Second Symphony* in 1957, and in 1958 the song cycle *Six Poems by Gerard Manley Hopkins* for contralto and string sextet. The choral suite *All Seasons Shall Be Sweet* appeared in 1959, commissioned by the BBC. Other song cycles were *Songs of Sleep* (1959), *Four Medieval Welsh Poems* (1962) and *The Billows of the Sea* (1969), written for the Swansea Festival. Grace's mother had died in 1962, aged 90, the same year that Grace wrote *Processional*, commissioned for the Llandaff Cathedral Festival.

At the age of 60, she wrote her only opera in 1966, *The Parlour*, an artistic success, and performed by the Welsh National Opera. In 1967 *Carmina Avium* (*Songs of Birds*) was a choral work based on three Latin texts. *Ballads for Orchestra* of 1970 is Grace Williams' last orchestral work. In collaboration with the great Saunders Lewis, Grace completed a powerful Latin mass, *Missa Cambrensis* in 1971. Second only to *The Parlour* in duration and scale, it was started in 1968, and is the culmination of her life's work. Grace now rejected commissioned works, as she wanted younger composers to benefit from them, and not have to struggle financially as she had done all her life.

1973 saw the recording of her works by the London Symphony Orchestra, but she advised against it, writing on 6 May 1972 'My immediate reaction... for I am nothing if not a realist... is that there will be no sales... practically none at all'. Then on 27 November 1973 she noted: 'I still feel I don't deserve to have a record to myself; nevertheless, it was quite an experience to hear such performances. It was a terrible ordeal beforehand and I almost expected to find the orchestra in a state of mutiny. Strangely enough they were very pleasant right up to the end. It now remains for the critics to tear the record to ribbons. Well, having had the goodwill of the performers, nothing else seems to matter now.'

In 1973 she wrote *Fairest of Stars*, for soprano and orchestra, based upon Book 5 of Milton's *Paradise Lost*, recorded in 1974. One critic has called it 'one of the most beautiful settings for soprano and orchestra of any text, and remarked that the final stanza 'is almost unbearably beautiful and has made grown men weep... The commercial recording with Janet Price as the superlative soloist is a real treasure. The orchestration is perfection - strong but subtle - shimmering strings with haunting support from the horns and nostalgic trumpet sounds in an impressive flow of sensuous, shifting exquisitiveness that is as beautiful as anything that Debussy or Vaughan Williams wrote.'

In 1974, Grace broke her resolution not to accept commissions to write *Ave Maris Stella* for the North Wales Music Festival, and in the same year wrote *My Last Duchess* based on a Browning poem, at the request of the baritone Louis Berkman. During her career, she wrote 15 pieces of music for the stage and ballet; 25 pieces of music for a full orchestra; 19 choral music suites; 22 arrangements for schools broadcasts; 18 pieces of instrumental and chamber music; 29 miscellaneous arrangements; and 34 pieces for solo vocals.

In 1976, Grace was fêted on her 70th birthday, with concerts across Wales, and many of her works being recorded for the first time. Just a few weeks later, she was diagnosed with cancer, and despite intensive treatment, she died just short of her 71st birthday. A letter of 30 July reads: 'The surgeon and his team are all delighted with their beautiful incisions - which reminds me that I too was well-pleased with the surgery I performed on the *Finale* of my *Symphony*. The dead-wood I'd cut out and the way I'd joined up the loose ends made the movement far more on-flowing.' It is typical of this unassuming, hard-working woman that she had been offered, and refused to accept, the OBE in 1966 and a Civil List pension in 1969 (the latter personally offered by the Secretary of State for Wales). Not even her closest friends and relatives knew of this until after her death.

* Elizabeth Maconchy wrote in a symposium for Grace in 1977, that Grace was her oldest friend. 'She acquired a first-class conversational technique and in

particular a mastery of the orchestra. Her songs and choral suites and her brilliant opera *The Parlour* are beautifully written for the voice. She invariably sang everything she wrote, vocal or instrumental, as she went along, and used to say that the real disadvantage of being a woman composer is not being able to sing the bass part at the right pitch, which she said made for a static bass-line.' Imogen Holst, Winifred Barocas, Mansel Thomas, Eiluned Davies and many others also paid tribute.

*Footnotes:*

1. *Grace Williams*, by Malcolm Boyd was published in 1980 as part of the *Composers of Wales Series* and contains examples of her scores. He concludes: ...in the history of music in Wales she occupies a position of the first importance. Although active as a teacher, it was mainly through personal example that her influence was felt. She showed younger composers that it was possible (even if it was not easy) to live in Wales as a freelance creative artist; she demonstrated to Welsh musicians the importance of cultivating the highest possible professional standards; she helped to place orchestral music in Wales on a new footing; and she brought to the concert hall for the first time a distinctively Welsh musical language. Above all, she left many works of the highest quality and originality which Welshmen, and not only Welshmen, will do well to cherish and to perform'.

2. This author, with Richard Booth MBE, 'King of Hay', responsible for 'booktowns' across the world, made a presentation to Barry Council to make Barry the first international Bookport. Booth would have supplied containers of books to the dozens of empty shops in its main street, and to the empty former bus depot. There was no interest or support, in the words of the committee chairman, because the 2006 commemoration of Grace Williams had not been a success. I also mentioned the opportunity of taking scrapped naval vessels to the docks, making them tourist attractions like HMS Belfast in London. There was no interest. Barry Council allowed Butlins holiday camp to be built upon Nell's Point, Barry Island, over St. Baruc's Holy Well of the 6th century and other archaeological remains, despite the headland being gifted to the townspeople for leisure in perpetuity. When the camp closed, houses were illegally built upon the best part of the site, on the headland overlooking Jackson's Bay and Barry Island. The papers relating to the gift of the land in perpetuity by the Romilly family to the people of Barry had predictably and conveniently disappeared.

## RUTH ELIZABETH 'BETTE' DAVIS 5 April 1908 - 6 October 1989

## FILM SUPERSTAR

Born in Lowell, Massachusetts, Ruth Elizabeth Davis was the daughter of a lawyer, Harlow Davis, of Welsh extraction*. Upon her parents' divorce, she lived with her mother and sister Barbara, in New York. During this time she became known as Bette, taking the spelling from Balzac's novel, *Cousin Bette*. She attended John Murray Anderson's Dramatic School, spent a summer season with George Cukor's stock company in Rochester, New York State and starred in Broadway, before she heard that Hollywood wanted her.

Aged just 22, she signed for Universal Studios in 1930, but an unimpressive debut in *Bad Sister* meant that she was dropped by them in 1931. However, Warner Brothers contracted Bette in 1932, and after a major role with George Arliss in *The Man Who Played God* (1932), people started taking notice of her. She made 5 pictures in 1932 for Warner Brothers, and her first good critical notices came with *Cabin in the Cotton* in which she plays a sexually-charged Southern belle, and slowly drawls 'Ah'd lurve t'kiss yew, but ah jes washed mah hair'. In 1934, she appeared with James Cagney in *Jimmy the Gent*. She ambitiously hoped for an Oscar with her performance of Mildred in *Of Human Bondage* in 1934, but the studio did not nominate her. However, aged 26 in 1935 she won an Oscar for *Dangerous*, playing a  self-destructive actress. Bette believed that it was a consolation prize for the Oscar that was 'rightfully' hers in 1934, and that Katherine Hepburn should have won in 1935.

Major films followed: *Dangerous* with Franchot Tone (1935); *The Petrified Forest* with Leslie Howard and Humphrey Bogart (1936); *Jezebel* with Henry Fonda (1938); *Dark Victory* with George Brent (1939 - Bette's favourite of all her films); and *The Old Maid* with Miriam Hopkins in 1939. Another star of Welsh extraction, Hopkins disliked playing the unsympathetic role of cousin Delia, and made the picture a 'living hell' for Bette by repeatedly attempting to upstage her, spoiling take after take of Bette's big scenes. Also in 1939, Bette brilliantly played Elizabeth I opposite Errol Flynn in *The Private Lives of Elizabeth and Essex*. In William Wyler's *The Little Foxes* (1941), Bette thought she gave one of the worst performances of her life. *Now Voyager* (1942) features the famous scene where Paul Henreid lights two cigarettes and gives one to Davis, and is a truly watchable movie, appealing to all generations even now. During the war years, she also starred in *The Man Who came to Dinner* (1942); *In This*

*Our Life* (1942); *Watch on the Rhine* (1943); *Old Acquaintance* (1944); and *Mr Skeffington* with Claude Rains (1944). In this picture she said 'A woman is only beautiful when she is loved'. In 1944, Joan Crawford joined Warner Brothers and asked for a dressing room next to Bette's. Also in this year, Bette's husband Arthur Farnsworth, who was rumoured to be a drunk, fell, hit his head and died in Hollywood Boulevard.

Bette had appeared in scores of movies, but after the War, opportunities began to dry up. She starred in *A Stolen Life* (1946); *Deception* (1946); *Winter Meeting* (1948); *June Bride* (1948) and *Beyond the Forest* (1949), her last film with Warner Brothers as her long contract finally ended. In 1949, Jack Warner had given her a 4-picture contract, paying Bette $10,285 a week, making her the highest-paid woman in the USA. Unfortunately he would not grant her script approval, and she walked out of Warner Brothers. However, the hoped-for 'good scripts' did not appear until she appeared for 20th Century Fox in 1950's *All About Eve*, one of the most scintillating screen comedies of all time, with Bette playing Margot Channing and receiving the *New York Film Critics Award* as Best Actress. She married Gary Merrill just prior to its release, and it stars Gary Merrill, Celeste Holm, Ann Baxter (who played Eve), George Sanders and features a very young Marilyn Monroe. Bette was nominated for her 3rd Oscar for playing the ageing Broadway star, and dramatically flounced out of a party in the film, saying 'Fasten your seatbelts, it's going to be a bumpy night'. The part helped resurrect Bette's career. It had previously been turned down by Marlene Dietrich, Claudette Colbert, Susan Hayward and Gertrude Lawrence.

Bette played alongside Sterling Hayden and a young Natalie Wood in *The Star* in 1953. She reprised her role as the *Virgin Queen* in 1955, and played Apple Annie in 1961 in *Pocketful of Miracles*. In 1962 we saw the excruciatingly interesting battle of the divas, *Whatever Happened to Baby Jane*, the famous teaming of her and Joan Crawford**. Crawford said 'I am not from the legitimate theatre as Ms Davis, but I am as much an actress as she is.' Davis responded 'I think Crawford's greatest performance is playing herself'. Crawford was rumoured to have campaigned amongst Academy members, not to vote for Bette when she was nominated for the Oscar for her role. A similar film was *Hush, Hush, Sweet Charlotte* with Olivia de Havilland in 1965, and Bette's last film role was as a character in *Death on the Nile* in 1978.

She died aged 81, and on 2 November 1989, the Hollywood community gathered to pay tribute to Bette, where scenes from her greatest films were shown. Among 350 celebrities were Clint Eastwood, Ann-Margret, Glenn Ford, Vincent Price and Robert Wagner. The Master of Ceremonies started the event by stating 'We are here to celebrate how much you matter to us, and recall the work that gave you such sweet joy and such dignity, not to mention so many damn awards.' Angela Lansbury said she left 'an extraordinary legacy of acting in the 20th century by a real master of the craft'. On Betty's crypt at the family mausoleum at Forest Lawns, Los Angeles, is inscribed what she wanted: 'She did it the hard way.'

\* James Davis sailed from Wales to the New World in the early 1600's, and helped found the city of Haverhill, Massachusetts, and became a 'selectman' of the community there. Another Welsh ancestor was Colonel Jabez Mathews, a Revolutionary War hero.

\*\* A wonderful film could be made of the battle of these two divas and the making of *Baby Jane*. From James Spada's *More Than a Woman - The Intimate Biography of Bette Davis,* we read these quotes from witnesses: 'Joan would arrive at the studio sharp at one minute to nine. Immaculately groomed, she'd come in with her entourage: a makeup man, a hairdresser, a secretary - there were always seven or eight people trailing after her. She would waft very regally into her dressing room and gently close the door. A moment or so later, you'd hear Bette clomping down the corridor, all by herself, using quite obscene language. She'd go thundering into her dressing room and slam the door. I really think her behaviour was just to shock Joan. She was definitely needling her. She put a little card up on her dressing room door which said "Of all my relations, I like sex the best". She knew it would horrify Joan, who was very strait-laced and didn't have much of a sense of humour... They came from totally different classes, and your roots come out. Bette had a stage background, Joan had maybe a burlesque show or two. When you got right down to it, Bette was a lady, and Joan Crawford was not.

It was ironic, because Bette would swear and lumber around, and Joan of course was all piety and refinement, but class will show. Joan would pretend to be drinking water when it was really vodka, and she'd drink herself stupid in public. Bette would never do that. And whenever Joan would call me all she'd talk about were the intimate details of her medical problems. She just didn't have any class...' There are some superb arguments and put-downs noted in the book, and the director Robert Aldrich said that 'they were like two Sherman tanks, openly despising each other'... 'Each tried to vex the other, put her off her stride, adversely affect her performance. As Joan acted out a solo scene, Bette turned to Walter Blake and said, loudly enough so that Joan could her, "She can't act, she stinks!" Afraid that Joan would stalk off the set, Aldrich piped up "I've got a terrible headache. We've got to get through this scene". When she had finished, Joan pulled Aldrich aside. "Did you hear what she said about me?"

Another scene, one of the script's most harrowing, called for Jane (Bette) to kick Blanche (Joan) senseless on their mansion's tiled floor. To obtain the proper sound effects, Bette first viciously kicked a dummy out of camera range. Then she repeated the shot with Joan, feigning the blows. She performed the stunt flawlessly - except for one kick that grazed Joan's head. "I barely touched her", Bette insisted, but Hedda Hopper reported that she had "raised a fair lump on Joan's head". Crawford got her revenge a few days later as Jane hauls the half-dead Blanche off her bed and drags her into the hallway. It was a difficult scene, and according to Aldrich, "Crawford wanted Bette to suffer, every inch of the way." Just prior to action, Joan strapped a lead-lined weight lifter's belt around her waist, adding considerably to her heft. "It was one continuous take," the screenwriter Lukas Heller recalled. "Bette carried her from the bed across the room and out of the door. Then, as soon as she got in the hallway, out of the camera's range, she dropped Joan and let out this bloodcurdling scream."

"My back! Oh God, my back!" Bette shrieked. Seemingly oblivious of Bette's agonies, Joan stood up, and as a small smile of satisfaction spread across her face, walked elegantly off the set. Joan had one last laugh on Bette. As Blanche nears death from starvation, there was no way that Joan could look anything but awful, and her make-up reflected that. But Bette noticed that Joan's bosom grew fuller every day. "Christ!" she bellowed. "You never know what size boobs that broad has strapped on! She must have a different set for every day of the week!...She's supposed to be shrivelling away while Baby Jane starves her to death, but her tits keep growing! I keep running into them like the Hollywood Hills!'

## LYNETTE ROBERTS 4 July 1909 – 26 September 1995

## WAR POET

Born Evelyn Beatrice Roberts in Buenos Aires, her parents were Welsh emigrants to Australia. Her Ruthin father had worked on the railways in Australia, and had been appointed manager of Western Railways in Argentina. Educated in at a convent in Buenos Aires, she was sent to a school in Bournemouth on her Pembroke mother's death, returning every two years to Argentina. She attended the Central School for Arts and Crafts in London, but gave up, disillusioned with her woodcarving and textile skills. She returned again to Buenos Aires, where her father had remarried, and finally studied at Constance Spry's Flower School in  London. She opened a flower studio ('Bruska'), catering for the hotel trade, but then made wreaths for soldiers who died in World War II, which affected her adversely. She did not wish to make money from grief.

At Llansteffan in 1940 she married the poet-editor Keidrich Rhys, born William Ronald Rees Jones, at Bethlehem, near Llandeilo. They settled in Llanybri, Carmarthenshire, Keidrych editing the literary magazine *Wales* that he founded, before he was called away to defend Dover, as a gunner with the London Welsh Regiment. Lynette worked as a cook for a time, as finances were desperately tight. Most of her poetry was written during the

Second World War, and has been called 'the last in the Modernist style of the 20th century and the first in the Magical Realist' (- *New Companion to the Literature of Wales*).

After visiting Keidrych at Dover in 1941, Lynette called to see the poet Alun Lewis in the Royal Engineers at Longmoor, Hampshire, on her way back to Wales. He had been in correspondence with Keidrych and Lynette, and she turned up wearing her red cloak and a copy of Gigli's recording of *Un Furtiva Lacrima* from Donizetti's *Elixir of Love*. There was mutual attraction, and she told him: 'I like your letters Alun, but I should be frightened if you came too near. I might fall in love with you, I might be disillusioned. Of the two I prefer the first. The second is horrible.' They exchanged poems, including an 'invitation' to him to visit her, in *Poem to Llanybri*:

'If you come my way that is...
Between now and then, I will offer you
A fist full of rock cress fresh from the bank
The valley tips of garlic red with dew
Cooler than shallots, a breath you can swank
In the village when you come! At noon-day
I will offer you a choice bowl of cawl
Served with a "lover's" spoon and a chopped spray
Of leeks or savori fach, not used now,
In the old way you'll understand!...
...You must come Alun, start this pilgrimage...'
Lewis' response was the poem *Peace*, which begins:
'The wind blows
Through her eyes,
Snow is banked
In her whiter thighs,
The birds are frantic with
Her last distress,
And flutter and chatter over
Her nakedness'

Lewis seems to have transferred his feelings for his girlfriend Gweno Ellice at this time to Lynette, but back home in Aberdare in April 1941 he disclosed that their love was over, and returned to Gweno, writing: 'Now it is "over". Thank God it has turned well. I am in love in love in love, the other girl who called me, she has withdrawn with a feminine prudence, making herself look rather silly, I think, sheathing in velvet fur the extended feline claws of disembodied imaginary love.'

After visiting Lynette and Keidrych, Keidrych being on 'unofficial leave' at Llanybri, and Brenda Chamberlain (q.v.) and John Petts at

Llanllechid, Lewis wrote in November 1941 to Brenda: 'Lynette is doing very fine work - her poems are becoming very rich & powerful & she is painting some fine things. She has a prodigal & worldflung imagination with a depth of personal & historical myth (she is South American by birth - Aztec) to draw on & a Catholic strain that provides ritual & mystique. It is interesting & exciting to read her poems & then yours - both of you utterly surpass any other woman poet I've read - yet you are so utterly utterly indifferent.'

Keidrych Rhys printed Lynette's *Village Dialect*, a study of the language of Llanybri, in 1944. In the same year T.S. Eliot, editor at Faber, published her *Poems*, and in 1951 published *Gods with Stainless Ears*, eight years after its completion. From *The Seasons* in her volume of *Poems* we read that Summer suggests:

'A romance that we have not received
Sunny balconies in the mind: the seldom
Forgotten perfect island summer with its
Warm haze on flesh, flower and hide.'

Keidrych had resumed editing *Wales* in his absence from the London Welsh Regiment, but then gave himself up and was imprisoned in Woolwich for some time. Lynette and the children were turned out of the cottage for non-payment of rent for a short while. The depressed Alun Lewis, in India now with the South Wales Borderers, killed himself, aged 28 in 1943. To what extent her relationship with the gifted Lewis had affected Lynette's marriage is unknown. She had Angharad in 1945 and Pridein in 1946, and with their mother the children used to wear bright red cloaks to keep warm. They were quite a sight in the small village, but Lynette explained that the material was cheap. She told Anthony Conran that T.S. Eliot was godfather to one of her children, and Robert Graves the other. The little cottage in Llanybri was damp and cold, with one of the tiny downstairs rooms was arranged as an air-raid shelter for the village.

Lynette is the probably most modernist of Welsh poets, along with the great (and underestimated David Jones (see *The 100 Greatest Welshmen*). *Gods with Stainless Ears* was 'A Heroic Poem' written between 1941 and 1943, which has been described as the greatest poem to come out of World War II (a parallel with David Jones and World War I)*. Its original title was *Cwmcelyn*, (Valley of Holly) but the new title was meant to indicate that the gods do not listen to the prayers of people in times of war. In its preface, she describes her seeing the scenes and visions for it 'like a newsreel'. Lines 28-38 of Part IV of this long poem describe the death of a baby:

'O love beaten. By loss humiliated

Stretched out in muslin distress. Bound
By an iron wreath scattered with coloured beads.
O my people immeasurably alone.
No ringfinger: with the tips of my fingers glazed
With sorrow with solemn gravity. Crown tipped sideways;
Ears blown back like lilac; with set face
And dry lids, waiting for Love's Arcade.
O love was there no barddionaeth?
No billing birds to be - coinheritor?
The night sky is braille in a rock of frost.'

In 1944 and 1945 drafts of Robert Graves' *The White Goddess* were published in Wales, and Lynette was the dedicatee in its first edition (1948),

**Lynette Roberts' painting of her Llanybri home, on postcard**

having provided much of the Welsh material used by him. The Poetry Foundation website reads: 'Roberts's poetry is known for its range and virtuosity. Her poems run the gamut from intimate descriptions of the Welsh village Llanybri where she lived to the difficult, shifting surfaces and scientific and epic themes of the long poem *Gods with Stainless Ears*. According to Drew Milne, the eponymous poem "deserves to be much read and admired as a long poem as important as Basil Bunting's *Briggflatts*, and a neglected classic in the history of writing produced by women working in the British Isles.'

Following her divorce in 1948, Lynette had moved to England with her two children, but suffered her first nervous breakdown. After this, she refused to write any more poetry, and for the rest of her life she was plagued by health problems. *The Endeavour*, her account of Captain Cook's first voyage, appeared in 1954. She returned to Llanybri in 1969, then to Carmarthen, where she began evangelising as a Jehovah's Witness. Lynette was elected to Yr Academi Cymraeg in 1984, and died at a retirement home in Ferryside, Carmarthenshire.

Later in life Roberts had repudiated her work and refused to permit it to be reprinted. An edition of her collected poems was issued by Seren after her death but was immediately withdrawn because of legal problems with the Roberts estate, but a new *Collected Poems*[1] appeared in 2006 from Carcanet. A volume of miscellaneous prose, diaries from her time in

Llanybri, correspondence with Robert Graves, memoirs of the Sitwells and T.S. Eliot, her essay on 'village dialect' and short stories appeared in 2008. An unpublished novel, *Nesta*, written in 1944, is apparently lost. Owen Sheers, in *A Poet's Guide to Britain* on BBC Radio 4 in 2013, devoted one of the six episodes to the almost forgotten Lynette Roberts.

\* The poet and critic Professor Anthony Conran has written in *The Anglo-Welsh Review* in 1979 an article on *Lynette Roberts: War Poet*: '...On the whole, then, the Second World War produced no major poets, certainly none of active service. The war poems of Dylan Thomas and Edith Sitwell have nothing really to say, though they say it with great pomp and ceremony and give the impression of lofty and compassionate utterance. If someone were to make out a case for claiming 'Gods with Stainless Ears' (or the first four parts of, anyway) as the greatest war-poem of the 1939-45 War, and, for that matter, as the war-poem to be expected from that war, then I, for one, would not know how to refute him.

Let me rehearse some of the reasons that could be advanced for making that extraordinary claim. Some, such as its passion, its sincerity, its fierce awareness of a particular time and place, its identification with the suffering of ordinary people under extraordinary circumstances, we have looked at already. Here are a few more. First, it is a heroic poem - and really heroic, not at all mock - about inactivity, punctuated from time to time by outbursts of mechanical violence that almost, but not quite, dwarf the human heartbreak that ensues....

Second, her poem obviously takes its place in the central tradition of modern poetry, to which contemporary English verse has been little more than a suburban backwater...Its very eccentricity and obscurity of language arise from a truly modern unwillingness to be less than totally open to experience, even the experience of war. Third, it is a heroic poem about being a woman. The Second World War was the first war in history where women were fully enfranchised citizens, and acted as such...Being a woman in the Second World War was as 'heroic' as being a man; and it therefore follows that muslin and work-baskets and coloured beads became suddenly part of the apparatus of heroism. Not simply giving birth - anyone can see "that" as in some sense a poetic, if not a heroic thing to do, to be celebrated in song - but the paraphernalia of birth. This startling fact accounts for a very great deal of the "oddity" of Lynette Roberts' poem: it is odd, at least partly, because it offends against the in-built sexism of our linguistic expectations built up over centuries of male dominance and self-esteem.'

## BRENDA CHAMBERLAIN 17 March 1912 - 11 July 1971

### POET-PAINTER

Born in Bangor, her father was an Inspector of Bridges for the LMS Railway Company, and her Manx/Irish mother became Bangor's first woman mayor. Brenda always wanted to be a writer and painter, and did not accept easily the constraints of Bangor County School for Girls. In the VI Form, she was sent for special lessons at the Royal Cambrian Academy in Conwy, such was her prowess in art. Upon leaving school, she went to Copenhagen to work as an *au pair*, where her eyes were opened to modern art by some Gauguin paintings at the Karlsberg Glyptotech. Her drawings in Copenhagen then helped her win a place at the Royal Academy Schools in London in 1931. In 1933, half-way

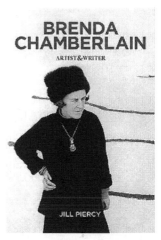

through her five-year training period, she moved into a studio-flat with a fellow, student John Petts. In 1935, Brenda married John, and they settled at Tŷ'r Mynydd, near Llanllechid, outside Bethesda, setting up the Caseg Press in 1937.

In the Second World War, John Petts was a conscientious objector, and was sent to carry out essential farm work in Surrey. Brenda stopped painting to concentrate upon poetry, and worked on *The Caseg Broadsheets*. Her first published poem was *The Harvester* in 1939, and from now on her articles and poems appeared in British and American periodicals). Alun Lewis had proposed that they should collaborate upon poems and engravings in inexpensive editions, to try and popularise their work. This series, *The Caseg Broadsheets,* contain works by Alun Lewis, Lynette Roberts (q.v.), Dylan Thomas, and translations of early Welsh poems by Harold Idris Bell. The poems, including some of her own, were illustrated by Chamberlain and Petts. A letter to her great friend Alun Lewis in 1941 reads: 'Quite frankly, I loathe contact with most people, I like men and women and children who are vital, standing alone in their own world, and not dependent on others for their happiness.'

She separated from John Petts (1914-1991) in 1943, and he blamed it upon her wish to develop her own recognition as an artist and poet. Petts was born in London, but is now considered a Welsh artist, best known for his engravings and stained glass. Alun Lewis had gone to India in 1942 and committed suicide in 1944, which greatly saddened her. During the war years, she spent a great deal of time with Esme Firbank at Dyffryn Mymbyr hill farm. Esme's husband Thomas was on active service, and wrote that wonderful book *I Bought a Mountain*. In 1946, she was taken to Bardsey Island\*, Enlli, for the first time by the German refugee Henry Michaslki (later Mitchell), and fell in love with it. After this visit she wrote 'I have found the home of my heart. I could not sit: I could not think straight any more; so I came to this solitary place and lay in the sun.' Brenda divorced Petts in 1946, and travelled to Germany to visit her friend Karl von Laer. She had met him in Bangor, when she was 20, and always kept in touch apart from the war years. He had lost his estates in East Germany with its Russian occupation.

1947 saw Brenda fall in love with Jean van der Bijl, a Frenchman nine years her junior, and they went to live on Ynys Enlli, at Carreg farmhouse. There were only a dozen islanders, no roads nor electricity, and

all supplies had to be ferried across dangerous waters. Her paintings, inspired by Gauguin, Picasso and Matisse, won Gold Medals at the National Eisteddfod in 1951 and 1953. Her first collection of poems, *The Green Heart* was dedicated to Karl von Laer when published in 1958. It had won an award from the Welsh Committee of the Arts Council in 1956. The book mainly consists of lyrics about fishermen and mountain-dwellers, along with a cycle of love-poems with a German background, and won an Arts Council award. Jean

**Blodeuwedd, by Brenda Chamberlain**

moved to the mainland to teach French in 1958, and Brenda started to tire of island life, only returning to Carreg in the summers from now on.

*The Tide Race*, a prose work, was published in 1962, an account of her austere life on Bardsey. It has been described as 'nightmarish' and 'close to poetry' as it explores the tensions of a small community surrounded by treacherous currents. In it she noted: 'I was in the habit of carrying scraps of paper with me, on which to put down word-gems, always cutting away; trying to make little express much; condensing, clarifying, and finally forging. Page after page of the notebook would become covered with countless variations of the one poem that might be taken up and laid aside over a period of weeks or months or even years. The making of a poem for me is an almost endless process; even when at last it sounds to be complete, it seems best to put it away for further ripening and a more dispassionate assessment at a later time.' This was her most popular work. In *The Tide Race* she notes: 'Life on a small island, I had found out at once and had been horrified by the discovery, is almost entirely public so far as one's outside movements are concerned.' Many islanders were offended by the work and its vivid descriptions of them, and the island's owner, Lord Newborough, asked her to give up the lease on Carreg in 1964.

In 1962, Brenda visited Athens, and then stayed in the house of a friend on the Greek island of Ydra (Hydra), near that of her friend Henry Mitchell. She lived there for most of the next five years. She worked on collaborations with the Greek dancer Robertus Saragas (performed in London in 1964), and with the composer Halim El-Dabh. Her novel *The Water Castle* appeared in 1964, a journal of love and disagreement over a period of six weeks in immediate post-war Germany, obviously based on her 1946 visit. She described her experiences in Greece in her journal *A Rope of Vines - Journal from a Greek Island* in 1965. In it she wrote: 'We invent our own lives, but there remains reality outside oneself, and these enduring boats, laden with melons and water pots, green peppers and cattle, point the way to life through abundant dying.' However, the 'colonels coup' of 1967 forced her to return to Bangor, where her mother had been transferred to a nursing home. Angered by a visit to the Greek detention centre on the Isle of Leros, she wrote a play condemning the coup, *The Protagonists*. It was performed in Bangor, but never published. For those readers interested in Brenda Chamberlain's poetry and writing, the finest introduction is Kate Holman's *Brenda Chamberlain* (1987).

From her 1962 move to the Greek island, her work had taken a new freedom and exuberance. She combined poetry and images, made drawings from music notations and wrote a play. However, upon moving back to North Wales in 1969 her work became increasingly stark, reflecting her mental state. Her last book, *Poems with Drawings* fused her writing and pictures, and was published in 1969, the year of her mental breakdown. Beset with financial problems and suffering from depression, she died in 1971. Three days previously, she had taken 18 sleeping tablets, and run to her neighbour saying that 'I have done a very foolish thing. This is a "*cri de coeur*".' She soon collapsed into a coma and never regained consciousness, and the inquest verdict was 'accidental death'. Anthony Conran translated the last piece she wrote as: 'The Creator who made me, he'll receive me / Among true folk of the parish of Enlli'.

* Bardsey Island, *Ynys Enlli* (- 'The Isle of 20,000 Saints'), can be reached from Aberdaron in a two mile sea trip. A monastery was founded there in 615 by St Cadfan. An important pilgrimage site since the 6th century, and the reputed burial place of Merlin, three pilgrimages were equivalent to one to Rome. A fourteenth century stone house, *Y Gegin Fawr* (the Big Kitchen), in Aberdaron was where pilgrims rested and ate their last meal before crossing the treacherous waters. In a rock at the foot of Mynydd Mawr facing Enlli is a well called *Ffynnon Fair* (Mary's Well) and the pilgrims used to walk down *Grisiau Mair* (Mary's Steps) to drink the sacred water and say their last prayers before setting off from *Porth Meudwy* (Hermit's Port) to the island. Many came here to die. St Deiniol, who founded the monastic site at Bangor, is also supposed to be buried

there. Apart from the remains of an abbey and some Celtic crosses, there are many nesting seabirds such as Manx Shearwaters, choughs, fulmars and guillemots on the island. Two types of dolphin, grey seals and leather-backed turtles can sometimes be seen. Wales' great poet, R.S. Thomas, was minister at the twelfth century Church of St Hywyn in Aberdaron, until he retired in 1978. The church had been founded in the 6th or 7th century.

This most holy of Welsh islands was given to St Cadfan by Einion, King of Llŷn. Saint Dyfrig and Saint Deiniol were buried here in the 6th century, and Saint Beuno in the 7th. In 1781, Thomas Pennant wrote of its 'halo of sanctity' when being rowed to visit the island: 'The mariners of Aberdaron seemed tinctured with the piety of the place: for they had not rowed far, but they made a full stop, pulled off their hats, and offered up a short prayer...'

Farming and fishing supported a population of a hundred until 1925, when there was a mass emigration. Its leader, Love Pritchard, had been declared unfit for military service in World War I because he was too old. In a fit of pique, this acknowledged 'King' of Enlli declared the island a pacifist enclave. The title of King probably went back to the Middle Ages when it was held by the Abbot, and then taken over by the islander who represented the islanders to the landlord, then Lord Newborough. The islanders were usually very late in paying their rents, despite which Lord Newborough had donated a crown to Love Pritchard. In response to the authorities' fears that the king and his Enlli subjects would side with the Kaiser, a boatload of police appeared, and took away everyone of military age.

In 1925, the King of Enlli led a mass exodus of farmers and their families, leaving only half a dozen people behind. Wynford Vaughan Thomas recounted a visitor's recollection of a 1910 meeting with Love Pritchard at suppertime... 'His Majesty sat in his grandfather's chair eating supper which consisted entirely of crabs and beer. On one side of the chair was a collection of good-sized crabs among seaweed in a wooden pail; on the other side an equally big pail of beer. The King was smoking but every now and then he reached down into the left-hand pail, pulled out a crab, put it on the back of his left hand and brought his right fist down on it with a crash. He took out the insides of the crab, dropped them in the beer, and swallowed the lot with one gulp.'

## TESSIE O'SHEA 13 March 1914 – 21 April 1995

### 'TWO-TON TESSIE'

Born in Plantagenet Street, Riverside, Cardiff, she watched variety acts as a four year-old, and determined upon the stage as a career. Aged 6, she took piano and elocution lessons, and at 7 years old won a Cardiff clog-dancing competition. From the age of 9, she had favoured a ukulele, which became a trademark of her act. Tessie won talent contests for singing and tap-dancing, and made her professional debut at 12 at the Bristol Hippodrome. This led to an appearance at the Chiswick Empire, and she was on her way on the variety circuit for the rest of her professional life.

At the start of her career, she dressed in comic clothes to disguise her weight, with boots, striped stockings and over-sized hats, basing her act on the legendary Welsh music-hall artiste, Lily Morris. Among her repertoire were the well-known *Josh-u-ah, Don't Have Any More, Mrs Moore, Why Am I Always the Bridesmaid and Hold Your Hand Out You Naughty Boy*. By the 1930's she had become a star, making fun of her weight and using it as part of her act, becoming an extremely warm and endearing

entertainer. She played summer seasons at Blackpool from 1934, and topped theatre bills across Britain, playing the banjo and singing such hits as *Nobody Loves a Fairy When She's Forty* (prefixing 'fat' in front of fairy, while prancing dreamily across the stage), and *I Met Him By the Withered Weeping Willows*. When the War broke out, she added *I Fell In Love with An Airman Who Had Big Blue Eyes, But I'm Nobody's Sweetheart Now.'* Her nick-name came from the number *Two Ton Tessie from Tennessee*. She toured with ENSA, entertaining the troops, starred in a revue at the Prince of Wales theatre, and topped the bill at the London Palladium in 1944 with Max Miller. With Tommy Trinder, she was invited to perform at a private party in Windsor Castle for King George VI and Queen Elizabeth.

In 1946 she was in a revue at the Palladium with Jimmy Jewel and Ben Warriss, and Nat Jackley. Making her entrance on a pregnant elephant, it threw her off after a few weeks, and she had to recuperate for 3 months, until a triumphal appearance in the Royal Variety Performance in that year. She then toured with Billy Cotton's Band, and the revue *Tess and Bill* was staged at London's Victoria Palace. 1950 saw Tessie touring South Africa, seventeen years after her first visit there. In the 1950's, theatres were decimated by the advent of television, but she continued in summer season and cabaret, as well as in plays such as *Romanoff and Juliet*. Her international fame was such, however, that the *Melbourne Argus* motoring review of the Holden FE car in 1956 reads - 'Next was the extra width of the front seat if you want to carry six. Those extra inches may not sound much, but they gave me the feeling that 'Two Ton' Tessie O'Shea could easily make a third.'

She became a regular on BBC TV's *The Good Old Days*, set in Leeds Music Hall. Her career faltered for a while, until she was taken to

America to play in Broadway's *The Girl Who Came To Supper* in 1963. Noel Coward especially wrote songs for her and she performed the show-stopper *London*, winning the prestigious *Tony* award as best supporting actress. In that year she appeared on the *Ed Sullivan Show*, and was so popular that she came back the following year on the same show as The Beatles. She also now appeared on America's vaudeville circuit, billed as 'London's Own Tessie O'Shea', and performed curtain-wheels on curtain-call. A year later she starred again on Broadway in *A Time For Song*, the adaptation of Richard Llewellyn's *How Green Was My Valley*. The ebullient, high-kicking, cart-wheeling 17-stone blonde singer was the toast of Broadway, appearing upon all the major TV chat shows. She also won an *Emmy* for her part in a TV version of *Dr Jekyll and Mr Hyde*.

In 1970, she appeared in Blackpool Opera House with Ken Dodd, starred in the TV comedy series *As Good Cooks Go*, and then went to the USA to live. She had a cameo role in Disney's film *Bedknobs and Broomsticks* and starred in a Las Vegas revue. Tessie also appeared in the films *Dr Jekyll & Mr Hyde* (in 1968, with Jack Palance starring); and *The Russians are Coming! The Russians are Coming!* (1966, with Alan Arkin). For the latter she received an *Oscar* nomination. From 1973 she starred in the Sands Hotel, Las Vegas, in *London Revue*, and became a US resident, although she occasionally returned to Britain. *The Times* stated that she was married to David Rollo in 1940, and the marriage was dissolved in 1950, but the *Western Mail's* obituary stated that she never married. Tessie died aged 82 in Leesburg, Florida, and the *South Wales Echo* commented that 'she was to Cardiff what Gracie Fields was to Lancashire'.


## SARA ADELINE ELUNED PHILLIPS 27 October 1914 - 10 January 2009

## THE ONLY WOMAN TO WIN THE BARDIC CROWN TWICE, 'QUEEN OF CENARTH'

Eluned Phillips was born in Cenarth, on the same day as Dylan Thomas in Swansea, and was only the second woman to win the Bardic Crown at the National Eisteddfod. She was educated at Abercych Primary School and Cardigan Grammar School, and lived in Cenarth all her life. She was known and loved as a wonderful storyteller and raconteur, and also for her outspoken opinions. Cenarth is a picturesque village famous for its coracles from which men fished the Teifi for Salmon and Sewin. Meic Phillips, in his *Independent* obituary, tells us: 'Her father was killed in the First World War while she was still a child and she never knew him, but she was brought up in a warm-hearted extended family, which included the aunt to whom she was devoted, and a grandmother who encouraged her to take up every challenge with the admonition, "Go for it, girl! Give it your best shot!"

From primary school at Abercych, a district renowned for its associations with the *Mabinogion*, she went to Cardigan Grammar School where, a dreamy child, she did not distinguish herself academically but began competing in local eisteddfodau.' She drew sustenance from the Congregationalist chapel in Cenarth and from hearing folk-stories. At Sunday school Phillips learned to read in Welsh, later becoming a fine public speaker and learning the rules of *cynghanedd*, the complex system of traditional prosody used by many Welsh poets to this day.

Eluned wrote for most of her life, publishing her first poem at age 7. At the time, a family friend accused her of not having written it by herself. Incensed, Phillips' mother told the friend her daughter would prove him wrong by writing a poem on the spot. Phillips obliged, but since she didn't much like the friend, she wrote a poem comparing him to a murderer (he cut down trees and had recently cut down one she loved to climb). He was impressed, but Phillips received a scolding from her mother for calling the man a murderer. By that age, however, Phillips was resigned to the fact that she was going to be in and out of trouble. The source of that trouble, and the embarrassment, she knew, was her hair colour.

'I was the only redhead in the family', she said. Red hair, back then and even now, has been associated with stubbornness and a fiery temper, and just four, she tried to dye her hated red hair black by dipping her head in a cask of tar. Had not it not been for a family friend it may well have cost her life. She wrote: 'They had to shave me - I was like Yul Brynner - I was quite happy but they told me when it grows back it will be redder still.' Eluned decided to accept it, going so far as using her red hair to justify her career decisions, because when she finished school, her parents wanted her to become a teacher. 'I was a redhead, I couldn't possibly do that,' she said. Instead, she became a professional writer, writing not just poems but plays, scripts, stories and articles. This work introduced her to bohemian circles and friendships with fellow Welsh writers and artists, including the painter Augustus John, who, she writes, 'had an ego at least double the size of a camel's hump.' She also became acquainted with poets Dewi Emrys and Dylan Thomas... 'I should have liked him, for I find most of his work truly inspiring,' she wrote in her memoirs. 'But I did not. The many times I met him, he was too drunk to hold a proper conversation.'

She was admitted into the Gorsedd of Bards as *Luned Teifi* at the age of 22, the blue robe being exchanged for the white, decorated with laurel leaves, after she had won her first crown. In 1965 she won a prize at Gŵyl Fawr Aberteifi (Cardigan) for a poem upon the Welsh poet and writer Dewi Emrys. In 1967 she first became a household name with Welsh-speaking families, when she won the Bardic Crown at the National Eisteddfod in Bala, becoming only the second woman to win the competition, after Dilys Cadwaladr. In 1971, she published a remarkable biography of her friend Dewi Emrys. Then in 1983 she repeated winning the Bardic Crown at Llangefni and remains the only woman to do so. Eluned's 1983 entry was influenced by the death on the Sir Galahad of Welsh Guardsman Michael Dunphy from neighbouring Llechryd. It traced the history of a fictitious Welsh family which emigrated to Patagonia in 1865. Blinded and badly wounded, a Welsh guardsman is cared for by a descendant of Welsh-Argentinians. Both her crowns are on display at the recently restored Cardigan Castle. Some of her work was published in *Cerddi Glyn-y-Mêl* (1985).

Consulted for *The Story of English*, we read: 'Eluned Phillips, winner of the Eisteddfod Crown, believes that Welsh-English speakers can always be identified by the lilt of their speech. She remarks that even with Richard Burton, who spoke almost perfect Standard English, his Welsh roots were recognizable in "the melodious lilt of his voice and the sing-song way he used to talk English, the resonance, the rounded vowels - in the music of the language". The Welshness of the English spoken in Wales also appears in sentence construction.

According to Eluned Phillips: "In Welsh we tend to invert our sentences, perhaps putting the adjective after the noun ... I was talking to a neighbour the other day. She is from the valleys and we were talking about a young Welshman who had died. What she said to me was, 'Pity it was that he died so early', which is really a literal translation of the Welsh ... We also have a habit of using throwaway words - like, indeed, look you - and I think this originally started because we couldn't finish the translation from Welsh in time. So a word like "indeed" became an important stop-gap. The Welsh contribution to English literature is also distinctive, and Eluned Phillips believes that this, too, has deep Celtic roots. "You can always tell when a Welshman is writing in English because of the flamboyance of the descriptions. I think that comes down from the old Celtic warriors who used to go into battle (against the Anglo-Saxons) not only with terror in their veins, but with red hot waves of ecstasy."

Born on the same day as Dylan Thomas, she mixed in the same Bohemian circles in the 1930s. She would often go to Paris to stay with Edith Piaf, and once visited Pablo Picasso's studios to see him working on

*Guernica* - a painting she declared 'a bit of a mess.' On another occasion, another of his paintings, *The Ugly Woman*, left her less than impressed. 'I told him I did not like it but he had the cheek to tell me that is how I would look when I was old.' She also knew Dylan Thomas, though she thought him 'a rude little man, always with drink taken and his hand out for a few bob.' Her stories of life in London and Paris, rubbing shoulders with such luminaries as Augustus John, Dylan Thomas, Jean Cocteau, Pablo Picasso and Edith Piaf – to whom she was a close friend – were legendary. Many of her stories are included in her memoir *The Reluctant Redhead* (2007), and written in a matter of weeks on her trusty computer, '*shenkin*', which she acquired at the age of 90. Eluned's memoir was published in 2007.

In a *Free Press* report we are told: 'As a young woman visiting Paris, she got to meet Pablo Picasso. She had managed to finagle an invitation to his studio but was suddenly paralyzed with shyness as she was about to cross the threshold. Part of that paralysis came from the doves hanging around (she was concerned they would land in her thatch of red hair), part from the large, bizarre canvas leaning against one wall and part from the man himself, whose gaze she compares to "a CAT-scan." She was about to apologize, then skitter away in shame. Luckily, the great artist was kind (and the fact that she was young, pretty and female probably didn't hurt) and convinced her to stay. They spent the afternoon drinking coffee and discussing art, and the large canvas, it turns out, was nothing less than *Guernica*. And she was one of the first to see it. Then there was the time when she tripped over what she thought was "a piece of bulky carpet" in friend Edith Piaf's apartment, and realized in shock it was actor Maurice Chevalier, sleeping off a party. Luckily, like Picasso, he did not take umbrage, and the two went on to become friends.' She wrote 'Someone I had great fun with was Maurice Chevalier - that was an odd thing because I trod all over him. I was at Piaf's house and I walked across this piece of carpet to get some music and he was sleeping underneath. He had a wonderful sense of humour... I was very lucky to be in amongst those people.'

A BBC website tells us: 'Archdruid Dic Jones said he understood she had been a member of the *Gorsedd* - an association whose members consist of poets, writers, musicians, artists and individuals who have made a contribution to Welsh language and culture - since the 1930s. "She was probably the oldest member of the Gorsedd and certainly the most faithful... She was a character, there's no doubt about that. She had the strange quality of being mysterious and accessible at the same time."... Andrew Gilbert, a good friend of the writer, was with her when she died. He said she picked up a cold after Christmas and developed pneumonia. "Eluned will be well missed, she was a lovely, lovely woman... She was like a mother to me and my partner Bernadette. We stayed with her when we first moved to Cenarth. We were blessed to have known her."

She published her memoirs in 2007 after her family persuaded her to share her memories of some of the world's most famous writers and artists. In her book - *The Reluctant Redhead* - she revealed that, although she shared a love of writing and poetry with Dylan Thomas, she did never really got on with him. She told the *BBC News* website, shortly before her 93rd birthday: "Either he was too drunk to talk or in a world of his own. "I was an ignorant girl from the country really and Dylan was a bit of a scrounger. I like most of his work - it's just I did not like his way of life." The pair met through their mutual friend the artist Augustus John, a man she had far more time for. "Augustus was so generous - but he had an ego and could get out of hand," she said. She also wrote of her friendship with Piaf, who she met after travelling to Paris. "When she sang I had never heard anything like it - it paralysed me... We talked a lot - she was wonderful, really a very nice person. She was a very capable person - quite religious - it was a marvellous time." Another anecdote she recalled was the time she travelled to Spain to meet Pablo Picasso. She told Piaf of her desire to meet the artist and the singer set the meeting up in Spain. "He had a sense of humour. He took me into his studio, made coffee and we spent an afternoon going through his pictures. He really was a kind person," she said.'

ELUNED PHILLIPS

She credited her American friends for encouraging her to write her memoir in the first place, during her last visit. "I had lots of embarrassing moments," she said. "It was America who told me to write them down." Looking back on her life, Eluned had no big regrets: 'I've been very, very lucky', she said, 'It's a great life'. Eluned Phillips passed away aged 94 in Glangwili Hospital in Carmarthenshire, and her funeral service was at St Brynach's Church, Llanboidy.

Upon the *Americymru website* Judy Duval wrote: 'Eluned Phillips was loved by so many in the world including those in Canada and in the U.S. She will be especially missed by *Cor Cymraeg De Califfornia* of which I'm a charter member. She loved us as we loved her. For many musical pieces that our founding director wrote, Eluned wrote her wonderful poetry in the form of lyrics just for us. She travelled many times over the years to Los Angeles for our opening concert seasons. We affectionately called her our "Groupie." She wrote about us in her book, *The Reluctant Redhead...* Eluned was a consummate story teller! When she told her stories she always had a twinkle in her eye. She gathered young and old alike around her as if she were a magnet and will be so missed by our choir members. As one very close friend of hers and former member of the choir said, "a light has gone out!"'

The life and work of Eluned was celebrated in a memorial concert at Rhos-y-Gilwen, near Cilgerran in 2012. The concert was centred around performances by the South Wales Male Choir, with whom Eluned was closely associated for many years. She was with the choir when they toured Australia in 2002, and climbed Sydney Harbour Bridge not once, but twice, and at the age of 87. The compére for the evening was Gwenno Dafydd, a close friend of Eluned's who sang at Eluned's 90th birthday celebrations in California in 2004. Readings of a selection of Eluned's poems and prose work were given by Menna Elfyn, the award-winning poet and playwright, and long-time friend Wyn Calvin related stories of many happy events he shared with Eluned.

As a vice President of the South Wales Male Choir, she had travelled the world and was dubbed Wales' best unofficial ambassador. Proceeds were distributed locally to part fund a sensory garden at the primary school in Cenarth and provide four Welsh oak stools, fashioned by local builder and entrepreneur, Emyr Thomas, from timbers recovered from an old property at Cwmcou. There is now a memorial garden and commemorative stone in Cenarth, and a message on the Eluned Phillips Facebook site reads: 'A Big Happy Birthday, 100 Years old. Our Queen of Cenarth A pity you are not with us to celebrate, but you're with us in our hearts. We drink to your memory, the garden is completed. My promise has been full filled you now have a fitting place for people to rest and gather their thoughts... pop goes the cork, and I drink to you...' Contributions were raised from across Britain and America, and the garden was completed in time for her centenary on 27 October 2014. Menna Elfyn (q.v.) is writing Eluned's biography, to be published by Gomer in 2016.

*Footnote:*

Her Obituary in *The Independent* 4 July 1913 by Meic Stephens reads: '... Eluned Phillips was unusual among Welsh writers of her generation in that she embraced a bohemian lifestyle which took her to pre-war London and Paris, where she made the acquaintance of such major artists as Augustus John, Dylan Thomas, Edith Piaf, Jean Cocteau, Maurice Chevalier and Pablo Picasso, the last of whom showed her the unfinished *Guernica* with the paint still wet on the canvas. She even made it to Casablanca, where she might easily have fitted in among the habitués of Rick's Bar. Nearer home, she was only the second woman to win the Crown, one of the major literary prizes awarded at the National Eisteddfod, and this she achieved on two occasions: first in 1967 and again in 1983. It was for this remarkable feat rather than her picaresque adventures in foreign parts that she was most admired in her native Wales.

Famously reticent about the details of her life, even in her memoir, *The Reluctant Redhead* (2007), she was always loath to reveal so much as the year of her birth. In the *Oxford Companion to the Literature of Wales* it was given as

"1915?", whereas in fact she had been born on 27 October 1914 – the same day as Dylan Thomas, whom she heartily disliked because of his fecklessness and scrounging habits. Nor does her book provide much information about the time she spent in the company of Picasso, Cocteau and Chevalier, though about Piaf, with whom she seems to have had more of a rapport, she wrote movingly. Instead, the book is largely the record (without many facts that can be checked) of the adventures this independent-minded woman had whenever she could shake off the confines of her native patch.

Many of her escapades and her short-fuse temper she attributed to the red hair she had as a young woman. Her introduction to the raffish milieu of London's Fitzrovia was made possible in the late 1930s by Dewi Emrys, the dissolute ex-preacher and talented poet whose life she treated in a biography published in 1971. Once described as "the Welsh Dylan Thomas" (as if Thomas were not Welsh because he wrote in English), Emrys was so tormented by the alcoholism that eventually killed him in 1952, that he immediately pawned the silver Crown he had won at the National Eisteddfod in order to buy more drink. Phillips's biography went some way to correcting Emrys's image as a *poète maudit* by debunking many of the apocryphal stories told about him and pointing to the very considerable qualities of his intricate verse.

Eluned's fascination with the life of the Left Bank was facilitated by a friend at her London boarding school whose mother worked in Paris: the two girls were exploring Montparnasse when hardly out of school uniform. In those days, as she was fond of pointing out, Paris was nearer London than west Wales, and she went there often. In 1939 she entered the University of London with the intention of becoming a journalist, an ambition in which she was encouraged by Hannen Swaffer, then at the height of his fame in Fleet Street, but her studies there were interrupted by the outbreak of war. The war also put paid to her love-affair with a Breton nationalist she had met in Paris, the only romance she was prepared to write about in her memoirs but over which she nevertheless drew a discreet veil, except to say that she knew him as Per, and that, although rescued from a French jail, he had later died of the injuries he had sustained while a prisoner.

After several years living as a pseudonymous writer for women's magazines in London, and penning a number of Mills and Boon-type romances to keep the wolf from her door, she returned to Newcastle Emlyn, where she took a job in a solicitor's office and served as a court translator. At about the same time she began writing scripts for the BBC in Wales and working as a roving reporter, but her thirst for adventure also took her to eastern Europe before the demise of the Soviet Union, to Ireland, where she became a friend of the folk-singer Seamus Ennis, to Australia and the U S, particularly to Los Angeles where, despite two serious car crashes in 1997, she celebrated her 90th birthday. She had a close connection with several of the leading Welsh male-voice choirs that visit California on a regular basis and was usually to be seen taking full advantage of the hospitality extended on those occasions.

Her only book of poems was *Cerddi Glyn-y-Mêl* ("Glyn-y-mêl Poems", 1985), which takes its title from the house in Cenarth she shared for many years with her aged aunt. Very few of her poems appeared in magazines and anthologies because she claimed never to send them off unless invited, which she seldom was. In her memoirs she provided an English translation of the long poem "*Clymau*" ("Bonds") with which she had won her second Crown in 1983. An exploration of the ancestral links between Wales and the Welsh colony in Patagonia, the poem focuses on two soldiers, one a Welshman in the British Army and the other a Patagonian in the Argentinian, and on the tragedy involved in their having to fight each other.

She explained that she had written her memoirs in English (and on a computer acquired in her 90th year) so that her many friends all over the world could read about the life of "a simple country girl with itchy feet". The book ends with her standing mischievously in the wet concrete of the Millennium Centre then under construction in Cardiff Bay and the typically spirited advice she gave to many a young writer: *"Try to make as many footprints in the concrete as you can – and treasure them."'* (reproduced by kind permission of the author)

## DOROTHY SQUIRES 25 March 1915 – 14 April 1998

### SINGING STAR, DIVA AND *CHANTEUSE REALISTE*

One of the brightest stars that Britain ever produced, died a poverty-stricken recluse, in a story of rags to riches to rags. She was born Edna May Squires, in a travelling van parked at Pontyberem outside Carmarthen, the daughter of a steelworker. Growing up in Dafan, she worked in the local tin-plate factory, and her first public performance was at the Ritz ballroom, Llanelli, as a crooner with the local dance-band. Dorothy moved to London in the 1930's and she worked as a nurse in Croydon. Being discovered by the legendary American pianist Charlie Kunz, in a West End cabaret in 1935, she joined his band at the Casani Club. In 1936 Dorothy made her first radio broadcast, which the composer and bandleader Billy Reid heard. She then

**Dorothy Squires with Roger Moore in the early 1960s**

made her recording debut with Reid and his Accordion Band in late 1936. In 1938 she joined the Billy Reid Band as his singer and lover, and the partnership, one of the most successful in British popular music, lasted until

1951. He was 12 years her senior, and they lived together from 1939-1951, although Reid's wife refused to divorce him.

Her first film was *Saturday Night Review*, and she toured with Reid as *The Composer and the Voice*. Her first hit was written by Reid, *Coming Home*, released in 1945, followed by *The Gypsy* and *I'll Close My Eyes* in the same year. She was at the peak of her career. In the War, their double-act was terrifically successful on the variety circuit, and their frequent broadcasts helped to sell her records. Resident star of *Variety Bandbox* on BBC radio from 1945, in 1946 she made her Palladium debut, and played pantomime principal boy across Britain. In the 1940's and 50's she packed theatres out, not only in Britain but in the USA. Dorothy was a dynamic, dramatic, highly emotional singer - a *chanteuse-realiste* - with an army of devoted fans. Hits included *Say It With Flowers* and *For Once in My Life.*

However, Reid became increasingly jealous of his young, glamorous blonde mistress, and after yet another violent row, she left him. She gave him Llanelli's Astoria Theatre, which they both owned, in return for their large Bexley home, St Mary's Mount. In 1952 Dorothy met the 25-year-old Roger Moore*, an unknown actor, who left his first wife for her. Her big chart hit *I'm Walking Behind You* coincided with her marriage in New Jersey in 1953, to Moore, 13 years her junior. They had met at a party at her house - Dorothy reminisced 'It started with a squabble, then he carried me off to bed.' *'Dot'* took Moore to Hollywood, introducing him to all the right people, partying with the likes of Gary Cooper, Grace Kelly, Doris Day and Rock Hudson. She helped him obtain the lead in a Broadway production. They returned to England where she had a hit with Edith Piaf's *If You Love Me*, which Piaf thought was better than their own version.

In 1954, the couple moved to Hollywood. Moore began filming with Elizabeth Taylor in *The Last Time I Saw Paris*. She starred in the film musical *Stars in Your Eyes* in 1956, as a music-hall star estranged from her husband. Returning to Hollywood, she was a success in cabaret at the *Moulin Rouge*, and then at the Coconut Grove. Here, her biggest fan was Elvis Presley, who attended most nights and repeatedly asked Dorothy to sing *'This Is My Mother's Day'.*

Roger Moore's career now started to take off, just as hers, in her 40's, began to slide, and her behaviour started to become erratic and obsessive. She was unable to have the children she wanted, and in 1959 Moore had shown great interest in his blonde leading lady and co-star in the TV series, *The Alaskans*. Dorothy and Roger argued publicly in a Hollywood night club. In 1961, she had another hit with *Say It With Flowers,* and was the first British singer to star at London's Talk of the Town. When she was there, Moore told her that he was leaving her for the Italian actress Luisa Mattioli. It was announced that Moore was to play Simon Templar in the long-running TV series *The Saint*, and three days later

Squires sued him for restitution of conjugal rights. He refused and stayed away.

In her 1977 autobiography *Rain Rain Go Away*, she recounted how she wished to fight her jealousy, and had decided to do anything to keep Roger Moore as her husband. However, they had parted bitterly in 1961. She refused him a divorce until 1968, despite the fact the Mattioli and Moore had a son and daughter. In 1968, the actor Kenneth More called Mattioli the wife of Roger Moore, and Dorothy sued for libel but lost the case. In 1969, Kenneth More was Roger's best man. A week later, *The News of the World* published an article purporting to be Dorothy's account of the marriage, and she sued and won £4,300 in damages. She insisted on including Moore's passionate love letters to Mattioli, that she had intercepted, in her autobiography but was prevented by a High Court injunction and the book could not be published. She sued Moore, Mattioli and the publishers for preventing publication, and lost the case and a great deal of money.

Her career was now on the rocks, but in 1970 at the age of 55 she decided to make a comeback, spending £5,000 of her own money to hire the London Palladium. Friends thought that she was mad, but the tickets sold out in ten hours, there was a 15-minute standing ovation and she had several new offers to work. Her recording of *My Way* hit the charts. On hearing it, Nancy Sinatra commented 'What a wow of an interpretation of that anthem. I think my father must have been half asleep when he recorded it.' The great man himself referred to Dot as 'Britain's only female singer with balls'. Dorothy filled concert halls again, and her fans chartered a jet to see her perform at Carnegie Hall in 1971. However she seemed to be mentally unstable by this time.

In 1974, she presented a concert at the London Palladium in tribute to Billy Reid, who had written hits for America's Ink Spots, Sinatra, Ella Fitzgerald and Eddie Fisher. Her under-insured mansion at Bexley burned down in this year. She barely escaped, clutching only her jewel box and a case of 400 love-letters from Roger Moore. She tried to sue so many times that she was named as a 'vexatious litigant' by the High Court in 1982. Over the previous ten years she had launched 20 strange legal actions claiming libel, assault, piracy of her autobiography, and misrepresentation in Roger Moore's biography.

In 1982 Dorothy was invited to open the new Barbican Centre with *An Evening with Dorothy Squires*, and in 1983 had her final hit with *I Am What I Am*. However, she had lost over £2 million in litigation. Her last great house was a 17-room mansion in Bray, Berkshire, the home of Edward VII's mistress, Lily Langtry. Her possessions were seized, and in 1988 she was evicted in bankruptcy proceedings. She went to live in a little cottage in Ackworth, near Pontefract. In 1992, she tried to sue her former trustee-in-bankruptcy but again lost, with heavy costs. She lived as a recluse, refusing to answer the door, leaving in 1995 hours before bailiffs arrived with a Crown Court Repossession order.

Luckily, she had been offered a rent-free home in Wales by a lifelong fan, Esme Coles, the owner of a Trebanog fish and chip shop. In 1996, Roger Moore paid for Dot's private room and for surgery to remove a bladder tumour. She died of lung cancer in Llwynypia Hospital, Mid-Glamorgan. Moore** had telephoned the hospital, and told her niece Emily-Jane Squires to 'Take hold of her hand, give it a little squeeze, and tell her Rog is thinking of her'. Dorothy's response was the single word 'Magic'. She said that her epitaph would be: 'She'd spit in the devil's eye before she'd lick her wounds and cry.' She was buried in Streatham in the same grave as her brother, Captain Frederick Squires, near her parents' grave, and Roger Moore's wreath read 'I've Said It With Flowers', referring to one of her hit records. The secretary of her fan club avers that she launched *Say It With Flowers* at Billy Smart's Circus in a cage with six tigers. Bruce Forsythe asked the on-looking Roger Moore, 'Have you taken out insurance?', and Moore responded, 'Yes... on the tigers.'

* Roger Moore's penchant for cardigans early in his career earned him the nickname in the acting profession of 'The Great Knit'. His RADA training gave him a mid-Atlantic accent, and he described his acting range as 'left eyebrow raised, right eyebrow raised'. His early TV roles were starring in series such as *Ivanhoe, The Saint* and *The Persuaders*, but he earned his millions from successfully succeeding Sean Connery in a series of *James Bond* films.

** Moore later left his 26-year marriage with Luisa Mattioli for a neighbour, 56 year-old Kiki Tholstrup, whom Mattioli described as 'old meat, a hungry hanger-on who has had two husbands and three facelifts.'

*Footnote:*
In January 17, 1998, an article in *The Times*, commenting upon Dusty Springfield's battle with cancer, Dorothy Squires is mentioned, along with another two Welsh women featured in this book: 'Petula has also long been an icon to gay men, rather as Dorothy Squires once was, and Shirley Bassey and Dusty Springfield are also. It's an interesting time for such women in British music. Bassey and Springfield share the honour of also being revered by a younger generation, the children of their original fans, which endorses their retro appeal. Clark, if not at the forefront of this revisionism, was re-discovered during the recent easy listening trend, thanks chiefly to her 1964 hit *Downtown*.'

## ELAINE MORGAN OBE FRSL 7 November 1920 – 12 July 2013

## AUTHOR, PLAYWRIGHT, EVOLUTIONIST

Elaine was born at Hopkinstown near Pontypridd, her father being a pumpsman for the Great Western Colliery Company. Like many others, he was unemployed for much of the 1930's. Elaine was an only child, and lived most of her life in Mountain Ash. After Trefforest Girls' School, Elaine studied English Language and Literature at Lady Margaret Hall, Oxford, graduating in 1942.

She became a lecturer for the Workers' Educational Association until her marriage in 1945, and took up freelance writing in the 1950's. Her husband, Morien Morgan, had fought in the International Brigade during the Spanish Civil War, and had spent a year in a Franco gaol as a prisoner-of-war. He taught French for many years in Pontypridd Grammar School, and they settled in the Cynon Valley, raising three sons, Dylan, Gareth and Huw Morien. Morien Morgan died in 1997. After her marriage, Elaine was extremely successful in working for television, specialising in serials, adaptations and documentaries. She sold her first play to BBC Television in 1952, and learned the ropes of scriptwriting when few established writers would have thought of contributing to the medium. She wrote hundreds of scripts - plays, serials, a sitcom, dramatised documentaries, adaptations, contributions to series - and won over a dozen national and international awards. She adapted for BBC Wales Richard Llewellyn's *How Green was my Valley* (1976), and Jack Jones's *Off to Philadelphia in the Morning* (1978). Among the best remembered are *Testament of Youth* (Writer of the Year Award), and the 9-part biography *The Life and Times of Lloyd George* in 1980. These were superb productions, and just the tip of the iceberg of her work for the genre. She also wrote for the long-running TV series, *Dr Finlay's Casebook* and *Z-Cars*, winning over a dozen national and international awards.

Her *Descent of Woman* was published in 1972, making Elaine a household name, and adding to the feminist debate by querying the role of women during evolution. A respected novelist and play-writer, she resented the odd Desmond Morris hypothesis in *The Naked Ape* that women had developed breasts purely to attract men. Her book was a feminist critique of the then popular books about human evolution featuring man's first ancestors as blood-thirsty hunters. Elaine retold the story from the angle of the hunter's mate, and attacked Morris's book as biased and far-fetched. This was at the very beginning of the Women's Lib movement, and its hard-hitting style was tempered with humour and irony to make it an international best-seller. It was Book of the Month Club choice in the USA and published in nine languages.

Her next four books on human evolution were addressed mainly to a scientific audience. She went on to develop her theories in *The Aquatic Ape* (1982), *The Scars of Evolution* (1990), *The Descent of the Child* (1994), *The Aquatic Ape Hypothesis* (1997) and *The Naked Darwinist* (2008). The controversial theme she has explored - that our ancestors must have spent some period of their evolutionary history in an aquatic or semi-aquatic environment to account for unique human characteristics such as walking on two legs, the loss of body hair, changes in respiration, fat babies, learning to speak – had been suggested by Oxford Professor Sir Alister Hardy in two brief papers, but had been neglected for 12 years before she revived it and began searching for new evidence to support it. She believed, unlike most biologists and paleoanthropologists, that mankind spent between one and two million years of its evolutionary life in water. Fat only occurs in two types of mammal, hibernating or aquatic. Unlike the apes, human infants are born fat and become fatter, as they had no need to live in trees. We have skin adapted for water, rather than layers of fur, human babies can swim from birth, and there appears to be no-one who can disprove this remarkable woman's theories. (Incidentally, it is a wonder that no socio-anthropologist has explored the rationale for Desmond Morris dyeing his hair and combing the strands carefully over his forehead, in a pathetic attempt to disguise his severe baldness). Elaine also wrote *Falling Apart: the Rise and Decline of Urban Civilisation* in 1976. Her work was at first ridiculed by professional anthropologists but now after 30 years it is winning support. The alternative scenario - that human anatomy evolved to cope with conditions on the African Savannah - has finally been renounced even by those who were its strongest supporters. Elaine died aged 92, a truly remarkable woman equally capable of writing film scripts and scientific research.

*Footnote:*
1. I was fortunate to meet Elaine, and the following two articles demonstrate Elaine Morgan's importance to the theory of human origin. From The Observer 10 December 2000, we read: ''First human learned to swim before she walked - The old notion that man evolved from the hot, dry plains is being swept aside by a feminist theory, reports Robin McKie: It was one of the most outrageous, improbable evolutionary ideas ever proposed: humans are amphibious apes who triumphed only when women started to stand on their own two feet at the water's edge. But now the idea, derided for most of

the past 30 years by academics, is becoming respectable. Key scientists, over recent months, have announced their support for Elaine Morgan's controversial aquatic ape hypothesis. Sympathisers include the US philosopher Daniel Dennett, the distinguished South African palaeontologist Philip Tobias, and the natural historian Sir David Attenborough, who is to deal with the theory in his next TV series, "*Mammals*". In addition the Norwegian Academy of Sciences has just awarded Morgan a medal in honour of her work, while *New Scientist* ran a feature supporting the theory. The aquatic ape theory was proposed in 1960 by British biologist Sir Alister Hardy, who argued that apes evolved into humans when they descended from the trees to live, not on the savannah as was then supposed, but beside the sea. To keep their heads above water, our ancestors evolved an upright stance, freeing our hands to make tools to crack open shellfish. Once safely in the swim of things, we lost our body hair and instead developed a thick layer of sub-cutaneous fat to keep warm in the water. This explains why new-born babies can float, unlike other apes, he said.

Hardy's ideas were ignored by mainstream scientists, but not by Morgan, a feminist writer and TV dramatist who had become enraged by popular anthropologists who claimed that apes evolved into humans when males, not females, began to hunt and kill. Men lost their fur to keep cool and evolved big brains to help co-ordinate hunts, ran the theory. Women followed in their wake. 'It was macho nonsense, and I hated it,' she told *The Observer* last week. 'Then I heard about Hardy's work and I thought that has got to be it, that makes sense.' Morgan transformed the ideas of a somewhat astonished Hardy in her book, *The Descent of Woman*. Females led the way to the beach, she said, arguing that women can 'survive immersion in cold water for longer, and the one athletic sport at which they outdo males is long-distance swimming'. She envisaged a group of apes becoming trapped on an island in a flooded valley or by the sea. To survive they became adept divers, and had to develop more complex ways of breathing - an adaptation that aided the evolution of human speech. Morgan pointed out that the patterns of fine hairs of our bodies - which sweep across our backs and down our spines - are consistent with those of a marine animal, not a land one. We are primates born of water, she says. Her ideas were ridiculed, however, and until recently were shunned by academics who insisted that humans evolved on the searing heat of North-East Africa's expanding savannahs. However, this idea was dealt a blow last year when Tobias, once a savannah supporter, announced that his research showed that Africa possessed little open grassland at the time, and was most probably covered with vast bodies of water.

Tobias's support for the aquatic ape hypothesis is also backed by Attenborough, who used his recent presidency of the British Association to organise the country's first full scientific debate of the theory. 'Five million years ago, north-east Africa was affected by techtonic rifting that would have created flooded forests and isolated islands. We also know now that when primates, such as proboscis monkeys and chimpanzees, get caught in flooded land they will wade and carry infants. So the idea makes sense.' The American philosopher Dennett is a convert. 'When in the company of distinguished biologists, evolutionary theorists and other experts, I have often asked them to tell me, please, why Elaine Morgan must be wrong. I haven't yet had a reply worth mentioning.' Not everyone has been turned to the cause. Many palaeontologists complain that Morgan's dating is vague. They also point out that there was a gap of several million years between the appearance of features like smooth skin and upright stance in humans, which suggests our stay by the sea would have had to have been an improbably long one. Professor Chris Stringer, of the Natural History Museum, London, accepts the theory's explanation for our upright stance is as good as any other. 'However, we don't have proof, and in combining this idea with so many other suggestions - about our voices, brains and tools - aquatic ape supporters are going too far.' But the theory has gained ground in recent years, much to Morgan's delight. 'The scientific establishment is retreating in good order,' she said. Or as *The New Scientist* put it: 'The tide is turning.'

2. From the *Johannesburg Mail and Guardian*, 14 January 1999, we read Ruben Mowszowski: 'In Search of Our Swimming Ancestors: Humans are the only primates able to hold their breaths. Our skin and body fat resembles that of animals that swim. Why? A theory that humans evolved from a swimming ancestor is arousing new interest among orthodox scientists gathering at a world archaeology conference in South Africa this week. If the proponents of a revolutionary theory of human origins are correct, our ancestors abandoned the trees not for the savannah, but for the water. The 3.5 million year old *Australopithicene* fossil found recently at Sterkfontein and billed as our ancestor is to be the subject of an opening talk at the World Congress of Archaeology in Cape Town this week. Inevitably the question will be asked: in what kind of environment did this 1.2 metre tall ancestor of ours live? A mural in the Sterkfontein tea-room makes it quite clear. A group of hominids holed up in a cave is beating off another group apparently intent on moving in, if not actually devouring them. The cave is located in the middle of savannah grassland. But evidence which has been accumulating since the discovery of the Australopithecus fossil nicknamed Lucy in the 1970's indicates that the environment in which the *Australopithicenes* and the earlier *Ardithecus ramidus* lived and died was not savannah at all. It was tropical forest. This means that the story of how our ancestors evolved the characteristics that distinguish us from the apes will have to change.

The version that most of us know is called *the savannah hypothesis* and it goes like this: a change in climate shrunk the forests and expanded the savannah, forcing a branch of tree-living apes into the open, so they stood up. The recently discovered 4.5 million year old, and already partly bipedal,

*Ardithecus ramidus* lived, not in the dry savannah, but in a forest environment. This means that the human origins story - the narrative that links the fossil evidence - has to be rewritten. In other words, we are in for a new paradigm. Paradigms are like cities within which, as long as everyone believes in the framework, social order prevails. It's when belief begins to wane that the voices of the heretics outside start to be heard. Every now and then the walls are breached and while the more determined defenders of the faith battle it out, the rest quietly change sides and the city is rebuilt. At the recent Dual 98 Congress on Palaeontology and Human Biology one of the delegates was Elaine Morgan. Morgan, a non-scientist, is the author of The Descent of Women, the best-seller that put the female gender back into the evolutionary story in the 70s. For the past 27 years she has been promoting an alternative hypothesis which was put forward by scientist Alistair Hardy in 1960.

Hardy noticed that humans share certain physiological attributes, which are not present in other land mammals, with aquatic mammals. It occurred to him that bipedalism might have been an adaptation to an environment that had become not dry, but wet. Hardy was advised by his academic mentors not to pursue the subject for fear of damaging his career. In the savannah hypothesis palaeontology already had a 'good-enough' story to explain bipedalism and it happens to be one that we are very comfortable with. The image of our ancestors coming down from trees, emerging stooped from the primeval damp forest and striding out into the open grasslands to become the erect humans that we are today is a vision of humankind triumphant. It finds biblical expression in the story of our expulsion from Eden. Who wants ancestors who stood up just so that they could breathe? Hardy let the theory lie for the sake of his career. Morgan took it up and it became her mission She gave it the provocative name *Aquatic Ape Theory* and it might have been ignored for longer if the savannah hypothesis had not begun to fail.

In 1995, the eminent South African palaeontologist Phillip Tobias delivered a lecture to the University of London. Foot bones from Sterkfontein , he said, showed that there was an "arboreal element" in the life of the hominids whose fossils were found there. His conclusion: the relatively scrubby trees one would find in savannah would not have been adequate for the size of *Australopithecines*.

New findings of fossil animals, plants and pollen and recent evidence by way of the 4.5 million year old *Ardipithecus ramidus* fossil, he said, indicated that hominids were upright before the forest shrunk, before they got big brained. End of hypothesis. Not entirely. There are all sorts of theories still being offered that seek to explain our physiological peculiarities as adaptations to the savannah environment. Standing on two legs, for instance, is said to reduce exposure to the sun at midday (though critics say any sensible hominid would be lying under a tree at that time) and to keep our overheated brain away from the hot ground. An older theory is that our ancestors needed to free their arms in order to reach food and carry it home, after which they progressed to throwing stones at predatory animals or, as the Sterkfontein mural shows, at each other. Another holds that we were forced into the savannah by biologically better-equipped monkeys eating the fruit off the trees before it was ripe enough for us to digest. None of these is particularly convincing. It seems like palaeontology has reached one of those difficult moments which science must every now and then face, when cherished beliefs that underpin established frameworks collapse and allow the heretics to pick their way across the fallen bodies of the defenders of the faith and enter the citadel.

Tobias has recognised that moment. "All the former savannah supporters (including myself) must swallow our earlier words in the light of the new results from the early hominid deposits... And the savannah hypothesis is washed out... if savannah is eliminated as a primary cause or selective advantage, of bipedalism, then we are back to square one and have to try to find consensus on some other primary cause," he said in his London lecture. Significant words that lead us to Hardy and Morgan's world of flooded forests where apes who live both on the ground and in the trees have to adapt to a wet environment or die. Which is why Morgan, who has been out in the cold for 30 years is now, at Tobias's invitation, taking her place on the rostrum in front of the brightest brains in evolutionary science. Morgan says that the adaptations that distinguish us from our closest primate cousins were forced on our ancestors by the presence of water. That, for a couple of million years, which is not very long as these things are measured, our ancestors lived like sea-otters in a semi-aquatic environment.

The aquatic hypotheses suggests that nakedness, bipedalism and many other distinctly human adaptations evolved long before our ancestors moved onto the savannah. It is founded on the observation that a number of the features that characterise our physiology, "though rare or unique among land mammals, are common in aquatic ones." Morgan thinks that the aquatic interlude lasted about two million years. Marc Verhaegan, a biologist who supports the theory, is more extreme. He thinks that humans may have remained semi-aquatic until as recently as 200 000 years ago. It would be a mistake to assume that the aquatic hypothesis is not good science. In Tobias's words: "...we owe a debt of gratitude to Morgan and Verhaegan for the comprehensive and rigorous way in which they have gathered together and sifted an enormous body of evidence based not only on Marc Verhaegan's own researches, but on those of a number of human biologists...." The suggestion that between 2.5 and 4.4 million years ago a small-brained, biped *Australopithecine* lived in a woodland or forest niche and not a savannah terrain he said, fitted in with the physiological and biochemical evidence, gathered by the two of them. He pointed out however that his rejection of the savannah hypothesis did not mean that he was "automatically" espousing the Aquatic Ape hypothesis.

A feature of the aquatic ape hypothesis is that it deals with a large number of physiological and structural features, the best-known of which is bipedalism. Morgan says perpendicular gait has many disadvantages. It is slower, unstable, needs to be learned and exposes vulnerable organs to attack. "Only some powerful pressure could have induced our ancestors to adopt a way of walking for which they were initially so ill suited" she says. We are still suffering the consequences of this adaptation in the form of backaches, varicose veins, haemorrhoids, hernias and difficult childbirths. Morgan points out that all the other primates that stand up on occasion have a habitat that is wet rather than dry. The proboscis monkey, which stands very readily, lives in mangrove swamps. The habitat of the *bonobo*, which, like dolphins, beavers, sea otters and humans, mates face to face, includes a seasonally flooded forest. She says that "the only animal that ever evolved a pelvis like ours, suitable for bipedalism, was the long-extinct *Oreopithecus* - known as the swamp ape." Then there is our nakedness. The only other mammals which are naked are swimmers like the whale and dolphin, wallowers like the hippopotamus and pig, and animals like the elephant and rhinoceros, which, she says, "bear traces of a watery past". Human hair direction (we are naked by virtue of thinner hair, rather than fewer, hair follicles) occurs in whorls corresponding to the movement of water against a swimming body. In all the other apes it points downward.

Humans are the fattest primate. We have 10 times as many fat cells in our body as any other animal of similar size. Unlike other primates, our children are born fat with a large proportion of white fat which is good for insulation and buoyancy but not for energy. Morgan thinks it is an adaptation that protected babies that had fallen out of trees. As with most aquatic animals, but unlike other primates, our fat is present all year and is stored, not deep within the body, but under the skin where it serves as an insulative layer. The only other mammals that store fat in this way are aquatic, like dolphins, seals and hippos.

Humans are the only primates which have the ability to hold their breath voluntarily. The only other mammals that are able to do this are aquatic diving animals like seals and dolphins. The descent of the larynx that occurs in the human infant at about three months is an adaptation that allows air to be gulped in large quantities through the mouth. The only other mammals that have a descended larynx are the sealion and the dugong. "Without voluntary breath control, it is very unlikely that we could have learned to speak," says Morgan. We have larger brains than any other ape. The building of brain tissue is dependent on availability of Omega-3 fatty acids which are abundant both in the marine food chain and in fresh-water fish. The mammal with the largest proportionate brain size after humans is, of course, the dolphin - a terrestrial animal that returned to the sea. Morgan's scenario for these evolutionary adaptations is based on known geological events. About six million years the low-lying section of land near the Red Sea known as the Afar triangle (where Lucy was found) was flooded and became the Sea of Afar. Some hominids, she says, would have been isolated in islands, others would have found themselves having to survive in flooded forests, among marshes and swamps.

Rapid speciation, such as occurred in the change from ape into homid, Morgan says, "is almost invariably a sign that one population from a species has become isolated by a geographical barrier such as a stretch of water. Survivors of such massive flooding would have been forced into adapting." When the sea became landlocked and evaporated their descendants would have followed the waterways of the Great Rift Valley upstream, towards the south, and emerged, as at Sterkfontein, erect, with no body hair, the ability to hold their breath and with a descended larynx , ready to speak. They were tied by their modified physiology to remain in places where water was plentiful; and, she imagines, they got a good proportion of their food from it for quite a long time. When did they snap the umbilical cord keeping them near the water? "Presumably when they got good at making containers." Tobias's invitation to Morgan to speak at a congress of professionals has brought her inside the walls of the citadel and scientific evolutionary theory, in so far as human origins are concerned, might never be the same'.

## RUTH BIDGOOD 20 July 1922 -

## ONE OF WALES'S FOREMOST ENGLISH LANGUAGE POETS

At the launch of the previous edition of this book, at the much-missed Oriel bookshop in Cardiff, I had the great pleasure of Ruth attending and reading some of her work, along with Amy Wadge giving a great performance of some of her songs. Living in Abergwesyn, near Llanwrtyd Wells, Ruth is probably the poet closest to the spirit of R.S. Thomas that Wales has today. Born Ruth Jones at Seven Sisters (Blaendulais) near Neath, she moved at the age of seven to Aberafan, where her Welsh-speaking North Wales father was vicar, and went to grammar school at Port Talbot. Ruth's mother was from the West Country, and the unease of a double heritage is the subject of her poem

*Gwlad yr Haf* ('Summer Country' is the old Welsh name for the county of Somerset). Her English master, who fostered his pupils' creativity and encouraged in them a sense of purpose, variety and excitement in life, was Philip Burton, the mentor of Richard Burton, another pupil at the grammar school.

After reading English at St Hugh's College, Oxford - often meeting other Welsh students at the Celtic Society - Ruth joined the WRNS, and after short postings at Devonport and Scotland was drafted to Alexandria, where she spent the latter part of the war years as a coder at HQ Flag Officer Levant and Eastern Mediterranean. Demobilisation, in Spring 1946, was followed by work in London as a sub-editor on the team bringing out a new edition of *Chambers Encyclopaedia*. During this time she married David Edgar Bidgood, and before long moved with her husband to Coulsdon in Surrey, where her two sons and one daughter were brought up. In the 1960's the family started coming for holidays to mid-Wales; Ruth Bidgood had never ceased to regard Wales as home.

It was this (then partial) return to Wales that sparked off her writing. At that time in her forties, she began to write and get published poems, and also articles on local history. She is convinced that this was no coincidence. Ruth divorced in 1974 and returned to settle permanently in the remote village of Abergwesyn, near Llanwrtyd Wells in Breconshire, until her move to Beulah in 2002. Here she continued writing her poetry, and also historical articles upon the counties of Brecon and Radnor. Although by no means all her poems are strictly about her '*bro*' (local area), the coming to Wales, this time rural Powys, was the trigger for her writing, and much of her work has been said to show a strong sense of place and Welsh identity. She put down roots in the district, and had her son Martin living with his family a few miles from her, her daughter Janet in South Wales, and her eldest son Anthony (Tony) just over the Border. Sadly, Janet died in 2007.

Steering away from the superficial and trendy, she writes of landscapes, time and the seasons. She often links the forces of nature with folk lore tales to evoke a strong Welsh feeling. Her publications include *The Given Time* (1972), *Not Without Homage* (1975), *The Print of Miracle* (1978), *Lighting Candles: New and Selected Poems* (1982), *Kindred* (1986), *Selected Poems* (with a selection of new work 1992) and *The Fluent Moment* (1996). *Not Without Homage* received an Arts Council Award, and she has twice been short-listed for the Welsh Arts Council's 'Book of the Year' for her 1992 and 1996 publications. Both were published when Ruth was over 70 years old.

From Ruth's eighth collection, *Singing to Wolves*, published by Seren in 2000, the poem *Enlli* reads:

'Faint and grey, Bardsey came out of the mist.
We could just catch, out there, what a poet saw

seven centuries back: the white waves leaping
around the holy island of Enlli.
No sound from them; the wind was too loud,
and the sea too loud, against the headland,
beating, tearing.

That's how the island
has stayed with me, a far silence
within storm, a shadow hardly seen,
beyond the clarity of gorse on the hill,
and the blurred singing of the autumn sea.

I have never landed there; the place
remains more visitant than friend.
Why it should be so loved, though,
I can sense, unclearly, as I still see
that shape far out in spume and rain,
beyond the silent waves that leap and leap
around the holy island of Enlli.'
*(reproduced by kind permission of the author)*

Ruth also wrote a *Trail* of the churches south and east of Builth Wells,
including those dedicated to St Cewydd (the original rain-saint) at Aberedw
(where Llywelyn the Last was killed), St Padarn at Llanbadarn-y-Graig, St
Dubricius (Dyfrig) at Gwenddwr and Mauricius (Meurig) at Alltmawr.
These are all 6th century foundations, the last being one of the smallest
churches in Wales, founded my Meurig ap Tewdrig in the sixth century. Her
local history work has in recent years been published mainly in the county
journals of Radnorshire and Breconshire, but in August 2000 Alun Books of
Port Talbot published her excellent illustrated book on her home area,
*Parishes of the Buzzard*. Ruth continues to write poems, and is engaged on
further historical research. Ruth denies that she is cut off from present-day
life because much of her poetry is about small, rural communities: 'I have
never wanted to escape from the world by coming here... this is the world.'
    In recent years, Ruth has had several articles published in the
*Carmarthenshire Antiquary*, the latest in collaboration with her son Martin.
Ruth has also had published *New and Selected Poems* (2004); *Symbols of
Plenty* (2006); *Hearing Voices* (2008); *Time Being* (2009) and *Above the
Forests* (2012). In April 2011 her collection, *Time Being*, was a Poetry Book
Society recommendation and was awarded the Roland Mathias Prize. The
chair of the judging panel, Glyn Mathias said: 'We felt this was the
crowning collection of her long career. It is so evocative of place and time,
and she packs such an emotional punch. The quality of writing is sustained
throughout, and yet she makes it look so easy'. Ruth was awarded the prize

during a ceremony in Roland Mathias' home town of Brecon, supported by BBC Wales and hosted by Nicola Heywood Thomas, presenter of Radio Wales' *Arts Show*. Ruth has a new collection of poems being published by Cinnamon Press in November 2016.

A book-length study of Ruth's work, written by Matthew Jarvis, was published in the *Writers of Wales* series in 2012. The book was launched together with her *Above the Forests* collection at Aberystwyth Arts Centre on 27 July 2012. Jarvis wrote: 'She deserves unequivocal recognition as one of Wales's foremost English-language poets of the last half-century.' Reviewing Matthew Jarvis's book, Jane Aaron wrote: 'With its persuasively argued thesis that Ruth Bidgood's twelve poetry collections compose one integrated epic poem in praise of mid-Wales - its history, its inhabitants, its traditions, and its landscape - this thoughtful and thoroughly researched book casts new light on its subject. Bidgood's achievement stands out clearly from its pages, which ring true, like her poems.'

From *The New Welsh Review* Summer 2001, *Lark Ascending* has been chosen to give a further flavour of Ruth's work - an enigmatic, threatening poem which brings in many themes and forces the reader to think about what is happening to modern society and the countryside:

How to tell the child
about skylarks? - the way,
as they climbed the sky,
the song too spiralled, not only
rising with the singer, but made
of notes with an upward curl?
How to tell her
about soft brownness, fragility
of a small bird, its nest
a treasure to find, out on the moor?

She knows 'bird'; kites have been back
for years now, over crumbling towns
(they find food enough) - but the word
means hugeness to her, swooping, rending,
something she crouches away from.

The high moor is out of bounds,
except to hunters; fields and woods
are feral, hazardous. Children
don't go outside the wall before
they can be trained to kill.
Since the virus, home means huddling
within the reassurance of streets. We patch,

we barricade; there are so few of us.

Rumour runs along nerves; out there,
in the risky lands of our cautious forays,
some sense impending change.
We are wary, knowing whatever comes
may not be enemy, but is not friend.

She has yet to know this, as she grows;
yet surely in crannies of her mind
I can plant images to flourish
of light-winged upward springing,
unthreatening vastness, horizons
attainable and worth the journeying.
*(by kind permission of the author)*

## LAURA ASHLEY 7 September 1925 – 17 September 1985

### FASHION DESIGNER, FOUNDER OF A GLOBAL FABRIC AND FURNISHINGS EMPIRE

Born Laura Mountney at 31 Staton Terrace, Dowlais Top, Merthyr Tudful, Glamorgan, she was a contemporary of Mary Quant (q.v.) and comes from the same home town as the current successful fashion designer, Julien McDonald. Her father was a civil servant, and she was brought up as a strict Baptist. Her parents were working in  London, but her mother returned to give birth in her own mother's home, in order that Laura was born in Wales. She attended the Welsh language Hebron Chapel attended in Dowlais, and although she could not understand the language, she loved it, especially the singing. It is noticeable how Welsh has all but disappeared from this area since this time. Educated at Marshall's School in Merthyr until 1932, she was then sent to the Elmwood School, Croydon, but was evacuated back to Wales aged 13. However, with so many World War II evacuees there were no school places left, and she attended Aberdare Secretarial School.

Trained as a secretary. Laura worked for the War Office, the WRNS then the National Federation of Women's Institutes. She had met her future husband, Bernard Ashley, at a local youth club, and the couple married in 1949 and went to London to work. In 1953, and pregnant, Laura started printing fabric with a silkscreen put together by Bernard, on the kitchen table of their small basement flat in Pimlico. Twenty scarves were immediately sold to the John Lewis department store, and more were immediately ordered. Laura now started using floral prints which Bernard and Laura made into table mats, napkins and tea towels.

The goods had now been successfully taken by some of the major London stores, initially by John Lewis, so Bernard gave up his job in the City and set up a family business, based upon Laura's design talent. The Ashley Mountney company produced her fresh natural designs in fabrics in their first factory in Kent in 1955. When the third of her four children was born, the family moved to Wales. Her natural fabrics were initially sold by mail order for women to 'make-up' in their own homes. Her dream was to use rustic, romantic fabrics with flowery patterns, to give the English country look to homes and fashions. Their first venture was designing smocks and aprons, but soon dresses, blouses and other clothes followed, and by 1967 they had opened their first shop in fashionable Kensington. She collected 18th and 19th century fabric patterns and designs from all over the world, scouring museums for fresh ideas. Her high-necked blouses, flowing skirts and floral patterns, using strong traditional materials, soon became an international look.

**Plaque for Laura Ashley in Merthyr Tydful**

Success for her 'country' look' creations led to factories being set up at a new headquarters in Carno, Powys, and soon shops were opened across the UK, USA and Europe. Laura had found a recipe for a 'brand-new version of the past', a feminine reaction against the sexist fashions of the 1960's. She wanted fashions that women and mothers at home could feel comfortable in, not the body-hugging contours of compatriot Mary Quant, but a softer look. By 1981 the Ashleys had 5,000 retail outlets across the world, and she had realised a long-held ambition of opening a shop in Wales' capital of Cardiff. In 1984 a new headquarters was opened in Newtown, bringing the couple back home to Wales, and in 1985 another factory opened at Gresford, near Wrexham, helping to alleviate colliery and steel closures in the area.

Her son David designed the shops and developed the North American business. Laura's children Nicholas and Emma designed dresses, and daughter Jane was the company photographer and contributed a contemporary collection. Bernard was the company chairman and Laura kept a close eye on fabrics. Laura herself dressed in Edwardian style, and although she and Bernard now lived abroad. The astonishing success of what proved to be the ultimate cottage industry meant that the Ashleys could afford a yacht, a private plane, a French château in Picardy, a town-house in Brussels, and a villa in the Bahamas. The yacht was later purchased from the estate for $8.5 million.

However, Laura still maintained her insistence upon simplicity of life-style, being called the 'Earth-Mother of the Alternative Society'. Her biography gives a comment by a friend: 'She knew what was right and wrong in fabrics just the same as she did in life, there were no grey areas'. In 1975, Laura turned down the offer of an OBE, upset that her husband had not been offered one. However, Bernard Ashley was knighted after her death. In 1985 Laura tragically died of a brain haemorrhage, a week after falling downstairs in an accident at her home. Aged only 60, she was buried in Carno. Her company now employed 4,000 staff in 11 factories and 225 shops, and was on the brink of further expansion. Valued at £200 million, it was 34 times over-subscribed and floated on the Stock Exchange. Soon turnover almost touched £300 million. There were shops in New York, Tokyo, Sydney, Madrid and Moscow. However, without her instinct for fashion, the company lost its way and began making losses in 1991.

Now, none of her five Welsh factories remains open. It seems that the basic flaw in the product offering was that more and more women were now going to work, and not having quality time at home, and their clothing requirements were very different to that offered by the Laura Ashley shops. Combined with this change in attitude and lifestyle, the company was badly hurt by manufacturing in Britain, rather than in far-East sweat-shops. Eleven Chief Executive Officers were appointed in quick succession in 14 years to turn the company around, one American woman in particular making some disastrous fashion choices. Since 1998 it has been Malaysian-owned. Sir Bernard Ashley later ran a successful hotel industry, his flagship being Llangoed Hotel, decorated with Laura Ashley fabrics. He died in 2009. The Laura Ashley Foundation gives 10 annual scholarships to music students at the Welsh College of Music and Drama in Cardiff.


## RACHEL ROBERTS 20 September 1927 - 26 November 1980

## FILM STAR, OSCAR NOMINEE

Roberts was born in Llanelli, undergoing a Baptist upbringing, against which she rebelled. A poorly child who suffered from bouts of nervous asthma, Rachel went to Llanelli Grammar School, then took an English degree at Aberystwyth, where she joined the drama society. She had dreamed of becoming an actress since she was 10, but had kept it a secret from her parents, as 'They thought it was a pipe dream, you see. And they were trying to be protective.' Her father Richard was a strict Baptist minister, and her mother Rachel Ann a frustrated housewife. Rachel was not close to either parent, and Rachel said that her mother's comment on her birth was 'Take her away, I don't want to see her', as she had only wanted a boy child. Rachel's upbringing was unhappy, and affected her badly throughout her life, giving Rachel low esteem, an inferiority complex that sat unhappily with an outgoing nature.

After university, Rachel secretly auditioned at RADA and won a scholarship. Supporting her studies in London, she worked in a hospital, but was sacked for being drunk. She turned to cleaning and nude modelling, and at RADA won several student prizes. Known to her friends all her life as 'Ray', she did not complete the course. However, the great Welsh actor Clifford Evans brought her to Swansea for 6 months repertory at the Grand Theatre (with  Richard Burton and Kenneth Williams), and she then played in Bristol and at London's Old Vic. One role was opposite the young Richard Burton in *The Tempest*. Rachel gained notice for her roles on the English stage, before her career moved into films.

She made her film debut in the Welsh-set comedy *Valley of Song* (1953), and then took a key role in J. Lee Thompson's *The Weak and the Wicked*. Aged 25, she married Alan Dobie, a fellow-actor at the Old Vic - 'He was serious and steady and 22 and I thought beautiful to look at - and I went for Alan because, on my own, I was personally adrift and promiscuous and unstable and getting to be 26'. Their Swansea wedding in 1955 was not auspicious, because after lunch at the Langland Bay Hotel they had a blazing row on the train to London. The impoverished young actor had bought 2nd-class tickets instead of 1st-class for his bride. They rowed more or less continuously until their 1961 divorce. Rachel commented I knew Alan wasn't the man I wanted. He said he didn't want affairs and if he did I wasn't the type of girl he'd want an affair with'.

Her portrayal of Brenda in Saturday Night and Sunday Morning (1960) won her a British Academy Film Award. In 1960, Rachel was playing in Chekhov at the Royal Court Theatre, and fell in love with her co-star Rex Harrison. He was the great love of her life: 'We were together all the time. Ease entered my life. Rex took all the decisions. I had nothing to live for but for him'. They married in Genoa in 1962, and the wedding was a semi-riot with 200 paparazzi trying to break into the closed-doors ceremony.

Rachel almost refused to go on with the wedding, Harrison hurled a camera out of the room, and reporters fought to gain entry to the registrar's office. The interest in their wedding was all the more intense because Roberts was also now a major name in films. She had starred with Alec Guinness and Ralph Richardson in *Our Man in Havana*, and in a terrific role opposite Richard Harris in *This Sporting Life*. For the latter she won a British Academy Film Award, as well as the 1963 Oscar nomination for leading actress, and a nomination for a Golden Globe. 'Ray' always referred to Rex as 'Reg', his real name being Reginald.

In theatre, she performed at the Royal Court and played the title role as the life-enhancing tart in Lionel Bart's musical Maggie May (1964).

Rachel's career now stagnated with her marriage to Harrison, living in luxury at their Portofino villa. She said 'with Rex I have the perfect life. If I get an offer that seems worth taking I accept it with his full blessing. Being with him is much more important than rushing around, working madly and generally playing the career woman.' However, she could not have a child, suffering a miscarriage. Sometime during the marriage, her role as Mrs Rex Harrison did not fulfil her any longer, and she began drinking heavily. Her self-doubts surfaced: 'I got to know all the right people with Rex and behaved like a clown. I felt equal to the rich and the beautiful and I wasn't. When he started to be embarrassed by it all, I drank more and got louder'. They tried to save their marriage, working together in Feydeau's *A Flea in Her Ear* in 1968. However, Harrison eventually could stand Rachel's behaviour no

**Rachel Roberts and her blue plaque, *courtesy Walesonline***

longer, and they separated in 1969 after she had tried to commit suicide by swallowing fifty aspirin tablets. The divorce came through in 1971, and Rachel turned even more heavily to alcohol.

Devastated by her divorce, she moved to Hollywood in 1975 and tried to forget the relationship, and started an affair with actor-director Val Meyer, before a Mexican dress-designer, Darren Ramirez, moved into her life. He was just 23, and she twice his age. She made two forgettable films, *Doctors' Wives* and *Wild Rovers* as well as the critically acclaimed *O Lucky Man* (1973), *Belstone Fox* (1973), *Picnic at Hanging Rock* (1975), *Foul Play* (1978), and *Yanks* (1979), receiving a British Academy Film Award for *Yanks*. However, her personal life was falling apart, and an appearance on *The Russell Harty Show* TV was scrapped because she was drunk and swearing. Ramirez said that he was attracted to her - 'I couldn't let this talented woman destroy herself.'

Mario Risoli recounted her last days (*Western Mail*, 4 November 1998): 'On November 26, 1980, Rachel Roberts was due to fly from Los Angeles to New York. There, she would audition for a part in Nabokov's *Lolita*. The 53-year-old actress never arrived at LAX airport. Later that day her body was found at her home in Hutton Drive, Beverley Hills. Wrapped in cashmere blankets, she was slumped in the bramble bushes behind her bungalow. Roberts had taken an overdose and washed down the pills with either weed killer or disinfectant. A heavy drinker, she had been divorced for some years, and had never really recovered from her divorce from actor Rex Harrison in 1971. The pair remained in contact after the split. Indeed, Harrison dined with Roberts at her home the evening before she committed suicide. Harrison described his ex-wife's mood as "bouncy and she was happy and extremely high".'

Rachel revealed her deep unhappiness in a journal she kept. Almost her last entry, dated 25 November 1980, the day before her death, said, 'I chose Rex over my craft. It happened. Not much of a sin, but I suffer for it dreadfully. I gave away my birthright. Therefore I cannot survive. More's the pity.' And her very last diary entry reads: 'Day after day, night after night, I'm in this shaking fear. What am I so terribly frightened of? Life itself I think.'

In 1980, a final attempt to win Harrison back proved futile, and, impulsive and insecure, she committed suicide on 26 November 1980, at her home in Los Angeles.

It was reported that her death was a result of swallowing lye, alkali, or another unidentified caustic substance, as well as barbiturates and alcohol, as detailed in her posthumously published journals. The corrosive effect of the poisonous agent was an immediate cause of death. Her gardener found her body on her kitchen floor, lying amidst shards of glass; she had fallen through a decorative glass divide between two rooms. Her cause of death was initially reported as cardiac arrest, but the coroner documented the cause of death as 'swallowing a caustic substance' and, later, 'acute barbiturate intoxication.' She was 53 years old.

She was cremated at the Chapel of the Pines Crematory in Los Angeles, and the faithful Darren Ramirez was the only person present at her cremation.

Her journals became the basis for *No Bells on Sunday: The Memoirs of Rachel Roberts* (1984). In 1992, Roberts' ashes, along with those of her very good friend Jill Bennett, who had committed suicide by poison in 1990, were scattered on the River Thames in London, by the director Lindsay Anderson, a friend of both women. Anderson had directed Rachel in This Sporting Life, almost 30 years earlier. Bennett had killed herself because of 'the brutalizing effects of her marriage to John Osborne, according to Osborne's biographer. On the boat trip to scatter the ashes, several of the actresses' professional colleagues and friends were aboard, and musician Alan Price sang *Is That All There Is?*

## PETULA SALLY OLWEN CLARK CBE 15 November 1932 -

## 'THE MOST SUCCESSFUL BRITISH FEMALE SINGER'

Her mother Doris's father James Phillips was a Welsh miner, and her mother was born and raised in David's Square, Abercanaid, outside Merthyr Tydfil. Although Pet was born in West Newell, near Epsom, she said in 1999, 'I was a real little Welsh kid. I used to run around the mountains, sliding down the tips. My childhood is about Wales. The things that are important to me happened in Wales'. Taught by her 'mam' to sing, Pet appeared on the stage aged just 5, and began broadcasting two years later. Her voice was called 'as sweet as chapel bells'. With her clear speaking voice, she had her own radio show, aged 11, in 1943 entertaining the troops. Petula had also appeared in over 200 war-time concerts for the forces by 1945. She was so popular that she was asked to sing at a national victory celebration at Trafalgar Square. In 1944, she made her first film, then signed for the J. Arthur Rank Organisation, appearing in over 20 feature films, starring with actors such as Alec Guinness and Anthony Newley.

She was something of a 'television pioneer' in Britain, first appearing on experimental TV in the 1940's, and then was host of her own series all through the early days, with *Pet's Parlour* being her longest-running show. Her recording career began in 1949, and throughout the 1950's had several hits, including *Where Did My Snowman Go* (1952), *The Little Shoemaker* (1954) and *Alone*. In 1957, she appeared at the Olympia Theatre in Paris, and after one song, the crowd went wild. Her success in France led to many concerts, and she recorded in France for the Vogue label. In 1959, unhappy with the inability of UK audiences to see her as anything but a sweet adolescent, she moved to France, aged 27. She married Vogue's PR man, Claude Wolff, and in 1960 introduced her 'new' sound. Still with clear vocals, there was a strong beat and electronic effects, and she had a massive hit with the *Ya Ya Twist*, for which she received the *Grand Prix du*

*Disque.* By 1962, she was France's favourite female vocalist, displacing the legendary Edith Piaf. During these early 1960's, she was 'reinvented' as a French 'chanteuse', and is still categorised as a French singer in French books and in French music stores.

Meanwhile, in Britain, her versions *of Romeo, My Friend the Sea* and *Sailor* were chasing Elvis Presley in the charts, with 'Sailor' reaching Number One. Also recording in Italian and German, Petula Clark became a household name across the Continent. Interestingly, each of her early European hits were with entirely different songs, a feat never achieved before or since, and testament to her voice and enunciation. She was then urged to sing something in English, and she allowed Tony Hatch to visit her in France with a song which he thought was just right for her.

Her recording of Tony Hatch's song *Downtown* in 1964 was a number one hit across Europe, selling 3 million worldwide, and also topping the charts in America. It gained a coveted *Grammy* award in the USA as the best rock'n'roll single. Her subsequent Hatch songs, *My Love, I Couldn't Live Without Your Love,* and *Don't Sleep in the Subway'* all made the US Top Ten, with *My Love* reaching Number One. *I Know a Place* reached No. 3 in the States, and gave her a second *Grammy* in 1965 (for best rock'n'roll performance). Her 1967 *This is My Song* broke into the US Top 5. Pet now toured the US, and had her own BBC TV series. She recorded a US NBC television special, *Petula* in 1968. This was marred by the programme sponsor's request for a sequence to be removed where she touched the arm of the black guest star, Harry Belafonte. However, the show was eventually transmitted uncut. Apart from another two US TV specials*, Pet had a sell-out season at the Cocoanut Grove in Los Angeles, attended by Sinatra and Streisand amongst others, and has also starred at the Copacabana and at Caesar's Palace in Las Vegas. The timing and popularity of her songs caused Petula in the USA to be dubbed the 'First Lady of the British Invasion.'

Also in 1967, she revived her dormant film career, appearing in *Finian's Rainbow* with Fred Astaire. In 1969, her appearance with Peter O'Toole in *Goodbye, Mr Chips,* marked her 30 years in entertainment. She was now playing in cabaret and concerts all over the world, her TV variety series made her the TV Times 'Most Popular TV Star', and she guest-starred on scores of American and European TV shows. In 1975, she was given the Waldorf Astoria Award, for breaking every attendance record in the 44-year history of its Empire Room, where all the American greats such as Sinatra and Crosby had played.

From 1981-82, 'Pet' appeared as Maria in the London revival of *The Sound of Music,* and later had another top 10 hit with the country-style *Natural Love.* 1989 saw a 'radically remixed' version of *Downtown* hit the UK charts, with an 'acid house' backing track. She has written scores of songs, sometimes under the pseudonym of Al Grant, and she wrote the music for *Someone Like You,* a musical which had a short West End run in

1990. In 1992, she made her first concert tour of the UK for 10 years, and in 1993 took over the starring role as Mrs Johnstone in *Blood Brothers* on Broadway (David and Shaun Cassidy, the sons of the Welsh Shirley Jones, were her co-stars). She then toured with it through 26 American cities. 1995 saw Pet star as Norma Desmond in *Sunset Boulevard* for a time when Elaine Paige took a 6-week holiday, and subsequently Pet starred until the show closed in 1997. At the final curtain, on April 5th, the 65-year-old entertainer received one of the greatest standing ovations ever seen in London's West End. On 1 January 1998, she received the CBE for 'services to entertainment', then embarked on another UK tour before starring in *'Sunset Boulevard'* on a major national US tour. She was interviewed in Houston before her appearance there, and asked what her parents did. Pet replied 'Oh, my parents were very sort of lower middle class, I think you'd call us. My mother and father were both nurses, and then my father was in the army. My mother was Welsh and had a very beautiful voice...the Welsh are like the Italians - they'll sing at the drop of a hat. And they sing very well, fortunately.' In 2000 Pet Clark began a one-woman show tour in Montreal.

No other British woman can match Pet's success. She has sold over 70 million records, and at one time had more Gold Discs than any other UK artiste. She has never stopped singing, despite making over 30 films in her 50 year career, and has over 1000 recordings to her credit. Pet has had 15 Top 40 hits in the USA, with two Number 1's, and has had 159 recordings in top 40's across the globe. Petula and Claude have three children, Barra, Kate and Patrick, and a grandson Sebastian. Her charity benefit concerts have included work for Broadway Cares/Equity Fights Aids, CRUSAID and UNICEF). Her titles in the press have been variously 'Britain's Most Popular Child Star', 'Britain's Leading Teenage Star', 'Juke Box Queen', 'First lady of Pop' and so on over her long and glittering career.

Petula Clark CBE is under-rated in Britain - how many other British performers have two *Grammies*? Aged 18, she was presented by the *Daily Mail* with the award of 'Most Outstanding TV Personality'. Them in 1964, she had Gold Discs for *Monsieur* (sung in German), *Chariot* (sung in French) and *Romeo* (sung in English). There was also a 'special gold disc' in Germany as Pet was the first foreign artist to achieve such a great success. In 1965, *Downtown* won US and UK Gold Discs, and *My Love, I Couldn't Live Without Your Love* and *This is My Song* gained gold discs in America, each selling a million records (remember, that discs can be awarded a gold disc today for 400,000 copies, not a million as in the 60's.) She also won Silver Discs for *Sailor* (1961), *Downtown* (1964), *My Love* (1966) and *This Is My Song* (1967) in Britain, each selling 250,000 copies. In 1964, she had a Silver Disk for her EP *Je Me Sens Bien* in Canada.

*Cash Box,* the leading American entertainment magazine, gave her International Gold Awards in 1965 and 1966 for *Downtown* and *I Know a Place*, and announced her 'The Top Female Artist in America' in 1966. The *Cash Box* DJ Awards made her 'Most Promising Female Vocalist' in 1965, followed by 'Most Popular Female Vocalist' in 1966, 1967 and 1968. In France, the French record industry awarded her *the Grand Prix National du Disque Francais*, for 1962's most successful singer. She was awarded the *Bravos du Music Hall* as the most popular French singer in 1965, and the Golden Rose in the same year by the French magazines *Jeunesse Cinema* and *Le Parisien*. In 1970, the City of Paris gave Pet *La Medaille de Vermel de la Ville de Paris* 'for bringing honour to Paris and increasing its fame'.

There are dozens more international awards, such as Austria's European Television Personality, Holland's *Grand Prix de la Chanson*, France's *Chevalier des Artes et des Lettres* and Italy's International Award for Outstanding World Sales by a European Artist.' She launched BBC TV's first ever colour transmission in 1969 with her Royal Albert Hall concert, and was the first woman to be featured twice on *This is Your Life*. In 1998 Petula was made a CBE and in 2012 was installed with the *Médaille du Commandeur de l'ordre des Arts et des Lettres de France* by the Republic of France's Culture Minister. She is still touring the globe, collaborating with singers and songwriters, and writing new music. From child-star to a polished singer/actress/songwriter, with a successful marriage, she is a role model for future generations. Petula Clark has sold more than 68 million records throughout her seven-decade career.

* Petula Clark became a household name in the USA by performing on dozens of top TV programmes. She has starred on *The Ed Sullivan Show* (11 times!), *The Dean Martin Show* (9 times), *The Andy Williams Show, The Carol Burnett Show, American Bandstand, The Tonight Show, The Danny Kaye Show, The Flip Wilson Show, The Hollywood Show, The Red Skelton Show, Here's Lucy* and on Bob Hope and Perry Como Specials, as well as at the Academy Awards and Golden Globe Awards.

# DAME BARBARA MARY QUANT DBE 11 February 1934 -

## INVENTOR OF THE MINI-SKIRT, FASHION DESIGNER AND ICON

Mary's father was from Merthyr Tydfil, and her mother from Cydweli, who both in Mary's words 'grew up surrounded by the hardships and deprivations of the mining communities during the 20's and early 30's and I realise, now that I am older, what tremendous courage and determination they must have had to have accomplished all they have done entirely by their own efforts. From their local schools, they went on to grammar school and from there to Cardiff University. Every step forward was made possible by their own scholarship. They were born with good brains and they have never stopped using and improving them. Both got firsts at university and both have dedicated their lives to teaching. The persistent habit of hard work is so ingrown in them now that to do less than work hard, always, all the time, is a mortal sin.' Mary was born in Kent, and left Tunbridge Wells for Tenby with her mother and father, to escape World War II's bombing. Mary and her brother Tony attended Tenby County School. However, when the bombing stopped, both her parents' schools were relocated back to the south-east of England.

She met her future husband and business partner, the 21-year-old Alexander Plunket Greene in 1953. Her biography begins with the words 'My life began for me when I saw Plunket' at Goldsmith's College. After graduating from Goldsmith's College of Art in 1955, Mary opened Bazaar, a stylish new clothing shop in London in 1957, with her soon-to-be husband, Alexander Plunket Greene, and Archie McNair. They were married from 1957 until his death in 1990, and had a son, Orlando (b. 1970).

Her first job after Goldsmith's was with a couture milliner, where she spent up to three days stitching a hat for one customer. She realised that fashion should be for the young as well as the privileged - 'I had always wanted young people to have a fashion of their own, absolutely 20th century fashion'. She searched for 'interesting' clothes for the new shop, and its first week's takings where five times what she expected. However, she still could not find the right products and decided to stock only clothes that she had made herself.

In *Quant by Quant* Mary writes: 'In 10 days, we hadn't a single piece of the original material in the place. Apart from hats, I designed only one original thing for the opening... a pair of mad house-pyjamas. These were snapped up by "*Harper's Bazaar*" who gave us our first fashion editorial. The only other recognition we got from the press was two or three paragraphs in the social columns...rather awful paragraphs headed something like "Alexander Plunket Greene, kinsman of the Duke of Bedford, opens shop in Chelsea". The trade ignored us. They laughed at us openly. They called us degenerate. They raised their eyebrows in mystified amazement. Later, when they realised how successful Bazaar was proving, they called our success a "flash in the pan". It was utterly impossible for them - or for us - to envisage that within 7 years the business would go well over the million mark and the clothes I was to design would be in 150 shops in Britain, 320 stores throughout America and also on sale in France, Italy, Switzerland, Kenya, South Africa, Australia, Canada and, in fact, in just about every country in the western world.'

Mary Quant had opened here Bazaar boutique in 1955 at a time when she said 'fashion wasn't designed for young people'. Quant was influenced by Chelsea beatniks and dance outfits she remembered from childhood. Famed for popularising, if not inventing, the mini skirt, her clothes were made up of simple shapes combined with strong colours. The shop 'made' King's Road, Chelsea, into the most famous shopping venue in the world. Vidal Sassoon said that her shop was 'a marvellous show...we'd come out of a horrendous war. There were still enormous shortages in the 1950's and suddenly - the 1960's! ... What was so invigorating about that 1960's thing was the innocence. There is a resurgence today of fashion... but a lot of cynicism goes with it now...In the 1960's, there was total innocence, people coming out of two decades of shortages, suddenly earning money of their own, young people with spending power. They wanted to spend it in their own way and people like Mary were there to lead them.' The 'Quant Look' came to be topped off by the strikingly functional and sexy statement that Vidal Sassoon brought to hair, and Quant's empire was iconised by the great photographers of the time, Brian Duffy, Terence Donovan and David Bailey. Catering to urban youth, she filled the shop with the exciting new clothes being worn by rock 'n' rollers - the bell bottoms, the bright patterns, and especially the thigh-climbing skirts. When she couldn't find the creative clothes she wanted, she started designing them herself. Her shop was an instant success and quickly drew a celebrity crowd of Beatles and movie stars. She'd keep the shop open late, and people would strip and try on clothes out in the open. 'Good designers know that to have any influence they must keep in step with public needs and that intangible 'something in the air.' They must catch the spirit of the day and interpret it in clothes before other designers begin to twitch at the nerve ends,' she said in *Blown Away*; 'I just happened to start when that something in the air was coming to a boil. The clothes I made happened to fit in exactly with the teenage trend, with pop records and espresso bars and jazz clubs.'

Quant later said 'It was the girls on the King's Road who invented the mini. I was making easy, youthful, simple clothes, in which you could move, in which you could run and jump and we would make them the length the customer wanted. I wore them very short and the customers would say, 'Shorter, shorter.'" She gave the miniskirt its name, naming it after her favourite make of car, the Mini.

In 1961, a second store was opened in Knightsbridge, and her company was exporting to the USA by 1963. In 1967 she said 'I love vulgarity. Good taste is death. Vulgarity is life. People call things vulgar when they are new to them. When they have become old they become good taste. The manufacturers who make my clothes and the people with financial interests in the things I design never like anything when I first show it to them. But the critical people, the people who understand fashion, they jump at the new thing, they're excited. In America, they never make anything without first having a market survey to ask the public what they want. People only ask for things that they already know about, so you don't get anything new that way. That's why American fashion is stuck... You would agree then that a great designer is one who gives people what they want before they know they want it?' For nearly the entire 1960's, Quant was at the centre of the fashion explosion that rocked the world. Even at the decade's end Mary kept inventing, kept igniting others with her ideas, and she even dropped another bombshell into the fashion world in '69 - hot pants, which did for shorts what her minis did for skirts. She brought her touch to hosiery and home linens and skin care products. Her famous daisy logo appeared on shoes and wallpapers. Mary was the first British designer to challenge the French successfully, and this fashion revolutionary was copied globally. She even started a fashion trend by announcing that she had shaved her hair into a heart shape, and recommended the use of hair dye to brighten up that area. She also wrote several books, among them her autobiography, *Quant by Quant* in 1966, followed by *Colour by Quant, The Ultimate Make-up and Beauty Book, Classic Make-up and Beauty,* and *Mary Quant's Daisy Chain of Things to Make and Do.* Today her Colour Concepts boutiques, which showcase her colour-saturated make-up, are located in world capitals like Paris, New York, and Tokyo. And Mary herself is still working in London, with jewellery and umbrellas and bags and socks among her latest creations.

Mary Quant defined the fashions of the 1960's across the world. In the '50s, young people had dressed in slightly modified and more colourful versions of the conservative clothes their parents owned: singers wore gowns, and actresses wore gloves - these were years of austerity and rebuilding after the War. Then came the '60s and a revolution not just in the clothes, but also in the people who created them. We tend now to associate the 60's with the rise of rock groups - the way that the Beatles revolutionised music, but a new breed of fashion designers such as Quant, inspired by the energy in the streets, drawing on influences from Op and Pop Art, and watching the triumphs of the space age, invented styles that were more daring, more colourful, and more exciting than ever before. She also directly changed the attitudes towards female shape in the latter half of the 19th century. Female icons were Marilyn Monroe, Gina Lollobrigida, Diana Dors - shapely women. Only Audrey Hepburn stood out among all popular actresses and singers of the day. Quant made it essential to be skinny, different, outrageous and noticed - jeans with holes arrived, and unisex

**Mary Quant in her 'trademark look'**

entered the language. The Chelsea Look became *de rigeur* across the world. The look was of a coquettish French schoolgirl - skinny rib polo-neck sweaters, miniskirts, bright tights and knee-high white, patent-plastic boots, with geometric Sassoon bobs and kohl-rimmed eyes. By 1969, up to 7,000,000 women had a Quant label in their wardrobe. Her slogan was 'brighter clothes make brighter people.'

The fashion revolution's catalyst was Mary Quant. She was the hippest designer in the hippest area of the world, the unrivalled Queen of Swinging London, and she was perfectly in sync with the spirit of her times. The Sunday Times commented, 'It is given to a fortunate few to be born at the right time, in the right place, with the right talents. In recent fashion, there are three: Chanel, Dior and Mary Quant.' Sparked by her design innovations, '60s fashions exploded in bursts of vibrant new colours, prints, and fabrics. Soon came other designers who introduced big geometric patterns, shades of purple and chartreuse, dresses made of shiny vinyl, or cellophane, or paper, dresses with pieces cut out, dresses made of metal or covered with mirrors, two-piece pantsuits, fur vests, go-go boots, prints from India, micro-mini skirts, midi skirts, maxi skirts, ruffled shirts, Nehru jackets, sharp Sassoon cuts, and enormous bellbottoms to the new vocabulary. As she explained in A.E. Hotchner's *Blown Away: The Rolling Stones and the Death of the Sixties*: 'I think that I broke the couture stranglehold that Chanel, Dior and the others had on fashion, when I created styles at the working-girl level. It all added up to a democratisation of fashion and entertainment. ... It was very gratifying to see that not only did the "mods" of the sixties want my clothes, but so did the grandees and the millionaires. They had everything else ... but they hadn't any fun clothes. ... Snobbery went out of fashion, and in the shops you found duchesses jostling with typists to buy the same dresses. Fashion had become the great leveller.'

Some sources credit French designer Andre Courreges with actually inventing the miniskirt ahead of Mary, as did Balenciaga with coloured patterned tights. That may or may not be true, but Mary was definitely the person who brought the styles to the masses by keeping prices affordable and fashionable (In the USA, J.C. Penney carried her designs as early as 1962) and by keeping the styles whimsical. By 1966, everyone had wanted to wear her clothes, because all their heroes did: Brigitte Bardot and Nancy Sinatra two of her famous customers, and when George Harrison married model Patti Boyd in the winter of 1966, they were both wearing clothes designed by Mary Quant. Fans could see her clothes on the silver screen, because Mary designed the costumes for several popular films, including the Oscar-nominated *Georgy Girl* in 1966 and Audrey Hepburn's *Two for the Road* in 1967. Quant was the first designer to use PVC as a fabric and when Anthony Armstrong-Jones was despatched by a magazine to take pictures of her in the hot new wet-look clothes, Princess Margaret wrongly became convinced they were having an affair – a case of the pot calling the kettle black, if ever there was one.

In 1966 Quant was awarded the OBE. In the early 1960s her designs were bought by the chain store J C Penney to be mass produced for the American market. The Quant label began to appear worldwide on accessories and make-up. A typical day's work for Mary was given in her autobiography:

| | |
|---|---|
| '10.00 am | Take last night's sketches to the workroom and discuss them with the cutters |
| 11.00 am-12.30 pm | See the ranges from 6 or 7 cloth merchants for a collection which will go into the shops 9 months later |
| 12.30 pm | Tom Wolsey to discuss the designs of labels and swing tickets for a new range for America |
| 1 pm | Choose trimmings from a selection made by our cloth buyer |
| 1.15 pm | Lunch in the restaurant round the corner with Archie, Alexander and the managing director of a hosiery firm who wants to produce Quant stockings |
| 2.30 pm | To Youthlines to look at the first samples of the new underwear made to my drawings |
| 3.15 pm | To the Ginger Group to meet Canadian journalists doing a piece about us |
| 4.00 pm | Vidal Sassoon |
| 5.15 pm | Back to workroom to see latest dresses tried on by Jan de Souza and Sarah Dawson |
| 5.30 pm | Austin Garrett brings some skins for the next furs |

| 6.30 pm | Home. Drinks with the design director of the Butterick pattern company who publish my things from time to time |
| 8.00 pm | Dinner chez Rendlesham |
| 10.00pm | The Purley Ball |

And - apart from this - I may have to talk to dozens of people on the telephone from journalists and licensees to cloth mills and scientists developing new material for us.'

Unlike previous fashion designers who were usually much older than the models who wore their clothes, Mary Quant was of the same generation as her clientele. This meant that Mary, who was petite and pretty with short, dark hair, could convincingly wear the new precision haircuts and the bold new eye shadows that all the models, celebrities, and stars were wearing. David Bailey, the decade's most famous photographer, was not just taking photos of Mary's models, including Twiggy* and Jean Shrimpton, in Mary's dresses, he was also taking photos of Mary herself. Although she is best known for the mini, her legacy is more than a single garment — it is an entire style which was known as the 'London Look', which by mid-decade meant clothes with simple lines, short/shorter/shortest skirts, bold colours, and flats. Photos of Mary in the '60s show her with the same short hair, the same short skirts, and the same tights and boots and blouses and eye shadow as any of her marvellous models. She is an expert on the subject of clothes and clothes history, of course: 'I grew up making my own clothes because I didn't like clothes the way they were,' she explained in *Blown Away*, 'I had a very strong idea of how I wanted to look. An innocent, child look -- that's what it was.' She started making her own clothes 'at the ludicrous age of five or six,' she added. In her teens the clothes she created were designed 'for people like myself -- skinny sweaters, black leotards, black patent leather shoes or tap-dancing shoes with white ankle socks -- that getup transfixed me. I was struck by the drama of dressing like that.'

When the Queen awarded Mary the Order of the British Empire (O.B.E.) in 1966, Mary accepted while wearing a miniskirt ... 'a woman,' Mary once said, 'is as young as her knees.' Two direct results of Mary's mini-revolution were the inventions of pantyhose and the maxi-coat (to keep those suddenly exposed legs warm). Mary said 'I wanted to make clothes that you could move in, skirts you could run and dance in.' She was always looking for new materials, solving the problems of making up vinyl dresses and boots. 'Then flannel caught my eye. I had been asked to design a dress in the Welsh stuff for a Swansea show during Eisteddfod week and I was shown some Welsh fabrics by Emrys Davies. Up till then, I had thought of flannel in terms of various shades of grey. I hadn't really considered other colours such as you see in club and school blazers as fashion possibilities. It was only when I saw the clear colours it is possible for the mills to produce that flannel became the theme of a winter collection. Lots of customers, bored with grey flannel dresses and suits, fell madly in love with it....

Rightly or wrongly, I have been credited with the Lolita Look, the Schoolgirl Look, the Wet weather Look, the Kinky Look, the Good Girl Look and lots of others and it is said that I was first with knickerbockers, gilt chains, shoulderstrap bags and high boots. I want to be first with a lot more. I want to invent new ways of making clothes in new materials, with new shapes and new fashion accessories that are up to date with the changing ways of life....One day I pulled on an 8 year-old boy's sweater for fun. I was enchanted with the result. And, in 6 months, all the birds were wearing the skinny-ribs that resulted. It was the same thing with string tops. As a joke, I put on a man's string vest over the dark dress I was wearing. The effect was electric. I bought up all the string vests I could put my hands on and had them dyed in the colours of the year. Fashion became a thing of tangled textures and stringy shapes, of hole-peppered stockings, crochet tops and fishnet gloves. I loved the look... In my own case, things like black boots, black stockings, embroidered and patterned stockings, pinafore and high-waisted dresses were all labelled "gimmicks" when they first appeared but some of them stuck and they became an integral part of the advance of fashion. The thing is that the true, dedicated designer is more likely to be right than anybody else.'

Famous quotes by Mary include: 'Having money is rather like being a blonde. It is more fun, but not vital'; 'Fashion is not frivolous. It is part of being alive today'; 'Fashion is a tool...to compete in life outside the home. People like you better, without knowing why, because people always react well to a person they like the looks of'; and 'The fashionable woman wears clothes. The clothes don't wear her'.

In December 2000, Mary was ousted from her company by its Japanese owners. Archie McNair commented 'As I understand it, the Japanese have made Mary an offer that's too good to refuse. She's a very famous girl and has still got plenty to offer.' Quant is in the Fashion Hall of Fame, and *Vogue* commented that 'Quant had a cataclysmic effect on London with her simple daisy motif, short skirts, mix of music and model, Twiggy...her international name and logo, associated with youth and freshness, enabled her to change direction and encompass kitchenware, stationery and fabulous make-up.' She was responsible for the mini-skirt, hot pants, the Lolita look, the slip dress, PVC raincoats, the wet look, smoky eyes and sleek bob haircuts, dresses with striking geometric patterns and strong colours, the mod look, the London look, the Biba look, the Chelsea look and vinyl boots but it was her make-up which eventually made her company the most money. When launched in 1966, they offered unprecedented colour ranges. The current licence is held by Mary Quant Cosmetics Japan, where there are 200 shops generating £100 million a year.

In 1999 she wrote her Classic Make-up and Beauty Book, and in 2011 Mary Quant: Autobiography, her second autobiography appeared. The book sheds light on the definitive relationship of Quant's life; her marriage to her business partner, Alexander Plunket Greene. She had the designs, while APG, as she calls him, had a knack for marketing ideas which fitted perfectly with the age. He named Quant's eye shadows Jeepers Peepers, called a range of gel cosmetics Jelly Babies and sold them in tiny baby bottles, dreamed up Pop Sox and called her new range of natural-shaped bras Booby Traps. She said: 'I mostly felt, my God, what a marvellous life you had, you are very fortunate. I think to myself, you lucky woman - how did you have all this fun?' Chief among her revolutionary innovations were tights for mini-skirts and waterproof mascara; all of a sudden women could cry, swim and run for the bus while still looking good. It appears that Mary is merely grateful for the opportunities that came her way: 'It was the spirit of the time. Yes, I worked very hard, but I loved the work, it was delicious.' Today, her Bazaar is just another coffee shop, selling hot pastries instead of hot pants.

A *Daily Mail* interview noted: 'Ironic really, given Mary Quant's trenchant fashion-world view on the eternal size zero debate. Mary said that 'It is the bones [of the woman wearing them] that make dresses look wonderful; it is the bones, when they jut out at the right place. 'There is no perfect size, it is all about the bones in the end. But if you are a size 14, I suggest, then you won't have many bones jutting out at all.

No. So it is worth getting them. Of course, I remember when everybody was thin. It wasn't until I went to America in the Sixties that I saw anyone who wasn't skinny thin. At the end of the war here, everyone was thin, thin, thin... I have been on a diet since 1962,' she said, citing black coffee, tomatoes, avocadoes, basil and olive oil as her slimming staples – 'You can gobble up as much of them as you like.

Originally her bob-cut was shaped by Vidal Sassoon himself, now she has it cut in a Vidal Sassoon salon in Chelsea by one of his employees. In her book, she describes APG as 'a 6ft 2in prototype for Mick Jagger and Paul McCartney rolled into one'.

He had long hair, played jazz trumpet and wore his mother's gold silk pyjamas to class in Goldsmiths.

The couple once hit the headlines when she revealed that he trimmed her pubic hair into a heart shape, and a waiter once served her a heart-shaped steak *tartare* in silent tribute. John Lennon also sent her sketches of suggestions for new shapes. APG adored Mary but was a dedicated womaniser who also drank too much. In 1988, Plunket Greene was told he had only two years to live, unless he stopped drinking. He died in 1990, at the relatively young age of 57. Mary said 'It was unbearable. Alexander drank too much, which had to do with his death. His doctors suggested he should stop drinking, but he didn't. He didn't want to. He loved wine and drinking. He drank too much but he said that life wasn't worthwhile without wine, that was his attitude. I am sure it killed him in the end. It killed his father, too. It is a very inherited thing. I don't know how much he drank, I never counted the bottles. But he loved wine and was always topping up.'

Mary says she never stopped loving APG, even though the marriage was difficult: 'Well, the word I would use is riotous, not difficult. He was a monstrous womaniser, so it was noisy and bumpy. We had great battles about it. Did he sleep with any of my friends? I am sure he did. I turned a blind eye as much as one could, then I would hurl things. It was wonderful, though. He was loyal at the same time, though. Unfaithful but loyal... He was such fun to be with. He was the best dancer that ever happened, he really was. And a terrific looker.'

After being ousted from her company, Quant has no direct involvement any more, just the occasional supply of an idea or a thought. All these years of success upon success, she claims, have not left her a fabulously wealthy woman. 'Well, I have a marvellous ability to get through money. And lawyers are quite good at removing it, too, aren't they?' she says. Today, she lives in the house in the country that was left to Alexander by one of his relatives, and she still sleeps in the bed that they bought when they first got married. Now she shares it with the man in her life, Antony Rouse. Originally a friend of both hers and Alexander's, Antonia Fraser once called him 'the most beautiful man at Oxford'. Mary was appointed Dame Commander of the Order of the British Empire (DBE) in the 2015 New Year Honours for services to British fashion.

* This coltish teenager from Neasden was transformed into the world's most famous model by a young Welshman who started his working life as a 16 year-old teaboy for Victor Sassoon. Nigel Davies changed Leslie Hornby's name to Twiggy, as she called her legs 'peculiar and thin like twigs'. He paid for her first modelling shots and taught her to pose. He changed his name to Justin de Villeneuve, became Twiggy's manager and mentor, and the couple were the Romeo and Juliet of the 'Swinging Sixties'. Twiggy's vital statistics were 32-22-32, a long way away from those of today's teenagers...

## DAME SHIRLEY VERONICA BASSEY 8 January 1937 -

### INTERNATIONAL DIVA, SINGER OF THREE *JAMES BOND* THEMES, 'BEST FEMALE SINGER IN THE LAST 50 YEARS'

Born at 182 Bute Street in the infamous and now-vanished Tiger Bay, the docks area of Cardiff, she was the youngest of six sisters and one brother. Her father, a ship's fireman from West Africa, was deported as an illegal immigrant when Shirley was just three, and her mother Eliza Jane Metcalfe remarried Nigerian merchant seaman. Moving to Portmanmoor* Road, Splott, in Cardiff, from the age of eight Shirley performed in the many clubs in Cardiff's Butetown. Leaving school in 1952, she worked for £3 a week packing enamel utensils in wood-shavings (other sources say that she wrapped sweets or sausages), and supplemented her income by singing in men's clubs in Cardiff. She started touring the country in reviews aged 15, and in the show *In Memory of Al Jolson* fell in love with another singer and became pregnant. Against his wishes, she decided to have the baby, and aged 16 gave her new daughter Sharon to her sister to bring up.

Shirley's career started to take off, and in 1955 she was spotted at London's Café de Paris by bandleader Jack Hylton. He booked her into that wonderful comedian Al Read's *Christmas Review* at the Hippodrome. 'The Tigress of Tiger Bay' had arrived. Al Read kept her in his succeeding revue, *Such is Life*, which ran for another year. She now had a recording contract with Philips, and reached the Top 10 with *The Banana Boat Song* in early 1957. This year was marred however, when a former boyfriend (Terence Clyde 'Pepe' Davies) held her hostage at gunpoint in her Cumberland Hotel room in London. Surrounded by armed police, he eventually released her and received 3 years in gaol.

By 1959, Shirley was hot property, with her powerful voice and expressive gestures. She had two No. 1 hits, *As I Love You* in 1959 and *Reach for the Stars/Climb Every Mountain* in 1961. In 1961, she married Kenneth Hume, a film-director. They separated in 1962 (he was a well-known homosexual), but were reconciled later that year. In 1962, teaming with orchestrator/band-leader Nelson Riddle, who resurrected Sinatra's career, helped her 'break' the States, and she headlined shows in New York and Las Vegas. Shirley had a daughter, Samantha in 1963, but Hume claimed that she was not his. 1964 saw the start of an affair with the hard-drinking actor Peter Finch. She later announced to the press that she and Finch would not be marrying, telling the press, 'It simply wouldn't work out. Just now I am not ready for marriage to anyone. I feel I have to be free.' In

1965, her powerful rendition of *Goldfinger* for the James Bond film reached the American Top 10, and became her 'signature tune' there. Shirley finally divorced Hume in this year, and he committed suicide in 1967.

In 1968, she married a 6 feet 5 inches Venetian hotelier, Sergio Novak in Las Vegas. He became her manager, and they went to live in Lugano, Switzerland, where a house was built for them. Shirley sang the Bond themes *Diamonds are Forever* in 1971 and *Moonraker* in 1979. Throughout the 1970's the hits kept coming, with *Something, For All We Know* and *Never, Never, Never*, and in 1977 she received the Britannia Award for the 'Best Female Solo Singer in the Last 50 Years'. In 1976, she went on a 22-day British tour to mark twenty years as a recording artist.

After her own BBC TV series, Shirley eased off her hectic schedule by 1981, and went to live permanently in Switzerland, divorcing in this year from Novak. Shirley then moved to Monaco, but still makes world tours. In 1984, her daughter Samantha Novak was discovered dead in the River Avon, near the Clifton Suspension Bridge. A 1994 poll in *Wales on Sunday* newspaper revealed that readers thought her 'The Sexiest Woman of the 20th Century'.

One of Shirley Bassey's many albums

Her relationships have often been stormy. Over the years, she has said 'I think men are afraid to be with a successful woman, because we are terribly strong; we know what we want and we are not fragile enough... It's hard for a man to live with a successful woman - they seem to resent you so much. Very few men are generous enough to accept success in their women... I've always been the breadwinner and men don't like that. They turn on you. They bite the hand that feeds them. Eventually, too, they become very jealous of the love one has with an audience. The first six months of a relationship are wonderful. I love that intensity, the passion, the "can't keep away from each other", then it all starts to taper off. They don't want to stay home and watch television, the want to go out. They don't want to listen to what I say, they start putting me down and I won't take that... No wedding bells for me any more. I've been happily married to my profession for years... Diamonds never leave you, men do. '

Shirley's many hits include *Climb Every Mountain, Kiss Me Honey Honey Kiss Me, As I Love You, I Who Have Nothing,* and *Big Spender*, all invested with her own unique delivery. After receiving her CBE in 1993 and then a DBE in 1999, Shirley commented 'Who would have thought a little girl from Tiger Bay would one day become a Dame?' In 1999 she also was awarded France's top honour, the Legion d'Honneur, as a mark of her popularity and importance in the culture of France. She was the star of the

1999 ceremony of the opening of the Rugby World Cup in Cardiff, dressed in a sparkling sack-dress of a Welsh Flag wrapped around her.

In 2001, Shirley was principal artiste at the Duke of Edinburgh's 80th Birthday celebration, and in 2002 performed at the Queen's 50th Jubilee Party at Buckingham Palace. In 2003, she celebrated 50 years in show business, releasing *Thank You for the Years*, yet another Top 20 album. A gala charity auction of her stage costumes at Christie's – 'Dame Shirley Bassey: 50 Years of Glittering Gowns', raised £250,000 for the Dame Shirley Bassey Scholarship at the Royal Welsh College of Music and Drama and the Noah's Ark Children's Hospital Appeal. She topped the bill at the 2005 Royal Variety Performance, and has hardly ever stopped touring, giving performances around the world. *The Living Tree* was released as a single on in 2007, marking her 50th anniversary in the UK Singles Chart, and the record for the longest span of Top 40 hits in UK chart history. Shirley performed a 45-minute set at the 2007 Glastonbury Festival, wearing customised Wellington boots and a pink Julien MacDonald dress. Her 2007 album, *Get the Party Started* entered the UK Albums Chart at No. 6, and the single of the title song reached No. 3 on the US Dance Chart.

Shirley was rushed to hospital in Monaco in May 2008 to have an emergency operation on her stomach after complaining of abdominal pains, and was forced to pull out of the Nelson Mandela 90th Birthday Tribute Concert. A biography, *Diamond Diva,* was published in 2008. In 2009, Shirley recorded the album *The Performance*, and a number of artists wrote songs expressly for her, including the Manic Street Preachers, Gary Barlow, the Pet Shop Boys, John Barry, Don Black and K.T. Tunstall. In 2011, she performed at a gala celebrating the 80th birthday of Mikhail Gorbachev. In June 2012 Shirley Bassey was one of a prestigious line-up of artists who performed at the Queen's 60th Jubilee Party at Buckingham Palace, singing *Diamonds Are Forever,* and she performed at the 2013 Academy Awards in 2013 to commemorate the 50th anniversary of the James Bond movie franchise. It was her first appearance at an Oscars ceremony as a performer, and she sang *Goldfinger* to a standing ovation. In 2014 Shirley Bassey performed *I'm Still Here* and *The Lady Is A Tramp,* and in that year released a new album, *Hello Like Before.* Her website claims that Shirley has spent more time in the UK charts than any other female performer.

* This seems to be a corruption of Porth Maen Mawr, the 'gateway of the great stone', which may date from the days when Cardiff was a Roman port, or from Roman-British times.

*Footnote:*
Just some of her awards, not noted above are as follows. The *NME* voted her Favourite British Female Singer in 1959, and *TV Times* made Best Female Singer her in 1972 and 1973. In 1974, she was the Best Female Entertainer according to the American Guild of Variety Artists, and *Music Week* made her

Best Female Singer in 1976. Shirley was given a BRIT Award in 1977 as the Best British Female Solo Artist in the previous 25 years, and in 1995 was Showbusiness Personality of the Year, according to the Variety Club of Great Britain. In 1997 she had a Grammy nomination for *The Birthday Concert* (recorded live at Althorp Park), and in 1998 had the longest run by a solo artist (ten shows), at the Royal Festival Hall, London. In 1999 her Madam Tussaud's waxwork unveiled in London (second model in Las Vegas). In 2000, the *Guinness Book of Records* stated she was the Most Successful British Female Singer, and in 2003 she received an Outstanding Contribution to Music Award in the National Music Awards. UNESCO gave her an Artist for Peace Award in 2004.

## GILLIAN CLARKE 8 June 1937 -

## THE NATIONAL POET OF WALES

Gillian was born in Cardiff to Welsh-speaking parents, was educated at St Clare's Convent, Porthcawl, and read English at Cardiff University. She lived in Cardiff, Barry and Penarth during her upbringing. In her childhood, she also spent a great deal of time in Pembrokeshire with her father's mother, her *mamgu*, known as *Ga*. She lived on the farm at Dinas Cross, with a farm-worker coming in to run it. Gillian spent all her school holidays there, and before school days when she was about three or four, and bombs were falling on Barry. In 1960 she returned to Cardiff, after two years working in News Information at the BBC in London, to marry her first husband. When her third child went to nursery school, she worked part-time lecturing in the department of Art History at Newport College of Art and Design. From 1971 to 1984 she was reviews editor, then editor of *The Anglo-Welsh Review*. In 1984 she moved to Ceredigion to take up a one-year appointment as Poet-in-Residence at St David's University College, Lampeter, where she has lived ever since as a free-lance poet and writer. She is probably the best-known poet currently working in Wales. Poet, writer, translator, editor, lecturer and broadcaster, she is President of Tŷ Newydd, Llanystumdwy, Gwynedd, the creative writing centre she co-founded in 1990.

She lives with her second husband, an architect, in Talgarreg near Llandysul, on an 18-acre small-holding run according to conservation principles. She has a daughter, Catrin (a writer) and two sons, Owain and

Dylan (both musicians). She was awarded the Glyndŵr Award for an Outstanding Contribution to the Arts in Wales at the 1999 Machynlleth Festival, her ninth collection of poems, *Ice,* was short-listed for the TS Eliot Award in 2013, and she was awarded the Queen's Gold Medal for poetry in 2013.

Meic Stephens published her early poems in *Poetry Wales,* and her first collection was the Triskel Poets pamphlet *Snow on the Mountain* in 1971. The first full collection of her poems, *The Sundial* appeared in 1978 and is now in its seventh edition. *The Irish Times* said that *Sundial* 'beautifully achieves an Edward Thomas-like perspective'. *Letter from a Far Country* (1982) is an important protest poem. *The Listener* commented: 'Her language has a quality both casual and intense, mundane and visionary. There is no gaudiness in her poetry; instead, the reader is aware of a generosity of spirit which allows the poems' subjects their own unbullied reality.' Gillian has been regarded from this time as one of the most important contemporary British poets. Her *Selected Poems* was published in 1985, and it is now in its 7th edition. In 1989, *Letting in the Rumour* was published, and was a Poetry Book Society Recommendation. *The King of Britain's Daughter,* also a Poetry Book Society Recommendation appeared in 1993, based on the story of the *Mabinogion's* Branwen (q.v.), and 'deserves to be read and re-read for the poet's brilliant wordcraft'. *Collected Poems* appeared in 1997, which *Book News* called 'a text that has the metaphoric and metamorphic power to astonish us into viewing life differently... from the most intensely sensuous of writers.' *The Times Literary Supplement* now called Gillian 'an impressively achieved and exceptionally rewarding poet.' *Five Fields* (1998) broke new ground for Gillian, after a time as writer in residence at Manchester's Bridgwater Hall. It was short-listed for the Arts Council of Wales 1999 Book of the Year Award, and was a Poetry Book Society recommendation. She had widened her rural Welsh themes to write about Bosnia, France and the Mediterranean coast. *The Times Literary Supplement* noted that the poems 'ring with lucidity and power... Her work is both personal and archetypical, built out of language as concrete as it is musical.'

A few lines from the disturbing poem *The City: The Bomb* in *Five Fields* reads:

'On the palm of a ledge outside the publisher's window
in the Corn Exchange is a clutch of broken eggs,
fledglings blown away twig-limbed and goggle-eyed.
I imagine a poem of love from the publisher's desk
afloat like a bright balloon against the wire.'

*The Field-Mouse,* from *Five Fields,* shows the breadth of Gillian's work. It was inspired by the Bosnian crisis and Srebrenica. The perceived traditional

347

British summer harvest of the first stanza moves from peripheral destruction, to central violence and horror in the second stanza:

'Summer, and the long grass is a snare drum.
The air hums with jets.
Down at the end of the meadow,
far from the radio's terrible news,
we cut the hay. All afternoon
its wave breaks before the tractor blade.
Over the hedge our neighbour travels his field
in a cloud of lime, drifting our land
with a chance gift of sweetness.

The child comes running through the killed flowers,
his hands a nest of quivering mouse,
its black eyes two sparks burning.
We know it will die and ought to finish it off.
It curls in agony big as itself
and the star goes out of its eye.
Summer in Europe, the field's hurt,
and the children kneel in long grass,
staring at what we have crushed.

Gillian has also written children's poetry, and *The Animal Wall and Other Poems* appeared in 1999. Her children's books include *One Moonlit Night* (1991); *I Can Move the Sea* (1996); and *The Whispering Room* (1996). An illustrated book of poems, *Nine Green Gardens* was commissioned for Aberglasney in 2000, 'the garden lost in time'. With a simple style, Gillian writes with a visionary lyricism, placing the recurring universal themes of childhood, womanhood and the fragility of life in terms of regional description and incident. Passionate about Wales and its future, Gillian sometimes makes use of the Welsh language in her poems, and also uses the seven-syllable traditional line and *cynghanedd*.

Gillian was appointed Capital Poet for Cardiff 2005-6. She travelled as a poet to the former Soviet Union and Yugoslavia; more recently has given poetry readings and lectures in India, Bangladesh, Mexico, Canada, Europe and the United States. Her poems have been translated into ten languages, most recently a bilingual collection in Italian, *Una Ricetta Per L'Acqua*. In 2008 she became Wales's third National Poet. In 2011 Gillian became the second Welsh winner of the Queen's Gold Medal for Poetry. She was quoted as saying 'So many wonderful poets have received the award, and I wondered if I belonged on such a distinguished list. I thought if RS Thomas can accept a medal from the Queen, so can I.' Only eleven women had received the award, and the medal was a 'gift for poetry and for Wales'.

348

Poet Laureate Carol Ann Duffy, who chaired the medal's judging panel, has described her as 'part of the literary landscape of this country.' In 2011, Gillian was honoured by the Gorsedd of Bards at the National Eisteddfod in Wrexham, and in 2012 received the Wilfred Owen Award.

Among Gillian's many publications are translations of two of Kate Roberts' novels, *Tegwch y Bore* (*One Bright Morning*, 2008) and *Y Lôn Wen* (*The White Lane*, 2009). Her later works are *Making the Beds for the Dead* (2004), *A Recipe for Water* (2009) and *Ice* (short-listed for the TS Eliot Award, 2012). Her prose memoir *At the Source: A Writer's Year* was published in 2008. Carol Ann Duffy wrote in *The Guardian:* 'Gillian Clarke's outer and inner landscapes are the sources from which her poetry draws its strengths...' Her poetry is studied by GCSE and A Level students throughout Britain and the *Times Literary Supplement* tells us 'Gillian Clarke's [poems] ring with lucidity and power... her work is personal and archetypal, built out of language as concrete as it is musical.'

*Footnote:*
This author sadly swapped Welsh for Spanish in Barry Grammar School, believing it in 1960 to be a 'useless language'. It was very much the feeling of the times, certainly in south-east Wales, and Gillian's interview with Kirsty McCrum, reported in *WalesOnline* on 26 October 2012 has a massive resonance. My mother grew up in a Welsh-speaking village, with a monoglot grandmother who could not communicate with my father, but she never spoke Welsh in my lifetime and has now, aged 94, virtually lost the language. Her village, Trefeglwys in Montgomeryshire, now has few, if any, Welsh speakers left, with many English people having moved in over the decades. Gillian lived in the same times, and McCrum reported her words: 'In the house when I was born lived my mother and father, my grandmother, my father's three sisters and the husband of one of them. There was a hell of a lot of noise in our house, everybody talking in two languages. Both my parents were Welsh speakers, but my mother thought it was posh to speak English, and she wouldn't let me speak Welsh' She didn't know it is better to have two languages. This is what it's like to be colonised, to be black in a white world. It was like that to be a Welsh speaker in those days.' Gillian made her first effort to learn Welsh when she reached her teens: '... it was greed for language. I'm a writer, I want all the words in the world.'

## DR. GWYNETH LEWIS FRSL 4 November 1959 -

## INAUGURAL NATIONAL POET OF WALES

Gwyneth Lewis was born into a Welsh-speaking family in Cardiff, and her father started teaching her English when her mother went into hospital to give birth to her sister. She said: 'I started writing poetry when I was seven years old. It had rained a good deal during a school holiday, preventing us from playing outside, so I decided to write a long poem about the rain instead. Many of my happiest moments since have been spent in the same way - sitting at a table, chewing the top of a pen, trying to let words take me where they want to. I think of writing as being a third eye which helps me to make sense of my life. Without it, and the routes it offers me into my subconscious, I seem to live less richly and certainly less wisely. Poetry requires an act of deep listening - to yourself, your body, to words and, even, to the silence which surrounds them. I don't know what I'd do without it.' (- British Council literature website author statement).

Gwyneth went to Ysgol Gyfun Rhydfelen, the first Welsh language comprehensive school in the south of Wales, and then studied at Girton College, Cambridge, where she was a member of *Cymdeithas y Mabinogi*. Gwyneth was awarded a double first in English literature, and the Laurie Hart Prize for outstanding intellectual work. She then studied creative writing at Columbia and Harvard universities, where she was taught by the Nobel Laureates Derek Walcott and Joseph Brodsky. The latter has said: 'Felicitous, urbane, heartbreaking, the poems of Gwyneth Lewis form a universe whose planets use language for oxygen and thus are inhabitable'. She then received her Doctorate in English from Balliol College, Oxford. Her thesis was upon Iolo Morganwg, and she kindly consented to this author reading it. She was made a Harkness Fellow at Harvard and then Columbia universities, and worked as a freelance journalist in New York for three years, before returning to Cardiff to work as a documentary producer and director at BBC Wales.

**Gwyneth Lewis,**
*courtesy of Keith Morris*

Lewis left the BBC in 2001 and was awarded a £75,000 grant by NESTA to carry out research and to sail to ports that were linked historically with the inhabitants of her native city, Cardiff. Lewis has been dubbed a 'bilingual virtuoso', writing in both Welsh, her first language, and in English. She has published many books of poetry in Welsh and English. Some of her Welsh volumes are: *Llwybrau bywyd* (1977); *Ar y groesffordd* (1978); *Sonedau Redsa a Cherddi Eraill* (1990); *Cyfrif Un Ac Un yn Dri* (1996); and *Y Llofrudd Iaith* (2000), which won the Welsh Arts Council Book of the Year Prize. Ruth McIlroy wrote in *Planet*: 'She is one of very few poets to be equally probing and technically sophisticated in both languages... intuitively sensitive to the peculiarities of each.'

Her first collection in English, *Parables & Faxes* (Bloodaxe, 1995) won the Aldeburgh Poetry Festival Prize and was short-listed for the

*Forward* award, as was her second, *Zero Gravity* (1998). The BBC made a documentary of *Zero Gravity*, inspired by her astronaut cousin's voyage to repair the Hubble Space Telescope. One critic noted: 'Lewis' originality is evidenced in her ability to sustain themes in longer poems or sequences of poems. Such exploration of themes through connected poems can be seen in Zero Gravity (1998) which explores modernity through poems ostensibly "to commemorate the voyage of my cousin Joe Tanner and the crew of Space Shuttle STS-82". Immediately from the *Prologue* section, we find that this is also a pioneering and philosophical piece when the speaker states:

My theme is change.
[...]
See how speed
transforms us? Didn't you know
that time's a fiction?'

*Y Llofrudd Iaith* ('The Language Murderer' 2000), won the Welsh Arts Council Book of the Year Prize and *Keeping Mum* (2003) was short–listed for the same prize in 2004. 'Formally, Lewis' sounds often echo the consonantal alliteration of Welsh poetry, and in one instance in *Consultant* she uses the Welsh half rhyme, the *proest* (where the consonants stay the same and the vowel sound changes), by ending a couplet with translate and tolerate'. Alex Pryce had noted: 'Lewis is a writer with a sense of adventure; all of her work probes the contemporary self with unflinching honesty, and she is a writer readers should allow to accompany them on their own voyages.'

Married to Leighton Davies, Lewis has been frank about her problems with clinical depression, which inspired her first book *Sunbathing in the Rain: A Cheerful Book on Depression* (2002), and the collection of poems *Keeping Mum – Voices from Therapy* (2003, republished in 2005 as part of *Chaotic Angels*). They bought the small yacht *Jameeleh*, taught themselves to sail and set out to cross the Atlantic Ocean to Africa. The journey inspired her 2005 book *Two in a Boat – The True Story of a Marital Rite of Passage*. The TLS reviewer wrote '...Lewis learns how the sea is an unanchored otherworld that tests everything that comes into its power... I have never read a better description of this process of discovery...'

Gwyneth Lewis's mark on the landscape of Welsh poetry since the publication of her first collection written in Cymraeg in 1977 is best evidenced on the impressive frontage of the Wales Millennium Centre. Six foot letters form verse in Welsh and English (what she calls her 'mother' and 'step-mother' tongues respectively) and indicate the stature she occupies in the poetry communities of those languages, and beyond.' The huge lettering reads: *Creu Gwir fel Gwydr o Ffwrnais Awen / In these Stones Horizons Sing*. The Welsh means 'Creating truth, like glass from inspiration's furnace', and the lettering is formed by windows in the upstairs bar areas and is internally illuminated at night. The centre opened in November 2004, and the same words form the title of Karl Jenkins' cantata, which is partly set to lyrics by Gwyneth.

The idea of this monumental inscription came from Roman classical architecture, and the centre's architect Jonathan Adams said: 'The Romans brought Christianity to these islands, along with the custom of engraving stone. The form of the Celtic cross embodies the cross-fertilisation of indigenous and Roman cultures, from which the Welsh nation first emerged. The monumental inscription is a familiar feature of Roman architecture. The inscription over the entrance of the Wales Millennium Centre is a revival of this classical tradition, and also a recognition of the formative influence of Roman culture upon our nation. We're lucky to have two languages; one that we share with half the world and one which belongs just to us.

**Gwyneth Lewis' words on the Wales Millennium Centre, Cardiff Bay**

Words in songs, stories and poems have helped to make Wales the proud country that it is'. The building iconic, and thankfully the original glass box design for a new opera house was abandoned.

The inscription is thought to be 'the biggest poem in the world', and Gwyneth explained: 'I wanted the words to reflect the architecture of the building. Its copper dome reminded me of the furnaces from Wales's industrial heritage and also Ceridwen's cauldron, from which the early poet Taliesin received his inspiration (*'awen'*). *Awen* suggests both poetic inspiration and the general creative vision by which people and societies form their aspirations. [...] It was important to me that the English words on the building should not simply be a translation of the Welsh, that they should have their own message. The strata of the slate frontage of the Wales Millennium Centre reminded me of the horizons just beyond Penarth Head. The sea has, traditionally, been for Cardiff the means by which the Welsh export their best to the world and the route by which the world comes to Cardiff. The stones inside the theatre literally sing with opera, musicals and orchestral music, and I wanted to convey the sense of an international space created by the art of music.'

In 2005 she was elected Honorary Fellow of Cardiff University, and in the same year was made the first National Poet of Wales. She is also a librettist, and has written two chamber operas for children and an oratorio, *The Most Beautiful Man from the Sea.*

It was given its world première at the Millennium Centre by the chorus of the Welsh National Opera and five hundred amateur singers. Later works include *A Hospital Odyssey* (2010); *The Meat Tree* (2010); *Sparrow Tree* (2011) and *Y Storm*, 2012 (her translation of *The Tempest*). The great poet Peter Porter RSL (1929-2010) tells us: '...Gwyneth Lewis has so many of the gifts required for good poetry: command of form, with improvisation enlivening tradition; supple rhythm; originality of subject-matter and the right eye to pin down detail; humour, both sardonic and direct; and; above all, commitment to human feeling...'

In 2010 Gwyneth was given a Society of Authors Cholmondeley Award recognizing a body of work and achievement of distinction. She is a Fellow of the Royal Society of Literature, and was a Vice President of the Poetry Society. On 6 August 2012 she won *Y Goron* (the Crown) at the National Eisteddfod at Llandow for a collection of poems on the set title of *Ynys* (Island).


## DAME GWYNETH JONES 7 November 1937 -

## ONE OF THE GREATEST WAGNERIAN SOPRANOS OF ALL TIME

Born at Pontnewynydd, Pontypool, her mother died when Gwyneth was only three, and after Pontypool's Twmpath Secondary School, she worked as a secretary at the Pontypool Engineering and Foundry Company, winning prizes at local eisteddfodau. She sang in the local Pontypool Cooperative Choir. Her father died just two hours after she discovered that she had been accepted as a student at London's Royal College of Music. Alone, she supported herself by singing at the Moo Cow Milk Bar, and won prizes and scholarships to enable her to continue her studies. She also studied voice in Sienna and Zurich, which is her present home. Later in her career, Gwyneth was a pupil of Dame Eva Turner, learning from her the role of *Turandot*, which became the greatest triumph of her career.

Her professional debut was as a mezzo-soprano in Zurich Opera House in 1962, and her first soprano role was Amelia in *Un Ballo in Maschera*. A representative of Covent Garden was impressed, and approached her to ask what her repertoire consisted of - the inexperienced Gwyneth answered 'You've just heard it!' She specialised in Italian opera in her early career, and 1962 saw her debut with the Welsh National Opera as *Lady Macbeth* in Cardiff. From 1963 she was a Principal Dramatic Soprano at the Royal Opera House, Covent Garden. In 1964 she replaced the ill Leontyne Price as Leonora in *Il Trovatore*, and was an overnight success. Gwyneth replaced another ailing soprano a few weeks later, playing Leonore in *Fidelio*. This role stimulated her interest in the German repertoire for which she has become celebrated, such as *Der Rosenkavalier* (for which Bernstein requested her) and *The Ring*. From 1966 she was Principal Dramatic Soprano at Berlin's Deutsche Oper, and from 1967 at the Bavarian State Opera.

She soon was singing regularly all over the world, from Tokyo to Buenos Aires, in the roles of Madame Butterfly, Desdemona, Aida, Lady Macbeth, Tosca, Santuzza and Elisabetta de Valois. From playing minor roles in *The Ring*, Gwyneth became one of the greatest of all the Brunhildes. At Bayreuth in 1972, she established a precedent for sopranos to double as Elisabeth and Venus, and she has sung all the leading Wagner roles except Elsa. Her greatest achievement was her Brunhilde in the Bayreuth Centennial Ring Cycle under Pierre Boulez, her performance of which can be seen on video. Her eight Strauss roles include a great performance in *'Die Frau Ohne*

Gwyneth Jones with one of her many Wagner recordings

*Schatten'* where she played both Barak's Wife, and the Empress. In 1976, Gwyneth was awarded the CBE.

After a quarter-century of performing, Gwyneth still pushed for new challenges, singing *Turandot* for the first time in the 1984 Olympics in Los Angeles, and for a decade was the world's greatest interpreter of this role. In 1986 Gwyneth was made a Dame of the British Empire (DBE). She also took new parts such as Minnie in *La Fanciulla del West*, the widow Begbick in *Mahogany* and the Mother in *Hansel und Gretel*. 1988 saw her triumphant return to the Royal Opera in *Turandot*, marking the 25th anniversary of her debut there, and she received the Royal Opera's Silver Medal. At the age of 59 she sang her first *bel canto* role as Norma. Since her first appearance in 1962 she has performed a punishing opera and concert schedule, with over 70 performances in 1997, when she was aged 60. She appeared at the Farewell Ceremony marking the end of British administration in Hong Kong in that year, and has given a one-woman show based upon Malvina Schnorr von Carolsfeld (the first Isolde). In 2003 Dame Gwyneth made her debut as director and costume designer, and appeared in the recent Dustin Hoffman film *Quartet*. She continues to perform, now taking on mezzo-soprano roles, including that of Herodias in *Salome*, which she performed in Malmö and Verbier in 2010. She gives master-classes in London and elsewhere. Gwyneth Jones is a *Kammersangrin* of both the Bavarian and Vienna

Operas, a recipient of the German Cross of Merit, and President of the British Wagner Society.


## DELIA ANN SMITH 18 June 1941 -

## BRITAIN'S BEST SELLING FOOD WRITER

Delia Ann Smith's mother was Etty Lewis, a Welsh-speaker from Gwynedd, who moved to London aged 16. Delia's brother is Glyn. Delia* failed her 11-plus examination, which she felt marked her out as a failure in life. She went on to fail at Secretarial College, where the Principal said that she was unlikely to be able to sit still for long enough to be a secretary. She then failed a hairdressing apprenticeship, and life looked fairly bleak for the young woman. She then became a shop assistant and worked in a travel agency. However, at the age of 22, she became a Roman Catholic, and ever since her religion has been vital to her everyday life. Shortly after, she became interested in cooking after asking for a recipe in The Singing Chef restaurant in Paddington. She was offered a job as a washer-up, then waitress, then started to assist in the cooking and discovered her true vocation in life. In her spare time, she read English cookery books in the British Museum Reading Room, trying them out on the family of a Harley Street doctor, with whom she was staying at the time.

In 1969, she began to write a column for the *Daily Mirror* magazine, and soon married its deputy editor, Michael Wynne-Jones in 1971. She published *'How to Cheat at Cooking'* in 1971, and also began long-running cookery columns in *The Evening Standard* and *The Radio Times*. From 1973, she has had a continual succession of cookery programmes on BBC TV. Her cookery books, usually spin-offs of TV series, had sold over 21,000,000 copies in Britain alone. Janet Clarke wrote (*The Guardian*, 4 November 2000) of Elizabeth David 'I regard her as the greatest writer on food in the second half of the 20th century. Elizabeth David and Jane Grigson could write, they had literary ability. They wrote about food and where it came from and their experiences of it. Delia Smith, on the other hand, writes recipe books. This is not to denigrate her. They are tried and tested and work. But it is different to what Elizabeth did.' Of course, no-one can hold a candle to Elizabeth David in her influence upon British cuisine, but Delia has been the great 'populariser' of good cooking for the general public, well before the current generation of Jamie Oliver, Gordon Ramsey and the like. Her books sell in millions, each new one jetting straight to the very top of the bestsellers list in hardback, and then repeating the feat in paperback.

Her biggest selling book, *Delia Smith's The Winter Collection* (1995) sold 2 million copies in hardback alone. In 1995, she was responsible for the 'cranberry crisis' which cleared supermarket shelves of the juice after her recommendation on TV. In 2003 Smith announced her retirement from television. However, she returned for an eponymous six-part series airing on the BBC in Spring 2008. Her television series, *Delia's How to Cook* (1998), had reportedly led to a 10% rise in egg sales in Britain. Her use of ingredients such as frozen mash, tinned minced beef and onions, certain brands of noodles and pasta, sea salt and fish sauce, as used in her 2008 TV series, or utensils such as an omelette pan or mini-chopper, could cause sellouts overnight. This phenomenon, known as the 'Delia Effect', was most recently seen in 2008, after her updated book *How to Cheat at Cooking* was published. Her fame has meant that her first name has become sufficient to identify her to the public and the 'Delia Effect' has become a commonly used phrase to describe a run on a previously poor-selling product, as a result of a high-profile recommendation. In 2010, *Delia through the Decades*, was broadcast in five episodes, with each episode exploring a new decade of her cooking. In March 2010, Delia Smith and Heston Blumenthal were signed up to appear in a series of 40 commercials on British television for the supermarket chain Waitrose, and in February 2013, Delia Smith announced that she had retired from television cookery programmes, and would concentrate on offering her recipes online.

She is more than simply a cook, she is a national icon with millions of followers and a reported fortune of over £30 million. Her religion has greatly helped Delia, and she wrote *A Journey to God*, a book on prayer, as well as *A Feast for Lent* and *A Feast for Advent*. Delia's only unfulfilled ambitions are to see Norwich City Football Club (which she saved from bankruptcy, and of which she and her husband own 60% of the shares) win the league and play in Europe. Delia's biography, by Alison Bower, appeared in 2000. Already an OBE, she was appointed a CBE in the 2009 Birthday Honours, 'in recognition of ... [her] contribution to television cookery and recipe writing'.

*Footnote:*
A website, *Pantheon Epicurium,* lists the greatest chefs such as David, Grigson and Escoffier, and its entry on Delia makes excellent reading: 'In an era of TV chefs, with cookery hailed as the new rock'n'roll, many people began to lose confidence in their kitchens. The foodies of course revelled in great flights of fancy, trying to outdo each other with Kiwi fruit *Tarte Tatin* and pork *sashimi* (don't try this at home!). But many competent everyday cooks found themselves lost in a mire of starfruit *coulis*. In addition to this an entire generation had by

now been raised on fish fingers, their mothers long since forsaking the mixing bowl for the microwave. Was there no one who could teach people the basics? Who could steer the nation through the minefield of Nouvelle Cuisine to the safer ground of good, honest cooking? Who would not be above explaining how to make a Victoria Sponge, a Steak and Kidney Pudding, how to use Coriander, or the difference between Olive and Sunflower oil? Fear not, for Saint Delia was at hand!

*Delia Smith's Complete Illustrated Cookery Course* is the biggest selling cookbook of all time. In it she carefully explained the techniques needed to create enjoyable food. She took nothing for granted, and her recipes were set out clearly and simply. Above all, if you do exactly as Delia tells you, you can be sure that her recipes will work and taste good which, at a time when you could never be sure whether half a cow in formaldehyde was a work of art or an entrée, were valuable attributes.

Delia's other works include *One is Fun, Delia Smith's Christmas* and her *Winter* and *Summer Collections*. Her latest venture, *How to Cook*, goes back to absolute basics such as how to boil an egg. The books sell in huge numbers because people know they can trust her recipes utterly. Her television series are watched by millions, and when Delia recommends a new ingredient you can bet the supermarkets will sell out of it the next day!

For all her popularity and power, Delia Smith is not without her detractors; she has been accused of patronising her audience, though usually by professional chefs who have no need of simplistic explanations. Her slightly gauche presentation style and insistence on mispronouncing the word *Chorizo* can be rather grating, too. Still, she is almost single-handedly responsible for restoring the Readymeal Generation's enjoyment in cooking and eating, and her place in the Pantheon is well deserved.'


## MENNA ELFYN FRSL 1 January 1951 –

## PROFESSOR OF POETRY


Menna Elfyn is an award winning poet, playwright and librettist and has published over twenty books consisting of collections of poetry, children's novels, libretti for UK and US composers as well as plays for television and radio. Her bilingual volume, *Murmur*, published in 2012 by Bloodaxe Books was selected as a Poetry Book Society Recommended Translation, the first volume in Welsh / English to be chosen. She is Professor of Poetry at University of Wales, Trinity Saint David, a Fellow of the Royal Society of Literature, Fellow of the Royal Literary Fund as well as Fellow of the Welsh Academi. Dr Menna Elfyn is the present director of the Masters programme in Creative Writing at University of Wales, Trinity Saint David, a course she co-directed with the late poet Nigel Jenkins from 1998-2004.

Menna Elfyn was born in Glanaman, Carmarthenshire, and lived in Pontardawe and Peniel, until where her father, the Rev. T. Elfyn Jones, a renowned hymnist was the minister. She was awarded an honours degree in Welsh at University College Swansea, before gaining a Diploma in Education at University College Aberystwyth. She taught at Cardigan Secondary School from 1973 until 1979, before being appointed to teach part-time in the Welsh department at St David's University College, Lampeter, 1979-1986. During those years she published her first volume of poetry, *Mwyara* (1976), and her second volume *Stafelloedd Aros* (1978) won a major literary prize at the National Eisteddfod of Wales for the most promising volume of unpublished poetry. Further collections followed: *Tro'r Haul Arno* (1982), *Mynd Lawr i'r Nefoedd*, (1986), and *Aderyn Bach mewn Llaw* (1990), *Selected Poems* which won a Welsh Arts Council prize for one of the best books of the year, all published by Gomer Press.

Following the demand for her work to be translated in 1995, Menna Elfyn published her first bilingual collection of selected poems *Eucalyptus* by Gomer Press. Tony Conran who was editor of the collection called her 'the first Welsh poet in fifteen hundred years to make a serious attempt to have her work known outside Wales'. Her second bilingual volume, *Cell Angel* by Bloodaxe Books was hailed by the same critic as the most significant collection of Welsh poetry for forty years.

In 1999, Menna co-wrote *The Garden of Light*, a choral symphony for the New York Philharmonic Orchestra, performed at the Lincoln Centre in New York. In the same year, she was commissioned to write the libretto *Hymn to a Welshman*, with the composer Pwyll ap Siôn, a tribute to R. S. Thomas and performed at Portmeirion. She received a Creative Arts Award in 2008, from the Arts Council of Wales to explore the subject of 'Sleep'.

Her work has been translated into eighteen languages including Italian, Spanish, Portuguese, Lithuanian, Hindi, Catalan and Chinese. In 2009, Menna was awarded the International Anima Istranza Foreign Prize for Poetry in Sardinia.

Some of the poet's other publications are: *Hel Dail Gwyrdd* (ed),1985; *Mynd lawr i'r nefoedd* (ed),1986); *O'r Iawn Ryw,* (ed), Gwasg Honno1991; *Madfall Ar Y Mur,* Gwasg Gomer (1993); *Trying the Line: A Volume of Tributes to Gillian Clarke* (1997) Gomer Press; *Camlas y Cwm: Pontardawe* (1999) Gregynog Press; *Ffŵl yn y Dŵr: Casgliad O Gerddi i Bobl Ifanc,* Gwasg Gomer (1999); *Cusan Dyn Dall: Blind Man's Kiss,*

Bloodaxe Books (2001); *Rana Rebel,* Gwasg Gomer (2002) *Caneri Pinc Ar Dywod Euraid: Cerddi Bardd Plant Cymru 2002-3 a Beirdd Ifanc Cymru* (2003) Hughes a'i Fab; *Perffaith Nam,* Gwasg Gomer (2005); *Perfect Blemish: New & Selected Poems 1995-2007,* Bloodaxe Books(2007); *Er Dy Fod,*Gwasg Gomer (2007); *Merch Perygl: Cerddi Menna Elfyn* (2011) Gwasg Gomer and *Murmur* Bloodaxe Books, (2012).

Her work in translation first appeared in *Seren Poets: The Bloodstream No. 1* (1989) Poetry Wales Press and subsequently appeared in *The Adulterer's Tongue: An Anthology of Welsh Poetry in Translation,* Carcanet Press (2003). In 2003, the definitive anthology of Modern Welsh Poetry in translation was published by Bloodaxe Books which she co-edited with John Rowlands. This volume also received the Poetry Book Society Recommended Translation for autumn 2003. In 2007, *Perffaith Nam/ Perfect Blemish: New & Selected Poems 1995-2007* appeared from Bloodaxe Books.

Her most recent libretto was *Gair ar Gnawd* with composer Pwyll ap Siôn (2015)—the first opera in the Welsh language to be commissioned and performed by the Welsh National Opera and later televised on S4C.

She travels the world for readings and residences and is the most travelled of all Welsh language poets. However, she is deeply committed to Wales and apart from literary work she is columnist with the Western Mail since 1994, and her journalistic writings often voice her deep political views. She was made Honorary President of Wales PEN Cymru in 2014, and is a tireless advocate of free expression and campaigns on behalf of minorities. During the Welsh language campaigns of the seventies and eighties she was imprisoned twice for taking part in non-violent action.

She also took part in peace protests and was an anti-apartheid activist.

Amongst the reviews on the Bloodaxe website are the following which affirm her international status: 'the international range of her subjects, inventiveness and generosity of vision place her among Europe's leading poets. Hayden Murphy called her 'one of the few great voice to emerge from Wales at the end of the 20th century. Mike Clement writes in reviewing her *Perfect Blemish: New & Selected Poems 1995-2007,* 'Elfyn releases her soul as song... it is deeply reflective, poignant, and empathetic of the dispossessed ... possibly, one of the best books of contemporary poetry there is, and has to be a must have for any reader of poetry. It is certainly one that you will read and re-read to unearth limitless gems of discovery.'

*Drws yn Epynt/* A Door in Epynt conveys one of her salient themes, in which a simple incident is part of the Epynt story where the inhabitants were uprooted and forced from their homes and community for military purposes in 1940.

## A Door in Epynt

*(before leaving Epynt, one woman asked if she could take her door with her)*

There's a door which closes by itself,
a door that deludes time,
one knock and there's fighting talk.

And although she lived in the back of beyond
this hearth was her harmony,
its underlay, the chill of tranquillity.

No stand-off or ford to cross,
no enemy but the purchase order:
'A perfect place, this, for a squaddies' mess.'

Armed with warrants, in haste they removed
the people from the land. Then the hills of refuge
surrendered to the combats' heavy outfits.

Not without a plea. Before turning her back:
'May I keep the door to the cottage?'
Empty handed, she left for the village.

Yet, when the east wind howls, I hear terror –
the door slam shut and, then, flung open.
Listen to its sounds. Earth shakes. Pleading.

*Trans. Elin ap Hywel from the Welsh*

From *Murmur,* Bloodaxe Books, 2012
(*Poetry Book Society Recommended Translation*)


## NANCI CAROLINE GRIFFITH 6 July 1954 -

## THE FIRST FOLK ARTIST TO PLAY CARNEGIE HALL

Born in Seguin, near Austin in Texas, her father is the Welsh Marlin (Griff)
Griffiths, and her mother Relene Strawser. They divorced in 1960, when
Nanci was just six. Griff was a singer in barber-shop quartets and a book
publisher. Suffering from dyslexia, Nancy moved from trying to learn piano,
to play guitar and wrote her own songs as a teenager, as she found that it was
more easy than learning how to play other people's songs correctly. Aged 14,

her first 'professional' performance at the Red Lion hotel in Austin, on Thanksgiving Day, made her $11. She took an education degree in the University of Texas and then taught kindergarten, while at the same time supporting herself for five years playing at the Hole in the Wall Bar in Austin. Her first recordings were released in 1977.

In *Sing Out!*, singer/songwriter Tom Russell remembered his first encounter with Nanci Griffith at a folk festival in 1976. One evening around a campfire, with people spread out on a grassy hill into the darkness, guitars and wine being passed around, a gruff voice yelled from the darkness, 'Let

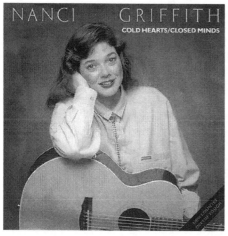

*her* play one.' From the edge of the campfire light came a waif-like young girl. She began to play and sing in a voice Russell said possessed 'a wild, fragile beauty'. When she finished and the echo of the applause drifted away, the voice spoke again: 'That was Nanci Griffith. She writes songs.' Married to singer-songwriter Eric Taylor from 1976 to 1982, she moved to a small farmhouse near Nashville in 1986, and also has a flat in Dublin, where she spends part of each year.

In 1986, she signed to the major label MCA/Nashville, and her debut album on that label went platinum, selling well in the British Isles as well as America. Her version of *From a Distance* became a number one hit in England and Ireland. Five years later Bette Midler would have a smash hit with the song, though it is Griffith's version that was used twice to awaken astronauts on space shuttle missions. Over the three two decades, Nancy has recorded with Lyle Lovett, Albert Lee, Hootie and the Blowfish, Phil Everly, Larry Mullen and Adam Clayton of U2, The Chieftains and Mark Knopfler, amongst others. Her greatest musical influences were Buddy Holly and Sonny Curtis (the latter wrote *I Fought the Law* and *Walk Right Back*), and she later worked with Curtis and Buddy Holly's Crickets.

An Autumn 1994 article in the USA's *National Forum* magazine tells us: 'Nancy Griffith, who has made eleven albums spanning more than 18 years, perhaps best personifies the contemporary folk artist. Her career could be a prototype for the new generation of folk singer-songwriters. But like most folk artists from any era, Griffith is first and foremost a musical storyteller, "The most important thing for me, my life, my goal from childhood on, is to be a good songwriter. That stamp of validation for that goal in my life comes to me every time someone records one of my songs, and every time someone takes one of my songs on as a companion."

Griffith's song-writing expertise has helped to bring intelligent music back into fashion. Inspired by such 20th-century novelists as Eudora Welty and Carson McCullers, her lyrics are as deeply rooted in literature as her melody is in folk... Griffith has extended her love of storytelling by writing two novels and numerous short stories.

Building a following month by month, and year by year, as she drove her Toyota station wagon from venue to venue, Griffith has become a folk success story without the benefit of radio play, or, until recently, much support from a major record label. Although she was with the record giant MCA for six years, the label failed to promote any of the five albums made under its auspices. Philo/Rounder, an independent record label which produced two of her early albums, said recently of Griffith: "No single artist has done more than this Texan songwriter to kick down the arbitrary marketing barriers that have separated musical genres and frozen folk out of the commercial marketplace" Her refusal to fit neatly into a conventional musical category has forged a path for such other contemporary folk-based artists as Mary Chapin Carpenter, Lyle Lovett, Shawn Colvin et al.

Stylistically, the songs that Griffith has written and performed are as varied as the genre of folk itself... In 1986 she was signed by MCA's country division and moved to Nashville. Her music adopted some elements from country music, and she termed this hybrid "folkabilly". After three albums she moved to MCA's Los Angeles division, and the next two albums demonstrated a distinctive pop component. Hoping for a record label that better understood her philosophy, Griffith moved to Elektra in 1993... In the span of her career, Griffith has gone from playing bars so rough that heads were smashed into cigarette machines* to headlining major folk festivals to selling out London's Royal Albert Hall for four consecutive nights. She is the first folk artist ever to play Carnegie Hall.'

Her Elektra debut, 1993's *Other Voices, Other Rooms,* won her the *Grammy* for Best Contemporary Folk Performance. Her interpretation of songs written by other artists, the album included Bob Dylan's *Boots of Spanish Leather,* a song that Dylan the previous year requested she perform at his historic Madison Square Garden 30th anniversary concert. After Nanci's 10th studio album, *Flyer,* the following year, her momentum suffered when she was treated for breast cancer in summer 1996, which caused her to exit from a tour with The Chieftains. In 1999, Griffith was diagnosed with thyroid cancer, but continued to be active as a touring and recording performer. She also lent her celebrity to various charitable organizations including Campaign for a Landmine-Free World. Apart from these few insights, Griffith seems to be guarded about her personal life.

Her long-time support band has been the Blue Moon Orchestra, and with Sheryl Crow she travelled to Cambodia in her work for the victims of landmines. Bob Dylan specifically asked that Nancy sang at his anniversary concert. *Rolling Stone* called her 'the Queen of Folkabilly', and the

*Telegraph Magazine* named her 'the torch-bearer of American folk music'. Griffith suffered from severe 'writers block' for a number of years after 2004, lasting until the 2009 release of her *The Loving Kind* album, which contained nine selections that she had written and composed either entirely by herself or as collaborations. In 2012, she released *Intersection*. She said that that a song off the album, 'Hell No (I'm Not Alright) is a huge hit. It's just become an anthem, you know, all over Europe and then the UK, and now in the States.' At 61 and with a 20-album, 37-year career behind her, she now suffers health issues, with incipient arthritis and recent hand surgery meaning that she now leans heavily on her band's guitarists.

Griffith offers songs of love, stories of broken dreams, observations of people living lives that are neither heroic nor pathetic. 'The people residing within the lines of her songs are the salt of the American earth', wrote *Connoisseur* reviewer Jared Lawrence Burden. And according to Stephen Holden of the *New York Times,* Griffith 'sings lyrics redolent of the American landscape.'

\* This was the only time that Nanci ever stopped in mid-song, when a cowboy was ramming someone's head against a Lucky Strike vending machine at the Hole in the Wall Bar in Austin.


## TRACY EDWARDS MBE 5 September 1962 -

## ROUND-THE-WORLD YACHTSWOMAN

She was born to Anthony Herbert Edwards and the former Patricia Bint at Battle Hospital, Reading. Her father was an electronics engineer and her mother a professional dancer, and they had met on the car rallying circuit when both were competing. Her brother Trevor arrived three years later. She says in her autobiography, *Living Every Second*: 'Dad's family was from Wales and was dominated by train drivers and miners. There was, however, a master mariner among them - my great-grandfather, Lewis Williams who was from Merthyr Tydfil in the valleys. He probably sailed on the coal ships coming out of Newport and Swansea at the turn of the century. My grandfather Lewis John Edwards was a fighter pilot in the First World War and a radio engineer afterwards. He put the first radio system into a public place in Britain, at Battle Hospital in reading. This led to the first hospital radio station.'

When she was 8, her father took Tracy and Trevor sailing for the first time, on a 25-foot yacht to the Isle of Wight. In a flat calm, both children were sick, and did not wish to return on the yacht to the mainland. Tracy wanted to be a ballerina like her mother or a show-jumping star when disaster struck. Her mother had been fighting Multiple Sclerosis since she had been pregnant with Tracy, and her condition was worsening. She was ten when her beloved grandmother died, and eleven when her father had a fatal heart attack. Her mother was just 37, ill, and with two young children. Tracy went to Arts Educational, a boarding school, where the comedienne Caroline Quentin was in the year above her.

Her mother remarried and aged 12, Tracy went to live at Llanmadoc, on the Gower Peninsula in Wales. In 1980, aged just 16, Tracy left for Athens, working as a nanny for a Greek family. She then spent 5 years delivering and working on charter yachts across the world. In the 1985 Whitbread Round-the-World yacht race, Tracy managed to secure a place on *Norsk Data* (previously *GBII*), with a fairly inexperienced crew, but disliked the lack of teamwork and leadership. Tracy had already completed four Atlantic crossings. After the first leg from Portsmouth, she swapped boats, managing to inveigle herself as cook  into the all-male crew of the maxi-yacht *Atlantic Privateer* from Capetown for the rest of the voyage. It beat the New Zealand boat into Auckland harbour by just 7 minutes, the narrowest winning margin in the history of the race. After another stop in Uruguay, Tracy decided on the homeward leg that a crew of women could compete in the race. Her fellow crew-members did not think that it was a good idea, but she persisted for the next four years in fund-raising and preparation.

She first went to see the chairman of the Whitbread Race Committee, who told her that there were no rules against her idea. In 1986, aged just 23, Tracy set about raising £1.8 million to take part in the Whitbread Round-the-World Yacht Race, with an all-women crew. The boat was to be named *Maiden, Great Britain*, a play on the words 'Made in Great Britain'. She had to mortgage her house, and bought a run-down 58-foot sloop called *Prestige*, in Cape Town, which had raced in the 1981-82 race as *Disque D'Or III*. It was small, dilapidated, covered with weeds and completely unseaworthy, and cost her £115,000 plus a few thousand pounds to strap in on top of a container to bring it back to England. When the crew celebrated its launch in Southampton, it promptly began to sink. Tracy now had to mortgage the boat for a complete refit. Money had run out, and she now needed £800,000 to actually take part in the race. She had a £350,000 overdraft and her bank manager was extremely nervous before King Hussein stepped in to help. He brokered a deal whereby Royal Jordanian Airways became *Maiden's* main sponsor. The Duchess of York officially launched the refitted *Maiden*, and Tracy decided to skipper the yacht as well as to navigate. The jobs usually went to separate people. The boat was not only small, but heavy. Other boats were made of carbon, and would be much quicker in light winds.

There was a 'warm-up' race for most of the Whitbread yachts, the 'Route of Discovery' race from Cadiz near Gibraltar, to Santo Domingo in the Dominican Republic. It would give the crew of 12 an opportunity to bond as a team. *Maiden* finished second overall and first on handicap, beating all the other Whitbread yachts and the winner of the 1985-86 race, Pierre Fehlmann. This was a marvellous and unexpected result, but there were still 8 months until the start of the Whitbread. The overdraft had crept up again to £100,000, and Tracy felt embarrassed asking Royal Jordanian Airlines for more money, especially as no British company would invest in *Maiden Great Britain*. Tracy managed to secure £450,000, enough to get halfway round in the race. The first leg was to Punta del Este in Uruguay. *The Daily Express* commented: 'Hardly rated to be in with even a prayer, despite trial success, the all girl crew in the round the world yacht race was given a stirring and "Britain expects" style send-off by the Duchess of York on the weekend... As most of the fleet disappeared over the horizon, *Maiden* was left trailing behind.' *Maiden* crossed the Atlantic 3rd from last in the fleet, but 3rd in its class. The Duchess of York, visiting her mother in Argentina, met the crew.

The next leg was the Southern Ocean, the hardest part of the race. In foul conditions, *Maiden* sailed to Fremantle, and arrived on 3 December 1989. Newspapers called it the longest, toughest leg in the history of the Whitbread. One man had died, and seven had gone overboard, including Claire Russell, the *Maiden's* medic. *Maiden* finished with an overall lead of 16 hours in its class, the best result by a British yacht for 12 years. It was first over the line in Division D, and first on handicap. The skippers and crews on the maxi-yachts stood as one and cheered the girls as they sailed into port. However, sponsorship money had once again run out. The British entry *Rothmans* had a budget five times larger than *Maiden's*, but the tobacco company was not getting its expected payback. However, Royal Jordanian Airlines officials were delighted, and again came to Tracy's rescue. The crew spent some time repairing the mast, stripping their 17 winches and re-splicing worn rigging and sheets affected by storm damage. A container had been sent to each stop-over with spares and equipment. There were 47 sails for *Maiden*, of which Tracy chose 26 for each leg, dependent upon prospective conditions. At the Fremantle presentation night, *Maiden* won more prizes than any other boat in the fleet.

The critics and cynics were starting to believe that the female crew could actually finish the race. Bob Fisher, called by Tracy 'the doyen of sailing journalists', apologised in *Yacht and Yachting*: 'OK, so I take it all back. I'll admit I was more than a touch cynical about the potential of the all girl crew on the *Maiden*, particularly their ability to handle the Southern Ocean legs. I formed my opinion without finding out that the *Maiden* ladies were a terribly determined bunch.

May 1990 Maiden crosses the finish line

Now, eating everything I have said, I praise them unreservedly for their efforts. It is 12 years since any British boat won anything in the Whitbread. For Maiden to take line honours and handicap first place for the second leg is a sterling effort which should make others who were even more critical than myself sit up and take notice... they proved beyond all doubt that they are quite an extraordinary group of women to whom I raise my glass.' However, the girls had other critics they wished to convert when they started the third leg. One of the rival skippers had called their success a fluke.

On this shortest leg of the race, *Maiden* just beat *L'Ésprit* by an hour into Auckland. 14,000 people were waiting at one in the morning around Prince's Wharf for *Maiden* to arrive and win the leg. The lead in Class D was extended to 18 hours, more than *Steinlager II's* lead in the 'Maxis' class. Tracy arrived to the news that she had been voted 'Yachtsman of the Year', the first woman in its 35 years history to win the award. The race restarted on 4 February, and *Maiden* suffered the loss of its generator, and a crew member was hurled across the wheel with such force that the wheel broke. The crew were cold and constantly wet, the weather charts were wrong, and Tracy had taken the boat too far south to try and catch up with *l'Ésprit*. They were to be the first all-woman crew to round Cape Horn. The yacht began to leak badly, and the repaired generator was flooded. The mast was shaking itself to pieces, and Tracy knew that their chances of winning Division D had all but evaporated as the boat limped towards Uruguay. They were now 17 hours behind *l'Ésprit*. The next leg was a short one, to Fort Lauderdale, Florida but a lack of wind lost the boat hours on its competitors. However, the team decided to arrive in Florida in style, arriving in their swimsuits to prove that they could lose both gracefully and with a sense of fun. There was a telephone call from Buckingham Palace announcing Tracy's MBE, as the team was repairing the yacht.

The last leg of 4,000 miles to Southampton left Fort Lauderdale on May 5, 1990. Tracy was already thinking of another attempt on the race, now she was sure that they could not win. She reckoned that Royal Jordanian Airlines had received around £26 million worth of publicity against its investment of £800,000. *Maiden* hit a tornado that literally spun it around facing the other way, and damaged the mast. Then the wind dropped to almost nothing and *Maiden* was virtually becalmed, before it hit storms in the last 800 miles to Southampton. The leak reoccurred, the generator broke down, and a halyard broke, before *Maiden* was just headed by Rucanor into Southampton. 600 boats followed *Maiden* in, and 20,000 people lined the quayside, chanting '*Maiden! Maiden! Maiden!*' The crew had finished second in Division D and 3rd in the combined division C and D. Her yacht was the first to win two legs of the race. She had desperately wanted to win, but was also furious that not one, of over 300 British companies she had approached, had helped the attempt. Tracy was on *This is Your Life* and feted across Britain. In 1989 she was the first woman to win the Yachtsman of the Year award. She was voted Sportswoman of the Year and Sports Personality of the Year, and married Simon Lawrence, but had to sell *Maiden* to pay off her massive debts, and give the crew a bonus of £8,000 each, on which Tracy paid the tax.

Dawn Riley recalled: '*Maiden* was a group of women who wanted to do the race at a time when there were very few opportunities for women to sail at any professional level racing. Skipper Tracy Edwards found the sponsorship, I joined as watch captain, and the entire crew did the boat work and the logistics and the sailing and the navigating and the cleaning... and the celebrating when we won the two Southern Ocean legs. Looking back, those were the two legs that many 'experts' had predicted we might die in. And that was before the course included ice gates.' (Ice Gates are compulsory crossing points for Vendée Globe racers in the southern seas. Their aim is to prevent skippers from sailing too deep in the South, in order to minimize the collision risks with drift ice.)

However, personal problems and the break-up of her marriage meant that Tracy fled the limelight and went to live in the lovely coastal village of Llangennith, back in the Gower. She bought the run-down College Mill, bought some horses, and settled into small-scale farming and showing horses. For two years, she had what she calls the best therapy of her life, until she met up with her old acquaintance Will Carling, who invited her to work for his comany Insights. It used sports people to teach teamwork, motivation and leadership skills to business people, and Tracy received glowing reports for her presentations. By the summer of 1993, she was thinking about the Whitbread once more, but its popularity meant that every city wanted to host it, with legs becoming as short as 350 miles. Instead, she decided that she wanted to break the world record for non-stop circumnavigation.

For *Maiden*, Tracy had needed to raise £1.2 million. For this new challenge she would need £3.2 million. In 1998 Tracy attempted to win the Jules Verne Trophy, in a 92-foot catamaran, the *Enza*. In 1993, it had been forced to abandon its attempt after 26 days, when it hit some floating debris. In 1994, it beat the record of 79 days 6 hours with a time of 74 days 22 hours. It was for sale in San Diego in 1995 and she mortgaged her farmhouse to part-pay it. After borrowing from friends, she was still £186,000 short, when a benefactor loaned her the remainder, interest-free. When Tracy handed over the final instalment in March 1996, she was the owner of the biggest, fastest, catamaran in the world. Tracy now spent £350,000 on refitting *Enza*, which she now called *Lady Endeavor*, but could not sail the boat away until she found the money. Her debts had spiralled up to £900,000. She said 'I owe more than a million pounds - I have two months to find the money, or I lose everything - even my friends.' Fortunately, Royal Sun Alliance agreed to sponsor the catamaran. In 1997, the Jules Verne Trophy had been taken by the Frenchman Olivier de Kersauson in 71 days 14 hours - it had taken him 4 years and 7 attempts to break the record. To test the boat, and the different

techniques needed for a catamaran, Tracy's 10-woman crew covered 1,516 miles in the first 4 days across the Atlantic in 1997, but were then becalmed and had to forget their attempt on the Atlantic record. The boat was now named the *Royal and Sun Alliance.*

In February 1998, they beat the record-holder's time to the Equator, and went on to sail seven consecutive 400+ mile days as well as one impressive 500 mile day. This feat has only been equalled by a handful of all-male crews. After 43 gruelling days at sea, the catamaran lost its mast. By harnessing the strength, experience and professionalism of her team, Tracy and the crew created a temporary rig and reached the safety of Chile without help. A media release reads: '*Royal & Sun Alliance*, the 92 foot catamaran skippered by Tracy Edwards with an all-female crew of ten, has been forced to abandon its attempt on the Round the World non-stop record for the Trophée Jules Verne. In pitch darkness at 0850 GMT this morning, on her 43rd day at sea having covered approximately 15,200 miles since setting off from Ushant, north-west France on 3rd February, disaster struck *Royal & Sun Alliance*. In 40-foot seas and winds gusting from 30 to 50 knots, a huge wave came up behind them, lifting the stern and burying both bows in the wave ahead bringing the boat to a shuddering halt.

About five minutes later, creaking could be heard from the top of the mast and the whole thing just crumpled over the port side and broke up as it hit the hull. The all-female crew, who are safe and well, are getting to grips with the new challenge of making the boat sailable and heading for land, some 2,000 miles away in South America. There is no possibility of pursuing the record. At the time of the disaster, the boat had covered about 350 miles in the last 24 hours, and had averaged 435 miles a day over the last 9 days in the relentless pursuit of the record of 71 days 14 hours, 22 minutes and 8 seconds set last year by the Frenchman Olivier de Kersauson. Speaking from the boat, Tracy Edwards said "We are disappointed beyond belief as we went so close to getting to Cape Horn is such good time against the record. Words cannot describe how we feel at the moment although the girls are once again pulling on their reserves of strength to get through this."' Before setting off the team had smashed the Channel record by 40 minutes at an average speed of 22.7 knots, which was the fastest ocean sailing record in the world. Tracy held the Australia to New Zealand record and the fastest time from Cowes to Fastnet Rock. Tracy gave birth to her daughter Mackenna in 1999, in the midst of planning for a second attempt on the Jules Verne Trophy in 2003. The crew was the same, except that Tracy was project manager rather than racing with the team. She now runs TEAM, a management motivation company, and raises money for the MS Society, notably in 2001 with Multiple Challenge for sufferers to raise money by sailing around the coasts of Britain.

Tracy began managing sailing programs, beginning with *Maiden II* in 2000. *Maiden II* was the first ever mixed professional racing crew aboard a Maxi Multihull, and they broke the Trans-Atlantic and 24-hour records in 2002. In 2003 she set up Quest International Sports Events and signed a £6 million sponsorship deal with the Crown Prince of Qatar to create two round-the-world races and a marina complex. HSBC sponsored the first event to the tune of £3 million. This was the first time a round-the-world has started and finished in the Middle East, based in Doha. Edwards had personally borrowed £8m from the bank to help fund the event, personally paying each boat $1 million to enter the race, and putting up her home as collateral, on the strength of a £6m sponsorship agreement. In the successful *Oryx Quest 05* in Qatar, four of the fastest multihulls in the world took part. The *Oryx Quest* 2005 was a huge success and created $46m worth of press coverage for the gulf state. However, Qatar refused to pay Tracy the £8 million she had borrowed to facilitate the event and pay the teams to enter. Qatar also refused to pay the $1 million prize money. Quest consequently went into receivership and Tracy was forced into bankruptcy in September 2005. Her ground-breaking project opened up the Middle East to first time sailing events in Oman, Abu Dhabi and Dubai and has paved the way for sponsorship in those countries. (Incidentally, 4,000 'guest workers' are predicted to die before the absurdly awarded football World Cup in Qatar. As of 2015, over 1,200 have already died, on an average wage of £40 a week, in the building programme estimated to finally cost $260 billion).

Tracy and her family were held against her will for 28 days in Qatar, whilst the authorities tried to force her to sign a waiver exonerating them from the sponsorship. Tracy refused to sign, exhibiting the strength of character that has characterised her sailing projects. Her refusal to sign and her fighting spirit ensured that legal action against Qatar could commence in the hope that she, her team and event suppliers could one day be compensated. She remembers the day she went bankrupt: 'It was my 43rd birthday and also the day my daughter started her new school. I managed to keep it together that morning but when I got back I just curled up into the corner of the kitchen floor and cried. But I knew if I didn't stop, I'd never stop. So I stood up.' She lost her home, had to put her mother, suffering from multiple sclerosis, into care and was raising her young daughter alone.

She left sailing and went to work for the Child Exploitation and Online Protection Centre (CEOP) as Project Manager for their International Youth Advisory Congress. Upon completion, despite leaving school at 15 with no qualifications, she attended Roehampton University and took a degree in psychology. She continued with her higly-rated motivational speaking and became a life coach. In 2013 she began teaching Internet Safety and Online Reputation to children and parents and works in schools and with youth groups. In 2014, Edwards discovered that *Maiden* was abandoned in poor condition in a marina in the Indian Ocean. She launched a public bid for funding to save the ship, with the intent to re-enact its Whitbread run before putting it in charitable use and displaying it in British maritime museums. She is now heavily involved with the Maiden Rescue charity.

Her three main charity commitments are as Patron of Regenerate UK, working in Roehampton with disadvantaged young people; to the NSPCC as an Ambassador; and as an Ambassador to Gingerbread which gives free advice and help to single parents. She is also involved with The Lady Taverners, The Prince's Trust, The Ahoy Centre, Emmaus, Action for Children and The Duke of Edinburgh Awards Scheme. Tracy's tumultuous childhood has given her a unique way to contribute to the organisations she helps and she is passionately committed to giving youngsters a second chance. Sailing gave Tracy a future at a time in her life when things could have gone badly wrong and now she uses that experience to help others. Her is a remarkable and inspirational story of battling against the odds and refusing to give up.

*Footnote:*
An all-female crew, TEAM-SCA has just won a leg in the Volvo Round-the-World race, the first to do so since Tracy Edwards in 1990. The yacht design for the class was amended to put less of a premium upon physical strength, which makes Edwards' achievement all the more remarkable.

# DR MERERID HOPWOOD 18 February 1964-

## THE FIRST WOMAN TO WIN THE BARDIC CHAIR*, AND THE ONLY WOMAN TO HAVE WON THE CHAIR, THE CROWN AND MEDAL RYDDIAITH (PROSE MEDAL)

Mererid Hopwood made history in 2001 by becoming the first woman ever to win the Bardic Chair at the National Eisteddfod. Although her family is from Pembrokeshire, she was brought up in Cardiff where she and her brother attended Bryntaf, Cardiff's first Welsh primary school, and then Ysgol Gyfun Llanhari. From there, Mererid took a year out to attend the Schiller Gymnasium in Heidenheim, Germany and teach English in a large secondary school in Malaga, Spain. Mererid then studied Modern Languages in Aberystwyth, graduating in 1987 with a first class honours in Spanish and German. Later that year she married and enrolled as a PhD student at University College London. Since 1993 she has lived in Llangynnwr, Carmarthen with her husband. They have two daughters and one son. With the exception of five years heading up the Arts Council of Wales office in Mid and West Wales, Mererid has spent her career in education. She has taught languages across the sector, mainly at university, but she has also run sessions from primary school to adults and evening classes.

In 2011 Mererid won the Chair at the National Eisteddfod for her poem *Dadeni* (Rebirth), the first female ever to achieve such accomplishment. Then, in 2003 Mererid won the Crown at the National Eisteddfod in Meifod, with her *pryddest* (a poem not in full strict metre) *Gwreiddiau* (Roots). In 2008 she was awarded the Eisteddfod's Prose Medal for her book O Ran. In August 2009, following the death of Dic Jones, Mererid was one of two nominated to follow him for the position of Archdruid of the National Eisteddfod, the first time a woman had been nominated, but withdrew, leaving T. James Jones to fill the vacancy.

Since 2010 she has worked in the University of Wales, Trinity St David where she is currently Reader and Director of Strategic Partnerships at the University's Centre of Teacher Education. The Centre builds on the University's historic strengths of working closely with schools and other partners in developing excellent learning and teaching, promoting the Welsh language and culture, and providing high levels of care and support to its students. Mererid works tirelessly to try and popularize *cynghanedd* (an intricate system of alliteration and rhyme) especially amongst girls and young people. She was the *Bardd Plant* (Children's Poet) in 2005. She has also presented programmes on S4C and Radio Cymru.

Her publications include: *Sarah Kirsch* (1997); *Singing in Chains: Listening to Welsh Verse* (2004); *Ar Bwys* (2007); *O Ran* (2008); *Trysor Mamgu* (2009); *Cynghanedd i Blant* (2010) and *Straeon O'r Mabinogi* (2011). She has edited, translated and contributed to many other publications. In 2012 she was awarded the Glyndŵr Award for her contribution to literature, by MOMA, Machynlleth. Mererid is an Honorary Fellow Literature Wales, Honorary Fellow UWTSD, Honrary President of the Waldo Williams Society, Board Member of *Gorsedd y Beirdd* and *Cymdeithas y Cymod*. In 2015 she was awarded a Literature Wales Writer's Bursary to give her the opportunity to work on her first volume of poems. Her readings in literary festivals include: The Hay Festival; Gŵyl Dinefwr Festival; Gŵyl Tŷ Newydd Festival; Children's Literature Festival, Cardiff; Gŵyl Gynganeddu, Tŷ Newydd; Leipzig Book Fair, Germany; Jaipur Literature Festival, Rajasthan, India; Argentina: Buenos Aires, University of Trelew and Austral University, Valdivia, Chile. She is currently working on *Aberfan*, a commemorative work with the composer Karl Jenkins, and *Wythnos yng Nghymru Fydd*, an opera with the composer Gareth Glyn.

Her poem *Wedi Cad Coludd ar Ddrain*, translated from the Welsh, was written for the *Peace News* 'The World is My Country' poster series. It takes as its title a line from Cynddelw Brydydd Mawr's work, a 12th Century Welsh poet, the line translates: 'After battle I saw entrails on thorns'. It was inspired by the WW1 pacifist campaigner, Charlotte Despard, who declared 'I should like the words "alien" and "foreign" be banished from the language. We are all members of the same family.'

*Wedi Cad Coludd ar Ddrain*
'The wind that shakes the memory tree wakes me.
It tears the flesh from the carcass of the mare that rides my night,
And howling, hurls it, skin and meat,
to dress the wounded branches, furious fright,
beside the entrails of my brother,
my father, my sister, my mother.
For there is no foreigner,
no alien, no other.
This is the mercy of memory.
And then before me, bold, bright,
dawn's first blade slits the day open –
and unforgotten
the tree now sliced with light's clean knife
shows me how it grieves for the leaves of life.'

A new Bardic Chair is specially designed and made for each eisteddfod and is awarded to the winning entrant in the competition for the *awdl*, poetry written in the strict metre form known as *cynghanedd*. The National Eisteddfod ceremony is presided over by the Archdruid, who reads the judges' comments before announcing the identity of the bard, using only the *nom de plume* that the winner has used to submit the work. Up to this point, no one knows the true identity of the bard, who is asked to stand and is then escorted to the stage. Local children perform a dance to honour the new bard. The other great award is the crowning of the bard. A new Bardic Crown is specially designed and made for each National Eisteddfod and is awarded to the winning entrant in the competition for the *pryddest*, poetry written in free verse. As with the chair, *nom de plumes* are used. The *Medal Ryddiaeth* is the third major literary award, for the best prose work. Sometimes these awards are not presented, because the standard is not considered high enough, so to achieve just one is a wonderful achievement.

## HELEN WYNNE THOMAS 16 August 1966 – 5 August 1989

## GREENHAM COMMON MARTYR

It is a little-known fact that the Greenham Common Women's Peace Camp began with a march of Cardiff women, from the Welsh capital to Berkshire, between 27 August and 5 September in 1981. They called themselves *Women for Life on Earth*. We must remember that this was the time of the Cold War and the constant threat of nuclear war. It was led by Ann Pettit of Llanpumsaint and three young mothers. The 110-mile walk was to protest against the NATO decision to  site Cruise Missiles at the RAF base there, which then became a base for the USAF. These missiles can travel over intercontinental distances, carrying nuclear as well as conventional payloads. 36 women, 4 babies and 6 men formed the initial march from Wales.

The 36 women, together with male supporters, delivered a letter to the Base Commander requesting a discussion on the expected arrival of the missiles.

However, when talks were refused, the group decided to remain at the base as a peace camp. From these humble beginnings there grew a series of camps surrounding the base, the last of which persisted for 19 years. The peace camp, which became women-only in 1982, saw thousands live in very basic conditions in all weathers with the constant threat of eviction, and ongoing harassment from police, military or vigilantes.

The women set up the first *Peace Camp* outside the base's main gate, which became known as 'Yellow Gate'. When other satellite peace camps sprang up around the 9-mile perimeter fence, each camp was given a name from the colours of the rainbow. The first act of civil disobedience was when the Welsh women chained themselves to the perimeter fence. On 14 November, 1983, 96 Ground Launch Cruise Missiles arrived. Women now joined the peace protest from all parts of the United Kingdom, determined upon non-violent direct action to rid the site of nuclear weapons.

It was a women-only movement, and the Campaign for Nuclear Disarmament commented: 'There was some opposition from within CND and the wider peace movement to the fact that men were barred from the camp, but this largely melted away as the determination, imagination and the energy of the Greenham Women became clear. In spite of press hostility and physical abuse including repeated, often quite brutal eviction, they stayed at the base, sometimes in their thousands, sometimes a few dozen only, but never giving up.' When Greenham Common was taken over by the military, it was not deregistered as a Common, so trespass laws could not be applied against the women.

However, probably illegal joint action by the Ministry of Defence, Newbury District Council and the USAF led to many evictions, arrests and imprisonment for the women around the base. Four years after the first peace camps, in 1985 the MOD introduced new by-laws (under the arcane 1892 Military Lands Act) to curtail women's intrusions into the base. Jean Hutchinson and Georgina Smith spent 4 years in litigation challenging these new by-laws as they interfered with 'commoners' rights', and in 1990 the by-laws were declared illegal in Crown Court. Undeterred, Michael Heseltine's department quickly made new laws which then allowed hundreds of the protesting women to be arrested and criminalised under RAF by-laws. (It is strange that some laws are passed more quickly than others. The author is still waiting for a law that enables him to physically evict burglars from his house, without the threat of imprisonment to the evictor).

Indeed, all construction carried out on the site under the USAF had been actually illegal, because it had no consent from the Secretary of State for the Environment. The MOD had set out to buy 'commoners' rights', from 1988. From 1996 their action was disputed by the Women's Peace Camp group at Reading Crown Court, and even as of July 2001 the case was still under appeal. There was some opposition from CND as men were barred from the peace camp, but the determination, energy and spirit of the women in the face of often brutal evictions ensured that it melted away. The overwhelming and constant press hostility towards these courageous women should be noted. Attempts to blacken the name of the Greenham Women was notably assisted by public taxation, in the form of counter-subversion units of MI5, and by generally unhelpful media coverage, including the BBC.

Declassified MOD documents confirm that there is radioactivity on the Common, leaving thousands of women contaminated, from when a nuclear weapon burned in a 1958 accident. Of course, the British people were not told about this - it is a secret footnote in history, disclosed 40 years later. An American B-47 bomber had caught fire, with its nuclear bomb aboard. The conventional explosive in the burning warhead exploded, releasing deadly uranium and plutonium oxide powder over an area several miles around the base. Several people were killed, and the fire of the plane and bomb burned for 5 days, reaching temperatures as high as 1,000 degrees Celsius because of the high magnesium content. It is not known what happened to the radioactive wreckage - was it simply buried?

Aldermaston recorded contamination on the Greenham Common runway in 1960 with uranium-235 and plutonium-239 present, and the Government confirmed the existence of the report, telling Parliament that the contents must remain secret. No clean-up operation took place, and 600,000 tons of concrete runway was broken up, causing dust to be spread over miles. The use of foam to try and control the inferno will have bonded radioactive particles to the concrete, which have now been released into Berkshire's atmosphere. There was a well-known cancer cluster in the area, with children suffering from leukaemia. Another 1987 Aldermaston report confirmed the nuclear accident, and the so-called *Saxby Report* was also classified as secret. (CND has further details - it appears that top politicians in any political party in any political system will always veer to the cover of secrecy rather than tell the truth).

Apart from the danger of radioactive causation cancers, and a heavy police activity, the campaigners also seem to have been targeted with other means to make their presence uncomfortable. In December 1985, the respected journal *Electronics Today* made a series of recordings and noted: 'Readings taken with a wide range of signal strength meters showed marked increases in the back-ground signal level near one of the women's camps at the time when they claimed to be experiencing ill effects. They noted that if the women created noise or a disturbance near the fence, the signals rose sharply.' And *The Guardian*, 10 March 1986 reported 'The American military at Greenham Common has an intruder detection system called BISS (Base Installation Security System) which operates on a sufficiently high frequency to bounce radar waves off a human body moving in the vicinity of this microwave perimeter fence.' The Americans had used a similar device in Vietnam.

The effects of non-ionising radiation on humans was known to the US military from *Project Pandora*, in that it can cause several types of cancer, possibly also to descendants of the recipient. Whether the women were irradiated by permanent proximity to the fence, or targeted by a microwave weapon, or both, they will never know. From late 1985, the women began suffering from unusual patterns of illness, ranging from 'severe headaches, drowsiness, menstrual bleeding at abnormal times, or after the onset of the menopause, to bouts of temporary paralysis and faulty speech co-ordination'. These led to the request to *Electronics Today* for an independent scientific survey. Tests taken revealed microwave radiation up to 100 times greater than in background readings away from the base. Protesters complained of headaches, paralysis, nausea and palpitations, the classic symptoms of microwave poisoning.

However, a participant in the camp had explained in 1983: 'What is really great about the movement and those who fight back, with everything to gain and nothing to lose, is that new human relations exist in it. People's values and attitudes change, they seem to move beyond the constraints and conditioning that society imposes on us. I think that inspires me above everything, to see the transformation in people'.

Several times women entered the camp. On New Year's Eve 1982 the women broke into the base for the first time; 44 women climbed over the military base's fence and climbed on top of the silos and danced around on them for hours. All the women were arrested, and 36 were imprisoned. The next major event was 'Reflect the Base' on 11 December 1983, when 50,000 women circled the base to protest against the Cruise missiles which had arrived three weeks earlier. The day started as a silent vigil, where women held up mirrors as to allow the base to symbolically look back at itself and its actions. The day ended with hundreds of arrests as the women pulled down large sections of the fence.

Against this background we can discuss Helen Thomas*, a young Welsh woman from Newcastle Emlyn, who saw no need for nuclear weapons in our country. Helen's involvement came about when she had finished her history degree at Lampeter University and decided she wanted to take a year out. After a stint of working for Women's Aid and various other charities while living in Cardiff, she became inspired by the women of Greenham. Her mother Janet, a magistrate, told *Wales on Sunday*: 'Helen went down at the beginning of 1989. They had been short of women at that time and she wanted to get involved. She wrote back to us and would tell us what an incredible inspiration the women were and how she really wanted to give her time to peace. At the time, Mrs Thomas said she was terrified for Helen, but her daughter's resolve was too strong. She turned to me and said "you don't really want me to go, do you?" I asked if it made any difference and she said it wouldn't. She was very determined. We communicated a lot and I would say to her, "why don't you come home, get a decent job and be involved at Greenham part time", but true to herself she said "working for peace and justice was not a part-time job."'

She left Cardiff to live at Yellow Gate in May 1989, and at the time of her death she was busy translating pamphlets produced at the camp into Welsh. She was a feminist, Welsh-speaker, and a supporter of Welsh and Irish independence. Between 25 and 27 May she painted protest slogans on the runway and Buildings 301, 302 and 303, for which she was arrested and charged under Section 1(1) of the 1971 Criminal Damage Act. If she had lived, at her trial upon 18 August, she would have set a historical precedent as being the first woman to have been tried in an English court in Welsh, her first language. She hitch-hiked to Cardiff, to collect a typewriter from friends to type-up a pamphlet on non-violent direct action. She told her friends how she had spent the night in Imber, and how she had 'decorated' a warplane and a hangar with some red paint ('Stop your killing', 'The treaty is a con') and was busily preparing for her court case. She told them she saw her defence as her opportunity to publicly discuss the parallels that she she saw between the Army unlawfully taking the village of Imber and the flooding of Capel Celyn (the Trywerin struggle), and linking that to the struggle in Ireland and the shortage of affordable housing in the UK. It was classic non-violent direct action, just a bit of property damage, estimated to be less than £2k.

Upon 15 August 1989, the Greenham women intended to occupy the village church at Imber, in Wiltshire. The West Midlands Police illegally attempted to stop them leaving the Yellow Gate camp. In the confusion, Helen was crushed by a police horse-box just outside the main gates of the Greenham Common USAF base. The protest was halted, but the protesters were left well alone by the police, when they decided to go ahead with the symbolic occupation just 11 days later, upon what would have been Helen's 23rd birthday. Helen had previously written the justification for the occupation of Imber Church, knowing full well how many Welsh villages in Pembroke and Brecon had been taken over by the armed forces forever:

'We want to draw attention to the relationship between the thousands that are homeless in Britain, and the millions of pounds that are spent on death - £15,000,000 at this moment in time on building FIBUA - a village on Salisbury Plain. FIBUA stands for "Fighting in Built-Up Areas". But nobody will live in this village. It will be used to prepare soldiers to fight on the streets of Germany. How much of this money could have been spent on building homes for Welsh-speaking Welsh people to enable them to have the choice of staying in their communities? There is another village on Salisbury Plain - IMBER - that was illegally seized by the military. Today IMBER is used to prepare soldiers for the oppression and killing in Northern Ireland. We want to reveal the evil and secret purpose of this village, and the real purpose of the military in Britain, which is to defend the oppressive state that steals our resources, and oppress our people every day through poverty and lack of services.'

A letter to *New Internationalist* from the Yellow Gate women, on 5 September 1991, reads: 'This day marks 10 years of non-stop women's resistance to militarism outside the main gates of RAF/USAF Greenham Common. Many will be surprised that we are still here; the British state met the camps' persistent, non-violent, non-aligned challenge to the military with strict censorship and police violence. And on August 5th, 1989 a young Welsh woman living and working at the base was killed by a West Midlands horse-box. Helen's mother, dissatisfied with the cursory inquest into her daughter's death, fought bravely to get to the truth of what happened. But recently a Judicial Review turned down her application for a re-opening of the inquest to examine more thoroughly the conflicting evidence

**Women surrounding the perimeter fences at Greenham Common**

which was presented. The camp has endured much censorship, harassment and violence over the past ten years, but the killing of Helen Thomas was the most tragic. Nevertheless we continue our campaign...'

Her parents John and Janet have long maintained there was a cover-up and that standard procedures were not followed. They have raised questions about why the driver was never breathalysed, why a crucial witness was not called to give evidence, and why the coroner instructed the jury to return an accidental verdict. But despite challenging the inquest verdict through a judicial review in the High Court, a judge refused to allow a fresh inquest. 'It is not the verdict itself that upset us but the way that verdict was reached,' Mrs Thomas said. 'I cannot help thinking that there was a cover-up, and that cover-up started immediately after my daughter was killed. Was it because my daughter was at Greenham Common that we did not get a fair inquest?'

Until recently**, there was a ring of Welsh stones and a memorial area for Helen at Greenham, and the Cardiff marchers are remembered in a £20,000 bronze statue in the National Assembly in Cardiff Bay. Another full-sizes bronze statue has been sculpted, 'of a woman who is every woman - who took part at Greenham: she is no particular woman'. Intended to commemorate the 20 years since the march began, the statue was cast in Narberth. A plaque was placed on 27 August 2001 at Cardiff's temple of Peace, and another at the Community Church in Newport where the marchers spent their first night.

The circumstances of Helen's death are mystifying. It was alleged that she was dancing on the road in front of police when the horsebox hit her, but her Greenham friends did not believe this. There was no protest going on at the time, and she had left her tent to post a letter. Her mother Janet said 'She wasn't involved in any protest when she died. She died when she crossed the road to post a letter.' Jean Hutchinson had been told by eye-witnesses: 'Helen was just waiting to cross the road to go to the Post Office - all kinds of lies were told about this - that she had been dancing in front of the vehicle. I was in town and I came back just a couple of minutes after it happened. It was a terrible shock. It was 75 yards from the main gate. A Ministry of Defence policeman told the truth and said Helen was just waiting and the vehicle swerved into her. The wing mirror hit her head and knocked her.'

Of course, the West Midlands Police Force at this time had the reputation as the most corrupt in Britain, and their standing among the Irish community has never recovered from their treatment of the innocent 'pub bombers'. Like Aberfan and so many other tragedies and miscarriages of justice in the history of Britain in the 20th century, the truth is never allowed to surface from the layers of official and political camouflage. We must also remember that the women were subject to daily abuse from local people and their children, as well as from the upholders of law and order. Helen's mother told *The Western Mail* (19 June 2000): 'It's hard to believe that people can be treated in this way. While the camp was still open, I visited and sat there many times (often on the anniversary of Helen's death), and I could see the buses of children going past with them putting their tongues out. They didn't know any better because this was the attitude they had learnt. I came to understand why the women stayed there, but there are a lot of people who don't understand why people do that kind of thing... We thought when the inquest comes we'll hear the truth, but we believed it couldn't have been much further from the truth. It was such an injustice that came out of it all. And that's what made us think this is what these women have lived with. We were shocked because we weren't used to it.

We realised on the day of the inquest that it was a cover-up - it was obvious. You couldn't help but realise it. The Ministry of Defence man who was watching - he said she wasn't even on the road and he did stand up and stick to his words in court. He left afterwards, he was getting all sorts of jibes. It was all decided before the inquest came. I want to believe that it was an accident, but there was too much cover-up. If it was an accident why cover it up at all? It was quite possible it was an accident. It was a big vehicle and a narrow part of the road - these things happen. But why the cover-up then? Why not say all these things? But instead they have to say that she stepped out into the road, making out as if she was responsible for her own death. There were so many different versions of the day, but the coroner decided to take the easier version, that she stepped out into the road.

She was a careful person. Why make out as if she was a careless person and not worried about her own safety? It belittled her somehow. Quite an issue was made at the time that the driver wasn't breathalysed. No-one suggested that he had been drinking, but on the other hand it's normal that everyone is breathalysed. It's a pity they didn't do all these things...It has opened my eyes to a lot of things.'

Janet Thomas challenged the inquest decision and took the issue for judicial review to the High Court a year after Helen's death. The High Court criticised the way that the inquest was handled but did not change the verdict. John and Janet Thomas decided to give up the costly process of appeal. Janet Thomas commented: 'It could have gone on forever, but we felt that Helen would not have wanted us to carry on. We are not the same people as we were before Helen died. We are not as strong as we were and there's only so far you can go. I feel that we have got to believe what we think is right and be satisfied that we will never get the truth.'

On 5 March 1991, the last Cruise Missile had left Greenham Common and upon 30 September 1992, the USAF left the site. The protesters stayed on the site to ensure that the (contaminated) land was returned to the Commoners, and the hated perimeter fence removed. Women turned their attentions to the nuclear sites - the Atomic Weapons Establishments - at nearby Aldermaston and Burghfield. In January 1994, the last of the satellite camps closed. This is yet another sad chapter involving lies from the untouchable military, police, judiciary, media*** and politicians, buried from the British people. Unfortunately, we tend to believe what we are told, which is often biased and partial information. Even the Wikipedia entry upon *Greenham Common Women's Peace Camp* as of 7 July 2014 makes no mention of Helen's killing. Helen and her parents John and Janet Thomas suffered for truth. Helen Thomas is a truly inspirational woman, whose intelligence, courage in the face of adversity, and above all desire to change things for a better future must always be remembered. She is a true twentieth century heroine of Cymru.

* Some of Helen's poems (which she performed at Chapter Arts Centre, Cardiff) can be found on the web, at a site called bitter.custard/beyond/poets/helen/helen.htm. Just one is included here:

'Rape
...is telling you

"you should be ashamed"
you feeling ashamed

you not being able to share your fears
feeling afraid

...is bulldozing carcasses
...is being able to tell people what to do
is them
'wanting' to do it

...is killing hope and ideals

scissors cutting skin.'

** Disgracefully, and obliterating meaningful history, the memorial was obliterated in 2013, bulldozed by the owners of the Greenham Common Enterprise Centre that owns the site. Bulldozers arrived at around 8am and began to rip up all the flowers and stones including even the memorial to Helen Thomas. The memorial was a garden of seven standing stones encircling the 'Flame' sculpture which represented a camp fire. A woman called the Greenham Common Trust which runs the site and was told that the memorial had 'been there long enough' and was 'a problem for local traffic'. The entire garden is now gone and the land is simply earth with all traces removed.

When the base closed, the women planned a garden on the site of the nuclear nightmare. The Peace Garden was established in 2002 to mark the action. 'It was an undeveloped piece of land when we put tents on it; now it has sculptures, stones and special plants.' Part of the garden was dedicated to Helen Thomas. Sarah Hipperson, one of the protesters, worked upon establishing it for 12 years. She raised £78,000 for the garden, most of it coming from small donations made by hundreds of people. Hipperson saw the handing over of the peace garden as her final act, completing the Greenham cycle. The land, handed back to the people. She recalled that at times during the protest, the local people were far from friendly.

The complete landscaping included Snowdrops, Snowflakes, Autumn Crocus, Wild Daffodils and Lily of the Valley. Other plantings included a variety of specially chosen British Native plants, and an Oak sapling, rescued from the Newbury Bypass, was also included. To honour Greenham's strong Welsh connections, they decided to use Pennant sandstone from Wales for the monument. 'It was a moving moment on 9 November 2002, when the Peace Garden was handed over to the Greenham Common Community Trust. In a fine drizzle of rain, a Japanese maple was planted to the haunting strains of *Mae gen i freuddwyd* (*I have a dream*), sung by Côr Cochion. Members of the choir, Sue Lent, Beaty Smith and Ray Davies were at the first march from Cardiff to Greenham, and Mary Millington devoted many years to the anti-nuclear struggle at the camp. Helen Thomas was represented at the ceremony by her mother and aunt.'

In 2011, a bench by the town clock in Newcastle Emlyn was dedicated to Helen's memory. Having travelled to Berkshire in 2011 to take part in the 30th Anniversary 'Women for Life on Earth' Celebration at Greenham Peace Garden Gathering, Janet Thomas said the protest was the action of so many brave women who put their political beliefs and hopes for peace before their own comfort: 'So many of them sacrificed their lives at home with their children to pursue their honourable cause'. Just two years later the peaceful garden was obliterated.

There is a quote on a peace site on the internet: 'The women of Greenham Common lit a flame for peace which inspired the world. We will never forget their wonderful determination, and the Peace Garden stands as a testament to their incredible victory.' Thank you the savages of Greenham Community Trust – as Santayana tells us: 'Progress, far from consisting in change, depends on retentiveness. When change is absolute there remains no being to improve and no direction is set for possible improvement: and when experience is not retained, as among savages, infancy is perpetual. *Those who cannot remember the past are condemned to repeat it.'*

\*\*\* 'Upon breaching the barriers and entering the camp, these women were making the statement that they would not stay at home and do nothing, as women are traditionally expected to do, while the men take care of the serious "male" issues. Their refusal to go home at the end of each day was a challenge against the traditional notion that a women's place was in the home - many media outlets even questioned the behaviour of the Greenham women stating that if their children were so important to them (as their protest suggested), then why were they not home with them? The media tended to ignore the Greenham women's collective identity of "women as mothers" protecting the children, and largely focused on the illegitimacy of the camp, describing it as a witches' coven laden with criminal activity, with the women posing a threat to family values and the state.' - Shepherd, Laura J., *Gender Matters in Global Politics* (2010)

*Footnote:*
This is a copy of a letter from Helen Thomas, published in *The Independent*, 20 July, 1989, just 16 days before her death: 'I'm writing in response to your article "Greenham women's parting shot to Missiles", written by Mike Prestage, 2 August 1989. Not only does the article trivialise the real issues involved in the 8 year struggle against the military at Yellow Gate, it also contains many inaccuracies. Before yesterday's flight there were 101, not 96 missiles inside the base.

Secondly, your treatment of an important issue of the warheads is very ambiguous. We have found that the I.N.F. treaty, signed 2 years ago this December, does not in fact cover the warheads at all - and have no proof that these will actually leave the base. The base is just as much a threat to life as it has always been. The money stolen from the work of the oppressed people throughout the world is still being misused to test more Nuclear Weapons in the Pacific and Canada, raping the land of the indigenous people of those countries. Your article takes no account of the real work going on at Yellow Gate to resist the military at Greenham Common, work which results in prison sentences for those who take non-violent direct action against the military. The military's publicity exercise at Greenham Common on August 1st was not a "moving moment" for us, but yet another reminder of the role of the British press in upholding the lies and propaganda of the military powers preparation for genocide.

We at Yellow Gate did not consider August the 1st to be a "great day" in any way. All that is leaving Greenham is the weapons casings, not the warheads. Every month cruise missile convoys still leave Greenham Common to practice on Salisbury Plain, and every month women are arrested for tracking and stopping them.

The article also claims that the I.N.F treaty was aimed to scrap "all U.S. land missile bases in Europe." There are no such plans. The I.N.F treaty covers the missile casings alone, not the warheads, not the bases. This treaty was basically designed to lull people into thinking that the world was actually a safer place. It is a victory for us though, that the world is seen as more secure "without" nuclear weapons, whereas before we heard about the need for the security of a nuclear deterrent.'

Helen Thomas
Yellow Gate
Women's Peace Camp
Greenham Common
Newbury
Berks

# KYLIE ANN MINOGUE 28 May 1968

## POP PRINCESS, 'WOMAN OF THE DECADE'

In a recent press article, 'The singer was controversially named as one of the greatest Welsh women of all time in 2001 due to her Welsh heritage. According to the records, Kylie's maternal great-grandmother Maggie Hughes was living with her Welsh-speaking parents, colliery labourer Elias and Margaret Hughes in Maesteg, but had been born in Blaenau Ffestiniog.' Of the 100 entries in my book, only this hit the headlines. The Daily Mirror of 29 December 2001 ran a two-page article: 'New Book: 100 Great Welsh Women contains some surprises! OZ Diva Kylie is a Valleys Girl!' And a long Sunday Express Books Review of January 2002 read: 'Women in the Hillside. 100 Great Welsh Women given 4-star review by Jonathan Hourigan. Terry Breverton's 100 Great Welsh Women has garnered media attention primarily because of the improbable inclusion of the diminutive Australian pop diva Kylie Minogue. Or perhaps that should be a Welshified La Minogue ... Breverton's breadth, generosity and sheer enthusiasm about Wales are compelling.'

The fact is that Carol Jones emigrated to Australia from Maesteg in 1955 when a youngster, and settled in Townsville, Queensland. There she met Ron Minogue, married him aged 20, and moved to Melbourne. Kylie was born in 1968, Brendan in 1970, and Danielle (Dannii) in 1971. Aged 11, and in her last year at primary school, Kylie won a part in a new soap, The

*Sullivans.* A neighbour was casting for the new series, and had asked Dannii to audition. To save arguments, Carol asked that her other daughter could also audition, and Kylie landed the part as Dannii was too young. Playing a Dutch girl, Kylie had to adopt a different accent. After success in this, she played alongside Jason Donovan in *Skyways* and they became great friends. After a few years of school, Kylie auditioned for a role in the popular series,

The Henderson Kids, in which she appeared for 6 months, while also passing her High School Certificate. Deciding that she wanted to be an actress, she secured an agent, and landed the part of Charlene Mitchell in the new soap, *Neighbours*, in February 1986. From an original 12-week contract, her character was so popular that she played in the show for around 30 months. In 1987, she had a memorable romance in *Neighbours* with her real-life boyfriend, Jason Donovan, playing Scott Robinson.

**KYLIE MINOGUE**

Fame came quickly, and in 1987 she was the youngest person to win the Most Popular Actress at the Australian TV Awards, the 'Logies'. By 1988 she was known across the world, and in that year became the first person to win four Logies in one night (Most Popular TV Personality, Victoria's Most Popular Personality, Most Popular Actress and Most Popular Video for *The Locomotion*). Her recording of *The Locomotion* was Number 1 in Australia for seven weeks in the summer of 1987, and the biggest-selling Australian single of the decade.

She was 're-invented' as a pop diva by the Stock-Aitken-Waterman combination after her girl-next-door role in Neighbours. In January 1988 they produced *I Should Be So Lucky*, which went straight to Number 1, and her first album *Kylie* sold 14 million copies across the world. Pete Waterman could not get a major record company to take the high-energy dance single, so released it (like *The Locomotion*) on his own label, PWL. It sold 2 million in the UK alone, and went to Number 1 in 12 countries. It was the first single to top the UK charts for 5 weeks for over a decade. PWL now re-mixed her Australian hit *The Locomotion*, which reached number 1 across Europe. It reached number 3 in America, and her follow-up hit *I Should Be So Lucky* established Kylie as a transatlantic star. Her next single, *Got To be Certain* was also a massive hit. In November 1988, she and Jason Donovan sang a duet, *Especially For You*, which again reached Number 1. With its release, Kylie became the first female artiste to have her first five singles all go silver, bringing her singles sales in the UK alone to 2 million copies in just one year. Just 5 feet and 1 inch in height, and weighing only 6 stone, Kylie had become one of Australia's biggest exports.

In 1989, Kylie starred in her first film role, *The Delinquents*, set in the outback of Australia. She had her third hit in the USA with *It's No Secret*, and the album *Kylie* went 'gold'. She was placed in Madame Tussaud's 'Hall of Fame' section alongside The Beatles and Mick Jagger, and won dozens of media and music awards across the world. The single *Hand on Your Heart* was her 3rd UK Number 1, and she dominated the Japanese charts. With the release of the single, *Wouldn't Change a Thing,* she created history with all of her 7 singles, album and video charting at either number 1 or 2 in the UK. Her second album *Enjoy Yourself* was launched, going 'triple-platinum' in the UK, and she switched on the Christmas lights on Regent Street. On New Year's Eve, Clive James presented her with an award as 'Woman of the Decade' - Kylie was just 21 years-old. In December, she sang on the Band Aid II single, *Do They Know It's Christmas.*

1990 saw her touring Australia, the Far East and Europe, with hit singles in *Tears on My Pillow* (another UK number 1) and *Better the Devil You Know*. Around this time, she moved to a more raunchy and sexy appeal, especially with a controversial video for the *Devil* release. With her 3rd album, *Rhythm of Love*, her new, more sophisticated look led to a 6-page fashion spread in *Vogue* magazine. 1991 saw another tour of the UK, Australia and Japan, and her new single *Shocked* made her the only artist ever to achieve 13 consecutive Top Ten hits with her first 13 releases. A fourth album appeared, *Let's Get To It*, and another hit, *Word is Out*. She co-wrote six of the album's songs with Pete Waterman. In 1992, after her *Greatest Hit'* album, her last under her PWL contract, she joined Deconstruction Records.

1994 saw Kylie with Claude van Damme in *Street Fighter*, which she admits was a mistake, as the movie was slammed by critics. 1994 saw another hit single, *Confide in Me*, followed by *Put Yourself in My Place* and *Where is the Feeling*, before the Nick Cave collaboration *Where the Wild Roses Grow*. Another US film, *Bio Dome* was also a flop in 1997, but there was another hit single in *Some Kind of Bliss*. In 1997, her former lover Michael Hutchence, of INXS, died. After a break from music, Kylie released the album *Impossible Princess* in Australia in 1998. It had to be renamed *Kylie Minogue* in the UK, because of the death of the Princess of Wales. She wrote most of the songs, and it sold well in Australia, but poorly elsewhere. However, the singles *Did It Again* and *Breathe* were hits. She then went on her 'Intimate and Live' tour in Australia. Unsure of her reception, she only booked 10 concerts, but they went so well that 24 concerts were eventually played, and the tour transferred to the UK. In 2000, she hit Number 1 again with *Spinning Round*, and had another successful tour, called *On a Night Like This* in 2001. Her *Light Year'* album on Parlophone charted, on which she co-wrote two of the numbers with Robbie Williams. Singing with Robbie Williams, the single *Kids* hit the UK Top 5. She is the most successful female solo act in UK music history, with 6 number 1 and 21 Top 10 singles. In Australia, she is 'bigger' than Madonna, breaking AC/DC's record of six consecutive concerts. Kylie did 9 in 2001.

Her 2001 single *Can't Get You Out of my Head* became one of the most successful singles during the 2000s, selling over ten million units, becoming recognized as her 'signature song' and being voted as the catchiest song ever. Her album *Fever* (2001) was a hit in many countries, including the US, a market in which Minogue had previously received little recognition. Along with two other Grammy nominations, Kylie received the award for Love at First Sight in 2003 and Come into My World in 2004. In 2005, while on her Showgirl: The Greatest Hits Tour, she was diagnosed with breast cancer. After treatment, she resumed the tour under the title Showgirl: The Homecoming Tour, reviewed as a triumph by critics. She has achieved worldwide record sales of more than 75 million and has received notable music awards.

Over time Kylie has become both a sex symbol and a gay icon, inspired by and compared to Madonna throughout her career. Her producer, Pete Waterman, recalled her during the early years with the observation: 'She was setting her sights on becoming the new Prince or Madonna ... What I found amazing was that she was outselling Madonna four to one, but still wanted to be her.' Dino Scatena wrote that 'A quarter of a century ago, a sequence of symbiotic events altered the fabric of Australian popular culture and set in motion the transformation of a 19-year-old soap actor from Melbourne into an international pop icon. Who could have imagined this tiny, unsophisticated star of *Neighbours*, with the bad '80s perm and questionable vocal ability, would go on to become Australia's single most successful entertainer and a world-renowned style idol?'

Throughout her career she has been known for reinventing herself in fashion and her musical content. *Fabulous Magazine* had labelled her a 'Master of Reinvention', and Larissa Dubecki in *The Age* had called her the 'Mother of Reinvention': 'This unveiling is as cleverly managed as every aspect of her career, and her illness, to date. Like sharks, celebrities cannot remain static; they must keep moving or die. Kylie has beaten her early detractors by inhabiting almost a dozen identities...' Fiona MacDonald in *Madison* said Kylie was 'an icon, one of the handful of singers recognised around the world by her first name alone. And yet despite becoming an international music superstar, style icon and honorary Brit, those two syllables still seem as Australian as the smell of eucalyptus or a barbeque on a hot day.' She and her sister both still have fond feelings for their mother's homeland. Dannii said 'I love Wales, it's a great place and because of my mother and my ties, it's always a special kind of feeling when I come here.'

## BARONESS CARYS DAVINA 'TANNI' GREY-THOMPSON DBE DL 26 July 1969 -

## THE WORLD'S MOST SUCCESSFUL PARALYMPIAN

'Tanni' Grey was born in the Heath, Cardiff, and now lives with her husband Ian Thompson (another wheelchair athlete) in Eaglescliffe, just north of Yarm-on-Tees. He helped with her road-training, and they were running the roads of Cardiff even on the morning of their wedding  in 1999. They have a daughter Carys, born in 2002. Dr Thompson is a research chemist, who was disabled in a road accident in his early twenties, and held the British 5000m record. In April 2001, this gifted and courageous sportswoman was voted onto the elite World Sports Academy. She had won four gold medals in the Sidney Paralympic Games, adding to the four she won in Barcelona four years previously, and won the London Wheelchair Marathon for the fifth time in 2001.

In the World Sports Academy she joined the likes of Pele, Michael Jordan, Jack Nicklaus, Martina Navratilova, Mark Spitz, Dawn Fraser, Seve Ballesteros, Boris Becker and Ian Botham. Her election as the first disabled athlete, to this elite group of 39 world sports stars, was both a breakthrough and a fitting reward for this wonderful sportswoman. In the Sidney 2000 Olympics, she took gold in the 100, 200, 400 and 800m wheelchair events, breaking three world records (and replicating her Barcelona haul). She held the course record for the London Marathon, has won five World Championships. In the Athens 2004 Paralympics, she won gold in the 100m and 400m.

Tanni won the 2001 London Marathon despite having a puncture on the cobbled section - she said 'I went off fast to join the men's field early on. It was nice winning here because I always have a nightmare after a Paralympics year. My ambition is to beat Ian (her husband) one day.' She won the London Marathon in 1992, 1994, 1996 and 1998, missing out on the gold after the Paralympics of 1992, 1996 and 2000, but nevertheless has eight medal placings in the event. She also has 4 Silvers and a Bronze in the Paralympics to go with her 11 Golds.

Her sister referred to her as 'tiny' when she first saw her, pronouncing it 'tanni' and the nickname stuck. Born with *spina bifida* and confined to a wheelchair from the age of 7, Tanni began wheelchair racing aged 13, inspired by the exploits of Chris Hallam (see footnote). At 17, after major surgery had grafted a metal rod onto her spine, she joined the Rookwood Paraplegic Club in Cardiff and began to compete. Aged 15, Tanni won the Junior National games, representing Wales in the 100m. She went on to train for the 1988 Paralympics in Seoul where she won a bronze in the 200m, aged 18. She then was forced to return to hospital for major surgery, as the metal rod on her spine had snapped off the bone grafts and was forcing its way through scar tissue, so she could not train or compete for a year.

Tanni had left school in Cardiff to study at Loughborough, where she took a politics degree. She won gold in Atlanta in 1992, and the rest is history. Often Tanni trained for 45 hours a week, but she commented on the worst point of her career: 'My low spot would be the Atlanta Paralympics for all the opposite reasons to Barcelona. The crowd was dreadful, not many people came and those that did were so biased to the USA that they booed good performances from other nations. It was a nasty place. I have competed in other parts of the States and it has never been quite as bad as the Atlanta crowd. It really didn't help that the organisation was dreadful. The food, the transport you name it, it was awful. At the time of competition it didn't affect me too much, because you have to deal with it, but I have to say that when I came back home I felt incredibly flat for some time afterwards. The experience was so bad I was considering not staying for the closing ceremony, in the end I stayed, then got the very next flight home.' Thankfully, the Sidney and Athens Paralympics were praised by all the competing athletes as being extremely well-organised and a fabulous experience.

There was a gaffe in the presentation of Tanni with the third place award in the BBC TV Sports Personality of the Year ceremony in 2000. Steve Redgrave, the Olympic rower won, with Denise Lewis the Olympic heptathlete placed second, but Tanni was unable to join them on the stage as there was no wheelchair ramp. She also won the Helen Rollason Award for outstanding courage and achievement in the face of adversity. Tanni played down the problem, saying 'I am very happy to have won two awards but there is a danger that the unfortunate error will be exploited as an issue and undo much of the work that has been achieved for disabled athletics. I want to carry on working with the BBC to encourage recognition and support for disabled people.' However, Bert Massie, chair of the Disability Rights Commission said 'This highlights how disabled people were prevented from fully participating in all sorts of ways. Tanni Grey-Thompson's experience shows even the most successful disabled people face discrimination.' Tanni said after the Sidney Olympics 'For many disabled people, life can be an uphill struggle - and that's not because they may be confined to a wheelchair. There is still a great deal of prejudice'.

She has been voted Welsh Sports Personality of the Year three times, *Sunday Times* Sports Personality of the Year, Variety Club Disabled Sportswoman of the Year and was awarded an OBE for services to sport in 2000. She has been featured on *This Is Your Life*. Tanni is chairperson of the Wheelchair Racing Association, Vice-President of the Women's Sports Foundation, President of Travel Freedom, Patron of the Youth Sport Trust, a member of the Sports Council for Wales, and a member of the national Disability Council, and works for UK Athletics, encouraging young people to take up sports, amongst other appointments. She was to retire after the 2002 Commonwealth games in Manchester, for which she is a member of the Games Organising Council. After beating a strong 400m field in her last Paralympics, and gaining her fourth gold of the Games, she was asked what she intended to do to celebrate, to which Tanni responded 'I'm going to pig out on ice cream'. She says 'I love my home country, the people and everything about it'. This is why she was not retiring until after representing Wales in the 2002 Commonwealth Games in England (like her inspiration, the great world record breaker, hurdler Colin Jackson of Cardiff). Her main reason for retirement was to see more of her husband.

Expecting a baby in February 2002, she vowed to compete in the London Marathon just two months later. (This author completed the London Marathon, aged 47, and can only be amazed at Tanni's grit, determination and fitness). The couple meant to wait until after the Manchester Commonwealth Games before starting a family. The author was lucky to speak to Tanni on BBC Radio Wales in 2001, and realises that she is not only a standard-bearer for disabled people, but a warm, natural and extremely kind-hearted lady. She has achieved everything by her own efforts, and fame has not affected her adversely in any way (unlike some other people the author has met). Tanni will take exactly the same approach to motherhood as she does to life: 'I have an 18-month-old niece who I pick up from the floor by her dungaree straps, she loves it. And that's the point. Disabled people can do what able-bodied people can do - it's just a case of doing it differently.' Tanni kept telling me she was not good enough to be included in this book. She is.

Tanni was persuaded to go to Athens in 2004, where she won two more Paralympic Golds. She then represented Britain at the World Championships in Essen in 2006, winning a gold, silver and bronze at the 'grand old age' of thirty-seven before finally retiring the following year from the sport she loved. Over her career she won a total of 16 Paralympic medals, including 11 golds, held over 30 world records and won the London Marathon six times between 1992 and 2002. In 1993 she was appointed an

MBE for 'services to sport', advanced in 2000 to OBE, and then in 2005 was DBE. Since the first book was published, Dame Tanni has been rewarded for her courage and intelligence with a career in television presenting, is on the panels of many advisory councils and charities. In July 2011 she was announced as the President of the Leadership 20:20 Commission, the Commission on the future leadership of Civil Society. She launched the Commission's recommendations in Parliament on 14 December 2011. On 23 March 2010, Grey-Thompson was created a Life Peer, and despite previously suggesting a desire for a title with a Welsh connection, her title was conferred as Baroness Grey-Thompson, of Eaglescliffe in the County of Durham. She swore the oath of allegiance in the House of Lords in both English and Welsh, and sits as a cross-bencher.

*Footnote: A Tribute to Chris Hallam MBE 1962-1913*
I taught Chris 'Shades' Hallam on an MBA course, went with him on a trip to Bordeaux, and respected him greatly. He needs to be remembered for many achievements, for pioneering diabled sports and especially for his influence upon Tanni. She says that Chris was the man who led the way for Paralympics, and upon his untimely death David Cameron tweeted 'Very sorry to hear of the death of Chris Hallam, a true pioneer of disabled sport and an inspiration to athletes everywhere.' Tanni said Chris Hallam had been 'hugely inspirational' to her and had 'broken down all the barriers' that enabled her and others to go into wheelchair athletics. She told the BBC News website he was also believed to be the first disabled athlete to get sponsorship. 'I remember watching him doing the London Marathon in 1985 with my parents and saying to mum and dad "I will do the London Marathon one day". He was an icon in wheelchair sport. He was edgy with this blond hair and he'd wear things like leopard print Lycra suits. He was very flamboyant and a real character - not at all bland. Without him we wouldn't have wheelchair racing. You have to realise that back then in the '80s, the word Paralympic hadn't been invented, nobody knew anything about disability sport, there was no coverage of it. It was as if it didn't exist...
I wouldn't have had my career without him. He was really close mates with my husband and was an usher at our wedding. He was amazing. He could be quite abrasive and rude and he would always have an opinion - he would say what he thought, which would often get him into trouble. He didn't suffer fools gladly and a lot of us wished we could be as direct as Chris. But he really cared about the people around him. He really helped me. In the Paralympic movement in Britain, he was the one who broke through. But a lot of people might not know about him because it was before social media. He broke down every barrier.' Fellow Paralympian John Harris said he got to know Chris Hallam after his accident and called him the 'ultimate hero' and the 'toughest man he had ever met'.
Tanni wrote Chris's obituary in *The Guardian*: 'The Paralympian Chris Hallam, who has died aged 50, was one of the most influential athletes in the development of disability sport. He was the first disabled athlete to receive widespread recognition for his athleticism rather than just his "courage" in

overcoming perceived adversity. Chris only ever saw himself as an athlete and he realised the power of the media to change public perceptions. At the time he began competing in the 1980s, the little coverage that existed was generally patronising and saw disabled people as "having a go". Chris had extremely forthright views on the management of sport and he stood up for what he believed to be right. On the track, he was known for his flowing blond hair, and an outrageous taste in Lycra body suits (most notably leopard prints)... Chris attended Llantarnam School. He became a competitive swimmer, and aspired to represent Wales.

At the age of 17, he broke his back in a motorcycle accident on the way to a training session. After rehabilitation he spent some time living and travelling in South Africa, before returning to the UK and becoming involved in wheelchair sport. His nickname was "Shades", due to the dark glasses he wore. Chris competed for Great Britain at four Paralympic Games – Stoke Mandeville (1984), Seoul (1988), Barcelona (1992) and Atlanta (1996) – and for Wales at the Commonwealth Games in Auckland (1990) and Victoria (1994). In 1984, he won a gold medal for the 50m breast stroke, but it was on the track and road where he had the biggest impact. He won a bronze medal in the 400m in Seoul, and repeated this in the 100m in Barcelona. During his career, he held world records in the 100m and 200m.

He was probably best known for competing in the London Marathon, where he won the men's wheelchair event and set course records in 1985 and 1987. The event was then only recently established but Chris's charismatic personality almost demanded coverage. For me, watching the 1985 London Marathon was a seminal moment. The way Chris dominated the field and his outlandish style convinced me that wheelchair racing was the sport for me. Throughout my career, Chris offered honest and helpful advice and support. He was a loyal friend. Without him there wouldn't have been the opportunities for other athletes to be treated as such. He broke down so many attitudinal barriers around disability, but also set a standard for training and athletic performance.

He won the Great North Run four times between 1986 and 1990 and was also the national road-racing champion on several occasions. He twice pushed around Wales (1987 and 1997) with his training partner John Harris, to raise money for a purpose-built wheelchair-accessible training centre at Cyncoed in Cardiff. Both resulted in an increased profile for Welsh disabled athletes. Chris was a perfectionist and he endlessly researched sports science and psychology, as he tried to find new ways to improve his performance. His knowledge of other athletes' performances was encyclopaedic... He held many coaching and mentoring positions and at the 2006 World Championships he was head wheelchair racing coach for the Great Britain team. In retirement from his competitive career, Chris returned to education and studied for an undergraduate degree and MBA at the University of Wales Institute, Cardiff (now Cardiff Metropolitan University), where he also worked with a number of younger athletes. He was made an MBE in the 1989 New Year's honours. Although he had a successful kidney transplant in 1999 (with a living donation from his father), in later years he experienced ill health. He was diagnosed with lymphoma in 2011 and received chemotherapy. He is survived by his parents,

John and Anne, and his sister, Julie. - Christopher Alexander Hallam, athlete, born 31 December 1962; died 16 August 2013.'

# A NOTE UPON THE TREATMENT OF WOMEN IN WALES

By 918, it appears that Hywel ap Cadell ap Rhodri Mawr (890-950) ruled Dyfed, and in 920 he took over Seisyllwg when his brother Clydog died, so his lands covered the kingdom of Deheubarth, South and West Wales from the Dyfi to the Tawe. His wife was Elen ap Llywarch, by which marriage he claimed Dyfed, and their child was Owain. Hywel made a pilgrimage to Rome in 928, and had gained control of Brecon by 930. In 942 Idwal Foel was killed by the Saxons, and from his power base in Deheubarth, Hywel Dda now added Powys and Gwynedd to his kingdom, to largely reunify Wales. Hywel was now acknowledged supreme among the Welsh princes, and in *Brut y Tywysogion*, Hywel was described as 'the chief and most praiseworthy of all the Britons.'

The only Welsh king to earn the epithet *Dda*, 'the good', he peacefully unified much of Wales by inheritance, marriage, alliances, and diplomatic relations with Alfred the Great of Wessex. He led no invasions into England, and coexisted peacefully with Aethelstan upon his succession after Alfred's death. It had helped that Alfred's chief advisor, Asser, was a former monk at St. David's. Hywel understood the power of his larger neighbour, despite extremely strong calls from the bards to ally against them. He had seen the death of Idwal Foel and witnessed the final extinction of the Brythonic kingdom of Cornwall, so wished to keep Wales intact. Hywel Dda's quiet diplomacy and conciliation helped give Wales another three centuries of independence against England. Hywel was the first Welsh ruler to issue his own coins.

The assembly called by Hywel in 930 at Y Hendy Gwyn (Whitland) was one of the first of its kind in Britain. In 942 the assembly finally established a legal code for all of Wales, *Cyfraith Hywel*, codifying the common laws of the different kingdoms of Wales. This legislation was only destroyed in 1536 with the Act of Union with England, where laws based upon the right of the individual of any sex were replaced by laws based upon male machismo, property ownership and class structure solidification. At Whitland today, one can visit the Hywel Dda Gardens and Interpretative Centre. *Cyfraith Hywel* was the name by which the native law was known to the Welsh in medieval times, and the extent of its use is reflected by the survival of around forty lawbooks dating from before 1536. The first generation of these books, some in Latin and some in Welsh, dates from the middle decades of the 13th century, and the laws themselves had accumulated for hundreds of years before their codification.

The outstanding quality of Welsh life, enshrined in the laws, was the equal position and treatment of women, possibly unique in Western civilisation. Welsh law gave precedence to the woman's claim in any rape case; marriage was an agreement, not a holy sacrament, and divorce was allowed by common consent, with an equal share of land and possessions. Illegitimate children had the same rights as legitimate children, and there was equal division of the land between all children upon the death of parents. Under Hywel's Laws, farming was a communal affair (reminiscent of Robert Owen eight hundred years later), and the man did not have unrestricted control over his wife as a possession, unlike all the other 'civilised' European countries.

In the Celtic Church, as well as outside, there was a tradition in Wales that women had a real social status - a woman's rights to property under *Cyfraith Hywel* were not granted in English law until 1883. A woman also had a right to compensation if her husband hit her without any cause. In English law, the woman was the property of the husband, a chattel, whereas a divorced Welshwoman received half the property. It is typical of the Laws that the queen had special privileges - there is no mention of a queen in early English, Irish or Germanic laws.

Also, doctors were liable for the death of patients unless the family had agreed to the course of treatment. Contracts were stronger than legislation in civil disputes. In criminal procedings, recompense by the offending family network, and reconciliation, took precedence over revenge. The laws tried to achieve social harmony, with none of the English elements of public whipping, trial by fire or boiling water, torturing, gibbetting, burning of witches or disembowelling being known in independent Wales. The rate of execution in 'primitive' 12th century Wales was proportionately less than a quarter than that endured under modern English law in the 19th century. Indeed the leaders of the Newport Chartists in 1839 were originally sentenced to be hung, drawn and quartered, later commuted to life transportation – this was for asking for democracy.

For theft there was no punishment whatsoever in Welsh law if the purpose was to stay alive, yet up to the late 18th century, children were hung in England for stealing a lamb. Children were of equal status - the law of *Gavelkind* meant shared inheritance amongst all children - a civilised and socially unique method of preventing massing of power and lands. Even more advanced was the law that illegitimate children received all the rights, including inheritance, of family offspring. *Cyfraith Hywel* states that the youngest son has equal rights to the oldest, and also that 'the sin of the father and his wrongdoing should not be set against the son's right to his patrimony', so illegitimate children had equal rights. A boy came of age at 14, free of parental control, and a father could be chastised for hitting him after this age. A girl came of age at 12, and like the boy could decide whether she wished to stay in the father's household. She could not be forced into marriage, nor arbitrarily divorced. Rhiannon, in the *Mabinogion* story of Pwyll, Prince of Powys, refuses to marry, saying 'every woman is to go the way she willeth, freely.'

Professor Dafydd Jenkins has noted that aspects of Hywel's laws, which were superseded by English law in 1536, were being reintroduced as enlightened reforms in the 1990's, such as reparation to the victims of crime. Compensation of the victim was more important than punishment of the offender. For damage unwittingly done, redress had to be made. Even for murder, Welsh judges were active in seeking compensation for the victim's family, to remove the need for vengeance and feud. Obviously, the far-extended Welsh family-clans exerted pressure on their members to toe the line, as if any of them offended, all had to pay something. All the checks and balances were in place under this ancient system to make society enforce its own social code.

Unlike many societies, there were no differences in morality requirements for the sexes - a Welsh woman could heavily fine her husband on an increasing scale for adultery, and also divorce him for it. A woman could even divorce her husband for 'stinking breath'. She had property rights not given under English law until the Married Woman's Property Act of 1870. In France and the rest of Britain, wife-beating was a recognised right of the husband, but in Wales there had to be a definite, very serious offence, and then the punishment was limited to just three strokes of a rod. The Welsh have possibly been the most civilised race in the world in their attitudes towards women from the European 'Dark Age' of the fifth and sixth centuries to the present day. (Indeed, this time was known as the 'Age of the Saints' in Wales, the only permanently Christian country in Europe, with over 900 named saints stating from that time.) The Laws were fair to all men and women - violence to the person was averted at all costs, and responsibility shared by the offenders' relatives, which made for social order. Not until the Act of Union in 1536 and after did we see the political/economic system that is known as British justice imposed on Wales. The 'torture until you confess' treatment was used to get a confession in IRA bomb cases - with never a comeback on corrupt policemen, politicians, lawyers and judges who use the system to their best advantage. The twin elements that define a nation are its language and legislation - the London government wiped out a humane system of laws based on social responsibility and replaced it with one based upon class, property, prestige, repression and violence. They almost wiped out the language by similar methods.

Hywel's death in 949 or 950 saw the resumption of Viking attacks, and the laws of *gavelkind* meant that princes fought against princes with no national unity until the accession of Gruffydd ap Llewellyn in 1039. There were ninety years of murder and mayhem and internal power struggles against a background of Saxon, Mercian and Norse invasions. But the Laws lived for six-hundred years, and their ethos of human equality is slowly replacing the property-based spirit of English laws. The finest book upon what was the finest legal framework in medieval history is by Dafydd Jenkins, *Hywel Dda, The Law*.

There is a tradition that the tribal laws and customs were codified by Dyfnwal Moelmud long before Hywel. However, the earliest manuscripts date from the 12th and 13th centuries, extracts made by practising lawyers, the earliest from the time of Llewelyn the Great. There were slight differences between North, West and South Wales, known as the Venetian, Dementian and Gwentian Codes, and they stayed in force in entirety until Edward I's Statute of Rhuddlan in 1283, with many provisions remaining until the period of the Tudors in the 16th century. Many Welsh laws and traditions are noted in the ancient *Triads*, expressions where objects are grouped in threes. We know of nothing similar in any other country, and some of these sayings may date back to the time of the Druids, who committed the old laws to memory. *Triads* are found in the oldest Welsh manuscripts such as the *Mabinogion*, bardic poems, the 12th century *Black Book of Carmarthen*, ancient versions of the Welsh Laws, and the 14th century *Red Book of Hergest*.

The amazing fact that the laws were written in Welsh as well as Latin helped ensure that the language thrived. To keep a Welsh culture, its history, laws, literature, religion, language and community must intertwine and be respected. These Welsh laws, first written down over a thousand years ago, according to Saunders Lewis fashioned: 'lively forms of the mind of every poet and writer in Wales until the sixteenth century, and also directly influenced the shape and style of Welsh prose. This implies that the language had already reached a philosophical maturity unequalled in its period. It meant that it had a flexibility and positiveness which are the signs of centuries of culture. This means that there is a long period of development behind the prose of the *Cyfreithiau* [Laws].'

Celtic women, such as Buddug (Boadicea) of the Iceni, and Cartimandua of the Brigantes, held real power. Queen Teuta fought the Greeks and Romans between 71 and 83CE. Women landowners in Ireland were expected to fight as warriors until Saint Adamnan forced a change of the laws in the sixth century. Women in Celtic Gaul were butchers, chemists, doctors and sellers of wine. This Celtic equality passed down and was enshrined in the *Laws of Hywel Dda*, who codified the old Welsh laws. In medieval times, Welsh women had amazing rights compared to all their European contemporaries. The union of marriage was a contract rather than a sacrament, whereby the woman received property which remained hers completely and in perpetuity, the exact opposite of the dowry system practised elsewhere. She had equal rights in a divorce case, and if married for seven years, could leave her husband with half of his property. The widow had the same right on a husband's death, and she could make a will leaving property. In England, women had no right to hold property apart from her husband until an act of 1882. In 1865, the Welsh colony in

Patagonia was the first society anywhere in the world to give women the vote.

In the 19th century, Ernest Renan noted the effect of the Welsh attitudes towards women upon the rest of Europe: 'It was through the *Mabinogion* that the Welsh influence influenced the Continent; it transformed, in the twelfth century, the poetic art of Europe and realised this miracle, that the creation of a small nation which had been forgotten had become a feast of imagination for mankind over all the earth........ Above all else, by creating woman's character the Welsh romances caused one of the greatest revolutions known to literary historians. It was like an electric spark; in a few years the taste of Europe was transformed.' He carried on to say that this was the first flowering of chivalry, which helped raised the status of women in Europe.

## BOOKS BY T.D. BREVERTON

AN A-Z of WALES and the WELSH (300 pages) March 2000 ISBN 0715407341 - published Christopher Davies – *'the first encyclopaedia of Wales'; 'a comprehensive anthology'*

THE SECRET VALE OF GLAMORGAN (230 pages) June 2000 ISBN 190352900X supported by a Millennium Commission grant for local parishes *'a historian's delight'*

THE BOOK OF WELSH SAINTS (606 pages) September 2000 ISBN 1903529018 hardback – *'this book is a really extraordinary achievement: a compilation of tradition, topography and literary detective work that can have few rivals. I have enjoyed browsing it immensely, and have picked up all sorts of new lines to follow up'* – Archbishop Rowan Williams; *'an enormous work of research'*

100 GREAT WELSHMEN (376 pages) May 2001 ISBN 1903529034 Welsh Books Council **Welsh Book of the Month** *'painstaking research'; 'a fascinating compendium'* (New Edition 2005)

100 GREAT WELSH WOMEN (304 pages) ISBN 1903529042 September 2001 *'an absolute must for all those who value their Welsh heritage'*

THE PATH TO INEXPERIENCE (158 pages) ISBN 1003529077 March 2002 *'magnificent, compassionate and moving'*

THE WELSH ALMANAC (320 pages) ISBN 1903529107 WBC **Welsh Book of the Month** July 2002 hardback *'a tremendous undertaking'; 'it will take its place on the bookshelf with other important works of reference'*

THE BOOK OF WELSH PIRATES AND BUCCANEERS (388 pages) ISBN 1903529093 WBC
**Welsh Book of the Month** April 2003 *'exemplary'; 'an immense work of great scholarship'; effectively a study of the whole genre of piracy'*

GLAMORGAN SEASCAPE PATHWAYS (144 pages) ISBN 1903529115 June 2003 supported by a Millennium Commission WCVA Arwain grant. **Fellow of the Millennium Award** (FMA) *'fascinating'*

BLACK BART ROBERTS – THE GREATEST PIRATE OF THEM ALL (254 pages) ISBN 1903529123 March 2004 (published abridged as BLACK BART ROBERTS – THE GREATEST PIRATE OF THEM ALL by Pelican

Publishing USA [166 pages] ISBN 1-58980-233) *a must read for anyone interested in pirates'*

THE PIRATE HANDBOOK (290 pages) ISBN 1903529131 Autumn 2004 (published abridged in USA by Pelican Publishing 2004 as THE PIRATE DICTIONARY [192 Pages] ISBN 9781589802438) - WBC **Welsh Book of the Month** *'this wonderful sourcebook is an absolute must'; 'a vitally important addition to the canon of naval literature'*

Introduction and 3 major poems in 600th anniversary commemorative book on Owain Glyn Dŵr, SONGS FOR OWAIN (98 pages) ISBN 0862437385 published by Y Lolfa June 2004.

SIR HENRY MORGAN – THE GREATEST BUCCANEER OF THEM ALL (174 pages) ISBN 1903529174 Spring 2005 – WBC **Welsh Book of the Month** - published abridged by Pelican USA as ADMIRAL SIR HENRY MORGAN – KING OF THE BUCCANEERS [120 pages] ISBN 9781589802773

WELSH SAILORS OF WORLD WAR II (with Phil Carradice) (448 pages) ISBN 9781903529195 March 1st, 2007 - WH Smith Welsh **Book of the Month** *'an account worthy of the pen of Xenophon'*

THE FIRST AMERICAN NOVEL: THE JOURNAL OF PENROSE, SEAMAN BY WILLIAM WILLIAMS, & THE BOOK, THE AUTHOR AND THE LETTERS IN THE LILLY LIBRARY BY TERRY BREVERTON (446 pages) ISBN 9781903529201 August 30th 2007. This is 'The Journal of Lewellin Penrose – Seaman', and an autobiography of William Williams - **Everett Helm Visiting Fellowship Award** of Indiana University.

Introduction and Annotated Edition of Exquemelin's 'THE BUCCANEERS OF AMERICA' (192 pages) August 2008 – commissioned July 2007 for Quarto Publishing. Consultant editor and writer: translation four different language versions of Exquemelin's Buccaneers of America as THE ILLUSTRATED PIRATE DIARIES: A REMARKABLE EYEWITNESS ACCOUNT OF CAPTAIN MORGAN AND THE BUCCANEERS, hardback for worldwide distribution by Apple Press (UK 9781845433000), New Holland (Australia) and Collins (USA 0061584487 and 9780061584480). *Das Piraten-Tagebuch* (trans. Karen Schuler & Henning Dedekind; *Dzienniki Piratow* etc.

IMMORTAL WORDS: HISTORY'S MOST MEMORABLE QUOTATIONS AND THE STORIES BEHIND THEM (978-1-84866-0045) 384pp hardback Quercus History/Borders – August 2009

OWAIN GLYNDŴR – THE STORY OF THE LAST PRINCE OF WALES (978-1-84868-3280) – 192pp July 2009 Amberley hardback 'Accessible and Highly Readable'
WALES - A HISTORICAL COMPANION – (978-1-84848-3264) 360pp November 2009 Amberley

BREVERTON'S NAUTICAL CURIOSITIES – A BOOK OF THE SEA (978-1-84424 – 7766) 384pp April 2010 Quercus hardback: published as BREVERTON'S NAUTICAL COMPENDIUM Globe Pequot USA 2010

IMMORTAL LAST WORDS – HISTORY'S MOST MEMORABLE DYING REMARKS, DEATHBED DECLARATIONS AND FINAL FAREWELLS (978-1-84916-478-8) 384pp Quercus/Borders hardback September 2010 (published in Holland as *Onsterfelikje Laatste Woorden*)

WALES' 1000 BEST HERITAGE SITES (978-1-84868-991-6) 224pp – Amberley – October 2010

BREVERTON'S PHANTASMAGORIA (978-0-85738-337-2) – A COMPENDIUM OF MONSTERS, MYTHS AND LEGENDS Hardback 384pp Quercus 7 July 2011

BREVERTON'S COMPLETE HERBAL – A BOOK OF REMARKABLE PLANTS AND THEIR USES – BASED ON NICOLAS CULPEPER'S THE ENGLISH PHYSITIAN OF 1652 AND COMPLEAT HERBALL OF 1653 (978-0-85738-336-5) Hardback 384pp Quercus 29 September 2011

I HAVE A DREAM – INSPIRING WORDS AND THOUGHTS FROM THE WORLD'S GREATEST LEADERS (978-1-84866-134-9) Hardback 384pp Quercus January 2012

BIRD WATCHING: A PRACTICAL GUIDE WITH PHOTOS AND FACTS (978-1-4454-8868-4) Parragon – the largest non-fiction illustrated book publisher in the world 2012

BACKYARD BIRDS – THE BIRDS OF AMERICA Parragon USA 2012

BREVERTON'S ENCYCLOPEDIA OF INVENTIONS – A COMPENDIUM OF TECHOLOGICAL LEAPS, GROUNDBREAKING DISCOVERIES AND SCIENTIFIC BREAKTHROUGHS THAT

CHANGED THE WORLD (978-1-7808-72391) Hardback 384pp Quercus May 2012

THE WELSH – THE BIOGRAPHY (978-1-4456-0808-2) *'Breverton's breadth, generosity and sheer enthusiasm about Wales are compelling'* 400pp Amberley – 28 November 2012

THE PHYSICIANS OF MYDDFAI – CURES AND REMEDIES OF THE MEDIEVAL WORLD – The first new and unexpurgated translation for 150 years, with a biography of physicians to the present day (978-0-9572459-9-0) 292pp Cambria Books November 2012

RICHARD III – THE KING IN THE CAR PARK: The Real Story of 'the Hunchback King' (978-1-4456-2105-0) Hardback 192pp Amberley 2013 [This is in fact a comparative analysis of Richard III and Henry Tudor]

THE JOURNAL OF PENROSE, SEAMAN - THE NEW ROBINSON CRUSOE (978-0-9576791-1-5) 548pp Cambria Books 2013/2014 – a rewrite of the original manuscript, with explanatory text

BREVERTON'S FIRST WORLD WAR CURIOSITIES (978-1-4456-3341-1) 320pp - Amberley June 2014

JASPER TUDOR – DYNASTY MAKER 320pp hardback Amberley September 2014

EVERYTHING YOU EVER WANTED TO KNOW ABOUT THE TUDORS BUT WERE AFRAID TO ASK 320pp Amberley hardback October 2014

RICHARD III – THE KING IN THE CAR PARK Feb 2014 paperback re-edition

THE TUDOR KITCHEN: HOW THE TUDORS ATE AND DRANK, WITH OVER 500 AUTHENTIC RECIPES OF THE TIMES Amberley hardback autumn 2015

THE TUDOR COOK BOOK: OVER 400 RECIPES FROM THE TIMES Amberley Spring 2016

JASPER TUDOR – DYNASTY MAKER 320pp paperback Amberley 2016
HENRY VII – THE MALIGNED TUDOR KING 320pp hardback Amberley 2016

OWEN TUDOR – FOUNDING FATHER OF THE TUDOR DYNASTY
320pp hardback Amberley 2017

100 GREATEST WELSHMEN (NEW EDITION) (490 pages) ISBN 9781903529294 2017 *'a veritable goldmine of a book'; 'a massive treasure chest of facts and figures which no collector of books on Wales can overlook'* 2006

THE CONFESSIONS OF WILLIAM OWEN, SMUGGLER, PRIVATEER AND MURDERER Gwasg Carreg Gwalch 2018

WELSH PIRATES AND PRIVATEERS Gwasg Carreg Gwalch 2018

A GROSS OF PIRATES Amberley 2018

BOOKS EDITED AND PUBLISHED BY TERRY BREVERTON
*The Dragon Entertains*, Alan Roderick 2001
*A Rhondda Boy*, Ivor Howells 2001
*Glyn Dŵr's War: The Campaigns of the last Prince of Wales'*, Gideon Brough 2002
*From Wales to Pennsylvania: the David Thomas Story'*, Dr Peter Williams 2002
*The Man from the Alamo*, John Humphreys 2004 WH Smith **Book of the Month**
*Heroic Science – the Royal Institution of South Wales and Swansea 1835-1865*, Ronald Rees 2005
*Gringo Revolutionary – The Amazing Adventures of Carel ap Rhys Pryce*, John Humphreys 2005

A big thanks to Dave Lewis of **Publish & Print**, who formatted the manuscript, designed the book cover and without whom this book could not have been published.

www.publishandprint.co.uk

78936863R00228

Made in the USA
Columbia, SC
23 October 2017